The Arab Charter of Human Rights:

A Voice for Sharia in the Modern World

The Arab Charter of Human Rights:
A Voice for Sharia in the Modern World

by

Ahmed Mohamed El Demery

Egypt

Chicago, 2015

©2015 by Ahmed Mohamed El Demery and the Council on International Law and Politics

All rights reserved. No part of this publication may be reproduced, stored in a retrieval system, or transmitted, in any form or by any means, without the prior permission in writing of the Council on International Law and Politics.

Published by	Council on International Law and Politics
	411 North LaSalle Street
	Suite 200
	Chicago, Illinois 60654
	http://www.cilpnet.org
Publications Coordinator:	Frank Emmert
Editorial Assistant:	Heather Leigh Grimstad
Cover Design:	Salma Taman
Cover Art:	©Hend Raafat Ismail, reproduced with permission
	Architect and Designer
	MSc. Sustainable Development
	E-mail hend.ismail@aucegypt.edu

Font Myriad Pro

Printed in the United States by CreateSpace

12 11 10 9 8 7 6 5 4 3 2 1

ISBN: 978-0-9858156-5-3

Table of Contents

Acknowledgments xi
Preface by Prof. Dr. M. Cherif Bassiouni xiii

Introduction 1

A. The Status of Human Rights in the Middle East 3
B. Research Problem 7
C. Research Questions 8
D. Research Methodology 9
E. The Significance of the Study 11
F. The Need for a Regional Charter 12
G. Roadmap 16

Chapter 1: The Sources and Methods of Application of Human Rights

A. Definition of Human Rights 19
B. Theories of Human Rights 22
C. Sources of Human Rights 22
    1. Treaties 23
    2. Jus Cogens 24
    3. Customary International Law 25
    4. General Principles of Law 27
    5. Judicial Decisions 27
    6. Other Possible Evidence of International Law 27
D. International System for the Protection of Human Rights 28
    1. Background and Evolution 28
    2. Internationally and Regionally Dividing Supranational Human Rights Systems 29
        a. The United Nations System 29
        b. Regional Human Rights Systems 32
    3. Comparison Between Universal and Regional Human Rights Systems 33

Chapter 2: Islamic Sharia Law as Key Legal Context of the Arab Charter

A. Introduction 37
B. The Foundations of Islamic Law 39
    1. Definition of Sharia 39
    2. Islam: An Introduction to the Religion 39
C. Sources of Islamic Law 40
    1. Primary Sources 41
        a. The Quran 41
        b. The Sunnah of the Prophet 44

    2. Secondary Sources: *Fiqh* and *Ijtihad* – Jurisprudential
       Methodologies of Islamic Law 47
       a. *Qiyas* and *Ijma* as Methodologies 49
       b. Istihsan and Istishab. 50
D. The Objectives and Purposes of Sharia Law 52
    1. What are the Objectives and Purposes of Sharia Law? 52
    2. The Pillars of Islam and the Philosophy of the Islamic Religion 53
    3. Peace and Justice in Islam 56
    4. Parental Rights 58
    5. General Obligations 59
E. The Effect of Diversity in *Fiqh* on the Application of Islamic Sharia 61
    1. The End of the Classical Era and its Effect on *Fiqh* 61
    2. The Door to *Ijtihad* Remains Open and Was Never Closed 62
    3. The Diversity of *Fiqh*. 73

Chapter 3: A Theory of Human Rights

A. Regional Systems for the Protection of Human Rights as Part of
   the Debate Between the Theories of Universalism and Cultural
   Relativism. 74
B. A Theory of Human Rights to Govern a Regional Human Rights System:
   A Brief Examination of Competing Theories of Human Rights 76
    1. Universalism 77
    2. Strict Cultural Relativism. 78
    3. Moderate Cultural Relativism 79
    4. Reverse Moderate Relativism 80
C. A New Theory of Human Rights Compatible with the Arab Human
   Rights System 81
D. The Stages of Evolution of Human Rights 87
E. Possibilities for Reconciliation Between International Human Rights
   Law and Islamic Law. 88
    1. Islam's *Zakat* and Social Security 89
    2. The Existence of Duties and Rights in Islam 95
    3. Gradualism in Islam and Human Rights Norms 99
    4. The Relationship Between the *'Umma* and the Individual in Islam
       and International Human Rights Law 105
    5. *Fitrah* and Natural Law Theory 111
    6. The Principle of Equality in Sharia Law and International Law 113
       a. Equality Between Men and Women 113
       b. Women's Experience in Arab Countries Before Islam 115
       c. Duties and Rights of Men and Women in Sharia Law 117
       d. Women and the Implementation of Gradualism 119
    7. Human Dignity in Islam and International Human Rights 121
    8. The Principle of the "Margin of Appreciation" as a Way of
       Reconciling Islamic Sharia Law and International Human
       Rights Law 126

Chapter 4: An Arab Regional Instrument for Human Rights: The Arab Charter on Human Rights

A. History of the Arab League and the Arab Charter on Human Rights 130
   1. The Arab League 130
   2. An Arab Charter on Human Rights 133
B. The Philosophy and Theory of the Arab Charter 139
C. The Scope of the Arab Charter 141
D. Rights Protected by the Charter 141
E. Incorporation of the Fundamental Principles into the Arab Charter 144
F. The Supervisory Mechanism of the Charter 148
G. An Interview with Dr. Nabil El Araby 150
H. An Arab Court for Human Rights? 154
   Bahrain's Proposal of Establishing an Arab Court on Human Rights
I. Is the Arab Charter an Important Step Forward? 160
J. The Evaluation of the Arab Charter in Comparison with the African Charter on Human and Peoples' Rights and the European Convention on Human Rights 163
   1. The European System 163
   2. The African System 164

Chapter 5: An Evaluation of Substantive Human Rights Protections in the Arab Charter

A. Introduction 168
B. The Right to Life 169
   1. The Death Penalty 170
   2. Abortion 191
C. Equality of Rights Between Men and Women 195
   1. Introduction 195
   2. Polygamy 215
   3. Discrimination Between Men and Women in Crimes of Passion 224
   4. Discrimination Between Husband and Wife in Initiating Divorce 226
D. The Right to Education 229
E. Private and Family Rights 238
   1. The Legal Framework 239
   2. Parental Rights 246
   3. Homosexuality 250
F. Torture and Cruel, Inhuman, or Degrading Treatment or Punishment 261
   1. Introduction 261
   2. *Hodood* Islamic Punishments 271
G. The Right to Freedom of Thought, Conscience and Religion 286
   1. Introduction 286
   2. Apostasy 293
   3. The Headscarf 298
H. The Right to a Fair Trial and the Rule of Law 306
I. The Right to Freedom of Movement and the Right to Seek Asylum 318
J. Prohibition of Slavery 326

Chapter 6: An Evaluation of the Procedural Human Rights Protections Through the Existing Arab Committee

A. Introduction 330
B. The Composition and Structure of the Existing Arab Human Rights Committee 333
   1. The Members of the Arab Committee on Human Rights 334
   2. The Secretariat of the Arab Committee on Human Rights 336
C. The State Reporting Mechanism 336
D. Documents Published by the Arab Committee on Human Rights to Guide the Committee and the Reviewed States 339
   1. Temporary Rules of Procedure of the Arab Committee on Human Rights 339
   2. The Mechanism to Examine the States Parties' Reports in the Arab Charter on Human Rights 342
   3. The Guidelines Regarding the Form and Content of Reports to Be Submitted by States Parties to the Arab Charter on Human Rights .. 345
E. The States Reports Submitted to and Examined by the Arab Committee on Human Rights 346
   1. Jordan 346
      a. The Report 346
      b. Conclusions and Observations of the Arab Human Rights Committee . 352
   2. Algeria 355
F. Implementation Review Mechanisms in the Arab League 360
G. Activities of the Arab Committee on Human Rights 362
   1. Algeria 362
   2. Libya 362
   3. Syria 363
   4. United Nations Human Rights Council 363
   5. Introductory Visits 364
H. Evaluation 365

Chapter 7: Recommendations for a Reformed Arab Committee on Human Rights Based on a Comparison with the African Commission on Human and Peoples' Rights

A. Creation and Composition 370
B. Mandate and Organization 374
C. Seat 375
D. Functions 376
   1. The Promotional Task 376
   2. The State Reporting System 378
E. Jurisdiction of the Arab Committee 387
F. Further Recommendations for the Arab Committee on Human Rights .. 390

Chapter 8: An Arab Court of Human Rights Based on a Comparison with the European Court of Human Rights

A. Institutional Structure and Composition 393
    1. Gradualism Within the European and Arab Courts of Human Rights 393
    2. Judges 395
        a. Structure of the Arab Court 401
        b. Immunity 406
        c. President and Vice-President of the Court 412
    3. The Registry 412
    4. Public Nature of the Proceedings 415
    5. Admissibility 417
        a. Who Can be Considered a Victim? 417
        b. Exhaustion of Domestic Remedies 418
        c. Sixth Month Limitation 421
    6. Handling of the Case After Registering the Application 422
    7. Judgment 428
    8. Enforceability – Comparison with the European Court of Human Rights 429
        a. Remedies Under Article 41 429
        b. Committee of Ministers 431
        c. General Measures 434
B. The Jurisprudence of the European Court on Human Rights, and the African Court and Commission on Human and Peoples' Rights as a Possible Guiding Light to the Functioning of the Arab Committee and Court 436
    1. The Principles Applied in the European Court on Human Rights 436
    2. Subsidiarity 436
    3. Living Instrument 438
C. Relationship with Other Human Rights Systems 440

Chapter 9 : Conclusion

A. The Arab Charter 444
B. Redefining Human Rights in the Arab Charter 449
C. The Door of *Ijtihad* is Open 450
D. The Arab Committee 450
E. An Arab Court 453
F. Summary 455

Annex

Arab Charter on Human Rights 461
Proposed 1st Optional Protocol to the Arab Charter on Human Rights 478
Proposed 2nd Optional Protocol to the Arab Charter on Human Rights 486
Bibliography 499
Index 511

Acknowledgements

I first want to thank Allah for the strength, patience, and endurance with which I was blessed while completing my book during this especially challenging time of change in my country Egypt. I quote a verse from the Quran that says, "My Lord! Grant me the power and ability that I may be grateful for Your Favours which You have bestowed on me and on my parents, and that I may do righteous good deeds that will please You, and admit me by Your Mercy among Your righteous slaves."[1]

This book, an edited and updated version of my J.S.D. thesis in Intercultural Human Rights at St. Thomas University School of Law in Miami, Florida, would not have been possible without the considerable assistance of several people, who contributed to the completion of this dissertation. I would like to thank my professors, as I have been blessed with the advice, support, and guidance of some of the best professors I have met in my life:

Professor Makdisi, thank you very much for all of your support and your ongoing feedback. You have been with me every single step of the way. You provided me with all the help you could; you were considerate of my circumstances and supported me with the best technical academic advice one could ask for. You gave me strength and motivation, especially when you would say, "As the expression goes, there is finally a light at the end of the tunnel!" Professor Makdisi, I will be forever indebted to you.

A very special thanks goes to Professor Wiessner, I would like to thank you for encouraging me to pursue this program and for your sincerity, patience, support, and encouragement. I will never forget when you told me that you did not want students to pursue graduate studies predominantly to make money, but rather because they are passionate about the law, human rights, and creating a difference for the good in the world.

I would like to express my gratitude to Professor Christopher McCrudden at Oxford University, School of Law. During my studies as a visiting research student at Oxford University School of Law, you provided me with direction regarding the cases and books that are related to the European human rights system. Also, I

---

1 QURAN chapter 27, verse 19, an electronic version of the Quran and its English translation is available at http://www.searchtruth.com (last visited Jan. 1, 2013). Each chapter in the Quran is composed of several verses, which vary in length. When citing the Quran in this book, the number of the chapter precedes the number of the verse. The chapter and the verse are separated by a colon.

want to extend my sincere appreciation to Bodleian Law Library at Oxford University where I found hundreds of thousands of books.

Despite the physical distance separating us, Professor Wiessner, Professor Makdisi, and Professor Pati you gave me clarifications and guidance that I needed. Without your great support and encouragement, I could not have been able to complete this book.

Professor Pati, I thank you deeply for your guidance, advice and feedback during the defence of my thesis. You are a model of how a professor should be. I would like to thank all of the panel members of the defence of my thesis; Professor Roza Pati (Chair), Professor Makdisi (the academic supervisor); and Professor Wiessner (the second evaluator). I am honored to have received a final grade of "high honors," *magna cum laude*. Thank you, I am grateful to you all!

I would like to thank each and every person that helped me in writing my book. I am grateful to all of the scholars that gave me the honor of conducting interviews with them. I thank everyone who gave me a book or an article or offered me guidance. I would like to thank my mangers at the Egyptian Public Prosecution and the Egyptian Ministry of Justice.

Lastly, my family:

I want to thank and dedicate this book to my late mother, Dr. Salwa, who has been my support, backbone and source of encouragement in completing this dissertation and throughout my Doctor of Juridical Science. Words fail to express how thankful I am to my mother. Mama, this goes to you.

To my father, Mohamed, and my sister, Dr. Yosra, your encouragement has kept me going and given me energy to complete this journey.

To the very special lady in my life, my wife Hagar, and to my daughter Talia and my son Ali, you have been very patient, understanding and supportive. You always make me happy. I love you and I cannot thank you enough.

Preface

This book by Ahmed El-Demery is a welcome addition to the literature on human rights in the Arab world.

The Arab world, like Africa, and before it Latin America and Europe, has seen the need over the last few decades to enhance regional human rights as a way of strengthening domestic human rights. The *European Convention on Human Rights and Fundamental Freedoms*, adopted in 1950, was the first document to have set the path towards the achievement of that goal. The establishment of a European Court of Human Rights produced effective results by enhancing human rights at the national and regional levels. Its counterpart in the Americas, though not as effective, nevertheless produced significant results. Africa and the Arab world are lagging behind. In 1970, the Arab League decided to establish a committee of experts to draft an Arab charter on human rights, but nothing came out of it for years. In 1985, I convened a high level committee of Arab Experts at the International Institute of Higher Studies in Criminal Sciences (ISISC) in Siracusa, Italy to draft an *Arab Charter of People's and Human Rights*. The highly dedicated expert group that produced the text deserves much credit, and the project was published by ISISC in 1986.[1] Thereafter ISISC formally submitted the text to the League of Arab States. Its secretary general, Dr. Esmat Abdel-Meguid, was instrumental in having the member-states agree to establish a committee of experts to review the text and eventually to have it adopted as an Arab regional instrument. It took many years for the Arab League's committee of experts to produce a text that was ultimately approved at a heads-of-state summit meeting in Tunis, Tunisia in 2005, where it was my privilege to be there as the official guest of the Tunisian government, the host country. There I saw the work that I started in 1985 come to fruition, even though it took 20 years to achieve that modest result. Even so, during the course of these 20 years a number of Arab states felt that the text was too progressive. They claimed that Islamic Law required less, and they proceeded to develop a more "conservative" text through a committee of experts, whose seat was in Jeddah, Saudi Arabia, they produced *The Cairo Declaration on Human Rights in Islam* (1990). That text was substantially less protective of human rights than that of the Arab Charter, which in turn was much less liberal than the European and the Inter-American Conventions.

One of the merits of Dr. Al-Demery's book is that in analyzing the Arab Charter it compares it with Islamic law, and more particularly with the *Shariᶜâ*, in order to show that the provisions contained in the Arab Charter, though drafted with

---

1 See International Institute of Higher Studies in Criminal Sciences (ISISC), http://www.isisc.org/dms/.

modern terminology, are in conformity with Islamic values and are not in violation of any of the norms of the *Sharīʿâ*. Thus the author not only contributes to the knowledge of human rights in the Arab world, but also links human rights in that part of the world with Islam and the *Sharīʿâ*. This in itself is a valuable contribution to human rights and to Islam. The author does not, however, address the contents of the OIC's Islamic Charter to compare the texts of both documents. That would have been an even more valuable contribution since the OIC's text is claimed by the more conservative Islamists to be more in conformity with Islamic law and the *Sharīʿâ* than the Arab Charter – I for one disagree with that conclusion.

The author of this book also addresses the enforcement of the Arab Charter. Initially those of us who drafted the draft *Arab Charter of People's and Human Rights* (1986) were hoping that there would be a Commission and a Court to enforce the provisions of the Charter, modeled after the European system, but that was not the case. Arab governments were satisfied with an instrument that did not have an enforcement mechanism. It took seven years since that Charter's adoption in Tunis for Bahrain, at the suggestion of this writer, to propose an initiative in the Committee of Ministers of Foreign Affairs of the League of Arab States to establish an "Arab Court of Human Rights" to enforce the provisions of the Arab Charter of Human Rights. The Kingdom of Bahrain deserves much credit for that initiative, particularly after King Hamad had taken the bold and courageous decision in 2011 to establish the Bahrain Independent Committee of Inquiry ("BICI"), which I had the honor of chairing.[2]

Within a short span of two years, a committee of experts was established under that chair of Professor Badria el-Awadi (Kuwait) who had also served on the BICI Commission. The text produced by the el-Awadi committee was completed at the beginning of 2014, but has not to date been formally adopted. The author of this book, to his credit, discusses this text and offers his own proposals for improvement in the hope that they may be taken into account before the text is submitted to the committee of experts once again and to the Committee of Ministers of Foreign Affairs (and also, as is expected, to the Committee of Ministers of Justice). This process is expected to take a few more years before one can hope to see a convention adopted and a court established. In the meantime, Bahrain has graciously offered to host the future Arab Court of Human Rights. But, in the interim, the proposed convention will have to be approved, by the league of Arab

---

2   See *Report of the Bahrain Independent Commission of Inquiry*, 23 November 2011, http://www.bici.org.bh/.

The Arab Charter on Human Rights: A Voice for Sharia in the Modern World

states, Arab states will have to join it, and their legislative bodies will have to ratify it and eventually adopt nationally implementing legislation.

The road to enforcing human rights in the Arab world is still a long one ahead, but as the Arabic proverb goes, "The longest journey starts with the first step."

At this historic stage of Arab transformation, what is more important than having another convention, is for Arab societies to make human rights part of their social values and the practice them. Accountability for human rights violations must be established and the judiciary must be more diligent in enforcing the rule of law.

Regrettably, governments fail to respect human rights in most Arab societies.[3] Nevertheless, the Arab peoples are keen on advancing the ideals of human rights, even though they have not yet incorporated them into their daily lives and into their individual and collective dealings with one another. Arab societies still have to learn that the road to democracy and social progress, as well as economic development, is through the respect for an observance of human rights. When the value of individual human dignity becomes paramount in Arab societies, these societies will progress.

Anyone following events in that part of the world during the last three years saw the "Arab Spring" turn into a bitter winter.[4] The latest and so far the worse conflict, in Syria, brought about, by July 2014, an estimated 200,000 persons killed in addition to an estimated 11,000 persons who were systematically tortured to death by the Assad regime.[5] Some three to four million persons have become refugees or internally displaced persons. Internationally prohibited weapons such as chemical weapons, barrel bombs, indiscriminate attacks upon civilian population, and the prevention of humanitarian relief remain common practice. These are not only violations of internationally protected human rights, they are also war crimes and crimes against humanity. Yet not a single international or regional organization is willing or capable to prevent this ongoing harm, let alone to hold its perpetrators accountable for such crimes. So much for Islamic values and

---

3 See for example in Egypt, M. Cherif Bassiouni, Chronicles of Egypt Revolution: Egypt Updates, at *http://mcherifbassiouni.com/egypt-updates/*.

4 Esam Al-Amin, *The Arab Awakening Unveiled: Understanding Transformations and Revolutions in the Middle East*, (American Educational Trust 2013) & Marc Lynch, *The Arab Uprising: The Unfinished Revolutions of the New Middle East*, (Public Affairs 2012). See also e.g. Eugene M. Fisher and M. Cherif Bassiouni, *Storm over the Arab World: A People in Revolution*, (Follett Publishing Company: Chicago 1972).

5 See Josh Rogin, *U.S.: Assad's 'Machinery of Death' Worst Since the Nazis*, The Daily Beast, 7 July 2014 (*http://www.thedailybeast.com/articles/2014/07/07/u-s-assad-s-machinery-of-death-worst-since-the-nazis.html*).

specific norms, that continue to be violated in the name of Islam by Muslim extremists and Muslim regimes.

The same tragedy has occurred in Iraq, and continues to unfold with new protagonists. Since Iraq was liberated by the "coalition of the willing" in 2003, an estimated 300,000 people have been killed in an internal conflict between *Sunni* and *Shīʿâ*, in the name of Islam. This resulted in the countless death of innocent civilians. In recent times, we have witnessed the emergence of the Islamic State of Iraq and Syria ("ISIS"), which has committed atrocities in both Syria and Iraq, also in the name of Islam.

These and other similar groups in the Arab world and elsewhere in the Muslim world, claim to act in the name of Islam, while at the same time committing violations of both the precepts and norms of Islam.[6] They indiscriminately kill civilians, prisoners, and children as well as indiscriminately attack civilian areas in violation of the specific norms of the *Sharīʿâ*.[7] They also claim some type of legitimacy arising out of their self-professed claims of being Muslim jihadists in total violation of what Islam dictates.[8] They act as if whatever ends they perceive to be legitimate justifies whatever means they engage in, no matter what the human rights violations may be.

Whether it is in Syria, Iraq, or to a much lesser extent in Yemen, Egypt, Tunisia, and Libya violent Islamist groups claim justification under Islam where none exists, while at the same time rejecting or ignoring the applicability of International Human Rights Law and International Humanitarian Law. The individuals that form these groups are a product of their environments and social experiences. What they have in common is a human development deficit, which is enhanced by misleading religious teachings. They come from or have lived in countries which they have been victimized by tyrannical regimes and exploited by corrupt ruling elites. The consequences of such environments, in which the powerless and oppressed have suffered for decades without a glimmer of hope that things might change, have certainly been a factor in breeding the violence we are witnessing. History teaches us that when human dignity and justice are trampled,

---

6   M. Cherif Bassiouni, *The Sharīʿâ and Islamic Criminal Justice in the Time of War and Peace.* (Cambridge University Press, 2014). See also Ahmed al-Dawoody, *The Islamic Law of War: Justifications and Regulations* (New York, USA: Palgrave, 2011).
7   Id.
8   M. Cherif Bassiouni, *Evolving Approches to Jihad: From Self-Defense to Revolutionary and Regime-Change Political Violence in Jihad: Challenges to International and Domestic Law*, co-edited with Amna Guellali (T.M.C. Asser Press 2010).

people rebel and they are likely to engage in indiscriminate violence when that is the only remaining alternative to what they experience.

Arab governments hardly address these human and social conditions, and hardly redress the inequities caused by their governments and the exploitation of their ruling elites. On occasion, they pay lip service to the postulates of human rights by ratifying international conventions, which are seldom enforced. But even these symbolic achievements are hard fought. Maybe the initiative of having an Arab Court of Human Rights will make a difference – and to that extent it deserves our support.

July 2014
M. Cherif Bassiouni

Emeritus Professor of Law, Depaul University;
President, International Institute of Advanced Studies in Criminal Sciences;
Honorary President, International Association of Penal Law
(*L'Association Internationale de Droit Penal*);
Former Visiting Professor of Criminal Law, The University of Cairo, Faculty of Law.

Ahmed Mohamed El Demery

Introduction

No one can deny that human rights are one of the significant achievements for the protection of human dignity. International human rights are the fundamental rights that empower human beings to shape their lives in accordance with liberty, equality, and respect for human dignity.[1] International human rights are the sum of civil, political, economic, social, cultural, and collective rights recognized by international law. Human rights are the achievements of natural law and positive law and include the powerful process of possible sanctions, under positive law, in case of violation.

Regional human rights systems are considered an important pillar for the safeguarding and protection of human rights internationally.[2] It is of significant importance to have regional human rights protection, as some countries may be unwilling or unable to protect human rights domestically.

The human rights situation in the Middle East is a very hot issue of debate. The United Nations and several specific countries criticize the human rights protection of people in Arab Countries. It was stated in one of the reports issued by the United Nations Development Program:

> Most Arab states have acceded to the major international charters pertaining to human rights which stipulate both the right to life and the right to freedom. Accession and ratification entail an obligation on the concerned Arab states to bring national legislation and practices in line with these conventions, an obligation that is however more honoured in the breach than the observance. At the regional level, the norms on human rights adopted by states and reflected in the Arab Charter on Human Rights (2004) are inconsistent with international standards. Indeed, the death penalty, which more than half the countries of the world have abolished and which the United Nations condemns, is applied liberally in several Arab countries, which do not limit it to the most serious crimes or exclude its imposition in cases of political crime.[3]

---

1   Manfred Nowak, Introduction To The International Human Rights Regime 1 (2003).
2   European Parliament Directorate-General For External Policies, Policy Department, The Role of Regional Human Rights Mechanism 1 (Nov. 2010), http://www.europarl.europa.eu/committees/de/droi/studiesdownload.html?languageDocument=EN&file=33385 (last visited May 27, 2012).
3   U.N. Development Programme, Regional Bureau for Arab States (RBAS), Challenges to Human Security in the Arab Countries, Arab Human Development Report 5 (2009), http://www.arab-hdr.org/contents/index.aspx?rid=5 (last visited May 26, 2012).

In the past years, human rights violations and abuses were common occurrences in the Middle East. Several Arab countries declared a state of emergency for many years to justify derogation of fundamental human rights principles. Torture, violence, and inhuman treatment were widespread throughout much of the Middle East.[4] On the other hand, many Arab and Western countries are criticizing the efforts of imposing a Western style of human rights on the Middle East. It was stated at the U.S. House of Representatives in the joint hearing before the Subcommittees on Europe and the Middle East and Human Rights and International Organizations of the Committee on Foreign Affairs:

> Over the years, government officials from the Middle East have suggested that given the profound differences in cultural and social norms and values, it would be unrealistic and inappropriate to impose western-style democracy in the Middle East. This may be true, but cultural and societal differences are no excuse for torture and repression. Many Middle Eastern countries have ratified key international human rights treaties, yet they have done little, if anything, to enforce them.[5]

An as example regarding women's rights, the kingdom of Saudi Arabia explained in one of its reports submitted to the United Nations that they are using a different perspective than that used by Western countries. It explained, "The Islamic Shariah respects these natural differences and accords woman a privileged position in order to achieve justice for her. For example, it charges the man with earning a living to provide for himself and his wife as compensation for the woman's role as conceiver, child bearer and mother."[6]

All of the previous points of views clearly show that there are different perspectives. I will give an in-depth explanation of the Arab system of human rights. My goal is to determine whether or not the Arab Charter on Human Rights is promoting human rights and how it can be promoted.

---

[4] Human Rights in the Middle East: Joint Hearing Before the Subcommittees on Europe and the Middle East and Human Rights and International Organizations of the Committee on Foreign Affairs, House Of Representatives, 102nd Cong., 2nd Sess. (Sept. 15, 1992) [hereinafter Human Rights in the Middle East].

[5] *Id.* at 1.

[6] U.N. Committee on the Elimination of All Forms of Discrimination against Women (CEDAW), Combined Initial and Second Periodic Reports of States Parties, Saudi Arabia,,U.N. Doc. CEDAW/C/SAU/2, at 11 (Mar. 29, 2007). http://www.unhcr.org/refworld/publisher,CEDAW,STATEPARTIESREP, SAU,467 bc0982,0.html (last visited May 1, 2012).

A. The Status of Human Rights in the Middle East

It has been stated that the Middle East and North Africa are considered fertile grounds for the infringements of human rights. In fact, there are several Middle Eastern countries currently seriously violating human rights.[7] A severe human rights situation exists in several countries parties to the League of Arab States. Several Arab countries used to rely on repression and inhuman treatment in order to maintain control over their nations.[8] Amnesty International's 2008 report regarding the state of the world's human rights states, "Indeed, it is only now, in the 60th anniversary year of the UDHR, that an Arab Charter on Human Rights is about to take effect. ... The international human rights system has been slow to develop in the Middle East and North Africa region for many and complex reasons."[9] For instance, in Iraq:

> Sectarian violence caused thousands of deaths, and gross mutilation and torture. Many Iraqis were forced to flee their homes – some 2 million refugees and a further 2.2 million internally displaced... More than 60,000 people were being detained without trial by the US-led Multinational Force and the Iraqi authorities; torture was common and used by Iraqi security forces with impunity; and those accused of attacks and killings were hauled before courts where they failed to get a fair trial, yet, increasingly, were sentenced to death.[10]

In Algeria, an attack by an armed group lead to the deaths of 130 people, including many civilians. With regards to the violence against women, the report explained that women remained in roles that were subordinate to men under family laws and other legislation in most of the region. In Egypt, it was reported that almost 250 women were killed by violent husbands or other family members in the first half of 2007. Thousands of people across the region were detained without trial for political reasons. In 2011, the Egyptian Ministry of Interior declared that there were no longer any administrative detainees in the prisons.[11]

---

7 Human Rights in the Middle East and North Africa, http://www.derechos.org/human-rights/mena/ (last visited Jan. 4, 2010); *see also* U.S. DEPARTMENT OF STATE: COUNTRY REPORT ON HUMAN RIGHTS PRACTICES (2007), http://www.state.gov/g/drl/rls/hrrpt/2007/ (last visited Jan. 4, 2010).

8 Human Rights in the Middle East, *supra* note 4.

9 AMNESTY INT'L, MIDDLE EAST AND NORTH AFRICA, HUMAN RIGHTS REPORT (2008), http://report2008.amnesty.org/eng/regions/middle-east-and-north-africa.html (last visited July 1, 2012).

10 *Id.*

11 AMNESTY INT'L, *supra* note 9. In 2008, the Egyptian Ministry of Interior stated that the number of detainees does not exceed one thousand. The Statement of the Assistant of Minister of Interior before the Human Rights Commission of the People's Assembly can be found at:

The 2007 Report on Human Rights Practices report by the US Department of State states that in Morocco "[t]he law does not prohibit arbitrary arrest or detention, and police use both practices."[12] The report also states that in Djibouti "[t]he law does not prohibit sexual harassment."[13] In 2012, in Egypt "[m]ore than 70 people have been killed in a Port Said stadium in the worst outbreak of football violence in Egyptian history."[14] In Egypt, the National Council of Human Rights states in its 2006/2007 report that complaints received by the Complaint Committee in the Council (in which citizens and different bodies asserted they have suffered from different sorts of infringements and violations of their rights) have increased by 25% in comparison with the year before.

In 2002, the concluding observation of the Human Rights Committee of the International Covenant on Civil and Political Rights (ICCPR) with respect to Egypt states, "the Committee notes that women are underrepresented in most areas of the public sector.... The Committee is disturbed by the fact that the state of emergency proclaimed by Egypt in 1981 is still in effect, meaning that the State party has been in a semi-permanent state of emergency ever since."[15] With respect to Lebanon, the Report of the Special Rapporteur on the human rights, which examines aspects of victims of human trafficking, especially cases involving women and children, states, "Discrimination must be regarded as one of the root causes of demand for trafficking. Many of the Special Rapporteur's interlocutors, including senior government officials, acknowledged that discriminatory attitudes on the basis of race, colour and ethnicity continue to be held by significant parts of Lebanese society."[16] With respect to Jordan, the Report of the Special

---

http://www.masrawy.com/News/Egypt/Politics/2008/June/1/inter.aspx (last visited Jan. 4, 2010).

12 US DEPARTMENT OF THE STATE, 2007 COUNTRY REPORT ON HUMAN RIGHTS PRACTICES MOROCCO (2007), http://www.state.gov/g/drl/rls/hrrpt/2007/100602.htm (last visited Jan. 4, 2010).

13 US DEPARTMENT OF THE STATE, 2007 COUNTRY REPORT ON HUMAN RIGHTS PRACTICES DJIBOUTI (2007), http://www.state.gov/g/drl/rls/hrrpt/2007/100478.htm (last visited Jan. 4, 2010).

14 Richard Spencer, *Egypt Football Riot: Dozens Killed in Egyptian Football Stadium Riot*, THE TELEGRAPH, (Feb. 2, 2012), http://www.telegraph.co.uk/news/worldnews/africaandindianocean/egypt/9055387/Egypt-football-riot-Dozens-killed-in-Egyptian-football-stadium-riot.html; *see also* Port Said Stadium disaster WIKIPEDIA.COM, http://en.wikipedia.org/wiki/Port_Said_Stadium_disaster (last visited May 1, 2012).

15 U.N. International Covenant on Civil and Political Rights, Concluding Observations of the Human Rights Committee: Egypt, U.N. Doc. CCPR/CO/76/EGY (Nov. 28, 2002), http://www.unhchr.ch/tbs/doc.nsf/(Symbol)/CCPR.CO.76.EGY.En?Opendocument (last visited Jan. 4, 2010).

16 U.N. Office of the High Commissioner for Human Rights, The Report of the Special Rapporteur on the human rights aspects of the victims of trafficking in persons, especially women and children, http://www.ohchr.org/EN/Issues/Trafficking/Pages/TraffickingIndex.aspx (last visited Jan. 4, 2010).

Rapporteur on torture and other cruel, inhuman or degrading treatment or punishment concludes "that the practice of torture persists in Jordan because of a lack of awareness of the problem, and because of institutionalized impunity."[17] The report that was issued by the United Nations Development Program on the Arab countries states:

> State constitutions do not adhere in several key respects to the international norms implicit in the charters to which Arab countries have acceded.... Arab countries' constitutions also routinely delegate the definition of rights to state regulation. In doing so, they allow freedoms and individual rights to be violated at the point when the latter are translated into ordinary law. While Arab laws and constitutions generally do not mandate discrimination between citizens on the basis of language, religion, doctrine, or confession, discrimination against women is quite evident on the law books of several states.[18]

A defect in the laws was highlighted in the concluding observation of the Human Rights Committee of the ICCPR with respect to Egypt; it was found that some articles of the Egyptian Penal Code include discrimination with respect to the unequal treatment of men and women with respect to issues of adultery.[19] In 2007, the concluding observation of the Human Rights Committee of the ICCPR with respect to Algeria stated that the state of emergency proclaimed in Algeria has been in place since 1992.[20] In 2006, the concluding observations of the Committee on the Elimination of Racial Discrimination with respect to Oman emphasized that "article 17 of the Basic Law of the State, on equality and non-discrimination, does not include 'race,' 'descent,' and 'national or ethnic origin' among the prohibited grounds of discrimination."[21]

---

17 U.N. Human Rights Council, Report of the Special Rapporteur on Torture and Other Cruel, Inhuman or Degrading Treatment or Punishment, Manfred Nowak: addendum: mission to Denmark, U.N. Doc. A/HRC/10/44/Add.2 (Feb. 18, 2009), http://www.unhcr.org/refworld/docid/49b794bb2.html (last visited Jan. 4, 2010).

18 ARAB HUMAN DEVELOPMENT REPORT, *supra* note 3, at 5.

19 U.N. International Covenant on Civil and Political Rights, Concluding Observations of the Human Rights Committee, *supra* note 15.

20 U.N. International Covenant on Civil and Political Rights, Concluding Observations of the Human Rights Committee on Algeria, U.N. Doc. CCPR/C/DZA/CO/3 (Dec. 12, 2007), http://daccess-dds-ny.un.org/doc/UNDOC/GEN/G07/457/74/PDF/G0745774.pdf?OpenElement (last visited Jan. 4, 2010).

21 U.N. Committee on the Elimination of Racial Discrimination (CERD), U.N. Committee on the Elimination of Racial Discrimination: Concluding Observations, Oman, U.N. Doc. CERD/C/OMN/CO/1 (Oct. 19, 2006), http://www.unhcr.org/refworld/docid/ 45c30bc70.html (last visited January 10, 2013).

Similarly, Human Rights Watch noted inadequacies in the justice system in Tunisia by stating, "[t]he Judiciary lacks independence. Prosecutors and judges usually turn a blind eye to torture allegation, even when the subject of formal complaint submitted by lawyers."[22] The 2007 concluding observations of the Human Rights Committee with respect to Libya explains, the "State party has not yet adopted legislation concerning the protection of women against violence, especially domestic violence."[23] The 2006 conclusions and recommendations of the UN Committee against Torture stated that in Qatar "there is a lack of comprehensive definition of torture in domestic law necessary to meet the requirements of article 1 of the Convention."[24] The 2002 conclusions and recommendations of the Committee against Torture with respect to Saudi Arabia provide that, "[w]hile noting the State party's indication that Shariah expressly prohibits torture and other cruel and inhuman treatment, the State party's domestic law itself does not explicitly reflect this prohibition, nor does it impose criminal sanctions."[25]

Human rights violations were noted in the Casablanca Declaration of the Arab Human Rights Movement (1999), which states:

> Despite the relative relaxation in the human rights situation in a number of Arab Countries, the general picture remains gloomy in comparison with the progress realized in other parts of the world. This is exacerbated by the failure of the League of Arab States to provide an effective regional conflict-resolution system and mechanisms for the protection of human rights in the Arab world.[26]

---

22 HUMAN RIGHTS WATCH, WORLD REPORT, TUNISIA (2008), http://hrw.org/englishwr2k8/docs/2008/01/31/tunisi17621.htm (last visited Jan. 4, 2010).

23 U.N. International Covenant on Civil and Political Rights, Concluding Observations of the Human Rights Committee on Libya, U.N. Doc. CCPR/C/DZA/CO/3 (Nov. 15, 2007), http://daccess-dds-ny.un.org/doc/UNDOC/GEN/G07/453/27/PDF/G0745327.pdf?OpenElement (last visited Jan. 12, 2013).

24 Convention against Torture and Other Cruel, Inhuman or Degrading Treatment or Punishment, Conclusions and recommendations of the Committee against Torture: Qatar, U.N. Doc. CAT/C/QAT/CO/1 (July 25, 2006), http://www.unhchr.ch/tbs/doc.nsf/898586b1dc7b4043c1256a450044f331/4b6bc620e633dfd1c12571ee00286e7f/$FILE/G0643239.pdf (last visited Jan. 4, 2013).

25 Convention against Torture and Other Cruel, Inhuman or Degrading Treatment or Punishment, Conclusions and recommendations of the Committee against Torture: Saudi Arabia, U.N. Doc. CAT/C/CR/28/5 (June 12, 2002), http://www.unhchr.ch/tbs/doc.nsf/(Symbol)/CAT.C.CR.28.5.En?Opendocument (last visited Jan. 4, 2010).

26 *The Casablanca Declaration of the Arab Human Rights Movement*, 17(3) N.Q.H.R. 363-369, (1999).

An Amnesty International report released in 2008 stated that the Universal Declaration of Human Rights was

> "depicted by many leaders as representing an attempt to impose 'Western' values in the aftermath of the Second World War. The UDHR's references to non-discrimination, for example, jarred with legal and customary systems in countries in the region, views on freedom of religion, and the different roles and positions of women and men."[27]

Also, some people may think that there is a hidden political agenda in the international human rights reports and some countries may use human rights as a way to interfere in the national affairs of other countries. The Egyptian National Council for Human Rights expressed this view in its 2007/2008 yearly report. It stated that some of the international reports (whether governmental or non-governmental) criticize the human rights situation in Egypt and that these reports use double standards and contain hidden political agendas. The report added that it seems necessary to examine these reports, as human rights are concerned with international as well as national affairs.[28] In addition, some Arab scholars doubt the attitude taken by some Western governments towards democracy and human rights in Muslim countries.[29]

B.   Research Problem

The idea of the protection of human rights knows no international boundaries. The international community has an obligation to ensure that governments guarantee and protect human rights wherever they are being violated. Therefore, international protection is an important final strategy for the protection of human rights. On the other hand, international protection is not always effective as countries may refrain from ratifying internationally binding treaties and protocols. Regional protection is more effective as it is supposed to balance international human rights and regional cultures and traditions.

The United Nations Charter and the Universal Declaration on Human Rights (UDHR) are considered important first steps towards the protection of human rights. There are three regional human rights systems: European, American, and African. The first-ever regional human rights system for the Middle Eastern

---

27 AMNESTY INT'L, MIDDLE EAST AND NORTH AFRICA, HUMAN RIGHTS REPORT, *supra* note 9.

28 THE YEARLY REPORT OF THE NATIONAL COUNCIL FOR HUMAN RIGHTS (2008), http://www.nchr.org.eg/popup_window.html?pdf_url=annual_pdf/07/report.pdf (last visited Jan. 4, 2010).

29 Azizah Al-Hibri, *ISLAM, LAW AND CUSTOM: REDEFINING MUSLIM WOMEN'S RIGHTS*, 12 AM. U. J. INT'L L. & POL'Y 4 (1997).

countries is the Arab Charter on Human Rights. The Charter entered into force in 2008. The Arab Charter on Human Rights is considered to be the only binding human rights instrument for many Arab countries that did not ratify other human rights treaties. Also, Arab countries consider the Charter to be the only human rights instrument that reflects and respects their own cultures and traditions. The Charter provides for the establishment of a committee that is responsible for examining reports submitted by states parties every three years. After examining these reports, the Committee includes its comments and recommendations in its annual report submitted to the Council of the League of the Arab States.

Although the Arab Charter on Human Rights is a late achievement in the realm of regional human rights systems, it has still made important progress that should be encouraged, implemented, and promoted in order to further develop an effective Arab regional human rights system for the Middle East. The Arab Charter on Human Rights strikes a balance between the protection of international human rights standards and respect for domestic cultures and traditions. Most of the Middle Eastern Arab cultures and traditions originated from Islamic Sharia.[30] Several Arab countries use Islamic Sharia law as a main component of the constitution. Therefore, Sharia law is not merely a religion to follow, but also a legal system to apply. The goal of the Arab Charter is to balance both respect of Sharia law and the implementation of international principles of human rights. However, the Charter still does not have an effective mechanism supervising the implementation of international human rights principles. This Charter should be implemented effectively and further developed in order to protect human rights in this region. It would be very useful to have effective supervisory bodies to oversee the implementation of the rights protected by the Charter. This supervisory body would be trusted more if its members would be expert nationals of the member countries of the League of Arab States.

C. Research Questions

Applying Sharia law as a main source of law may raise questions with respect to universalism and cultural relativism. Can we find common ground between Sharia law and international human rights standards? Is there a minimum universal core of human rights that is compatible with Sharia law? What should we consider to be the essence of Sharia law and where should we look for guidance with respect to the development of a new consensus between Sharia law and

---

30 As to the transliteration, Arabic words have certain transliteration rules. For instance, the correct transliteration of some Arabic words are Shari͑â, Qur'ân and Ijma͑. However, for ease of reading of the book I have not made the proper transliteration.

international human rights? Can we have a moderate Islamic human rights theory that is the common ground between Sharia principles and international principles on human rights?

These questions continue: Does the Charter not need further amendments? Or is it still in an embryonic stage that requires further solidification and greater coherence? How can it be made more effective? Does the Arab Charter allow for the amendment of its articles to enable the establishment of an Arab Court and to modify the structure and role played by the Committee? Does the Charter have rights that are in extreme contradiction with international human rights principles? Does the Charter include rights that are contrary to views associated with Western human rights? Does success of the Charter require the imitation of another regional system that already has proven itself as successful? Or can the Charter still be effective and successful while reflecting and respecting the national and regional cultures and traditions on the condition that they are not contrary to the international minimum standards of human rights? Does the Arab Charter already protect and promote human rights in the Arab region? If not, what can be done to promote and protect human rights through the Arab Charter? Does the Charter have an effective mechanism that can supervise the implementation of the rights protected by the Arab Charter? Is Sharia law the standard for the Arab Charter? Or is Sharia used to evaluate the rights outlined in the Arab Charter?

D. Research Methodology

The goal of this book is to find answers to all of the previous questions through a comparative study. Determining how best to improve the efficiency of the Arab Charter must be done through a comparative analysis between the Charter and other regional human rights systems. The European system is considered to have the best regional human rights mechanisms. While not considered the most effective, the African human rights system is still very important because some Arab countries are parties to both the African Charter and the Arab Charter. In addition, the African and the Arab systems have some cultures and traditions in common.

Due to the fact that many Arab countries apply Sharia law as a legal system, it will be necessary to explain the nature, source, goals, and purpose of Sharia law in a subsequent chapter. The chapter will examine the possibility of reconciliation between Sharia law and human rights. The chapter will outline interpretations of Islam that demonstrate alignment with the core of shared human rights principles. Through the use of evidence, I will show that there is no need to reject

Sharia law in order to secure human rights.³¹ This common ground between international human rights principles and Islam will establish the possibility for greater dialogue between the two. This idea is expressed by the Council of Europe in the conclusions adopted by the Interregional Meeting in advance of the World Conference on Human Rights: The Council stated:

> We must go back to listening. More thought and effort must be given to enriching the human rights discourse by explicit reference to other non-Western religions and cultural traditions. By tracing the linkages between constitutional values on the one hand and the concepts, ideas and institutions which are central to Islam or Hindu-Buddhist traditions or other traditions, the base of support for fundamental rights can be expanded and the claim to universality vindicated. The Western World has no monopoly or patent on basic human rights. We must embrace cultural diversity but not at the expense of universal minimum standards.³²

This discussion will draw from the decisions of different Arab domestic courts, but will focus particularly on cases from the Egyptian courts.

Recognizing that there are parts of the Charter that reflect the rights of the cultures and traditions of the Arab countries and seem to be in contradiction with international human rights principles, this book will provide suggestions and recommendations as to how the Arab Charter can be improved through amending articles and additional protocols. In its most recent report, Amnesty International states that "this Charter has positive features which enlarge on the rights enshrined in international human rights treaties, but it also has severely negative aspects – such as failing to outlaw the executing of children – that states could seek to use to undermine their obligations under binding global standards."³³ Weak points, such as these, need to be addressed.

---

31   KATERINA DALACOURA, ISLAM, LIBERALISM AND HUMAN RIGHTS 39 (3d ed. 2007).

32   Conclusions by the General Rapporteur, Mary Robinson, President of Ireland, *Human Rights at the Dawn of the 21st Century*, Council of Europe Doc. CE/CMDH (93), at 16 (January 1993) (citing World Conference on Human Rights, *Status of Preparation of Publications, Studies and Documents for the World Conference*, U.N. Doc. A/CONF.157/PC/62/Add.11/Rev.1 (Apr. 22, 1993), http://www.bayefsky.com/expertreport/expertreport_1993.pdf (last visited Jan. 16, 2010)).

33   AMNESTY INT'L, MIDDLE EAST AND NORTH AFRICA, HUMAN RIGHTS REPORT, *supra* note 9.

E. The Significance of the Study

This book seeks to achieve certain specific goals. First, through comparing Western and Arab societies, it will explain the primary concepts within Western society and Western views on human rights in such a way that they can be clearly understood by the Arab countries. At the same time, it will try to assist Western society in the development of a deeper understanding of the Arab view on human rights and Arab cultures, traditions, as well as religious beliefs related to human rights. Second, it will highlight the history of human rights violations in Arab states. In addition, it will clarify how the Arab Charter on Human Rights will help in rectifying the human rights situation in Arab countries. This will assist the League of Arab States in improving the effectiveness of the Charter, which can be particularly enabled through the enactment of the necessary amendments that it proposes upon a comparative study of other regional human rights systems.

Third, I hope to help the states parties of the League of Arab States understand the rights protected by the Arab Charter such that these rights can be applied on the national level in cases where they are matching Sharia law. In addition, this book will provide a detailed explanation of the different mechanisms for the supervision of the protection of human rights in order to help legislators issue additional optional protocols for the improvement of the Arab Charter. Both the comparative studies and the theoretical discussion will guide states parties to become more acquainted with the best procedures, rules, and theories relevant to the promotion and the protection of human rights. The theoretical discussion will help uncover the theory that best balances compliance with international human rights standards and respect to the Middle Eastern cultures and traditions. The discussion will focus not only on substantive rights, but also on procedural rules. The discussion of the procedures related to the other regional human rights treaties will contribute to ensuring the solidity and concreteness of the Arab Charter. This is because most countries in the world (both developed and developing) have ratified most of the international and regional human rights treaties. As a result, there are many treaties and many domestic laws guaranteeing human rights. However, there still are continuing human rights violations by countries that have ratified these treaties. This means that the treaties and how they deal with human rights are not the only, or even the primary, issue. Instead, the primary issue is the implementation of the rights enshrined within in these treaties, which can only be done through effective procedures. Indeed, the implementation is the heart and soul of the success of every treaty. In this way, it is also vitally important to focus on implementation.

Fourth, many people in the Middle East do not have full knowledge of their human rights. This book should help to expand the knowledge of the peoples living in the Middle East such that they have a better understanding of their rights and duties, as much it hopes to be a positive contribution to the literature on human rights and for professionals seeking to improve the Arab Charter on Human Rights.

F. The Need for a Regional Charter

There is a long-standing debate about the right of the international community to protect individuals of other states from human rights violations. In 1924, the Permanent Court of International Justice determined that "it is an elementary principle of international law that a State is entitled to protect its subjects, when injured by acts contrary to international law committed by another State."[34] The idea of protecting individual rights in international law began to develop more formally on August 8, 1945, with the Charter of the International Military Tribunal. The Charter of the International Military Tribunal established the Nuremberg Tribunal whereby individuals, not states, could be tried for:

> a. Crimes Against Peace: namely, planning, preparation, initiation, or waging of a war of aggression, or a war in violation of international treaties, agreements, or assurances, or participation in a common plan or conspiracy for the accomplishment of any of the foregoing;
>
> b. War Crimes: namely, violations of the laws or customs of war. Such violations shall include, but not be limited to, murder, ill-treatment or deportation to slave labor or for any other purpose of civilian population of or in occupied territory, murder or ill-treatment of prisoners of war or persons on the seas, killing of hostages, plunder of public or private property, wanton destruction of cities, towns or villages, or devastation not justified by military necessity;
>
> c. Crimes against humanity: namely, murder, extermination, enslavement, deportation, and other inhumane acts committed against any civilian population, before or during the war, or persecutions on political, racial or religious grounds in execution of or in connection with any crime within the jurisdiction of the Tribunal, whether or not in violation of the domestic law of the country where perpetrated.[35]

---

34 Mavrommatis Palestine Concession, 1924 P.C.I.J. (ser A) No. 2, at 12 (Aug. 30 1924).

35 International Committee of the Red Cross, *Agreement for the Prosecution and Punishment of the Major War Criminals of the European Axis, and Charter of the International Military Tribunal.* London, (Aug. 8 1945), http://www.icrc.org/ihl.nsf/WebART/350-530014?OpenDocument (last visited May 21, 2012).

In 1946, the judgment of the Nuremberg Tribunal confirmed the non-positivist norm that both individuals and states are subject to international law. The Nuremberg judgment states:

> It was submitted that international law is concerned with the actions of sovereign states, and provides no punishment for individuals; and further, that where the act in question is an act of state, those who carry it out are not personally responsible, but are protected by the doctrine of the sovereignty of the State. In the opinion of the Tribunal, both these submissions must be rejected. That international law imposes duties and liabilities upon individuals as well as upon states has long been recognized. In the recent case of Ex Parte Quirin (1942, 317 U.S. 1, 63 S.Ct. 2, 87 L.Ed. 3), before the Supreme Court of the United States, persons were charged during the war with landing in the United States for the purposes of spying and sabotage. The late Chief Justice Stone, speaking for the Court, said:
>
> "From the very beginning of its history this Court has applied the law of war as including that part of the law of nations which prescribes for the conduct of war the status, rights and duties of enemy nations as well as enemy individuals."
>
> He went on to give a list of cases tried by the Courts, where individual offenders were charged with offences against the law of nations, and particularly the laws of war. Many other authorities could be cited, but enough has been said to show that individuals can be punished for violations of international law. Crimes against international law are committed by men, not by abstract entities, and only by punishing individuals who commit such crimes can the provisions of international law be enforced.[36]

The Nuremberg Judgment clearly showed that human rights of individuals are protected under international law and that persons committing these violations are legally responsible under international law. The Charter of the United Nations also mentioned the same principle. The Charter states that the United Nations shall promote "universal respect for, and observance of, human rights and fundamental freedoms for all without distinction as to race, sex, language, or religion."[37]

---

36   The Nuremberg Trial, 1946, 6 F.R.D. 69, 110 (1946); *see also*, Judgment: The Law of the Charter, LAW.YALE.EDU, http://avalon.law.yale.edu/imt/judlawch.asp (last visited May 21, 2012).

37   United Nations, *Charter of the United Nations*, 1 UNTS XVI, art. 55 (c) (Oct. 24, 1945),

Article 1 of Rome Statue of the International Criminal Court mentions explicitly that the jurisdiction of the International Criminal Court extends over individuals as they are responsible under international law. It provides that,

> An International Criminal Court ('the Court') is hereby established. It shall be a permanent institution and shall have the power to exercise its jurisdiction over persons for the most serious crimes of international concern, as referred to in this Statute, and shall be complementary to national criminal jurisdictions. The jurisdiction and functioning of the Court shall be governed by the provisions of this Statute.[38]

The Crimes within the jurisdiction of the International Criminal Court are the most serious crimes. Article 5 of Rome statue provides that,

> 1. The jurisdiction of the Court shall be limited to the most serious crimes of concern to the international community as a whole. The Court has jurisdiction in accordance with this Statute with respect to the following crimes:
> (a) The crime of genocide;
> (b) Crimes against humanity;
> (c) War crimes;
> (d) The crime of aggression.[39]

The jurisdiction of the International Criminal Court clearly shows that individuals are currently subject to the international jurisdiction. "The development of a body of international criminal law which imposes responsibilities directly on individuals and punishes violations through international mechanisms is relatively recent."[40]

Cherif Bassiouni, listed twenty-five categories of international crimes, that is crimes which affect a significant international interest or consist of egregious conduct offending commonly shared values which involve more than the State where they are committed because of differences of nationality of victims or perpetrators or the means employed, or which concern a lesser protected interest which cannot be defended without international criminalization.[41]

---

http://www.un.org/en/documents/charter/index.shtml (last visited Feb. 2, 2013).

38 Article 5 of Rome Statue of the International Criminal Court (*opened for signature July. 17, 1998*) (*entered into force July. 1, 2002*), http://www.icc-cpi.int/NR/rdonlyres/ADD16852-AEE9-4757-ABE7-9CDC7CF02886/283503/RomeStatutEng1.pdf

39 Article 5 (1) of Rome Statue of the International Criminal Court.

40 ROBERT CRYER ET. AL., AN INTRODUCTION TO INTERNATIONAL CRIMINAL LAW AND PROCEDURE (2nd ed. 2010).

41 Id. (Citing. M. CHERIF BASSIOUNI (ED.), INTERNATIONAL CRIMINAL LAW, 3 (3RD ed. 2008)).

Professor William A. Schabas explained that the Rome Statute safeguards international human rights. He elaborates that,

> The Rome Statute provides for the creation of an international criminal court with power to try and punish for the most serious violations of human rights in cases when national justice systems fail at the task. It constitutes a benchmark in the progressive development of international human rights, whose beginning dates back more than sixty years, to the adoption on 10 December 1948 of the Universal Declaration of Human Rights by the third session of the United Nations General Assembly.[42]

Although it may seem that both the international criminal law and international protection of human rights are two branches of law independent of each other, there is a direct link between them. The international criminal law is based mainly on the criminalization of violations of fundamental human rights.[43] "The growth and expansion of international and national human rights protection have impacted ICL through the criminalization of violations of fundamental human rights, providing for victims' rights (including accountability) and by means of establishing standards of fairness and due process."[44]

The UDHR, which is not a binding instrument for states, was the first international declaration to deal with the issue of human rights. Since it is non-binding, the rights outlined in the Declaration are not enforceable. The ICCPR was very important for the ratifying countries because it is a binding instrument. The European Convention on Human Rights was similarly important for the protection of human rights in Europe because it, too, is a binding instrument.[45] On the other hand, some of the Arab countries have still not ratified many of the international treaties. The Committee of the United Nations Convention on Elimination of All Forms of Discrimination against Women mentioned:

> States' adherence to the nine major international human rights instruments enhances the enjoyment by women of their human rights and fundamental freedoms in all aspects of life. Therefore, the Committee encourages the Government of Saudi Arabia to consider ratifying the treaties to which it is not yet a party, namely, the International Cove-

---

42 WILLIAM A. SCHABAS, AN INTRODUCTION TO THE INTERNATIONAL CRIMINAL COURT, ix (4th ed. 2011).
43 M. CHERIF BASSIOUNI & KHALED M. AHMED, INTERNATIONAL AND REGIONAL INSTRUMENTS ON CRIMINAL JUSTICE, PART II, INTERNATIONAL CRIMES AND COOPERATION IN CRIMINAL MATTERS, 1 (2007).
44 M. CHERIF BASSIOUNI, INTRODUCTION TO INTERNATIONAL CRIMINAL LAW, cxxii (2nd ed. 2012).
45 MARK W. JANIS & RICHARD S. KAY, EUROPEAN HUMAN RIGHTS LAW 21 (1990).

nant on Civil and Political Rights, the International Covenant on Economic, Social and Cultural Rights, the International Convention on the Protection of the Rights of All Migrant Workers and Members of Their Families, the International Convention for the Protection of All Persons from Enforced Disappearance, and the Convention on the Rights of Persons with Disabilities.[46]

Even some of the Arab countries that have ratified the international treaties have put many reservations on the rights protected by these treaties. Therefore, it is better and more efficient to have an effective regional treaty that is ratified by the countries of the entire region.

G. Roadmap

Chapter 1 of this book focuses on broadly defining human rights. This chapter explains the meaning and origins of human rights and also briefly highlights sources and theories of human rights.

Chapter 2 of this book focuses on Sharia law. This chapter explains how understanding Sharia law is important to being able to understand the Arab Charter and the role it plays in interpreting the Charter. Nearly all member countries of the Arab League apply Sharia law as a foundational component of their constitution. As such, in my book I will focus on the explaining that the Sharia law (Islamic law) does not contradict the values of Western societies. It has also been also argued that Sharia law facilitates authoritarianism and opposes many human rights principles.[47] Similarly, it has been argued that democracy is contrary to Islam because democracy permits the adoption of laws that are incompatible with Islam.[48] On the other hand, many Muslim scholars demonstrate there is a direct link between Sharia law and human rights and that the misunderstanding of Islam (which prevents others from seeing this connection) is because of a lack of knowledge and the strong influence of the media.[49] This could also be due to

---

46   U.N. Committee the Elimination of All Forms of Discrimination against Women, Concluding Comments of the Committee on the Elimination of Discrimination against Women: Saudi Arabia, U.N. Doc. CEDAW/C/SAU/CO/2, at 9 (Apr. 8, 2008), http://www2.ohchr.org/english/bodies/cedaw/docs/CEDAW.C.SAU.CO.2_en.pdf (last visited March 10, 2012).

47   DANIEL E. PRICE, ISLAMIC POLITICAL CULTURE, DEMOCRACY, AND HUMAN RIGHTS: A COMPARATIVE STUDY xi (1st ed. 1999).

48   David F. Greenberg & Valerie West, *Siting the Death Penalty Internationally*, 33 LAW & SOC. INQUIRY 295 (2008).

49   El-Ghirani, *The Legal Concept of Human Rights in Islam*, http://www.theses.com/idx/scripts/it.asp?xml=F:\index\idx\docs\all\37\it00154142.htm&subfolder=/search (last visited Jan. 4, 2010); *See also Advice from a Muslim: Don't stereotype Muslims as bombers, billionaires or belly*

acts of Islamic extremists that misrepresent the religion, which results in a misunderstanding of Islam by the West. For instance, if a terrorist who is a Muslim becomes a suicide bomber and kills innocent civilians, Western society may believe that Islam has encouraged Muslims to commit such an act. However, according to Islamic Sharia, this act is entirely forbidden and against Sharia law. This chapter, which focuses entirely on Sharia law, will speak to all of these issues by highlighting the pillars of Islam and the principles, objective, and purpose of Sharia law. This chapter also explains the origins of Sharia law and outlines what is considered against the public order of Sharia law. The Arab Charter on Human Rights strikes a balance between the protection of international human rights standards and respect for domestic cultures and traditions.

Chapter 3 shows how Sharia law fits with my own theory of human rights. Furthermore, this chapter explains different theories of human rights, such as moderate cultural relativism, universalism, strict cultural relativism, and reverse moderate relativism. These human rights theories will, in an important way, help in explaining the need for human rights. I am here suggesting a new theory of human rights that justifies the evaluation process used in my dissertation. In addition, this chapter mentions the possibilities of reconciliation between international human rights and Islamic law.

Chapter 4 outlines the Arab Charter on Human Rights. The chapter explains the history of the Arab League and the background, philosophy, and scope of the Arab Charter. Furthermore, this chapter details the rights protected by, and the supervisory mechanism within, the Arab Charter. In addition, I refer to an interview that I conducted with Dr. Nabil El Araby, the Secretary General of the Arab League and I mention his opinion regarding several important topics.

Chapter 5 offers an evaluation of substantive human rights protections in the Arab Charter. In addition, this chapter outlines a comparison between the Arab Charter on Human Rights and other international and regional instruments. It examines the rights incorporated in the Arab Charter through a comparative lens (by contrasting it with international and regional human rights instruments). Specific rights from the Arab Charter (such as the right to life, the right to not be tortured, equality between men and women, freedom of religion, prohibition of slavery, and freedom of movement) are reviewed and evaluated to determine whether they do, or do not, promote human rights. This chapter analyzes various

---

dancers, http://www.news.cornell.edu/stories/Feb06/bajwa.cover.cp.html (last visited Feb, 3, 2013).

problematic substantive human rights guarantees whereby Arab concepts may seem to collide with 'universal' concepts.

Chapter 6 offers an evaluation of the procedural human rights protections outlined by the Arab Human Rights Committee. I will explain the duties of the existing Committee. I will highlight the work being done by the Arab Committee. I will briefly highlight the Jordanian and the Algerian reports that were submitted by the governments of Jordan and Algeria to the Arab Committee on Human Rights. I will also state the conclusions and recommendations of the Committee with respect to the report of Jordan.

In Chapter 7, I will explain and suggest what can be done to improve the work of the Committee to make it more effective and efficient. For instance, I will suggest that the Committee should have a method through which to receive complaints from states and individuals. This is a very important chapter, as it will focus on procedural aspects. It compares the existing mechanisms of the Arab Charter's Committee with the Committee of African Charter on Human and Peoples' Rights. This comparison extends to the jurisdiction and jurisprudence. I will also propose a protocol that includes all of my recommendation for establishing an Arab Committee on Human Rights.

Chapter 8 offers an evaluation of the procedural human rights protections in the Arab Charter through an Arab Court on Human Rights. The existing Arab Charter does not have such a Court, nor did it outline the establishment of one. I will suggest a proposal for an optional protocol to establish an Arab Court. This chapter is an important evaluation of the Charter and it suggests the considerable value of an Arab Court. I will suggest the ways in which the court judges should be chosen and will outline the immunities they could be given. I will also propose a protocol that includes all of my recommendation for establishing an Arab Court on Human Rights. My suggestions and proposals will be based on a comparative analysis with the European Court of Human Rights.

Chapter 1: The Sources and Methods of Application of Human Rights

A. Definition of Human Rights

Over the last three decades the revolutions that have taken place around the world have led to an increased understanding of the importance for the protection of human rights. Human rights have become the globally established framework of values, whereby democracy within any country is assessed on the extent to which these rights are protected. While human rights do not provide universally applicable ready-made solutions, they do, however, outline the minimum requirements and regulations for human relations.[50]

Under the international human rights framework, "all human beings have them simply because they are human."[51] These rights, which are primarily moral rights, focus mainly on preserving the life and dignity of all human beings, which means ensuring that all humans are allowed access to a minimum amount of food and accommodation; have access to education, economic, social and cultural rights; and are not tortured.[52] Hence, international human rights are the basic minimum rights required for human beings to live freely, as equals, and with respect to their dignity. Human rights are comprised of the political, economic, social, cultural and collective rights to which human beings are universally entitled.[53]

A "right" could refer to the liberties or freedoms to which a person and other fellow human beings have access. A "right" may refer to being entitled to be fed if you are hungry and cannot pay for or get food. Members of society arguably have the responsibility to help those in need. The focus is on the relationship between the right holder and the duty bearer.[54] Rights place right holders and duty bearers in a relationship that is largely under the control of the right holders, who may ordinarily exercise their rights as they see fit.[55]

The international human rights system witnessed its major launch with the establishment of the international organization, the United Nations, which gathers all of the countries of the world. Through the United Nations, all of the countries in the world, along with governmental and nongovernmental organizations, started to play an important role on the international human rights

---

50 Nowak, *supra* note 1.
51 Jack Donnelly, International Human Rights 18 (1998).
52 Nowak, *supra* note 1.
53 *Id.*
54 Donnelly, *supra* note 51, at 21.
55 *Id.*

scene.[56] The combined ideas of protecting human rights irrespective of international boundaries and that nations had an obligation to ensure governments protected and endorsed these rights wherever they were viewed as being violated has both intrigued humankind and have been cause for debate.[57]

The traditional concept of international law refers to the legal relationships between countries. According to it, individuals were not given legal rights and are not protected by international law if their moral, or natural, rights were violated. In other words, countries did not have any international legal obligations to people. In addition, according to the traditional concept of international law, stateless people are not protected against any rights abuses committed against them.[58] With time, amendments were made to the traditional theory of international law. For instance, humanitarian law gave the right of access to humanitarian protection to all people.[59]

Also, this traditional theory was expanded by the ratification and accession of treaties, according to which states parties were obliged to fulfill the obligations listed within these treaties. The sovereignty of states is not absolute, as it is limited by treaties. Each state is obliged to implement the treaties that it has ratified. If treaties protected by certain human rights norms and principles are ratified without reservations by many states and ensuing state practice is coupled with *opinio juris*, these rights become customary international law.[60] I agree with Jerome J. Shestak,[61] who states, "While the modern human rights theories have been articulated largely by Western philosophers, the moral concepts are not exclusively Western … It is significant that the key human rights instruments starting with the Universal Declaration of Human Rights were drafted by Western States alone."[62]

Although I am in full agreement with this quote, I would add that non-Western countries should not be bound by each and every norm and principle that is stated in the treaties drafted by Western countries alone, such as the European Convention on Human Rights. It is unwise to criticize countries that do not agree

---

56 THOMAS BUERGENTHAL & JANUSZ SYMONIDES, HUMAN RIGHTS CONCEPT AND STANDARDS 4 (2000).
57 Id.
58 Id. at 5.
59 Id. at 6.
60 Id.
61 Jerome J. Shestack is the Chairman of the International League for Human Rights, the former United States Ambassador to the United Nations Commission on Human Rights, and a former member of the Executive Committee of the American Society of International Law.
62 BUERGENTHAL & SYMONIDES, *supra* note 56, at 32.

with each and every rule included in the regional treaties that are drafted and ratified by both Western and non-Western countries. On the other hand, it is very wise to consider the international treaties that are drafted and ratified by countries from different regions all over the world as an international principle or standard through which we can judge other regional treaties. Also, it is unfair to bind Western or non-Western countries to new interpretations of certain articles without obtaining wide acceptance on these new interpretations. For instance, the right of homosexuals to marry is not declared as such by the Universal Declaration of Human Rights or the ICCPR. The European Court of Human Rights did not protect this right for years until a new interpretation of the European Convention was made on the basis of a right to private life, which arguably gave individuals this right. This new interpretation did not originate from, nor was it accepted by, many countries around the world. Therefore, it is not wise to criticize or force all countries to accept this new interpretation of the European Court of Human Rights.

It is very important to define "human rights." Understanding human rights will undoubtedly assist in the development of an understanding of the rights that can, or cannot be, derogated. Also, it will help to know which of these rights should be given highest priority.[63]

---

63 Such a hierarchy may be seen in the establishment of certain non-derogable rights. Derogation means removing and limiting the implementation of certain rights. For example article 4 (1) of the International Covenant on Civil and Political Rights allows derogation in time of public emergency. Article 4 (1) states that "in time of public emergency which threatens the life of the nation and the existence of which is officially proclaimed, the States Parties to the present Covenant may take measures derogating from their obligations under the present Covenant to the extent strictly required by the exigencies of the situation, provided that such measures are not inconsistent with their other obligations under international law and do not involve discrimination solely on the ground of race, colour, sex, language, religion or social origin." On the other hand, derogation is not absolute; there is framework for it. Article 4 (2) of the ICCPR limits the application of derogation to specific rights; for instance, derogation is prohibited in relation to the right to life and the prohibition of slavery. *See* International Covenant on Civil and Political Rights, G.A. Res. 2200A (XXI), U.N. Doc. A/6316 (*opened for signature* Dec. 16, 1966) (*entered into force* Mar. 23, 1976), http://www.ohchr.org/EN/ProfessionalInterest/Pages/CCPR.aspx (last visited Aug. 9, 2013) [hereinafter ICCPR].

B. Theories of Human Rights

Human rights were defined and put in place not to only guarantee that which humans need for survival, but to guarantee that humans can lead a life of dignity. Human rights, which are derived from human nature, are based mainly on the moral position of human possibility.[64] The development of an understanding of human rights comes from different sources, such as natural law, religion, etc.[65] In addition, there are human rights theories that are based on natural rights, for instance theories based on equality, dignity, and justice. Human rights are justified by different rationales. Opinions differ about the bodies legislating and requiring the adoption of human rights, but nonetheless there is unanimous international agreement regarding the existence of these rights.[66]

C. Sources of Human Rights

The United Nations Charter established the International Court of Justice in 1946. It is considered to be the main judicial body of the United Nations. Article 38 of the Rome Statute of the Court states:

> 1. The Court, whose function is to decide in accordance with international law such disputes as are submitted to it, shall apply:
> a) international conventions, whether general or particular, establishing rules expressly recognized by the contesting states;
> b) international custom, as evidence of a general practice accepted as law;
> c) the general principles of law recognized by civilized nations;

---

64 *Id.* at 22.
65 *See* Roger P. Alford, *In Search of a Theory for Constitutional Comparativism*, 52 UCLA L. REV. 639 (2005). The author defines natural law as the "certain principles of right and justice which are entitled to prevail of their own intrinsic excellence, altogether regardless of the attitude of those who wield the physical resources of the community. . . . They are external to all will as such and interpenetrate all reason as such. They are eternal and immutable. In relation to such principles, human laws are . . . merely a record or transcript, and their enactment an act not of will or power but one of discovery and declaration." Edwin S. Corwin, *The Higher Law Background of American Constitutional Law* HARVARD LAW REV. 42 149, 152-153 (1928). *See also* Robert P. George, *Natural Law, The Constitution, and the Theory and Practice of Judicial Review*, 69 FORDHAM L. REV. 2269, 2268 (2001). The author states that natural law generally refers to a "higher" law accessible by human reason. *See also*, Jens C. Dammann, *The Role of Comparative Law in Statutory and Constitutional Interpretation*, 14 ST. THOMAS L. REV. 513, 526 (2002). The author clarifies that natural law represents an "absolute standard of justice." Robert P. George *Colloquium Natural Law: Colloquium Natural Law, the Constitution, and the Theory and Practice of Judicial Review*, 69 FORDHAM L. REV. 2269 (2001).
66 DONNELLY, *supra* note 51, at 24.

d) subject to the provisions of Article 59, judicial decisions and the teachings of the most highly qualified publicists of the various nations, as subsidiary means for the determination of rules of law.
2. This provision shall not prejudice the power of the Court to decide a case ex aequo et bono, if the parties agree thereto.[67]

It is worth noting that Paragraph 1 of the Article does not construct a hierarchy of sources. While being exercised, the court may be required to take the order in which the sources are written into consideration. For instance, the first source is of major importance because it refers to a legal international obligation. The second is also important because customary law refers to international consensus on a certain matter.[68]

1. Treaties

Treaties are the main major source of international law. Treaties emerge from agreements to create legal obligation between two or more countries. The parties of a treaty can be countries and/or international organizations.[69] The definition of a treaty was stated by the Vienna Convention on the Law of Treaties as follows: "'treaty' means an international agreement concluded between states in written form and governed by international law, whether embodied in a single instrument or in two or more related instruments and whatever its particular designation."[70] Countries parties to a treaty are required to fulfill their obligations under the treaty. The advisory opinion of January 21, 1925 of the Permanent Court of International Justice stated that "a principle which is self-evident, according to which a State which has contracted a valid international obligation is bound to make in its legislation such modifications as may be necessary to ensure the fulfillment of the obligation undertaken."[71] From the moment of ratifying or acceding a treaty, states parties are obliged to fulfill their international obligations in that treaty. The parties of the treaty are the states that ratified or acceded the treaty.[72]

67　United Nations, *Statute of the International Court of Justice*, art. 38 (April 18, 1946), http://www.unhcr.org/refworld/docid/3deb4b9c0.html (last visited Feb. 2, 2010).

68　IAN BROWNLIE, LAW AND CIVIL WAR IN MODERN WORLD 5 (1974).

69　NIHAL JAYAWICKRAMA, THE JUDICIAL APPLICATION OF HUMAN RIGHTS LAW NATIONAL, REGIONAL AND INTERNATIONAL JURISPRUDENCE 5 (2002).

70　United Nations, *Vienna Convention on the Law of Treaties*, U.N. Treaty Series, vol. 1155, art. 2 (1-A) (May 23, 1969), http://www.unhcr.org/refworld/docid/3ae6b3a10.html (last visited Feb. 2, 2010).

71　A. H. ROBERTSON, HUMAN RIGHTS IN NATIONAL AND INTERNATIONAL LAW 12 (1968).

72　DONNELLY, *supra* note 51, at 8.

Although treaties are legally binding for states parties, widespread ratification of a treaty and the acceptance of its rules as legally binding can lead to the creation of customary international law. States that do not wish to comply with all the rules of treaties at hand may accept the provisions of a multilateral convention as representing general international law.[73] If a certain right is protected in several treaties, and it reflects state practice and is backed by *opinio juris*, it can be considered customary international law. The court can apply and implement this right even against countries that are not party to the treaties that protected this right provided that they are not persistent objectors to this right under international law[74]

2. Jus Cogens

There are some rights that are considered to be supreme and cannot be violated. A treaty will be considered null and void if it violated a peremptory norm (*jus cogens*).[75] Article 53 of the Vienna Convention on the Law of Treaties states, "A treaty is void if, at the time of its conclusion, it conflicts with a peremptory norm of general international law."[76] Also, the Vienna Convention on the Law of Treaties defined the meaning of peremptory norm by stating that "a peremptory norm of general international law is a norm accepted and recognized by the international community of States as a whole as a norm from which no derogation is permitted and which can be modified only by a subsequent norm of general international law having the same character."[77] The Special Rapporteur of the United Nations International Law Commission Gerald Fitzmaurice explained the difference in meaning between ordinary rules and a peremptory norm. He stated:

> The rules of international law in this context fall broadly into two classes-those which are mandatory and imperative in all circumstances (jus cogens) and those (jus dispositivum) which merely furnish a rule for the application in the absence of any other agreed regime or, more correctly, those the variation or modification of which under an agreed regime is permissible, provided the position and rights of third States not affected.[78]

---

73 BROWNLIE, *supra* note 68, at 13.
74 *Id.* at 14.
75 JAYAWICKRAMA, *supra* note 69, at 5-6.
76 United Nations, *Vienna Convention on the Law of Treaties*, *supra* note 70, at art. 53.
77 *Id.*
78 Sir Gerald Fitzmaurice, *Third Report on the Law of Treaties*, YBILC, vol II, at 40 (1958).

3. Customary International Law

A law that has emerged from practiced customs, traditions, or cultures is called customary law. In addition, if a general practice implemented by countries is believed to be obligatory, it then becomes an international custom.[79] There are specific conditions that must be fulfilled before a norm of behavior becomes a rule of customary international law. According to the Special Rapporteur of the ILC, the following requirements of the law must be fulfilled:

> "(1) A concordant practice by a number of states with reference to a type of situation falling within the domain of international relations, (2) a continuation or repetition of practice over a considerable period of time, (3) a conception that the practice is required by, or consistent with, prevailing international law, and (4) a general acquiescence in the practice by other states."[80]

The sources of the customs are many and the value of each of these sources is different and depends on their circumstances.[81]

The rules of *jus cogens* are implemented regardless of the will of the concerned states. Therefore, *jus cogens*, or peremptory norms, prevail over treaties. In other words, the rights that are considered jus cogens started as customary law and were promoted to a higher level until they reached the level of *jus cogens*.[82]

Regarding the prohibition of torture, the International Criminal Tribunal for the former Yugoslavia stated that "a practically high status in the international normative system, a status similar to the principles such as those prohibiting genocide, slavery, racial discrimination, aggression, the acquisition of territory by force and the forcible suppression of the right of peoples to self determination."[83] The Inter-American Court affirmed, "The principle of equality before the law, equal protection before the law and nondiscrimination belongs to jus cogens, because the whole legal structure of national and international public order rests on it."[84]

---

79 Jayawickrama, *supra* note 69, at 6.
80 Mark Villiger, Customary International Law and Treaties, A Manual on the Theory and Practice of Interrelation of Sources 15 (2nd ed. 1997).
81 Brownlie, *supra* note 68, at 6.
82 Alexander Orakhelashvili, Peremptory Norms in International Law 8 (2006).
83 *Prosecutor vs. Anto Furundzija*, Case no IT-95-17/I-T, para 147 (December 10, 1998); *see also* Orakhelashvili, *supra* note 81, at 54.
84 *Advisory Opinion on Juridical Condition and Rights of the Undocumented Migrants*, OC-18/03, Inter-American Court of Human Rights (IACrtHR), para 101 (September 18, 2003), http://www.refworld.org/cgi-bin/texis/vtx/rwmain?page=country&category=&publisher=IACRTHR&type=&coi=MEX&rid=&docid=4f59d1352&skip=0 (last visited July 24, 2013);

Public order is one of the major issues that is taken into consideration in international and national law. Public order, which comes from either written or unwritten clauses, is crucial to every legal system. For example, in Germany no private transactions can be made if they violate good morals.[85] Also, according to the German law no foreign laws can be applied in Germany if they go against the good morals of the German law.[86] The English legal system applies similar principles to those used in Germany. Foreign transactions, even if they are valid outside the United Kingdom, cannot be implemented automatically in the United Kingdom unless they are not offending the morals of the United Kingdom.[87]

Public order and international law are directly connected. In other words, through private international law conventions, countries are permitted to make use of their public order clauses. If countries were not given this right, the ratification of conventions would be in danger. Conversely, the public order clauses can easily threaten the objectives and purposes of conventions. The public order clauses cease if their applications are in contradiction with the treaty obligation.[88] The Human Rights Committee stated:

> Accordingly, a State may not reserve the right to engage in slavery, to torture, to subject persons to cruel, inhuman or degrading treatment or punishment, to arbitrarily deprive persons of their lives, to arbitrarily arrest and detain persons, to deny freedom of thought, conscience and religion, to presume a person guilty unless he proves his innocence, to execute pregnant women or children, to permit the advocacy of national, racial or religious hatred, to deny to persons of marriageable age the right to marry, or to deny to minorities the right to enjoy their own culture, profess their own religion, or use their own language. And while reservations to particular clauses of Article 14 may be acceptable, a general reservation to the right to a fair trial would not be.[89]

---

see also ORAKHELASHVILI, *supra* note 82, at 54-55.
85 Bürgerliches Gesetzbuch [BGB] [Civil Code], Aug. 18, 1896, at art. 138.
86 ORAKHELASHVILI, *supra* note 82, at 12-13.
87 Id. at 13.
88 Id. at 25.
89 U.N. Human Rights Committee, General Comment 24 (52): Issues Relating to Reservations Made upon Ratification or Accession to the Covenant or the Optional Protocols Thereto, or in Relation to Declarations Under Article 41 of the Covenant, U.N. Doc. CCPR/C/21/Rev.1/Add.6, para. 8 (1994), http://www1.umn.edu/humanrts/gencomm/hrcom24.htm (last visited Feb. 16, 2010).

4. General Principles of Law

General principles of law include rather abstract principles or rules common to all major legal systems, including, e.g. the right to a fair trial and equality. For instance, according to this general principle of law, all parties of a case should be heard justly and fairly and compensation should be given to any injured victim.[90]

5. Judicial Decisions

Judicial decisions are not formal sources of international and human rights law, rather they are considered to be evidence of it. No one can deny that judicial decisions have major consequences on law, but they do not have the force of *stare decisis*, even if they emanate from the International Court of Justice.[91]

6. Other Possible Evidence of International Law, in Particular the Resolutions of International Conferences, the International Law Commission, the International Law Association and the UN General Assembly

The conclusions and the final reports of international conferences of states can be important evidence of rules of international law. If the results and conclusions of the international conferences are applied very widely, they may mature into customary international law on the concerned subject matters. On the other hand, the resolutions of the International Law Commission and the International Law Association, by themselves, can be seen as evidence of international law.[92] The reaching of a consensus with respect to these resolutions would reflect customary international law. The Resolutions of the United Nations General Assembly, on the other hand, by themselves, are non-binding for states parties. However, the wide acceptance, by a majority of votes, of these resolutions concerned with general principles and norms of international law can be evidence of the opinions of countries on this matter.[93]

---

90 JAYAWICKRAMA, *supra* note 69, at 66-67.
91 IAN BROWNLIE, PRINCIPLES OF PUBLIC INTERNATIONAL LAW 19 (2003).
92 AMERICAN LAW INSTITUTE, THIRD RESTATEMENT OF THE FOREIGN RELATIONS LAW OF THE UNITED STATES, § 103 Reporters' Notes No. 1 (1987); Wolfgang Graf Vitzthum, *Begriff, Geschichte und Quellen des Völkerrechts, in* VÖLKERRECHT (Wolfgang Graf Vitzthum ed., 3rd ed. 2004), at 72, para. 147.
93 BROWNLIE, *supra* note 91, at 15. *See also* the judgment in the case of *Nicaragua vs. United States* (Merits), ICJ Reports (1986), 98-104, paras. 187-95; 107-8, paras. 203-05.

D. International System for the Protection of Human Rights

1. Background and Evolution

Since the adoption of the Universal Declaration on Human Rights (UDHR) in 1948, human rights began to be protected by the international community. International human rights principles were adopted so as to encourage the international community to afford individuals minimum international legal protection through a floor of fundamental rights[94] below which countries should not go.

The adoption of the UDHR is considered to be a revolutionary step forward for the protection of human rights. Despite the fact that the UDHR was adopted as a declaration and not a binding charter or convention, it has become extensively agreed upon worldwide.[95] The Declaration "aims not merely to assure individuals their international rights, but it aims also to impose on all nations a standard of conduct towards all men, including their own nationals."[96] The UDHR is considered to be the first declaration adopted by universal international organizations that states and defines the basic fundamental individuals rights and principles.[97] International human rights law was established and evolved after World War II due to the extreme and severe human rights violations that occurred during World War II.[98] The international community insisted on establishing an international system for human rights protection in order to prevent any future such violation of human rights.[99] Starting from this point, the international community believed that human rights could not be considered a private domestic matter. After that, the protection of human rights was promoted with the adoption of the International Bill of Rights (the Universal Declaration of Human Rights, followed by the International Covenant on Civil and Political Rights (ICCPR) and the International Covenant on Economic, Social, and Cultural Rights (ICESCR)).[100] Both the ICCPR and the ICESCR are legally binding for States parties. Although the

---

94 George William Mugwanya, *Realizing Universal Human Rights Norms Through Regional Human Rights Mechanisms: Reinvigorating the African System*, 10 IND. J. GLOBAL LEGAL STUD. 35 (1999).
95 Thomas Buergenthal, *The Evolving International Human Rights System*, 100 AJIL 783 (2006).
96 *Id.* at 784 (citing Philip Marshall Brown, *The New York Session of the Institut de Droit International*, 24 AJIL 126, 127 (1930)).
97 *Id.*
98 *Id.* at 783.
99 Melissa Robbins, *Powerful States, Customary Law and the Erosion of Human Rights Through Regional Enforcement* 35 CAL. W. INT'L L.J. 275 (2005).
100 Mugwanya, *supra* note 94, at 35.

UDHR is not in itself binding, it is considered to be the initial spark in the field of human rights.[101]

2. Internationally and Regionally Dividing Supranational Human Rights Systems

a. The United Nations System

The United Nations Charter states that the United Nations shall promote "universal respect for, and observance of, human rights and fundamental freedoms for all without distinction as to race, sex, language, or religion."[102] With the launch of the Universal Declaration on Human Rights (UDHR), human rights developed from being a matter of domestic, often constitutional law, to becoming an international issue. The UDHR set and launched human rights standards at the level of international law. The General Assembly of the United Nations adopted the first international declaration, the Universal Declaration on Human Rights, which focuses entirely on the protection of human rights.[103]

The Universal Declaration of Human Rights provided further details regarding the minimum protection of human rights to protect human rights due to the fact that the United Nations Charter included somewhat ambiguous references to human rights. The preamble to the Charter of the United Nations states,

> "the peoples of the United Nations ... to reaffirm faith in fundamental human rights, in the dignity and worth of the human person, in the equal rights of men and women and of nations large and small...to employ international machinery for the promotion of the economic and social advancement of all peoples."[104]

Article 1 of the Charter explains, "The Purposes of the United Nations are: To achieve international co-operation in solving international problems of an economic, social, cultural, or humanitarian character, and in promoting and encouraging respect for human rights and for fundamental freedoms for all without distinction as to race, sex, language, or religion."[105] Article 1 of the Universal Declaration on Human Rights states, "All human beings are born free and equal in dignity and rights..."[106] As previously explained, while not a binding convention,

---

101 Janis & Kay, *supra* note 45, at 15. It does, however, in many articles, reflect customary international law.
102 United Nations, *Charter of the United Nations*, *supra* note 37.
103 Janis & Kay, *supra* note 45, at 15.
104 United Nations, *Charter of the United Nations*, *supra* note 37, preamble.
105 Robbins, *supra* note 99, at 279.
106 Universal Declaration of Human Rights, G.A. Res. 217A, art. 15, U.N. GAOR, 3d Sess., 1st plen.

the UDHR, in its key provisions, has risen to the level of customary international law.[107] The UDHR states, "All human beings are born free and equal in dignity and rights."[108] In addition, the UDHR includes a list of human rights that can be enjoyed by every person regardless of his or her sex, religion, race, nationality, etc.[109]

Supervisory bodies are needed to monitor the protection of rights listed in the treaties. There must be an effective supervisory body to guarantee the implementation of these rights. For instance, the Arab countries that have agreed to the Arab Charter on Human Rights have a supervisory body, the Arab Committee on Human Rights. This committee monitors the protection of human rights by receiving annual reports from states parties. Two bodies supervise the International Bill of Rights (which includes the ICCPR and the ICESCR). The Human Rights Committee (HRC) was adopted by Article 28 of the ICCPR to monitor the implementation of rights stated in the convention. Also, the ICESCR states that the Economic and Social Council is the main body responsible for supervising the implementation of the Covenant.[110]

Furthermore, various United Nations bodies successfully increased the protection and respect of human rights. For example, the United Nations established the Human Rights Committee in order to monitor respect for and application of the human rights articles listed in the ICCPR. The first Optional Protocol to the ICCPR provides that ratifying states parties "recognizes the competence of the Committee to receive and consider communications from individuals subject to its jurisdiction who claim to be victims of a violation by that State Party of any of the rights set forth in the Covenant. No communication shall be received by the Committee if it concerns a State Party to the Covenant which is not a Party to the present Protocol."[111] This Protocol gives access to individuals to submit complaints against any human rights violations. In addition, the United Nations established a Committee on Economic, Social, and Cultural Rights to monitor and guarantee the implementation of the rights listed in the ICESCR. Furthermore, the United Nations established the Committee on the Elimination of Discrimination Against Women. The duties of the Committee were to monitor the implemen-

---

mtg., U.N. Doc. A/810 (Dec. 10, 1948), http://www.un.org/en/documents/udhr/ (last visited Feb 2, 2013). [hereinafter UDHR].

107 Robbins, *supra* note 99, at 280-281.
108 UDHR, *supra* note 106, at art. 1.
109 Robbins, *supra* note 99, at 280-281.
110 *Id.* at 281.
111 U.N. General Assembly, *Optional Protocol to the International Covenant on Civil and Political Rights*, U. N. Treaty Series, vol. 999, art. 1 (Dec. 16, 1966), http://www.unhcr.org/refworld/docid/3ae6b3aa0.html (last visited Feb 2, 2013).

tation of the rights protected by the Convention on the Elimination of All Forms of Discrimination Against Women (CEDAW).[112]

To complement and reinforce the treaties, the United Nations bodies may also assign special rapporteurs to investigate the human rights infringements in certain regions or to supervise the protection of certain rights from violation.[113] Furthermore, the Human Rights Council examines and monitors the states' annual reports on the protection and implementation of human rights.

To ensure effective supervision of states there should be also another mechanism to ensure state compliance, other than the states reporting system, for example receiving, and reviewing, complaints directly from individuals. That being said, it is challenging to encourage all states to endorse treaties that include the right of individuals to submit complaints against their own states. The use of the principle of gradualism is important in any treaty. This step should be taken later in an amendment or in additional protocol in order not to discourage states from ratifying the convention at its inception. Over time, states will gain confidence in the treaty and will render their domestic laws and regulations in compliance with the rights protected in treaties they ratified. For instance, Australia ratified the ICCPR in 1980. Following that, it ratified Optional Protocol 1 to the ICCPR in 1991, which gives the right to individuals to submit complaints against states. France ratified the ICCPR in 1981 and then ratified the Optional Protocol in 1984. However, other countries ratified the ICCPR, but did not ratify the Optional Protocol, such as the United States of America[114] and Egypt.[115]

The issue about whether the international community has the right to protect individuals of other countries has been very controversial. The prevailing theory in international law during the 19th and early 20th centuries was that of legal positivism, which states that international law deals solely with states. A state only had the right to safeguard the rights of its own nationals against violations by other states.[116] Regional human rights treaties were formulated to supplement the United Nations treaties on human rights. Globally there have been four regional systems for human rights. The regional treaties that were signed are the

---

112 Mugwanya, *supra* note 94, at 36.
113 Robbins, *supra* note 99, at 283.
114 The USA ratified the ICCPR in September 1992.
115 Egypt ratified the ICCPR in April 1982. *See* http://treaties.un.org/Pages/ViewDetails.aspx?src=TREATY&mtdsg_no=IV-4&chapter=4&lang=en (last visited Feb. 2, 2013).
116 JANIS & KAY, *supra* note 45, at 9.

European, American, African, and Arabian Charters and Conventions. Asia is the largest remaining region that does not have a regional human rights charter.[117]

b. Regional Human Rights Systems

Regional human rights charters were established because countries in the same region share common challenges, cultures, and traditions. This takes into account the assumption that countries located geographically close to one another probably also have similar traditions and cultures. As a result, there are currently the European, African, Inter-American, and Arab systems on human rights. The regional charters require that each region have its own supervisory mechanisms and lists of rights, which are often also safeguarded globally through international organizations.[118]

The establishment of regional systems does include advantages that distinguish them from, and occasionally make them more successful in their application, than international systems. The effectiveness of regional systems stems from the fact that they attempt to apply and protect human rights at the grassroots. Thus, the regional systems provide the institutional and normative foundations, as well as tools, to achieve human rights goals. Regional systems are used as a subsidiary body for national systems that are unwilling or unable to protect and safeguard human rights of individuals. In addition, the majority of the regional systems have established human rights courts to safeguard human rights in their regions. The European system is the first regional system that established an effective court that is accessible to individuals. Following that, the Inter-American and the African systems established regional courts. On the other hand, there is no universal human rights court. Therefore, the regional human rights system plays a vitally significant role in protecting the rights of individuals against any human rights abuses by member states. One of the major achievements of the regional systems is that they complement the international human rights instruments. The success of the regional human rights systems comes from their ability to influence and stimulate the practice of human rights among the members that ratified their regional human rights charters and conventions.[119]

Regional systems can be more effective than universal systems because countries in the same region share common challenges, values, traditions, and cultures. In addition, one of the main advantages of regional systems is that they are flexible

---

117 Seth R. Harris, *Asian Human Rights: Forming a Regional Covenant*, 1 Asia-Pacific L. & Pol'y J. 17, 2 (2000).
118 Robbins, *supra* note 99, at 283.
119 Mugwanya, *supra* note 94, at 40–41.

enough to be amended more quickly than the global systems; in doing so, they are more able to face changes or challenges. One of the reasons of the effectiveness of regional systems is that, because change is proposed locally, it is less likely to be met with as much resistance as changes coming from the universal international system.

Universal human rights systems face a diversity of traditions and cultures that exist within the global system. As a result, the enactment of any rules is more complex. Conversely, countries that, because of their geographical and regional settings, share the same legal, socioeconomic, intellectual, political, and cultural values and objectives are very likely to enable effective human rights protection within their region. Furthermore, the large number of countries participating in the universal conventions makes it more difficult to effectively implement those treaties.[120]

Due to the lack of effective enforcement mechanism to force states to comply with universal human rights obligations, extra-, or para-legal methods, such as disgrace, pressure, and name and shame, are used against non-complying states. In addition, sanctions and other measures that can be taken to force recalcitrant states to comply with human rights obligations can be considered. These methods are probably more effective with respect to regional human rights, as countries in the same region share the same cultures and traditions and are fewer in number than the countries in global systems. This illustrates some of the advantages that enable regional systems to have a greater capacity to apply pressure and ensure the protection of human rights more successfully than the universal systems.[121]

3. Comparison Between Universal and Regional Human Rights Systems

There are people who oppose the idea of establishing regional human rights systems, as they believe that the establishment of international human rights law was put in place to ensure consistency in the understanding and protection of human rights worldwide. Hence, some believe that the presence of regional systems is contradictory to having universal human rights. To further elaborate, regional human rights law establishes segregating lines between nations and regions. The states and regions that have the power to lead the establishment of customary international law have the authority to outline and describe human rights. In this way, should the decentralization process of rights and laws continue

---

120 *Id.*
121 *Id.*

to develop on the existing trend, the rights that are deemed valuable and worthy of protection by the less influential countries of the developing world will most likely vanish from the universal human rights system.[122]

The existence of more than one human rights system globally gives rise to the possibility that one set of rules might take superiority over the other. For instance, if the Inter-American, European, and African human rights systems together became the main source of human rights, they might take superiority over the universal systems. Therefore, the global human rights system ought to be centralized through the umbrella of the United Nations.[123]

People who oppose the idea of having regional human rights systems believe that if the strength of the European human rights systems continues to increase, non-European and non-Western rights will no longer be viewed as part of human rights. The dominance of the Western states on the international legal discourse would allow them to develop the customary norms towards which the remainder of the world would need to orient itself. On the other hand, the human rights that are viewed by the non-Western world as important would cease being a part of the global human rights regime.[124]

Nonetheless, there are still people who believe that the presence of regional human rights systems is crucial as they cater more to the local traditions and challenges of their regions. As a result, the regional systems are likely to be more effective and fruitful as compared to global human rights systems. It cannot be denied that the inspiration of the substantive articles of the regional human rights treaties comes from the Universal Declaration of Human Rights, the International Bill of Rights (ICCPR and ICESCR) and different global human rights treaties. The basic values and laws of regional human rights treaties are inherently based on the global human rights regime.[125]

There are certain rights that are accepted and acknowledged universally by regional and universal treaties, such as those forming part of *jus cogens*. Both regional and universal systems include the prohibition of torture, the right to not be subject to slavery, and the right to fair trial. The rights that are globally agreed upon by all nations are seen as basic minimum human rights that must be protected universally — a floor below which no state should go.

---

122 Robbins, *supra* note 99, at 276.
123 *Id.* at 301.
124 *Id.* at 301-302.
125 Gabriel M. Wilner, *Status and Future of the Customary International Human Rights Law: Reflections on Regional Human Rights Law*, 25 Ga. J. Int'l & Comp. L. 407 (1996).

It is worth noting that there may be different interpretations of human rights that are accepted by the regional and worldwide systems. For instance, the right to a private life is a right that is universally protected. In some countries, the right to a private life is broad enough in its interpretation to allow for, and protect, homosexuality. Meanwhile, in the Arab world this is not an acceptable interpretation of the right to a private life. Hence, as a result of the varying interpretations, some nations have resorted to not ratifying conventions providing such broad interpretations. This could be the reason why countries located in the same regions have a preference for regional charters that are both in accordance with the global standards and conform to their religious and cultural values.

Countries in the same geographical region have common historical and cultural roots, traditions, legal and intellectual backgrounds, which ultimately result in each regional charter being different, or slightly different, from those belonging to other regions. Consider equality between men and women. Article 3 (3) of the Arab Charter on Human Rights states:

> "Men and women are equal in respect of human dignity, rights and obligations within the framework of the positive discrimination established in favour of women by the Islamic Shariah, other divine laws and by applicable laws and legal instruments. Accordingly, each State party pledges to take all the requisite measures to guarantee equal opportunities and effective equality between men and women in the enjoyment of all the rights set out in this Charter."[126]

Furthermore, article 20 (2) of the African Charter states, "Colonized or oppressed peoples shall have the right to free themselves from the bonds of domination by resorting to any means recognized by the international community."[127]

The challenges and objectives encountered among the regions will differ across the regions of the world. These challenges can be reflected in the regional charters. For example, the issue of illiteracy is a major challenge in the Arab region and Arab governments put a lot of money towards the eradication of illiteracy. In addition, they have to develop strategies to face this big challenge. This

---

126 Arab Charter on Human Rights, (*entered into force* March 15, 2008), see Annex, pp. 461 et seq., also *available at* http://www.lasportal.org/wps/wcm/connect/c93eba804a7 c700c8 ca19c 526 698d42c/ %D8% A7%D9%84%D9%85%D9%8A%D8%AB%D8%A7%D9%82+%D8%A7%D 9%86%D8%AC% D9%84%D9%8A%D8%B2%D9%8A.pdf?MOD=AJPERES (last visted Feb. 3, 2013). [hereinafter ACHR].

127 African [Banjul] Charter on Human and Peoples' Rights, OAU Doc. CAB/LEG/67/3 rev. 5, 21 I.L.M. 58 (1982), http://www.africa-union.org/root/au/Documents/Treaties/Text/Banjul%20-Charter.pdf [hereinafter African Charter].

challenge was demonstrated in the Arab Charter, which states: "The eradication of illiteracy is a binding obligation upon the State and everyone has the right to education."[128] Thus, the regional systems can perform a significant role in illustrating the challenges and realize the goals of the individual regions. Conversely, the universal systems will not be able to review and debate each and every issue that faces each region; rather global systems can only discuss the general issues that are encountered internationally. Hence, it is essential to have regional systems which are able to highlight problems encountered regionally and support the states involved in successfully resolving them.

In addition, my human rights approach, which will be explained later in greater detail, can be best reflected and implemented in the regional system. My proposed theory will fit well within the Arab regional system. The theory strikes a balance between global human rights standards and respecting cultures and traditions of the region. In order to understand the regional Arab human rights system, it is important to understand the main source of its legal context. Sharia law is the main source of legislation in most Arab countries. Therefore, it is important to know why the Arab Charter on Human Rights was written from this basis and how it can be evaluated from the Sharia point of view. Understanding the philosophy behind the articles of the Arab Charter cannot be achieved except by an understanding of the Sharia.

---

128   ACHR, *supra* note 126, at art. 41(1).

Chapter 2: Islamic Sharia Law as Key Legal Context of the Arab Charter

A. Introduction

Some legitimate questions must be answered. For example, why am I writing a full chapter on Sharia law? Why is the Sharia important for this book? Is there is a relationship between the Sharia and my new proposed theory for human rights? What is the object and purpose of Sharia? How is Sharia law in accordance with international documents on human rights? Can Sharia law be used as a standard to evaluate the Arab Charter or as a reason to explain why some of the articles of the Arab Charter were written the way they were?

It is important to know the origins of the legal systems of the states parties of the Arab League that adopted the Arab Charter. For instance, Article 7 of the Constitutional Law of the United Arab of Emirates,[129] Article 2 of the Arab Republic of Egypt,[130] Article 2 of the Bahrain Constitution,[131] Article 2 of the Kuwait Constitution[132], and the preamble of the Union of the Comoros[133] explicitly state that the Islamic Sharia is a principal source of legislation. In addition, most of the Arab countries make reservations and declarations to the United Nations treaties on human rights. These reservations emphasized the accordance of these treaties with Sharia law. For instance, many Arab countries have reservations with respect to Article 2 of the Convention on the Elimination of All Forms of Discrimination against Women (CEDAW). Bahrain voiced reservations regarding Article 2 "in order to ensure its implementation within the bounds of the provisions of the Islamic Shariah."[134] Egypt expressed reservations about Article 16 by stating that "concerning the equality of men and women in all matters relating to marriage and family relations during the marriage and upon its dissolution... The provi-

---

129 M. CHERIF BASSIOUNI, A COMPILATION OF ARAB CONSTITUTIONS, A COMPARATIVE STUDY OF INTERNATIONAL HUMAN RIGHTS STANDARDS (2005), http://www.law.depaul.edu/centers_institutes/ihrli/publications/iraqi_constitutions/index.html (last visited June 1, 2012).
130 *Id.*
131 *Id.*
132 *Id.*
133 *Id.*
134 United Nations Division for the Advancement of Women, Department of Economic and Social Affairs, Convention on the Elimination of All Forms of Discrimination against Women, Declarations, Reservations and Objections to CEDAW, http://www.un.org/womenwatch/daw/cedaw/reservations-country.htm (last visited Feb. 2, 2013).

sions of the Sharia lay down that the husband shall pay bridal money to the wife and maintain her fully and shall also make a payment to her upon divorce…"[135]

Therefore, Arab countries will not apply articles, laws, or treaties that are against the objectives and purposes of Sharia law. The Arab Charter is as a vital human rights instrument specifically for the Arab countries. The intent of the Charter is to reflect Arab cultures and traditions. Therefore, it is not expected that parties will have reservations regarding the extent to which Sharia law is included the Charter. It is important to understand Sharia law to be able to evaluate and interpret the articles of the Arab Charter. In addition, understanding the Sharia helps to enable an understanding of why the Arab Charter was written as it was. Therefore, Sharia is used to appraise and comprehend the Charter. Furthermore, having even a brief understanding of Sharia law clarifies how Sharia law is in accordance with universal documents on human rights. For example, Saudi Arabia stated in its report submitted to the CEDAW:

> Islam affirms many values which promote the family, which is not limited to husband and wife but extends to include children, siblings, parents and relatives. These values include filial piety, the bond of kinship and the raising of children. Women enjoy a more favourable share of these than men: the Islamic Sharia has more to say about the virtue of caring for daughters than for sons, a mother's right over her children is three times that of a father's and a woman's right to custody of her infant child takes precedence over a man's, in principle.[136]

There is a direct link between Sharia law and my new proposed theory of human rights, which I will explain in detail in the next chapter. Understanding Sharia law will definitely help in the evaluation of domestic laws and treaties. Through this understanding, we will also be able to determine whether or not the roots of domestic law are related to Sharia law. In other words, the Arab Charter can be used as a minimum standard to amend the laws that constitute extreme violations of human rights that are not related to the Sharia. Therefore, the Arab Charter can guide the countries parties to the Charter to promote and amend their laws.

---

135   *Id.*
136   U.N. Committee the Elimination of All Forms of Discrimination against Women, U.N. Committee on the Elimination of Discrimination against Women: Combined Initial and Second Periodic Reports of States Parties, Saudi Arabia, *supra* note 6.

B. The Foundations of Islamic Law

1. Definition of Sharia

Sharia is an Arabic word that means the right way to be followed. Literarily it means the "the way to a watering place,"[137] or "right path"[138] or the "path to be followed."[139] This path not only leads to Allah (God), but is also the path shown by him. Sharia is the way of Allah for the godliness of all mankind. It liberates people from servitude under anyone else other than Allah.[140]

Fiqh has a different meaning than Sharia. It is the understanding of Islamic law. Sharia law comes from Islamic law. The meaning of the word *Islamic* is the submission to the will of God. Sharia law is not just a legal system to be implemented, it is the legal system that is adopted and issued by God.[141] Sharia comes from the word Shra'a, which means sail. Sharia is the sail that guides Muslims to the correct path.

2. Islam: An Introduction to the Religion

It is important to clarify the difference between "Islam" and "Muslim." "Islam" is the religion of Muslims. "Muslim" is the name of the people who believe in Islam. The word Islam literally means "submission to the will of God."[142] The root of the word *Islam* comes from the word *slm* or *salam* which means peace.[143] It has been stated, "Islam is part of more than one billion people's lives. Its legacy spans more than fourteen centuries, and today Islam is the fastest growing religion on Earth."[144] Muslims believe that God is the only one who is incomparable.[145] The

---

137 ABDUR RAHMAN I. DOI, SHARIAH: THE ISLAMIC LAW, 3 (1984).
138 MASHOOD A. BADERIN, INTERNATIONAL HUMAN RIGHTS IN ISLAM 33 (2005).
139 Irshad Abdal-Haqq, Islamic Law: An Overview of its Origin and Elements, 7 J. ISLAMIC L. 7 (1996) (citing ABDUR RAHMAN I. DOL, SHAR'AH: THE ISLAMIC LAW 12 (1984)).
140 DOI, *supra* note 137.
141 Joëlle Entelis, *International Human Rights: Islam's Friend Or Foe?* 20 FDMILJ 1267 (1997); *see also* David A. Jordan, *The Dark Ages Of Islam: Ijtihad, Apostasy, And Human Rights In Contemporary Islamic Jurisprudence*, 9 WASH. & LEE RACE & ETHNIC ANC. L.J. 68 (spring 2003).
142 Entelis, *supra* note 141, at 1267.
143 Abdal-Haqq, *supra* note 139, at 15.
144 Hamid M. Khan, *Nothing Is Written: Fundamentalism, Revivalism, Reformism and the Fate of Islamic Law*, 24 MICH. J. INT'L L., 276 (2002); *see also Islam*, WIKIPEDIA.COM, http://en.wikipedia.org/wiki/Islam (last visited Oct. 31, 2011).
145 QURAN Chapter 112 "Say (O Muhammad): He is Allah, (the) One. Allah-us-Samad [Allah the Self-Sufficient Master, Whom all creatures need, (He neither eats nor drinks)]. He begets not, nor was He begotten. And there is none co-equal or comparable unto Him."; *see also* Quran 2:255 "Allah! La ilaha illa Huwa (none has the right to be worshipped but He), Al-Hayyul-Qayyum

purpose of existence of people on earth is to worship God.[146] However, this does not mean that the only duty of Muslims is to do religious worship. I will explain this issue later when discussing the pillars of Islam.

C. Sources of Islamic Law

There are primary and secondary sources of Islamic law. The primary sources of Islamic law are the Quran and the Sunnah. There is consensus between all Muslims Islamic scholars that the Quran and Sunnah are the primary sources of Islamic law.[147] There are just fewer than twenty additional secondary sources. There is consensus between all Muslims Islamic scholars regarding some, but not all, of these secondary sources.[148]

The Quran is the first primary source of Sharia law. The Sunnah is the second main source of Sharia law. Sunnah is the teaching and the sayings of Prophet Mohammed. There are additional sources (for instance, *Qiyas*, *Ijma*, and *Ijtihad*) in addition to these two main sources of Sharia law.[149]

The Quran is neither a legal code nor a treaty or a convention that provides a detailed explanation for everything. However, the Quran provides general guidance and principles for moral behavior.[150] On some matters, the Quran states detailed rules on legal issues, such as inheritance. On other matters, the Quran provides general principles, leaving the details to the legislator. For instance, the Quran provides general guidance[151] concerning trusteeship by stating the following general rule: "Verily! Allah commands that you should render back the trusts to those to whom they are due... "[152]

(the Ever Living, the One Who sustains and protects all that exists). Neither slumber nor sleep overtakes Him. To Him belongs whatever is in the heavens and whatever is on the earth. Who is he that can intercede with Him except with His Permission? He knows what happens to them (His creatures) in this world, and what will happen to them in the Hereafter. And they will never compass anything of His Knowledge except that which He wills. His Kursi extends over the heavens and the earth, and He feels no fatigue in guarding and preserving them. And He is the Most High, the Most Great." [This verse is called Ayat-ul-Kursi].

146 *Islam*, supra note 144.
147 Professor Saad Al-Din Helaly, *Magless el Fiqh* [Council of Fiqh] (Channel One, Dec. 4, 2012).
148 Id.
149 Entelis, *supra* note 141, at 1262.
150 Kimberly Younce Schooley, Cultural Sovereignty, Islam, And Human Rights--Toward A Communitarian Revision, 25 Cumb. L. Rev. 661 (1994-1995).
151 Entelis, *supra* note 141, at 1264-1265.
152 Quran 4:58.

The Sunnah is considered to be the second main source of Sharia. Sunnah means the spoken words, acted practices, and habits of Prophet Mohammed.[153] In the Quran, God said, "Nor does he speak of (his own) desire. It is only a Revelation revealed."[154]

Ijtihad is applied if the Quran and the Sunnah do not mention some issues or if they do not answer some questions.

1. Primary Sources

As indicated, the primary sources of Sharia law are the Quran and the Sunnah.

a. The Quran

The Quran is the first primary source of Sharia law and the last book of Allah.[155] The Quran is the words of God that were revealed to Prophet Mohammed.[156] The Quran guides followers towards the right path. In addition, the Quran mentions stories from the past, present, and the future, which include advice, lessons, and warnings of the Day of Judgments, on which day all people will be lead either to heaven or hell.[157] The Quran was not revealed all at once to Prophet Mohammed, but was done so gradually over a period of twenty-two years.[158]

The stories in the Quran give practical advice. The Quran explains, "We relate unto you (Muhammad) the best of stories through Our Revelations unto you, of this Qur'an. And before this (i.e. before the coming of Divine Revelation to you), you were among those who knew nothing about it (the Qur'an)."[159] Also, the Quran states,

> "Indeed in their stories, there is a lesson for men of understanding. It (the Qur'an) is not a forged statement but a confirmation of (Allah's existing Books) which were before it [i.e. the Taurat (Torah), the Injeel

---

153 Jordan, *supra* note 141, at 57.
154 QURAN 53:3-4.
155 Khan, *supra* note 144, at 286.
156 *The Quran: To Get to Know The Quran*, WHATISQURAN.COM, HTTP://WHATISQURAN.COM/THE-QURAN-WHAT-IS-THE-QURAN (last visited Oct. 4, 2011).
157 Khan, *supra* note 144, at 287.
158 Leila P. Sayeht & Adriaen M. Morse, Jr *Islam and the Treatment of Women: An Incomplete Understanding of Gradualism*, 30 TEX. INT'L L.J. 311 (1995), http://www.law-lib.utoronto.ca/Diana/fulltext/saye.htm (last visited Jan. 20, 2013).
159 QURAN 12:3

(Gospel), and other Scriptures of Allah] and a detailed explanation of everything and a guide and a Mercy for the people who believe."[160]

With respect to the Quran, Allah stated, "This is the Book (The Quran), whereof there is no doubt."[161] Also, God said, "Month of Ramadan in which was revealed The Quran, a guidance for mankind and clear proofs of guidance and the Criterion…"[162] The greatness of this book is demonstrated by it being from Allah, the creator of the universe. Therefore, it is impossible to find any mistakes or contradictions in the verses of the book.[163] God said, "Do they not then consider the Qur'an carefully? Had it been from other than Allah, they would surely have found therein many a contradiction."[164]

Muslims all over the world, whether they are Arab, African, Asian, American, or European, have only one book. There are not multiple editions of this book. This is what is special about the Quran. It cannot be falsified; no one can write a book and indicate that it is a different edition of the Quran.[165] This is because, in the Quran, God said, "Verily, We, it is We Who have sent down the Dhikr (i.e. the Qur'an) and surely, We will guard it (from corruption)."[166]

The reason for the Quran is explained in the Quran itself,[167] which states: "a Book which We have revealed to you that you may bring forth men, by their Lord's permission from utter darkness into light — to the way of the Mighty, the Praised One."[168] The Quran is divided into 114 chapters, which vary in length. It is explained:

> The Quran is a record of the exact words revealed by God through the Angel Gabriel to the Prophet Muhammad. It was memorized by Muhammad and then dictated to his Companions, and written down by scribes, who cross-checked it during his lifetime. Not one word of its 114 chapters, Suras, has been changed over the centuries, so that the

---

160 *Id.* at 12:111
161 *Id.* at 2:2
162 *Id.* at 2:185
163 *The Quran: To Get to Know The Quran, supra* note 156.
164 QURAN 4:82.
165 *The Quran: To Get to Know The Quran, supra* note 156.
166 QURAN 15:9.
167 *Allah & the Holy Qur'an*, AL-ISLAM.ORG, http://www.al-islam.org/allah/info/Quran.html (last visited September 26, 2011.
168 QURAN 14:1.

Quran is in every detail the unique and miraculous text which was revealed to Muhammad fourteen centuries ago.[169]

The Quran is the primary source for Sharia law. It not only regulates the relationship between God and people, but it also regulates all matters relating to human beings. For instance, the Quran explains the relationships between people with respect to human rights, morals, parents' rights, inheritance, orphans rights, right to fair trial, etc. In addition, the Quran warns human beings that the world will come to an end.[170] The Quran is not just a law or a treaty that lists a number of articles; it is a living instrument that provides guidelines for believers to follow.[171]

The Quran states that Muslims believe in previous books and prophets starting from Adam and ending with Mohammed.[172] In the Quran, God said, "The Messenger [Mohammed] believes in what has been sent down to him from his Lord, and (so do) the believers. Each one believes in Allah, His Angels, His Books, and His Messengers. (They say): We make no distinction between one another of His Messengers."[173]

The Quran effectively applies the principle of freedom of speech. For instance, it discusses what disbelievers say about the Quran in the following way:

> Those who disbelieve say: "This (the Qur'an) is nothing but a lie that he (Muhammad) has invented, and others have helped him at it. In fact they have produced an unjust wrong (thing) and a lie." And they say: "Tales of the ancients, which he has written down: and they are dictated to him morning and afternoon." Say: "It (this Qur'an) has been sent down by Him (Allah) (the Real Lord of the heavens and earth) Who knows the secret of the heavens and the earth. Truly, He is Oft-Forgiving, Most Merciful."[174]

The Egyptian former *Mufti* said that all those who are diligent to Islam have reached a conclusion that the Quran is the main source of legislation of Sharia.[175]

---

169 *Understanding Islam and Muslims*, ISLAMICITY.COM, http://www.islamicity.com/mosque/uiatm/un_islam.htm (last visited 5 Oct. 2011).
170 Khan, *supra* note 144, at 287-288.
171 *Interpreting Koran as the source of living fatwas*, http://www.thejakartapost.com/news/2010/08/03/interpreting-koran-source-living-fatwas.html (last visited Feb. 3 2013).
172 *Id.*
173 QURAN 2:285.
174 *Id.* at 25:4-6.
175 *The Egyptian Mufti Aly Gomaa, Civilized Rooting of Islamic Legislation*, ALMASRYALYOUM.COM, http://www.almasry-alyoum.com/article2.aspx?ArticleID=321839&IssueID=2357 (last visited

The Quran states, "This is the Book (the Qur'an), whereof there is no doubt, a guidance to those who are Al-Muttaqun [the pious believers of Islamic Monotheism who fear Allah much (abstain from all kinds of sins and evil deeds which He has forbidden) and love Allah much (perform all kinds of good deeds which He has ordained)]."[176]

b. The Sunnah of the Prophet

The Sunnah is the secondary primary source of Sharia. It is the way the Prophet lived and practiced his life.[177] We should differentiate between the Sunnah, which mean all of the spoken words and acted practices of the Prophet, and the word Sunnah, which means "recommended." For example, since the Prophet used to pray two rak'at after Magrib prayer, it is not mandatory to pray these two rak'at, but it is recommended. Sunnah, as the second main source of Islamic legislation, is the sayings of the Prophet, and the recommended actions.[178]

The Sunnah is considered to be the traditions and the *hadith* (the sayings of the Prophet), both of which are seen as the second main source of the Sharia. The Sunnah is the approvals, actions, and sayings of the Prophet. The Sunnah also explains the acts that the Prophet prohibits.[179] In the Quran, God stated, "And whatever the Messenger gives you, take it, and whatever he forbids you, leave it. And fear Allah: truly Allah is severe in punishment."[180] In the Quran, God also said, "Your companion (Muhammad) is neither astray nor being misled. Nor does he speak of his own desire. It is (only) the revelation with which he is inspired."[181]

Obeying the Prophet means obeying God. In the Quran, God stated: "But no, by your Lord, they can have no faith, until they make you (O' Muhammad) judge in all disputes between them, and find in themselves no resistance against your decisions, and accept them with full submission."[182] The Quran states general guidance and principles. On the other hand, the Sunnah gives more detailed

---

Jan. 1, 2012).

176 QURAN 2:2.

177 *What is Sunnah and Hadith?*, ISLAMICITY.COM, http://www.islamicity.com/forum/printer_friendly_posts.asp?TID=7907 (last visited Oct. 5 2011); *see also Authority of the Sunnah*, AL-ISLAMI.COM, http://www.al-islami.com/islam/authority_of_sunnah.php (last visited Oct. 5 2011).

178 *Authority of the Sunnah*, supra note 177.

179 Khan, supra note 144, at 289; *see also What is Sunnah?*, ISLAAMNET.COM, http://www.islaamnet.com/whatissunnah.html (last visited Oct. 5 2011); *see also* Irshad Abdal-Haqq, *Islamic Law: An Overview of its Origin and Elements*, 1 J. ISLAMIC L. 7 (1996).

180 QURAN 59:7.

181 *Id.* at 53:2-4.

182 *Id.* at 4:65.

explanations and clarifications."[183] The Quran says, "We have revealed the reminder (Quran) to you (Muhammad) in order that you explain to the people what has been revealed to them, that perhaps they may reflect."[184]

The Egyptian former *Mufti* indicated that the Sunnah is a source of Sharia law. He mentioned several Quranic verses that support this idea. The *Mufti* also added that God requested from Muslims to obey Mohammed.[185] With respect to Mohammed, the Quran said, "Nor does he speak of (his own) desire."[186] Also, the Quran provides: "And We have sent you (O Muhammad): not but as a mercy for the 'Alamin (mankind, jinn and all that exists)."[187] Furthermore, the Quran states, "Indeed in the Messenger of Allah (Muhammad) you have a good example to follow for him who hopes for (the Meeting with) Allah and the Last Day, and remembers Allah much"[188] and "O you who believe! Obey Allah, and obey the Messenger (Muhammad) and render not vain your deeds"[189], as well as "Say (O Muhammad to mankind): 'If you (really) love Allah then follow me (i.e. accept Islamic Monotheism, follow the Qur'an and the Sunnah), Allah will love you and forgive you your sins. And Allah is Oft-Forgiving, Most Merciful.'"[190]

The Sunnah of Prophet Mohammed guides Muslims to know, understand, and practice the Quran.[191] In the Quran, God said, "Indeed in the Messenger of Allah you have the most beautiful pattern of conduct."[192] Together, the Sunnah and the Quran are the main primary source of Sharia.[193] The Sunnah is not collected in one book, like the Quran. The Sunnah is several books, which are collected by different scholars. The *Hadith* is neither written nor collected by Prophet Mohammed. However, the *Hadith* was collected and written over many years. The Sunnah can play three different roles in relation to the Quran:

> Confirming Sunnah: This is the part of the Sunnah that confirms what is in the Qur'an, and reinforces it.

---

183   Khan, *supra* note 144, at 289.
184   QURAN 16:44.
185   *The Egyptian Mufti Aly Gomaa, Civilized Rooting of Islamic Legislation, supra* note 175.
186   QURAN 53:3.
187   *Id.* at 21:107.
188   *Id.* at 33:21.
189   *Id.* at 47:33.
190   *Id.* at 3:31.
191   *What is Sunnah?, supra* note 179.
192   QURAN 33:21.
193   *What is Sunnah?, supra* note 179.

Explanatory Sunnah. This part of the Sunnah explains the holy Qur'an and the various Shariah injunctions that come in the holy Qur'an. It includes four parts: expanding on what is mentioned only briefly in the holy Qur'an, explaining difficult verses or issues, putting limits on general statements in the Qur'an and finally specifying generalities in the Qur'an.

Sunnah that brings new legislation. This part of the Sunnah is the one that brings new legislation, and new Shariah that is not in the holy Qur'an.[194]

Therefore, the Sunnah can play a role in confirming the Quran. In addition, it can clarify and explain what is stated in the Quran. For instance, it can explain how to fast during the month of Ramadan and how to make *hajj* and pay *zakat* to the poor. Finally, it can make judgments about issues not mentioned in the Quran, such as the prohibition of a murderer receiving the inheritance of the murdered person.[195]

Not every *hadith* was said by the prophet Mohammed. It is recognized that, "some *hadith* were fabricated...Scholars were forced to verify a chain of transmission (*isnad*). The process of authenticating *hadith* involved examining the narrators who propagated a particular version of a tradition and scrutinizing the subject matter in order to determine whether it was in conflict with the Koran."[196] Furthermore:

The Sunna of the Prophet is "the normative model behavior of Muhammad." Muslims look to the *hadith*, the "narrative reports or traditions" of the "Prophetic words and deeds." *Hadiths* multiplied throughout the years after the Prophet's death and were not codified until the ninth century. This lack of codification led to many questions about which traditions were genuine; therefore, "*hadiths* were evaluated through a painstaking attempt to evaluate credibility which produced the new Muslim science of *hadith* criticism (mustalah al-hadith)." Varied criteria were developed to evaluate the credibility of the narrators of the hadiths such as "moral character, reputation for piety, intelligence, and good memory." After evaluating the narrator, "a link (sanad) by link examination of the transmissional chain was made to trace the continuity of the tradition back to the Prophet." Hadiths were also judged

---

194 *Authority of the Sunnah, supra* note 178.
195 Muhammed Selim El-Awa, *Approaches to Shari'a: A Response to N. J. Coulson's 'A History of Islamic Law'*, 2 J. Islamic Studies 143 (1991).
196 Khan, *supra* note 144, at 290.

in terms of their matn (subject matter). The question was whether the subject matter contradicts "the Quran, a verified tradition, reason, or the consensus of the community." Having undergone evaluation of the narrator and the subject matter, the hadiths were classified as either sahih (authentic), hasan (good) and daif (weak).[197]

Also, the sayings of Prophet Mohammed were not written during his life. They were written after his death over a period of 300 years by different scholars. There are several Islamic scholars who are very famous and professional for authenticating *hadith*,

> Concern about the accuracy and authenticity of the Hadiths resulted in the advent of the *sahih* movement (meaning authentic, sound or genuine), between 850 C.E until 915 C.E., during which time dedicated scholars attempted to authenticate each hadith.[198] From this movement came *The Six Books*, six acclaimed Hadiths compiled by recognized scholars of high character. These compilers are Al-Bukhari, Muslim, Abu Dawud, alTirmidhi, al-Nasai, and Ibn Majah Muhammad bin Yazid.[199]

2. Secondary Sources: *Fiqh* and *Ijtihad* – Jurisprudential Methodologies of Islamic Law

"Sharia law" or "Islamic law" includes individual and collective rights; moral behavior of the person; and the rights, responsibilities, and duties of the community. In short, Sharia law or Islamic law is a very broad term.[200] *Fiqh* means knowledge of legal provisions by way of *ijtihad*.[201] Fiqh is "the process of deducing and applying Shari'ah principles and injunctions in real or hypothetical cases or situations is called *fiqh* or Islamic jurisprudence."[202]

The root of the word *ijtihad* is from the word *Johd* which means "effort." *Ijtihad* means putting in the extra effort to know the legitimate rules.[203] Scholars who

---

197 Schooley, *supra note* 150, at 662-663.
198 Abdal-Haqq, *supra* note 139, at 23 (citing ABDUR RAHMAN I. DOI, SHAR'AH: THE ISLAMIC LAW 12 (1984)).
199 *Id.*
200 Abdal-Haqq, *supra* note 139, at 5.
201 *Al mawso'aa Al-shamlah* (comprehensive encyclopedia), ISLAMPORT.COM, http://islamport.com/d/2/usl/1/84/768.html?zoom_highlightsub=%22%CA%DA%D1%ED%DD+%C7%E1%DD%DE%E5%22 (last visited Jan. 4, 2013).
202 Abdal-Haqq, *supra* note 139, at 10.
203 *Ijtihad*, QARADAWI.NET, http://www.qaradawi.net/2010-02-23-09-38-15/4/619.html (last visited Jan. 4, 2013).

make *ijtihad* are called the *moj'tahdeen*. The person that makes *fiqh* is called *faqih*. Sheikh Yousef Alkaradawy, said that not every person who is an eloquent orator and preacher and who can influence emotions and stir hearts is considered a *faqih*. *Faqih* is a person who is becoming fully informed with respect to the legitimate rules.[204] In order to be a good *faqih*, a scholar should make good *ijtihad*. In order to be a good *faqih* and *moj'tahd* the scholar should have vast knowledge of Islamic sharia and the ability to elicitate Islamic rules. Elicitation needs a special talent and enough knowledge in the *moj'tahd* in order to be able reach the legitimate rule in the light of the objectives and purposes of Sharia law.[205]

The *fiqh*, or the jurisprudence of Sharia law, is a far-reaching term that includes both the primary and secondary sources of Sharia, or Islamic, law. *Fiqh* refers to the "collective body of laws deduced from Shariah through the use of fiqh methodology... It covers all the subject areas of law including religious, political, civil, criminal, procedural..."[206] In other words, *fiqh*, or Islamic jurisprudence, includes issues that are not mentioned or stated explicitly in the Sunnah and the Quran. Sharia applies the methodology of reasoning in order to reach decisions on matters and questions that are not answered explicitly by Quran and Sunnah.[207] A judge was appointed to Yemen by Prophet Mohammed. Prophet Mohammed asked the judge about the method that he would use when judging a case before him, to which the judge replied:

> "According to what shalt thou judge? [Mohammed] replied: According to the Book of Allah. And if thou findest nought therein? According to the Sunnah [traditions] of the Prophet of Allah. And if thou findest nought therein? Then I will exert myself to form my own judgment. Praise be to God who has guided the messenger of His prophet to that Which pleases His prophet,"[208]

This conversation clearly shows the importance of individual reasoning in Islam; in fact, individual reasoning plays a major role in the Islamic jurisprudence. The jurisprudence can be used to answer questions upon which the Quran and Sunnah are silent. There are several Islamic schools of jurisprudence that use the

---

204 Id.
205 Id.
206 Abdal-Haqq , *supra* note 139, at 10.
207 Jason Morgan-Foster, *Third Generation Rights: What Islamic Law Can Teach The International Human Rights Movement,*, 8 YALE HUM. RTS. & DEV. L.J. 103 (2005).
208 HISHAM M. RAMADAN, IRSHAD ABDAL-HAQQ, HISHAM M. RAMADAN, AHMED ZAKI YAMANAI, NOOR MOHAMMED, MAHMOUD HOBALLAH, HAFIZ NAZEEM GOOLAM & ALI KHAN, UNDERSTANDING ISLAMIC LAW: FROM CLASSICAL TO CONTEMPORARY 5 (2006); *SEE ALSO* Morgan-Foster, *supra* note 200 (citing Irshad Abdal-Haqq, *Islamic Law: An Overview of its Origin and Elements*, 1 J. ISLAMIC L. 1, 9 (1996)).

legal reasoning, or *ijtihad*. The four most popular schools of *ijtihad* are Hanafi, Maliki, Shafii, and Hanbali. These four schools were established in the first centuries of Islam. There are many other Islamic scholars who used *ijtihad*, but these four schools are very widely recognized by Sunni Muslims. [209]

One of the best things about Islam is the different schools of interpretation. However, interpretation cannot change the objectives and purposes of the Quran. There are not different versions or authors of the Quran; there is only one book. Therefore, interpretations cannot change the objectives and purposes of the book. The different interpretations are focused on the details of the objectives and purpose. This chapter will explain the objectives and purpose of Islam and how they can be attained.

a.   Qiyas and Ijma as Methodologies

If a certain issue is stated clearly in the Quran and/or Sunnah, it should be respected. For instance, if it is stated in the Quran that Muslims should pray, this should be implemented. However, if a certain matter is not answered clearly in the Quran and/or Sunnah, then Islamic scholars must use *ijtihad* to determine the opinion that complies with the objectives and purposes of the Quran. However, "there is no guarantee that the ruling he/she reaches will be identical with that which is lodged in God's mind."[210] *Ijtihad* makes Sharia a living instrument that can adapt to new circumstances. Prophet Mohammed said, "Difference of opinion within my community is a sign of the bounty of Allah."[211] A clear example of *ijtihad* is organ transplantation, which is very new medical treatment that did not exist centuries ago at the beginning of Islam. Islamic scholars use *ijtihad* to determine whether the organ transplantation is considered a sin or is in compliance with Sharia.

If a certain legal issue has no direct answer in the Quran or Sunnah, *ijtihad* will be used to establish a solution. *Ijtihad* can be reached by *ijma* or *qiyas*. *Ijma* is the consensus of Islamic schools and scholars on a certain issue. Prophet Mohammed said, "My community will never agree on an error."[212] *Qiyas* and *ijma* are kinds of *ijtihad*. *Qiyas* "is an intellectual striving to arrive at one's own judgment. *Ijtihad* is

---

209   *Understand Islam: The Four Schools of Law in Islam*, FREE-ISLAMIC-COURSE.ORG, http://www.free-islamic-course.org/Stage1TheFourSchoolsOfLawInIslam.html (last visited Nov. 14, 2011).
210   Khan, *supra* note 144, at 292-293.
211   Schooley, *supra* note 150, at. 665.
212   Khan, *supra* note 144, at 291 (citing CYRIL GLASSÉ, THE CONCISE ENCYCLOPEDIA OF ISLAM 182 (1989)); *see also Sources of Islamic Law*, WIKIPEDIA.COM, http://en.wikipedia.org/wiki/Sources_of_Islamic_law (last visited 19 Nov. 2011).

a process by which well-trained scholars adapt Islamic law to changing societies."²¹³ Qiyas is defined as "analogical deduction based on the provisions laid down by the appropriate verse(s) in the Qur'an and/or a corresponding matter within the Sunnah. Qiyas was created in response to a growing need to resolve problems which were not explicitly addressed in the Qur'an or the Sunnah."²¹⁴ *Qiyas* is more specifically a form of striving that operates by way of analogical reasoning. *Qiyas* cannot be used to permit an act that is against the objectives and purposes of Sharia. *Qiyas* must only be applied in light of the objectives and purposes of Islamic law. Islamic scholars "use qiyas today to apply Islamic principles to modern-day problems."²¹⁵ For instance, alcoholic drinks are prohibited explicitly in the Quran because of their intoxicating property. Therefore, *qiyas* can be used to prohibit all intoxicants, including wine.²¹⁶

b. *Istihsan and Istishab*

Istihsan means "'to consider something good.' Muslim scholars may use it to express their preference for particular judgments in Islamic law over other possibilities. It is one of the principles of legal thought underlying personal interpretation or ijtihad… Technically it has been defined in several ways by Muslim jurists."²¹⁷ There are several interpretations by Islamic scholars regarding the meaning of *istihsan*. *Istihsan* "involves a departure from *qiyas* in the first place, and then the departure in question often means giving preference to one *qiyas* over another."²¹⁸

Istihsan is

> an important branch of ijtihad, and has played a prominent role in the adaptation of Islamic law to the changing needs of society. It has provided Islamic law with the necessary means with which to encourage flexibility and growth. Notwithstanding a measure of juristic technicality which seems to have been injected into an originally simple idea, *istihsan* remains basically flexible, and can be used for a variety of purposes. Yet because of its essential flexibility, the jurists have discouraged an over-reliance on istihsan lest it result in the suspension of

---

213 Entelis, *supra* note 141, at 1266.
214 Khan, *supra* note 144, at 291.
215 Entelis, *supra* note 141, at 1266.
216 *Sources of Islamic Law*, *supra* note 212.
217 *Istihsan*, WIKIPEDIA.COM, http://en.wikipedia.org/wiki/Istihsan (last visited Oct. 12, 2012).
218 M. H. KAMALI, PRINCIPLES OF JURISPRUDENCE (CHAPTER FIFTEEN), http://ar.scribd.com/doc/28679295/22/Chapter-Fifteen-Istishab-Presumption-of-Continuity (last visited Oct. 12, 2012).

the injunctions of the Shari'ah and become a means of circumventing its general principles. Istihsan literally means 'to approve, or to deem something preferable'. It is a derivation from hasuna, which means being good or beautiful. In its juristic sense, istihsan is a method of exercising personal opinion in order to avoid any rigidity and unfairness that might result from the literal enforcement of the existing law. 'Juristic preference' is a fitting description of istihsan, as it involves setting aside an established analogy in favor of an alternative ruling which serves the ideals of justice and public interest in a better way."[219]

On the other hand, *istishab* means the presumption of continuity.[220] It is the "presumption of existence or non-existence of facts. It can be used in the absence of other proofs."[221] *Istishab* means the assumption of the "continuation of a fact till the contrary is proved."[222] For instance, everyone is presumed innocent until evidence proves the contrary. Similarly, a marriage contract is valid until its annulment, for example, in a situation where it is proven that there has been a divorce.[223]

Istishab differentiates between the previous certainty and the present doubt,

> Istishab means the principle or rule of continuity. This principle is used in a case in which a person has "a previous certainty" and "a present doubt" about the same thing. For example, there is a glass of water on my table. I am sure that it was ritually pure (tahir) in the morning, but now I doubt in its ritual purity. The principle of istishab says that act on your previous certainty and ignore your present doubt because doubt cannot over-ride certainty.[224]

---

219 *Istihsan or Equality in Islamic Law*, THE MESSAGE OF ISLAM, http://english.islammessage.com/articledetails.aspx?articleId=625 (last visited Oct. 12, 2012).

220 Istishab means the presumption of continuity. *See Istishab* [Presumption of Continuity], http://thequranblog.files.wordpress.com/2010/04/istishab.pdf (last visited Oct. 12, 2012).

221 *Id.*

222 *Id.*

223 *Id.*

224 *An Introduction to the Islamic Shari Shari'ah*, AL-ISLAM.ORG, http://www.al-islam.org/introduction-islamic-shariah-smrizvi/6.htm (last visited Oct. 12, 2012).

D. The Objectives and Purposes of Sharia Law

Many people are interested in knowing more about Islamic Sharia law. Many scholars are curious about the objectives and purposes of Islamic law and the opinion of Islam regarding human rights, the right not to be tortured, the right to life, etc. Nearly all constitutions of the Arab countries apply Islamic Sharia as the main source of law. For instance, in Article 7 of the Constitution of the United Arab Emirates and Article 2 of the Egyptian Constitution, Bahrain Constitution, and Kuwait Constitution explicitly state that the Islamic Sharia is the principal source of legislation. It is important to know whether Sharia encourages violence or discrimination between men and women. Even the Arab Charter on Human Rights states, "Men and women are equal in respect of human dignity, rights and obligations within the framework of the positive discrimination established in favour of women by the Islamic Shariah, other divine laws and by applicable laws and legal instruments…"[225] I have been asked many times how a judge in a court could enact the objectives and purposes of Sharia.

It is important for the reader of this book, especially when reading the following chapters, to understand the objectives and purposes of Sharia. By doing so, I may be more able to convince the reader of my explanation regarding the correctness of the Arab Charter. To have a full picture of Sharia law, one must fully understand its objectives and purposes. It will be difficult to include everything that could be said about the objectives and purposes of Sharia in this section; doing so would require another book. However, I will do my best to highlight the main principles and norms that constitutes the objectives and purposes of Sharia law.

1. What are the Objectives and Purposes of Sharia Law?

The objectives and purposes of Sharia law transcend the literal meaning of the words; they also refer to the reasons for Sharia and the interpretation of what is inferred.[226] Most Western scholars and people raised in Western cultures do not know the purposes of Sharia law. People sometimes understand the literal meaning only. For instance, in Arab countries before the existence of Islam, women were not allowed to receive inheritance; only men could receive inheritance. After Islam, the situation became different. With respect to inheritance, the Quran states, "Allah commands you as regards your children's (inheritance): to the male, a portion equal to that of two females."[227] This literal meaning is dis-

---

225 ACHR, *supra* note 126, at art. 3 (3).
226 Yousf Alkaradawy, Derasah Fi Fkh Makasd AlSharia [Study in the Jurisprudence of the purposes of Sharia] 15 & 20 (3rd ed. 2008).
227 Quran 4:11.

criminatory against women, in that a man is worth double that of a woman with respect to inheritance.

Is a woman in Islam perceived to be at a level lower than a man? The answer is absolutely no. The purpose of the previous verse of the Quran is related to the difference in financial obligations and duties imposed on men and women. This can be explained in the following scenario: A father who had a son and a daughter dies. He left 150,000 Egyptian pounds in inheritance to his children. His son will inherit 100,000 Egyptian pounds and the daughter will inherent 50,000 Egyptian pounds. However, this is not the end of the story, it is the beginning. In Islam, the husband is responsible for paying for almost everything. If the son wants to get married he has to pay. For example, a son might pay 25,000 Egyptian pounds as a dowry for his wife. Therefore, the money that he inherited is reduced to 75,000 Egyptian pounds. However, when his sister gets married, she will receive a dowry from her husband (e.g. 25,000 Egyptian pounds). Therefore, the money she has will increase to 75,000 Egyptian pounds. As such, her wealth is now equal to that of her brother; they both have 75,000 Egyptian pounds. On the other hand, her brother's 75,000 Egyptian pounds will continually decrease, because the husband has to buy or rent an apartment to live in with his wife. Also, he has to pay for his wife's food, clothes, medicine, medical insurance, etc. However, his sister will not pay for anything because her husband is financially responsible for all of her expenses.[228]

The previous example clearly explains the reason and the goal of the previous verse of the Quran, which gave men double that which was given to women in inheritance. Some Islamic scholars have even said that Sharia gives women more privileges than men.[229] I will explain the perspectives on inheritance in further detail in Chapter Five.

2. The Pillars of Islam and the Philosophy of the Islamic Religion

There are five pillars of Islam, which are considered to be the basic ways in which Muslims worship.[230] First, the testimony of faith, which outlines that "there is no deity but Allah and Mohammed is His Prophet." The second pillar is praying, which is done five times a day for a few minutes. The third pillar is *Zakat*, which means supporting those in need. All Muslims that acquire a certain amount of wealth are obliged to give 2.5% of their wealth to the poor. The fourth pillar is for

---

228 Alkaradawy, *supra* note 226.
229 Alkaradawy, *supra* note 226 (citing the women's privileges regarding inheritance and expenses).
230 *Islam, supra* note 144.

Muslims who meet certain conditions to fast for the month of Ramadan. This entails refraining from eating and drinking anything between sunrise and sunset. The fifth pillar is pilgrimage to Makkah (Saudi Arabia) for Muslims who can afford it.[231]

A deep understanding of the pillars of Islam is not just about engaging in certain acts and refraining from others. The philosophy of the Islamic religion and the reasons behind these pillars is the "stability of ethics."[232] Prophet Mohammed said, "I was sent to perfect good character."[233] He also said, "The best amongst you are those who are best in morals."[234] As explained previously, hadith of the prophet is considered to be the second primary source in Islam. The two previous hadith clearly show that good morals are the heart of Islam. The previous hadith did not say the best amongst you is the white or the black. The hadith discusses morals regardless of the color and sex. In the Quran, the primary source of Sharia law, Allah said, "And We have not sent you [Mohammed] but as a mercy to the worlds."[235]

The profound interpretation of the five pillars of Islam is not just to pray, fast, pay zakat, and go to makkah. The pillars of Islam call for the protection of human rights, dignity, ethics, and morals. For instance, praying is not about doing aerobic acts. It is stated in the Quran that "surely prayer keeps (one) away from indecency and evil."[236] Therefore, God may not accept the prayers of a Muslim who is involved in lewdness and iniquity, as this would be considered to be engaging in aerobics, not praying.

The third pillar of Islam is *Zakat*. It is stated in the Quran to "Take Sadaqah (alms) from their wealth in order to purify them and sanctify them with it... "[237] Paying *zakat* makes a Muslim person generous, merciful, nearer to God, and kind to the poor. It is different than taxes, because people may try to find illegal ways not to

---

231 Walter R. Schumm and Alison L. Kohler, *Muslims Social Cohesion and the Five Pillars of Islam: A Comparative Perspective*, 23 AMERICAN JOURNAL OF ISLAMIC SOCIAL SCIENCES, 126 (2006).

232 AMR KHALED, AKHLAAK ALMO'MEN [Ethics of Believers] 7 (5th ed. 2005). (citing Mostafa sadeek el Refaey, mn wahy el kalam)

233 *Imam Malek, Book 47, Hadith 8*, SEARCHTRUTH.COM, http://www.searchtruth.com/book_display.php?book=47&translator=4&start=0&number=0 (last visited Oct. 16, 2011).

234 *Sahih Muslim, Book 30, Hadith 5740*, SEARCHTRUTH.COM, http://www.searchtruth.com/search Hadith.php?keyword=moral&translator=2&search=1&book=&start=0&records_display=10&search_word=all (last visited Oct. 16, 2011).

235 QURAN 21:107.

236 *Id.* at 29:45.

237 *Id.* at 9:103.

pay taxes or reduce the amount that should be paid. However, with respect to *zakat*, a believer knows that God will see his actions and knows everything.

The fourth pillar in Islam is fasting. Muslims who meet certain conditions are obliged to fast in the month of Ramadan from sunrise to sunset. It is stated in several verses in Quran: "O you who believe! Observing As-Saum (the fasting) is prescribed for you as it was prescribed for those before you, that you may become Al-Muttaqun (the pious)."[238] The Quran explicitly states that the main purpose of fasting is to be *muttaqun*. The meaning of *muttaqun* is described in the same chapter as the previous quote in the following way:

> This is the Book (the Qur'an), whereof there is no doubt, a guidance to those who are Al-Muttaqun [the pious believers of Islamic Monotheism who fear Allah much (abstain from all kinds of sins and evil deeds which He has forbidden) and love Allah much (perform all kinds of good deeds which He has ordained)]. Who believe in the Ghaib and perform As-Salat (Iqamat-as-Salat), and spend out of what We have provided for them [i.e. give Zakat, spend on themselves, their parents, their children, their wives, etc., and also give charity to the poor and also in Allah's Cause-Jihad].[239]

The previous verse is very important because it defines the term *Al-Muttaqun*, which means the pious. This term will be repeated several times throughout this book.

One of the main reasons for fasting is

> to develop and strengthen our powers of self-control, so that we can resist wrongful desires and bad habits, and therefore "guard against evil." In fasting, by refraining from the natural human urges to satisfy one's appetite, we are exercising our ability of self-restraint, so that we can then apply it to our everyday life to bring about self-improvement… Fasting in Islam does not just consist of refraining from eating and drinking, but from every kind of selfish desire and wrong-doing. The fast is not merely of the body, but essentially that of the spirit as well. The physical fast is a symbol and outward expression of the real, inner fast.[240]

---

238 *Id.* at 2:183.
239 *Id.* at 2:2-3.
240 *Ramadan and its Significance: Purpose of Fasting in Islam*, THE LAHORE AHMADIYYA MOVEMENT, http://www.muslim.org/islam/ramadan.htm#3 (last visited Oct. 29, 2011).

In addition, fasting teaches people how to be generous to their parents, family, friends, and those who are needy and poor. In the month of Ramadan, people do an increased amount of good deeds, because the rewards from God are increased many times during this period.

The last pillar is *Hajj* or the pilgrimage to Makkah. Every adult Muslim who can afford, at least one time in his or her life, must travel to Mecca (Saudi Arabia) to make *Hajj*.[241] With respect to *Hajj*, Allah said in the Quran: "The pilgrimage is (in) the well-known months, and whoever is minded to perform the pilgrimage therein (let him remember that) there is (to be) no lewdness nor abuse nor angry conversation on the pilgrimage."[242] There is a very great reward for Muslims who perform Hajj, "the Prophet (p.b.u.h) said, 'Whoever performs Hajj for Allah's pleasure and does not have sexual relations with his wife, and does not do evil or sins then he will return (after Hajj free from all sins) as if he were born anew.'"[243] *Hajj* is an important opportunity to teach Muslims how to be ethically disciplined. When going to *Hajj*, all Muslims should demonstrate good morals, not raise their voices, and not offend or let alone insult anyone in the crowded place that becomes inhabited by several million Muslims for a few days of the year.[244]

3. Peace and Justice in Islam

The five previous pillars are the only pillars of Islam. However, we can say that, in a deeper way, the backbone of Islam is peace and justice. It has been said, "The very word Islam comes from the same verbal root as *salaam* meaning 'peace' and, since the religion is based upon total submission to the will of God, Muslims believe that real peace is out of reach unless it is based upon this submission within the universal order."[245]

Justice is outlined in several verses in the Quran. For instance, the Quran states, "Verily! Allah commands that you should render back the trusts to those to whom they are due; and that when you judge between men, you judge with justice. Verily, how excellent is the teaching which He (Allah) gives you! Truly, Allah is Ever All-Hearer, All-Seer."[246] Also, it is stated in the Quran to "make peace between

---

241 Schooley, *supra* note 150, at 668 (citing JOHN L. ESPOSITO, ISLAM: THE STRAIGHT PATH 89-90 (1988)).
242 QURAN 2:197.
243 *Sahih Bukhari, Volume 2, Book 26, Number 596,* HADITSBUKHARIONLINE, http://haditsbukhari-online.blogspot.com/2010/10/pilgrimmage-hajj.html (last visited May 22, 2012).
244 KHALED, *supra* note 232.
245 Charles Le Gai Eaton, *The Concept of Justice in Islam*, THEBOOK.ORG, http://thebook.org/tbf-articles/article_55.shtml (last visited Oct. 30, 2011).
246 QURAN 4:58.

them with justice and be fair: for Allah loves those who are fair (and just)."[247] Furthermore, it is stated in the Quran, "O you who believe! Stand out firmly for Allah as just witnesses; and let not the enmity and hatred of others make you avoid justice. Be just: that is nearer to piety; and fear Allah. Verily, Allah is Well-Acquainted with what you do."[248]

Islam insisted on implementing justice without discrimination, even against parents and beloved persons. In the Quran, God states:

> "O you who believe! Stand out firmly for justice, as witnesses to Allah, even though it be against yourselves, or your parents, or your kin, be he rich or poor, Allah is a Better Protector to both (than you). So follow not the lusts (of your hearts), lest you avoid justice; and if you distort your witness or refuse to give it, verily, Allah is Ever Well-Acquainted with what you do."[249]

In another verse in the Quran, God said to His prophet, "(They like to) listen to falsehood, to devour anything forbidden. So if they come to you (O Muhammad), either judge between them, or turn away from them. If you turn away from them, they cannot hurt you in the least. And if you judge, judge with justice between them. Verily, Allah loves those who act justly."[250]

Prophet Mohammed talked about the relationship between inequitable justice and the collapse of nations. He said, "What destroyed the nations preceding you, was that if a noble amongst them stole, they would forgive him, and if a poor person amongst them stole, they would inflict Allah's Legal punishment on him. By Allah, if Fatima, the daughter of Muhammad stole, I would cut off her hand."[251] Islam also stated that justice should be applied in time of war and peace and should always be the main goal. The Quran states,

> "And if two parties or groups among the believers fall to fighting, then make peace between them both. But if one of them outrages against the other, then fight you (all) against the one that which outrages till it complies with the Command of Allah. Then if it complies, then make

---

247 Id. at 49:9.
248 Id. at 5:8.
249 Id. at 4:135
250 Id. at 5:42.
251 Raghed El-Sergany, *Justice in Islam...Its importance and Reality*, Islamsotry.com, http://en.islamstory.com/justice-islam-importance-reality.html (last visited Oct. 30, 2011) (citing Sahih al-Bukhari, Kitab al-Anbiyaa (Book of the Prophets)).

reconciliation between them justly, and be equitable. Verily! Allah loves those who are the equitable."[252]

4. Parental Rights

Currently, many people say that women have no rights in Islam, be they a mother, wife, sister, or daughter. Islam does not differentiate between the parents. Mothers and fathers are given the same rights by the Quran. Parents' rights in Islam are superior to those of any other person. Parents' rights are extremely important in Islam, they are highly ranked and they are referred to in Quran just after the verses discussing belief in God. In the Quran, it is written:

> And (remember) when Luqman said to his son when he was advising him: "O my son! Join not in worship others with Allah. Verily joining others in worship with Allah is a great Zulm (wrong) indeed. And We have enjoined on man (to be dutiful and good) to his parents. His mother bore him in weakness and hardship upon weakness and hardship, and his weaning is in two years – give thanks to Me and to your parents. Unto Me is the final destination."[253]

In Islam, mothers are given more care than fathers. Mothers raise children; in addition, they suffer pain during pregnancy and at the time of delivering the baby. One of the Companions of Prophet Mohammed asked of him, "Who deserves my good treatment most?", to which the Prophet responded, "Your mother." "Who next?" asked the Companion. "Your mother," responded the Prophet. The interaction continued: "Who next?" "Your mother." "Who after that?" "Your father." Therefore, mothers receive three times the care from their children, which is more than the father deserves.[254]

The Quran states, "And your Lord has decreed that you worship none but Him. And that you be dutiful to your parents. If one of them or both of them attain old age in your life, say not to them a word of disrespect, nor shout at them but address them in terms of honour."[255] The Quran also states, "And lower unto them the wing of submission and humility through mercy, and say: 'My Lord! Bestow

---

252 QURAN 49:9.
253 *Id.* at 31:13-14.
254 Dr.I. A. Arshed, *Parents-Child Relationship in Islam*, ISLAM101.COM, http://www.islam101.com/sociology/parchild.htm (last visited Oct. 21, 2011).
255 QURAN 17:23.

on them Your Mercy as they did bring me up when I was young.'"[256] It is also stated in Quran,

> "And when We made a covenant with the children of Israel: You shall not serve any but Allah and (you shall do) good to (your) parents, and to the near of kin and to the orphans and the needy, and you shall speak to men good words and keep up prayer and pay the poor-rate. Then you turned back except a few of you and (now too) you turn aside."[257]

Muslims must be kind to their parents, even if their parents do not believe in God or they want their son or daughter not to believe in God or to convert to other religion. It is said in Quran, "But if they (both) strive with you to make you join in worship with Me others that of which you have no knowledge, then obey them not; but behave with them in the world kindly, and follow the path of him who turns to Me in repentance and in obedience. Then to Me will be your return, and I shall tell you what you used to do."[258]

Parents still have rights even after their death. There is a *hadith* for the prophet that states,

> "While we were with Prophet Muhammad of God a man of Banu Salmah came to Him and said: Apostle of God is there any kindness left that I can do to my parents after their death? He replied: Yes, you can invoke blessings on them, forgiveness for them, carry out their final instructions after their death, join ties of relationship which are dependent on them, and honour their friends."[259]

5. General Obligations

There are general obligations that are imposed by Allah. These obligations enable us to develop an understanding of the objectives and purposes of Islam. It is stated in Quran:

> And render to the kindred their due rights, as (also) to those in want, and to the wayfarer: But squander not (your wealth) in the manner of a spendthrift. Verily spendthrifts are brothers of the Evil Ones; and the

---

256 *Id.* at 17:24
257 *Id.* at 2:82.
258 *Id.* at 31:15.
259 Mir Fateh Shah, *Parent's Rights in Islam*, QURAN AND SCIENCE, http://www.Quranand-science.com/fakes-about-islam/171-parents-rights-in-islam.html (last visited Oct. 21, 2011).

Evil One is to his Lord (himself) ungrateful. And even if thou hast to turn away from them in pursuit of the Mercy from thy Lord which thou dost expect, yet speak to them a word of easy kindness. Make not thy hand tied (like a niggard's) to thy neck, nor stretch it forth to its utmost reach, so that thou become blameworthy and destitute. Verily thy Lord doth provide sustenance in abundance for whom He pleaseth, and He provideth in a just measure. For He doth know and regard all His servants. Kill not your children for fear of want: We shall provide sustenance for them as well as for you. Verily the killing of them is a great sin. Nor come nigh to adultery: for it is a shameful (deed) and an evil, opening the road (to other evils). Nor take life — which Allah has made sacred — except for just cause. And if anyone is slain wrongfully, we have given his heir authority (to demand qisas or to forgive): but let him nor exceed bounds in the matter of taking life; for he is helped (by the Law). Come not nigh to the orphan's property except to improve it, until he attains the age of full strength; and fulfill (every) engagement, for (every) engagement will be enquired into (on the Day of Reckoning). Give full measure when ye measure, and weigh with a balance that is straight: that is the most fitting and the most advantageous in the final determination. And pursue not that of which thou hast no knowledge; for every act of hearing, or of seeing or of (feeling in) the heart will be enquired into (on the Day of Reckoning). Nor walk on the earth with insolence: for thou canst not rend the earth asunder, nor reach the mountains in height. Of all such things the evil is hateful in the sight of thy Lord. These are among the (precepts of) wisdom, which thy Lord has revealed to thee. Take not, with Allah, another object of worship, lest thou shouldst be thrown into Hell, blameworthy and rejected."[260]

In addition, Islam focuses on the rights of neighbors and the rights of guests. Also, Islam encourages every Muslim to have a pure heart, which means that a Muslim should love for people what he or she loves for himself or herself. The Prophet said, "None of you [truly] believes until he loves for his brother that which he loves for himself."[261] Also he said, "Let him who believes in Allah and the Last Day speak good, or keep silent; and let him who believes in Allah and the Last Day be generous to his neighbour; and let him who believes in Allah and the Last Day be generous to his guest."[262] Also, he said, "He is not a perfect Muslim who eats his

---

260 QURAN 17:26-39.
261 Abu Zakaria An-Nawawi, *Hadeth Number 13*, Rasoulallah.net, http://www.rasoulallah.net/v2/document.aspx?lang=en&doc=3993 (last visited Oct. 21, 2011).
262 Abu Zakaria An-Nawawi, *Hadeth Number 15*, Rasoulallah.net, http://www.rasoulallah.net/

fill and lets his neighbor go hungry."[263] Another *hadith* about behaving well with people states, "have *Taqwaa* (Fear) of Allaah wherever you may be, and follow up a bad deed with a good deed which will wipe it out, and behave well towards the people."[264]

Islam encourages doing good deeds, such as reconciling with people and judging other people justly regardless their sex, religion, etc. The Prophet said,

> "Every joint of a person must perform a charity each day that the sun rises: to judge justly between two people is a charity. To help a man with his mount, lifting him onto it or hoisting up his belongings onto it, is a charity. And the good word is a charity. And every step that you take towards the Prayer is a charity, and removing a harmful object from the road is a charity."[265]

E. The Effect of Diversity in *Fiqh* on the Application of Islamic Sharia

Every Muslim is permitted to freely choose the school of jurisprudence that he or she finds convenient.[266] A Muslim could even choose a combination of different schools. In other words, a Muslim could choose parts from different schools that fit him or her, as long as he or she is convinced that each school fits his or her personality.[267] There are two opinions regarding *ijtihad*. The first opinion states that *ijtihad* has come to an end. The other opinion states that *ijtihad* did not come to an end and the door is still open.

1. The End of the Classical Era and its Effect on *Fiqh*

There is an opinion that states that the interpretation (*ijtihad*) of the Quran and Sunnah has come to an end.[268] This opinion argues that Muslims are satisfied with the predominant schools of *ijtihad* and claims that all of the interpretation scenarios of Sharia have already been resolved.[269] Muslims subscribing to this

---

v2/document.aspx?lang=en&doc=3995 (last visited Oct. 21, 2011).
263 *Prophet Muhammad's Kindness*, ISLAMWEB.NET, http://www.islamweb.net/emainpage/index.php?page=articles&id=136183 (last visited Oct. 21, 2011).
264 Abu Zakaria An-Nawawi, *Hadeth Number 18*, Rasoulallah.net, http://www.rasoulallah.net/v2/document.aspx?lang=en&doc=4000 (last visited Oct. 21, 2011).
265 Abu Zakaria An-Nawawi, *Hadeth Number 26*, Rasoulallah.net, http://www.rasoulallah.net/v2/document.aspx?lang=en&doc=4009 (last visited Oct. 21, 2011).
266 AL-HIBRI, *supra* note 29, at 6.
267 Professor Saad Al-Din Helaly, Lecture at Al-Sedeeq Mosque, (Mar. 17, 2012).
268 Khan, *supra* note 144, at 295.
269 Jordan, *supra* note 141, at 56, 59 & 60.

opinion have decided to "close the door to ijtihad."²⁷⁰ Islamic scholars are not developing any new *ijtihad* for the Quran and Sunnah. The withholding of interpretation of Quran and Sunnah is marked by the phrase, "the closing of the door of ijtihad."²⁷¹ Scholars have stated:

> The premise behind such conclusory sentiments like closing the doors to ijtihad is based on the idea that a reopening of interpretation still would require a fidelity to the whole of the Islamic legal tradition, which means that in order to reinterpret the primary sources, one had to be qualified in some sense. Reinstitution of ijtihad requires a rationale for why this right was qualified in the first place. Arguably, the right to conduct ijtihad was limited for functional reasons: if everyone possessed such a right for any enduring length of time, especially in light of trying to formulate working precedents, nothing would remain of Islamic law.²⁷²

2. The Door to *Ijtihad* Remains Open and Was Never Closed

Most Islamic scholars believe that the diversity of Islamic schools and different opinions emerging from *ijtihad* make Sharia law a living instrument. The legitimacy of the perspective that the door of *ijtihad* remains open has its roots in Sharia law.²⁷³ For instance, there is a hadith from the Prophet that encourages *ijtihad*. Prophet Mohammed said, "If a judge gives a verdict according to the best of his knowledge and his verdict is correct (i.e. agrees with Allah and His Apostle's verdict) he will receive a double reward, and if he gives a verdict according to the best of his knowledge and his verdict is wrong, (i.e. against that of Allah and His Apostle) even then he will get a reward."²⁷⁴ This hadith is clear proof that *ijtihad* is encouraged and welcomed in Sharia law. The hadith indicates that if a person makes *ijtihad* and it was correct he or she will receive double the reward, because he or she made *ijtihad* and because it was correct. On the other hand, if a person makes *ijtihad* and it was not correct, the person will still receive a reward. Therefore, the very act of making *ijtihad* provides a reward. In short, Sharia encourages people to think and analyze.

---

270   Khan, *supra* note 144, at 295.
271   Id.
272   Id. at 296.
273   Prof. Saad Al-Din Helaly, Hokook Alinsan Fi Alislam [Human Rights in Islam] 228 (1st ed. 2010).
274   *Shahi Bukhari, Volume 009, Book 092, Hadith Number 450*, http://www.luvu4luv.com/Hadith_Bukhari_Book92.html (last visited Apr. 22, 2012).

In order to gain a deeper understanding and to hear different opinions with respect to my book I requested to hear the perspective of the office of the Egyptian *Mufti* with respect to this issue. The office informed me that I would meet with the Academic Consultant of the Egyptian *Mufti*.[275] I asked the Academic Consultant about the opinion that states that 'the door of *ijtihad* is closed'. He said that the door is never closed rather it is still open. He advised me to read a book entitled 'Respond to who clung to the earth and ignorantly did not know that diligence is obligatory in every era.'[276] The author, Galal Al-Syooty, was born in 1445 and died in 1505.[277] He wrote about, and cited the opinions of, famous Islamic scholars to ensure that diligence, or *ijtihad*, continues in all eras and not only in the beginning of Islam. He added that it is a religious duty in every era to have a group of scholars working on *ijtihad*.[278] In his book Al-syooty cited *Al-Hawy Al-Kabeer,* a book by Abo Hassan Al-Mawardy. In this book, the Shafi said that there is a religious duty entitled *Fard Al-Kifayah*, which means that *ijtihad* is "not required to be performed as long as a sufficient number of community members fulfill it."[279] The Quran explains, "if a contingent from every expedition remained behind, they could devote themselves to studies in religion, and admonish the people when they return to them, that thus they (may learn) to guard themselves (against evil)."[280] The previous verse shows clearly that there must be scholars who make *ijtihad*. If all scholars imitated and copied their predecessors there would be no knowledge or *ijtihad*. Therefore, in every era there must be a group of scholars to make *ijtihad* from whom other Muslims can get advice.[281]

I would like to note that some of the verses of the Quran are *Muhkam*, while others are *Mutashabih*. The Quran states,

> "It is He Who has sent down to you (Muhammad) the Book (this Qur'an). In it are Verses that are entirely clear, they are the foundations of the Book [and those are the Verses of Al-Ahkam (commandments), Al-

---

275 The meeting was in February 2012 at Dar Al-Ifta in Cairo.
276 AL IMAM ALHAFEZ ALSHEIKH GALAL ALDIN ABDAL-RAHMAN ABN-ABY BAKR AL-SEYOOTY, AL-RAAD ALA MN AKHLAD ELAA AL-ARAD WA GAHL AN AL-IJTIHAD FI KOL ASR FARD [RESPOND TO WHOM CLUNG TO THE EARTH AND IGNORANTLY DID NOT KNOW THAT DELIGANCE IS OBLIGATORY IN EVERY ERA] 67 (Shekh Khalel ed.,1st ed. 1983). Sheikh Gala El Din el Seyooty was born in 1445 and died in 1505.
277 Al-Suyuti, WIKIPEDIA.ORG, http://en.wikipedia.org/wiki/Al-Suyuti (last visited Mar. 19, 2012).
278 AL-SEYOOTY, *supra* note 276.
279 *Fard*, WIKIPEDIA.COM, http://en.wikipedia.org/wiki/Fard (last visited Mar. 19, 2012).
280 QURAN 9:122.
281 Al-Seyooty, *supra* note 276.

Fara'id (obligatory duties) and Al-Hudud (legal laws for the punishment of thieves, adulterers)]; and others not entirely clear."[282]

The verses that are entirely clear and decisive are called *Muhkam* and the verses that are not decisive and clear are called *Mutashabih*. The *Muhkam* can help with the interpretation of the *Mutashabih*. The reason for which all of the verses of the Quran are not *Muhkam* is as follows:

> Al-Shaykh al-Tusi, in his tafsir, Tibyan (p. 11), has said: "Wisdom has required that the Qur'anic words and phrases be used in a way that their understanding should require investigation, effort and exertion, so as to result in the growth of knowledge." That is, since human development and growth, on the level of the individual as well as of society, is a law of God embedded in nature, God has set forth the verses of the Qur'an in such a profound and rich fashion so as to afford human beings to benefit from them and seek inspiration from them in step with their growing intellectual, spiritual and material needs in their individual and social lives, and thus traverse the Divinely-envisaged path of development and perfection without encountering any stagnation.[283]

Although the verses of *Muhkam* are thought to be clearer and more decisive than the verses of *Mutashabih*, they both need interpretation.[284] As an example of the verses of *Muhkam*, the Quran provides, "The Creator of the heavens and the earth. He has made for you mates from yourselves, and for the cattle (also) mates. By this means He creates you (in the wombs). There is nothing like Him; and He is the All-Hearer, the All-Seer."[285] The previous verse is clearly decisive, in that it states that there is nothing like or comparable to God and that God is the creator of everything. As another example, Quran states about God, "He begets not, nor was He begotten."[286] On the other hand, as an example of *Mutashabih* the Quran states, "Divorced women shall wait concerning themselves for three monthly quruu."[287] There are two different interpretations for the word *'quruu;'* The first meaning is menstruation and the second is purity from menses."[288]

---

282 QURAN 3:7.
283 *The Holy Quran as the First Source of Ijtihad*, AL-ISLAM.ORG, http://www.al-islam.org/al-tawhid/ijtihad/2.htm (last visited Mar. 19, 2012).
284 Helaly, *supra* note 267.
285 QURAN 42:11.
286 *Id.* at 112:3.
287 *Id.* at 2:228.
288 Helaly, *supra* note 267.

The total number of verses of ahkam (*Muhkam*) is five hundred verses and five hundred hadith.[289] The verses of ahkam need to be understood clearly as "the ayat al-'ahkam lay down the Islamic laws and rules concerning social, penal and economic matters."[290] Currently, there is a need for Islamic scholars who can interpret the Quran. The Quran will always need to be interpreted. One of the main reasons for this is that new issues arise that need the Sharia perspective. For instance, what is the point of view with respect to transplantation of organs? If a person needs a kidney, can another person donate a kidney to him? Is this to be considered against, or compatible with, Sharia law? Another example is banks and stocks. The old Jurisprudential Schools of Islam did not write about this issue. To be able to determine the compatibility of such matters with the Quran and the Sunnah, there is a need for deep understanding of the Quran. The Quran "contains hidden meanings. That is, besides the literal meanings of the words and their apparent, ordinary sense, other meanings and concepts underline the same that are beyond the grasp of many."[291]

As mentioned earlier, there are only five hundred verses that are *Muhkam*. There is a need for interpretation to understand the other verses, which constitute the majority of the Quran. There is a need for new interpretations to answer all of the new questions that have arisen during the past two centuries, such as the transplantation of organs, etc.

People may think that the verses that are *Mukham* do not need interpretation. Yet, they definitely do. I will give an example of a verse of the Quran about the *Muhkam* to show that it needs interpretation.[292] For instance, the Quran provides,

> "The only reward of those who make war upon Allah and His messenger and strive after corruption in the land will be that they will be killed or crucified, or have their hands and feet on alternate sides cut off, or will be expelled out of the land. Such will be their degradation in the world, and in the Hereafter theirs will be an awful doom."[293]

A clear example of a *Muhkam* verse is that gangsters must be "killed or crucified, or have their hands and feet on alternate sides cut off, or will be expelled out of

---

289 Helaly, *supra* note 267; *see also The Holy Qu'ran as the First Source of Ijtihad*, AL-ISLAM.ORG, http://www.al-islam.org/al-tawhid/ijtihad/2.htm (last visited Mar. 19, 2012).
290 *The Holy Qu'ran as the First Source of Ijtihad*, *supra* note 283.
291 Id.
292 Helaly, *supra* note 267.
293 QURAN 5:33.

the land."[294] Yet, there are different interpretations by different Islamic jurisprudential schools regarding the meaning of "gangsters."[295] For instance, some Islamic scholars indicate that gangsters must have a weapon in order for the hudood punishment to be applied. Also, there are different interpretations regarding the word "or" that is written in the previous verse of the Quran. Does it mean diversification or does it mean to choose between any of the punishments regardless of the kind of crime committed? Also, there are different opinions of Islamic jurisprudential schools as to whether the previous punishment can be applied to a woman or if gangsters can only be men.[296]

From these examples, we can come to the conclusion that both *Muhkam* and *Mutashabih* need interpretation. In other words, all of the Quran can require further interpretation. Interpretations of the Quran make it a living instrument. God created people and also created their minds. If God wanted people not to think, He would write all of the Quran clearly in order to not require people to think. Yet, people are not created to be machines. The most important thing that distinguishes human beings from animals is the mind. People have minds and they should think with their minds. The first word that was revealed to Mohammed in the Quran is "Read".[297] The first verse that was revealed to Mohammed is "Read! In the Name of your Lord Who has created (all that exists)."[298]

On the other hand, Professor Saad Al-Din Helaly, Professor of Comparative Islamic Jurisprudence at Al-Azhar University, has indicated that there are some Islamic scholars who are against *ijtihad*. One of them is the famous Islamic scholar Ibn Hazm. Professor Saad Al-Din Helaly states that it should be noted that in his book entitled *Al-Moha'la*, Ibn Hazm (a very professional scholar) analyzed the opinions of different scholars and then defended his opinion. He criticized the diversity of *fiqh* to defend his opinions because he has *ijtihad* skills and he believes that his *ijtihad* is correct. Professor Saad said that scholars are against *ijtihad* because they have no *ijtihad* skills. They cannot defend their reasoning and so criticize different Islamic opinions.[299] Professor Saad added that we cannot apply the Quran and Sunnah without *ijtihad* because the Arabic vocabulary is very rich and each Arab word can have different meanings.[300]

---

294 Id.
295 Helaly, *supra* note 267.
296 Id.
297 QURAN 96:1.
298 QURAN 96:1.
299 HELALY,*supra* note 273, at 230
300 Id.

Some scholars, such as Sheikh Aly Al-Khafeef, state that there was no *ijtihad* during the life of the Prophet.[301] They add that even if any issue was raised with respect to *ijtihad*, Prophet Mohammed would immediately state the opinion of Sharia law.[302] Therefore, there was no *ijtihad* in the life of the Prophet. However, I agree with the opinion of Professor Saad Al-Din Helaly regarding the existence of *ijtihad* even during the life of Prophet Mohammed. The methodology of Sharia is to encourage thinking. The doctrinal diversity in opinions is a method applied by Sharia.[303] During his life, the Prophet left some issues that were not explicitly explained to encourage *ijtihad*. During the life of the Prophet:

> It is related that Ibn Umar said, "When the Prophet may Allah bless him and grant him peace, returned to us from the Battle of the Parties (Ahzab), he said, No one should pray Asr before they get to Banu Qurayza. For some of them Asr became due on the way." Some people said, We will not pray until we get there. Others said, No, we should do the prayer. That was not what he meant." This was mentioned to the Prophet and he did not rebuke any of them.[304]

In the previous hadith, Prophet Mohammed requested that a group of Muslims travel to a city. He requested for them to hurry and to not pray Asr[305] until they got to Banu Qurayza. Along their way the Asr was due. Some of them decided to pray Asr and not to wait since praying is obligatory as the second pillar of Islam. In addition, the Quran provides that praying is to be done at fixed times. The Quran states, "Verily, As-Salat (the prayer) is enjoined on the believers at fixed hours."[306] They decided to pray Asr because if they did not pray Asr until they arrived, the Asr time would have passed and it would be time for Magrib prayer. They interpreted what the Prophet had said not as a request not to pray, but a request to hurry as much as possible. The other group decided to wait because, although praying is mandatory, the decisions of the Prophet should be respected. Sharia requests that Muslims obey God and Prophet Mohammed. For instance, the Quran provides: "And obey Allah and the Messenger (Muhammad) that you

---

301 *Id.*
302 *Id.*
303 *Id.* at 230.
304 Imam Bukhari, *Book of the Fear Prayer*, Hadith 904, SUNNYPATH.ORG, http://www.sunni-path.com/Library/Hadith/H0002P0018.aspx (last visited Apr. 22, 2012).
305 Asr is the third prayer in the day. The time of this prayer differs from city to city. However, it tends to occur between noon and sunset.
306 QURAN 4:103.

may obtain mercy."[307] This group decided to pray Asr after they arrived at Banu Qurayza. After both groups returned to the Prophet, he did not criticize any of them. He did not say that one of the groups was better than the other. This means that Sharia accepts the diversity of opinions and did so even during the life of the Prophet. The two groups used jurisprudential reasoning. The Prophet did not criticize any of them, which means that both opinions are correct.[308]

Sharia encourages thinking and understanding; it does not accept imitation or that the door of *ijtihad* is closed. There are many verses in the Quran that encourage, and call for, thinking and understanding. For instance, the Quran states, "When it is said to them: 'Follow what Allah has sent down.' They say: 'Nay! We shall follow what we found our fathers following.' (Would they do that!) even though their fathers did not understand anything nor were they guided?"[309] Also, the Quran states:

> Verily! In the creation of the heavens and the earth, and in the alternation of night and day, and the ships which sail through the sea with that which is of use to mankind, and the water (rain) which Allah sends down from the sky and makes the earth alive therewith after its death, and the moving (living) creatures of all kinds that He has scattered therein, and in the veering of winds and clouds which are held between the sky and the earth, are indeed Ayat (proofs, evidence, signs, etc.) for people of understanding.[310]

As another example, the Quran states:

> And in the alternation of night and day, and the provision (rain) that Allah sends down from the sky, and revives therewith the earth after its death, and in the turning about of the winds (i.e. sometimes towards the east or north, and sometimes towards the south or west sometimes bringing glad tidings of rain etc., and sometimes bringing the torment), are signs for a people who understand.[311]

The Quran also states, "And He it is Who spread out the earth and placed therein firm hills and flowing streams, and of all fruits He placed therein two spouses

---

307   *Id.* at 3:132.
308   Helaly, *supra* note 267.
309   QURAN 2:170.
310   *Id.* at 2:164.
311   *Id.* at 25:5.

(male and female). He covereth the night with the day. Lo! herein verily are portents for people who take thought."[312] As well as,

> Verily, the likeness of (this) worldly life is as the water (rain) which We send down from the sky; so by it arises the intermingled produce of the earth of which men and cattle eat: until when the earth is clad in its adornments and is beautified, and its people think that they have all the powers of disposal over it, Our Command reaches it by night or by day and We make it like a clean-mown harvest, as if it had not flourished yesterday! Thus do We explain the Ayat (proofs, evidence, verses, lessons, signs, revelations, laws, etc.) in detail for the people who reflect.[313]

Ijtihad is from *fitrah*, which "is a philosophical and legal belief that all humans are governed by basic innate laws, or laws of nature, which are separate and distinct from laws which are legislated."[314] *Ijtihad* requires thinking and analyzing. God created a brain in each and every person. If God wanted people not to think, it would have been easy for Sharia to come with each and every detail explained, without requiring interpretation. However, thinking comes from *fitrah*, therefore *ijtihad* is also from *fitrah*. There are many verses that request people to think, understand, etc. From these verses we can easily recognize that Sharia wants people to understand, think, and make *ijtihad*. For instance, with respect to women's rights, the Quran states:

> O you who believe! You are forbidden to inherit women against their will; and you should not treat them with harshness, that you may take away part of the Mahr [dowry] you have given them, unless they commit open illegal sexual intercourse; and live with them honourably. If you dislike them, it may be that you dislike a thing and Allah brings through it a great deal of good.[315]

In the previous verse it is said, "and live with them honourably."[316] The Arabic word said live with them is *belma'roof*. There are different interpretations of *ma'aroof* as it was mentioned in the verse. For instance, scholars have said that a woman came to Prophet Mohammed complaining about her husband because he is niggard and scarce and does not give her sufficient money for herself and

---

312   *Id.* at 13: 3.
313   *Id.* at 10:24.
314   *What is Natural Law Theory*, WISEGEEK.COM, http://www.wisegeek.com/what-is-natural-law-theory.htm (last visited Apr. 14, 2012).
315   QURAN 4:19.
316   *Id.*

her child. She added that she takes money from him without telling him. The Prophet replied by instructing her to take the money that satisfies you and your child *belma'roof*.[317] With respect to the meaning of *belma'roof*, Islamic scholars have said that there is no fixed amount for every wife. If the wife is a princess married to a prince, the amount will be greater than for a rural woman married to a farmer. Therefore, the door of *ijtihad* is not closed and cannot be closed.

Imam Abo-Hamed Al-Gazaly writes about whether a student can travel to seek knowledge without the permission of his parents. He said that if there are no people who are making *ijtihad* in a country, a student in this country can travel to seek knowledge without the permission of his parents.[318] Iman Gazally gives priority to people who make *ijtihad* without the permission of their parents. Imam Negm Al-Din Abn-ALraf'a said that if the student is travelling to seek knowledge, it is preferable to go with the permission of the parents.[319] Parents are considered to be on a unique level in Sharia law, but some scholar give priority to *ijtihad*, if there are no other people who are making *ijtihad* in the country.

Al-kady abo-Alhassan says that Imam Malik and many Islamic scholars mentioned that *ijtihad* is obligatory and there should be revocation for imitation.[320] They referred to the Quranic verse that says, "So keep your duty to Allah as best ye can... "[321] Imam Nawawy refers to the following Quranic verse that encourages, and calls for, *ijtihad*: "whereas if they had referred it to the messenger and to such of them as are in authority, those among them who are able to think out the matter would have known it."[322] He said that it is important to determine and analyze each issue, because the clear verses in Quran can solve only a few life matters.[323] Al-Kady Abd-Alwahab referred to several Quranic verses that encourage people to think deeply to fully understand the Quran.[324] The Quran states, "Do they not then consider the Qur'an carefully?"[325] Also it explains, "So learn a lesson, O ye who have eyes!"[326]

---

317 Islamic Fatwa, ISLAMWEB.NET, http://www.islamweb.net/fatwa/printfatwa.php?Id=125360 &lang=A (last visited Mar. 19, 2012).
318 AL-SEYOOTY, *supra* note 276.
319 *Id.* at 78.
320 *Id.* at 80
321 QURAN 64:16.
322 *Id.* at 4:83.
323 AL-SEYOOTY, *supra* note 276.
324 *Id.*
325 QURAN 82:4; AL-SEYOOTY, *supra* note 276.
326 *Id.* at 59:2; AL-SEYOOTY, *supra* note 276.

Professor Kamal Abo Al-Magd,[327] a member of the Islamic Research Academy, a professor of law at Cairo University and one of the famous Islamic philosophers in Egypt and the Arab World, said in his article *Hewar la Mowagaha* [Dialogue, not Confrontation][328] that there are many people who fear and refuse the opening of the door of *ijtihad*. They think that any renewal of Islamic jurisprudence will lead to the dissolution of Sharia law in other civilizations. They believe that the opening of the door of *ijtihad* aims to destroy Islamic jurisprudence in other civilizations that are not in compliance with the objectives and purposes of Sharia law. He added that he respects the concerns of the people who fear *ijtihad* and the renewal of Sharia. However, the non-renewal of Islamic jurisprudence leads to the risk of stagnation and infertility of Sharia.[329] He added that bearing the consequences of *ijtihad* requires bravery and patience. He also added that if Arabs remain as they are, without *ijtihad*, their concerns will cause them to continue to be in less powerful positions in relation to other nations.[330] He added that there is a thin line between renewing ones faith and *ijtihad* on one hand and not following the direction of Sharia law and Islam on the other hand. He suggested that *ijtihad* should be used with respect to ways of thinking and behaviors and not with respect to the religion itself. He wrote the hadith of the Prophet Mohammed, which states that, "God will send renewers of the faith every 100 years."[331] This hadith clearly shows that the *ijtihad* will never end and God did not request that people should ever close the door of *ijtihad*.

Professor Kamal Abo Al-Magd also said that one of the important conditions of *ijtihad* is the fulfillment of its requirements by the person who makes it. The person making *ijtihad* must have knowledge of the Quran and its interpretations. This person should have full knowledge of the reasons for each verse and the stories behind them. There should be full knowledge of the Sunnah, etc.[332] The most important thing suggested by Professor Abo Al-Magd is that an individual

---

327 Professor Kamal Abo Al-Magd is a professor of law at Cairo University, a former Minister in Egypt, and the former vice-president of the National Council of Human Rights in Egypt. He is a member of the Islamic Research Academy and a consultant lawyer at Baker & McKenzie law firm in Egypt.
328 Dr. Kamal Abo Al-Magd, Hewar la Mowagaha [Dialogue, not Confrontation] 43-44 (3rd ed. 2006).
329 *Id.*
330 *Id.*
331 *Id.*
332 *Id.* at 48.

cannot make the *ijtihad*. He said that it must be made through institutions, by a group of people. In other words, *ijtihad* must be made collectively.[333]

From all that I have outlined, we can come to the conclusion that the door of *ijtihad* is still open and it will never be closed. The real question is not whether the door of *ijtihad* is still open or closed, this question has already been answered. The question that remains is regarding who can make this *ijtihad*. Later in the book, I will further explain the different opinions of Islamic schools of jurisprudence, such as Imam Malik, Imam Shafi, Imam Hanbali, and Imam Hanafi. When we read the jurisprudence of these schools and the reasons for each opinion they wrote, we find that they demonstrate profoundly deep thinking. They analyzed each issue thoroughly. To this day, it is not easy to find this sort of trusted man with such knowledge. However, we have more privileges in this century than was the case in previous centuries. For instance, if a scholar wanted to learn at the beginning of Islam, he would travel by horse for months in order to reach an Islamic scholar and begin learning from him. However, nowadays, we can get easily access to libraries, books, and different opinions of Islamic scholars.

I agree with Professor Kamal Abo Al-Maged that the door of *ijtihad* is open and that we need an institution to make *ijtihad*. Professors at these institutions need to work collectively to do this. Al-Azhar, as one of the most famous and oldest Islamic institutions and universities, can do this effectively. There are many professors and scholars at Al-Azhar who are very capable of these tasks. Furthermore, Al-Azhar is a moderate Islamic university; they are not on the extreme right or left. Also, the scholars at Al-Azhar are highly qualified. In addition, and most importantly, the four main schools of Islamic jurisprudence are taught at Al-Azhar. In other words, it does not favor one school and ignore the others. In this way, a diversity of knowledge is important to having diversity in opinions. Due to the great importance of Al-Azhar, it is protected in a separate article in the Egyptian Consitution of 2014. Article 7 of the Constitution states,

> "Al-Azhar is an independent Islamic scientific institution, with exclusive competence over its own affairs. It is the main reference for religious sciences and Islamic affairs. It is responsible for calling to Islam, as well as, disseminating religious sciences and the Arabic language in Egypt and all over the world.
>
> The State shall provide sufficient financial allocations thereto so that it can achieve its purposes.

---

333   Id.

Al-Azhar's Grand Sheikh is independent and may not be dismissed. The Law shall regulate the method of appointing the Grand Sheikh from amongst the members of Council of Senior Scholars."[334]

The fact that the door of *ijtihad* is still open offers a great advantage. Because of this, there is the need for new interpretations to be made by honest and trusted institutions. These interpretations will enable new understandings of the Sharia view with respect to international human rights. It is important to have an examination and evaluation by Islamic scholars, who are professional scholars of law and Sharia, of the articles of the Arab Charter and other international and regional treaties. This will lead to a large revolution of the Sharia interpretation that will protect and respect the Sharia objectives and purposes, while also complying with international standards.

3. The Diversity of *Fiqh*

The diversity in *fiqh* offers some lenience for followers. Different scholars who make *ijtihad*, the *moj'tahdeen* have different kinds of personalities and represent different cultures and traditions from different societies. Therefore, each *moj'tahd* has a group of people that supports and are convinced of his ideas.[335] It should be noted that, while schools of Islamic law are very much alike with respect to the core principles, there is variation with respect to the details.

Even the same Islamic scholar can change his *ijtihad*. For instance, Imam Shafii, who established one of the four most popular Islamic schools of jurisprudence, made *ijtihad* while he was living in Iraq. After he moved to Egypt, he changed his opinion on some matters and made another *ijtihad*. Beside every opinion or *ijtihad* in Shafii's book, the sentences "in the old" or "in the new" are written. "In the old" indicates his opinion while he was living in Iraq. "In the new" indicates his opinion while he was living in Egypt.[336]

It should be noted that the legal reasoning of the Islamic scholars is called *fat'wa*. Any *fat'wa* is not legally binding for people and countries. Instead, they can choose between different *fat'wa* according to their interests.[337]

---

334 Egyptian Const. art. 7. http://www.sis.gov.eg/Newvr/Dustor-en001.pdf (last visited May 14, 2014).

335 HELALY, *supra* note 273, at 228 & 229.

336 Ahas, Hlayhel, *Did Egyption Customs Lead to a New Shafi'i School?*, muslimmatters.org, http://muslimmatters.org/2010/04/19/did-egyptian-customs-lead-to-a-new-shafii-school/ (last visited May 21, 2012).

337 BADERIN, *supra* note 138, at 72.

Chapter 3: A Theory of Human Rights

A. Regional Systems for the Protection of Human Rights as Part of the Debate Between the Theories of Universalism and Cultural Relativism

There is an ongoing debate between people who believe that human rights are universal thus everywhere in the world and those who believe that human rights are culturally based and can differ from one place to another. Those in favor of the universality of human rights believe that rights should be applied to all people regardless of their cultural differences, region, nationality, color, sex, etc. Universalists believe that human rights should be accessible to all people, simply because they are human.[338] Louis Henkin, a universalist scholar, states:

> To call them human suggests that they are universal: they are the due of every human being in every human society. They do not differ with geography or history, culture or ideology, political or economic system, or stage of development. They do not depend on gender or race, class or status. To call them "rights" implies that they are claims "as of right," not merely appeals to grace, or charity, or brotherhood, or love; they need not be earned or deserved. They are more than aspirations, or assertions of "the good," but claims of entitlement and corresponding obligation in some political order under some applicable law…[339]

People in favor of universality believe that human rights are rights that must be accessible to all people, regardless of whether or not they live in a certain region. This perspective advocates that, around the world, all people share the desire to live in peace and justice without any discrimination or cruel and inhuman treatment.[340]

On the other hand, cultural relativists believe that different cultures and traditions do not share a common ground. This perspective advocates that cultures and traditions differ from place to another. Therefore, universality of human rights does not, and cannot, exist. The cultural relativist theory also believes that cultures and traditions of specific country or region cannot be imposed on other countries or regions. The Chinese delegate at the World Conference on Human Rights in Vienna stated, "One should not and cannot think the human rights standard and model of certain countries as the only proper ones, and demand all other countries to comply with them."[341] Furthermore, this delegate stated that

---

338 Robbins, *supra* note 99, at 277.
339 *Id.* (citing Louis Henkin, *Rights: Here and There*, 81 COLUM. L. REV. 1582, 1582 (1981)).
340 *Id.* at 278.
341 Robbins, *supra* note 99, at 278 (citing Patrick D. Curran, *Universalism, Relativism, and Private*

any attempt to define rights in terms of universality "infringes on a State's right to autonomy."[342] In addition, cultural relativists emphasize that cultures and traditions of a certain country or region cannot be imposed on other countries or regions because this constitutes violation to the states sovereignty. They state, "[T]he push to universalization of norms [will arguably] destroy diversity of cultures and hence...amount to another path toward cultural homogenization in the modern world."[343]

Neither of these two theories is superior to the other. No one can deny that human rights are universal around the world and must be protected regardless of country, region, sex, etc. For instance, the Arab Charter explains, "The present Charter seeks, within the context of the national identity of the Arab States and their sense of belonging to a common civilization, to achieve the following aims: To entrench the principle that all human rights are universal, indivisible, interdependent and interrelated."[344] Most of the human rights that are protected in the Universal Declaration on Human Rights, ICCPR, ICESCR, and the Arab Charter on Human Rights are the minimum level below which a state should not go. These rights are considered universal and should be protected. On the other hand, the expansion of the interpretations of some rights by some courts or scholars should not be imposed on other states and regions as universal, unless there is widespread acceptance across the world of these new interpretations. Therefore, instead of having a debate as to whether to follow universalism or cultural relativism, it is better, from my point of view, to draw from both theories. For instance, the right to privacy is universal because it is protected by all international and regional human rights treaties. However, we cannot force other countries to follow the European Court of Human Rights in its interpretation that the right to privacy extends to the right to abortions and homosexual marriage. Also, we cannot categorize countries that do not follow this interpretation as violating international human rights law. The best way is to recognize the commonalities between countries that respect the right to privacy, instead of criticizing these countries that do not follow some of the interpretations.

There are some rights that are considered universally protected. No country is permitted to suspend or derogate from these rights. Cultural diversity cannot be

---

Enforcement of Customary International Law, 5 CHI. J. INT'L L. 311 (2004)).

342 *Id.* (citing Patrick D. Curran, *Universalism, Relativism, and Private Enforcement of Customary International Law*, 5 CHI. J. INT'L L. 311 (2004)).

343 *Id.* at 279 (citing HENRY J. STEINER & PHILIP ALSTON, COMMENT ON THE UNIVERSALIST-RELATIVIST DEBATE, IN INTERNATIONAL HUMAN RIGHTS IN CONTEXT 366, 367 (2nd ed. 2000)).

344 ACHR, *supra* note 126, at art. 1(4).

used to suspend the protection of these rights, such as the right to fair trial and the right not to be tortured.[345]

On the other hand there are rights that are not internationally protected, with respect to which cultural diversity should be respected. For instance, there is no international consensus as to whether to, or not to, abolish the death penalty. Even in a single country, such as the United States of America, some states do not have the death penalty while others do. No one can say that countries and states that have not abolished the death penalty are violating human rights. Instead of naming and shaming, it is better to encourage countries and states that apply the death penalty towards putting more restrictions and guarantees with respect to the application of the death penalty.

B. A Theory of Human Rights to Govern a Regional Human Rights System: A Brief Examination of Competing Theories of Human Rights

In his article, *A New Perspective on the Universality Debate: Reverse Moderate Relativism in the Islamic Context*, Jason Morgan-Foster tries to find the ideal regional human rights theory. After examining the three most well known theories of human rights, previously reviewed by Kimberly Younce Schooley, Morgan-Foster suggested a fourth theory as ideal.[346] He focused on the following three theories: strict cultural relativism, moderate cultural relativism, and universalism. The strict cultural relativist theory believes that human rights are invalid because they are Western centered.[347] The moderate cultural relativist approach believes that although cultural diversity and cultural differences exist, there are some shared universal human rights principles.[348] The universalist theory believes that the only human rights principles that should be applied universally are the Western principles.[349] It has been stated:

> One of the most pertinent issues of the past twenty years has been the conflict between two different ideologies of human rights on a national scale, universalism, and cultural relativism. Universalism holds that more "primitive" cultures will eventually evolve to have the same

---

345 Doi, *supra* note 137, at 419.
346 Jason Morgan-Foster, *A New Perspective on the Universality Debate: Reverse Moderate Relativism in the Islamic Context*, 10 ILSA J. INT'L & COMP. L. 35, 36 (2003).
347 Schooley, *supra* note 150, at 679.
348 *Id.*
349 Morgan-Foster, *supra* note 346, at 36, 40 (citing Kimberly Younce Schooley, *Cultural, Sovereignty, Islam, and Human Rights-Toward a Communitarian Revision*, 25 CUMB. L. Rev. 651, 691-698 (1994-1995).

system of law and rights as Western cultures. Cultural relativists hold an opposite, but similarly rigid viewpoint, that a traditional culture is unchangeable.[350]

1. Universalism

The universalist approach "embraces the notion that human rights belong to everyone wherever he or she resides."[351] This approach recognizes that human rights are not a gift from a government, a president, or a king. Human rights are universal around the world to all people, merely because they are human.[352] In addition, "Universalism holds that more 'primitive' cultures will eventually evolve to have the same system of law and rights as Western cultures."[353] Universalism is criticized by opponents, who state that it perpetuates "colonialist practices" and that, under such an approach "one group assumes superiority over the other and bases values, ethics, power on that assumption."[354] The acceptance of this theory undermines human rights. Following this theory would create false universalism, as large numbers of countries ratify treaties but in fact do not fully implement them because of the reservations made in these treaties. For example, if we suppose that a large number of countries from all different regions of the world ratified a certain treaty after making reservations to this treaty, theoretically this treaty would be considered universally accepted. However, in practices this treaty would be useless because of the large number of reservations on its articles.[355] Universalism has also been criticized because "[i]t is not possible to impose a universal system of human rights if the effects of social change stemming from modernization are not understood or worse yet, ignored. In non-Western societies, industrialization, capitalism, and democracy might not have been the eventual outcome of the process of cultural evolution."[356]

---

350 *Human Rights: The Pursuit of an Ideal*, THINKQUEST.ORG, http://library.thinkquest.org/C0126065/issuniversalism.html (last visited May 18, 2012).

351 Elisabeth Reichert, *Human Rights: An Examination of Universalism and Cultural Relativism*, J. COMP. SOC. WELFARE, 22 No. 1, 24 (April 2006), http://socialwork.siu.edu/resourcecenter/RJCS_A_152282.pdf (last visited May 18, 2012).

352 Shashi Tharoor, *Are Human Rights Universal?*, NEW INTERNATIONALIST MAGAZINE, Mar. 2001, http://www.thirdworldtraveler.com/Human_Rights/Are_HR_Universal%3F.html (last visited May 18, 2012).

353 *Human Rights: The Pursuit of an Ideal, supra* note 350.

354 Reichert, *supra* note 351, at 27.

355 Morgan-Foster, *supra* note 346, at 42.

356 *Human Rights: The Pursuit of an Ideal, supra* note 350.

2. Strict Cultural Relativism

According to Elisabeth Reichert, "Cultural relativism refers to a view that all cultures are equal and universal values become secondary when examining cultural norms. No outside value is superior to that of the local culture."[357] This theory of strict cultural relativism "oppose[s] any discussion of international human rights consensus as an affront to culture."[358] In addition, it believes that "local cultural traditions…properly determine the existence and scope of… [human] rights enjoyed by individuals in a given society…[and] that no transboundary legal or moral standards exist against which human rights practices may be judged acceptable or unacceptable."[359] Also, "strict cultural relativists believe that human rights advocates impose a hegemonic set of values that are anathema to other equally valid cultural traditions."[360] Strict cultural relativism believes that it is impossible to change cultures, because they are unchangeable.[361] Those who advocate for cultural relativism and against universalism say:

> There is no universal culture, therefore there are no universal human rights… The Universal Declaration was adopted at a time when most Third World countries were still under colonial rule. 'Human rights' are only a cover for Western intervention in the affairs of the developing world… In addition, some religious leaders argue that human rights can only be acceptable if they are founded on transcendent values of their faith, sanctioned by God.[362]

Cultural relativism does not only refer to non-Western countries. Cultural relativism can exist even in Western countries. Different cultures exists even in the same region:

> "People may think that cultural discussions of universalism vs. cultural relativism often focus on a Western tendency toward universalism and a non-Western tendency to highlight… However, cultural relativism also occurs in Western countries like the USA. The reality is that no

---

357 Reichert, *supra* note 351, at 27.
358 Morgan-Foster, *supra* note 346, at 36, 42 (citing Kimberly Younce Schooley, *Cultural, Sovereignty, Islam, and Human Rights-Toward a Communitarian Revision*, 25 Cumb. L. Rev. 651, 678 (1994-1995)).
359 *Id.* (citing Fernando R. Teson, *International Human Rights and Cultural Relativism*, 25 Va. J. Int'l L. 869, 870-71 (1985)).
360 Robert E. Sinnott, *Universalism and Cultural Relativism in Roper vs. Simmons*, 14 Willamette J. Int'l L. & Dispute Res. 136 (2006).
361 *Human Rights: The Pursuit of an Ideal, supra* note 350.
362 Tharoor, *supra* note 352.

country or culture readily accepts the imposition of a 'universal' human right when that right clashes with indigenous viewpoints."[363]

Strict cultural relativism is criticized because it is believed that this theory will lead to peoples' rights differing from one place to another, depending on cultures and nationalities. In addition, cultural relativism is also criticized because cultures change over time. Opponents of cultural relativism indicate that countries should not request derogation from human rights because of their cultures, rather cultures should be changed to accommodate human rights.[364]

3. Moderate Cultural Relativism

According to Robert E. Sinnott, "[m]oderate cultural relativists posited that all cultures recognize a universal core set of rights, and those rights should be discovered and enforced."[365] The theory of moderate cultural relativism emphasizes that there is space for shared principles related to human rights and that these shared core human rights shape the universal principles of human rights. This approach tries to determine the rights that are held in the common and tries to expand the number of rights that are held in common. The scholar An-Na'im is one of the famous proponents of this theory.[366] An-Na'im advocated that "the scope of ijtihad be expanded to enable modern Muslim jurists not only to change rules settled through *ijma*, but also to substitute previously enacted texts with other, more general, texts of Qur'an and Sunna despite the categorical nature of the prior texts."[367] Schooley criticized An-Na'im's theory, stating,

> "Although An-Na'im advocates a cross-cultural dialogue to define 'rights,' he actually adopts as 'rights' those already considered the norm in international law and advocates that the Shari'a be reformed to meet these standards. This approach seems conceptually inconsistent with An-Na'im's cultural legitimacy theme. Moreover, this concept is 'foreign' to Islam and excludes all discussion of community."[368]

---

363 Reichert, *supra* note 351, at 23, 24.
364 *Id.* at 29-30.
365 Sinnott, *supra* note 360, at 137.
366 Morgan-Foster, *supra* note 346, at 43.
367 Abdullahi Ahmed An-Naim, *Human Rights in Muslim World: Socio-Political Conditions and Scriptura l Imperatives, A Preliminary inquiry*, 3 HARV. HUM. RTS. J. 13, 49, (1990).
368 Schooley, *supra* note 150, at 690; *see also* Morgan-Foster, *supra* note 346, at 46.

Morgan-Foster states, "An-Na'im's approach to reach common ground with international norms on some issues by a plausible reading of local texts, such a theory based on international norms is likely to offend local culture frequently."[369]

Moderate cultural relativism, is not the best solution. Under An-Naim's theory, international law is always the base from which Shari'a should be reformed. Yet, there should be a balance between protecting international human right norms on one hand and respecting cultures and traditions on the other. Even An-Na'im himself said,

> "Such a modern 'Shari'a' could be, in my view, entirely consistent with current standards of human rights. These views, however, are appreciated by only a tiny minority of contemporary Muslims. To the overwhelming majority of Muslims today, Shari'a is the sole valid interpretation of Islam, and as such ought to prevail over any human law or policy."[370]

I agree with An-Na'im's diagnosis that Sharia law is aligned with current standards of human rights. However, I do not agree with his prescription that any conflict between international human rights standards and Sharia law should be only resolved by a modification or reinterpretation of Sharia law. Reinterpretation is very important and useful in some cases. However, reinterpretation of Sharia law should not be advocated as the only solution. In another words, I do not reject the theory of An-Na'im entirely, but I do suggest that a balance be achieved as much as possible in order to have a theory that is widely accepted both within the West and by Muslims. Due to the disadvantages of moderate cultural relativism, Morgan-Foster introduced a theory of reverse moderate relativism.

4. Reverse Moderate Relativism

The theory of reverse moderate relativism shares some similarities with the theory of moderate relativism. Reverse moderate relativism believes that there are opportunities for common shared human rights principles across different cultures. These principles are considered universal. The difference between the reverse moderate relativism and moderate relativism is that the reverse theory approaches the issue in reverse. In other words, according to reverse moderate

---

369 Morgan-Foster, *supra* note 346, at 46.
370 An-Naim, *supra* note 367, at 21.

relativism, cultures and traditions are the benchmark that should be reached by international human rights law.[371]

Morgan-Foster proposed the theory of reverse moderate relativism as a new theory of the universality of all human rights. This theory assures that it is impossible to reach the universality of human rights. However, the theory admits that there are core human rights that can exist and that are universally applicable. The key to this theory is to determine the shared core values in way that is the reverse of the approach used by moderate cultural relativism. Morgan-Foster stated, "Instead of starting with the international value as the neutral benchmark and reinterpreting local law to draw it closer to the international norm, reverse moderate relativism takes a given local law as the neutral standard, and exposes ways in which international law has drawn closer to that standard."[372]

C. A New Theory of Human Rights Compatible with the Arab Human Rights System

It is not wise to ignore Sharia as the legal system that exists in nearly all countries that are members of the Arab Charter. In addition, it is not practical to focus on criticizing the Sharia legal system. It is not realistic to believe that the Sharia legal system will imitate another specific system exactly. Rather, it is practical and wise to recognize that different legal systems share commonalities. We have to understand the philosophy, objectives, and purposes of Sharia law before judging it. For example, the Kingdom of Saudi Arabia stated in its combined initial and second periodic report of states parties, which was submitted to the Committee on the Elimination of Discrimination against Women, that "Islamic Shariah respects these natural differences and accords woman a privileged position in order to achieve justice for her. For example, it charges the man with earning a living to provide for himself and his wife as compensation for the woman's role as conceiver, child bearer and mother."[373] In this way, we should follow a theory that does not ignore Sharia law. However, the theory should understand the objectives and purposes of Sharia and then examine the articles of the domestic laws to determine whether they operate in congruence or against Sharia law. Furthermore, we should examine Islamic jurisprudence to determine whether

---

371 Jason Morgan-Foster, *Reverse Moderate Relativism Applied: Third Generation International Human Rights from an Islamic Perspective*, BEPRESS LEGAL SERIES 5 (2004), http://law.bepress.com/cgi/viewcontent.cgi?article=1569&context=expresso (last visited May 19, 2012).

372 Morgan-Foster, *supra* note 346, at 49.

373 U.N. Committee on the Elimination of Discrimination against Women: Combined Initial and Second Periodic Reports of States Parties, Saudi Arabia, *supra* note 6.

there is any Islamic interpretation that is compatible with the international human rights standards. These previous examinations will help to establish a common area of shared values and principles that should not be derogated. In short, we should decide what kind of theory we want. Do we want a reasonable and logical theory that can be implemented practically? Or are we looking for a fake theory written in nice books kept on the shelf, which cannot be accepted by Arab Countries.

I do agree with Morgan-Foster when he stated, "An-Na'im's moderate cultural relativism, which first appears the most attractive, is perhaps the most dangerous of all: In attempting to create and expand a list of core shared rights, moderate cultural relativism treats the international norm as the neutral benchmark to be achieved, with dangerous neo-colonialist implication."[374] Respecting human rights does not mean imitating specific civilizations. Even within the same civilization, what is considered right differs from one era to the next. Even in the same country, there are differences in opinion. For example, in the United States of America the death penalty is applied in some states, while it is prohibited in others. An-Naim's theory could never gain wide acceptance from both decision makers and the community in the Middle East.

Jason Morgan-Foster's theory of reverse moderate relativism is the most suitable theory for many reasons. This theory seeks to find a common ground of shared values and principles for human rights. His theory is realistic as compared to the other theories. He seeks to find the commonalities between both Sharia law and international law. Unlike moderate relativism, reverse moderate relativism seeks to position domestic and national law as the benchmark that should be achieved by human rights law. Morgan-Foster's theory will be highly respected in the Middle East and Arab countries as it respects cultures, traditions, and domestic national laws. In contrast, the theory of universalism ignores the diversity in cultures and traditions[375] and the theory of strict cultural relativism believes that Western principles are fundamental.[376]

On the other hand, as mentioned earlier, I do not agree entirely with Morgan-Foster's theory of reverse cultural relativism. While his theory is the best of those examined, it should be amended. According to his theory, "instead of starting with the international value as the neutral benchmark and reinterpreting local law to draw it closer to the international norm, reverse moderate relativism takes a given local law as the neutral standard, and exposes ways in which international

---

374 Morgan-Foster, *supra* note 346, at 66.
375 Id.
376 Id.

law has drawn closer to that standard."[377] The amendment that I propose is that Sharia law should be recognized as a base and the neutral benchmark from which to examine, and alter, international law. There are commonalities between Sharia law and international law. There should be an examination of the rights upheld by both sets of laws in order to show the common ground between Sharia law and international law.

The local law should not always be the base used to gauge international law, rather there should be a balance between the theories of universalism, strict cultural relativism, moderate cultural relativism, and reverse moderate relativism. All of the theories can be applied together as one theory. In other words, parts of the universalist theory should be applied in order to ensure a core of shared rights that are protected everywhere in the world. As I have outlined above, there are shared principles between international law and Sharia law. From these shared principles we can establish shared rights that are respected by both Sharia law and international law. These shared principles should be applied because they are universally accepted and constitute rights that should be applied across all cultures. On the other hand, each region and even each country should be given some flexibility in the implementation of the details. Doing so respects the diversity within different cultures and traditions. From this understanding, the theories of universalism, strict culture relativism, and moderate culture relativism are applied in my proposed theory.

The Vienna Convention on the Law of Treaties defined 'jus cogens' and considered any treaty to be null and void if it conflicts with jus cogens rules. Article 53 of the Vienna Convention on the Law of Treaties states,

> "A treaty is void if, at the time of its conclusion, it conflicts with a peremptory norm of general international law. For the purposes of the present Convention, a peremptory norm of general international law is a norm accepted and recognized by the international community of States as a whole as a norm from which no derogation is permitted and which can be modified only by a subsequent norm of general international law having the same character."[378]

There are only very few international crimes that form part of *jus cogens* — such as slavery, genocide, torture, and other crimes against humanity. The international human rights courts and committees play an important role in interpreting these universal rights to be free from such scourges of humankind. For instance,

---

377 Id. at 49.
378 United Nations, Vienna Convention on the Law of Treaties, *supra* note 70, art. 53.

the Human Rights Committee stated that: "a State may not reserve the right to engage in slavery, to torture, to subject persons to cruel, inhuman or degrading treatment or punishment, to arbitrarily deprive persons of their lives, to arbitrarily arrest and detain persons, to deny freedom of thought, conscience and religion, to presume a person guilty unless he proves his innocence..."[379]

It important to determine whether international human rights law, including *jus cogens* principles, contradicts principles of Sharia law. People who have been raised in Western culture may think that Sharia law violates human rights including *jus cogens* rights. Western scholars may say that Sharia law is against freedom of religion, freedom of thought, equality between men and women, prohibition of torture, right to life, etc. All of the principles of Sharia law, however, are, properly interpreted, absolutely compatible with international human rights law. I support applying my proposed theory even if it faces some criticism. It is impossible to have a theory that will not face any criticism. In my book, Sharia law will be evaluated in depth. I will rely not only on the opinions of Islamic scholars but also on the main sources of Sharia law. I will prove with evidence from the Quran and Sunnah that Sharia complies and is entirely compatible with international human rights law.

The theory that I will apply is based on the possibilities of reconciliation between international law and Sharia principles. In other words, the theory aims to create space for shared values and principles. There should not be conflicts between cultures. My goal is to enable constructive dialogue between cultures. The constructive dialogue should be based on respect. People are created with minds and every person has his own way of thinking, even within the same family. However, before judging anything harshly, we should think quietly. The first word that was revealed to Prophet Mohammed in the Quran is "Read." The first chapter revealed to Prophet Mohammed in the Quran is entitled "Read." The first verse that was revealed to Prophet Mohammed is "Read! In the Name of your Lord Who has created (all that exists)."[380] In addition, there is another full chapter in the Quran entitled "The Pen."[381] In short, we cannot force people who do not agree with our opinions to obey and follow certain cultures. Respecting the opinions of others should be done not only when evaluating other cultures but even

---

379 U.N. Human Rights Committee (HRC), CCPR General Comment No. 24: Issues Relating to Reservations Made upon Ratification or Accession to the Covenant or the Optional Protocols thereto, or in Relation to Declarations under Article 41 of the Covenant, U.N. Doc. CCPR/C/21/Rev.1/Add.6 (Nov. 4, 1994), http://www.unhcr.org/refworld/docid/453883fc11.html (last visited Feb. 3, 2013).

380 QURAN 96:1.

381 *Id.* at 68.

within the same culture, where there can also be different opinions. My aim is to open a dialogue about human rights between the West and the East by finding common ground between these different cultures, while respecting the basic fundamental principles of Islamic law.

Regional human rights charters encourage countries in these regions to ratify these treaties. There is no ideal regional human rights system, rather the human rights system of every region has special features that distinguish it from that of other regions. According to my proposed theory, the theory of strict cultural relativism can be applied when the principle of the "margin of appreciation" can be applied. An important principle like this needs to be addressed in this book. It should be noted that my new proposal outlines that neither the theory of reverse moderate relativism nor the theory of strict cultural relativism should be applied automatically. It will not be applied if the rights protected in the local law do not reflect any culture or religious beliefs. Furthermore, the theory of reverse moderate relativism or the theory of strict cultural relativism should not be applied automatically if the culture contradicts the religious beliefs. In addition, the local law should not automatically be the standard. If we think a particular law is against international human rights and standards then we should examine the roots of this law and whether or not it reflects cultures, traditions, or Sharia law. For instance, the Egyptian criminal law states that if a husband killed his wife because he saw her committing adultery, his sentence can be reduced.[382] However, this law did not grant the same right to the wife. The Kuwaiti criminal law further expanded this article. It reduced the punishment not only for the husband, but also for the son, brother, and father.[383] In this case, the law is discriminatory without reason. Sharia law supports equality and justice. Therefore, neither Egypt nor Kuwait can say that this law provision, which discriminates women, is from Sharia. Therefore, this article should be amended or deleted to ensure equality. So we should fully examine the article for any possible amendments. At the same time, religious scholars should do more to find new interpretations of Sharia that are compatible with the international human rights norms and are not contrary to the objectives and purposes of Sharia. This will encourage an examination of the core premises of the Sharia to find possible compatibility with international norms.

An argument, which is mostly put forth by Western human rights scholars, states that because of the fact that human rights developed from Europe and Western

---

382 Egyptian Code of Criminal Law, art. 237
383 Kuwaiti Penal Code, art. 153.

traditions and cultures,[384] there should be a Western interpretation of these principles. It is neither realistic nor wise to say that international human rights do not exist or cannot develop within non-Western civilizations.[385] To apply and protect human rights does not mean to copy a specific human rights system. Human rights can be protected and applied effectively and successfully, while reflecting and respecting the national and regional cultures and traditions on the condition that they are not contrary to the international minimum standards of human rights. A moderate Islamic human rights theory can stand as common ground between Sharia principles and international principles of human rights.

Human rights find inspiration from Sharia law. However, most Islamic scholars often refer to the 'double standards' of Western states and their discriminatory response to the human rights violations of 'Islamic' and 'non-Islamic' regimes. In other words, there is a lack of consistency in the agenda of international human rights.[386] For example, I will restate the example that I referred to previously, i.e. the 2007/2008 yearly report of the Egyptian National Council for Human Rights that stated that some of the international reports (whether governmental or nongovernmental) criticize the human rights situation in Egypt and that these reports use double standards and contain hidden political agendas.[387] In addition, some Arab scholars question the attitude taken by some Western governments towards democracy and human rights in Muslim countries.[388]

Can we have a moderate Islamic human rights theory that stands as the common ground between Sharia principles and international principles of human rights? Many of the theories that were written by various scholars either advocate the Western concept of human rights as the base which the Islamic concept should follow or advocate the Islamic concept of human rights and ignore the Western concept. The theory presented in this section attempts to strike a balance between the Western concept of human rights and Islamic human rights principles. My aim is to open a dialogue about human rights between the West and the East by finding common ground between them, while respecting the basic fundamental principles of Islamic law. The theory that I will apply is based on the possibilities of reconciliation between international law and Sharia principles. I seek to

---

384 Bassam Tibi, *International Law and Islamic Law, Islamic Law/Shari'a, Human Rights, Universal Morality and International Relations*, 16 HUM. RTS. Q. 278 (1994).

385 Mashood A. Baderin, *Human Rights and Islamic Law: The Myth of Discord*, 10 EUR. HUM. RTS. L. REV. 168 (2005).

386 *Id.*

387 THE YEARLY REPORT OF THE NATIONAL COUNCIL FOR HUMAN RIGHTS (Fourth Report, 2008), http://nchr-egypt.org/ar/images/files/4thannualreport(1).pdf (last visited Feb. 3, 2013).

388 AL-HIBRI, *supra* note 29, at 4.

take fundamental principles that appear in both sets of standards, such as social security, duties, gradualism, community, and natural law, to show how differences between existing human rights in Islam and the West can be deciphered, understood, and perhaps even accepted as legitimate. It is important to make it clear that rights must fulfill certain requirements in order to be legally protected. I will explain this in the following section.

D. The Stages of Evolution of Human Rights

Having discussed the structure of human rights, it is important to discuss the different stages of evolution of a right, so we can understand the significance that this right has attained in world community values. Professor Mahmoud Cherif Bassiouni explained that this pattern of emergence and development usually occurs in the five following stages:[389]

> First, the enunciative stage is the emergence and shaping of internationally perceived shared values through an intellectual and social process.
>
> Second, the declarative stage is the declaration of certain identified human values, interests or rights in an international document or instrument.
>
> Third, the prescriptive stage. The articulation of these human rights in some prescriptive form in an international instrument (general or specific) generated by an international body; or the elaboration of specific normative prescriptions in binding international conventions.
>
> Fourth, the enforcement stage. The search for, or the development of, modalities of enforcement.
>
> Fifth, the criminalization stage. The development of international penal proscriptions.
>
> Rights in the declarative stage (stage 2) frequently are framed in general terms. In the prescriptive stage (stage 3), rights are more specifically articulated in general international instruments having some legally binding effect. In the final stage, international criminalization, rights are

---

[389] M. Cherif Bassiouni, *The Proscribing Function of International Criminal Law in the Processes of International Protection of Human Rights*, 9 YALE J. WORLD PUB. ORD. 195 (1982); *see also* M. CHERIF BASSIOUNI, THE PROTECTION OF HUMAN RIGHTS IN THE ADMINISTRATION OF CRIMINAL JUSTICE: A COMPENDIUM OF UNITED NATIONS NORMS AND STANDARDS xxv (1994).

always expressed in specific international conventions which deal exclusively with the rights and proscribe violation of them.[390]

Human rights may not necessarily evolve through each of these stages or in the order listed above. Nevertheless, there is a sufficient similarity in the pattern of development and evaluation of many international human rights principles, norms, and standards to validate this classification.[391] To be universally protected, a right should be protected by a universal, not a regional, treaty. For instance, the right to engage in homosexuality and the right to homosexual marriage are not explicitly and universally protected by international treaties; it is only protected through a broad interpretation of the right to private life. Another example is the abolition of the death penalty, which is not widely accepted as a right that fulfills the five stages. While the European Convention on Human Rights accepts this right, it has not been affirmed internationally. Although the death penalty has been abolished by Protocol Two of the International Covenant on Civil and Political Rights, this has not been widely accepted because not many countries have accepted this treaty. A last example is the right to abortion, which is a right that has not been fully developed. It is not even a regional right. There is a widespread debate, as I will mention, as to whether it is a right or not. Therefore, no one can claim that Sharia law violates women's rights regarding abortion, as abortion has not been fully developed as a right.

E. Possibilities for Reconciliation Between International Human Rights Law and Islamic Law

Many commonalities exist between Islamic law and international law. For instance, the legal concept of "[t]he principle of pacta sunt servanda is recognized by all Muslim jurist-theologians."[392] The Quran explains, "But if they seek your help in the cause of the true Faith, it is your duty to assist them, except against a people with whom you have a treaty."[393] An essential aspect of Sharia law is its morally binding influence on Islamic countries to respect and implement the treaties they have signed, even if the national domestic laws provide easy ways to violate these treaties.[394] For example, a famous Islamic treaty is the treaty of

---

390 Id.
391 Id.
392 Khan, *supra* note 144, at 327 (citing MAJID KHADDURI, WAR AND PEACE IN THE LAW OF ISLAM 204 (AMS Press 1979) (1955)). "Pacta sunt servanda" means that treaties obligation must be respected and fulfilled.
393 QURAN 8:72.
394 Id. at 328 (citing HASAN MOINUDDUN, THE CHARTER OF THE ISLAMIC CONFERENCE AND LEGAL FRAMEWORK OF ECONOMIC CO-OPERATION AMONG ITS MEMBER STATES 48 (1987)).

"Hudaybiya," which was signed between Prophet Mohammad and the tribes of Mecca. Its aim was to achieve "a truce between the warring sides."[395]

> "Even after repeated breaches by the Meccans, Muhammad's entry into Mecca was without incident. The Treaty of Hudaybiya offers two important points of consideration. First, the treaty, at that time, was in fact an international treaty of peace between Muslims and some of the more aggressive tribes of Arabia. Second, although a military reprisal was justified under the terms set forth in the treaty, an extreme counter response never materialized."[396]

Furthermore, Islamic law applies custom as the second main source of Sharia. The Sunnah of Prophet Mohammed, which includes his practices and acts, are considered to be the second main source of Sharia.[397]

There are several principles that are shared between Islamic law and international human rights. Jason Morgan-Foster states four areas where we can find a shared values and principles between human rights law and Islamic law.[398] I will add the following four principles to the four areas mentioned by Morgan-Foster: the principle of "*fitrah* and natural law"; the principle of equality in international law and Sharia; the principle of human dignity; and the principle of margin of appreciation. The four areas outlined by Morgan-Foster are Islam's *Zakat* and Social Security, the existence of duties and rights in Islam, gradualism in Islam and human rights norms, the relationship between the *'umma* and the individual in Islam and international human rights law.

1. Islam's *Zakat* and Social Security

As previously explained, there are five pillars of Islam. The third pillar is the *zakat*. *Zakat* is a very broad term meaning supporting the needy. This includes giving money to orphans or financing the medical costs for ill people who cannot afford to pay. This also includes giving money and/or food to poor people and widows and financing debtors and students who cannot afford to complete their education.[399] There are eight kinds of *zakat*. The Quran explains:

---

395 *Id.* (citing M. Cherif Bassiouni, *Protection of Diplomats Under Islamic Law*, 74 Am. J. Int'l L. 609, 611-612 (1980)).
396 *Id.* (citing Christopher A. Ford, *Siyar-ization and its Discontents: International Law and Islam's Constitutional Crisis*, 30 Tex. Int'l L.J. 499, 519 (1995)).
397 Khan, *supra* note 144, at 328.
398 Morgan-Foster, *supra* note 346, at 51.
399 Schooley, *supra* note 150, at 668 (citing John L. Esposito, Islam: The Straight Path 89-90 (1988)).

Alms are for the poor and the needy, and those employed to administer the (funds); for those whose hearts have been (recently) reconciled (to Truth); for those in bondage and in debt; in the cause of Allah; and for the wayfarer: (thus is it) ordained by Allah, and Allah is full of knowledge and wisdom.

The believers, men and women, are Auliya' (helpers, supporters, friends, protectors) of one another; they enjoin (on the people) Al-Ma'ruf (i.e. Islamic Monotheism and all that Islam orders one to do), and forbid (people) from Al-Munkar (i.e. polytheism and disbelief of all kinds, and all that Islam has forbidden); they perform As-Salat (Iqamat-as-Salat), and give the Zakat, and obey Allah and His Messenger. Allah will have His Mercy on them. Surely Allah is All-Mighty, All-Wise."[400]

One of the main objectives and purposes of Sharia law regarding *zakat* is to prevent the concentration of wealth in the hands of the rich. Islamic law aims to enable the redistribution of wealth by requesting that the rich give an amount of their money and wealth to the poor and needy. Islam requests and puts the duty on each Muslim to donate a very small percentage (2.5%) of his or her excess wealth to the poor every year.[401] Every Muslim should pay the zakat once the amount of his wealth reach a certain amount. "The amount of wealth which makes one liable for *Zakat* is called Nisab. The payment of Zakat is compulsory on the excess wealth which is equal to or exceeds the value of Nisab, and which is possessed for a full Islamic year."[402] In addition, *zakat* aims at "removing the love of wealth from one's heart, a spiritual disease that could be detrimental to one's Iman."[403] The Quran provides, "And they give food, in spite of their love for it (or for the love of Him), to the Miskin (the poor), the orphan, and the captive. (Saying): 'We feed you seeking Allah's Countenance only. We wish for no reward, nor thanks from you.'"[404] In light of the previous verse and the reasons that are mentioned, we can understand that *zakat* is not just a way to give money and food to the needy. It seeks to develop and promote bestowal and tenderness in the behavior of Muslims. Furthermore, Sharia law aims to instill a sense of duty on every Muslim to be generous towards the poor.

---

400 QURAN 9:60&71.
401 Morgan-Foster, *supra* note 346, at 51.
402 *How Should I calculate Zakat?,* HIDAYA.ORG, http://www.hidaya.org/publications/zakat-information/how-should-i-calculate-zakat (last visited Nov. 17, 2012).
403 Shaykh Muhammad ibn Adam al-Kawthari, *Purpose and Benefit of Zakat,* QIBLA.COM, http://qa.sunnipath.com/issue_view.asp?HD=1&ID=2361&CATE=5 (last visited Apr. 19, 2012).
404 QURAN 76:8-9.

Sharia offers Muslims a large reward for giving money to the poor and feeding the hungry. Furthermore, the Quran requests that Muslims be humble while giving money. The Quran explains:

> The likeness of those who spend their wealth in the Way of Allah, is as the likeness of a grain (of corn); it grows seven ears, and each ear has a hundred grains. Allah gives manifold increase to whom He wills. And Allah is All-Sufficient for His creatures' needs, All-Knower. Those who spend their wealth in the Cause of Allah, and do not follow up their gifts with reminders of their generosity or with injury, their reward is with their Lord. On them shall be no fear, nor shall they grieve. Kind words and forgiving of faults are better than Sadaqah (charity) followed by injury. And Allah is Rich (Free of all needs) and He is Most-Forbearing.[405]

There is a hadith that shows the large reward in the Day of Judgment to the people who pay *zakat* and give money to the poor. The Prophet said that "seven people will be shaded by Allah under His shade on the day when there will be no shade except His. They are….(6) a person who practices charity so secretly that his left hand does not know what his right hand has given (i.e. nobody knows how much he has given in charity)."[406] On the other hand, the Quran threatens those who refuse to give money to the poor. For example, the Quran states:

> And those who hoard up gold and silver [Al-Kanz: the money, the Zakat of which has not been paid] and spend them not in the Way of Allah, announce unto them a painful torment. On the Day when that (Al-Kanz: money, gold and silver the Zakat of which has not been paid) will be heated in the Fire of Hell and with it will be branded their foreheads, their flanks, and their backs, (and it will be said unto them): "This is the treasure which you hoarded for yourselves. Now taste of what you used to hoard."[407]

Sharia law uses a moderate approach in its request that people give a minimum amount of their wealth to the poor. While Sharia law does not request that believers give all their wealth to the poor, it also does not request that believers do not give any money to the poor. Instead, Sharia law requests that people give a small amount of money to the poor yearly. There is a very profound story in the Quran with respect to a person named *Qaron* who refused to give money to the

---

405   *Id.* at 2:261-263.
406   *Sahih Muslim, Book 24, Hadith 504*, SEARCHTRUTH.COM, http://www.searchtruth.com/book_display.php?book=24&translator=1&start=19&number=502 (last visited May 5, 2012).
407   QURAN 9:34-35.

poor, claiming that he possessed his money because of his knowledge. *Qaron* was a very rich man, it was even difficult for a group of strong men to bear the weight of holding the keys to his safety boxes. In the Quran, it states:

> Verily, Qarun (Korah) was of Musa's (Moses) people, but he behaved arrogantly towards them. And We gave him of the treasures, that of which the keys would have been a burden to a body of strong men. Remember when his people said to him: "Do not exult (with riches, being ungrateful to Allah). Verily Allah likes not those who exult (with riches, being ungrateful to Allah)." "But seek, with that (wealth) which Allah has bestowed on you, the home of the Hereafter, and forget not your portion of lawful enjoyment in this world; and do good as Allah has been good to you, and seek not mischief in the land. Verily, Allah likes not the Mufsidun (those who commit great crimes and sins, oppressors, tyrants, mischief-makers, corrupters)." He said: "This has been given to me only because of the knowledge I possess." Did he not know that Allah had destroyed before him generations, men who were stronger than him in might and greater in the amount (of riches) they had collected? But the Mujrimun (criminals, disbelievers, polytheists, sinners) will not be questioned of their sins (because Allah knows them well, so they will be punished without being called to account). So he went forth before his people in his pomp. Those who were desirous of the life of the world, said: "Ah, would that we had the like of what Qarun (Korah) has been given! Verily he is the owner of a great fortune." but those who had been given (religious) knowledge said: "Woe to you! The Reward of Allah (in the Hereafter) is better for those who believe and do righteous good deeds, and this none shall attain except those who are As-Sabirun (the patient in following the truth)." So We caused the earth to swallow him and his dwelling place. Then he had no group or party to help him against Allah, nor was he one of those who could save themselves. And those who had desired (for a position like) his position the day before, began to say: "Know you not that it is Allah Who enlarges the provision or restricts it to whomsoever He pleases of His slaves. Had it not been that Allah was Gracious to us, He could have caused the earth to swallow us up (also)! Know you not that the disbelievers will never be successful. That home of the Hereafter (i.e. Paradise), We shall assign to those who rebel not against the truth with pride and oppression in the land nor do mischief by committing crimes. And the good end is for the Muttaqun (the pious – See V.2:2). Whosoever brings good (Islamic Monotheism along with righteous deeds), he shall have the better thereof; and whosoever brings evil (polytheism

along with evil deeds), then those who do evil deeds will only be requited for what they used to do." [408]

Sharia law threatens people who do not pay *zakat*. On the Day of Judgment, God will speak with every individual separately. There is a *hadith* by the Prophet Mohammed explaining the accountability of each Muslim on the Day of Judgment:

> And (no doubt) each one of you will stand in front of Allah and there will be neither a curtain nor an interpreter between him and Allah, and Allah will ask him, "Did not I give you wealth?" He will reply in the affirmative. Allah will further ask, "Didn't I send a messenger to you?" And again that person will reply in the affirmative Then he will look to his right and he will see nothing but Hell-fire, and then he will look to his left and will see nothing but Hell-fire. And so, any (each one) of you should save himself from the fire even by giving half of a date-fruit (in charity). And if you do not find a half date-fruit, then (you can do it through saying) a good pleasant word (to your brethren). [409]

This hadith shows clearly that Allah will ask every person about his actions.

Zakat is not just about deducting a certain amount of money from a person's wealth; *zakat* contributes to building a model and ideal society. *Zakat*

> "is a minimum acceptable moral standard for a working human community. Zakât plays a key role in bringing about such a ideal society. It not only enshrines the right of help for the community's needy, facilitating ongoing support from the rich to the poor, but, in so doing, it builds a relationship of consideration and appreciation between society's members."[410]

Zakat also builds and strengthens social security. *Zakat* aims to ensure peace, justice, and the distribution of wealth. In this way,

> "Zakat spreads tranquility and peace in society because it secures the weak and their dependents with the guarantee of certain provision, shelter, and access to essential communal facilities. The magic of *Zakat* is not only that it links one to others by a sense of personal responsi-

---

408 *Id.* at 28:76-84.
409 *Sahih Muslim, Book 24, Hadith 94*, SEARCHTRUTH.COM, http://www.searchtruth.com/book_display.php?book=24&translator=1&start=10&number=493 (last visited May 5, 2012).
410 *Zakat and Social Justice*, ZAKAT.ORG, http://www.zakat.org/zakat_in_islam/faqs/category/zakat_and_social_justice/ (last visited Apr. 19, 2012).

bility, but that it binds everyone to the individual through an obligation of sufficiency. There is no greater bulwark against social disintegration."[411]

Prophet Mohammed said, "The believers—in their kindness, compassion, and empathy for one another—are as a single body. When one limb is afflicted, the whole body responds to it with sleeplessness and fever."[412]

Morgan-Foster found an area of shared values between Sharia law and human rights standards. He referred to the adequate standard of living and social security that are stated in the International Covenant on Economic, Social, and Cultural Rights (ICESCR). Article 9 of the ICESCR states, "The States Parties to the present Covenant recognize the right of everyone to social security, including social insurance."[413] Article 11(1) provides, "The States Parties to the present Covenant recognize the right of everyone to an adequate standard of living for himself and his family, including adequate food, clothing and housing, and to the continuous improvement of living conditions…"[414] Article 11 (2) states, "The States Parties to the present Covenant, recognizing the fundamental right of everyone to be free from hunger…"[415] The General Comments of the United Nations Committee on Economic, Social and Cultural Rights provides:

> The human right to adequate food is recognized in several instruments under international law. The International Covenant on Economic, Social and Cultural Rights deals more comprehensively than any other instrument with this right. Pursuant to article 11.1 of the Covenant, States parties recognize "the right of everyone to an adequate standard of living for himself and his family, including adequate food, clothing and housing, and to the continuous improvement of living conditions", while pursuant to article 11.2 they recognize that more immediate and urgent steps may be needed to ensure "the fundamental right to freedom from hunger and malnutrition". The human right to adequate food is of crucial importance for the enjoyment of all rights. It applies to everyone; thus the reference in Article 11.1 to "himself and his family"

---

411 *Id.*
412 *Id.* (citing hadith of Prophet Mohammed).
413 International Covenant on Economic, Social and Cultural Rights, G.A. Res. 2200A (XXI), entered into force Jan. 3, 1976, http://www.ohchr.org/EN/ProfessionalInterest/Pages/CESCR.aspx (last visited Aug. 9, 2013) [hereinafter ICESCR].
414 *Id.* at art. 11 (1).
415 *Id.* at art. 11 (2).

does not imply any limitation upon the applicability of this right to individuals or to female-headed households.[416]

The Arab Charter on Human Rights confirmed the right for social security. It provides, "The States parties shall ensure the right of every citizen to social security, including social insurance."[417] The Arab Charter also mentioned the importance of the eradication of poverty, stating:

> The right to development is a fundamental human right and all States are required to establish the development policies and to take the measures needed to guarantee this right. They have a duty to give effect to the values of solidarity and cooperation among them and at the international level with a view to eradicating poverty and achieving economic, social, cultural and political development. By virtue of this right, every citizen has the right to participate in the realization of development and to enjoy the benefits and fruits thereof.[418]

In addition, the Arab Charter refers to the right to an adequate standard of living, which provides, "Every person has the right to an adequate standard of living for himself and his family, which ensures their well-being and a decent life, including food, clothing, housing, services and the right to a healthy environment. The States parties shall take the necessary measures commensurate with their resources to guarantee these rights."[419]

2. The Existence of Duties and Rights in Islam

Human rights are not always absolute; there are limits. In other words, every individual can enjoy his right freely on the condition that he or she does not prevent other people from freely enjoying their rights. It has been said that "your right to swing your arm ends just where the other person's nose begins. One person's right is another person's duty."[420]

---

416 U. N. Committee On Economic, Social And Cultural Rights, General Comment 12: The Right to Adequate Food (art. 11) (20th session, April 26-May 14, 1999), http://www.unhchr.ch/tbs/doc.nsf/0/3d02758c707031d58025677f003b73b9 (last visited Apr. 19, 2012).
417 ACHR, *supra* note 126, at art. 36.
418 *Id.* at art. 37.
419 *Id.* at art. 38.
420 KATHRYN ENGLISH & ADAM STAPLETON, THE HUMAN RIGHTS HANDBOOK: A PRACTICAL GUIDE TO MONITORING HUMAN RIGHTS 5 (1995).

Morgan-Foster stressed the fact that Sharia law balances individual rights and duties.[421] Professor Sherman Jackson stated that, "the relative dominance and sanctity in Islamic law of *individual rights* gives rise to a formidable high burden of proof for alienating private rights in pursuit of broader social interests. [emphasis added]"[422] Article 1 of the Cairo Declaration on Human Rights in Islam provides that:

> a) All human beings form one family whose members are united by submission to God and descent from Adam. *All men are equal in terms of basic human dignity and basic obligations and responsibilities,* without any discrimination on the grounds of race, colour, language, sex, religious belief, political affiliation, social status or oilier considerations. True faith is the guarantee for enhancing such dignity along the path to human perfection.
>
> b) All human beings are God's subjects, and the most loved by Him are those who are most useful to the rest of His subjects, and no one has superiority over another except on the basis of piety and good deeds. [emphasis added][423]

Sharia law emphasizes the importance of individual duties in society. Sharia law does not isolate duties from rights. In other words, in order to have rights, a duty must be fulfilled. For instance, with respect to *zakat*, poor people will not be given their rights if other people are not fulfilling their duty to pay *zakat*. In this way:

> Islam builds its community out of human obligation toward each other, making each Muslim accountable for the wellbeing of every other Muslim. This concept of reciprocal social obligation is called takâful, meaning "mutual responsibility," and it is strongly bolstered by the fact that the Zakât-Charity is an act of mandatory worship. The tenet of mutual responsibility helps Muslims envision their society like an extended family.[424]

Morgan-Foster mentioned that *zakat* imposes religious duties and obligations on Muslims. In contacts, the ICESCR only creates general rights and does not focus

---

421 Morgan-Foster, *supra* note 346, at 59.
422 *Id.* (citing Prof. Sherman A. Jackson, *Fiction and Formalism: Towards a Functional Analysis of Us l al-Fiqh*, in STUDIES IN ISLAMIC LEGAL THEORY 177, 410 (Bernard G. Weiss ed., 2002)).
423 Cairo Declaration on Human Rights in Islam, Aug. 5, 1990, U.N. GAOR, World Conf. on Hum. Rts., 4th Sess., Agenda Item 5, U.N. Doc. A/CONF.157/PC/62/Add.18, art. 1 (1993).
424 *Zakat and Social Justice, supra* note 410.

on individual duties.[425] In this way, Sharia law is more effective at protecting human rights because it imposes duties and responsibilities on all Muslims. In other words, if there are no duties, rights will not be fulfilled. Furthermore, since Muslims believe that the Quran is from God, they are supposed to implement it happily. *Zakat* is the duty not only of the government, but also of each and every Muslim. This is different than, and unique from, most international human rights treaties. We cannot have right without a duty. In this way, it is the duty of every Muslim to pay the poor.

In addition, the Quran threatens people who illegally take money from orphans. In other words, the Quran gives people the duty of keeping the money that belongs to orphans safe. The Quran provides, "Verily, those who unjustly eat up the property of orphans, they eat up only fire into their bellies, and they will be burnt in the blazing Fire!"[426] As another example, the Quran provides, "Until, when death comes to one of them (those who join partners with Allah), he says: 'My Lord! Send me back, So that I may do good in that which I have left behind!' No! It is but a word that he speaks; and behind them is Barzakh (a barrier) until the Day when they will be resurrected."[427]

There is a famous hadith for the prophet, which states that every person, whether a man or a woman has this responsibility. This hadith states:

> Narrated 'Abdullah bin 'Umar: That he heard Allah's Apostle saying, "Everyone of you is a guardian and is responsible for his charge; the ruler is a guardian and is responsible for his subjects; the man is a guardian in his famlly and responsible for his charges; a woman is a guardian of her husband's house and responsible for her charges; and the servant is a guardian of his master's property and is responsible for his charge." I definitely heard the above from the Prophet and think that the Prophet also said, "A man is a guardian of his father's property and responsible for his charges; so everyone of you is a guardian and responsible for his charges."[428]

This hadith clearly shows that every individual, regardless of his or her position or employment, has a responsibility and duty.

---

425 Morgan-Foster, *supra* note 346, at 51-53.
426 QURAN 4:10.
427 *Id.* at 23:99 and 100.
428 *Sahih Muslim, Book 46, Hadith 94*, SEARCHTRUTH.COM, http://www.searchtruth.com/book_display.php?book=46&translator=1&start=37&number=729 (last visited May 5, 2012).

Morgan-Foster demonstrates the common values that are shared between Islamic law and international human rights with respect to rights and duties. He states that traditionally, international human rights have focused mainly on rights, not on obligations and individual duties. Yet, recently international law has started to focus on duties.[429] He clarified that it has only been in the past few years that duties and obligations have begun to be recognized in the field of international human rights (e.g. the Universal Declaration of Human Responsibilities, UNESCO, 1997).[430] In 1998, the United Nations issued the Declaration on the Right and Responsibility of Individuals, Groups and Organs of Society to Promote and Protect Universally Recognized Human Rights and Fundamental Freedoms.[431] Another similar example is the United Nations Resolution on Human Rights and Human Responsibilities.[432] Furthermore, the United Nations appointed a Special Rapporteur to write a report on human responsibilities and duties. The report was completed and released in 2002.[433] In the report, it stated that the:

> Special Rapporteur starts out from the premise that the idea that there can be rights without ethical duties or responsibilities, or rights not based on equity and human solidarity, constitutes a patent breach of logic, as well as a social impossibility. The proof is the thousands of millions of human beings in the world who today suffer from all sorts of deprivations, and the generalized crisis in the economy, the environment and governance that visibly marks today's world should serve as a clear warning to all. Freedoms recognized only generically and in the abstract are simply useless. On the other hand, to argue that social

---

429 Morgan-Foster, *supra* note 346, at 60-61.
430 *Id.* at 61-62.; UNESCO, Universal Declaration of Human Responsibilities of 5 April 1997, http://globalethic.org/Center/unesco.htm (last visited Nov. 23, 2011).
431 Declaration on the Right and Responsibility of Individuals, Groups and Organs of Society to Promote and Protect Universally Recognized Human Rights and Fundamental Freedoms G.A. Res. 53/144 U.N. Doc. A/RES/53/144 (Mar. 8, 1998), http://www.unhchr.ch/huridocda/huridoca.nsf/(Symbol)/A.RES.53.144.En (last visited Nov. 24 2011).
432 Morgan-Foster, *supra* note 346, at 62; U.N. Commission on Human Rights, 56th Sess., U.N. Doc. E/CN.4/RES/2000/63(2000); *see also* Special Rapporteur on the Study requested by the Commission in its resolution 2000/63 and submitted pursuant to Economic and Social Council decision 2002/277, *Promotion and Protection of Human Rights*. U.N. Doc. E/CN.4/2003/105 (Mar. 17, 2003) (by Miguel Alfonso Martínez), http://www.unhchr.ch/Huridocda/Huridoca.nsf/0/52c520c7be26d11dc1256d040055f1b0/$FILE/G0312023.pdf (last visited Nov. 23, 2011).
433 *Id.*: *see also* Special Rapporteur on the Study requested by the Commission in its resolution 2000/63 and submitted pursuant to Economic and Social Council decision 2002/277, *Promotion and Protection of Human Rights*. U.N. Doc. E/CN.4/2003/105 (Mar. 17, 2003) (by Miguel Alfonso Martínez), http://www.unhchr.ch/Huridocda/Huridoca.nsf/0/52c520c7be26d11dc1256d040055f1b0/$FILE/G0312023.pdf (last visited Nov. 23, 2011).

duties can exist without individual rights is not only unimaginable, but absolutely unacceptable under the principles of ethics and equity. For these reasons he considers that all persons have, at the same time, rights, obligations and duties in all aspects of life touching on the promotion, effective realization and protection of all human rights. Neither from a legal point of view, nor on the ethical plane, is it possible to conceive of rights without such a logical correlation. Every right, in one way or another, is linked to some obligation or some responsibility, and every time that a duty is fulfilled, it is very likely that the violation of some right is prevented.[434]

3. Gradualism in Islam and Human Rights Norms

Sharia law applies the very important method of "gradualism." Gradualism is considered to be

> "a method of interpretation that proceeds by degrees, over time, advancing slowly but regularly. Gradualism is ideally suited to Islam because, while the Qur'an does enumerate certain legal standards, it consists primarily of very broad and general moral directives. The idea of gradualism complements the notion that Islam is a further step along the path to a greater understanding of God."[435]

The principle of gradualism helps to ensure the efficient, step-by-step implementation of Islamic law. This approach also means to "proceed by degrees, over time, advancing slowly but regularly."[436]

Gradualism is related to *fitrah* and "is one of the laws of nature that Allah Almighty has created. It is also needed in applying the rulings of the Shari`ah to make a change in people's life."[437] Gradualism is a law of nature that also applies to humans. For instance, a baby cannot walk immediately after it is born, it takes

---

434 Special Rapporteur on the Study requested by the Commission in its resolution 2000/63 and submitted pursuant to Economic and Social Council decision 2002/277, *Promotion and Protection of Human Rights*. U.N. Doc. E/CN.4/2003/105 (Mar. 17, 2003) (by Miguel Alfonso Martínez), http://www.unhchr.ch/Huridocda/Huridoca.nsf/0/52c520c7be26d11dc1256d0400 55f1b0/$FILE/G0312023.pdf (last visited Nov. 23, 2011).

435 Sayeht & Morse, *supra* note 158, at 318 (citing John L. Esposito, Islam: The Straight Path 79 (1988)).

436 Morgan-Foster, *supra* note 346, at 63 (citing Leila P. Sayeh & Adriaen M. Morse, Jr., *Islam and Treatment of Women: An Incomplete Understanding of Gradualism*, 30 Tex. Int'l L.J.. 311 (1995)).

437 *Gradualism in Applying Shari'ah*, Islamawareness.net, http://www.islamawareness.net/Shariah/sh_fatwa010.html (last visited Apr. 20, 2012).

time for the baby to learn how to take steps. Gradualism applies not only to human relations, but also to nature. For example, the principle of gradualism can be applied to our ability to eat vegetables and fruits. We have to plant the seeds and wait until the plant matures. This process can take months or even years depending on the kind of plants. For example, we cannot eat an orange immediately, we must wait until it ripens in the tree. When the orange fruit is green on the tree it is not mature, we have to wait for its color to change to orange.

The method of gradualism cannot be used in all instances. It depends on the circumstances. For instance according to Sharia law, it is forbidden to charge interest on a loan when a debtor is unable to pay the debt on time. According to Sharia law, Muslims are not permitted to charge usurious interest on debts. Islam prohibits this practice, without any need to apply the method of gradualism. It was stated only once in the Quran:

> Those who eat Riba (usury) will not stand (on the Day of Resurrection) except like the standing of a person beaten by Shaitan (Satan) leading him to insanity. That is because they say: "Trading is only like Riba (usury)," whereas Allah has permitted trading and forbidden Riba (usury). So whosoever receives an admonition from his Lord and stops eating Riba (usury) shall not be punished for the past; his case is for Allah (to judge); but whoever returns [to Riba (usury)], such are the dwellers of the Fire – they will abide therein. Allah will destroy Riba (usury) and will give increase for Sadaqat (deeds of charity, alms, etc.) And Allah likes not the disbelievers, sinners. Truly those who believe, and do deeds of righteousness, and perform As-Salat (Iqamat-as-Salat), and give *Zakat* they will have their reward with their Lord. On them shall be no fear, nor shall they grieve.[438]

On the other hand, some cultural habits and practices cannot be modified immediately; in which cases, the method of gradualism should be applied.[439] For example, before Islam, Arabs were used to drinking alcohol and gambling. Islam did not prohibit these practices immediately, but used a gradual approach. The Quran states, "They ask you (O Muhammad SAW) concerning alcoholic drink and gambling. Say: 'In them is a great sin, and (some) benefit for men, but the sin of them is greater than their benefit…'"[440] This was the first step in which the Quran stated, while there are benefits and sins, the sins are greater.[441] Then in the next

---

438 QURAN 2:275-278.
439 Sayeht & Morse, *supra* note 158, at 320.
440 QURAN 2:219.
441 Id.

stage the Quran prohibited it during prayers, stating, "O you who believe! Approach not AsSalat (the prayer) when you are in a drunken state until you know (the meaning) of what you utter... "[442] The final stage was "an outright and absolute interdiction of all intoxicants and of gambling in all circumstances."[443] The Quran states:

> "O you who believe! Intoxicants (all kinds of alcoholic drinks), gambling, AlAnsab, and AlAzlam (arrows for seeking luck or decision) are an abomination of Shaitans (Satan) handiwork. So avoid (strictly all) that (abomination) in order that you may be successful." "Shaitan (Satan) wants only to excite enmity and hatred between you with intoxicants (alcoholic drinks) and gambling, and hinder you from the remembrance of Allah and from As-Salat (the prayer). So, will you not then abstain?" "And obey Allah and the Messenger (Muhammad SAW), and beware (of even coming near to drinking or gambling or AlAnsab, or AlAzlam, etc.) and fear Allah. Then if you turn away, you should know that it is Our Messengers duty to convey (the Message) in the clearest way."[444]

Gradualism is practical and effective in "certain cultural practices and habits common in Arab Society [which]...were less amenable to instant change [by preparing them] little by little [for the] full Word of God."[445]

Gradualism is an important method that was established and implemented by Sharia law from the earliest days of Islam.[446] The example of alcohol and gambling is perfect to explain gradualism. Muslims believe entirely in the Quran and believe that it is from God. Although God has the right to forbid anything immediately, these practices were not prohibited outright at the beginning. It was forbidden "by a series of verses that were revealed over a period of years."[447] Then, it was forbidden to pray while drunk. This limited the drinking hours because there are five prayers daily (at sunrise, noon, after noon, sunset, and night). The final stage was absolute prohibition of drinking and gambling. Before Islam, drinking and gambling were habits in the Arab world. The application of gradualism by the Quran was perfect because it would be very difficult to stop Arab people from

---

442 *Id.* at 4:43.
443 Sayeht & Morse, *supra* note 158, at 320.
444 QURAN 5:90-92.
445 Morgan-Foster, *supra* note 346, at 63 (citing Leila P. Sayeh & Adriaen M. Morse, Jr., *Islam and Treatment of Women: An Incomplete Understanding of Gradualism*, 30 TEX. INT'L L.J.. 320 (1995)).
446 Sayeht & Morse, *supra* note 158, at 320 (citing JOHN L. ESPOSITO, ISLAM: THE STRAIGHT PATH 80 (1988)).
447 *Id.*

drinking alcohol suddenly. Therefore, gradualism was introduced with Sharia law, which helped people develop new customary practices of not drinking or gambling. The following is an important example of applying gradualism by the fifth Caliph of Muslims Omar Ibn Abdul Aziz:

> `Umar ibn `Abdul-`Aziz's son, `Abdul-Malik, who was a firm pious young man, said to his father one day, "O father! Why you do not implement the rulings firmly and immediately? By Allah, I would not care if all the world would furiously oppose us so long as we seek to establish the right [that Allah Almighty has enjoined]." These words show how zealous that young man was to destroy all signs of corruption and deterioration immediately and without delay whatever the consequences. But the wise father said to his son, "Do not deal with matters hastily, son. Allah Almighty [Himself] despised drinking alcohol twice in the Qur'an and did not declare it forbidden but in the third time. I am afraid that if I enjoined the right on people at one stroke, they would give it up all at once, which might lead to sedition."[448]

Morgan-Foster established connections between Sharia law and international human rights law by stating that, similar to Sharia law, the ICESCR also applies gradualism. For example, Article 2 of the ICESCR states,

> "Each State Party to the present Covenant undertakes to *take steps*, individually and through international assistance and co-operation, especially economic and technical, to the maximum of its available resources, with a view to achieving progressively the full realization of the rights recognized in the present Covenant by all appropriate means, including particularly the adoption of legislative measures. [emphasis added]"[449]

From the previous article it is clear that the ICESCR requires a gradual process in order to fulfill the obligations stated in the Convention.[450] The method of gradualism is not only stated in the International Covenant on Economic, Social and Cultural Rights, but is also applied by the ICCPR. For example, Article 2 (2) of the ICCPR requires that "each State Party to the present Covenant undertakes to *take the necessary steps,* in accordance with its constitutional processes and with the provisions of the present Covenant, to adopt such laws or other measures as may

---

448 *Gradualism in Applying Shari'ah, supra* note 437.
449 International Covenant on Economic, Social and Cultural Rights, G.A. Res. 2200A (XXI), entered into force Jan. 3, 1976, http://www.ohchr.org/EN/ProfessionalInterest/Pages/CESCR.aspx (last visited Aug. 9, 2013) [hereinafter ICESCR].
450 Morgan-Foster, *supra* note 346, at 65-66.

be necessary to give effect to the rights recognized in the present Covenant. [emphasis added]"[451] Also the ICCPR states, "States Parties to the present Covenant shall take appropriate steps to ensure equality of rights and responsibilities of spouses as to marriage..."[452]

Professor Saad Al-Din Helaly recognized that the Universal Declaration on Human Rights applied the principle of gradualism. He said that Universal Declaration did not explicitly prohibit occupation and did not mention the right to self-determination. He added that the Universal Declaration applied the policy of gradualism by leaving this issue to the United Nations General Assembly resolution number 1514, which was adopted on December 15, 1960. This resolution confirmed the right of states to self-determination.[453]

Gradualism was also applied by the European Convention on Human Rights, which made it optional, not compulsory, for states parties to accept individual complaints against the states. After states parties became accustomed to individual complaints, it became compulsory for all states to accept the individual complaints. It took approximately fifty years to make optional complaints compulsory. Without a gradual approach, states and people may reject changes and not respect or apply new changes that are introduced to them.

The Arab Charter on Human Rights applies the principle of gradualism. The Charter provides:

> 1. The State Parties shall recognize the right of everyone to the enjoyment of the highest attainable standard of physical and mental health and the right of every citizen to enjoy free and non-discriminatory access to health services and health care centres.
>
> 2. *The steps to be taken by* the State Parties shall include those necessary to:
> a. Develop basic healthcare and ensure the free and non-discriminatory access to the services of health care centres.
> b. Make every effort to fight disease by means of prevention and cure in order to reduce mortality.
> c. Take action to increase awareness and promote health education.
> d. Fight against traditional practices which are harmful to an individual's health.
> e. Ensure basic nutrition and clean water for everybody.

---

451 ICCPR, *supra* note 63, at art. 2.
452 *Id.* at art. 23 (4).
453 HELALY, *supra* note 273, at 412, 415.

    f.   Fight environmental pollution and supply sanitation systems.

    g.   Fight against tobacco, drugs, and psychotropic substances. [emphasis added][454]

The Arab Charter can be promoted and developed by using the principle of gradualism. Muslims will accept the use of gradualism as a method because it has already been applied by the Quran and Sharia. Furthermore, gradualism is from *fitrah* and the law of nature. In other words, if the Arab Charter is applied smoothly and gradually, it will not face objections. In addition, applying gradualism will encourage the governments of Arab countries to ratify and implement the Charter and its future protocols without further obligations. In addition, the countries that did ratify the Charter that want to go further and adopt additional protocols to the Charter will also be able to do so. In this way, the Arab Court of Human Rights can be established through the use of the principle of gradualism. Within a few years, more countries will have ratified the additional protocols and Arab countries will gain confidence in the Arab Charter. Furthermore, Arab countries will become better acquainted with the Arab Charter. The principle of gradualism will best promote and develop the Arab Charter.

The culture of human rights needs years to develop and mature in the world. The United Nations website includes the following statement by Antônio Augusto Cançado Trindade, the Former President of the Inter-American Court of Human Rights:

> When the General Assembly of the United Nations adopted, on 10 December 1948, the Universal Declaration of Human Rights, in one of the brief spells of enlightenment in the twentieth century, one could hardly anticipate that a historical process of generalization of the international protection of human rights was being launched, on a truly universal scale. Throughout the last six decades, of remarkable historical projection, *the Declaration has gradually acquired* an authority which its draftsmen could not have foreseen. This happened, not only because of the persons who participated in its elaboration, nor because of the form which was given to that historical document, nor because of the circumstances of its adoption*: it happened mainly because successive generations of human beings,* from distinct cultures and all over the world, recognized in it a "common standard of achievement" (as originally proclaimed), which corresponded to their deepest and most legitimate aspirations.[455] [emphasis added]

---

454   ACHR, *supra* note 126, at art. 39.

455   Antônio Augusto Cançado Trindade, *Universal Declaration of Human Rights*, Untreaty.un.org,

This statement mentions that gradualism played an important role in the development of the Universal Declaration on Human Rights and also outlined that successive generations of human beings are required (i.e. we need gradualism) in order for human rights to become fully developed.

Gradualism is applied even in the adoption of international human rights treaties. For example, the Universal Declaration on Human Rights, which was adopted in 1948,[456] was just a declaration, not a binding treaty. In 1966 the International Covenant on Civil and Political Rights and the International Covenant on Economic, Social and Cultural Rights were adopted. These covenants did not enter into force immediately, but did so after several years, in 1976.[457] These examples show that there is a need for gradualism in order to protect and promote human rights.

4. The Relationship between the *'Umma* and the Individual in Islam and International Human Rights Law

Morgan-Foster emphasizes an important issue of the strong relationship between the individual and the *'umma* (the nation). Morgan-Foster mentioned that Mohammed 'Amara, an Egyptian religious scholar and author, stated:

> Islam doesn't think either that the human being is the supreme being in creation, or that he is indistinguishable from the rest of creation. Man is the representative (khalifa) of God, and human beings have liberties that reflect their nature as God's representatives. These liberties are not absolute, they are bounded. So the individual as civil and social being is free, but all this is limited by the need for the freedom of the society. There has to be a balance between what is good for the individual and good for the group-they are not mutually exclusive. This…is very different from the Western view where, in the democratic state, the ruling class's interests take precedence; or where, in the authoritarian state, the state's interests take precedence. In Islam, the 'Umma's interests take precedence, not those of the ruling class, not those of the state and not those of the individual. So in this sense, Islam has a moderate

---

http://untreaty.un.org/cod/avl/ha/udhr/udhr.html (last visited July 10, 2012).
456 *History of the document*, UN.ORG http://www.un.org/en/documents/udhr/history.shtml (last visited Apr. 28, 2012).
457 For the date of adoption and entry into force of the ICESCR *see* U.N. Office of the High Commissioner for Human Rights, *International Covenant on Civil and Political Rights*, http://www2.ohchr.org/english/law/ccpr.htm (last visited Apr. 28, 2012).

view of the individual: the individual is free in so far as it is of benefit to the community.[458]

The concept of the 'umma and the individual are also applied on the Day of Judgment. For instance, it is at this point that the community of each prophet comes together. Morgan-Foster cited Salah ed-Din Jorshi, a religious Tunisian scholar, who states that

> "in Islam the individual exists: on the Day of Judgment, God does not speak with the 'umma, He speaks with each individual....So, at one and the same time there is the 'umma and there is the individual. And in order to have an Islamic view of freedom, of the individual, of human rights, you have to have a vision of the whole society and also of the rights of the individual."[459]

The Quran demonstrates a balances between 'umma and individual. There are many verses of the Quran that speak to 'umma and there are many verses that refer to individuals and people. George C. Decasa outlines that "The term umma appears sixty-four times in the Qur'an, in thirteen of these appearances the plural, umam, is used…umma is the term that the Qur'an uses to refer to bodies of people who are the objects the divine plan of salvation."[460]

Examples of the verses of 'umma' in the Quran include, "Thus, have We made of you an Ummat justly balanced, that ye might be witnesses over the nations, and the Messenger a witness over yourselves…"[461] Also, the Quran explains, "And there may spring from you a nation who invite to goodness, and enjoin right conduct and forbid indecency. Such are they who are successful."[462] The Quran provides examples of what will happen on the Day of Judgment, by asking, "How (will it be) then, when We bring from each nation a witness and We bring you (O Muhammad) as a witness against these people?"[463] In addition, the Quran states, "And for every Ummah (a community or a nation) there is a Messenger; when

---

458   Morgan-Foster, *supra* note 346, at 54-55 (citing Kevin Dwyer, Arab Voices: The Human Rights Debate in the Middle East 78 (1991)).
459   *Id.* at 63 (citing Kevin Dwyer, Arab Voices: The Human Rights Debate in the Middle East 78 (1991) (quoting personal interview with Salah ed-Din Jorshi).
460   George C. Decasa, Svd, The Quranic Concept of Umma and its Function in Philippine Muslim Society 13-14 (Editrice Pontifica Universita Gregoriana, 1999).
461   Quran 2:143.
462   *Id.* at 3:104.
463   *Id.* at 4:41.

their Messenger comes, the matter will be judged between them with justice, and they will not be wronged."[464]

The Quran also speaks about individuals. For instance, the Quran describes, "Everyone shall taste death. And only on the Day of Resurrection shall you be paid your wages in full. And whoever is removed away from the Fire and admitted to Paradise, he indeed is successful. The life of this world is only the enjoyment of deception (a deceiving thing)."[465] The Quran also instructs, "And perform As-Salat (Iqamat-as-Salat), and give *Zakat* and whatever of good (deeds that Allah loves) you send forth for yourselves before you, you shall find it with Allah. Certainly, Allah is All-Seer of what you do."[466] Also the Quran teaches, "And fear the Day (of Judgment) when no person shall avail another, nor shall compensation be accepted from him, nor shall intercession be of use to him, nor shall they be helped."[467] Furthermore, the Quran states, "And fear the Day when ye shall be brought back to Allah. Then shall every soul be paid what it earned, and none shall be dealt with unjustly."[468] In addition the Quran explains:

> And We have fastened every man's deeds to his neck, and on the Day of Resurrection, We shall bring out for him a book which he will find wide open. (It will be said to him): "Read your book. You yourself are sufficient as a reckoner against you this Day." Whoever goes right, then he goes right only for the benefit of his ownself. And whoever goes astray, then he goes astray to his own loss. No one laden with burdens can bear another's burden. And We never punish until We have sent a Messenger (to give warning).[469]

Morgan-Foster outlines that Islam balances the interests of individual and the interests of 'umma. He stated that Mohammed Hashim Kamali mentioned that sometimes "rights of the community and those of the individuals are combined."[470] The combination of Individual and community rights protects individual rights, such as:

---

464 *Id.* at 10:47.
465 *Id.* at 3:185.
466 *Id.* at 2:110.
467 *Id.* at 2:123.
468 *Id.* at 2:281.
469 *Id.* at 17:13, 14, 15.
470 Morgan-Foster, *supra* note 346, at 55 (citing MOHAMMED HASHIM KAMALI, PRINCIPLES OF ISLAMIC JURISPRUDENCE 349 (rev. ed. 1991)).

relation (*qisas*), and blood-money (*diyah*) of any kind, whether for life or for grievous injury…The community is entitled to punish such violations, but the right of the heirs in retaliation and in *diyah* for injuries for erroneous killing, and the right of the victim in respect of diyah for injuries, is preponderant in view of the grievance and loss that they suffer as a result. The guardian (*wali*) of the deceased, in the case of *qisas*, is entitled to pardon the offender or to accept compensation from him. But the state, which represents the community, is still entitled to punish the offender through a *ta'zir* punishment even if he is pardoned by the relatives of the deceased.[471]

The Arab Charter refers to the *'umma* both directly and indirectly; it is stated in the preamble of the Charter that

"Based on the faith of *the Arab nation* in the dignity of the human person whom God has exalted ever since the beginning of creation and in the fact that the Arab homeland is the cradle of religions and civilizations whose lofty human values affirm the human right to a decent life based on freedom, justice and equality… Believing in the unity of the Arab nation. [emphasis added]"[472]

In addition, the Arab Charter provides:

The present Charter seeks, within the context of the *national identity of the Arab States* and their sense of belonging to a common civilization, to achieve the following aims:

1. To place human rights at the centre of the key national concerns of *Arab States,* making them lofty and fundamental ideals that shape the will of the individual in Arab States and enable him to improve his life in accordance with noble human values…

3. To prepare the *new generations in Arab States* for a free and responsible life in a civil society that is characterized by solidarity, founded on a balance between awareness of rights and respect for obligations, and governed by the values of equality, tolerance and moderation. [emphasis added][473]

---

471 *Id.* (citing MOHAMMED HASHIM KAMALI, PRINCIPLES OF ISLAMIC JURISPRUDENCE 350 (rev. ed. 1991)).
472 ACHR, *supra* note 126, at preamble.
473 ACHR, *supra* note 126, at art. 1(1), 1(3).

According to Morgan-Foster, unlike Islam, international human rights law focuses mainly on the individual.[474] For instance, Henry J. Steiner and Philip Alston stated that "[o]bservers from different regions and cultures can agree that the human rights movement…stems principally from the liberal tradition of Western thought…[and that] [n]o characteristic of the liberal tradition is more striking than its emphasis on the individual."[475]

In addition, 'first generation rights' constitute civil and political rights of *individuals*.[476] There are many rights that are considered first generation rights "first-generation rights include, among other things, freedom of speech, the right to a fair trial, freedom of religion and voting rights."[477] First generation rights are also "known as negative rights… These human rights include due process, freedom of speech and religion."[478] For instance, the ICCPR focuses on individual rights and states,

> "Each State Party to the present Covenant undertakes to respect and to ensure to all individuals within its territory and subject to its jurisdiction the rights recognized in the present Covenant, without distinction of any kind, such as race, colour, sex, language, religion, political or other opinion, national or social origin, property, birth or other status."[479]

Second generation rights are:

> positive rights,[they] attempt to ensure each individual an adequate standard of living. Under this second set of human rights, everyone "has the right to a standard of living adequate for the health and well-being of himself and of his family, including food, clothing, housing and medical care and necessary social services." In addition, "motherhood and childhood are entitled to special care and assistance" and everyone has the right to a free education at the elementary level (United Nations, 1948; Art. 16–27).[480]

---

474 Morgan-Foster, *supra* note 346, at 57.
475 *Id.* (citing Henry J. Steiner & Philip Alston, International Human Rights In Context, 361-362 (2d. ed. 2000)).
476 *Id.* (citing David J. Bederman, International Law Frameworks 95-96 (2001)).
477 *Three Generations of Human Rights*, Wikipedia.org, http://en.wikipedia.org/wiki/Three_generations_of_human_rights (last visited Apr. 21, 2012).
478 Reichert, *supra* note 351.
479 ICCPR, *supra* note 63, at art. 2 (1).
480 Reichert, *supra* note 351, at 25.

Other examples of second generation rights are "a right to be employed, rights to housing and health care, as well as social security and unemployment benefits."[481]

International human rights law has recently become more similar to Sharia law in terms of recognizing group rights or *'umma* rights, by applying third generation rights. Examples of third generation rights include:

- Group and collective rights
- Right to self-determination
- Right to economic and social development
- Right to a healthy environment
- Right to natural resources
- Right to communicate and communication rights
- Right to participation in cultural heritage
- Rights to intergenerational equity and sustainability.[482]

First and second generation rights are mainly concerned. In addition:

> The list of internationally recognised human rights has not remained constant. Although none of the rights listed in the UDHR has been brought into question in the 50 or so years of its existence, new treaties and documents have clarified and further developed some of the basic concepts that were laid down in that original document. These additions have been a result of a number of factors: they have partly come about as a response to changing ideas about human dignity, partly as a result of technological changes and often as a result of new threats emerging. In the case of the specific new category of rights that have been proposed as a third generation, these have been the consequence of a deeper understanding of the different types of obstacles that may stand in the way of realising the first and second generation rights. Increasing globalisation has also revealed the possibility for resources to be diverted towards the removal of these obstacles.[483]

From all that has been mentioned and explained, it is clear that a common ground exists between Sharia law and international human rights law. In addition to the four areas of similarity between international law and Islamic law that are mentioned by Morgan-Foster, I will explain the relationship between *fitrah* and

---

481 *Three Generations of Human Rights*, supra note 477.
482 Id.
483 Manual on Human Rights Education with Young People – Council of Europe, *The Evolution of Human Rights*, http://eycb.coe.int/compass/en/chapter_4/4_2.html (last visited Apr. 21, 2012).

natural law. In addition, I will explain the principle of equality in international law and Sharia law. Furthermore, I will explain the inclusion of an understanding of human dignity. Finally, I will explain the principle of the "margin of appreciation" as a way of reconciling Islamic Sharia law and international human rights law.

5. *Fitrah* and Natural Law Theory

Fitrah is the order of nature. It recognizes that there are some acts that go against the order of nature and, as such, are prohibited by nature. They need no law of regulations to criminalize them. Every person regardless of his or her sex, religion, or race knows that some acts go against nature. For instance, acts such as bribery, rape, murder, and robbery all go against nature. Any person knows these acts should not be done, even if the law does not prohibit them. The roots of morals come from *fitrah*. *Fitrah* is: "an inborn natural predisposition which cannot change, and which exists at birth in all human beings. What makes our religious understanding positive is that it not only acknowledges *fitrah* as a natural predisposition, but also one which is inclined towards right action and submission to Allâh, the One God."[484] Natural law theory is defined as "a philosophical and legal belief that all humans are governed by basic innate laws, or laws of nature, which are separate and distinct from laws which are legislated."[485] For instance, natural law theory prohibits murder because it is against natural law.[486] However, *fitrah* does not mean morals, because morals can differ across countries and regions. Morals can even be different across cities within the same country. On the other hand, *fitrah* means that all people all over the world are born with the same principles. The Quran, states that all people are born with the *fitrah*, "And a soul and Him Who perfected it. And inspired it (with conscience of) what is wrong for it and (what is) right for it. He is indeed successful who causeth it to grow, And he is indeed a failure who stunteth it."[487] This is why there can be universal principles that govern everyone, regardless of his or her religion, sex, race, etc. In this way, core principles should be governed by universalism theory and strict cultural relativism can be applied to the other details. In other words, the details are the specific applications of the universal principles, which can vary in different cultures; these differences do not mean that the specific applications

---

484 Yasien Mohamed, *The Definition of Fitrah*, ANGELFIRE.COM, http://www.angelfire.com/al/islamic-psychology/fitrah/fitrah.html (last visited Mar. 7, 2012).

485 *What is Natural Law Theory*, WISEGEEK.COM, http://www.wisegeek.com/what-is-natural-law-theory.htm (last visited Apr. 14, 2012).

486 *Natural Law Ethics*, WISEGEEK.COM, http://topics.wisegeek.com/topics/natural-law-ethics.htm# (last visited Apr. 14, 2012).

487 QURAN 91:7-10.

are wrong. My proposed theory seeks a combined universalist and relativist approach with respect to the standards that should be used to evaluate the treatment of human rights in the Arab Charter. It is also true that the core principles in Islamic schools of jurisprudence are very much alike, while there is more variation with respect to other principles.

Fitrah is very similar to natural law. *Fitrah* means the "natural constitution with which a child is created in his mother's womb in a state of happiness or misery..."[488] *Fitrah* has been defined as,

> "The Laws or the sharî'ahs, which the prophets were sent with, are guiding lights to the essential faith in Allâh which is created in every human being. Furthermore, since this faith comes from Allâh, it naturally follows that only laws capable of guiding man back to it must also come from Allâh, hence Islâm is also called *dîn al-fitrah*, the religion of human nature."[489]

Prophet Mohammed said, "Every new-born child is born in a state of *fitrah*. Then his parents make him a Jew, a Christian or a Magian, just as an animal is born intact. Do you observe any among them that are maimed (at birth)?"[490] The Quran, which states that all people are born with the *fitrah*, continues,

> "So set you (O Muhammad) your face towards the religion (of pure Islamic Monotheism) Hanif (worship none but Allah Alone). Allah's *Fitrah* (i.e. Allah's Islamic Monotheism) with which He has created mankind. No change let there be in Khalq-illah (i.e. the religion of Allah — Islamic Monotheism): that is the straight religion, but most of men know not."[491]

Since Islam is the religion of *fitrah*, the objectives and purposes of Sharia law is in conformity with *fitrah*. This is because, according to the belief of Muslims, Sharia law came from God, who created the *fitrah*. In another words, Sharia law permits anything that is in compliance with *fitrah* and prohibits anything that is against *fitrah*. The theory that I will use will be based in the *fitrah*. If we want to apply the principle of *fitrah* to the Arab Charter, we will easily come to the conclusion that

---

488   Yasien Mohammed, *Fitrah and its Bearing on the Principles of Psychology*, 12 THE AM. J. OF ISLAMIC SOC. SCI. 1, 2, http://i-epistemology.net/attachments/408_V12N1%20Spring%2095%20-%20Mohamed%20-%20Fitrah%20and%20its%20Bearing%20on%20Islamic%20Psychology.pdf (last visited May 1, 2013).

489   Mohamed, *supra* note 484.

490   *Id.* (citing I. M. Hanîf, *Sahîh Muslim bisharh al-Nawawî*, Book of Qadr, Vol. 16 (al-Matba'at al-Misriyyah bi al-Azhari, 1930) at 207.).

491   QURAN 29:30.

homosexuality is forbidden in Sharia law, because it is against *fitrah* and against the order of nature. Not only does Sharia law consider homosexuality to be against the order of nature, but it also considers it to be against several domestic laws (for instance, the Tasmanian Criminal Code (1924), as amended, criminalizes homosexual acts). Section 122 provides:

> Any person who:
> - has sexual intercourse with any person against the order of nature;
> - has sexual intercourse with an animal; or
> - consents to a male person having sexual intercourse with him or her against the order of nature,
>
> is guilty of a crime.[492]

When the words "against the order of nature" were used in the previous law, this meant against *fitrah*. In addition, I would like to shed light on important issue. The previous article established a connection between sexual intercourse with any person of the same sex and sexual intercourse with an animal (which is discussed in the subsequent article) as they are both being against the order of nature. In addition, both homosexuality and sexual relations with animals have equal punishment in law. In another words, the law did not make the sexual relation with an animal more punishable, but rather gave equal punishments for them both, because they are both against nature.

6. The Principle of Equality in Sharia Law and International Law

a. *Equality Between Men and Women*

Equality between men and women is one of the basic international principles mentioned in every human rights instrument. Evadne Grant recognized that "The bold assertion in the Universal Declaration of Human Rights (UDHR) that '[a]ll human beings are born free and equal in dignity and rights [article 1]'"[493] placed equality at the top of the international human rights agenda more than fifty years. Since then the right to equality and the prohibition of discrimination have been incorporated into an array of constitutional and international instruments."[494] Equality between men and women is stated in all of the human rights treaties. For example, the ICCPR states, "The States Parties to the present Cove-

---

492 Wayne Morgan, *Sexuality and Human Rights: The First Communication by an Australian to the Human Rights Committee under the Optional Protocol to the International Covenant on Civil and Political Rights*, 14 AUSTRALIAN Y.B. INT'L L. 277, 278 (1992).
493 UDHR, *supra* note 106.
494 Evadne Grant, *Dignity and Equality*, 7 H.R.L REV. 299, 300 (2007).

nant undertake to ensure the equal right of men and women to the enjoyment of all civil and political rights set forth in the present Covenant."[495] Furthermore, the ICESCR explains, "The States Parties to the present Covenant undertake to ensure the equal right of men and women to the enjoyment of all economic, social and cultural rights set forth in the present Covenant."[496]

This is also true of regional human rights conventions; for instance, Article 14 of the European Convention on Human Rights states, "The enjoyment of the rights and freedoms set forth in this Convention shall be secured without discrimination on any ground such as sex, race, colour, language, religion, political or other opinion, national or social origin, association with a national minority, property, birth or other status."[497] The Arab Charter on Human Rights, which is inspired by Sharia law, provides:

> 1. Each State party to the present Charter undertakes to ensure to all individuals subject to its jurisdiction the right to enjoy the rights and freedoms set forth herein, without distinction on grounds of race, colour, sex, language, religious belief, opinion, thought, national or social origin, wealth, birth or physical or mental disability.
>
> 2. The States parties to the present Charter shall take the requisite measures to guarantee effective equality in the enjoyment of all the rights and freedoms enshrined in the present Charter in order to ensure protection against all forms of discrimination based on any of the grounds mentioned in the preceding paragraph.
>
> 3. Men and women are equal in respect of human dignity, rights and obligations within the framework of the positive discrimination established in favour of women by the Islamic Shariah, other divine laws and by applicable laws and legal instruments. Accordingly, each State party pledges to take all the requisite measures to guarantee equal opportunities and effective equality between men and women in the enjoyment of all the rights set out in this Charter.[498]

---

495 ICCPR, *supra* note 63, at art 3.
496 ICESCR, *supra* note 449, at art 3.
497 Council of Europe, *European Convention for the Protection of Human Rights and Fundamental Freedoms, as amended by Protocols Nos. 11 and 14*, 4 November 1950, ETS 5, available at: http://www.unhcr.org/refworld/docid/3ae6b3b04.html (last visited Feb. 3, 2013) [hereinafter ECHR].
498 ACHR, *supra* note 126, at art. 3.

In addition to this article which directly qualifies the idea of "equality between men and women" by the idea of "positive discrimination," the Arab Charter explains, "All persons are equal before the courts and tribunals. The States parties shall guarantee the independence of the judiciary and protect magistrates against any interference, pressure or threats. They shall also guarantee every person subject to their jurisdiction the right to seek a legal remedy before courts of all levels."[499] The previous examples clearly show that both the Arab Charter and other international and regional human rights conventions outline the importance of equality between men and women.

On the other hand, we have all read, watched, and heard about how women in Islam are treated different than men. I will explain this topic, but I use the Quran and hadith as the main sources of Sharia law, because they are the most trusted sources for the real opinion of Islam. Before writing about men and women in Islam, I first have to explain what women faced prior to the development of Islam in Arab countries. I will cite what the Quran says about this important issue. This will not only show what women faced, but it will also provide an important understanding of the objectives and purposes of the Quran in relation to women.

b.   Women's Experience in Arab Countries Before Islam

Before Islam, women in Arab countries had no rights. This was also true of other women in most parts of the world in this era. Before Islam, most Arab people hated girls and did not want to have daughters. Women faced discriminatory cultures and traditions.[500] The Quran outlined the rights of women in order to ensure that women were given the rights that had been stolen from them. The Quran condemned fathers who hated their daughters. The Quran states,

> "And when the news of (the birth of) a female (child) is brought to any of them, his face becomes dark, and he is filled with inward grief! He hides himself from the people because of the evil of that whereof he has been informed. Shall he keep her with dishonour or bury her in the earth? Certainly, evil is their decision."[501]

The following is also mentioned, in another chapter of the Quran:

> And if one of them is informed of the news of (the birth of a girl) that which he sets forth as a parable to the Most Gracious (Allah), his face

---

499   *Id.* at art. 12.
500   RASHAD HASSAN KHALEEL, NAZAREYT AL-MOSAWAH FI AL-SHARIA AL-ISLAMEYAH [Theory of Equality in Islamic Sharia, part two] 19 (2007).
501   QURAN 16:57-59.

becomes dark, and he is filled with grief! (Like they then for Allah) a creature who is brought up in adornments (wearing silk and gold ornaments, i.e. women), and who in dispute cannot make herself clear? And they make the angels who themselves are slaves of the Most Gracious (Allah) females. Did they witness their creation? Their testimony will be recorded, and they will be questioned!"[502]

In addition, the Quran also shamed the custom that existed before Islam of burying females. It stated, "And when the female (infant) buried alive (as the pagan Arabs used to do) is questioned: For what sin, was she killed?"[503]

There is a long chapter in the Quran entitled *The Women*, which reflects the importance of women in Islam. There are many issues that are mentioned in this chapter, some of which I will mention. For instance, while women had no inheritance right before Islam, Islam stressed the right of women to inheritance. The Quran stated, "There is a share for men and a share for women from what is left by parents and those nearest related, whether the property be small or large — a legal share."[504] Islam forcibly prohibited that women could be part of an inheritance against their will. It was stated in Quran, "O you who believe! You are forbidden to inherit women against their will; and you should not treat them with harshness..."[505]

Sharia law gives respect to and honors women. There is a chapter in the Quran entitled *Maryam*, which means Mary.[506] Jesus' mother is given tremendous amount of respect and placed in a position of superiority in the Quran. In addition to the full chapter about Mary, there is another chapter entitled *Aal-e-Imran*,[507] which is Mary's family name. This shows the compassion that was given to a woman like Mary. The Quran states, "And (remember) when the angels said: 'O Maryam (Mary)! Verily, Allah has chosen you, purified you (from polytheism and disbelief), and chosen you above the women of the 'Alamin (mankind and jinn) (of her lifetime).'"[508]

The Quran also discusses what men used to do before Islam, in that they would mistreat their wives and steal the dowry from their wives and then divorce them.

---

502 *Id.* at 43:17-19.
503 *Id.* at 81:8-9.
504 *Id.* at 4:7.
505 *Id.* at 4:19.
506 *Id.* at 4.
507 *Id.* at 3.
508 *Id.* at 3:42.

The Quran states, "But if you intend to replace a wife by another and you have given one of them a Qintar (of gold i.e. a great amount as Mahr) take not the least bit of it back; would you take it wrongfully without a right and (with) a manifest sin?"[509] Before Islam, if a woman's husband died, she was forbidden to marry for one year. In addition, she could not beautify herself and or present herself in a good-looking manner, and she should exhibit grief for one year. After Islam, this custom was forbidden; Islam states that, after the death of their husband, women must wait only for a short period of time before they marry. The Quran states:

> And those of you who die and leave wives behind them, they (the wives) shall wait (as regards their marriage) for four months and ten days, then when they have fulfilled their term, there is no sin on you if they (the wives) dispose of themselves in a just and honourable manner (i.e. they can marry). And Allah is Well-Acquainted with what you do. And there is no sin on you if you make a hint of betrothal or conceal it in yourself, Allah knows that you will remember them, but do not make a promise of contract with them in secret except that you speak an honourable saying according to the Islamic law. And do not consummate the marriage until the term prescribed is fulfilled. And know that Allah knows what is in your minds, so fear Him. And know that Allah is Oft-Forgiving, Most Forbearing.[510]

c. *Duties and Rights of Men and Women in Sharia Law*

The Quran is not only a book of rights, it is also a book of duties. Islam applied equality and justice with respect to the duties and rights of both men and women. For instance, the Quran states, "Verily, those who give Sadaqat (i.e. Zakat and alms), men and women, and lend Allah a goodly loan, it shall be increased manifold (to their credit), and theirs shall be an honourable good reward (i.e. Paradise)."[511] The Quran also states, "Whosoever doeth right, whether male or female, and is a believer, him verily we shall quicken with good life, and We shall pay them a recompense in proportion to the best of what they used to do."[512] Furthermore, the Quran states, "For men there is reward for what they have earned, (and likewise) for women there is reward for what they have earned..."[513]

---

509   *Id.* at 4:20.
510   *Id.* at 2:234-235.
511   *Id.* at 57:18.
512   *Id.* at 16:97.
513   *Id.* at 4:32.

Does Sharia law discriminate against women? Does the Quran place men at a higher level than women? The answer is that the Quran emphasizes the fact that men and women are the same. The Quran states, "And among His Signs is this, that He created for you wives from among yourselves, that you may find repose in them, and He has put between you affection and mercy. Verily, in that are indeed signs for a people who reflect."[514] Sharia law states that men and women are equal: "O mankind! We have created you from a male and a female, and made you into nations and tribes, that you may know one another. Verily, the most honourable of you with Allah is that (believer) who has At-Taqwa. Verily, Allah is All-Knowing, All-Aware."[515]

Sharia law emphasizes the fact that there is no differentiation between men and women with respect to duties and states that men and women are created from a single soul. The Quran states,

> "O mankind! Be careful of your duty to your Lord Who created you from a single soul and from it created its mate and from them twain hath spread abroad a multitude of men and women. Be careful of your duty toward Allah in Whom ye claim (your rights) of one another, and toward the wombs (that bare you). Lo! Allah hath been a watcher over you."[516]

The Quran also encourages the romantic life of husbands, wives, and children stating: "And those who pray, "Our Lord! Grant unto us wives and offspring who will be the comfort of our eyes, and give us (the grace) to lead the righteous."[517] Furthermore, Sharia did not say that husbands exist at a higher level than women, but that they will both enter paradise together. The Quran states, "Enter Paradise, you and your wives, in happiness."[518] Furthermore, with respect to being in paradise together, the Quran states, "They and their wives will be in pleasant shade, reclining on thrones."[519]

Men have to pay dowry to women in order to marry them. It should be noted that Sharia law did not consider the dowry as a gift, but as a woman's right with respect to marriage. The marriage contract cannot be completed without a dowry. The Quran, which is the primary source of Sharia law, states, "And give to the women (whom you marry) their Mahr (obligatory bridal-money given by the

---

514   *Id.* at 30:21.
515   *Id.* at 49: 13.
516   *Id.* at 4:1.
517   *Id.* at 25:74.
518   *Id.* at 43: 70.
519   *Id.* at 36:56 .

husband to his wife at the time of marriage) with a good heart..."[520] It is important to explain that the previous verse did not say that the dowry is given to the father of the woman, but is given to the woman who will be getting married. There are a lot of verses of the Quran and many hadith stated by Mohammed regarding the rights of women. I have mentioned but a very few of them to give an overview of the objectives and purposes of Sharia law regarding equality between men and women.

d. Women and the Implementation of Gradualism

Sharia protected women's rights. It applied both immediate changes to combat the excesses of bad habits and customs during Jahiliyah, as well as gradual changes. It was stated, "Islam contains within it the seeds for fundamental change in the treatment of women."[521]

Before Islam, women during the Jahiliyyah were very severely discriminated against. Prophet Mohammed faced a lot of obstacles and extremely discriminatory practices. For instance, during Jahiliyyah, polygamy was unlimited. In other words, men were permitted to marry an unlimited number of wives. After a husband's death, his wives are included in his wealth. In other words, his heirs could take these women.[522]

At the beginning of Islam, Sharia law started to apply the principle of gradualism in order to change the culture and impose new rights for women. The Quran informed people that men and women are created from the same soul and that one is not better than the other. The Quran states, "O mankind! Be careful of your duty to your Lord Who created you from a single soul and from it created its mate and from them twain hath spread abroad a multitude of men and women..."[523] Prophet Mohammed emphasized the important position of women in the society. In addition, he showed the vital role that can be played by wives. For instance, he considered his wife A'isha to be a religious scholar, he said "take half of your religion from this ruddy-complexioned woman."[524] Sharia law and Prophet Mo-

---

520 *Id.* at 4:4.
521 Sayeht & Morse, *supra* note 158, at 321.
522 Sayeht & Morse, *supra* note 158, at 321.
523 QURAN 4:1.
524 Sayeht & Morse, *supra* note 158, at 322 (citing MOHAMMED KOTB, BAY'AT AL-NISSA, THE WOMEN'S RATIFICATION 101 (n.d). It must be noted that this particular hadith is considered to be weak. Hadiths may be strong or weak depending on the strength of their attribution to the Prophet through contemporaneous accounts from several sources and similarity between these accounts.)

hammed started planting the seeds of respecting women and wives. Gradually, this led to changes in the unfair discriminatory cultures and traditions of Jahliyah against women. A'isha was one of the important scholars of Islam. She even taught many Islamic scholars about Sharia law.[525] After the Prophet, A'isha was the person who narrated the greatest number of hadith. She narrated more than two thousands hadith of the Prophet.[526] Leading by example, Mohammed showed Muslims the important role that can be played by women. In addition, he demonstrated the potential beauty of the relationship between a husband and wife.

Another practical example of gradualism can be seen in an approach to education. The illiteracy of women was widespread in the Arab world during Jahiliyyah. Yet, women need to be educated, in order for them to recognize and claim their rights and respect for their dignity. In short,

> "The education of women was part of Islam's revolutionary progress out of Jahiliyyah and, together with other measures, helped to mold a new society which was to be more faithful to the pattern laid out for it by God. The evolution of Muslim society was not completed in the Prophet's era, but his example was meant to guide future generations of Muslims in further completing God's will."[527]

Prophet Mohammed used Sharia law when applying the doctrine of gradualism with respect to the education of women. According to Sharia law, education is not just a privilege or a right, but it is a religious obligation for all Muslim men and women.[528] There are a lot of verses that encourage education. The Quran states, "Say: 'Are those equal, those who know and those who do not know? It is those who are endued with understanding that receive admonition.'"[529] In conclusion, we can recognize that Sharia law is compatible with international human rights regarding equality and non-discrimination.

---

525 Sayeht & Morse, *supra* note 158, at 322 (citing 2 MUHAMMAD, ENCYCLOPAEDIA OF SEERAH 174 (Aftalur Rahman ed., 1982)).
526 Sayeht & Morse, *supra* note 158, at 322.
527 *Id.* at 324.
528 *Id.* (citing MOHAMMED KOTB, BAY'AT AL-NISSA, THE WOMEN'S RATIFICATION 101 (n.d)).
529 QURAN 39:9.

7. Human Dignity in Islam[530] and International Human Rights

There are scholars who believe that non-Western cultures do not recognize human rights. For instance, Jack Donnelly stated:

> However, it will be argued here that human rights present only one path to the realization of human dignity. Although there are indeed close connections between the two concepts, I shall argue that there are conceptions of human dignity which do not imply human rights, and societies and institutions which aim to realize human dignity entirely independent of human rights. This view, which was once rather common, seems to be ignored or rejected in most of the recent literature specifically devoted to the topic. The argument that "human rights are not a Western discovery" (Manglapus 1978), that "all societies have human rights notions" (Pollis and Schwab 1980, p. xiv), and that "all societies cross culturally and historically manifest conceptions of human rights" (Pollis and Schwab 1980, p. 15), is a common feature of a contemporary discussions of human rights in non-Western settings. I shall argue to the contrary that most non-Western cultural and political traditions lack not only the practice of human rights but the very concept of human rights is an artifact of modern Western civilizations.[531]

Islam respected human dignity and made it a main principle in Sharia law. According to the Quran, God states that He has honored every human being. The Quran did not differentiate between human beings depending on their race or their belief in Islam. The Quran stated human beings, which means any human beings. The Quran states, "And indeed We have honoured the Children of Adam, and We have carried them on land and sea, and have provided them with At-Tayyibat (lawful good things), and have preferred them above many of those whom We have created with a marked preferment."[532]

Rights are given to people because of their dignity and because they are honored. Human beings are honored and respected above many of God's creatures. For instance, the Quran explains "See this one whom You have honoured above me..."[533]

---

530 HELALY, *supra* note 273, at 101-149.
531 Jack Donnelly, *Human Rights and Human Dignity: An Analytical Critique of Non-Western Conceptions of Human Rights*, 76 AM. POL. SCI. REV. 303 (1982).
532 QURAN 17:70.
533 *Id.* at 17:62.

Several rights are included under the principle of dignity. For instance, freedom of speech is attached to human dignity. In other words, without freedom of speech, human dignity does not exist. The Quran respected freedom of speech, for instance, it states:

> "O mankind! We have created you from a male and a female, and made you into nations and tribes, that you may know one another. Verily, the most honourable of you with Allah is that (believer) who has At-Taqwa [i.e. he is one of the Muttaqun (the pious. See V.2:2)]. Verily, Allah is All-Knowing, All-Aware."[534]

Revoking promises is considered to be a kind of disrespect to the human dignity. Sharia law requests that Muslims fulfill their promises to others, regardless of their sex, race, religion, etc. Sharia law also requests that Muslims do not revoke their agreements. The Quran explains, "And fulfill (every) covenant. Verily, the covenant, will be questioned about."[535]

The right of human dignity includes the right to private life. The Quran requests that believers do not violate the right to private life. It states,

> "O you who believe! Avoid much suspicion; indeed some suspicions are sins. And spy not, neither backbite one another. Would one of you like to eat the flesh of his dead brother? You would hate it (so hate backbiting). And fear Allah. Verily, Allah is the One Who forgives and accepts repentance, Most Merciful."[536]

Sharia law respects the dignity of people, while they are in their home. The Quran requests that believers not enter any private place without permission. Furthermore it explains that if they are not given permission, they should leave. The Quran explains:

> O you who believe! Enter not houses other than your own, until you have asked permission and greeted those in them; that is better for you, in order that you may remember. And if you find no one therein, still, enter not until permission has been given. And if you are asked to go back, go back, for it is purer for you. And Allah is All-Knower of what you do. There is no sin on you that you enter (without taking permission) houses uninhabited (i.e. not possessed by anybody), (when) you have

---

534 *Id.* at 49:13.
535 *Id.* at 17:34.
536 *Id.* at 49:12.

any interest in them. And Allah has knowledge of what you reveal and what you conceal.[537]

It was said by one of the famous interpreters of the Quran, Ibn-Kasser, that the reason for the previous verse was that a woman came to the Prophet Mohammed one day and told him that while she is in her home, one of her relatives suddenly entered her home without requesting to do so or receiving her permission. She added that she did not want anyone to enter her home without permission as she felt that this was disrespectful of her privacy. As a result of this story, the previous Quranic verse was included in the Quran.[538]

There is a special respect paid to the honour and dignity of women in Sharia law, which forbids divulging women's secrets. There is a hadith for the Prophet Mohammed in which he indicates, "The most wicked among the people in the eye of Allah on the Day of Judgment is the man who goes to his wife and she comes to him, and then he divulges her secret."[539] This hadith shows clearly that God threatens the husband that divulges any of his wife's secrets. This clearly shows the respect that is given by Sharia law to the right to private life. It also shows that Sharia respects the dignity of women. All of the previous Quranic verses and hadith clearly show that the Sharia law honors human beings and respected their dignity, regardless of their race, language, sex, etc.

The first paragraph of the Arab Charter shows clearly that the Arab Charter highly respects human dignity and connected it to Sharia law. The preamble of Charter explains, "*Based on the faith of the Arab nation in the dignity of the human person whom God has exalted ever since the beginning of creation and in the fact that the Arab homeland is the cradle of religions and civilizations whose lofty human values affirm the human right to a decent life based on freedom, justice and equality ....[emphasis added]*"[540] In addition, Article 2 of the Arab Charter established the connection between human dignity and the right to self-determination and resistance of occupation. Article 3 (3) of the Arab Charter clearly shows that the dignity of men and women should be respected. This article explains, "Men and women are equal in respect of human dignity."[541]

---

537 *Id.* at 24:27, 28, 29.
538 HELALY, *supra* note 273, at 122 (citing Ibn-Kasser's interpretation).
539 *Sahih Muslim, Book 8, Hadith 3369*, SEARCHTRUTH.COM, http://www.iium.edu.my/deed/hadith/muslim/008_smt.html (last visited May 5, 2012).
540 ACHR, *supra* note 126, at preamble.
541 *Id.* at art. 3 (3) of the Arab Charter.

Article 1 of the Cairo Declaration on Human Rights in Islam provides:

> (a) All human beings form one family whose members are united by submission to God and descent from Adam. *All men are equal in terms of basic human dignity* and basic obligations and responsibilities, without any discrimination on the grounds of race, colour, language, sex, religious belief, political affiliation, social status or other considerations. True faith is the guarantee for enhancing such dignity along the path to human perfection.
>
> (b) All human beings are God's subjects, and the most loved by Him are those who are most useful to the rest of His subjects, and no one has superiority over another except on the basis of piety and good deeds. [emphasis added][542]

The international human rights treaties are entirely compatible with Sharia law with respect to the respect for human dignity. The preamble of the United Nations Charter refers to the term dignity. It states, "We the peoples of the United Nations determined…to reaffirm faith in fundamental human rights, in the dignity and worth of the human person, in the equal rights of men and women and of nations large and small…"[543] Furthermore, the Universal Declaration on Human Rights mentions the word dignity several times. For instance, Article 1 explains, "All human beings are born free and equal in dignity and rights. They are endowed with reason and conscience and should act towards one another in a spirit of brotherhood."[544] The preamble of the ICCPR also refers to the word dignity. It explains, "Recognizing that these rights derive from the inherent dignity of the human person."[545] In addition, the articles of the ICCPR states, "All persons deprived of their liberty shall be treated with humanity and with respect for the inherent dignity of the human person."[546] Not only is dignity mentioned with respect to civil and political rights, but also with respect to economic, social, and cultural rights. For instance, it explains:

> The States Parties to the present Covenant recognize the right of everyone to education. They agree that education shall be directed to the full development of the human personality and sense of dignity, and shall strengthen the respect for human rights and fundamental

---

542 Cairo Declaration on Human Rights in Islam, *supra* note 423.
543 United Nations, *Charter of the United Nations, supra* note 37, preamble.
544 UDHR, *supra* note 106.
545 ICCPR, *supra* note 63, at preamble.
546 *Id.* at art. 10 (1).

freedoms. They further agree that education shall enable all persons to participate effectively in a free society, promote understanding, tolerance and friendship among all nations and all racial, ethnic or religious groups, and further the activities of the United Nations for the maintenance of peace.[547]

Regarding the right to food, the United Nations Committee on Economic, Social and Cultural Rights states, "The Committee affirms that the right to adequate food is indivisibly linked to the inherent dignity of the human person and is indispensable for the fulfillment of other human rights enshrined in the International Bill of Human Rights."[548]

Dignity is not only mentioned in international and regional treaties, but is also mentioned in national constitutions. For instance, the Articles 51 and 55 of the Egyptian Constitution of 2014 states, "Dignity is the right of every human being and may not be violated. The State shall respect and protect human dignity. Every person who is either arrested, detained, or his freedom is restricted shall be treated in a manner that maintains his dignity. ."[549] The Saudi Arabian Constitution explains, "Information, publication, and all other media shall employ courteous language and the state's regulations, and they shall contribute to the education of the nation and the bolstering of its unity. All acts that foster sedition or division or harm the state's security and its public relations or detract from man's dignity and rights shall be prohibited. The statutes shall define all that."[550] The Lebanon Constitution states, "Education is free insofar as it is not contrary to public order and morals and does not interfere with the dignity of any of the religions or creeds."[551] The Arab region is not the only region that mentions dignity in its national constitutions; across the world several countries have done likewise. For instance, the German Constitution states:

---

547 ICESCR, *supra* note 449, at art. 13.
548 United Nations Committee on Economic, Social and Cultural Rights, Twentieth session, 26 April-14 May 1999. http://www.unhchr.ch/tbs/doc.nsf/0/3d02758c707031d58025677f003b73b9 (last visited Feb.. 3, 2013).
549 The Arab Republic of Egypt Const., 11 Sept. 1971, as amended, May 22, 1980, May 25, 2005, March 26, 2007, December 25, 2012, January 18, 2014, http://www.sis.gov.eg/Newvr/Dustor-en001.pdf (last visited May 14, 2014).
550 Saudi Arabia Const., art. 39, http://www.servat.unibe.ch/icl/sa00000_.html (last visited Apr. 26, 2012).
551 Lebanon Const., art.10, http://www.servat.unibe.ch/icl/le00000_.html (last visited April 26, 2012).

> (1) Human dignity shall be inviolable. To respect and protect it shall be the duty of all state authority.
>
> (2) The German people therefore acknowledge inviolable and inalienable human rights as the basis of every community, of peace and of justice in the world.
>
> (3) The following basic rights shall bind the legislature, the executive, and the judiciary as directly applicable law.[552]

It is very clear from all that I have mentioned above that there is international consensus on the direct link between dignity and human rights. Human dignity comes from *fitrah* and is from natural law theory. Natural law theory is not only related to Islam, but also to other religions. Evadne Grant explains:

> A view of dignity similar to that of the Stoics derives from the Jewish and Christian belief in God and the view of God as the father of mankind. In this view, man shares a common humanity and occupies a unique position within the universe. Moreover, since man is created in the image of God, each individual is seen as valuable in his or her own right. The ideas of Stoic philosophy transmitted via Cicero and combined with Jewish and Christian beliefs were developed into natural law theory by mediaeval Christian philosophers such as Thomas Aquinas…[553]

In short, we can say that Sharia law and international human rights law are compatible regarding human dignity. The West and the East are not two different planets. We are all human beings, we all live on the same Earth. As stated by Professor Siegfried Wiessner, "We don't live on a totally different planet, and Western rights are relatively recent. The common concept appears to be respect for human dignity."[554]

8. The Principle of the "Margin of Appreciation" as a Way of Reconciling Islamic Sharia Law and International Human Rights Law

There are many commonalities that exist between Islamic law and international law. However, the principle of the margin of appreciation can play an important role for cases where Western scholars and people raised in Western cultures still

---

552 GRUNDGESETZ FÜR DIE BUNDESREPUBLIK DEUTSCHLAND [GRUNDGESETZ] [GG] [BASIC LAW], May 23, 1949, BGBl. I at art. 1 (Ger.), http://www.iuscomp.org/gla/statutes/GG.htm#1 (last visited April 26, 2012).

553 Evadne Grant, *Dignity and Equality*, H.R.L REV. 304 (2007).

554 Prof. Siegfried Wiessner, email to author, June 6, 2012.

believe that there are insufficient commonalities between Sharia law and international human rights. The margin of appreciation is a doctrine the Court uses to interpret certain Convention provisions. It generally refers to the amount of discretion the Court gives national authorities in fulfilling their obligations under the Convention.[555] Thus, the margin of appreciation leaves the door open for the national judges to balance between the interest of the right of the individual and the right of the public in ways that may differ from other Member States of the Council of Europe and the approach taken by the Court in Strasbourg. At the same time, the margin of appreciation does not mean that there are no commonalities at all or that the national authorities have unlimited discretion. The extent of the margin of appreciation varies in accordance with the type of right the state authorities are interfering with and also depends on the circumstances and merits of the individual case.[556]

The margin of appreciation has been developed by the European Court of Human Rights in many cases. The first case that mentioned the margin of appreciation is that of *Handyside vs. the United Kingdom*.[557] *Handyside* is a successful example of applying the margin of appreciation. The case

> Involved the publication of a book called the Little Red Schoolbook. The book targeted young readers and mixed generally liberal social advice with controversial encouragements to smoke marijuana and experiment sexually. After receiving complaints about the book, the Director of Public Prosecutions asked the Metropolitan Police to investigate the premises of the book's publisher, Richard Handyside. The Police searched his premises and his books were seized and ultimately destroyed. The local Magistrate's Court convicted him of possessing obscene books for gain.[558]

The Court ruled:

> According to the Government and the majority of the Commission, the Court has only to ensure that the English courts acted reasonably, in good faith and within the limits of the margin of appreciation left to the Contracting States by Article 10 para. 2... Consequently, Article 10 para.

---

555   Jeffrey A. Brauch, The Margin of Appreciation and the Jurisprudence of the European Court of Human Rights: Threat to the Rule of Law, 11 COLUM. J. EUR. L. 113, 115 (2004).

556   Margin of appreciation, http://www.ukessays.com/essays/law/margin-of-appreciation.php (last visited October 29, 2012).

557   Handyside vs. the United Kingdom, (5493/72) [1976] ECHR 5 (7 December 1976).

558   Brauch, *supra* note 555.

2 (art. 10-2) leaves to the Contracting States a margin of appreciation. This margin is given both to the domestic legislator ("prescribed by law") and to the bodies, judicial amongst others, that are called upon to interpret and apply the laws in force.[559]

The Court added:

It is not possible to find in the domestic law of the various Contracting States a uniform European conception of morals. The view taken by their respective laws of the requirements of morals varies from time to time and from place to place, especially in our era which is characterised by a rapid and far-reaching evolution of opinions on the subject. By reason of their direct and continuous contact with the vital forces of their countries, State authorities are in principle in a better position than the international judge to give an opinion on the exact content of these requirements as well as on the "necessity" of a "restriction" or "penalty" intended to meet them.[560]

In the case of *S.H. and Others vs. Austria* the "applicants alleged in particular that the provisions of the Austrian Artificial Procreation Act prohibiting the use of ova from donors and sperm from donors for in vitro fertilisation, the only medical techniques by which they could successfully conceive children, violated their rights under Article 8 of the Convention read alone and in conjunction with Article 14."[561] Furthermore,

In the Government's view, the central issue in the case was not whether there could be any recourse at all to medically and technically assisted procreation and what limits the State could set in that respect, but to what extent the State must authorise and accept the cooperation of third parties in the fulfilment of a couple's wish to conceive a child. Even though the right to respect for private life also comprised the right to fulfil the wish for a child, it did not follow that the State was under an obligation to permit indiscriminately all technically feasible means of reproduction or even to provide such means. In making use of the margin of appreciation afforded to them, the States had to decide for themselves what balance should be struck between the competing

---

559 Handyside vs. the United Kingdom, *supra* note 557.
560 *Id.*
561 S.H. and Others vs. Austria [GC], (57813/00) ECHR (3 November 2011), http://hudoc.echr.coe.int/sites/eng/pages/search.aspx?i=001-107325 (last visited October 28, 2012).

interests in the light of the specific social and cultural needs and traditions of their countries.[562]

Realistically it should be noted that the majority of rights that are stated in the Convention are not absolute. In other words, "the convention says it gives these rights to the individual, but then it immediately places those rights back in hands of the government…governments would never have agreed to be bound by the Convention if such scenario had not been followed – and without governments' signature and ratification, the Convention would never have come into being."[563]

It should be noted that the doctrine of margin of appreciation does not allow the governments to escape from any supervision. It was stated in the *Handyside* case, "The domestic margin of appreciation thus goes hand in hand with a European supervision. Such supervision concerns both the aim of the measure challenged and its 'necessity;' it covers not only the basic legislation but also the decision applying it, even one given by an independent court."[564]

The flexibility given to countries to apply the margin of appreciation is measured case by case. For instance, countries are given wider margin of appreciation in cases of protection of national security. Countries are given more power to put more restrictions on rights and freedoms in order to protect national security. For instance, in *Klass vs. Germany*, the European Court gave Germany wider margin of appreciation in order for Germany to combat terrorism.[565]

The principle of the margin of appreciation can be used as a way of reconciliation between Sharia and international human rights law. It can be used to give respect to Sharia law and at the same time non violation to the international human rights law. For instance, I explained in this chapter and will explain in details in Chapter 5 the principle of equality between men and women according to Sharia law. The meaning of the positive discrimination in favor of women will be explained in this book. For instance, according to Sharia law, husbands are financially responsible to their wives even if the salary of the wife is more than her husband. In this example, there is no equality between men and women as men have to pay to women. Therefore, the margin of appreciation can be used to protect the rights given to women according to Sharia law.

---

562 *Id.*
563 Marie-Benedicte Dembour, Who Believes in Human Rights, Reflection on the European Convention 36 (2006).
564 Handyside vs. the United Kingdom, *supra* note 557.
565 Brauch, *supra* note 555.

Chapter 4: An Arab Regional Instrument for Human Rights: The Arab Charter on Human Rights

A. History of the Arab League and the Arab Charter on Human Rights

1. The Arab League

Although the Arab Charter on Human Rights was a late-comer to the club of regional systems protecting human rights, it is not the last, as an Asian human rights system has not yet been adopted. The Arab Charter on Human Rights is considered to be the fourth regional human rights system that came into force after the European, American, and African systems. The Arab Charter is considered to be a considerable step towards establishing a regional human rights system in the Middle East and North Africa. It is an important and major step towards improving the effectiveness of the protection of collective human rights in the Middle East.

Similar to the European Convention on Human Rights, the inspiration for the creation of the Arab Charter on Human Rights was the Universal Declaration of Human Rights; however, the Arab Charter does not duplicate the rights referred to in the Universal Declaration of Human Rights. The European Convention was adopted mainly for two reasons. First, it was developed and adopted in response to the extreme human rights violations that had happened during the Second World War. Thus, the goal of the European Charter was to avoid any further human rights violations from happening in the future. Second, the European Convention was issued and adopted to safeguard European states from communism.[566] On the other hand, the Arab Charter was adopted for different reasons, including: the desire of the Arab region to have an effective regional human rights system similar to those of Europe, the Americas, and Africa; the increase in international awareness of issues of human rights in the Arab countries; and the growth of Arab human rights movements that arose out of an interest in more effective human rights protection.

The Arab Charter reflects the objectives and purposes of the Pact of the League of Arab States. The goal and purpose of this pact was, and still is, the "strengthening of the relations between the member states; the co-ordination of their polices in order to achieve co-operation between them and to safeguard their independence and sovereignty; and a general concern with the affairs and interests of the Arab countries."[567] One of the ways that this goal has been achieved

---

566 Francis G. Jacobs & Robin C. A. White, The European Convention on Human Rights 2 (4th ed. 2006).
567 League of Arab States, *Charter of Arab League*, (Mar. 22, 1945), at art. 2, http://www.un-

is through the adoption of charters and amendment of the pact to give more strength to the relations between states parties and to establish the Arab Court of Justice.[568]

The idea of adopting a new Arab League was mentioned not only by Arab countries, but also by non-Arab countries. On May 29, 1941 at the Mansion House, the British Secretary of State, Antony Eden, said in a speech:

> The Arab World has made strides since the settlement reached at the end of the last war, and many Arab thinkers desire for the Arab peoples a greater degree of unity than they now enjoy. In reaching out towards this unity, they hope for our support. No such appeal from our friends should go unanswered. It seems to me both natural and right that the cultural and economic ties, too, should be strengthened. His Majesty's government for their part will give their full support to any scheme that commands general approval.[569]

There were continuous efforts on the part of the Arab states to work towards achieving unity and independence. An example of these efforts was the idea of establishing the Arab League and the Arab Charter. Nahas Pasha, the Prime Minister of Egypt, undertook one of the important initiatives in 1943. Nahas Pasha coordinated several meetings with Arab leaders. In June 1944, he organized a preliminary meeting in Egypt to which he invited the government officials of Iraq, Syria, Lebanon, Transjordan, Saudi Arabia, and Yemen.[570]

On September 25, 1944, the Preparatory Committee of the General Arab Congress was held in Alexandria, Egypt. The preparatory committee adopted the Alexandria Protocol on October 7, 1944. The protocol expressed the desire of the signatories "to strengthen and consolidate the ties which bind all the Arab countries and to direct them towards the welfare of the Arab World, to improve its conditions, insure its future, and realize its hopes and aspirations".[571] The Alexandria Protocol was considered to be the principal document that laid the

---

hcr.org/refworld/docid/3ae6b3ab18.html (last visited Feb. 3, 2013).

568 Id. at preamble.

569 Majid Khadduri, *Towards an Arab Union: The League of Arab States*, 40 (1) AM. POL. SCI. REV. 90 (1946); *see also Presentation of the Arab League*, ARABLEAGUEONLINE.ORG, http://www.arab-leagueonline.org (last visited Aug. 1, 2010).

570 I. Pogany, *The League of Arab States: An Overview*, 21 BRACTON L. J. 43 (1989).

571 Id. at 44.

basis of the League of Arab Countries. The Protocol stated the following principles:[572]

1. The establishment of 'the league of Arab States', to be comprised of independent Arab Countries that accept accession to it, while at the same time forming a council, in which all member states enjoy equal rights.

2. The Arab League Council would be entrusted with the implementation of agreements, the holding of periodical meetings, and enhancing the relations between various Member States.

3. The resolutions adopted by the Arab League Council are binding upon all states, save that in cases implying differences between two League Member States who will refer to the Council to settle conflicts between them. In such cases, the resolutions will be binding upon all parties.

4. It is illegal to use power to settle conflicts that may arise between two League Member States. It is also illegal to follow a foreign policy that would harm the policy followed by the League of the Arab States or any of its Member's policies.

5. Declaring the sovereignty and independence of the organizing countries and their present borders, the Protocol implied two resolutions relating to the following items;

a. Respect of Lebanon's independence and sovereignty;

b. To consider Palestine as an important element in the Arab Countries set up.

6. The Protocol stated the formation of a subsidiary political committee, formed by members of the former Preparatory Committee, to draft an order and discuss political matters, where agreements can be concluded between Arab Countries.

Today the League of Arab states is an umbrella organization for 17 specialized agencies, dealing with functions such as maritime transport, civil aviation, economic and social development, educational, cultural and scientific affairs. There

---

[572] KEIR STARMER & THEODARA A. CHRISTOU, HUMAN RIGHTS MANUAL AND SOURCEBOOK FOR AFRICA 50-51 (Beattie et al. eds., 2005).

are also 15 permanent committees for matters concerning human rights, oil, and women, etc.[573]

In February 1945, the Egyptian Government requested that the Arab Foreign Ministers meet in Cairo to draft the Pact of the Arab States.[574] The Pact was approved on March 22, 1945.

The League of Arab States is a vital official governmental body, which includes representatives from all of the Arab States. The League currently consists of twenty two states parties located mainly in North Africa and the Middle East. The League was founded by Egypt, Iraq, Lebanon, Saudi Arabia, Syria, Transjordan (Jordan, as of 1950), and Yemen. Countries that joined later include Algeria (1962), Bahrain (1971), Comoros (1993), Djibouti (1977), Kuwait (1961), Libya (1953), Mauritania (1973), Morocco (1958), Oman (1971), Qatar (1971), Somalia (1974), Southern Yemen (1967), Sudan (1956), Tunisia (1958), the United Arab Emirates (1971), and the Palestine Liberation Organization (which was admitted in 1976).[575] The summit of the heads, presidents, kings, and princes of Arab states is organized on a yearly basis.

2. An Arab Charter on Human Rights

The idea of adopting an Arab Charter on Human Rights goes back to 1969, when the Council of the Arab League issued Resolution 2486 on March 16, agreeing to the declaration and resolutions of the Arab Human Rights Conference, which had been held in Beirut in December 1968. These resolutions included inviting the Secretariat of the Arab League to take the necessary measures to arrange the meeting of the Permanent Arab Committee for Human Rights, which would observe and monitor the outcomes of the execution of these resolutions.[576]

On March 11, 1970, the Council of Arab League issued Resolution 2605, accepting the recommendations of the Permanent Arab Committee for Human Rights in its fourth meeting. One of the main recommendations was to invite the Secretariat to organize a forum of experts to develop a proposal for an Arab Charter of Human Rights. This charter of human rights would take both the international

---

573 *Id.* at 52.
574 This meeting is in accordance with the Alexandria Protocol, which had envisaged the establishment of a committee to prepare the text of the pact. *See* The League of Arab States, *The Alexandria Protocol*, Res. 1., Oct. 7, 1944.
575 *Presentation of the Arab League, supra* note 569.
576 WAEL ALLAM, AL MESAQ AL AABY LEHOKOOK AL EN'SAAN DERASAAH HWL DOR EL MESAQ FI TAZEZ HKOOK AL EN'SAAN FI GAMET AL DEWAL AL ARABEYAH [The Arab Charter On Human Rights, Study on its Role in Strengthening Human Rights in the Arab League] (2005).

declarations of human rights and the cultural heritage and the historical circumstances of the Arab nations into consideration.[577]

In September 1970, the Arab Council established the committee of experts to write the proposal for the Arab Charter within six months. The Committee convened from April to July 1971. After the proposal was completed, it was submitted to the Secretariat of the Arab League, which then sent it to the states parties for comments and observations. Only a few countries replied and wrote comments; most of the countries did not reply. In addition, the circumstances facing Arab countries in the 1970s and 1980s led to this process being suspended for an indefinite period of time.[578] The idea of adopting an Arab Charter reappeared in 1981, when the Secretariat requested that a group of experts of international law write a proposal for an Arab Charter. The Arab Permanent Committee of Human Rights revised the final draft of the proposal in its meetings between May and August of 1981.[579] On March 31, 1983, the Council of Arab League issued a resolution to send the final draft of the proposal to the states parties for their comments. The Committee introduced some changes to the draft after receiving the comments from the States parties. However, it postponed making a decision on the proposal until the Organization of Islamic Conference finished its studies on Human Rights in Islam.[580] In 1994, a special committee revised the final draft of the proposal in light of the Cairo Declaration of Human Rights in Islam, which was issued by the Organization of Islamic Conference in 1990.[581] The document was revised based on the observations and suggestions of the member countries.[582]

Parallel to the initiatives done by the League of Arab States, some personal efforts were undertaken to adopt a draft Arab Charter on Human Rights. It goes back to 1986 when Professor M. Cherif Bassiouni, the Godfather of the Arab human rights system, organized and chaired a meeting of experts to work on preparing a draft Charter on Human Rights in the Arab World.[583] The meeting took place at the International Institute of Higher Studies in Criminal Sciences (ISISC) in Siracusa,

---

577   Id.
578   For example, the Egyptian-Israeli war in 1973, the peace agreement between Egypt and Israel, and the murder of the president of Egypt Anwar el Sadat in 1981.
579   AHMED SHWKEY ET AL., LA HEMAYAH L'AHAD DOOR GAMET AL DEWAL AL ARABEYAH FI HEMAYAT HKOOK AL EN'SAAN [No Protection for Any One, Role of the Arab League in Protecting Human Rights] (2006).
580   ALLAM, *supra* note 576.
581   Cairo Declaration on Human Rights in Islam, *supra* note 423.
582   SHWKEY ET AL *supra* note 579.
583   CHERIF BASSIOUNI, DRAFT CHARTER ON HUMAN AND PEOPLE'S RIGHTS IN THE ARAB WORLD (1987).

Italy, December 5 – 12, 1986. It was attended by seventy-six Arab experts from more than 10 Arab countries. They included prominent personalities from all the Arab World. Many of them were highly ranked judges, law professors, lawyers and representatives of nongovernmental organizations.[584]

In a comparative approach, the experts examined many documents presented to the conference such as a draft Arab Charter prepared by the General Administration for Legal Affairs of the Secretariat of the League of Arab States. In addition, they examined also many other regional and international conventions in order to reach the ideal draft for the Charter.

The draft Charter was composed of 65 articles, including all three generations of rights. The draft Charter also provided for the establishment of an Arab Commission on Human Rights and an Arab Court on Human Rights.

Professor Bassiouni submitted the draft Charter to all Arab Heads of State, Ministers of Justice, Ministers of Foreign Affairs, the Secretary General of the League of Arab States, etc. The League of Arab states established a committee of experts. The committee of experts used the Siracusa Draft as its model."[585]

Regarding the draft Charter, Professor Bassiouni stated

> The Arab Charter's origin is in the "Draft Arab Charter of People's and Human Rights," published in 1986 by ISISC. It was developed by a group of experts who are listed in the ISISC publication. They included prominent personalities from Egypt and other Arab states. The text was then sent by me to the League of Arab states and a committee of experts was established. The committee of experts used the Siracusa Draft as its model. The same was done with the organization of the Islamic Conference, and they came out with another text that is less progressive that the Arab League's text.[586]

Leila Zerrougui confirmed that there were many efforts done by nongovernmental organizations to adopt the draft charter for human rights in the Arab World,

> The first draft declaration on Arab human rights was drafted in 1971 by a committee of experts established by the Council of the League of Arab States, but the project did not materialize. In view of the lack of enthusiasm on the part of the States, the text was reworked and a draft

---

584 *Id* at 1.
585 Prof. Cherif Bassiouni, email to author, June 26, 2014.
586 *Id.*

treaty was again submitted to the States in 1983. The League then decided to temporize and await the adoption of the Declaration on Human Rights in Islam by the Organization of the Islamic Conference. It should be noted that parallel to the initiatives of the League of Arab States toward the adoption of an Arab Charter on Human Rights, various initiatives undertaken by Arab non-governmental organizations resulted in draft texts or critically examined the projects of the League.[587]

It should be noted that the text of the Cairo Declaration on Human Rights in Islam that was adopted by Organization of Islamic Conference is different from the text of the Arab Charter on Human Rights adopted by the Arab League. Professor Bassiouni highlighted this issue by stating that,

> The fact that the OIC came out with a different text than the Arab League was because some of the Muslim states disagreed with some of the progressive language in the Arab Charter. There is a question therefore with some Arab states and scholars about whether or not the Arab Charter is entirely consistent with the Shari⁣â or not. Certainly for those in the OIC who drafted that charter's text, they believe that they are more in keeping with the Shari⁣â than the Arab Charter.[588]

On September 15, 1994, the Council of Arab League adopted the Arab Charter on Human Rights.[589] Article 42, Paragraph 2 of the Charter states, "The present Charter shall enter into effect two months after the date of deposit of the seventh instrument of ratification or accession with the Secretariat of the League of Arab States." The Charter did not enter into force, as none of the Arab countries ratified or signed the Charter, except Iraq. It was surprising that no other Arab countries signed the Arab Charter as it neither included any new rights nor had any effective supervisory mechanisms. While it would have been easy for the Arab countries that already ratified both the ICCPR and the ICESCR to ratify the Charter, they refrained from doing so.[590] Mervat Rishmawi noted that "[a]lthough it was widely criticized at the time by many human rights organizations both within the region

---

587 LEILA ZERROUGUI, ARAB CHARTER ON HUMAN RIGHTS, http://projects.essex.ac.uk/ehrr/V7N2/Zer-rougui.pdf (last visited July 2, 2014).
588 Prof. Cherif Bassiouni, email to author, June 26, 2014.
589 Council of the League of Arab States, Arab Charter on Human Rights, September 15, 1994, *reprinted in* 18 HUM. RTS. L.J., 151 (1997).
590 WAEL ALLAM, ALMISAQ AL-ARABY LEHOKOOK ALINSAN [Arab Charter on Human Rights] 1(2005).

and beyond as failing to meet international human rights standards not one Arab League State was prepared to ratify it."[591]

The Council of the Arab League adopted Resolution 6809 on March 12, 2001, which encouraged states parties to sign, ratify, and modernize the Charter to correspond with international human rights standards. The idea of the modernization of the Charter started before September 11, 2001. This shows that the modernization process came purely from a feeling of national responsibility and was not affected by international circumstances.[592] After September 11, 2001 and the resulting international changes, members of the Arab Permanent Committee on Human Rights accelerated their efforts regarding the adoption of a new Arab Charter.

Establishing a Human Rights Office in the Arab League under the Secretariat was a good step forward in modernizing the Charter. In 2003, the Secretary-General of the Arab League, Amr Mousa, clarified that "the term 'modernization' should be understood as being the process required to bring Charter provisions into compliance with international standards for human rights."[593] On March 24, 2003, the Council of Arab League requested that the Arab Permanent Committee of Arab States work with a group of law and human rights experts to modernize the Charter based on the comments from Arab countries. In October 2003, the Committee wrote its proposal.[594] There was a need for the proposal of the Charter to be developed and revised by a group of experts who were both highly qualified in the field of human rights and had full knowledge of, and background in, Arab cultural heritage, culture, and traditions. The Arab Permanent Committee of Human Rights agreed on this in its exceptional session in October 2003. The Arab League reached a bilateral agreement with the Office of the High Commissioner for Human Rights (OHCHR) to gather a group of 'independent Arab experts' as the Committee of Experts to carry out the task. All of the Committee's members, who consisted of two women and three men from Algeria, Egypt, Qatar, Saudi Arabia, and Tunisia, were drawn from the United Nations human rights treaty bodies.[595]

---

591 Mervat Rishmawi, *The Revised Arab Charter on Human Rights: A step Forward?* 5 HUM. RTS. L. REV 5(2) 361-376 (2005) (Mervat Rishmawi is the legal advisor for the Middle East and North Africa at the International Secretariat of Amnesty International).
592 ALLAM, *supra* note 590.
593 Rishmawi, *supra* note 591.
594 ALLAM, *supra* note 590.
595 *Id.*

The Charter was finally adopted in May 23, 2004. It entered into force in March 15, 2008 after the seventh ratification. As of December 1, 2014, sixteen countries have signed the Charter and it has been ratified by the following fourteen Arab countries:[596] Jordan,[597] Algeria,[598] Bahrain,[599] Libya,[600] Syria,[601] Palestine,[602] the Emirates,[603] Yemen,[604] Qatar,[605] Saudi Arabia,[606] Lebanon,[607] Sudan, Kuwait, and Iraq.[608] It is very surprising that many of the Arab countries that ratified many international and regional conventions and protocols refrained from ratifying the Arab Charter, including five Arab countries that have already ratified the First Optional Protocol of the ICCPR. This Optional Protocol permits submission of individual communications to the Human Rights Committee.[609] Although, Tunisia, Djibouti, and Somalia ratified the First Optional Protocol, they refrained from ratifying the Arab Charter. Furthermore, although Djibouti ratified the Second Optional Protocol of the ICCPR (which abolished the death sentence), it did not ratify the Arab Charter. Furthermore, Egypt, Djibouti, Somalia, and Mauritania ratified the African Charter on Human and Peoples' Rights, but they did not ratify the Arab Charter. Thus, one has to conclude that, even though the Arab Charter is supposed to reflect the cultures and traditions of the Arab region, it was not

---

596 Article 49 (2) of the Arab Charter states, "The present Charter shall enter into effect two months from the date on which the seventh instrument of ratification is deposited with the secretariat of the league of Arab States." The first seven Arab Countries that ratified the Charter are Jordan, Algeria, Bahrain, Libya, Syria, Palestine, and the United Arab Emirates. The list of signing and ratifying countries can be found at http://www.arableagueonline.org (last visited Apr. 30, 2012).

597 Jordan ratified the Charter on October 28, 2004.

598 Algeria ratified the Charter on June 11, 2006.

599 Bahrain ratified the Charter on June 18, 2006.

600 Libya ratified the Charter on August 7, 2006.

601 Syria ratified the Charter on February 6, 2007

602 Palestine ratified the Charter on November 28, 2007.

603 Emirates ratified the Charter on January 15, 2008.

604 Yemen ratified the Charter on November 12, 2008.

605 Qatar rarified the Charter on January 11, 2009.

606 Saudi Arabia ratified the Charter on April 15, 2009.

607 Lebanon ratified the Charter on May 8, 2011.

608 Sudan ratified the Charter on May 21, 2013. Kuwait ratified the Charter on September 5, 2013. Iraq ratified the Charter on April 4, 2013.

609 The Arab countries that ratified the First Optional Protocol to the ICCPR are Algeria, Tunisia, Libya, Somalia, Djibouti. *See* Optional Protocol to the International Covenant on Civil and Political Rights, G.A. res. 2200A (XXI), 21 U.N. GAOR Supp. (No. 16) at 59, U.N. Doc. A/6316 (1966), 999 U.N.T.S. 302, entered into force March 23, 1976, http://treaties.un.org/Pages/View-Details.aspx?src=TREATY&mtdsg_no=IV-5&chapter=4&lang=en (last visited Apr. 17, 2012).

ratified by many Arab countries. Usually, regional charters are ratified more quickly than international charters, because they reflect the cultures and traditions of the states parties. For example, all African Union states parties ratified the African Charter.[610] Regarding the European Convention on Human Rights, all the states parties of the European Council were parties to the European Convention.[611]

The principle of gradualism has been applied smoothly in the case of the Arab regional human rights system. The old charter did not enter into force. The new Arab Charter was adopted in 2004. It took approximately four years until it entered into force. From its adoption until December 2014, only fourteen member countries of the Arab League had ratified the Arab Charter. Even though several Arab countries did not ratify the Arab Charter, they ratified many international and regional treaties that included stricter articles and more effective supervisory mechanisms. Over time, the Arab countries will gain confidence in, and awareness of, the Arab Charter. The Arab Charter stated that one of its aims is "to place human rights at the centre of the key national concerns of Arab States, making them lofty and fundamental ideals that shape the will of the individual in Arab States and enable him to improve his life in accordance with noble human values."[612]

After the Arab Charter entered into force and according to Article 45 of the Charter, an Arab Human Rights Committee was established consisting of seven members. The aim of that Committee was to ensure the human rights protection in the member countries that had signed on to the Arab Charter.[613]

B. The Philosophy and Theory of the Arab Charter

The uniqueness of the Arab Charter, which reflects the uniqueness of the Arab regions, can be easily recognized. The Arab Charter is relevant to my proposed theory. In fact, the Charter simultaneously combines different theories. The Charter applies the universalism theory, while also respecting the identity of the Arab states. The Charter states, "The present Charter seeks, within the context of the national identity of the Arab States and their sense of belonging to a common civilization, to achieve the following aims: To entrench the principle that all

---

610 As of January 1, 2014, 53 Countries have ratified the African Charter, *see* http://www.africa-union.org (last visited May 1, 2014).
611 *European Convention on Human Rights*, WIKIPEDIA.ORG, http://en.wikipedia.org/wiki/European_Convention_on_Human_Rights (last visited May 17, 2012).
612 ACHR, *supra* note 126, at art. 1 (1).
613 ALLAM, *supra* note 590, at 3.

human rights are universal, indivisible, interdependent and interrelated."[614] However, this does not mean that the Charter accepts the theory of universality as the only theory that should be used. The Charter strikes a balance between universality and the special and regional requirements of the Arab states. The first paragraph of the preamble states that the Charter is

> "based on the faith of the Arab nation in the dignity of the person whom God has exalted ever since the beginning of creation and in the fact that the Arab homeland is the cradle of religions and civilizations whose lofty human values affirm the human rights to a decent life based on freedom, justice and equality."[615]

Also, it is mentioned in the preamble that the Charter has "regard to the Cairo Declaration on Human Rights in Islam."[616]

The Charter effectively respects regional Arab cultures and protects the international human rights norms and standards. It focuses on international human rights standards that should be respected and protected, such as the right to life and the right to not be tortured while also focusing on regional cultures and traditions. For instance, Article 1(2) of the Charter states that it seeks

> "to teach the human person in the Arab States pride in his identity, loyalty to his country, attachment to his land, history and common interests and to instill in him a culture of human brotherhood, tolerance and openness towards others, in accordance with universal principles and values and with those proclaimed in international human rights instruments."[617]

The Charter also explains that "men and women are equal in respect of human dignity, rights and obligations within the framework of the *positive discrimination* established in favour of women by the Islamic Shariah, other divine laws and by applicable laws and legal instruments... " [emphasis added][618]

---

614 ACHR, *supra* note 126, at art. 1 (4).
615 *Id.* at preamble.
616 *Id.* at preamble.
617 *Id.* at art. 1 (2).
618 *Id.* at art. 3 (3).

C. The Scope of the Arab Charter

With the exclusion of Article 3, the Arab Charter, like the Universal Declaration on Human Rights, lists all the guaranteed rights and freedoms and takes the form of a declaration of rights. The Charter gives binding effect to the rights guaranteed in the Charter and provides:

> 1. Each State Party to the Present Charter undertakes to ensure to all individuals subject to its jurisdiction the right to enjoy the rights and freedoms set forth herein, without distinction on grounds of race, color, sex, language, religious belief, opinion, thought, national or social origin, wealth, birth or physical or mental disability.
>
> 2. States parties to the present Charter shall take the requisite measures to guarantee effective equality in the enjoyment of all the rights and freedoms enshrined in the Present Charter in order to ensure protection against all forms of discrimination based on any grounds mentioned in the preceding paragraph.
>
> 3. Men and women are equal in respect of human dignity, rights and obligations within the framework of the positive discrimination established in favor of women by Islamic Sharia, other divine laws and by applicable laws and legal instruments. According, each State party pledges to take all the requisite measures to guarantee equal opportunities and effective equality between men and women in the enjoyment of all rights set out in this Charter.[619]

Article 44 of the Charter explains, "The states parties undertake to adopt, in conformity with their constitutional procedures and with the provisions of the present Charter, whatever legislative or non-legislative measures that may be necessary to give effect to the rights set forth herein."[620]

D. Rights Protected by the Charter

The Charter includes the three generations of rights. First generation rights are the civil and political rights, such as freedom of thought,[621] the right to life,[622] and the right to liberty.[623] Second generation rights are the economic, social, and

---

619 *Id.* at art. 3.
620 *Id.* at art. 44.
621 *Id.* at art. 30.
622 *Id.* at art. 5.
623 *Id.* at art. 14.

cultural rights, such as the right to work,[624] the right to own private property,[625] and the right of every citizen to social security. Third generation rights include the right to development.[626] The Charter includes specific provisions on women, children, and the disabled. On the other hand, the Charter includes rights that are not stated in either the International Covenant on Civil and Political Rights or the International Covenant on Economic, Social, and Cultural Rights. For example, it guarantees human dignity to people with mental and physical disabilities[627] and prohibits human trafficking.[628]

The Charter not only includes a list of rights, but it also clearly requests that the states parties "undertake to adopt, in conformity with their constitutional procedures and with the provisions of the present Charter, whatever legislative or non-legislative measures that may be necessary to give effect to the rights set forth herein."[629] In addition, the Charter also provides,

> "Each State party to the present Charter undertakes to ensure to all individuals subject to its jurisdiction the right to enjoy the rights and freedoms set forth herein, without distinction on grounds of race, colour, sex, language, religious belief, opinion, thought, national or social origin, wealth, birth, or physical or mental disability."[630]

In exceptional situations that threaten the life of the nation, the Charter gives states parties the right to derogate their obligation under the Charter. However, this right is not absolute and there are three conditions that must exist for it to be allowed: First, the derogation of rights must not be inconsistent with the obligations under international law and must not involve discrimination solely on the grounds of race, colour, sex, language, religion, or social origin.[631] Second, the Charter includes a list of rights that cannot be derogated in any exceptional cases of emergency. These rights are the right to life,[632] the right not to be subjected to torture of cruel or inhuman treatment,[633] the right not to be subjected to medical

---

624 *Id.* at art. 34.
625 *Id.* at art. 31.
626 *Id.* at art. 37.
627 *Id.* at art. 40.
628 *Id.* at art. 10.
629 *Id.* at art. 44.
630 *Id.* at art. 3(1).
631 *Id.* at art. 4.
632 *Id.* at art. 5.
633 *Id.* at art. 8.

or scientific experimentation without free consent,[634] the right not to be held in slavery and servitude under any circumstances,[635] the right to fair trial,[636] the right not to deprive any person of his liberty except on such grounds and in such circumstances as are determined by law,[637] no crime and no penalty without a prior provision of law,[638] the right not to be imprisoned if you are unable to pay a debt arising from a contractual obligation,[639] the right not to be tried twice for the same offence,[640] the right for all persons deprived of their liberty to be treated with humanity and respect to their human dignity,[641] the right to recognition as a person before the law,[642] the right to not arbitrary or unlawfully prevented from leaving or residing in any country,[643] the right to nationality,[644] the right to freedom of thought,[645] and the right to seek political asylum.[646] Third, the Charter explains that the previous rights should not be derogated from in any circumstances and the judicial guarantees required for the protection of the aforementioned rights cannot be suspended.[647] In addition, the Charter states that

> "nothing in the Charter may be construed, or interpreted as impairing the rights and freedoms protected by the domestic laws of the States parties or those set forth in the international and regional human rights instruments which the States parties have adopted or ratified, including the rights of women, the rights of the child and the rights of persons belonging to minorities."[648]

---

634 *Id.* at art. 9.
635 *Id.* at art. 10.
636 *Id.* at art. 13.
637 *Id.* at art. 14.
638 *Id.* at art. 15.
639 *Id.* at art. 18.
640 *Id.* at art. 19.
641 *Id.* at art. 20.
642 *Id.* at art. 22.
643 *Id.* at art. 27.
644 *Id.* at art. 29.
645 *Id.* at art. 30.
646 *Id.* at art. 28.
647 *Id.* at art. 4(2).
648 *Id.* at art. 43.

E. Incorporation of the Fundamental Principles into the Arab Charter

The Preamble of the Arab Charter and Article 1 refer to the relationship between the *'umma* and the individual in Islam. For instance, the preamble states, "Based on the faith of the Arab nation... Being proud of the humanitarian values and principles that the Arab nation... Believing in the unity of the Arab nation."[649] In addition, Article 1 of the Charter also refers to the *'umma*, stating "To prepare the new generations in Arab States..."[650] These examples show clearly that the Charter refers to the *'umma*.

Regarding *Zakat* and social security, the Arab Charter explains, "The States parties shall ensure the right of every citizen to social security, including social insurance."[651] The Charter also states,

> "Every person has the right to an adequate standard of living for himself and his family, which ensures their well-being and a decent life, including food, clothing, housing, services and the right to a healthy environment. The States parties shall take the necessary measures commensurate with their resources to guarantee these rights."[652]

Furthermore, the Charter explains:

> The States parties recognize the right of every member of society to the enjoyment of the highest attainable standard of physical and mental health and the right of the citizen to free basic health-care services and to have access to medical facilities without discrimination of any kind. The measures taken by States parties shall include the following: (a) Development of basic health-care services and the guaranteeing of free and easy access to the centres that provide these services, regardless of geographical location or economic status.[653]

In addition, the Charter states, "The States parties shall provide social services free of charge for all persons with disabilities."[654] Also, the Charter states, "The States parties shall guarantee their citizens free education at least throughout the

---

649 *Id.* at preamble.
650 *Id.* at art. 1.
651 *Id.* at art. 36.
652 *Id.* at art. 38.
653 *Id.* at art. 39(1), (2)(a).
654 *Id.* at art. 40(2).

primary and basic levels. All forms and levels of primary education shall be compulsory and accessible to all without discrimination of any kind."[655]

Concerning gradualism, the Arab Charter mandates that "*[t]he States parties shall take all necessary legislative, administrative and judicial measures* to guarantee the protection, survival, development and well-being of the child in an atmosphere of freedom and dignity…[emphasis added]"[656] The Charter also states that "*[t]he States parties shall take all the necessary* measures to guarantee, particularly to young persons, the right to pursue a sporting activity. [emphasis added]"[657] Furthermore, the Charter states that "[t]he right to development is a fundamental human right and all States are required to establish the development policies and *to take the measures needed* to guarantee this right… " [emphasis added][658]

With respect to all of these provisions, it is very clear that the requisite measures cannot all be taken in one day or one month. These steps should be taken gradually; it can even take several years or generations for some of these steps to be achieved. Article 1 (3) of the Arab Charter explains:

> The present Charter seeks, within the context of the national identity of the Arab States and their sense of belonging to a common civilization, to achieve the following aims: *To prepare the new generations* in Arab States for a free and responsible life in a civil society that is characterized by solidarity, founded on a balance between awareness of rights and respect for obligations, and governed by the values of equality, tolerance and moderation. [emphasis added][659]

This article shows that some measures cannot be taken immediately. Preparing new generations cannot be done in one month or even one year; it takes a very long time.

Regarding the principle of equality, Article 3 of the Arab Charter provides:

> 1. Each State party to the present Charter undertakes to ensure to all individuals subject to its jurisdiction the right to enjoy the rights and freedoms set forth herein, without distinction on grounds of race, colour, sex, language, religious belief, opinion, thought, national or social origin, wealth, birth or physical or mental disability.

---

655 *Id.* at art. 41(2).
656 *Id.* at art. 33(3).
657 *Id.* at art. 33(4).
658 *Id.* at art. 37.
659 *Id.* at art. 1(3).

2. The States parties to the present Charter shall take the requisite measures to guarantee effective equality in the enjoyment of all the rights and freedoms enshrined in the present Charter in order to ensure protection against all forms of discrimination based on any of the grounds mentioned in the preceding paragraph.

3. Men and women are equal in respect of human dignity, rights and obligations within the framework of the positive discrimination established in favour of women by the Islamic Shariah, other divine laws and by applicable laws and legal instruments. Accordingly, each State party pledges to take all the requisite measures to guarantee equal opportunities and effective equality between men and women in the enjoyment of all the rights set out in this Charter.[660]

In addition, the Arab Charter provides, "All persons are equal before the courts and tribunals. The States parties shall guarantee the independence of the judiciary and protect magistrates against any interference, pressure or threats. They shall also guarantee every person subject to their jurisdiction the right to seek a legal remedy before courts of all levels."[661]

The Arab Charter does not discriminate between people; it is neutral. For instance, the articles of the Charter use words such as, "Every human being," "no one," "every individual," etc. All of these words clearly show that the Charter is neutral. For example the Charter states, "*Every human being* has the inherent right to life. [emphasis added]"[662] Also the Charter states, "Each State party shall protect every individual subject to its jurisdiction …"[663] In addition, the Charter explains, "All forms of slavery and trafficking in human beings are prohibited and are punishable by law. No one shall be held in slavery and servitude under any circumstances."[664] In addition, the Arab Charter states, "All persons are equal before the law and have the right to enjoy its protection without discrimination."[665] All of the previous articles clearly show that the Arab Charter treats human beings equally regardless of sex, race, etc.

Concerning *fitrah* and natural law theory, the Arab Charter explains, "The family is the *natural* and fundamental group unit of society; *it is based on marriage*

660　*Id.* at art. 3.
661　*Id.* at art. 12.
662　*Id.* at art. (1).
663　*Id.* at art. 8.
664　*Id.* at art. 10(1).
665　*Id.* at art. 11.

between a man and a woman." [emphasis added][666] The previous article clearly shows that, by *fitrah* and nature, families are considered the fundamental group unit of society. The Article also states clearly that the definition of family, by *fitrah* and nature, is based on a marriage between a man and a woman. In other words, the Charter considers it neither a family nor a marriage if the parties to the marriage are of the same sex.

In another example, the Arab Charter provides:

> The right to work is a *natural* right of every citizen. The State shall endeavor to provide, to the extent possible, a job for the largest number of those willing to work, while ensuring production, the freedom to choose one's work and equality of opportunity without discrimination of any kind on grounds of race, colour, sex, religion, language, political opinion, membership in a union, national origin, social origin, disability or any other situation.[emphasis added][667]

This article clearly shows that the Arab Charter considers the right to work as deriving from *fitrah*. The right to work is a basic right, one that does not even need to be stated in the laws. For instance, beginning thousands of centuries ago, members of each family or tribe would have to work in order to get their food. People went hunting in the woods and deserts to gather their food. Therefore, work came from *fitrah* even before the existence of written laws. It is from nature.

The Arab Charter did not follow Sharia law regarding duties. The Arab Charter was affected by international and regional human rights treaties, which focus mainly on rights. The Arab Charter did not create a balance between rights and duties. For instance, the Arab Charter mentions duties, whereby it states "… The laws in force regulate the rights and duties of the man and woman as to marriage, during marriage and at its dissolution."[668]

The first paragraph of the Arab Charter clearly shows that the Arab Charter highly respects human dignity and connects human dignity to Sharia law. The preamble of Charter explains, *"Based on the faith of the Arab nation in the dignity of the human person whom God has exalted ever since the beginning of creation and in the fact that the Arab homeland is the cradle of religions and civilizations whose lofty human values affirm the human right to a decent life based on freedom, justice and equality…* [emphasis added]"[669] In addition, Article 2 of the Arab Char-

---

666 *Id.* at art. 33(1).
667 *Id.* at art. 34(1).
668 *Id.* at art. 33(1).
669 *Id.* at preamble.

ter connects human dignity and the right to self-determination and the resistance to occupation. Article 3 (3) of the Arab Charter clearly shows that both men and women possess dignity that must be respected. The article states, "men and women are equal in respect of human dignity."[670] From the perspective of Sharia law, all of the human rights in the Arab Charter exist because of human dignity. For example, the Arab Charter outlines:

> 1. All forms of slavery and trafficking in human beings are prohibited and are punishable by law. No one shall be held in slavery and servitude under any circumstances.
>
> 2. Forced labor, trafficking in human beings for the purposes of prostitution or sexual exploitation, the exploitation of the prostitution of others or any other form of exploitation or the exploitation of children in armed conflict are prohibited.[671]

In addition, the right to life exists in the Arab Charter because of human dignity, as does the right to religion, the right to freedom of speech, the right to fair trial, and the right not to be tortured or subjected to inhuman treatment.

F. The Supervisory Mechanism of the Charter

The Charter establishes a supervising committee, entitled the "Arab Human Rights Committee."[672] This Committee is composed of seven members who are nominated by the states parties.[673] They are elected for a four-year term.[674] The members of the Committee serve in a personal capacity and are fully independent and impartial.[675] Each States party submits an initial report to the Committee within one year of the date upon which the Charter enters into force and a periodic report every three years thereafter.[676] The Committee discusses the report and makes necessary recommendations[677] The Committee includes these recommendations in its annual report, which is submitted to the Council of the Arab League.[678]

---

670   *Id.* at art. 3(3).
671   *Id.* at art. 10.
672   *Id.* at art. 45
673   *Id.* at art. 45(1).
674   *Id.* at art. 45(4).
675   *Id.* at art. 45(2).
676   *Id.* at art. 48(2).
677   *Id.* at art. 48(4).
678   *Id.* at art. 48(5).

The supervisory mechanism in any international or regional treaty is vital to guaranteeing the protection and the implementation of the rights of the treaty. The reporting system is the only supervisory mechanism by which the Arab Committee can monitor the implementation of the treaty. The recommendations of the Committee can be a very useful guide for the states parties. Article 48 (2) of the Arab Charter provides, "Each State party shall submit an initial report to the Committee within one year from the date on which the Charter enters into force and a periodic report every three years thereafter. The Committee may request the States parties to supply it with additional information relating to the implementation of the Charter."[679] Jordan, which was the first country to ratify the Arab Charter, was also the first State party to submit its first report to the Arab Committee.[680] The Head of the Arab Committee declared that the members of the Committee examined the report in 2012 and they will send their concluding observations and recommendations to Jordan.[681] In addition, he added that the Committee met with the Jordanian non-governmental organizations and examined the shadow reports submitted by these NGOs.[682]

Unlike other international and regional treaties, the Arab Charter has only one supervisory system, which is the reporting system. The European Convention on Human Rights, for example, has a court to which both individuals and states can submit complaints against states. The African Charter has a court and a committee. In addition, the African Charter has Special Rapporteurs, who are responsible for specific duties.

The Arab League made an agreement with the United Nations Office of the High Commissioner for Human Rights (OHCHR). As part of this agreement, a group of Arabian experts was chosen from the United Nations Human Rights Treaty Bodies to write a proposal for an Arab Charter on Human Rights. The Arabian experts recommended in their proposal that the Arab Charter should permit individuals,

---

679   *Id.* at art. 48(2).

680   The annual reports of States Parties, http://www.lasportal.org/wps/portal/las_ar_human-rights/inpage/!ut/p/c5/vc9NDoIwEAXgs3AAM60SqkuQ_4YasaJ2Q8AYpIBoJFQ9vZi41ZVxZjGLl7wvAwKGPWV9WWRd2Z6yGrYgjBThmK-ph5Gn2xYKyJKOjSSIUDiGDWyRnq7k_Rw8qkcsSRx11ZFy6ajIdiZMCtZJizJ7rVZI3XiFaZfPVeRM73g_w4m7dEy_viyuUw1CEEXd5i_VGorFN5rr7_zDmAiY3zYH2IEgH1sYAf7DB75arv5Hy_ipdW76ZhaMvH64halpT6gAw1w!/dl3/d3/L2dBISEvZ0FBIS9nQSEh/?pcid=9c8bcd0047335c82a506ad3ebe8887b5 (last visited May 1, 2014).

681   *Alittihad*, http://www.alittihad.ae/details.php?id=33085&y=2012 (last visited Apr. 23, 2012); *see also* el-balad, http://www.el-balad.com/125069/lgnh-arbyh-tnaksh-tkryr.aspx (last visited Apr. 23, 2012).

682   *Alittihad*, http://www.alittihad.ae/details.php?id=33085&y=2012 (last visited Apr. 23, 2012).

groups of individuals, and NGOs to submit complaints to the Arab Committee on Human Rights after exhausting domestic solutions. The Arabian experts added that these complaints should be binding only for states that declared their acceptance of the individual complaints.[683] The Arab Charter of 2004 was adopted with no supervisory mechanism except state reports.

Scholars have different opinions regarding the success and effectiveness of the Charter. For instance, Mervat Rishmawi, a legal advisor at the International Secretariat of Amnesty International, said:

> The success of the Charter will depend on how seriously Arab states and Arab human rights organizations decide to take it. Aside from the obvious question of whether Arab states will follow through in making actual changes in law and practices to conform to the Charter, there is the question of whether Arab civil society organizations will engage in the process in the same way they do with other regional and international systems. For the Charter to succeed in furthering human rights, Arab governments would have to be willing to re-open the debate on some provisions that clearly contradict international standards. Another measure of the significance of the Charter will be whether, once states submit their reports on measures they have taken to conform to the Charter, serious debates on human rights start to take place within the walls of the Arab League.[684]

The success of the Arab Charter depends on the political will and effectiveness of the supervisory mechanism of the Charter. The head of the Arab Committee on Human Rights told the media that the Arab Committee could not force Arab countries to submit their periodic reports.[685] To achieve real progress in the implementation of human rights, the Arab Charter should examine all the supervisory mechanisms of international and regional instruments and then adapt the best mechanisms for the region.

G. An Interview with Dr. Nabil El Araby

I conducted an interview with Dr. Nabil El Araby, the Secretary General of the Arab League, on March 13, 2012 at the Arab League in Cairo. He has had a wide-

---

683 SHWKEY ET AL., *supra* note 579, at 311.
684 Mervat Rishmawi, *The Arab Charter on Human Rights,* http://carnegieendowment.org/2009/10/06/arab-charter-on-human-rights/6cj1 (last visited Apr. 16, 2012).
685 *Alittihad,*http://www.alittihad.ae/details.php?id=33085&y=2012 (last visited Apr. 23, 2012), *supra* note 681.

ranging and outstanding amount of experience.[686] For instance, he is a law graduate and has an LL.M. degree as well as a J.S.D. (Doctor of Juridical Science). He was member of the International Court of Justice and was the former Egyptian Minister of Foreign Affairs. In addition, he was the permanent representative of Egypt to the United Nations in New York and Geneva. He has both an academic and a professional background. His comments were as follows:

> International law, with all of its treaties and conventions, covers the individual issues in all fields, on land, sea, sky, etc. However, there is a gap between the international law system, on one hand, and its implementation on the other hand.
>
> For instance, if there is a country that committed a violation of an international law norm, how could we implement that international law rule in that country?
>
> We cannot automatically refer a case to a court. The international courts cannot at their own motion examine a case. The accused country must accept such a referral. For instance, if a country violated the Fourth Geneva Convention of 1949 regarding the Protection of Civilian Persons in Time of War, how could we implement the convention, prevent this violation, and judge the country?
>
> No case can be referred to the International Court of Justice without the consent of the country involved. Of the 193 countries of the world, only 62 countries have accepted the referral of cases to the International Court of Justice. Even these 62 countries did not accept absolute referral. They put their conditions and limitations on their acceptance. For instance, Egypt accepted the referral of Egyptian cases to the International Court of Justice in 3 cases, one of which was addressing the administration of the Suez Canal.
>
> The International Criminal Court cannot accept a case against nationals of non-states parties except if the Security Council refers the case. The

---

686 The CV of Dr. Nabil El Araby the Secretary General of the Arab League, http://www.lasportal.org/wps/portal/las_en/inner/!ut/p/c5/vZLLcoJAEEW_hQ9lzfAQclkIMgryGkZgQw1qBvEt BISvD1ZlkY1mk7Lvpqtu3z6bC1Iw6ESbHaP17nyiBxCDVM6mYz8gUiBCNTTGEAIT5DoLQYC uOPjJc19V_kivQDIB4fY0LOmr08ejhw-fjAZBAILIV35k8hD5oepP ZrqAiAAwiKGUhWV3Qf2-D8o-mGPsiLh0WmdqdBiTRW3c7Wrf3vFt6Sz3zNQLRmfkdh315-uClS33TKtkHPeaZfJvZInvYxH4r6 w5SNnhnA8VW9lrpkwr1JpaHNQ0IPKNXMvb8gILjXbirGJu-KlqriVGm4RGqYUUz8Fj0mlray U0BZW-im7irZOIxbYrZ0N34-tNLP0R9T-uuJU3I0jZ2rWb2Dp_z5gh7EjGewFpsJdnI9gqr F4IKC80vTcTUnFgaZ2PW3A5Rs0uUPkfiUzjuG-J4IHv/dl3/d3/L2dBIS EvZ0FBIS9nQ SEh/?pcid= 4ef73f00425e2a9fb9d3f9c0e4251219 (last visited Feb. 3, 2013).

case can only be referred by the Security Council if the members of the Security Council accept to do so and none of the permanent members vetoes it. It is very rare to have such consensus of the permanent members.

The jurisprudence of the international law states that if a country commits a violation against a national of another country, the second country can sue the first country using diplomatic protection.

There is a weakness in the international judicial system. Even if there are implementation mechanisms in some systems, it is still weak and not very effective.

The international judicial system is still weak. For instance, we cannot stop the human rights violations that are happening in Syria. The international judicial system is not effective enough.

There is no mechanism for implementing the decisions of the International Court of Justice. If a country does not implement a court decision, the other country will complain to the Security Council.

The European System of Human Rights is currently the best regional human rights system.

The international and regional systems cannot be used except after the exhaustion of national complaint mechanisms.

All of the treaties and conventions that are adopted by the Arab League cannot be automatically implemented in the Arab countries because the Arab countries do not use the concept of self-implementation. However, in European countries, treaties are often self-implemented.

He preferred the universalism theory, because all human rights are universal everywhere in the world. He mentioned Article 1 (4) of the Charter, which states, "The present Charter seeks, within the context of the national identity of the Arab States and their sense of belonging to a common civilization, to achieve the following aims: To entrench the principle that all human rights are universal, indivisible, interdependent and interrelated."[687]

The President of Syria, Bashar, told him that the human rights of Syria are a national issue. Dr. Nabil replied to him by referring to Article 1 of

---

687 ACHR, *supra* note 126, at art. 1(4).

the Arab Charter on Human Rights, which states that all human rights are universally indivisible and interdependent.

The women's rights in Sharia are equal to women's rights in Western countries. The Quran indicates that men receive double the inheritance of women, yet Sharia law permits the writing of wills. In addition, a brother could give more to his sister through his own will. For instance, if there are two apartments inherited from a father, the brother can give his sister one apartment and take the other.

It is easy for a woman to get divorced using *khul*.

Homosexuality is not an issue to talk about; it is from cultures and traditions in the West.

The Arab Charter is still not effective and needs a supervisory mechanism. Bahrain submitted a proposal to the Arab League to establish an Arab Court of Human Rights. However, this will take time."[688]

I agree entirely with Dr. Nabil that there are large gaps in the international human rights system. There is no possibility of automatically referring a case to an international court. In addition, if a country refused to ratify the statute of a certain court, there is no way to force the country to be a party to the court. Even with the supervisory mechanisms that are established by charters and conventions, we cannot force states parties to comply with the requirements of a charter. For instance, the head of the Arab Committee said that there are no mechanisms to force states parties to submit their periodic reports. He added that forcing states to submit reports is contrary to the sovereignty of states.[689] More steps should be taken not only in the regional human rights systems but also in the universal human rights systems. In other words, in order to stop human rights violations, the human rights system must be truly binding for states.

In addition, there is a lack of full independence in some of the international and regional courts. The international human rights system is not fully independent. Many steps should be taken to ensure independence. In light of what Dr. Nabil said, there is a need for many changes to the human rights systems. However, it is currently impossible for the Arab human rights system to take the lead in improving the international and regional human rights systems. The Arab human

---

[688] Interview with Dr. Nabil El Araby, the Secretary General of the Arab League, at the Arab League in Cairo (Mar. 13, 2012).

[689] *Alittihad*, http://www.alittihad.ae/details.php?id=33085&y=2012 (last visited April 23, 2012), *supra* note 681.

rights system is still in its infancy. It needs time to get more mature. In addition, it needs to be supported by the will of the states, which seems to be missing not only in the Arab region, but also in the international community. For instance, in October 2012, I was a member of the Egyptian delegation that attended and participated in the Conference of the Parties to the United Nations Convention against Transnational Organized Crime.[690] One of the purposes of this annual meeting was to adopt an implementation review mechanism of the Convention and its three protocols.[691] Despite the fact that the Convention against Transnational Organized Crime entered into force in 2003, the conference of the states parties failed to adopt an implementation review mechanism for the convention. Dr. Nabil Al-Araby mentioned gradualism indirectly. He said that it will take time for the establishment of an Arab Court of Human Rights. Gradualism is needed for the development of any mechanism. By applying gradualism, success can be achieved.

H. An Arab Court for Human Rights?[692]

The idea of establishing an Arab Court is not new. It dates back to 1945, the year the Pact of the Arab League was adopted. The Pact of the Arab League permitted the amendment of the Pact in three cases, one of which was the establishment

---

690 U.N. Office on Drugs and Crime, Sixth session of the Conference of the Parties to the United Nations Convention against Transnational Organized Crime, Vienna, 15-19 October 2012, http://www.unodc.org/unodc/en/treaties/CTOC/CTOC-COP-session6.html (last visited October 28, 2012).

691 The first protocol is the Protocol to Prevent, Suppress and Punish Trafficking in Persons, Especially Women and Children, supplementing the United Nations Convention against Transnational Organized Crime. The second protocol is the Protocol against the Smuggling of Migrants by Land, Sea and Air, supplementing the United Nations Convention against Transnational Organized Crime. The third protocol is the Protocol against the Illicit Manufacturing of and Trafficking in Firearms, Their Parts and Components and Ammunition, supplementing the United Nations Convention against Transnational Organized Crime, *see* U.N. Office on Drugs and Crime, Signatories to the United Nations Convention against Transnational Organized Crime, http://www.unodc.org/unodc/en/treaties/CTOC/signatures.html (last visited October 28, 2012).

692 *Lam'ha Tarekheya* [A Brief History], http://www.lasportal.org/wps/portal/las_ar/inner/!ut/p/c5/vZLBkoIwEES_xQ-wkgiiHtGgiAJLCEi4WICIggKiIObrF2sPe3K9bDI9maqe6Xdp4INOedAck-B2LPLgBDzgS1s8sYgrEgFCakpwOVAxMZAhjKdS57PXvobefG8AU4AdVN3i_3X6DHr68MXIEBhqcY4BA_7oN2VhrUS4tOyhodlfSF5AQIEHxa2dPsolzzhJOTFoBIsaKncdKw9KnZZC6WFjw7SdK6dQ5LZTrihICI0nyJ1biozrdtQ6vTeswQdZwgdZ6F9ZGvCTUxF2Rduo0bHFVz3BikfCcX5HtwO_9Ue7OiW7TDOTaZLd5TTO9qivDeOqgNI6zVy_Zipu9tawOqc7Q5w1c0GfnaRkFLcR6bdMF3gccOg1iZ5fpuo2yk2ICCN3Pb3WISfMD2pghnDy5ehNoZf7S1hiTiw5Yj1Qnp3mSMbG_kf6N9tHB94!/dl3/d3/L2dBISEvZ0FBIS9nQSEh/?pcid=5ced5d80425e47cb8f3dff7cf4bbec57 (last visited Feb. 6, 2013).

of the Arab Court of Justice. This clearly shows that the Arab states are keen to promote the protection of justice regionally. In 1964, at the Alexandria Summit, a resolution was adopted establishing the Arab Court of Justice. In 1980, sixteen years later, the Council of the Arab League established a committee to write the Statute of the Arab Court of Justice. In 1982, the committee wrote the Statute. However, it did not state the mandatory areas of jurisdiction of the Court. Therefore, another committee was established during the Arab Summit of 1982. This new committee issued a draft proposal of the Statute of the Arab Court. In 1994, twelve years later, the Council of Arab League examined the draft proposal. In 1995, the draft proposal was forwarded to the Permanent Legal Committee at the Arab League to draft the final proposal. The main points of the Statute were:

1. The Court consists of seven judges that should be nominated by secret ballot for three years. Judges can be re-elected.

2. The Court has to examine cases that are referred to it by either by State Parties or according to international and bilateral treaties.

3. The Court will decide in the cases according to the principles stated in the Pact of Arab League and according to the rules of International Law.[693]

In April 2012, the head of the Arab Committee on Human Rights, which is established by the Arab Charter, told the media that one of the main proposals that is emerging nowadays is the idea of establishing an Arab Court in order to enhance human rights.[694] The Arab Charter on Human Rights did not mention the idea of establishing an Arab Court. However, Article 52 of the Charter provides that any State party can propose the idea of establishing any additional protocol. Article 52 outlines, "Any State party may propose additional optional protocols to the present Charter and they shall be adopted in accordance with the procedures used for the adoption of amendments to the Charter."[695] In addition, the Charter also determines that it can be amended, stating, "Any State party may submit written proposals, though the Secretary-General, for the amendment of the present Charter. After these amendments have been circulated among the States members, the Secretary-General shall invite the States parties to consider the

---

693   Id.
694   Alittihad http://www.alittihad.ae/details.php?id=33085&y=2012 (last visited Apr. 23, 2012), *supra* note 681.
695   ACHR, *supra* note 126, at art. 52.

proposed amendments before submitting them to the Council of the League for adoption."[696]

Bahrain's Proposal of Establishing an Arab Court on Human Rights

In my interview with Dr. Nabil El Araby, the Secretary General of the Arab League, he stated that Bahrain submitted a proposal to the Arab League to establish an Arab Court of Human Rights. His office provided me with Bahrain's proposal, of which there is both an Arabic and an English version. Dr. Nabil El Araby informed me that the Arab League will submit this proposal to the yearly summit of the Arab League. The participants of this summit are presidents, kings, princes, and prime ministers. The summit was held in Bagdad, Iraq in March, 2012. At the summit, it was requested that a committee of experts write a report that includes the proposal of the committee. Bahrain is a state party to the Arab Charter on Human Rights. It ratified the Charter on June 18, 2006. According to Article 52 of the Charter, any state party can propose the idea of establishing additional protocol.

The English version of the proposal is six pages long. I will highlight its main points. The proposal states, "In this short paper we outline how we may establish an Arab Court of Human Rights for the region [as] the Arab region is the only major region in the world without a human rights court."[697] This proposal was submitted directly to the Arab League. The proposal also mentioned that the three regional human rights courts (European, American and African) have key features that are already existing in the Arab region. The proposal stated the following examples:

> The three regional courts are part of regional organizations. The Arab Court on Human Rights could be a part of the Arab League. As another example, Bahrain's proposal referred to the three regional courts' implementation of regional human rights conventions. The Arab Court on Human Rights could also apply the Arab Charter on Human Rights.
>
> Both the African Court and the Inter-American Courts are working with commissions that are responsible for fact finding and for determining the admissibility of cases. The Arab Human Rights Committee can play this role.
>
> The financing of the three regional courts is done through contribution of states parties. The proposal mentioned that the "scale of assessment

---

696 *Id.* at art. 50.
697 Proposal submitted by Bahrain to the Arab League to establish an Arab Court of Human Rights.

used by the League of Arab States could be applied to the funding of an Arab Court of Human Rights."

Each of the states parties to the three regional courts automatically agrees to be under the compulsory jurisdiction of the regional court. On the other hand, the additional protocol of the Arab Court would be compulsory for the states that ratified it.

The jurisdiction of the three regional courts is subsidiary. The Courts examine whether or not there is a violation of human rights protected in the Charter. States, individuals, or NGOs can submit a complaint. In addition, all of the three regional courts can give an advisory opinion to regional bodies upon their request. The proposal added, "This means that the highest domestic courts such as the Supreme Court of each country is no longer the 'final word' on human rights issues covered by the relevant regional treaty as appeals can be made to the regional court."

The decisions rendered by the three regional courts are compulsory and binding for the State parties concerned in each case. The court's judgment varies from paying damages to the victim to amending domestic law that constitutes a violation of the human rights protected by the Charter. The proposal added, "This is an important guarantee to ensure that individuals have effective remedies where violations occur. It has been controversial where the court has been considered to be adopting expansive interpretations of rights that affect areas traditionally considered to be within the sphere of national sovereignty e.g. the UK Attorney General has challenged the ruling by the European Court of Human Rights that the UK must give prisoners the right to vote." [698]

The proposal stated the challenges and opportunities facing the establishment of an Arab Court on Human Rights. The proposal mentioned that the Arab Charter is being criticized because of its substance and the lack of an effective supervisory and enforcement mechanism. The proposal added:

> The Arab Human Rights Committee is mandated to monitor compliance with the Charter by receiving periodic reports from States Parties. Such reports have not been forthcoming. The Committee has no means for addressing the non-submission or delayed submission of reports. Clearly, something more than periodic reporting is required for genuine

---

[698] http://www.guardian.co.uk/politics/2012/jul/15/uk-prisoner-voting-rights-europe (last visted Feb. 6, 2013).

accountability under the Charter. Unlike other regional human rights systems, the Arab Charter has no provision for individual or State communications. Providing access to justice for victims of human rights violations is an obligation of every State under international law. An Arab Court of Human Rights would form a vital part of fulfilling this obligation. A Court with the power to receive individual and State communications and to dispense a range of remedies should form the centerpiece of the Charter-system. Without such an enforcement body, the rights guaranteed in the Charter will remain theoretical. An Arab Court of Human Rights would help to create a common approach to human rights in the region and make the Arab Charter of Human Rights a genuinely operational document. Such a strengthened regional approach to human rights would also assist in conflict prevention.[699]

The proposal that was submitted by Bahrain to the Arab League is a major step forward for the protection of the human rights by the Arab Charter. The proposal declares that the Arab Charter is lacking an effective supervisory enforcement mechanism. The proposal aims to establish an Arab Court that can guarantee the enforcement of human rights. The proposal mentioned a very important issue; it stated:

The Court could reflect cultural values in a manner that is human rights-compliant. An Arab Court of Human Rights would allow Arab States to address human rights concerns in a regional context, paying special attention to regional practices that may not be as well-understood at the international level. For instance, many Arab governments have felt the need to vary their international human rights obligations under UN treaties to take into account Shariah law. The Arab Charter is considered to reflect such cultural values already and therefore may be a more appropriate forum for enforcing individual rights than UN treaty-monitoring bodies such as the Human Rights Committee.[700]

With respect to the Arab Committee, the proposal stated:

The committee should be strengthened. The requirements and appointment procedures for the Committee members should be made more stringent to guarantee that elected members have legal experience, knowledge of subjects relevant to the Charter, and an understanding of the various legal systems in the region. This would help to

---

699 Bahrain proposal submitted to the Arab League to establish an Arab Court of Human Rights.
700 *Id.*

ensure that the Committee's work is more efficient and valuable. The Committee should also have a website in Arabic and English that explains its procedures and work and posts key documents that have been filed.[701]

Finally, Bahrain's proposal suggested that the League of Arab States should organize a conference in 2012. It was stated, "The conference should involve high-level government representatives and experts in human rights law and court administration. Representatives of existing regional human rights courts could share best practices and lessons learned."[702] Bahrain offered to host the League conference and explained,

> "The aim of the conference would be to achieve consensus on establishing a regional human rights court, with a report drawn up following the conference detailing current levels of support and next steps. Working group could be formed to draft provisions of judicial membership, judicial appointment, jurisdiction, and other key aspects of the court's functioning."[703]

Bahrain's proposal indirectly mentioned the principle of gradualism. It stated that the Arab Court "cannot be created overnight. But many of the structures are in place to start moving on the path to establish an Arab Court of Human Rights. Now is the time to launch a focused discussion on the issue of a court. This should be led by governments, in partnership with NGOs, academics and other interested parties."[704]

On February 25 and 26, 2012, Bahrain hosted a conference for the Arab States in Manama to discuss the idea of establishing an Arab Court on Human Rights. The recommendations of the conference included the idea of establishing the Court. Bahrain requested officially from the League of Arab States to host the Arab Court on Human Rights in Manama. On 1 September 2013 the League accepted the request of Bahrain.[705]

On March 26, 2013, the resolution of the twenty forth summit of the Arab League, held in Qatar, agreed to assign to high-level committee of legal experts of the member states of the Arab League the task to establish a statute of the Arab

---

701   Id.
702   Id.
703   Id.
704   Id.
705   The Kingdom of Bahrain host the Arab Court on Human Rights, http://62.3.35.36/Human-RightsOffice/index.php?action=News&Sub=ShowOne&ID=8 (last visisted May 19, 2014).

Court on Human Rights. A draft statute was written and circulated to the states parties to the Arab League for further study and consideration of amendments. The Arab League also started to organize a series of several meetings for the Arab states in order to study the proposal submitted by the committee of legal experts with a view toward drafting further amendments.

I. Is the Arab Charter an Important Step Forward?

There are both proponents and opponents of the Arab Charter; there are others who criticize the delay in ratification and implementation on the part of the Arab countries. For instance, there is criticism against the Arab countries that have not yet ratified the Arab Charter.[706] On the other hand, there are people who support the Arab Charter, believing that it is an important step forward for the Arab human rights system. For instance, it has been said that the Arab Charter on Human Rights is the first Arab regional instrument for human rights and that it is both compatible with international human rights standards and congruent with Sharia law.[707] Professor Mohammed Mattar, the Executive Director of the Protection Project at Johns Hopkins University, said that the Arab Charter imposes obligations on Arab countries regarding human rights and that, in addition, the Charter is consistent with Sharia law. He said that the most important thing is the implementation and application of the articles of the Charter. He added that implementation and application is more important than the wording of the articles of the Charter.[708] Mahmud Rahed, the former director of the Human Rights Office at the League of Arab States, mentioned the importance of the Arab Charter. He said that the Charter calls for the development of a culture in respect for human rights in the Arab world. He added that the media should focus on introducing the Arab Charter to the Arab world in order to promote the implementation of the Arab Charter in the Arab world.[709]

I agree with Professor Mohammed Mattar. The application and implementation of the rights is more important than the articles themselves. Now the most important thing is the implementation of the rights. Over time, the rights can be amended. For example, the European Convention was amended by several protocols to make it stricter with respect to the protection human rights. We should

---

706 Abd Al-Kader Anees, *Reading in the Arab Charter of Human Rights*, AHEWAR.ORG, http://www.ahewar.org/debat/show.art.asp?aid=194996 (last visited Apr. 23, 2012).

707 *Can the Arab Charter Protect Human Rights?*, IRAQHURR.ORG, http://www.iraqhurr.org/content/article/1779953.html (last visited Apr. 23, 2012).

708 *Id.*

709 *Saudi Arabia Ratified the Arab Charter on Human Rights,* http://www.alriyadh.com/2009/04/17/article422970.html (last visited Apr. 23, 2012).

not always criticize the Charter, nor should we say that it is the best human rights instrument in the world. Instead, we should recognize both sides. In this way, while the Charter does not have efficient supervisory mechanisms and some of the rights in the Charter could be more effective, no one can deny that the Charter is an important step forward in the protection of human rights in the Arab world. The Arab Charter faces several challenges, for example, many countries did not ratify the Charter. In addition, there are no effective supervisory mechanisms for the Charter. There are obstacles facing the establishment of the Arab Court, which include:

- The economic situation facing Arab countries.
- The wars and national conflicts that faced and are still facing some Arab countries.
- The lack of experience regarding regional human rights systems.

All of the previous obstacles are real, but can be overcome. From the time of the adoption of the Arab Charter until 2014, it was always possible to establish a Court. The adoption of the African Court has faced, and is still facing, similar problems, including some that are financially based, but the Court has been successfully established. In addition, the African countries also faced, and are still facing, wars and conflicts, but they succeeded in establishing the Court. In its beginning, the European human rights system faced many problems. For example, the Second World War was just finishing, from which many European countries took several years to recover. Over time, the Arab Charter will better promote human rights.

It is difficult to understand why Arab countries did not achieve the same success, maybe because there was no *will* to do so. The European and African Countries have had enough will to establish a human rights system. This does not mean that the Arab countries have no will to establish an effective mechanism to supervise the implementation of the Arab Human Rights Charter. Most of them have the will, as demonstrated by the fact that they have already ratified the main universal and regional human rights treaties. For example, sixteen Arab countries had already ratified the International Covenant on Civil and Political Rights and the International Covenant on Economic, Social and Cultural Rights.[710] The Arab

---

710 The sixteen Arab countries that ratified the International Covenant on Civil and Political Rights and the International Covenant on Economic, Social and Cultural Rights are Djibouti, Egypt, Iraq, Libya, Jordan, Kuwait, Lebanon, Morocco, Syria, Somalia, Sudan, Yemen, Tunisia, Algeria, Bahrain, and Mauritania. The official link of the ratifying countries of the ICESCR is http://treaties.un.org/Pages/ViewDetails.aspx?src=TREATY&mtdsg_no=IV-3&chapter=4&lang=en; the official link of the ratifying countries of the ICCPR is http://treaties.un.org/Pages/ViewDetails.aspx?src=TREATY&mtdsg_no=IV-4&chapter=4&lang=en (last visited Apr. 15, 2012).

Charter, which was supposed to reflect the cultures and traditions of the Arab region, should be ratified by a number of Arab countries that is equal or greater than the number of Arab countries that had ratified the ICCPR and the ICESCR. However, only fouteen Arab countries have ratified the Arab Charter. As another example, Egypt ratified most of the United Nations conventions and additional protocols that are related to human rights. In addition, Egypt is a member of the African Committee. Yet, for reasons that seem incomprehensible, Arab countries did not achieve the same success. After the spark of the Arab Spring, the situation will be different and there will be more awareness towards the promotion of human rights protection. In the last few years people living in the Arab World started claiming their human rights, both those known as civil and political rights, and those commonly referred to as social, economic and cultural rights. Even in the countries that did not experience revolutionary upheavals, governments started to take positive steps for the respect of equality, justice and human rights. Although the Arab Spring has not brought about immediate success with regard to general improvements to the rights of the people across the region, people have started to claim their rights without fear. This is considered a great positive sign. We should expect that human rights standards and protection will not revolutionary change immediately overnight. It will require gradual change over years.

The application of the principle of gradualism in the context of the Arab Charter can be an important component of its success. For instance, in April 2012, the head of the Arab Committee on Human Rights, which is established by the Arab Charter, said that one of the main current proposals is the establishment of an Arab Court. Furthermore, he said that, after two years, the Arab Committee will issue a report that will include the challenges and obstacles facing the enhancement of the culture of human rights in the Arab world. In addition, the report will mention the obstacles to the implementation of the Arab Charter.[711] This can be considered gradualism. Gradualism starts with an idea, and then steps are taken towards achieving this idea.

---

[711] Alittihad, http://www.alittihad.ae/details.php?id=33085&y=2012 (last visited Apr. 23, 2012), *supra* note 681.

J. The Evaluation of the Arab Charter in Comparison with the African Charter on Human and Peoples' Rights and European Convention on Human Rights

I will evaluate the substantive rights in Chapter 5 and the procedural mechanisms in Chapters 6, 7, and 8. There will be a comparison of the Arab Charter with other mechanisms, including the International Covenant on Civil and Political Rights, the Cairo Declaration of Human Rights in Islam, the European Court on Human Rights, and the African Court and Commission on Human and Peoples' Rights. The aim of doing this comparative evaluation is to fashion practical recommendations as to how to develop the Arab Charter. In this way, the book will propose what *can* be done to promote human rights. Before beginning the evaluative comparative study, it is important to mention the reasons for choosing to compare the Arab system with the Cairo Declaration of Human Rights in Islam and both European and African systems. The Cairo Declaration of Human Rights in Islam is an Islamic Declaration that reflects the Sharia point of view on human rights.

1. The European System

For many reasons, the European system is the most effective regional system. First, it is the oldest working regional court; the compulsory jurisdiction of the European Court of Human Rights was accepted by declarations made by eight states on January 21, 1959. Second, the decisions of the Court are legally binding on states parties. Third, the decisions of the European Court not only provide a remedy, but they also provide clear guidance to the contracting parties as to whether or not their laws and practices are compatible with the European Convention.[712] Fourth, the European Court has a worldwide reputation and different courts around the world cite judgments of the Court. Fifth, the European Court has a larger scope of personal jurisdiction than any other regional court in the world; its jurisdiction covers over 800 million people. Sixth, non-nationals, non-residents, and even stateless people have the right to submit cases to the court regarding matters within the Court's jurisdiction.[713] In addition to all the reasons that are mentioned, the most important part of the European Convention is its supervisory mechanisms. The Convention created the European Court of Human

---

712 DAVID HARRIS, MICHAEL O'BOYLE, COLIN WARBRICK, & ED BATES, LAW OF THE EUROPEAN CONVENTION ON HUMAN RIGHTS 648 (1995).

713 JACOBS & WHITE, *supra* note 566, at 472; *see also* Article one of the European Convention, which provides that "the high contracting parties shall secure to everyone within their jurisdiction the rights and freedoms defined in Section I of this Convention.

Rights. The Committee of Ministers of the Council of Europe supervise the execution of the judgments of the Court.[714] For all of these reasons it is important to focus on the European Court of Human Rights. It will be important for the Arab Charter to learn from other human rights systems in order to build on the approach that was developed over years by other regional and international systems.

2. The African System

There are several reasons for choosing to also focus on the African Charter on Human and Peoples' Rights. First, the African Charter is the only human rights system for most of the African region that interacts geographically with the Arab region. Some of the countries that are member to the Arab Charter are also members of the African Charter, because these Arab countries are geographically located in Africa. Second, many of the cultures and traditions of the Arab countries are closer to African cultures and traditions than to the European cultures and traditions. Third, some of the domestic human rights issues and challenges in the African countries are similar to those of the Arab countries.

The reason that regional treaties are widely ratified and accepted is because they reflect the traditions and cultures of certain region. The African Charter reflects the cultures and traditions and the needs of the African region.[715] The Charter combines civil and political rights with social and cultural rights. All of these rights are treated equally in the Charter.[716] Nearly all African Union states parties ratified the African Charter.[717] The reason behind this wide acceptance and ratification of the African Charter is its reflection of the challenges, traditions and cultures of the African region.

The African Charter emphasizes the duties of the individual towards the regional and international community, his nation, his family, and other individuals.[718] The Arab Charter, which is inspired by Sharia law, also mentions individual duties as I explained in detail in Chapter 3. For example, as to the duties of men and women, it states:

---

714 Explanatory Report of Protocol 14 to the European Convention on Human Rights is available at http://conventions.coe.int/Treaty/EN/Reports/Html/194.htm (last visited Dec. 1, 2013).
715 Dr. Rachel Murray, The African Commission on Human and Peoples' Rights and International Law 10 (2000).
716 *Id.*
717 As of June 1, 2014, fifty-three countries have ratified the African Charter, *see* http://www.africa-union.org (last visited June 1, 2014).
718 Frans Viljoen, International Human Rights Law in Africa 248-249 (2007).

> The right to development is a fundamental human right and all States are required to establish the development policies and to take the measures needed to guarantee this right. They have a duty to give effect to the values of solidarity and cooperation among them and at the international level with a view to eradicating poverty and achieving economic, social, cultural and political development. By virtue of this right, every citizen has the right to participate in the realization of development and to enjoy the benefits and fruits thereof.[719]

The duties are considered to be one of the important parts of the Arab Charter because they reflect cultures, traditions, and Sharia law. The Arab Charter also mentions the 'obligations' of generations. The Arab Charter explains:

> The present Charter seeks, within the context of the national identity of the Arab States and their sense of belonging to a common civilization, to achieve the following aims: To prepare the new generations in Arab States for a free and responsible life in a civil society that is characterized by solidarity, founded on a balance between awareness of rights and respect for obligations, and governed by the values of equality, tolerance and moderation.[720]

Sharia law is similar to the African Charter, which also focuses on individual duties as an important aspect of achieving progress and welfare. The Arab Charter can use this approach to duties in order to protect the rights guaranteed in the Charter. It is impossible to guarantee rights if there are no obligations and duties, because rights are the result of obligations.

The African Charter

> "strives to secure certain flexibility, equilibrium, and to emphasize certain principles and guidelines of our Organization as well as the aspirations of the African peoples. It seeks not to isolate man from society but as well that society must not swallow the individual. Such is the African wisdom that was to be recalled from the very beginning of the proceedings."[721]

---

719 AHCR, *supra* note 126, at art. 37.

720 *Id.* at art. 1 (3).

721 N.S Rembe, *The System of Protection of Human Rights under the African Charter on Human and Peoples' Rights: Problems and Prospects*, 6 HUMAN AND PEOPLES' RIGHTS MONOGRAPH SERIES (1991), 1 (citing OAU Doc. AHG/102/XVII, June 1981, at p. 22).

This statement clearly explains the idea and philosophy behind the African Charter. The African Charter reflects the traditions and cultures of the African states; this was stated explicitly in the preamble of the Charter. The Charter takes into consideration "virtues of their historical tradition and the values of African civilization which should inspire and characterize their reflection on the concept of human and peoples' rights."[722]

Similar to the African Charter, the preamble of the Arab Charter reflects the cultures and principles of the Arab countries, as it states that

> "being proud of the humanitarian values and principles that the Arab nation has established throughout its long history, which have played a major role in spreading knowledge between East and West, so making the region a point of reference for the whole world and a destination for seekers of knowledge and wisdom."[723]

However, the preamble of the Arab Charter also focuses on Sharia law and Islam. This is important because Sharia law evaluates the rights in the Arab Charter and the standard of the Charter is Sharia law. The preamble emphasizes:

> Based on the faith of the Arab nation in the dignity of the human person whom God has exalted ever since the beginning of creation and in the fact that the Arab homeland is the cradle of religions and civilizations whose lofty human values affirm the human right to a decent life based on freedom, justice and equality,

> In furtherance of the eternal principles of fraternity, equality and tolerance among human beings consecrated by the noble Islamic religion and the other divinely-revealed religions.[724]

The preamble of the Arab Charter also reflects the struggle and challenges faced by the Arab nations. It states:

> Believing in the unity of the Arab nation, which struggles for its freedom and defends the right of nations to self-determination, to the preservation of their wealth and to development;believing in the sovereignty of the law and its contribution to the protection of universal and interrelated human rights and convinced that the human person's

---

722 African Charter, *supra* note 127, at preamble.
723 Id.
724 Id.

enjoyment of freedom, justice and equality of opportunity is a fundamental measure of the value of any society."[725]

The Arab Charter is well aligned with the Arab region. If it is promoted and developed by effective mechanisms, it can play an important role in the improvement of human rights in the Middle East. The Arab Charter reflects the religion, cultures, and traditions of the Arab world, because it has been issued, adopted, and implemented by the region. No one from the Arab region will fear it because they have created it. Therefore, its role in the Middle East can be more effective than any other regional or international systems.

The Arab Charter contains eloquent phrases, but no effective mechanisms. The Arab Charter emphasizes, "All persons are equal before the courts and tribunals. The States parties shall guarantee the independence of the judiciary and protect magistrates against any interference, pressure or threats. They shall also guarantee every person subject to their jurisdiction the right to seek a legal remedy before courts of all levels."[726] The Charter does not say how it can protect these rights. As explained in detail earlier, the Arab Charter does not mention the idea of establishing an Arab Court for Human Rights. The idea of establishing an Arab Court was mentioned in the Pact of the Arab League. However, according to Article 52 of the Arab Charter, states parties may propose additional protocols. The Charter explains, "Any State party may propose additional optional protocols to the present Charter and they shall be adopted in accordance with the procedures used for the adoption of amendments to the Charter."[727] The Charter does not have an effective supervisory mechanism to supervise the states parties in their implementation of the Charter. The Arab Charter can examine other regional and international mechanisms in order to determine which mechanism is most suitable.

This book will explain the substantive rights of the Arab Charter through comparison. I will evaluate them from the Sharia law point of view and I will explain why they are written in that way. My goal is to determine how we can make the Charter more effective and efficient in order to protect and promote human rights in the Arab World.

---

725 Id.
726 ACHR, *supra* note 126, at art. 12.
727 Id. at art. 52.

Chapter 5: An Evaluation of Substantive Human Rights Protections in the Arab Charter

A. Introduction

It is important to know that, throughout my discussion, this book will provide many examples from Egypt. This is due to the nature of my work in the judicial system in Egypt, which gave me thorough academic and practical knowledge of it. In addition, Egypt is a member country of the Arab League and has signed the Arab Charter. Therefore, a focus on Egypt will enable an examination of the legal system of one key country of the region. Furthermore, articles developed by Egyptian scholars are copied by many of the legislations of the Arab countries, so there is a similarity between Egypt and other countries. In addition, there are agreements between the Egyptian Supreme Judicial Council and several Arab countries that grant Egyptian judges and prosecutors work in the judicial system of other Arab countries (by being temporarily transferred to a post in another country). Because of all of these factors, Egypt is an effective model of other Arab countries.

In my explanation, I will always give examples from Sharia law and provide the Sharia law point of view. Sharia law is the foundation of the Arab Charter. It can be used as a primary instrument to help understand and interpret the Arab Charter. In addition, Sharia law can be used to evaluate the rights in the Arab Charter. This book will provide an overview of what has been done by international and regional instruments on human rights. Then, it will evaluate the Arab Charter with respect to the Sharia law principles. This comparative evaluation will help deepen understandings of the articles of the Arab Charter from the perspective of the Sharia law. In addition, by doing so, we will be able to comprehend why the Arab Charter was written as it was.

B. The Right to Life

The right to life is a basic and fundamental peremptory right that is stated in all of the regional and international conventions on human rights.[728]

---

728 For example: The 1950 European Convention for the Protection of Human Rights and Fundamental Freedoms states: "Everyone's right to life shall be protected by law. No one shall be deprived of his life intentionally save in the execution of a sentence of a court following his conviction of a crime for which this penalty is provided by law. Deprivation of life shall not be regarded as inflicted in contravention of this article when it results from the use of force which is no more than absolutely necessary: in defence of any person from unlawful violence; in order to effect a lawful arrest or to prevent the escape of a person lawfully detained in action lawfully taken for the purpose of quelling a riot or Insurrection. (Y.B. Eur. Conv. on H.R, (1950))." Also, Article 1 of Protocol No. 6 to the 1983 Convention for the Protection of Human Rights and Fundamental Freedoms states: "The death penalty shall be abolished. No-one shall be condemned to such penalty or executed" and in Article 2: "A State may make provision in its law for the death penalty in respect of acts committed in time of war or of imminent threat of war; such penalty shall be applied only in the instances laid down in the law and in accordance with its provisions. The State shall communicate to the Secretary General of the Council of Europe the relevant provisions of that law." Furthermore, Article 1 of Protocol No. 13 to the Convention for the Protection of Human Rights and Fundamental Freedoms states: "The death penalty shall be abolished. No one shall be condemned to such penalty or executed" (Council of Europe, *European Convention for the Protection of Human Rights and Fundamental Freedoms, as amended by Protocol No 13*, art. 1, May 3 2002, http://conventions.coe.int/Treaty/en/Treaties/Html/187.htm (last visited Feb. 6, 2013) and Article 2 states: "No derogation from the provisions of this Protocol shall be made under Article 15 of the Convention" (*Id.* at art. 2). Article 4 of the 1969 American Convention on Human Rights states: "1. Every person has the right to have his life respected. This right shall be protected by law and, in general, from the moment of conception. No one shall be arbitrarily deprived of his life. 2. In countries that have not abolished the death penalty, it may be imposed only for the most serious crimes and pursuant to a final judgment rendered by a competent court and in accordance with a law establishing such punishment, enacted prior to the commission of the crime. The application of such punishment shall not be extended to crimes to which it does not presently apply. 3. The death penalty shall not be reestablished in states that have abolished it. 4. In no case shall capital punishment be inflicted for political offenses or related common crimes. 5. Capital punishment shall not be imposed upon persons who, at the time the crime was committed, were under 18 years of age or over 70 years of age; nor shall it be applied to pregnant women. 6. Every person condemned to death shall have the right to apply for amnesty, pardon, or commutation of sentence, which may be granted in all cases. Capital punishment shall not be imposed while such a petition is pending decision by the competent authority. (Organization of American States, American Convention on Human Rights, "Pact of San Jose", Costa Rica, art. 4, Nov. 22, 1969, http://www.unhcr.org/refworld/docid/3ae6b36510.html (last visited Feb. 6 2013). Article 1 of the 1990 Protocol to the American Convention on Human Rights to Abolish the Death Penalty states: "The States Parties to this Protocol shall not apply the death penalty in their territory to any person subject to their jurisdiction" (Organization of American States, Protocol to the American Convention on Human Rights to Abolish the Death Penalty ("Pact of San Jose"), June 8, 1990, OAS Treaty Series, N°.73, art. 1, http://www.unhcr.org/refworld/docid/3de4b4884.html (last visited- Feb. 6 2013) and Article 2 states: "No

Its most controversial issues, to be discussed here, surround the end of life and its beginning, in particular, the death penalty and abortion.

1. The Death Penalty

In its General Comment No. 6, the United Nations Human Rights Committee assured that the right to life is a "supreme right from which no derogation is permitted even in time of public emergency which threatens the life of the nation."[729] In the case of *McCann and Others vs. the United Kingdom*, the Grand Chamber of the European Court of Human Rights stated,

> "Article 2 ranks as one of the most fundamental provisions in the Convention – indeed one which, in peacetime, admits of no derogation under Article 15. Together with Article 3 of the Convention [the prohibition of torture], it also enshrines one of the basic values of the democratic societies making up the Council of Europe."[730]

---

reservations may be made to this Protocol. However, at the time of ratification or accession, the States Parties to this instrument may declare that they reserve the right to apply the death penalty in wartime in accordance with international law, for extremely serious crimes of a military nature" (*Id*. at art 2).

Article 4 of the 1981 African Charter on Human and People's Rights states: "Human beings are inviolable. Every human being shall be entitled to respect for his life and the integrity of his person. No one may be arbitrarily deprived of this right" (African Charter, *supra* note 120 at art. 4). Article 5 of the 1990 African Charter on the Rights and welfare of the Child states: "1. Every child has an inherent right to life. This right shall be protected by law; 2. States Parties to the present Charter shall ensure, to the maximum extent possible, the survival, protection and development of the child; 3. Death sentence shall not be pronounced for crimes committed by children." (African Charter, *supra* note 127 at 5).

The Second Optional Protocol to the International Covenant on Civil and Political Rights states: "1. No one within the jurisdiction of a State Party to the present Protocol shall be executed; 2. Each State Party shall take all necessary measures to abolish the death penalty within its jurisdiction" (Second Optional Protocol to the International Covenant on Civil and Political Rights, aiming at the abolition of the death penalty, G. A. Res. 44/128 of Dec. 15, 1989).

The 1989 Convention on the Rights of the Child states: "1. States Parties recognize that every child has the inherent right to life; 2. States Parties shall ensure to the maximum extent possible the survival and development of the child" (UN General Assembly, *Convention on the Rights of the Child*, Nov. 20, 1989, U. N. Treaty Series, vol. 1577, p. 3, http://www.unhcr.org/refworld/docid/3ae6b38f0.html (last visited Feb. 6 2013).

729 United Nations Human Rights Committee, General Comment No. 6: The Right to Life, http://www.unhchr.ch/tbs/doc.nsf/0/84ab9690ccd81fc7c12563ed0046fae3 (last visited May 16, 2012).

730 McCann and others vs. the United Kingdom, GC judgment of 5 September 1995, § 147, with reference to Soering vs. the United Kingdom, judgment of 7 July 1989, para 88; *see also* DOUWE KORFF, THE RIGHT TO LIFE: A GUIDE TO THE IMPLEMENTATION OF ARTICLE 2 OF THE EUROPEAN CONVENTION

Also, Protocol 13 of the European Convention calls for the complete abolishment of the death penalty. As of March 13, 2012, forty-seven countries of the Council of Europe have ratified the Protocol.[731] This absolute abolition of the death penalty did not enter into force immediately rather it was applied gradually. It took more than fifty years for this idea to become legally binding. First, in 1950 it was Article 2 of the European Convention that stated that the right to life is protected except "in the execution of a sentence of a court following his conviction of a crime for which this penalty is provided by law."[732] Second, the Sixth Protocol to the Convention was adopted approximately thirty years later and then it entered into force in 1985 through the modification of Article 2 of the Convention. The new Article 2 abolished the death penalty during peacetime. Third, on July 1, 2003, Protocol 13 entered into force. This Protocol abolished the death penalty in all circumstances with no right to any derogation even during wartime. We can come to the conclusion that it took more than fifty years for the European Human Rights system to prohibit the death penalty in all circumstances. This means that it is not easy for any system to achieve all its goals in a few months or even in few years; rather it requires patience and reasonable steps forward in the right direction. Therefore, it is not quite fair to criticize the Arab Charter by saying that it did not provide more guarantees to the right to life in its initial manifestations, as we can see that these processes happen gradually.

Article 3 of the Universal Declaration of Human Rights of 1948 states, "Everyone has the right to life, liberty and security of person."[733] The International Covenant on Civil and Political Rights (ICCPR), which is considered the first United Nations treaty that has binding obligations on States, was adopted eighteen years later, in 1966.[734] Article 6 of the ICCPR permits the death penalty as an exception to the right to life, but does so with many stipulations. Article 6 states:

> 1. Every human being has the inherent right to life. This right shall be protected by law. No one shall be arbitrarily deprived of his life.
>
> 2. In countries which have not abolished the death penalty, sentence of death may be imposed only for the most serious crimes in accordance

---

ON HUMAN RIGHTS (Council of Europe Handbook Series, 2006), http://echr.coe.int/NR/rdonlyres/16D05FDF-4831-47EC-AE6D-A2C760B0B630/0/DG2ENHRHAND082006.pdf (last visited May 16, 2012).

731 Official link for signatories and ratifications, http://conventions.coe.int/Treaty/Commun/ChercheSig.asp?NT=194&CM=7&DF=13/03/2012&CL=ENG (last visited Mar. 13, 2012).
732 ECHR, *supra* note 497, at art. 2.
733 UDHR, *supra* note 106, at art. 3.
734 ICCPR, *supra* note 63.

with the law in force at the time of the commission of the crime and not contrary to the provisions of the present Covenant and to the Convention on the Prevention and Punishment of the Crime of Genocide. This penalty can only be carried out pursuant to a final judgment rendered by a competent court.

3. When deprivation of life constitutes the crime of genocide, it is understood that nothing in this article shall authorize any State Party to the present Covenant to derogate in any way from any obligation assumed under the provisions of the Convention on the Prevention and Punishment of the Crime of Genocide.

4. Anyone sentenced to death shall have the right to seek pardon or commutation of the sentence. Amnesty, pardon or commutation of the sentence of death may be granted in all cases.

5. Sentence of death shall not be imposed for crimes committed by persons below eighteen years of age and shall not be carried out on pregnant women.

6. Nothing in this article shall be invoked to delay or to prevent the abolition of capital punishment by any State Party to the present Covenant."[735]

Article 6 places several restrictions on the implementation of the death sentence. It states that the death sentence can only be applied in cases of the most serious crimes in accordance with the law enforced at the time of the commission of the crime and not contrary to the provisions of the present Covenant and to the Convention on the Prevention and Punishment of the Crime of Genocide. In addition, the death sentence punishment should be carried out pursuant to a final judgment rendered by a competent court. Furthermore, Article 6 stipulates that capital punishment cannot be carried out on persons under eighteen years old or on pregnant women. Article 6 gives the right to seek pardon or commutation of the sentence to anyone sentenced to death. Amnesty, pardon, or commutation of the sentence of death may be granted in all cases.

General Comment Number 6 of the Human Rights Committee (HRC) indicates, "States parties are not obliged to abolish the death penalty totally they are

---

735   ICCPR, *supra* note 63, at art 6.

obliged to limit its use and, in particular, to abolish it for other than the 'most serious crimes'."[736]

The National Report of Egypt submitted to the Working Group on the Universal Periodic Review of the Human Rights Council explained the Egyptian view regarding the death sentence and the reasons for applying it. The report states:

> In response to the rising incidence of violence in society, the legislature has decided to retain capital punishment for the most serious offences, such as murder accompanied by other serious offences like rape. The purpose is to serve as a deterrent, an objective which deprivation of liberty does not always achieve. The alternative to capital punishment is a "life sentence," which might last no longer than 15 years if parole is granted, or 20 years if the prisoner is eligible for conditional release. The view has been expressed in some quarters that the courts should be given the power to prevent persons convicted of serious crimes from being paroled or from being granted a conditional release, as this would encourage the courts to hand down fewer death sentences, given that deprivation of liberty would serve its real purpose of acting as a deterrent.[737]

Article 4 of the American Convention on Human Rights (ACHR) imposed the following restrictions on the implementation of the capital punishment: [738]

> Art 4 (3) provides that the death penalty shall not be re-established in states that have abolished it;
> Art 4 (4) requires that in no case capital punishment be inflicted for political offences or related common crimes;
> Art 4 (5) provides that capital punishment shall not be imposed upon persons who, at the time the crime was committed, were under 18 years of age or over 70 years of age; nor shall it be applied to pregnant women.

---

736 U.N. Human Rights Committee (HRC), CCPR General Comment No. 6: Right to Life (art. 6), *supra* note 729.

737 The National Report of Egypt submitted to the Working Group on the Universal Periodic Review of the Human Rights Council, Seventh Session, 8–19 February 2009 http://daccess-dds-ny.un.org/doc/UNDOC/GEN/G09/170/69/PDF/G0917069.pdf?OpenElement (last visited Feb. 6, 2013).

738 STARMER & CHRISTOU, *supra* note 572, at 84.

> Art 4 (6) adds another legal safeguard, that capital punishment shall not be imposed while a petition (amnesty, pardon, commutation) is pending decision by the competent authority.[739]

Although Article 4 of the African Charter on Human and Peoples' Rights safeguards the right to life, it does not cover the issue of the death penalty.[740] In addition, it does not put any restrictions or limitations on the death penalty.[741] The Arab Charter on Human Rights includes the following three articles dealing with right to life and the death penalty:[742]

> Article 5, which states, "Every human being has the inherent right to life. This right shall be protected by law. No one shall be arbitrarily deprived of his life;"[743]

> Article 6, which states that the "sentence of death may be imposed only for the most serious crimes in accordance with the laws in force at the time of commission of the crime and pursuant to a final judgment rendered by a competent court. Anyone sentenced to death shall have the right to seek pardon or commutation of the sentence;"[744] and

> Article 7, which states, "Sentence of death shall not be imposed on persons under 18 years of age, unless otherwise stipulated in the laws in force at the time of the commission of the crime" and "The death penalty shall not be inflicted on a pregnant woman prior to her delivery or on a nursing mother within two years from the date of her delivery; in all cases, the best interests of the infant shall be the primary consideration."[745]

In this way, the Arab Charter prohibits the use of the death penalty for pregnant women. However, unlike the American Convention on Human Rights and the ICCPR, the Arab Charter does not give full exclusion from death penalty for crimes committed by persons under the age of eighteen, in that (as stated in Article 7)

---

739   Id.
740   Article 4 of the Arab Charter of Human Rights states, "Human beings are inviolable. Every human being shall be entitled to respect for his life and integrity of his person. No one may be arbitrary deprived of this right" (ACHR, supra note 119, at art. 4).
741   STARMER & CHRISTOU, *supra* note 572, at 84.
742   ACHR *supra* note 126, at arts. 5-7.
743   Id. at art. 5
744   Id. at art. 6.
745   Id. at art. 7.

exceptions are given in cases where this is prescribed by law.[746] This means that after ratifying the Charter, the ratifying country cannot execute people under 18 unless the law that permits execution was enforced prior to the ratification. For example, Saudi Arabia permits the execution of people under 18 years old and Saudi Arabia ratified the Arab Charter in 2009. In this case, its domestic law that permits execution of people under 18 is compatible with the Charter because it was enforced before ratification of the Charter. Exceptional clauses, such as these, help to reduce the number of reservations in a treaty. The exception clause in Article 7 was added in order not to have any reservations to this article by any state, as in a few Arab countries the provisions of domestic law do not exclude people who are under 18 from being subjected to the death penalty. As much as possible, the intention of the legislator was to write the article in a way that all the countries would agree to it without reservation. It is preferable to encourage all of the state parties to sign the Charter without any reservation rather than to have many countries place reservations on it. In addition, only two countries apply the death penalty to persons under the age of 18,[747] and the countries using this practice do so on a very limited basis. For instance, in 2007, Saudi Arabia executed only one person who was under eighteen years of age and Yemen executed only one person who was under eighteen years of age.[748]

It is understood that Sharia law inspired the Arab Charter. Within Sharia law, there is a legitimate reason for the exception clause of the previous article. According to Sharia law, there is no specific age set for execution. Instead, it is outlined that any person can be executed if he or she is an adult and not suffering from insanity.[749] In addition, the person must be mature. For instance, when girls start to menstruate, they are considered to be adults. The Arab Charter tried to strike a balance between countries that mention a minimum age for the application of the death penalty and countries that apply Sharia law. The Arab Charter tried to

---

746 Article 7 (1) of the Arab Charter of Human Rights states, "Sentence of death shall not be imposed on persons under 18 years of age, unless otherwise stipulated in the laws in force at the time of the commission of the crime" (ACHR, supra note 126, at art. 7(1)).

747 Saudi Arabia and Yemen are the two Arab countries that apply the death penalty to persons under the age of 18.

748 For the death sentences and executions in 2007, see Amnesty International, *Death Sentences and Executions in 2007*, http://www.amnesty.org/en/library/asset/ACT50/001/2008/en/b43a1e5b-ffea-11dc-b092-bdb020617d3d/act500012008eng.pdf (last visited Feb. 6, 2013).

749 *Kuwaiti Jurisprudence Encyclopedia* (comprehensive encyclopedia), ISLAMPORT.COM, http://islamport.com/d/2/fqh/1/35/900.html?zoom_highlightsub=%22%D4%D1%E6%D8+%C7%E1%DE%D5%C7%D5%22 (last visited Mar. 30, 2012).

create an article that would gain acceptance by all Arab countries such that no reservations would be placed on the Charter.

On the other hand, Article 7 introduced a new aspect that had never been mentioned in any regional or international treaty before regarding nursing mothers. Article 7 (2) explained, "The death penalty shall not be inflicted on a pregnant woman prior to her delivery or on a nursing mother within two years from the date of her delivery; in all cases, the best interests of the infant shall be the primary consideration."[750] In this article, the legislator was inspired by the Islamic Sharia law. This article explicitly pointed out that the interest of the infant shall be of primary consideration. This provision is actually from the Quran and the Sunnah.

Similar to Article 2 of the European Convention and Article 6 of the ICCPR, Sharia law considers the right to life to be a fundamental rule. There are many Quranic verses, in different chapters, that exemplify this, such as,

> "take not life, which Allah hath made sacred, except by way of justice and law: thus doth He command you, that ye may learn wisdom"[751] and "Nor take life — which Allah has made sacred — except for just cause. And if anyone is slain wrongfully, we have given his heir authority (to demand *qisas* or to forgive): but let him not exceed bounds in the matter of taking life; for he is helped (by the Law)."[752]

Similarly, the Quran states, "… if any one slew a person — unless it be for murder or for spreading mischief in the land — it would be as if he slew the whole people: and if any one saved a life, it would be as if he saved the life of the whole people…" Also, Article 2 of the Cairo Declaration of Human Rights in Islam states:

> (a) Life is a God-given gift and the right to life is guaranteed to every human being. It is the duty of individuals, societies and states to safeguard this right against any violation, and it is prohibited to take away life except for a shari'ah prescribed reason.
>
> (b) It is forbidden to resort to any means which could result in the genocidal annihilation of mankind.
>
> (c) The preservation of human life throughout the term of time willed by Allah is a duty prescribed by Shari'ah.

---

750 ACHR, *supra* note 126, at art. 7(2).
751 QURAN 6:151.
752 *Id.* at 17:33.

(d) Safety from bodily harm is a guaranteed right. It is the duty of the state to safeguard it, and it is prohibited to breach it without a Shari'ah-prescribed reason.[753]

Both Article 2 and the previous verses of the Quran show that Islam put strict regulations on the death penalty and state that it must be done within the due process of law. This is shown in the provisions of the Quran that state, "except by way of justice" and "except for just cause."

The objectives and purposes of Islam regarding the death sentence are to protect peoples' lives. The Quran explains, "And there is (a saving of) life for you in Al-Qisas (the Law of Equality in punishment)."[754] This verse of Quran has a very profound meaning. It clearly shows the main objectives and purposes of the Quran regarding the death penalty and the equality in punishment. It advocates that the killer will be deterred if there is equality in punishment. Sharia law seeks to apply Al-Qisas (the Law of Equality in Punishment) to ensure that people are assured to have a safe life. This approach emphasizes that no individual will think of committing murder because he or she will be punished by the death sentence. Therefore, the life of both of them (the potential killer and the killed) is saved because the criminal will be deterred by the punishment.[755] For instance, in some parts of Egypt and other Arab countries, if someone is killed from a certain family, all of his relatives and family members take revenge on the family of the killer, as a result of which many people die. Therefore, if we apply equality in punishment by law, we will save the lives of many people.[756] The objective of Al-Qisas is not to punish and put severe pain on the criminal after having committing a crime. Rather, the goal is to prevent the crime from being committed. If the punishment is not effective, people will commit the crime without fear of punishment. Likewise, if the punishment deters people, they will be afraid of committing the crime.[757]

---

753 Cairo Declaration on Human Rights in Islam was adopted and Issued at the Nineteenth Islamic Conference of Foreign Ministers in Cairo on 5 August 1990 by the Member States of the Organization of the Islamic Conference, on 5 August 1990; see Cairo Declaration on Human Rights in Islam, supra note 423.

754 QURAN 2:179.

755 ALY ALY MANSOUR, NEZAM AL-TAGREEM WA AL-AKAAB FI AL-ISLAM MOKARANAN BEL KAWANEEN AL-WAD'IYAA [The system of criminsalization and punishment in Islam comparing to manmade law] 69 (1976).

756 HOKOOK AL-INSAN FI AL-KETAB WA EL-SUNNA [Human Rights in Quran and Sunna] 110 (first ed. 2006).

757 MANSOUR, supra note 755, at 73.

During the autumn session of the of the General Assembly, the Sudanese delegate affirmed, "Capital Punishment was a divine right according to some religions, in particular Islam...[C]apital punishment was enshrined in the Koran and millions of inhabitants of the Muslim world believed that it was teaching of God."[758] There is not a unanimous decision by all of the countries of the world to abolish the death penalty. In fact, there is not even customary international law that abolishes and forbids the death penalty. Ninety-seven states have abolished the use of the death sentence for all crimes. Eight states have abolished the death penalty for ordinary crimes. In addition, there are thirty-six states which permit the application of the death penalty in their laws, but where the death penalty has essentially been abolished, as it has not been applied during the last ten years.[759] Furthermore, the execution of minors was not prohibited in the United States of America until the United States of America Supreme Court recently declared it unconstitutional. In the case of *Roper vs. Simmons*, the Supreme Court of the United States of America held that it is unconstitutional to impose capital punishment for crimes committed while under the age of 18.[760] It held the juvenile death penalty to be unconstitutionally cruel and unusual in violation of the Eighth and Fourteenth Amendments and reversed seventeen-year-old Christopher Simmons' death sentence.[761] Therefore, we can come to the conclusion that there is not a worldwide consensus as to whether the application of the death sentence is, or is not, against international law. Each country can determine whatever it will operate within restrictions that protect and safeguard the human rights of individuals, including the right to fair a trial. As the death penalty is related to Sharia law and to the Quran, it would be difficult, if not impossible, for all the Arab countries to abolish it in all circumstances. However, the death penalty can be restricted through the use of Sharia law, which encourages pardoning and forgiveness by the family of the victim. For instance, in Egypt there is no such thing as blood money, which is the payment of a specific amount of money to the family of the victim by the accused in order to seek forgiveness.

Sharia law cannot be separated from the legal regime of many of the Arab countries. Nearly all of the Arab countries apply Sharia law as the primary law. For instance, Article 7 of the Constitutional Law of the United Arab Emirates,[762] Article

---

758 WILLIAM A. SCHABAS, THE DEATH PENALTY AS CRUEL TREATMENT AND TORTURE (1996).

759 Amnesty International, *Death Penalty: Abolitionist and Retentionist Countries,* http://www.amnesty.org/en/death-penalty/abolitionist-and-retentionist-countries (last visited May 16, 2012).

760 Roper vs. Simmons, 125 S. Ct. 1183 2005.

761 *Id.*.

762 BASSIOUNI, *supra* note 129.

2 of the Arab Republic of Egypt,⁷⁶³ Article 2 of the Bahrain Constitution,⁷⁶⁴ Article 2 of the Kuwait constitution⁷⁶⁵, and the preamble of the Constitution of the Union of the Comoros⁷⁶⁶ explicitly state that the Islamic Sharia law is a principal source of legislation. However, this does not mean that all of the Arab countries practice the death penalty. While on paper the majority of Arab countries retain the use of the death penalty for crimes such as murder, it can be considered abolished in practice in those countries that have not executed anyone over the past ten years and are believed to have a policy, or established practice, of not carrying out executions.⁷⁶⁷ For instance, in Morocco and Algeria the last execution happened in 1993 and in Tunisia the last execution happened in 1991.⁷⁶⁸ Therefore, we can presume that these three Arab countries have established a policy of not carrying out the death penalty.

At the same time, Islamic jurists would consider any legislation that abolishes the death penalty as contrary to Sharia law.⁷⁶⁹ From the Islamic perspective, the reasons for the death penalty are related to retribution and deterrence. This is shown clearly in the Quran, which states, "And there is (a saving of) life for you in Al-Qisas (the Law of Equality in punishment), O men of understanding, that you may become Al-Muttaqoon (the pious — see V.2:2)."⁷⁷⁰ On the other hand, Sharia law requires strict evidentiary requirements in order to apply the death penalty. Similar to other human rights treaties, the Arab Charter requires that the death sentence be carried out only "pursuant to a final judgment rendered by a competent court."⁷⁷¹ On the other hand, Sharia law requires to "take not life, which Allah hath made sacred, except by way of justice and law."⁷⁷² According to the Egyptian legal system, it is necessary that before rendering its decision regarding the use of the death sentence, the court requests the Sharia law opinion regarding the application of the death sentence in the particular circumstances of the case. While the opinion of the *Mufti* is not binding for the court, it is required that

---

763   Id.
764   Id.
765   Id.
766   Id.
767   *Death Penalty: Abolitionist and Retentionist Countries*, supra note 759.
768   Id.
769   MASHOOD A. BADERIN, INTERNATIONAL HUMAN RIGHTS AND ISLAMIC LAW 70 (2005).
770   QURAN 2:179.
771   ACHR, *supra* note 126, at art. 6.
772   QURAN 6:151.

the court knows the opinion of the *Mufti*, which will definitely affect the discretionary authority of the court.

The 2011 report by Dar Al-Ifta, the main Egyptian official body that gives religious point of view in all aspects to both government and people, stated that 145 cases have been referred to it as an institution.[773] Dar Al-Ifta accepted the application of the death sentence for 136 of the cases and rejected its application for nine of the cases. I tried to get more information and details about these cases in order to trace them in the court, but Dar Al-Ifta stated that they are not allowed to give detailed information about these cases. The objection of Dar Al-Ifta to applying the death sentence in these nine cases shows clearly that Sharia law seeks to apply justice. The 145 cases that were referred to Dar Al-Ifta in 2011 should be understood as not being a very large number, as a final decision was not reached in all of these cases. Practically speaking, this number will be reduced because Dar Al-Ifta objected to the application of the death sentence in some of the cases. In addition, the Supreme Court of Cassation must review all of these cases and can order a retrial of the cases. After retrial, the Court of Cassation has full discretionary authority to reduce the punishment or even render a decision that the accused person is innocent. If the Court imposed a death sentence, the case will be again referred to Dar Al-Ifta and then to the Supreme Court of Cassation. The Court of Cassation has full discretionary authority to reduce the punishment or even render a decision that the accused person is innocent. Furthermore, this number of 145 cases is not large in when compared with the Egyptian population, which is nearly 90 million.

The Egyptian *Mufti* stated that, due to the graveness of the punishment of the death sentence, any death sentence decision must be referred to the *Mufti* for the opinion on Sharia law.[774] It should be noted the death sentence is applied strictly to the most serious crimes. In addition, it is applied through very strict and complicated regulations. For instance, in Egypt the death sentence is not imposed by a majority vote by the judges. In Egypt, the death sentence can only be imposed when there is unanimous agreement by all of the judges hearing the case. In another words, if only one judge in the court rejected the application of the death sentence it would not be applied. In its National Report of Egypt submitted to the

---

773 Statement, Dar Al-Ifta http://www.dar-alifta.org/Viewstatement.aspx?ID=460&type=0 (last visited Mar. 17, 2012).

774 Mufti: I feel pain when I accept the implementation of each death sentences, Almasry-alyoum.com, http://www.almasry-alyoum.com/article2.aspx?ArticleID=223357&IssueID=1505 (last visited Mar. 17, 2012).

Working Group on the Universal Periodic Review of the Human Rights Council, the Egyptian Government stated:

> The legislature has established powerful safeguards for capital punishment, as described here below:
>
> 1. A death sentence may only be pronounced by a criminal court following a fair trial in which the accused was afforded all means of a defence and a defence lawyer was appointed, if the defendant did not have one.
>
> 2. A death sentence must be imposed unanimously by all the judges hearing the case.
>
> 3. A Mufti must be consulted before the sentence is pronounced.
>
> 4. All death sentences must be referred to the Court of Cassation by the Office of the Public Prosecutor, even if the condemned person does not appeal.
>
> 5. It is illegal to pass a death sentence on a child.
>
> 6. It is illegal to execute a woman who is pregnant.[775]

On the other hand, there is another Islamic point of view that, according to Sharia law, the death sentence can be waived if there is a payment of blood money by the criminal to the heirs of the victim.[776] During the consideration of its second periodic report on the ICCPR, the Sudanese government stated, "since 1973… execution had been avoided in cases involving the death sentence, either because the higher court or the President had not confirmed the sentence or because the blood money–the diy'a had been paid instead."[777]

Sharia law, which encourages pardoning and forgiveness, can be used to limit the application of the death sentence. In addition, Sharia law requires that many conditions be met to legitimately establish the criminal evidence. For instance, Sharia law requires that four witnesses saw an illegal sexual relationship in order for the accused to be punished. It is nearly impossible that four people could witness an act of sexual intercourse unless it happened in a public place. For instance, during the Caliphate of Muslims, Omar Ibn El-Khattab asked a question

---

775 The National Report of Egypt submitted to the Working Group on the Universal Periodic Review of the Human Rights Council, *supra* note 737.

776 BADERIN, *supra* note 138, at 71.

777 U.N. International Covenant on Human Rights, 1628th Mtg, at para. 15, U.N. Doc. CCPR/C/SR/1628 (Oct.2, 1998).

to Aly Ibn Aby Talb, who is one of the closest relatives and companions of Prophet Mohammed, with respect to whether is it legitimate to punish people who engage in illegal sexual relations if the sexual intercourse was seen by the Caliph himself? Aly replied by saying that anyone witnessing such an act that does not gather three more witnesses will be punished.[778] According to Sharia law, evidence cannot be gathered in an illegal manner. For instance:

> It is reported that during the Caliphate of Omar Ibn el-Khatab he used to go, himself, on round patrol of the city of Medina. One night while on patrol he heard some noise of drunkenness coming from a house, he knocked on the door but no one answered him. He then climbed over the wall and saw a drunken party inside. He shouted down and accused the homeowner of breaking the law prohibiting the intoxicants. The man replied back by saying that, if I have committed one sin you have committed four sins to find out. First, you spied on us against God's command "spy not."[779] Second, you climbed over the wall despite God command "It is not Al-Birr (piety, righteousness, etc.) that you enter the houses from the back but Al-Birr (is the quality of the one) who fears Allah. So enter houses through their proper doors, and fear Allah that you may be successful."[780] Third, you entered without announcing yourself nor greeting in violation of God's Command that "Enter not houses other than your own, until you have asked permission and greeted those in them."[781] Fourth, you entered without permission in violation of God's command that "enter not until permission has been given."[782] The caliph Omar was abashed and he said you are right and I am must forgive your sin. The man then indicated the caliph saying "that is your fifth sin, you claim to be the caliph and protector of Islamic law, how can you then say you forgive what God has prohibited."[783]

One of the famous Islamic schools of jurisprudence stated that Muslim women should not be punished by the death sentence. They made *ijtihad* by using the principle of *Qiyas*, which is based on a hadith for Prophet Mohammed in which he prohibited killing non-Muslim women in times of war.[784] This Islamic school

---

778 MANSOUR, *supra* note 755, at 69.
779 QURAN 49:12.
780 *Id.* at 2:189.
781 *Id.* at 24:27.
782 *Id.* at 24:28.
783 Baderin, *supra* note 385, at 117.
784 Prof. Saad Al-Din Helaly, Makased Al-Sharia Al-Islameyah wa Kadayaa Al-Asr [The Objectives

stated that as long as it is prohibited to kill non-Muslim women, therefore it is also prohibited to kill Muslim women. [785]

Sharia law can be used to limit, and sometimes prevent, the use of the death penalty. In fact, Sharia law encourages refraining from the use of the death penalty and calls for forgiveness and mercy. To further illustrate this point, I will give the example of a murder case in the state of the United Arab Emirates.[786] The Court of First Instance and the Court of Appeal sentenced a criminal to death because he was convicted of killing a woman. The accused appealed to the Supreme Court. The Supreme Court stated that the Court should wait to communicate its decision until it asked the father of the murdered woman whether he wanted retribution or was going to pardon the criminal. The Supreme Court stated that if the Court of First Instance decided to use the death penalty it should always ask the heirs whether they want retribution or want to pardon the criminal. Then the court wrote the following Quran verses to support its opinion: "And if anyone is slain wrongfully, we have given his heir authority to demand qisas or to forgive"[787] "But if the killer is forgiven by the brother (or the relatives, etc.) of the killed against blood money, then adhering to it with fairness and payment of the blood money, to the heir should be made in fairness. This is an alleviation and a mercy from your Lord."[788] The court also stated that Sharia law encourages reconciliation and pardoning "if a person forgives and makes reconciliation, his reward is due from Allah."[789] In the end, the Court of First Instance rejected the death sentence.

The Supreme Court rejected the death sentence in another murder case in the Emirates.[790] The Supreme Court stated that the heir has the right to pardon in return exchange for money (compensation) or even without receiving anything in return.

---

of Islamic Law (Shari'ah) and Issues of The Contemporary Age] 507 Research and Proceedings: The 22nd General Conference of the Supreme Council for Islamic Affairs, part one, (Cairo, February 22-25, 2010 [hereinafter Makased Al-Sharia Al-Islameyah wa Kadayaa Al-Asr]; *see also* HELALY, *supra* note 273, at 225.

785 Makased Al-Sharia Al-Islameyah wa Kadayaa Al-Asr, *supra* note 784, at 733; *see also* HELALY, *supra* note 273, at 225.
786 Case No. 157 for the year 1991, 5/12/1992. Supreme Court of the United Arab Emirates.
787 QURAN 17:33.
788 *Id.* at 2:178.
789 *Id.* at 42:40.
790 Case no 82 of the judicial year 19, 27/12/1997. Supreme Court of Emirates.

On the other hand, pardoning is not applied in several Arab countries. For instance, in Egypt, the penal law does not mention that the heir has the right to pardon. From the above cases, we can see that the Arab Charter can use the influence of Sharia law to encourage people and countries to give pardon and limit the use of the death penalty. For instance, the Quran states,

> "and We ordained therein for them: 'Life for life, eye for eye, nose for nose, ear for ear, tooth for tooth, and wounds equal for equal.' But if anyone remits the retaliation by way of charity, it shall be for him an expiation. And whosoever does not judge by that which Allah has revealed, such are the Zalimun (polytheists and wrong-doers — of a lesser degree)."[791]

Furthermore, the Quran states:

> And do not kill anyone whose killing Allah has forbidden, except for a just cause. And whoever is killed wrongfully (Mazluman intentionally with hostility and oppression and not by mistake), We have given his heir the authority [to demand Qisas, — Law of Equality in punishment — or to forgive, or to take Diyah (blood money)]. But let him not exceed limits in the matter of taking life (i.e. he should not kill except the killer). Verily, he is helped (by the Islamic law).[792]

The application of the death penalty in Arab countries comes not only from Sharia law, but also from cultural influences. As David F. Greenberg and Valerie West explain, "Cultures define the seriousness of criminal offenses and provide the values that shape crime policies. Decisions makers take into account the values and policy preferences of their populations. It is usually expected that a people's culture influences a government's use of the death penalty."[793] For instance, many people who live in Upper Egypt believe in retribution and revenge. It has been reported, "'*Tar*' vendettas are deeply rooted in southern Egyptian tradition, with some feuds often linked to disputes over money and land lasting for more than half a century. '*Al-Tar Wala Al-'Aar*' (Vendetta is better than disgrace), is a common saying associated with these vendettas…In Upper Egypt, family vendettas can sometimes turn into mass murders."[794] In general, in the Middle East the well-known principle of an 'eye for eye and tooth for tooth' is

---

[791] QURAN 5:45.

[792] *Id.* at 17:33.

[793] David F. Greenberg &Valerie West, *Siting The Death Penalty Internationally*, 33 LAW & SOC. INQUIRY 295, (2008).

[794] Reem Nafie, *We'll Get Them*, AHRAM.ORG, (Feb. 26 – Mar. 3, 2004), http://weekly.ahram.org.eg/2004/679/eg11.htm (last visited Jun. 2, 2012).

deeply rooted in the minds of many people. Therefore, decision makers and governments should take these cultural beliefs and traditions into account before thinking of abolishing the death penalty.

Some Western scholars believe that the intransigence of Islamic States on the issue of the death sentence raises issues of cultural relativism.[795] If we look to the situation in the Middle East (for example, Libya, Yemen, Syria, Sudan, Lebanon, and Iraq), we can see that the situation is unstable not only between countries, but even within countries. Countries that are not currently in the midst of war are facing national problems, such as strikes, unstable conditions, and potential terrorist bombings. For instance, there is a large increase in the number of crimes in several Arab Countries. The increase in the number of crimes, such as murder, leads to an increase in the number of death sentences.

The question of capital punishment is subject to an open and endless debate. People have strong reactions to it; for the most part, they are either strongly for or strongly against it. This is true not only in the Arab world, but also in other regions. People who are proponents of abolishing capital punishment argue that scientific studies have proven that the death penalty does not deter criminals more effectively than other forms of punishment.[796] In addition, they say that the criminal is a human being and, as such, he or she should be given mercy and forgiveness. People who support the use of death penalty argue that, since the criminal who committed murder did not show any kind of forgiveness or mercy to the victim, they should not be given mercy and should be treated as they treated others.[797] Even if we could overcome the question of whether we can give mercy and forgiveness to a criminal, we could not determine whether a 'society' can give mercy and forgiveness to criminals and other offenders.[798]

There is not worldwide acceptance of the abolishment of capital punishment. The United Nations General Assembly adopted a resolution for "a moratorium on the death penalty."[799] One hundred and four states voted in favor of the resolution, fifty-four states voted against the adoption of the resolution, and twenty-nine

---

795 Henry J. Steiner, Philip Alston & Ryan Goodman, International Human Rights in Context, Law, Politics, Morals 22 (3rd. ed. 2007).
796 Id. at 19.
797 B. Moxley, Capital Punishment: Right or Wrong? 46 (1995).
798 Id. at 49.
799 U.N. Department of Public Information. *General Assembly Adopts Landmark Text Calling for Moratorium on Death Penalty.* Sixty-second General Assembly Plenary, 76th & 77th mtg, GA/10678, (Dec. 18, 2007), http://www.un.org/News/Press/docs/2007/ga10678.doc.htm (last visited Mar. 17, 2012).

states abstained.[800] The representative of Barbados stated that "the European Union and other main sponsors were trying to impose their will on other countries."[801] After the vote, the United Nations determined that "[c]apital punishment remains legal under international law and Barbados wishes to exercise its sovereign right to use it as deterrent to the most serious crimes."[802] The representative of Egypt stated:

> His delegation had voted against the resolution because it was in contradiction to religious, practical and legal norms that were agreed upon. The death penalty was only imposed according to due process of law and the provisions of Islamic law. This was done in such a way as to ensure that the punishment was in line with legal and religious obligations. Moreover, the death penalty was only imposed for the most serious of crimes, in accordance with laws applicable at the time of the crime, he said. There were provisions to seek pardon or to appeal. The key element there, he said, should have been due process and sound implementation of legal measures, instead of the imposition of a restriction on the use of the penalty. Its use in Egypt reflected the belief that capital punishment could only be imposed against adults cognizant of their responsibility. The prohibition of the death penalty against pregnant women was a recognition that death should not be imposed against those who had no choice, and who should not be deprived of their right to life. In the same vein, Islamic Sharia law also prohibited abortion, he noted.[803]

A number of cases in the Human Rights Committee (HRC) have dealt with the issue of capital punishment. These cases clearly show how the judgments are gradually changing towards providing more guarantees and restrictions in favor of protecting the right to life. For example, in the case of *Judge vs. Canada*,[804] concerning the deportation of an American citizen from Canada to the United States of America, "The HRC reversed its previous jurisprudence in *Kindler vs. Canada* and found that people may not be deported to countries where they face the death penalty."[805] In this case the HRC mentioned that ten years have passed since its decision in *Kindler vs. Canada* and added that, during the ten years, there

---

800 *Id.*
801 *Id.*
802 *Id.*
803 *Id.*
804 Judge vs. Canada, July 17, 2002, Comm. No. 829/98. U.N. Doc. CCPR/C/78/D/829/1998, (2003).
805 Sarah Joseph, *Human Rights Committee: Recent Cases*, 5 HUMAN RIGHTS LAW REVIEW 105 (2005).

was a general broadening of the international consensus in favor of the abolition of the capital punishment. The Committee stressed the fact that, according to Article 6 of the ICCPR, the abolitionist states should protect the right to life in all circumstances. Therefore, they must not extradite or deport any person before have accurate guarantees that the capital punishment will not be carried out.[806]

Sharia law balances the needs of the criminal, victim, and society (public order). In other words, as already outlined in Chapter 3, Sharia law strikes a balance between the individual and 'umma. In this way, the criminal must be punished because he committed murder. The family of the victim will not seek revenge because either:

> The rule of law is implemented efficiently by punishing the criminal or;
> The victim's family forgives the criminal or they take blood money in return from the criminal.

It should be noted that, according to Sharia law, if the family of the victim forgives the criminal, the judge has the authority to apply *Ta'zir* punishment, which can take the form of verbal threatening, imprisonment, expulsion, etc.[807] For example, if a rich person has performed repeated killings, after which he or she has given blood money to the heir, the judge can apply the death sentence even if the family of the victim accepts the blood money, because the judge always has the right and duty to protect society. Therefore, criminals will know that equality and justice is applied and whoever kills intentionally can be executed. As a result, members of society will feel that they are safe and that the rule of law is equitable. It is not fair that the rule of law favors the criminal. Instead, the rule of law should favor the criminal and the victim equally. This is the correct balance between the individual and 'umma, whereby the criminal can take all of his rights of defense and the victim's rights will also not be ignored.

The Quran indicates that no compassion should be given to persons who commit crimes: "Let not compassion move you in their case, in a matter prescribed by Allah…"[808] Sheikh Mohamed Metwally Shaarawy, one of the most popular Egyptian and Arab Islamic religious Imams, said that one of the mistakes of the domestic laws is the slow litigation process. The trial of an accused murderer may take many years. Yet, the trial should not take a long period of time in order to ensure equality between the criminal, the victim and the people within the society. If the trial takes a long time, people will have already forgotten the victim, who may

---

806 STARMER & CHRISTOU, *supra* note 572, at 87.
807 Helaly, *supra* note 267.
808 QURAN 24:2.

have been dead for ten years by the time the trial occurs, and remember only the accused criminal. Because this person is alive, the general public will be inclined to feel sympathy toward him. Sheikh Mohamed Metwally Shaarawy added that the crime and the court decision should follow each other more directly. In this way, if the people think of the graveness of the death penalty they will remember the graveness of the crime committed.[809]

Many Western countries use the death penalty. For instance, the death penalty is legal in in thirty-eight of the fifty United States of America states. The death penalty is also included in the United States of America's federal military and civilian law. As of January 2006, approximately three thousands four hundred prisoners were being held under death sentence.[810] No one can say that applying the death sentence will bring an end to crimes entirely. Crime is present in all societies all over the world. Yet, it can be limited or increased depending on the social and legal system around with the society is organized. However, applying the death sentence effectively will most likely limit crimes to a minimum.[811]

Sharia law cannot stop implementing the death sentence absolutely. In addition, the death sentence is not against international law as long as it is applied for the most serious crimes after a fair trial. Many Western and non-Arab countries apply the death sentence. In addition, the death sentence has not been abolished by the ICCPR, the African Charter, the American Convention, or the Arab Charter on Human Rights. Therefore, the implementation of the death sentence for the most serious crimes complies and is compatible with international human rights standards as long as it comes after a fair trial. Sharia law advocates human rights more strongly than international human rights law because Sharia law encourages pardoning and the giving of blood money, if accepted by the family of the victim instead of applying the death penalty. Sharia law strikes a balance between the victim, the society, and the criminal. In other words, there should be deterrents for criminals to not commit murder so that society is protected from criminals and the victim's rights are protected by equality in punishment. In addition, Sharia law encourages pardoning and forgiveness of the victim's family or the payment of blood money to the victim's family. Therefore, the rights of the victim are protected and, at the same time, the death penalty is not applied on the criminal. Furthermore, the death sentence cannot be applied except on the most serious crimes and after a fair trial. Therefore, the rights of the criminal are pro-

---

809 *Sheikh Sha'rawy* (one of the most popular Egyptian and Arab religious people in the Middle East), YOUTUBE.COM, http://www.youtube.com/watch?v=MuUJizHacSU (last visited Mar. 14, 2012).
810 STEINER, ALSTON & GOODMAN, *supra* note 795, at 21.
811 MANSOUR, *supra* note 755, at 74.

tected and even the rights of society are protected because justice is applied. The Western concept of human rights focuses mainly on the rights of the criminal. In other words, the Western concept focuses more on rights than on duties. The Sharia law concept of human rights should be respected and applied in the Arab world on the other hand, the Western concept should be respected and implemented in the Western world. There should be a constructive dialogue based on respect between the East and the West. It is premature to determine whether the abolition of the death penalty is a universally protected principle of international human rights; further discussion, in an atmosphere of open debate based on respect, is required in order to come to a resolution.

In short, it is more practical and reasonable to encourage Arab countries to limit the death penalty by encouraging pardoning from the victim's family and the giving of blood money to the victim's family. In addition, death penalty should not be applied unless the Court believes 100% that the person who will be punished by death sentence is the one who committed the murder. The countries that carry out the death penalty should publish the category of crimes for which the death penalty is authorized and should publish the number of people that are sentenced to death. In resolution 1989/64, adopted on May 24, 1989, the United Nations Economic and Social Council urged United Nations member states:

> To publish, for each category of offence for which the death penalty is authorized, and if possible on an annual basis, information about the use of the death penalty, including the number of persons sentenced to death, the number of executions actually carried out, the number of persons under sentence of death, the number of death sentences reversed or commuted on appeal and the number of instances in which clemency has been granted, and to include information on the extent to which the safeguards referred to above are incorporated in national law.[812]

Similarly, in resolution 2005/59, adopted on April 20, 2005, the United Nations Commission on Human Rights called upon all states that still maintain the death penalty "to make available to the public information with regard to the imposition of the death penalty and to any scheduled execution."[813]

The Arab Charter on Human Rights can be used to help reduce the use of the death sentence. As previously outlined, the Arab Charter is inspired by Sharia law,

---

812   E.S.C. Res.1989/64, 1989 U.N. ESCO, U.N. E/1989/89.
813   U.N. Commission on Human Rights, E/CN.4/RES/2005/59, adopted April 20, 2005.

which is the primary source of law in nearly all of the Arab countries. Sharia law encourages pardoning the accused and calls for very strict requirements in order to establish that a crime has been committed. Not all of the Arab countries have replaced the death sentence with pardoning. Also several Arab countries do not use the strict requirements related to gathering evidence advanced by Sharia law. Therefore, the Arab Charter can be a model way for promoting human rights and limiting the death sentence in the Middle East. In addition, the Arab Charter outlines further rights and privileges related to the death sentence. For instance, Egypt prohibits executing pregnant women until two months after the delivery of the child. On the other hand, the Arab Charter prohibits executing pregnant women until two years after the delivery of the baby.[814] The Arab Charter on Human Rights states,

> "Sentence of death shall not be imposed on persons under 18 years of age, unless otherwise stipulated in the laws in force at the time of the commission of the crime [and] The death penalty shall not be inflicted on a pregnant woman prior to her delivery or on a nursing mother within two years from the date of her delivery; in all cases, the best interests of the infant shall be the primary consideration."[815]

A focus on ensuring that a baby is breastfed for two years comes from the Quran. The Quran states, "The mothers shall give suck to their children for two whole years, (that is) for those (parents) who desire to complete the term of suckling, but the father of the child shall bear the cost of the mother's food and clothing on a reasonable basis."[816] In this way, the Arab Charter can help in improving the rights of women and babies.

In the light of my proposed theory, the death penalty should be applied even if it faces some criticism. However, it should be applied only for the most serious crimes and after fair trial. In addition, Sharia law can be used to reduce its implementation by encouraging pardoning and forgiveness from the victim's family. In addition, the giving of blood money can also be encouraged in order to reduce the implementation of the death penalty.

---

814   Article 476 of the Egyptian Code of Criminal Procedures.
815   ACHR, *supra* note 126, at art. 7.
816   QURAN 2:233.

2. Abortion

Although abortion is not mentioned in the Arab Charter, it is considered a violation of the right to life from the Sharia law point of view. According to Sharia law and the penal laws of Arab countries, abortion constitutes violation to the right to life of the embryo. Abortion is prohibited in many Arab countries; as I will explain in this section, there are strict limitations on permitting it.

Abortion is a hotly debated issue all over the world, that is, not only in the Arab world, but also in Western countries. Abortion is a controversial subject even in the Council of Europe. European states have not reached a consensus with respect to abortion. For instance, abortion in Ireland is almost prohibited. On the other hand, abortion is entirely permitted in some European countries.[817] The European Court of Human Rights applied the margin of appreciation with respect to the issue of abortion. For example, the German Constitutional Court struck down a law concerning abortion in Germany as unconstitutional.[818] The Constitutional Court permits abortion within the first twelve weeks of pregnancy without any grounds of necessity, after which the use of abortion is limited to particular situations. The Commission reached a conclusion that this legislation is not considered violating or interfering with the applicant women's rights with respect to her private life. It concluded that abortion was permissible and the health of the mother is taken into account.[819]

In *H vs. Norway*, the Commission mentioned that laws on abortion in the European states differ from one country to another. The Commission added that states parties should be given discretion to determine their approach to this issue.[820] Both the Court and the Commission did not answer the question of whether an unborn child, or the fetus, is considered protected by the right to life (Article 2 of the European Convention). This question remained unanswered in *Bos vs. Italy*, wherein abortion was prohibited except on the grounds of risk to the mother. The Commission stated that if we suppose that the fetus could be protected under Article 2 of the European Convention, the state did not exceed the margin of appreciation.[821]

---

817 KAREN REID, A PRACTITIONER'S GUIDE TO THE EUROPEAN CONVENTION ON HUMAN RIGHTS 215 (3rd ed. 2008).
818 8416/79, (Dec.) May 13, 1980, 19 D.R. 244.
819 REID, *supra* note 817, at 217.
820 *Id.*
821 *Id.* at 216.

The Egyptian criminal law criminalizes abortion. The criminal is considered to be the person who performed the abortion on the pregnant women, either without her consent (by force) or with previous consent. A pregnant woman who requested an abortion would also be punished.[822] The Egyptian Supreme Court states that the consent of the pregnant woman to receive an abortion does not give the doctor the right to perform an abortion. The Court added that there is sanctity of human life.[823] It should be noted that abortion is similarly not encouraged in Middle Eastern culture. In this way, abortion is criminalized unless necessary to save the life of a pregnant woman. It is not only Egypt that prohibits abortion; many other member countries of the Arab League prohibit it except in certain circumstances. For instance, in the concluding observation of the United Nations Human Rights Committee on Morocco, it was stated, "The Committee notes with concern that abortion is still a criminal offence under Moroccan law unless it is carried out to save the mother's life."[824] Similarly, Kuwait's penal law punishes the person who performs an abortion on a pregnant woman, regardless of whether it is done with or without her consent.[825] The law also punishes the pregnant woman who either performs an abortion on herself or gives permission to someone else to perform an abortion on her.[826] On the other hand, the law does not criminalize abortion if it was done to save the life of a pregnant woman.

According to Sharia law, abortion is prohibited except in very limited cases. The Sharia law point of view is that abortion is considered an extreme violation of the right to life. In the hierarchy of rights, the right to life of the unborn baby is higher than the right to private life of his mother. Sharia law balances between the rights of the woman and the rights of the child. Abortion is allowed if the life of the woman is at risk because of the pregnancy. On the other hand, the abortion is forbidden if a woman just wants to abort her baby without any serious reason for doing so.

In 2010, Egypt's Parliamentary Health Committee requested the opinion of Dar Al-Ifta with respect to abortion. Dar Al-Ifta replied by saying that all of the Islamic scholars have stated that abortion is entirely forbidden if the embryo is more than 120 days old. The reason is that, according to Sharia law, the soul enters the body

---

822 Egyptian Code of Criminal Law, art. 260, 261, 262, 263.
823 Egyptian Supreme Court, Case Number 1127 for the Judicial year 40 k, 27/12/1970.
824 U.N. International Covenant on Human Rights, 82th Sess. Concluding Observations of the HRC on Morocco, U.N. Doc. CCPR/CO/82/MAR (Dec. 1, 2004), http://tbinternet.ohchr.org/_layouts/treatybodyexternal/TBSearch.aspx?Lang=en&TreatyID=8&DocTypeID=5 (last visited May 2, 2014).
825 Kuwaiti Penal Code 16/1960, art. 174.
826 *Id.* at 176.

after the first 120 days, and if an abortion is performed it would be considered to be the killing of a human being. Dar Al-Ifta added that it is not acceptable to perform an abortion even before the embryo has reached 120 days unless in cases that doctors determine that this is the only way to save the life of the mother.[827]

In 1980, the former Egyptian *Mufti* and the former Egyptian Sheikh Azhar, Gad Al-Haq,[828] stated it is forbidden for an abortion to be performed after the embryo has reached 120 days. However, if an abortion is performed before 120 days, there are the following four different opinions of Islamic jurists:[829] The first opinion is supported by group of scholars of Abu Hanifa School. According to this first opinion, it is accepted to perform an abortion before the completion of the first four months even if there is no serious reason to do so.[830] The second opinion is that abortion can happen before the completion of the first 120 days if there is a serious reason for doing so.[831] If there is no reason, performing an abortion is considered to be hated and distasteful. This opinion is supported by a group of Hanafi scholars and a group of Shafi scholars. The third opinion is that it is always hated and distasteful to perform an abortion.[832] This is the opinion of some scholars of Imam Malik School. The fourth opinion is that abortion is entirely *Haram* (forbidden).[833] This is the opinion of the Malik School.

The diversity of opinions in Sharia law is one of the best things in Islam. It provides flexibility to enable people and a country to choose what best suits their interests. The difference in opinions is not only between different schools of Islam; different opinions can exist within the same school. On the other hand, we cannot say that there is utter confusion within the differences in opinions. There is a frame through which the opinions are understood. The frame is that, while there are different opinions regarding abortion before the embryo reaches 120

---

827 *Official Answer of Dar Al-Ifta*, DAR-ALIFTA.ORG, http://www.dar-alifta.org/Viewstatement.aspx?ID=229&text=%D8%A7%D9%84%D8%A5%D8%AC%D9%87%D8%A7%D8%B6 (last visited Mar. 17, 2012).

828 Tim Winter, *Obituary: Sheikh Gad al-Haq Ali Gad al-Haq*, THE INDEPENDENT, http://www.independent.co.uk/news/people/obituarysheikh-gad-alhaq-ali-gad-alhaq-1342744.html (last visited Mar. 17, 2012).

829 *Almawsoo'aa Al-sha'melah* (comprehensive encyclopedia), ISLAMPORT.COM, http://islamport.com/d/2/ftw/1/11/484.html?zoom_highlightsub=%C7%CC%E5%C7%D6 (last visited Mar. 17, 2012).

830 *Id.*
831 *Id.*
832 *Id.*
833 *Id.*

days, all of the Islamic schools prohibit abortion after the embryo reaches 120 days. The difference in opinion makes the Sharia law, as a legal system, a living instrument that will be compatible in any era for all generations to come.

Sharia law gives the fetus the rights given to human beings; for instance, the Egyptian Supreme Court of Cassation rendered a decision regarding the rights of an unborn child in his father's death compensation. The Court mentioned Article 163 of the Egyptian Civil code, which provides that "a perpetrator should pay compensation for every mistake which caused harm to others."[834] The Court added:

> There is no civil liability unless the harm was caused by the mistake…It is commonly known that a child has personal rights that flow from the wrongful death of his father even if his birth date is subsequent to the date of the action that caused his father's death. So a child has rights even as an embryo…the inheritance law keeps [for the unborn child] her/his share of inheritance like other rights guaranteed by law. The right to nationality, the right of inheritance under his father's will are all determined after his birth since his gender can only be determined then.[835]

The previous example shows that Egyptian Court of Cassation protected the rights of the unborn child. Sharia law strikes a balance between the mother's rights and the rights of the unborn child. Abortion is permitted in Sharia law in order to save the life of mother otherwise the right of the unborn child to life is protected. Several Western legal systems may not give the same protection to unborn children. Yet, we cannot criticize these legal systems saying that they undermine the rights of the unborn child. We should not say that the Western legal systems should be modernized and apply the Egyptian style of human rights with respect to the protection of the rights of unborn child. We cannot impose the Egyptian legal system on other legal systems. Likewise, the Western legal systems cannot be imposed on other countries. In light of my proposed theory, abortion cannot be permitted unless it is in situations that comply with the principles of Sharia law explained above and in accordance with the opinions of Islamic scholars, some of which have been highlighted in this text. In short, there should be a constructive dialogue between different legal systems in order to find commonalities. It may be premature to determine whether the abolition

---

834 The Egyptian Supreme Court of Cassation, Civil Chamber, petition for Cassation no; 6891 J.Y 78, Hearing Session Saturday 22 October 2007, Quarterly Review, *Judgments and Legal Research*, Volume 6.

835 *Id.*

of abortion should be a universal principle of human rights; it needs discussion in an atmosphere of open debate in order to come to a resolution. The principle of margin of appreciation that is explained in my proposed theory can be applied regarding abortion; this permits each Arab country the right to choose between the opinions of the Islamic schools of jurisprudence.

Abortion in Sharia law is aligned with international human rights standards, as there is no unanimous opinion in the international community regarding abortion. Therefore, any country can choose what is deemed to best fit its public interest. Abortion is, and will be, the subject of endless debate in Western countries because there are two rights competing against each other: the right of the private life of the woman and the right to life of the unborn child.

C. Equality of Rights Between Men and Women

1. Introduction

The equality between men and women is a fundamental principle that must be protected and safeguarded. The Human Rights Committee (HRC) of the ICCPR observed:

> Inequality in the enjoyment of rights by women through the world is deeply embedded in tradition, history and culture, including religious attitude…States parties should ensure that traditional, historical, religious or cultural attitudes are not used to justify violations of women's right to equality before the law and to equal enjoyment of all covenant rights. States parties should furnish appropriate information on those aspects of tradition, history, cultural practices and religious attitudes which jeopardize or may jeopardize, compliance with Article 3, and may indicate what measures they have taken to overcome such factors.[836]

Similarly, the HRC has observed that "equality during marriage implies that husband and wife should participate equally in responsibility and authority within the family."[837]

---

836 U.N. International Covenant on Human Rights, General Comment No. 28: Equality of Rights Between Men and Women (art. 3), para. 5, U.N. Doc. CCPR/C/21/Rev.1/Add.10 (Mar. 29, 2000), http://tbinternet.ohchr.org/Treaties/CCPR/Shared%20Documents/1_Global/CCPR_C_21_Rev-1_Add-10_6619_E.pdf (last visited May 2, 2014).

837 General Comment 29, para 25, 29 March 2000, http://tbinternet.ohchr.org/Treaties/CCPR/Shared%20Documents/1_Global/CCPR_C_21_Rev-1_Add-10_6619_E.pdf (last visited May 2, 2014).

There are many cases concerning gender equality before the European Court on Human Rights. For instance, in *Leyla Sahin vs. Turkey*,[838] the applicant complained that banning the wearing of an Islamic headscarf in higher education institutions constituted a violation of her rights and freedoms, including the right to gender equality. The Court noted that gender equality is "one of the key principles underlying the Convention and a goal to be achieved by member States of the Council of Europe."[839] In addition, "The Court did not explicitly discuss the meaning of gender equality and how the applicant's actions threatened women's rights, or how the principle could justify prohibiting an adult woman from following what seemed to be freely adopted and personally important practice."[840] The European Court concluded that there was no violation of the human rights of the applicant. The Court did not highlight the consequences of the prohibition of the headscarf on thousands of other women in Turkey.[841] The approach of the Court, however, has been criticized:

> [T]he formula that the Court applies in assessing sex discrimination claims asks the wrong set of questions. The question should not be whether there is unjustified differential treatment or unjustified non-accommodation of differences, but rather whether the law or practice at issue perpetuates or produces the subordination of women (as defined by other identity characteristics) and unequal gender (and other) relations. Instead of asking the question about the illegitimacy of the distinction under the dominant standard, the Court should ask the question about disadvantage, in its multiple forms determined by the intersectionality of discrimination, as assessed from the perspective of the disadvantaged... The way the principle was applied in the *Leyla Sahin* case – as a justification of restrictions on women's freedom – undermines rather than enhances gender equality.[842]

Many Arab countries are expressing reservations to Article 2 of the Convention on the Elimination of Discrimination against Women (CEDAW).[843] For example,

---

838 Leyla ªahin vs. Turkey [GC], no. 44774/98, § 107, ECHR 2005-XI, http://hudoc.echr.coe.int/sites/eng/pages/search.aspx?i=001-70956 (last visited Sept. 22, 2012).
839 *Id.*
840 Ivana Radacic, *Gender Equality Jurisprudence of the European Court of Human Rights*, 19 Eur. J. Int'l L. 841, 852 (2008).
841 *Id.*
842 *Id.* at 857.
843 Article 2 of the CEDAW provides: "States Parties condemn discrimination against women in all its forms, agree to pursue by all appropriate means and without delay a policy of eliminating discrimination against women and, to this end, undertake:

Bahrain voiced reservations to Article 2 "in order to ensure its implementation within the bounds of the provisions of the Islamic Shariah."[844] Also, Egypt has reservations to Article 16, "concerning the equality of men and women in all matters relating to marriage and family relations during the marriage and upon its dissolution...The provisions of the Sharia lay down that the husband shall pay bridal money to the wife and maintain her fully and shall also make a payment to her upon divorce..."[845]

In the past, Egypt had reservations to Article 9, paragraph 2 concerning granting equal rights to women and men with respect to the nationality of their children. Nowadays, Egypt has withdrawn its reservation to Article 9, paragraph 2 as the Egyptian law was amended[846] and children can have the nationality of their mothers.[847] Saudi Arabia also expressed reservations concerning Article 9, paragraph 2. Yet, the Committee of CEDAW requested from Saudi Arabia "to amend the Nationality Code so as to bring it in conformity with Article 9 of the Convention and to withdraw its reservation concerning article 9, paragraph 2."[848]

(a) To embody the principle of the equality of men and women in their national constitutions or other appropriate legislation if not yet incorporated therein and to ensure, through law and other appropriate means, the practical realization of this principle;
(b) To adopt appropriate legislative and other measures, including sanctions where appropriate, prohibiting all discrimination against women;
(c) To establish legal protection of the rights of women on an equal basis with men and to ensure through competent national tribunals and other public institutions the effective protection of women against any act of discrimination;
(d) To refrain from engaging in any act or practice of discrimination against women and to ensure that public authorities and institutions shall act in conformity with this obligation;
(e) To take all appropriate measures to eliminate discrimination against women by any person, organization or enterprise;
(f) To take all appropriate measures, including legislation, to modify or abolish existing laws, regulations, customs and practices which constitute discrimination against women;
(g) To repeal all national penal provisions which constitute discrimination against women."

844 United Nations Division for the Advancement of Women, *supra* note 134.
845 *Id.*
846 Law number 154 for the year 2004.
847 U.N. Committee on the Elimination of Discrimination Against Women, Responses to the List of Issues and Questions with Regard to the Consideration of the Combined 6th and 7th Periodic Reports: Egypt, Nov. 23, 2009, CEDAW/C/EGY/Q/7/Add.1, http://www.unhcr.org/cgi-bin/texis/vtx/refworld/rwmain?page=publisher&docid=4b792f41d&skip=0&publisher=CEDAW&querysi=egypt&searchin=title&display=10&sort=date (last visited Jun. 10, 2012).
848 U.N. Committee the Elimination of All Forms of Discrimination against Women, Concluding comments of the Committee on the Elimination of Discrimination against Women on Saudi Arabia, *supra* note 46.

Article 9 is not related to Sharia law, since Sharia law does not call for discrimination between men and women. Article 29 (2) of the Arab Charter on Human Rights provides, "States parties shall take such measures as they deem appropriate, in accordance with their domestic laws on nationality, to allow a child to acquire the mother's nationality, having due regard, in all cases, to the best interests of the child."[849] The Charter can be used as an effective instrument to encourage Saudi Arabia, which ratified the Charter, to amend the Nationality Code to grant women equal rights to men with respect to the nationality of their children.

In Arab countries, women are not granted equal rights to those of men with respect to the nationality of their children; but, this discrimination also exists in non-Muslim countries. For instance, a case was submitted to the Committee on the Elimination of Discrimination against Women against the United Kingdom.[850] The author of the communication claimed to be a victim as she was prevented from transmitting her British nationality to her son:

> Constance Ragan Salgado, a British citizen born on 24 November 1927 in Bournemouth, United Kingdom of Great Britain and Northern Ireland, currently residing in Bogotá, Colombia … claims to have been a victim of violations by the United Kingdom of Great Britain and Northern Ireland of articles 1, 2 (f) and 9, paragraph 2, of the Convention on the Elimination of All Forms of Discrimination against Women by having been prevented from transmitting her British nationality to her eldest son by descent.[851]

Although the communication concluded that the communication was inadmissible, it stated:

> The Committee considers that the alleged discrimination complained of originated at the time of the birth of the author's eldest son (16 September 1954), well before the Optional Protocol or even the Convention were adopted. In those days, British nationality law did not grant women — the author included — the right to pass on British citizenship to their children, whereas their husbands, had they been British, would have had such a right. The Committee notes that on 7 February 1979 there was a change in government policy, which allowed

---

849 ACHR, *supra* note 126, at art. 29 (2).
850 Constance Ragan Salgado vs. United Kingdom of Great Britain and Northern Ireland, Comm. No. 11/2006, http://www1.umn.edu/humanrts/cedaw/decisions/11-2006.html (last visited Feb. 6, 2013).
851 *Id.*

applications by British women to have their minor children born on or after 7 February 1961 registered as British citizens.[852]

This communication shows that women in different regions of the world face similar discrimination.

Iraq expressed reservations concerning Article 2 by stating , "The reservation to this last-mentioned article shall be without prejudice to the provisions of the Islamic Shariah according women rights equivalent to the rights of their spouses so as to ensure a just balance between them."[853] Also, Kuwait made reservations to Article 16 by stating, "The Government of the State of Kuwait declares that it does not consider itself bound by the provision contained in article 16 (f) inasmuch as it conflicts with the provisions of the Islamic Shariah, Islam being the official religion of the State."[854] Libya has made reservations to Article 16 by stating, "The implementation of paragraph 16 (c) and (d) of the Convention shall be without prejudice to any of the rights guaranteed to women by the Islamic Shariah."[855] Saudi Arabia made a general reservation stating that "[i]n case of contradiction between any term of the Convention and norms of Islamic law, the Kingdom of Saudi Arabia is not under obligation to observe the contradictory terms of the Convention."[856]

The Arab Charter uses the term 'positive discrimination' regarding the equality between men and women, which may seem to be vague and unclear from the Western point of view. In Article 3(3), the Arab Charter states:

> Men and women are equal in respect of human dignity, rights and obligations within the framework of the positive discrimination established in favour of women by the Islamic Shariah, other divine laws and by applicable laws and legal instruments. Accordingly, each State party pledges to take all the requisite measures to guarantee equal oppor-

---

852 *Id.*
853 Reservation made by Iraq on the CEDAW Convention, http://www.un.org/womenwatch/daw/cedaw/reservations-country.htm (last visited Feb. 6, 2013).
854 Reservation made by Kuwait on the CEDAW Convention, http://www.un.org/womenwatch/daw/cedaw/reservations-country.htm (last visited Feb. 6, 2013).
855 Reservation made by Libya on the CEDAW Convention, http://www.un.org/womenwatch/daw/cedaw/reservations-country.htm (last visited Feb. 6, 2013).
856 Reservation made by Saudi Arabia on the CEDAW Convention, http://www.un.org/womenwatch/daw/cedaw/reservations-country.htm (last visited Feb. 6, 2013).

tunities and effective equality between men and women in the enjoyment of all the rights set out in this Charter.[857]

Also, in Article 6 of the Cairo Declaration on Human Rights in Islam, it states, "Woman is equal to man in human dignity, and has rights to enjoy as well as duties to perform; she has her own civil entity and financial independence, and the right to retain her name and lineage [and] the husband is responsible for the support and welfare of the family."[858]

My aim is to explain the equality between men and women from the Islamic point of view in order to show that the Western concept of equality is not the only, nor the most ideal, approach. Many people may think that Sharia law abuses the rights of women and discriminates against their rights and freedoms in favor of those of men. Azizah al-Hibri explains, "secular feminists tend to blame Islam for laws in Muslim countries which are oppressive to women. Muslim women tend to defend Islam in light of their familiarity with the 'ideals of Islam'."[859] Here it is important to recognize that, in Islam, equality is recognized on the principle of equivalence but not formal equality.[860] Although males and females are equal, they may not be equivalent in their duties and roles, especially in family matters.[861] Sharia law gives very precise details with respect to family matters and relationships between men and women. This is because the family is considered to be the backbone of society. Instead of criticizing Sharia as a legal system, there should be emphasis on deepening understandings of the philosophy of Sharia law regarding women rights. It is more worthwhile to understand the objectives and purposes of Sharia law and then encourage the implementation of its norms and principles, as they actually favor women.

The Kingdom of Saudi Arabia stated the following in its combined initial and second periodic reports of states parties submitted to the Committee on the Elimination of Discrimination against Women:

> Islam's view of woman derives from her shared humanity with man: they are equal in respect of a basic humanity which is unaffected by division into sex. It views both woman and man in a social framework governed by relations of reciprocal rights, exemplified in practice by human morality, mutual understanding and love, not by confrontation

---

857 ACHR, *supra* note 126, at art. 3(3).
858 Cairo Declaration on Human Rights in Islam, *supra* note 423, art. 6.
859 AL-HIBRI, *supra* note 29, at 2.
860 BADERIN, *supra* note 138, at 60.
861 *See e.g.* LOIS LAMYA AL-FARUQI & ISMAIL RAJI' AL-FARUQI, THE CULTURAL ATLAS OF ISLAM 150 (1986).

and disruption. However, proceeding from a basis of realism, Islam holds that full likeness between men and women is contrary to the reality of their being, to which the facts attest (it is the woman who conceives, gives birth and nurses, not the man). Scientific studies attest to the physiological difference between them and the Convention acknowledges this in article 4, considering the protection of maternity to be a woman's right and not discriminatory. The Islamic Shariah respects these natural differences and accords woman a privileged position in order to achieve justice for her. For example, it charges the man with earning a living to provide for himself and his wife as compensation for the woman's role as conceiver, child bearer and mother.[862]

In the previous example, Saudi Arabia explained the idea of equivalence, but not formal equality. Women are given more care. Saudi Arabia used the words 'natural differences,' which refer to the *fitrah* that is explained in my theory. Since Islam is the religion of *fitrah*, therefore the objectives and purposes of Sharia law is in conformity with *fitrah*. Saudi Arabia referred again to the *fitrah* in the report when it explained how Sharia law sees the relationship between man and woman. It stated:

> Islam views the relationship between man and woman as a complementary one, with each forming the complement of the other. Our Prophet Muhammad said: "Women are the sisters of men." By this complementariness, the social structure is given a human face through a cooperative blending which proceeds from intimacy, amity and mutual respect, with each playing the part he/she can in the absence of the strife and self-containment which are incompatible with the nature of being. It is by means of the complementary relationship between man and woman that the family, which represents the basic building block of Muslim society and civilization as a whole, is built.[863]

The report referred to *fitrah* by using the words 'incompatible with the nature of being.' Many people think that Sharia law results in discrimination against women and an oppression of women's rights. The CEDAW commented on the report submitted by Saudi Arabia by saying that "[t]he Committee calls upon the State party to enact a comprehensive gender equality law and intensify its efforts

---

862 U.N. Committee on the Elimination of Discrimination against Women: Combined Initial and Second Periodic Reports of States Parties, Saudi Arabia, *supra* note 6.

863 *Id.*

to raise awareness about the Convention among the general public."[864] The Committee should understand the philosophy of Sharia law and encourage the implementation of its norms. There are many shared values between Sharia law and the international human rights standards. The reservations expressed by Arab countries that are based on Sharia law should be examined article by article from the perspective of Sharia law.

The CEDAW noted that Egypt expressed "reservations incompatible with the object and purpose of the Convention [that] were not permitted according to its article 28."[865] The CEDAW also stated that it "hoped for an early withdrawal of the reservations."[866] The Egyptian representative to the committee stated:

> Under Islamic law, the marriage was entered into by contract, and it was obligatory for the spouses to abide by its terms. The husband had the primary responsibility for all financial expenditures. That provision was even discriminatory against men, as women were allowed to spend their own money freely. Under Islamic law, a woman had the right to divorce her husband at any time if such a stipulation was made in the marriage contract. In addition, a woman could divorce her husband under certain conditions. Some of those conditions were that her husband had married a second wife, he was concealing a first marriage, he did not give his wife any money or that he was in a prison for a period of three years. With regard to the granting of the same rights and responsibilities during marriage and at its dissolution, Egypt had made a reservation on article 16 of the Convention.[867]

The reservations expressed by Egypt do not mean that there is discrimination against women, but rather that, as stated by the Arab Charter on Human Rights, there is "positive discrimination established in favour of women by the Islamic Shariah."[868] This can be shown clearly in the judicial cases regarding women's and family rights. For instance, the International Cooperation and Human Rights Division at the Egyptian Public Prosecution Office is doing great work with respect to the protection of women rights. Because of the work done in this

---

864 U.N. Committee the Elimination of All Forms of Discrimination against Women, Concluding comments of the Committee on the Elimination of Discrimination against Women on Saudi Arabia, *supra* note 46.

865 CEDAW Committee, Concluding Observations, Egypt, CEDAW A/39/45 (1984),34th and 39th Mtgs (Mar. 30 & Apr. 3, 1984), http://www.bayefsky.com/html/egypt_t4_cedaw.php (last visited March 10, 2012).

866 *Id.*

867 *Id.*

868 ACHR, *supra* note 126, at art. 3.

office, where I worked from 2006 until 2012, many children have been returned to their mothers. For example, an Egyptian father escaped with his two children (aged seven and eight years old) to Malaysia.[869] The mother of the children submitted a complaint to the Family Public Prosecution Office, claiming that she is the one who had custody of the children according to the Egyptian Family Law, which is based on Sharia law and gives the right of child custody to the mother. The Family Public Prosecution Office rendered a decision stating that the mother had the right to the custody of her children. The International Cooperation and Human Rights Division filed a judicial assistance request to the judicial authorities in Malaysia. Finally, the two children were returned to their mother.[870]

An example of a similar case is that of a father who escaped with his child to Kuwait. The wife submitted a complaint to the Family Public Prosecution Office, claiming that she has the right to custody of her son. In the light of Egyptian Family Law, which (as outlined above) is based on Sharia law, the Family Public Prosecution Office rendered a decision given the right to have custody of the child to the mother. The International Cooperation and Human Rights Division at the Public Prosecutor Office sent a judicial assistance request through diplomatic channels to the judicial authorities in Kuwait, requesting the safe return of the child to his mother. The judicial authorities in Kuwait accepted the decision for the safe return of the child to his mother. His mother traveled to Kuwait and happily brought her child back with her to Egypt.[871] The previous examples clearly show that, based on Sharia law, positive discrimination is established in favor of women. People should not rush to quick conclusions against Sharia law before they fully read, and understand, this law and its objectives and purposes.

Another example is the case of *Aziz vs. Aziz*,[872] wherein the Supreme Court of New York rendered a decision accepting to grant a divorced wife the postponed *mahr* (dowry) that is due after divorce. The Court rejected the ex-husband's argument that, as the *mahr* is a religious document, it should not be enforceable.[873] From the Western point of view, the *mahr* may appear discriminatory because the principle of "positive discrimination" is not applied in the West.

---

869 Judicial assistance request 56 for the year of 2010, September 27, 2010.
870 *Id.*
871 Judicial assistance request 63 for the year of 2008, December 12, 2008.
872 Aziz vs. Aziz, 127 Misc. 2d 1013; 488 N.Y.S.2d 123 (1985) Court: Supreme Court of New York, Special Term, Queens County (cited in KARAMAH.ORG, http://www.karamah.org/cases/aziz-v-aziz (last visited Mar. 9, 2012)).
873 *Id.*

Many people, and even many scholars, examine the literal meanings of the Quran and hadith and from that understand that Sharia law advances discrimination against women. For instance, the concluding comments of the Committee on the Elimination of Discrimination against Women on Morocco stated:

> The Committee calls upon the State party to ensure equality between women and men in marriage and upon its dissolution, by giving women equal rights in marriage and family relations. The Committee urges the State party to amend without delay all remaining discriminatory provisions including provisions relating to divorce, custody and legal guardianship of children and inheritance. The Committee further calls on the State party to enact legal provisions to ensure that, upon dissolution of marriage, women have equal rights to property acquired during marriage, in line with article 16 paragraph 1 (h) of the Convention and the Committee's general recommendation 21. The Committee encourages the State party to bring those amendments in consultation with women's organizations.[874]

Yet, the Quran and hadith are always in favor of equality and justice. The prima facie reading of the Quran gives the impression that women are at a lower level than men, such as when the Quran states, "Allah commands you as regards your children's (inheritance): to the male, a portion equal to that of two females."[875] In this way, the 'positive discrimination' mentioned in the Arab Charter is vague for many people and, as a result, they are doubtful of it. In Islam, women are not considered to be at a lower social level, but at a unique level. According to Sharia law, the husband has primary responsibility for all financial expenditures, as stipulated in the marriage contract. Even after the dissolution of marriage, the husband has to make a payment to his wife upon divorce. I will repeat the example I mentioned in the Chapter 2, because it is an important example. This example explains the reasons for giving a brother double the amount of the inherited money that is given to his sister. If a father left 150,000 Egyptian pounds to his son and daughter, upon his death the son would inherit 100,000 pounds and the daughter would inherit 50,000 pounds. Later, if the brother wanted to get married, he would have to pay 25,000 Egyptian pounds as the dowry for his wife. Therefore, the money that he inherited is reduced to 75,000 Egyptian pounds. However, when his sister gets married she will receive a dowry from her husband

---

874 U.N. Committee the Elimination of All Forms of Discrimination against Women, Concluding Comments of the Committee on the Elimination of Discrimination against Women: Morocco, U.N. Doc. CEDAW/C/SMOR/CO/4, at 9 (Apr. 8, 2008), http://www2.ohchr.org/english/bodies/cedaw/docs/CEDAW.C.MAR.CO.4_en.pdf (last visited March 10, 2012).

875 QURAN 4:11.

because, according to Sharia law, the husband is responsible for paying for everything. Therefore, the combined amount that she has received from her inheritance and from her dowry would be 75,000 Egyptian pounds. Therefore, she now has an equal amount to her brother; they both have 75,000 Egyptian pounds. But, her brother still has to buy or rent an apartment to live in with his wife. Also, he has to pay for the expenses related to food, clothes, and medication for his wife. He is still responsible for these expenses even if his wife is working and has her own salary. The husband cannot claim that he should stop paying for these expenses by stating that his wife's salary is greater than his salary. Therefore, his 75,000 Egyptian pounds will be further reduced. However, his sister will not have to pay anything because her husband is financially responsible for everything.[876]

This example clearly explains the purpose behind giving men double the inheritance than that of women. Even some Islamic scholars have said that Sharia law provides women with more privileges than men.[877] The Kingdom of Saudi Arabia explained the purposes and objectives of Sharia law with respect to inheritance in its report submitted to CEDAW. It stated:

> A son in relation to daughters and a brother in relation to sisters, the male receives double the share of the female. The reason for this is that a man will provide for his wife and children while his sister, by virtue of the fact that she is not burdened with outlay but will herself be provided for, will invest her share, thus making the outcome, after a short time, equal or even favourable to the woman.[878]

Another important example, that was also previously outlined, is regarding wives financial rights in Islam, which is demonstrated by the story of a woman who came to Prophet Mohammed complaining that her husband was niggard and scarce and did not provide her with enough money for herself and her child. She added that she takes money from him without telling him. The Prophet told her to take all the money that satisfies you and your child *belma'roof*.[879] When Islamic scholars interpreted the word *belma'roof*, they indicated that there is not one fixed amount that every wife should receive. This amount differs between social

---

[876] YOUSF ALKARADAWY, DERASAH FI FKH MAKASD ALSHARIA [Study in the Jurisprudence of the purposes of Sharia] 22-23 (3rd ed. 2008).

[877] *Id.* at 23 (citing the privileges of women on men regarding inheritance and expenses).

[878] U.N. Committee the Elimination of All Forms of Discrimination against Women, U.N. Committee on the Elimination of Discrimination against Women: Combined Initial and Second Periodic Reports of States Parties, Saudi Arabia, *supra* note 6.

[879] *Fatwa*, ISLAMWEB.NET, http://www.islamweb.net/fatwa/printfatwa.php?Id=125360&lang=A (last visited Mar. 19, 2012).

classes. For instance, if the wife is a princess married to a prince, the money will be greater than in the case of a rural woman married to a farmer.

It is better not to come to hasty conclusions about any legal system until we understand it deeply. Therefore, we must fully understand the logic of Sharia jurisprudence before judging whether or not it violates women's rights. Furthermore, this understanding must be accompanied by a deep analysis of the Quranic verses. The Quran explains, "Allah commands you as regards your children's (inheritance): to the male, a portion equal to that of two females."[880] The deep understanding of the verse shows that a brother takes only one-sixth more than a sister. For instance, let us take the example of a father, whose wealth amounts to 6,000 Egyptian pounds. If we imagine that, when he dies, the sister and her brother inherit equal portions, each one of them will inherit 3,000 pounds. However, according to Sharia law, the brother will inherit 4,000 pounds and the sister will inherit 2,000 pounds. Therefore, the sister will give her brother one sixth of the total amount that she inherited. In return, he has financial responsibilities towards her, as I previously explained.[881]

It should be noted that, according to Sharia law, women do not always inherit less than men.[882] We should understand the objectives and purposes of Sharia law regarding inheritance. The media portrayal of inheritance in Sharia law is that it is based on gender and the majority of Western scholars think this to be true. In other words, it is believed that females receive smaller portions than males. This important issue has to be clarified. The details about inheritance as they are stated in the Quran should be noted clearly. This issue is not left to the discretionary authority of the legislators; rather all of the possible scenarios for inheritance are outlined in the Quran. From the reading of the Quranic verses, it is very clear that the general rule of inheritance in Sharia is not merely based on the gender. Professor Mohamed Amara, an Egyptian religious scholar, stated that the philosophy of Sharia law and the objectives and purposes of Sharia law regarding inheritance is governed by the following three criteria:[883]

– First, the degree of familial relationship between the heir and the person who is receiving the inheritance. In other words, the closer the link between the heir and the person receiving the inheritance there is

---

880 QURAN 4:11.
881 RASHAD HASSAN KHALEEL, NAZAREYT AL-MOSAWAH FI AL-SHARIA AL-ISLAMEYAH [Theory of Equality in Islamic Sharia, part two] 192 (2007).
882 *Id.* at 93.
883 PROF. MOHAMED AMARA, SHOBOHAT WA IGABAT HAWL MAKANT AL-MAR'AA FI AL-ISLAM [Suspicions and Answers about the Status of Women in Islam] 96-97 (2001).

a greater share of the inheritance and vice versa. If we suppose that the people with closer connections to the heir are women, women will receive larger portions than men.

– Second, young generations receive a greater share than older generations, regardless of gender. If women are part of the young generations and men are in the older generation, the women will receive larger portions than men.

– Third, the financial burden, which is the only criteria that is based on gender. In other words, men are given larger portions than women because of the financial burden imposed on men. The financial burden, according to Sharia law, is the responsibility of men as I previously explained.[884]

These three criteria govern the rule of inheritance. Therefore, if a woman is a closer relative to the heir, the woman will inherit a greater share than the man. On the other hand, if there were both men and women who were equally close to the heir and were of the same generation, the men would inherit more than the women, because men have greater financial responsibilities than their female relatives.[885] Professor Mohamed Amara added that, according to Sharia law, there are only four cases in which women inherit half of the portion of men and there are many scenarios in which women inherit an equal portion. Also, there are ten or more scenarios in which women inherit more than men. Furthermore, there are scenarios in which women inherit whereas men do not inherit anything.[886]

In conclusion, there are thirty scenarios in which women either inherit equal portions to, or more than, men or inherit money when men do not. There are only four scenarios in which women inherit half of the portions of men.[887] For instance, the Quran explains, "For parents, a sixth share of inheritance to each if the deceased left children."[888] In this example, a wife receives a portion equal to her husband's when they inherit the estate of their son. Furthermore, if a brother dies and he has no living parents or children, his brother and sister receive equal portions of inheritance. The Quran states, "If the man or woman whose inheritance is in question has left neither ascendants nor descendants, but has left a brother

---

884 *Id.*
885 *Id.* at 96-97.
886 *Id.* at 98.
887 *Id.* at 98.
888 QURAN 4:11.

or a sister, each one of the two gets a sixth."[889] As another example, let us look at the scenario of what happens if a mother dies who has a brother and sister in addition to a husband and one daughter. The husband will only receive 25% percent of his wife's wealth. On the other hand, the daughter will receive 50% of her mother's wealth. The sister and the brother of the mother will divide 25% of the wealth equally. In this example, the daughter (who is female) receives more than her father and the mother's brother (who is male). In addition, the sister (who is female) will receive an equal portion to her brother (who is a male).[890]

The Supreme Constitutional Court of Egypt rendered many decisions in favor of women that are in compliance with women's rights in Islam. An example is a case concerning the financial obligations of the father to pay for guardianship.[891] In 1989, a court decided that a father had to make payments to a mother for her guardianship of their infant child dating back to 1973 and continuing forward until the date at which the mother no longer was the guardian of their child. The ruling of the court shows clearly that the objectives and purposes of Sharia law are in favor of women's rights. International conventions that combat crime result in the existence of a long statute of limitations or provide a suspension of the statute of limitations when the alleged offender has evaded the administration of justice.[892] Sharia law is in compliance with international conventions, as it safeguards the existence of a long statute of limitations in order to protect the financial rights of wife. In this case, the father claimed that subsection 4 of Article 18 of the Personal Status Law was unconstitutional with respect to its stipulation that the father was obliged to pay for guardianship beginning at the date that he stopped doing so. He asserted this violated Article 2 because of the Hanafi religious doctrine.[893]

The Hanafi doctrine stated that payment for the upbringing of children was only due from the date of the court's ruling. The court stated that the long existence

---

889 *Id.* at 4:12.
890 Telephone interview with Shekh Fekry Hassan Ismail, the former under Minster of Awqaf in the Ministry of endowments, which is in charge of religious endowments (Nov. 19, 2012).
891 Case No. 29, Judicial Year 11, 26th Mar. 1994.
892 For example, Article 29 of the United Nations Convention against Corruption states, "Each State Party shall, where appropriate, establish under its domestic law a long statute of limitations period in which to commence proceedings for any offence established in accordance with this Convention and establish a longer statute of limitations period or provide for the suspension of the statute of limitations where the alleged offender has evaded the administration of justice"; *see* U.N. Office on Drugs and Crime, United Nations Convention against Corruption (2004), http://www.unodc.org/documents/treaties/UNCAC/Publications/Convention/08-50026_E.pdf (last visited Mar. 12, 2012).
893 Hanafi religious doctrine is the official doctrine that is followed in Egypt.

of one of these rules does not mean that it could not be substituted by a new rule provided that the new rule was in the best interest of the society and not contrary to the main purposes and norms of the Sharia. The Court added that the view of the Hanafi was that the child had been otherwise provided for during this period and therefore no longer required the costs claimed. The court asserted that this view was neither consistent with what actually occurred in practice nor was in the best interests of the family. Furthermore, the court added that the father was the only person responsible for the costs of guardianship of his child in accordance with the words of the Prophet: "it is a great sin for the person to abandon whom he feeds."[894] The court also clarified that the child's rights do not lapse until full payment has been made. The payment was necessary for both the mother and the child. The court clarified that the Quran states, "neither shall a mother be made to suffer harm on account of her child, nor a father on account of his child."[895]

The legislature should do whatever is required to ensure that the mother receives the payments over the length of time that complies with the Sharia law, which states that the responsibility is on the man. As according to God's pronouncement: "The duty of feeding and clothing nursing mothers in a seemly manner is upon the father of the child."[896] The delay of the father in paying the money to his children was an injustice and caused them harm. This delay in time should not, in and of itself, nor without taking any other factor into consideration, lead to forfeiture of the right to receive guardianship costs. Rights should only be forfeited by their holders if they desire to relinquish them. In the end, the court ruled that the amendment of Article 18 (4) of the Law No 25 of 1929 by law No 100 of 1985 was constitutional and dismissed the case.

These examples clarify the attitude of Islam toward women and that the role and duty of spouses are not equal. A man has more responsibilities to his wife and children than they do towards him. From the Islamic point of view, this is not considered discrimination against men; it is a form of respect toward women. Another important example is that of the right of a married woman to ask for divorce in the event of her husband marrying another woman. This right was granted under Article 11 of the Family Law No 29 of 1929. It legally requires a man who wants to marry to declare his status on the official marriage certificate. If the man is already married, it places him under a legal obligation to notify his first wife of his new marriage. Within a period not exceeding one year from the date

---

894 Case No. 29, Judicial Year 11, 26th Mar. 1994.
895 QURAN 2:233.
896 *Id.*

of notification, the first wife has the right to ask her husband for a divorce providing that she can prove that she has been harmed materially or morally as a result of the new marriage. If both parties fail to reconcile and he refuses to divorce her, then a divorce will be granted by a judge.

A case regarding this issue was presented to the Supreme Constitutional Court.[897] The plaintiff husband challenged the constitutionality of Article 11, claiming that it contradicts Article 2 of the Constitution, which states that the principles of Islamic Sharia law are the principal source of the legislation and the right to have more than one wife is granted by Islamic Sharia law. The Supreme Constitutional Court ruled that the plaintiff's claim had no basis in Islam. According to Sharia law, the right of a husband to have more than one wife is granted in respect to the needs of each individual. The exercise of that right is conditional upon a guarantee of fair and equal treatment for all wives. A woman's right to ask for a divorce due to her husband getting married to another woman is not based merely upon dislike of her husband, but upon objective grounds involving her suffering real harm, either materially or morally. This harm leads to the impossibility of the maintenance of a decent life between them. The wife has the burden of proving this harm. In cases where the two parties are unable to reconcile, the judge will render a decision permitting the wife to divorce her husband.

Finally, the Court concluded that a woman's right to seek divorce as a result of the harm that she is suffering from a new marriage of her husband is accepted by Sharia law standards. Therefore, the legislation in question was neither in violation of Sharia law or the Constitution. On the other hand, Article 5 of Protocol 7 to the European Convention on Human Rights states: "Spouses shall enjoy equality of rights and responsibilities of a private law character between them, and in their children, as to marriage, during marriage and in the event of dissolution. This article shall not prevent States from taking such measures as are necessary in the interest of children."[898] This article clearly shows that there is a difference between the European Charter and the Arab Charter, the latter of which states, "Men and women are equal in respect of human dignity, rights and obligations within the framework of the positive discrimination established in favour of women by the Islamic Shariah."[899] The Prophet of Islam (Mohammed) stressed the importance of respecting the rights of women. In his last public speech, He said,

> "O People it is true that you have certain rights with regard to your women, but they also have rights over you. Remember that you have

---

897 Case No 35, Judicial Year 9, 15 August 1994.
898 ECHR, *supra* note 497, at art. 5 of Protocol 7.
899 ACHR, *supra* note 126, at art. 3 (3).

taken them as your wives only under Allah's trust and with His permission. If they abide by your right then to them belongs the right to be fed and clothed in kindness. Do treat your women well and be kind to them for they are your partners and committed helpers."[900]

Many people would think that if it is true that Islam does not tolerate discrimination against women, why are some Muslim women in the Arab world actually seen to be discriminated against and abused? This is due to factors such as patriarchal conservatism, illiteracy, and poverty.[901] For example, the concluding comments of the Committee on the Elimination of Discrimination against Women on Morocco focused on poverty and education. It stated that

> [the] Committee recommends that the State party implement measures to ensure access to girls and women to all levels of education. Such measures could include canteens, boarding facilities, proper sanitation, water and electricity, which have a direct impact on the realization of their right to education, especially in rural areas. The Committee also recommends the State party to adopt temporary special measures in accordance with article 4, paragraph 1, of the Convention and the Committee's general recommendation 25, to ensure the retention of girls in school. The Committee calls on the State party to continue to strengthen its efforts to improve the literacy level of girls and women through the adoption of comprehensive programs of formal and non-formal education, adult education and training and increase training and employment of teachers, the development of gender-sensitive educational materials and the monitoring and evaluation of progress achieved towards time-bound targets. The Committee recommends that special attention be given to girls who are domestic workers, in order to ensure that they are not employed below the age of 15, allowing them to continue their education, at least until that age. The Committee urges the State party to raise general awareness of the importance of education as a human right and as a basis for the empowerment of women, and to take steps to overcome traditional attitudes that perpetuate discrimination.[902]

---

900 Farewell Sermon, http://en.wikipedia.org/wiki/Farewell_Sermon (last visited May 2, 2014).
901 BADERIN, *supra* note 138, at 61.
902 U.N. Committee the Elimination of All Forms of Discrimination against Women, Concluding Comments: Morocco, *supra* note 874.

Another important reason for this is the aggressive interpretation of Sharia law. These interpretations lead to this discrimination against women.

The Arab Charter on Human Rights can be used as an effective instrument to urge, encourage, and request from governments to work on the eradication of illiteracy. Article 41 of the Arab Charter provides:

> 1. The eradication of illiteracy is a binding obligation upon the State and everyone has the right to education.
> 2. The States parties shall guarantee their citizens free education at least throughout the primary and basic levels. All forms and levels of primary education shall be compulsory and accessible to all without discrimination of any kind.
> 3. The States parties shall take appropriate measures in all domains to ensure partnership between men and women with a view to achieving national development goals.
> 4. The States parties shall guarantee to provide education directed to the full development of the human person and to strengthening respect for human rights and fundamental freedoms.
> 5. The States parties shall endeavour to incorporate the principles of human rights and fundamental freedoms into formal and informal education curricula and educational and training programmes.
> 6. The States parties shall guarantee the establishment of the mechanisms necessary to provide ongoing education for every citizen and shall develop national plans for adult education.[903]

The Arab Charter could play a vital role not only in the eradication of illiteracy, but also in the development and increased awareness of human rights in the member countries of the Arab League. Furthermore, the effective and precise implementation of Article 41 can build a new strong culture and awareness of human rights in the Middle East. The eradication of illiteracy is an effective and rapid way to increase awareness on human rights issues. In addition, the eradication of illiteracy will lead to knowledge that will limit the aggressive interpretation of Sharia law. This will happen because knowledge is increased through reading and understanding the objectives and purposes of Sharia law.

The principle of equality between men and women held by the Sharia law point of view clearly shows that there is no discrimination between men and women in Islam. Women are given their full rights and respect. The interpretation of Sharia law is compatible with international human rights norms. The moderate

---

903   ACHR, *supra* note 126, at art. 41.

Islamic human rights theory is compatible with international human rights law with respect to the basic fundamentals of Islamic law.

The conclusion is that it is better not to come to rapid conclusions regarding the different laws, cultures, and traditions that are adhered to by other nations, unless we deeply understand the reasons for their existence. For instance, Egypt made a reservation to Article 16 (which is focused on equality between men and women in all matters relating to marriage and family matters during the marriage and after its dissolution) and Article 2 (which is about equality between men and women in general) of the Convention on the Elimination of All Forms of Discrimination against Women (CEDAW).[904] Regarding its reservations to Article 16, the Egyptian government said:

> Reservation to the text of article 16 concerning the equality of men and women in all matters relating to marriage and family relations during the marriage and upon its dissolution, without prejudice to the Islamic Sharia provisions whereby women are accorded rights equivalent to those of their spouses so as to ensure a just balance between them. This is out of respect for the sacrosanct nature of the firm religious beliefs which govern marital relations in Egypt and which may not be called in question and in view of the fact that one of the most important bases of these relations is an equivalency of rights and duties so as to ensure complementarity which guarantees true equality between the spouses, not a quasi-equality that renders the marriage a burden on the wife. The provisions of the Sharia lay down that the husband shall pay bridal money to the wife and maintain her fully and shall also make a payment to her upon divorce, whereas the wife retains full rights over her property and is not obliged to spend anything on her keep. The Sharia therefore restricts the wife's rights to divorce by making it contingent on a judge's ruling, whereas no such restriction is laid down in the case of the husband.[905]

The prima facie reading of the previous reservation made by Egypt gives the impression that Sharia law is against women's rights and discriminates against them. However, in light of what I explained, it is easy to understand the object and purpose behind this reservation.

---

904 The reservation that Egypt made on the CEDAW convention: http://www.un.org/womenwatch/daw/cedaw/reservations-country.htm (last visited Aug. 9, 2013).

905 Id.

On the other hand, not every reservation is made because of incompatibility with Sharia law. For instance, Egypt had made before a reservation to Article 9, paragraph 2, wherein it stated:

> Reservation to the text of article 9, paragraph 2, concerning the granting to women of equal rights with men with respect to the nationality of their children, without prejudice to the acquisition by a child born of a marriage of the nationality of his father. This is in order to prevent a child's acquisition of two nationalities, since this may be prejudicial to his future. It is clear that the child's acquisition of his father's nationality is the procedure most suitable for the child and that this does not infringe upon the principle of equality between men and women, since it is customary for a woman to agree, upon marrying an alien, that her children shall be of the father's nationality.[906]

This reservation made by Egypt on Article 9, paragraph 2 is not related to Sharia law. Currently, this law has been amended and children have the nationality of their mothers. As previously mentioned with respect to my proposed theory, we should examine the law itself to fully understand its objectives and purposes and whether it reflects any religious beliefs. It should be noted that Muslim women are not looking forward to be "'Super moms' who are eternally exhausted and turned female sexuality into a commodity."[907] Similarly,

> it is important to keep in mind that most Muslim women tend to be highly religious and would not want to act in contradiction to their faith…The majority of Muslim women who are attached to their religion will not be liberated through the use of a secular approach imposed from the outside by international bodies or from above by undemocratic governments. The only way to resolve the conflicts of these women and remove their fear of pursuing rich and fruitful lives is to build a solid Muslim feminist jurisprudential basis which clearly shows that Islam not only does not deprive them of their rights, but in fact demands these rights for them.[908]

Also,

> Women's rights in Islam must be preserved by the world community and not simply brushed aside because of ignorance concerning how Islam, as a religion, treats women. Islam has been presented to the West

---

906 *Id.*
907 AL-HIBRI, *supra* note 29, at 4.
908 *Id.* at 3.

in a negative fashion, both by governments in the Muslim world that deny fundamental rights to women, as well as by the Western press, which is quick to pin the blame on the religion itself rather than on the misogynists who use it as a pretext for persecution.[909]

2. Polygamy

Before explaining polygamy according to Sharia law, it is important to examine some of the Western points of views regarding polygamy. It is important to know whether or not polygamy is considered a problem with respect to the protection of human rights. For instance, the Canadian Department of Justice said that polygamy in the sense of one man being married to several women (polygyny) is considered to be a violation of women's human rights. It states:

> International human rights standards for the elimination of all forms of discrimination against women are essential to Canada's foreign and domestic policy as well as its jurisprudence. The Canadian Department of Foreign Affairs has publicly noted that, "the human rights of women remain a central foreign policy priority for Canada, both in bilateral discussions and in multilateral fora. In this sense, when Canada fails to address the domestic human rights violations of women through practices such as polygyny, its foreign policy legitimacy is undermined."[910]

It also states:

> The right of women and children to be free from the various forms of discrimination that polygyny perpetuates should be given a similar level of protection under Canada's Charter equality and security of the person provisions that it would receive under the Women's and Children's Conventions… an argument that the prohibition, or at the very least growing restriction, of polygyny is part of international customary law as evidenced by state practice and opinio juris would not require a further transformation analysis to have effect in Canadian law.[911]

Furthermore, the Canadian department of Justice provides, "Given that the HRC has expressly stated that polygamy violates the equality of men and women

---

909 Sayeht & Morse, *supra* note 158, at 333.
910 *Polygyny and Canada's Obligations under International Human Rights Law*, JUSTICE.GC.CA, http://www.justice.gc.ca/eng/dept-min/pub/poly/chap7.html (last visited Mar. 10, 2012).
911 *Id.*

guaranteed in the Political Covenant, legally legitimizing polygamous unions within Canada could be challenged by individual petitions."[912]

The General Comment No. 28 on Article 3 (Equality of rights between men and women) of the International Covenant on Civil and Political Rights provides that "[i]t should also be noted that equality of treatment with regard to the right to marry implies that polygamy is incompatible with this principle. Polygamy violates the dignity of women. It is an inadmissible discrimination against women. Consequently, it should be definitely abolished wherever it continues to exist."[913] Also, in 2011, the report of the working group on the Universal Periodic Review of the Human Rights Council on Libya recommended that Libya should "ensure equality, under the law and in practice, of women, and amend all discriminatory legal provisions concerning marriage (including polygamy)."[914]

Sharia law permits polygamy in that men can marry up to four wives at the same time. However, it is forbidden in Islam for women to be married to more than one husband at a time. After she has divorced or her husband dies, a wife can marry another man if she so desires. The Quran explains,

> "And if you fear that you shall not be able to deal justly with the orphan-girls then marry (other) women of your choice, two or three, or four; but if you fear that you shall not be able to deal justly (with them), then only one or (the slaves) that your right hands possess. That is nearer to prevent you from doing injustice."[915]

It is important to explain that, first of all, Islam did not create polygamy. Polygamy was rampant before Islam; any man could marry as many women as he wanted. Sharia law used the principle of gradualism regarding polygamy, in that it regulated and controlled polygamy such that men could only have up to four wives. The Prophet of Islam requested that after his companions converted to Islam they only have four wives and divorce any others.[916] It should be noted that polygamy

---

912 Id.
913 U.N. International Covenant on Human Rights, General Comment No. 28: Equality of Rights Between Men and Women, *supra* note 836.
914 U.N. Human Rights Council, Rep. of the Working Group on the Universal Periodic Review on Libya,; GAOR, 16th Sess.(2011), http://www2.ohchr.org/english/bodies/hrcouncil/docs/16session/A-HRC-16-15.pdf (last visited Mar. 10, 2012).
915 QURAN 4:3.
916 *Women and Her Rights [sic]*, SHIAMASJID.COM, http://www.shiamasjid.com/books/WomenAndHerRights/page-0031.htm (last visited Mar. 4, 2012); *see also Al-rad 3ala shobhat ta'adod Al-zawgat* [Reply to Suspicion of Polygamy], YOUTUBE.COM, http://www.youtube.com/watch?v=8Ej6ZJAomSE (last visited Mar. 4, 2012).

is allowed only on three conditions.[917] First, the husband must be able to ensure the application of justice and equality in the treatment of all of his wives.[918] The Quran explains that "but if you fear that you shall not be able to deal justly (with them), then only one."[919] Therefore, it is forbidden to marry more than one wife if the husband is not certain that he will apply justice to all of his wives. Justice means equality in everything, including expenses. For instance, if he buys a villa or a car for one wife then he must buy another one for his second wife, etc. In addition, the days of the week should be divided equally between his wives. In another words, if he is married to two wives, he should stay at the home of the first wife half of the week and the second wife the other half of the week, turn by turn. In short, the husband is required to treat his wives equally. However, he is not required to provide the same amount of love to all of his wives, since he has no control over his heart. The Quran mentions that there will be never be equality in love even if the husband tries to do so.[920] The Quran provides,

> "You will never be able to do perfect justice between wives even if it is your ardent desire, so do not incline too much to one of them (by giving her more of your time and provision) so as to leave the other hanging (i.e. neither divorced nor married). And if you do justice, and do all that is right and fear Allah by keeping away from all that is wrong, then Allah is Ever Oft-Forgiving, Most Merciful."[921]

The second condition of polygamy is that the husband must be able to afford to spend money on all of his wives.[922] The Quran states, "A husband has the right of having more than one wife, provided his financial condition allows him to do so."[923] With respect to people who cannot afford to get married, the Quran states, "And let those who find not the financial means for marriage keep themselves chaste, until Allah enriches them of His Bounty... "[924] The third condition is the "physical and sexual potentialities."[925] They are another pre-requisite.

---

917 *Hokm Ta'adod Al-zawgat wa Al-Hekmah Menhoo* [The Rule of Polygamy and the Wisdom Behind it], ISLAMQA.INFO, http://islamqa.info/ar/ref/14022 (last visited Mar. 4, 2012).

918 *Women and Her Rights*, supra note 916; *see also* Al mawso'aa Al-shamlah (comprehensive encyclopedia), Islamport.com, http://islamport.com/w/fqh/Web/5127/17.htm (last visited Aug. 14, 2013).

919 QURAN 4:3.

920 *Hokm Ta'adod Al-zawgat wa Al-Hekmah Menhoo*, supra note 917.

921 QURAN 4:129.

922 *Hokm Ta'adod Al-zawgat wa Al-Hekmah Menhoo*, supra note 917.

923 *Women and Her Rights*, supra note 916.

924 QURAN 24:33.

925 *Women and Her Rights*, supra note 916.

Professor Saad Al-Din Helaly said that polygamy is permissible according to Sharia law. In other words, it is not encouraged or discouraged. Every man has the right to choose between marrying one wife or up to four wives. However, if a man wants to marry more than one woman, he must comply with the conditions stated by Sharia law.[926] Sheikh Khaled Al-Gendy said that governments cannot interfere by either prohibiting or forcing men to marry more than one wife. Polygamy depends on each man; sometimes polygamy can be prohibited, hated, permitted, highly recommended, and obligatory. Each individual could feel anyone of these things with respect to polygamy. Sheikh Khaled explained his point of view by giving the following examples. Polygamy is prohibited if a man is entirely certain that he will not apply justice if he marries more than one wife. Polygamy is obligatory in cases where the wife of a married man gets sick to the point to which she cannot have sex with him. In this example, if the husband is entirely certain that he will have illegal sexual relations with other women to fulfill his sexual desires, it is obligatory for him to marry a second wife instead of having illegal sexual relations. As third example, polygamy is recommended if the husband is afraid that he may have illegal sexual relations with other women. On the other hand, polygamy is detestable if the husband feels that if he gets married to another woman he may not be able to apply justice to his wives. According to Sheikh Khaled, governments should not interfere with respect to polygamy. Every man knows himself and is the best one to choose what he wants. He added that polygamy does not foster sexually transmitted diseases. According to him, sexually transmitted diseases happen if a woman has sexual relations with more than one man. However, if a man marries more than one wife, there will usually be no sexually transmitted diseases.[927]

The Academic Advisor of the Egyptian Mufti said that Islamic scholars have different opinions regarding polygamy. Some of them indicate that marrying one wife is the exception. Other Islamic scholars said that marrying more than one wife is the exception. In other words, some said that marriages to one wife are predominant. Others state that marriages to more than one wife are predominant and the exception are marriages to one wife. He added that governments should not interfere by forcing men to marry more than one wife or prohibiting polygamy. He said that, for example, if the government prohibited polygamy, some men would seek out illegal sexual relations to fulfill their sexual desire.[928]

---

926 A telephone interview with Prof. Saad Al-Din Helaly, professor of Comparative Islamic Jurisprudence at Al-Azhar University (Aug. 20, 2012).
927 A telephone interview with Sheikh Khaled Al-Gendy (Aug. 29, 2012).
928 An interview with Prof. Magdy Ashore, the Academic advisor of the Egyptian Mufti (Sep. 23, 2012).

In light of my proposed theory, polygamy cannot be prohibited completely in the Arab world even if it faces some criticism from Western scholars. The Eastern people cannot force the Western people to prohibit prostitution. Therefore, Western people cannot force Eastern people to prohibit polygamy and legalize prostitution. There should be a constructive dialogue between the East and the West. Practically speaking, polygamy is very rare in comparison to the cases of marriage to one wife. There are several reasons for this. One of the main reasons is the husband's financial obligations. Due to the global economic situation, it is very difficult for the average husband to be financially responsible for two wives in the way that husbands are financially obligated in accordance with Sharia law. In addition, the husband must equally apply justice to all of his wives, which is not easy to accomplish.

Some scholars who are advocates for polygamy explain, "The fact is that polygamy is vehemently opposed by male-dominated Western society because it would force men to fidelity. It would encourage them to take socio-economic responsibility for the fulfillment of their polygynous desires and provide protection for the weaker members of society, women and children from mental and physical abuse."[929] Sharia law strikes a balance between men, women, and society. On the other hand, "the monogamous marriage system, clearly, does not take into consideration the real needs of human society."[930] Sharia law is a living instrument that is not only relevant for one era or one century. For instance, Sharia law protects the society from prostitution. In other words, if Sharia law prohibited polygamy, the door of prostitution would be opened. Polygamy is prohibited in the West, but prostitution and illegal sexual relations are widespread. In some Western countries polygamy is legal and prostitutes have annual medical supervision in order to make sure that they do not have sexually transmitted diseases, since prostitutes have sexual relations with different men. Sharia law protects women. Sharia prohibits illegal sexual relations in order to encourage men who want to fulfill their sexual desires to get married. Therefore, women get married and start having a family and babies. Sharia law believes that we cannot have a strong united country unless we have strong united families. Therefore, prohibiting illegal sexual relations and encouraging marriage will build a strong healthy environment and children will grow up in a united family. "Every child has a natural desire to know its parents."[931] The child should know his father by the fact that he married his mother not by checking the DNA of the child and

---

929   *Islam's Women Jewels of Islam*, ISLAMSWOMEN.COM, http://www.islamswomen.com/marriage/monogamy_and_polygamy.php (last visited Nov. 19, 2012).
930   *Id.*
931   *Id.*

the DNA of all the men with whom his mother had sexual relations in order to determine the father of her baby.

A strong society and community cannot be established without a strong family. A family cannot be established strong and rooted without a legal frame of marriage. Women should have their full rights to fulfill their psychological rights and sexual desire in the legal frame of marriage.

> Women as a whole live longer than men; not to mention the large numbers of men who die daily in the various wars around the world. Thus, although the ratio may vary from country to country the results are still the same; women outnumber men. This apparent imbalance has been further aggravated by the fact that homosexuality appears to be more frequent among men than among women. Hence there are more females competing for a diminishing number of males. Consequently, there will always remain a large segment of women unable to fulfill their sexual and psychological needs through legitimate means in monogamous societies. Their presence in an increasingly permissive society also contributes to the break down of Western family structure. A strong family structure is an absolute requirement for a strong and a healthy society. And, the only way that the family can remain strong and responsive to the needs of its male and female members is through the Islamic form of marriage of which polygamy is a part.[932]

The Human Rights Committee's review of Uganda stated that "[r]educing a woman to a state of polygamy was inadmissible; it was an attack on the dignity of women and offended all human individuals."[933] What really reduces and diminishes a woman's dignity are illegal sexual relations. It is unjust for a wife to have an unfaithful husband who has sexual relations with others. It is better for a wife that her husband marries a second woman, rather than he being unfaithful to her through having illegal sexual relations with another woman. It is also better for the woman involved in the sexual relations to be a second wife receiving respect and dignity, rather than to be engaging in illegal relations. "Females have a

---

932 *Id*; see also *Al mawso'aa Al-shamlah* (comprehensive encyclopedia), Islamport.com, http://islamport.com/w/fqh/Web/5127/23.htm (last visited Aug. 14, 2013).

933 Press Release, Human Rights Committee, Polygamy, Female Genital Mutilation Unacceptable, Says Chairman As Human Rights Committee Concludes Review Of Uganda's Report, U.N. Press Release HR/CT/651, http://www.un.org/News/Press/docs/2004/hrct651.doc.htm (last visited Mar. 10, 2012).

vested interest in institutional polygamy because of the obvious socio-economic protection it provides."[934]

People may question that if both men and women "have equal rights, either both of them should be allowed to practice polygamy or neither of them. It is a pure and simple discrimination to allow man to have several wives and not to allow woman to have several husbands. To allow man to have up to four wives means that the value of a woman is only one-fourth that of man."[935] It is important to know that, in nearly all countries, there is no regular medical supervision regarding sexually transmitted diseases for married women. Such medical supervision exists only for prostitutes. For instance, in countries where prostitution is legal, prostitutes are registered and there is regular medical supervision of prostitutes in order to prevent the transmission of sexually transmitted diseases to the men with whom the prostitutes are having sexual relations. However, there is no regular medical supervision of men that have sexual relations with the prostitutes. The reason for this is because sexually transmitted diseases can happen to women when they are having sexual relations with more than one man. It is written in several medical reports that "cancer of the uterine cervix has its highest incidence in prostitutes, and its lowest in nuns."[936] An Egyptian doctor conducted a medical study on this issue. He concluded that if a woman got pregnant after having sexual relationships with two different partners, the embryo can carry a part of the genetic traits of the both the first and the second partner.[937]

---

934 *Islam's Women Jewels of Islam, supra* note 929.
935 *Women and Her Rights, supra* note 916.
936 Ira Pilgrim, *Everything You Want to Know About Sex and Cancer*, http://irapilgrim.mcn.org/toc14.html (last visited Aug. 11, 2013). "Bacterial vaginosis (BV) is the name of a condition in women where the normal balance of bacteria in the vagina is disrupted and replaced by an overgrowth of certain bacteria. The cause of BV is not fully understood. BV is associated with an imbalance in the bacteria that are normally found in a woman's vagina. The vagina normally contains mostly "good" bacteria, and fewer "harmful" bacteria. BV develops when there is an increase in harmful bacteria. Any woman can get BV. However, some activities or behaviors can upset the normal balance of bacteria in the vagina and put women at increased risk including: i) Having a new sex partner or multiple sex partners, ii) Douching. There are some serious risks from BV including: Having BV can increase a woman's susceptibility to HIV infection if she is exposed to the HIV virus. Having BV increases the chances that an HIV-infected woman can pass HIV to her sex partner. Having BV while pregnant may put a woman at increased risk for some complications of pregnancy, such as preterm delivery. BV can increase a woman's susceptibility to other STIs, such as herpes simplex virus (HSV), chlamydia and gonorrhea." Be aware of Sexually Transmitted Infections, even during Carnival, http://www.sintmaartengov.org/Health/Pages/Be-aware-of-Sexually-Transmitted-Infections,-even-during-Carnival.aspx (last visited Aug. 11, 2013).
937 Dr. Gamal Ibrahim, http://digital.ahram.org.eg/articles.aspx?Serial=605599&eid=986 (last

Sheikh Mohammed Metwally Shaarawy, who is a famous and popular Islamic scholar in Egypt and the Middle East, said that in countries that have legalized prostitution, female prostitutes have two medical examinations per week. During his visits to these countries, he asked some people that are raised in these cultures whether they also applied this medical examinations to married women. They were astonished by his question and replied no. He asked them: did you ever ask yourselves why you do not apply the same medical examination to married women? They replied by saying that there was no need to discuss this issue. He said that if they found there was a need to discuss this issue they would resolve it by conducting medical examinations on all married women. He said that reason that this medical examination is conducted on prostitutes and not on married women is because sexually transmitted diseases occur when there are sperms of different men in one woman. However, sexually transmitted diseases do not occur if the sperm of one man is inside a woman. He said that we did not reach this conclusion by medical experiments but because God issued the command by prohibiting polygamy for women, not for men. Therefore, we did not suffer from the pain of these kinds of diseases because God gave us the prescription. Furthermore, he added that we did not know the reason and the logic of prohibiting polygamy for women and not for men. However, after we discussed this issue thoroughly, we understood the wisdom behind it. Finally, he explained that for each issue for which Islam created a rule with respect to which our minds do not understand the underlying reasons and logic, God will bring our minds to know the reasons in order to increase our faith and believe in God. The Quran says, "We will show them Our Signs in the universe, and in their own selves, until it becomes manifest to them that this [the Qur'an] is the truth…"[938] I am wondering about the general recommendations that are made by the Committee on the Elimination of Discrimination against Women, which stated that "[h]armful traditional practices, such as… polygamy …may also expose girls and women to the risk of contracting HIV/AIDS and other sexually transmitted diseases."[939] I have never heard of a case wherein a wife became infected by

---

visited Aug. 11, 2013); *see also* Dr. Zaglol Al-Nagar, http://www.youtube.com/watch?v=UW7RBQPyFLs (last visited Aug. 11, 2013); A telephone interview with Sheikh/ Khaled Al-Gendy (Aug. 29, 2012); *see also* Sheikh/Mohammed Metwally Shaarawy, YOUTUBE.COM, http://www.youtube.com/watch?v=CtaZWKLXvZ8 (last visited Nov. 19, 2012).

938 QURAN 41:53. Sheikh Mohammed Metwally Shaarawy, *supra* note 937.

939 United Nations Division for the Advancement of Women, Department of Economic and Social Affairs, Convention on the Elimination of All Forms of Discrimination against Women, General recommendations made by the Committee on the Elimination of Discrimination against Women, General Recommendation No. 24 (20th session, 1999), http://www.un.org/womenwatch/daw/cedaw/recommendations/recomm.htm (last visited Mar. 10, 2014).

HIV/AIDS because of polygamy. If this was true, the highest percentage of infected people by HIV/AIDS should be in the Middle East. If polygamy leads to infection by HIV/AIDS, why is there no medical supervision of men before they engage in sexual intercourse with prostitutes? In short, it is impossible for a wife or husband to become infected by HIV/AIDS because of polygamy.

The general recommendations that are made by the Committee on the Elimination of Discrimination against Women criticized polygamy, declaring that it is unfair as it is only permitted by husbands. These recommendations explain:

> States parties' reports also disclose that polygamy is practised in a number of countries. Polygamous marriage contravenes a woman's right to equality with men, and can have such serious emotional and financial consequences for her and her dependents that such marriages ought to be discouraged and prohibited. The Committee notes with concern that some States parties, whose constitutions guarantee equal rights, permit polygamous marriage in accordance with personal or customary law. This violates the constitutional rights of women, and breaches the provisions of article 5 (a) of the Convention.[940]

In addition, if a woman is allowed to marry more than one man at the same time, it would take time to identify the father of her children. She would have to check the DNA of her baby and also the DNA of all the men with whom she had sexual relations in order to try to determine the father of her baby. In short, it is very harmful to allow women to marry more than one man at the same time. On the other hand, sexually transmitted diseases are not spread when a man marries more than one woman at the same time. There is no regular medical supervision of men that marry more than one woman at the same time. Therefore, one of the objectives and purposes of Sharia law, in prohibiting polygamy for women, is to protect peoples health. Furthermore, the psychology of women refuses to be married to more than one man at the same time. Polygamy, as it is applied from an understanding of the conditions stated by Sharia law, is not contrary to the principles of equality between men and women. Sharia law does not permit polygamy in an absolute way without any conditions, nor does it prohibit it absolutely. Sharia law allows polygamy under very strict conditions.

On the other hand, cases that are submitted to the HRC or the CEDAW regarding polygamy or the equality between men and women in any Arab country should not be focused on determining whether HRC or the CEDAW are for or against polygamy. The HRC or the CEDAW should supervise and ensure that women's

---

940   *Id.* General Recommendation No. 21 (13th session, 1994).

rights are not violated in any country. Regarding equality between men and women, they should judge whether women's rights are being guaranteed or infringed upon from the perspective of the objectives and purposes of Sharia law. The Western style of equality should not be cloned exactly. For instance, according to Sharia law, women are given dowry and the husband is financially responsible for everything. Even after the dissolution of a marriage, the husband has to pay money to his divorced wife. It is not fair and just to say that this is not equality and that the wife must pay just as the husband does. The principle of the margin of appreciation can be used in order to prevent husbands from saying that their rights to equality are being violated. Generally, the margin of appreciation can play an important role in reconciling the differences between Sharia law and international law. The most important thing is to make sure that women's rights are protected. In other words, women are given their dowry and husbands pay their financial responsibilities towards their wives. It is important to make sure that husbands treat wives in a good manner and polite way as this is requested by Sharia law. Both Western and Arab approaches should be respected because they come from different cultures and traditions. Countries and nations should get to know each other to better understand their different cultures and traditions. The Quran states the following: "O mankind! We have created you from a male and a female, and made you into nations and tribes, that you may know one another. Verily, the most honourable of you with Allah is that (believer) who has At-Taqwa [i.e. he is one of the Muttaqun]. Verily, Allah is All-Knowing, All-Aware."[941]

3. Discrimination Between Men and Women in Crimes of Passion

Not every law in Arab countries is based on Sharia law. Some laws are based on customs and traditions that are not related to Sharia law. Therefore, as I mentioned in my theory, we should examine the purposes and origins of the national law. If we think a law is entirely against international human rights standards then we should understand its roots and understand whether or not it reflects cultures, traditions, and/or Sharia law. For instance, Article 237 of the Egyptian Penal Law states that if a husband kills his wife because he saw her committing adultery, his sentence can be reduced. The court implements this article to reduce the punishment on the husband. However, the law did not give the wife the same right. The Kuwaiti criminal law even expanded this article. It reduced the punishment not only for the husband, but also in cases where a son, brother, or father kills their mother, sister, or daughter. In this case, the law is discriminatory for no reason. Sharia law supports equality and justice. Therefore, neither Egypt nor Kuwait can

---

941 Quran 49:13.

say that this law provision, which discriminates against women, is from Sharia law. Therefore, this article should be amended or deleted to ensure equality. In this way, we must examine each article individually.

The Human Rights Committee of the ICCPR on Egypt stated that some articles of the Egyptian Penal Code are discriminatory with respect to the treatment of men and women equally in matters of adultery,[942] in that husbands were given more rights. The legislator should apply equality between husbands and wives either by reducing the punishment on both of them or by giving them the same punishment without reduction. Article 237 completely violates the obligations of the government regarding equality between men and women. Also this article violates the obligations of Egypt toward the implementation of the Convention on the Elimination of all Forms of Discrimination Against Women. Article 237 constitutes explicit discrimination between men and women.

Article 237 also violates Article 2 of the Egyptian constitution, which states that the Islamic law is the main source of the legislation: "The Holy Quran in many verses, reveals that God Almighty has addressed both men and women alike as far as their obligations."[943] The Quran stresses equality between men and women, stating: "O mankind! Lo! We have created you male and female, and have made you nations and tribes that ye may know one another. Lo! the noblest of you, in the sight of Allah, is the best in conduct. Lo! Allah is Knower, Aware."[944] In addition, Article 3 (3) of the Arab Charter on Human Rights provides, "Men and women are equal in respect of human dignity, rights and obligations within the framework of the positive discrimination established in favour of women by the Islamic Shariah..."[945] The Arab Charter, which states that men and women are equal from the perspective of Sharia law, can be used in order to improve the legislation within the Arab countries. The Charter can be used as an effective instrument to amend laws that are discriminatory and are also contrary to Sharia law.

---

942 U.N. International Covenant on Human Rights, Concluding Observations of the Human Rights Committee: Egypt, *supra* note 15.

943 THE FORMER GRAND IMAM DR. MUHAMMAD SAYED TANTAWAY, SHEIKH AL AZHAR, MANIFESTATIONS OF ISLAM'S REVERENCE FOR WOMEN 7 1995.

944 QURAN 49:13.

945 ACHR, *supra* note 126, at art. 3 (3).

4. Discrimination Between Husband and Wife in Initiating Divorce

In order for a wife to divorce her husband, she has to have a judicial decision to enforce the divorce. However, the husband can divorce his wife without need for a judicial decision. The prima facie reading of the law shows that it is very discriminatory. It would be discriminatory if the financial obligation of the husband were equal to that of the wife before, during, and after dissolution marriage. In fact, it is not discriminatory because there is a financial responsibility of the ex-husband toward his divorced wife. For instance, the ex-husband has to pay his divorced wife something called Mot'aa, which is an amount of money that depends on number of things including the length of the marriage in years and the economic status of the husband. The wife can sue her ex-husband, claiming Mot'aa. Also, in addition to the Mot'aa, the ex-husband has to pay for the period of 'Iddah,'[946] which is a three-month period starting from the first day of divorce, calculated by the number of menses had by the woman. During this period the wife may not marry another man.[947] Although the ex-husband has divorced his wife, he has to pay her during these three months as if they are married. Furthermore, she can claim postponed dowry, which is an amount of money that is written in the marriage contract. It is due if the wife gets divorced. In the case of *Aziz vs. Aziz*, the Supreme Court of New York stated:

> Husband and Wife were married in 1981 in the U.S.. The marriage certificate included a "mahr" (dowry) agreement of $5,032 ($32 immediate payment and $5,000 postponed payment). In 1984, divorce was granted to the Wife on the ground of constructive abandonment. Husband argued that the mahr is a religious document and is not enforceable as a contract in a matrimonial action. The Wife argued that the mahr is enforceable. The court found that the mahr document conformed to the requirements of New York contracts law and its secular terms are enforceable. It did not matter that the contract was entered into as a part of a religious ceremony. The court granted judgment to the Wife against the Husband for $5,000 and awarded an additional $2,050 for legal counsel fees.[948]

---

946 Iddah is a period of three months. During this time, the husband and the wife can return to each other again without signing a new marriage contract as if they were still married. This period exists for several reasons: to let the husband and the wife think quietly with respect to whether they can return to each other and to make sure that the wife is not pregnant before getting married to a new man, such that the father of the fetus can be known.
947 *Iddah*, Wikipedia.org, http://en.wikipedia.org/wiki/Iddah (last visited Mar. 9, 2012).
948 Aziz vs. Aziz, *supra* note 872.

The Supreme Court of New York accepted the application of the same notion that is applied by Arab Courts, that of 'equivalent but not equal.' It rejected the argument of the husband that the mahr is a religious document and is not enforceable. The wife can sue her ex-husband, claiming the expenses she paid for the delivery of her baby. The mother of the baby can also request 'ag'r reda'aa' from the court, which is the cost of feeding her child until the child turns two years old. This amount of money is paid even if she is breastfeeding the baby. The divorced woman can also claim 'Nafakah' for her children, which is the financial expense incurred by the children, including food, etc. The husband has to pay all of the expenses related to his children while they are with their mother. In addition, she can claim other expenses related to her children, such as beds, mattresses, pillows, etc. She can also claim 'mas'kan zawgeyah' before the court, which is the cost of housing. She can request from the ex-husband the purchase of an apartment for her children or she can request that the court force her husband to pay the rent of the apartment where she and her children live. He is responsible for paying all of these costs until his children reach fifteen years of age. When the children reach fifteen years old, the mother can request that the court extend her custody of her female child until the time that this daughter marries. The divorced wife can also sue her ex-husband, claiming the educational and health related expenses of her children. Furthermore, the divorced wife can claim 'ag'r hadanah,' which is a cost paid by the ex-husband to her because she is taking care of her children.

The decision of the court depends on the economic standard and the income of the husband. The wife can claim any of the rights that are explained above once her ex-husband divorces her. Sharia law regulates these rights. If she wants to get divorced and enjoy all of these rights, she has to sue her husband and request that the court grant her a divorce. She must convince the court that she should be granted a divorce. For instance, she could prove that her husband was causing her harm, which means any act that was done by the husband to the wife that caused her moral or physical harm as a result of which she cannot bear staying with her husband.[949] Moral harm differs from one case to another and the court has discretionary authority to determine the presence of moral harm.

The court can reject granting a divorce for the wife if it was not convinced of the wife's reasons. For instance, the family court in Cairo rejected granting a divorce to a woman in the case of a thirty-six year old woman who sued her husband and

---

949 TA'LEMAT EL NAEB EL AAM BESHA'N TATBEEK KANOON MAHKAMET EL OSRAA AL SADER BEL KANON RAKAM 10LESANAAT 2004 [The Prosecutor General, The Instructions of the Prosecutor General Regarding the Establishment of the Family Court by the Law No. 10, 2004] 58 (2004).

asked the court to grant her a divorce due to harm that had been inflicted on her. She claimed that she married her husband when she was twenty nine years old and he was sixty four years old and stated that, after being married, she realized that her husband had many diseases, including diabetes. She said that her husband forced her to give him daily injections because of his diabetes and that she could not bear living with him because she could not stand giving him insulin injections every day. The husband told the court that his diabetes was only diagnosed three years ago and that he takes tablets and has never taken injections (he gave the court his medical papers as proof). He told the court that the real reason that his wife was seeking a divorce was because his wife had written a condition into the marriage contract in case of divorce, which stated that the husband must pay her 120,000 Egyptian pounds in case of divorce (postponed dowry). The court refused to grant a divorce to the wife, stating that the woman knew from the beginning that her husband was old (and, as such, there is a greater probability that he may have age-related diseases). The court added that any person could have a disease and, therefore, the disease of the husband could not be considered to harm her as his wife.[950]

On the other hand, if any wife would like to get divorced without any reason, she can request divorce using 'khul.' For instance, in the above case, the woman is not prevented from ending the relationship with her husband, because she can sue him through the use of khul. Yet, if the court grants her a divorce due to harm, she can claim all of her financial rights, as explained above. Azzizah Al-Hibri explains:

> 'Khul' was meant to be an equitable solution. According to Prophetic precedent, a woman who does not like her husband through no fault of his own has the option of leaving him, so long as she returns to him the mahr (usually translated as dowry) he gave her. The actual story goes as follows: a woman developed a great dislike for her husband, through no fault of his own. She went to the Prophet seeking a way out of the marriage. The Prophet instructed her to return to the man his mahr (in this case, a garden). She was so pleased by the prospect of ending the marriage.[951]

From what I have explained above, we can see that the husband holds a lot of responsibility before, during, and after marriage. Because of this, he is given some rights in return. Therefore, we should not say that women are discriminated

---

950 ALGOMHURIA.NET, http://www.algomhuria.net.eg/algomhuria/today/accedents/detail08.asp (last visited May 2, 2006).
951 AL-HIBRI, *supra* note 29, at 24.

against. Women are protected and respected. In my work as a Chief Prosecutor at the Office of the Prosecutor General, I experienced many cases where we requested extradition and where we extradited many ex-husbands who did not fulfill their obligations towards their wives. Therefore, we should differentiate between two different perspectives: First, the Western style, which applies equality between men and women in all matters. Second, the approach taken by Sharia law, which applies equality from a different perspective. Sharia law gives more rights to women and more responsibilities (and so too more privileges) to men. The principle of the margin of appreciation can be used as a way of reconciling the differences between international human rights law and Sharia law.

D. The Right to Education

The right to education is a basic fundamental right for the success of any region and nation. Education is the sign of development. The level of development of any country can be measured by the quality of education in that country. The United Nations issued several reports regarding the level of education in the Arab world. It is stated that, "A recent UN report suggests that less than 2% of the population in the Arab world reads even one book a year and that one-third of Arabs are illiterate."[952] The right to education is stated in all of the main international and regional human rights instruments. The right to education is one of the few rights that are mentioned precisely and in detail. For example, the word 'education' is mentioned eighteen times in the ICESCR.[953]

---

952 Lack of Reading the Arab World, THEWORLD.ORG, http://www.theworld.org/2010/04/lack-of-reading-in-the-arab-world/ (last visited May 01, 2012).

953 Article 13 of the ICESCR provides: "1. The States Parties to the present Covenant recognize the right of everyone to education. They agree that education shall be directed to the full development of the human personality and the sense of its dignity, and shall strengthen the respect for human rights and fundamental freedoms. They further agree that education shall enable all persons to participate effectively in a free society, promote understanding, tolerance and friendship among all nations and all racial, ethnic or religious groups, and further the activities of the United Nations for the maintenance of peace. 2. The States Parties to the present Covenant recognize that, with a view to achieving the full realization of this right: (a) Primary education shall be compulsory and available free to all; (b) Secondary education in its different forms, including technical and vocational secondary education, shall be made generally available and accessible to all by every appropriate means, and in particular by the progressive introduction of free education; (c) Higher education shall be made equally accessible to all, on the basis of capacity, by every appropriate means, and in particular by the progressive introduction of free education; (d) Fundamental education shall be encouraged or intensified as far as possible for those persons who have not received or completed the whole period of their primary education; (e) The development of a system of schools at all levels shall be actively pursued, an adequate fellowship system shall be established, and the material conditions of teaching staff shall be continuously improved. 3. The States Parties to

The concluding comments of the Committee on the Elimination of Discrimination against Women on Morocco focused on poverty and education. It stated that the:

> Committee recommends that the State party implement measures to ensure access to girls and women to all levels of education. Such measures could include canteens, boarding facilities, proper sanitation, water and electricity, which have a direct impact on the realization of their right to education, especially in rural areas. The Committee also recommends the State party to adopt temporary special measures in accordance with article 4, paragraph 1, of the Convention and the Committee's general recommendation 25, to ensure the retention of girls in school. The Committee calls on the State party to continue to strengthen its efforts to improve the literacy level of girls and women through the adoption of comprehensive programmes of formal and non-formal education, adult education and training and increase training and employment of teachers, the development of gender-sensitive educational materials and the monitoring and evaluation of progress achieved towards time-bound targets. The Committee recommends that special attention be given to girls who are domestic workers, in order to ensure that they are not employed below the age of 15, allowing them to continue their education, at least until that age. The Committee urges the State party to raise general awareness of the importance of education as a human right and as a basis for the empowerment of women, and to take steps to overcome traditional attitudes that perpetuate discrimination.[954]

The right to education imposes negative and positive obligations on countries. It requests that states refrain from interfering with the right to education. In addition, it imposes obligations on countries to take the necessary steps, strategies, and measures to fulfill, safeguard, and protect this right from any violation.

---

the present Covenant undertake to have respect for the liberty of parents and, when applicable, legal guardians to choose for their children schools, other than those established by the public authorities, which conform to such minimum educational standards as may be laid down or approved by the State and to ensure the religious and moral education of their children in conformity with their own convictions. 4. No part of this article shall be construed so as to interfere with the liberty of individuals and bodies to establish and direct educational institutions, subject always to the observance of the principles set forth in paragraph I of this article and to the requirement that the education given in such institutions shall conform to such minimum standards as may be laid down by the State.

954 U.N. Committee the Elimination of All Forms of Discrimination against Women, Concluding Comments of the Committee on the Elimination of Discrimination against Women: Morocco, *supra* note 874.

The positive obligation of the right to education finds its adherents in the Supreme Court of the United States of America. In *Plyler vs. Doe* the United States of America Supreme Court "struck down a state statute denying funding for education to illegal immigrant children and simultaneously struck down a municipal school district's attempt to charge illegal immigrants."[955] In this case, "a Texas statute denying free public education to illegal immigrants violated the Equal Protection Clause of the Fourteenth Amendment, because discrimination on the basis of illegal immigration status did not further a substantial state interest."[956] The case of *Plyler vs. Doe* clearly shows that the right of education is an important governmental interest. It should be protected, respected, and fulfilled without any kind of discrimination.

The Arab Charter on Human Rights demonstrates great appreciation of the right to education. The Arab Charter provides:

> 1. The eradication of illiteracy is a binding obligation upon the State and everyone has the right to education.
>
> 2. The States parties shall guarantee their citizens free education at least throughout the primary and basic levels. All forms and levels of primary education shall be compulsory and accessible to all without discrimination of any kind.
>
> 3. The States parties shall take appropriate measures in all domains to ensure partnership between men and women with a view to achieving national development goals.
>
> 4. The States parties shall guarantee to provide education directed to the full development of the human person and to strengthening respect for human rights and fundamental freedoms.
>
> 5. The States parties shall endeavour to incorporate the principles of human rights and fundamental freedoms into formal and informal education curricula and educational and training programmes.
>
> 6. The States parties shall guarantee the establishment of the mechanisms necessary to provide ongoing education for every citizen and shall develop national plans for adult education.[957]

---

955 *Plyler vs. Doe*, WIKIPEDIA.ORG, http://en.wikipedia.org/wiki/Plyler_v._Doe (last visited Jun. 7, 2012).

956 *Id.*

957 ACHR, *supra* note 126, at art. 41.

Although the right to education is stated in detail in the Arab Charter, it is not implemented effectively in the Arab world. As I have said repeatedly, there is a need for effective supervisory mechanisms to monitor the implementation of the rights of the Arab Charter. Illiteracy in the Arab world is increasing drastically. For instance: the Algerian report on human rights that was submitted to the Arab Committee on Human Rights mentioned that the illiteracy rate was 25% in 2002. In 2005, there were more than 6 million illiterate people. It is important to note that the Algerian population is more than 34 million.[958] As another example:

> The Kingdom of Bahrain, Egypt, The Sultanate of Oman, Kingdom of Saudi Arabia, Sudan, Syria and Yemen. The number of youth and adults, 15 years and over, who are basically illiterate is estimated at 68 million, of which 63% are females. 70 percent of the 68 million illiterates are found in five countries in the Region: Egypt, Algeria, Sudan, Morocco and Yemen. A common feature which these five countries share, besides the high rate of illiteracy, is the fact that they all have to deal with high rates of population growth, poverty and a concentration of population in rural areas.[959]

The illiteracy rate must be controlled. According to Hassan R. Hammoud:

> Great variations exist among the Arab states in their literacy rates for the age group 15 and over. The most recent data ... reveals that such literacy rates range from 80% and above in nine countries (Jordan, United Arab Emirates, Bahrain, Saudi Arabia, Syria, Kuwait, Lebanon, Qatar, and Libya), which are relatively small states with the exception of Saudi Arabia, to less than 75% in nine other countries with large

---

958 *The Arab Human Rights Committee, Countries reports*, Lasportal.org, http://www.lasportal.org/wps/portal/las_ar_humanrights/inpage/!ut/p/c5/vc9NDolwEAXgs3AAM60SqkuQ_4YasaJ2Q8AYpIBoJFQ9vZi41ZVxZjGLI7wvAwKGPWV9WWRd2Z6yGrYgjBThmK-ph5Gn2xYKyJKOjSSIUDiGDWyRnq7k_Rw8qkcsSRx11ZFy6ajldiZMCtZJizJ7rVZI3XiFaZfPVeRM73g_w4m7dEy_viyuUw1CEEXd5i_VGorFN5rr7_zDmAiY3zYH2IEgH1sYAf7DB75arv5Hy_ipdW76ZhaMvH64halpT6gAw1w!/dl3/d3/L2dBISEvZ0FBIS9nQSEh/?pcid=9c8bcd0047335c82a506ad3ebe8887b5 (last visited May 23, 2014).

959 Abdelwahid Abdalla Yousif, *Adult Literacy and Adult Education in the Arab States: Bahrain, Egypt, Oman, Saudi Arabia, Sudan, Syria and Yemen* 2 (2007). Research paper prepared for the UNESCO Regional Conferences in Support of Global Literacy(Doha, 12 – 14 March 2007), http://unesdoc.unesco.org/images/0016/001611/161145e.pdf (last visited Apr. 27, 2012).

populations, with Iraq, Mauritania and Yemen standing as low as 40% and 41.2% and 49% respectively.[960]

The Egyptian Constitution gives great concern to the right to education, the constitution states,

> Every citizen has the right to education. The goals of education are to build the Egyptian character, preserve the national identity, root the scientific method of thinking, develop talents and promote innovation, establish cultural and spiritual values, and found the concepts of citizenship, tolerance and non-discrimination. The State shall observe the goals of education in the educational curricula and methods, and provide education in accordance with international quality standards.
>
> Education is compulsory until the end of the secondary stage or its equivalent. The State shall provide free education in the various stages in the State's educational institutions according to the Law.
>
> The State shall allocate a percentage of government spending to education equivalent to at least 4% of the Gross National Product (GNP), which shall gradually increase to comply with international standards.
>
> The State shall supervise education to ensure that all public and private schools and institutes abide by its educational policies.[961]

In addition the Egyptian Constitution focuses on combating illiteracy, the constition provides that "The State shall develop a comprehensive plan to eradicate alphabetical and digital illiteracy among citizens of all ages. The State shall develop its implementation mechanisms with the participation of civil society organizations within a definite timeline."[962]

In May 2012, the head of the education committee of the Egyptian parliament said that the school dropout rate is one of the main reasons for the increase in illiteracy. Many students, especially in villages and countryside, do not continue their primary education. The Chief Executive of the General Authority for Adult Education and Literacy in Egypt said there are more than 17 million Egyptians

---

960 Hassan R. Hammoud, *Illiteracy in the Arab world*, 3 (2005). Background paper prepared for the Education for All Global Monitoring Report 2006 *Literacy for Life*, http://unesdoc.unesco.org/images/0014/001462/146282e.pdf (last visited Apr. 27, 2012).

961 Unofficial translation of the Egyptian Const, art. 19. http://www.sis.gov.eg/Newvr/Dustor-en001.pdf (last visited May 14, 2014).

962 Unofficial translation of the Egyptian Const, art. 25. http://www.sis.gov.eg/Newvr/Dustor-en001.pdf (last visited May 14, 2014).

who are illiterate, which is to say they cannot read or write.[963] The Egyptian population is approximately 90 million; having 17 million people who are illiterate is a very large percentage of the Egyptian population!

The Egyptian President Abdel-Fathah El-Sisi said that there is an immediate need to build, as soon as possible, twenty thousand schools in Egypt. He added also, there is a need to appoint two hundred thousand teachers to work in the twenty thousand schools.[964]

How can we think that people will be able to ask for their human rights if they cannot read or write? How can we hope that people will go to the Arab Court and the Arab Committee if they do not know the meaning of human rights? How can we ask that people defend their rights if they cannot read or write to be able to know, let alone claim, their rights? How can we expect that others will not have hostile interpretations of Sharia law if they cannot even read the Quran and Sunnah in order to know Sharia law? How can we expect that people who cannot read or write will not be brainwashed and commit terrorist attacks, killing innocent civilians including women and children? How can we expect that sons and daughters will respect parents' rights if they are not able to read Sharia law, such that they can become aware of these rights? How can we expect to be able to protect women's rights if men and women cannot read or write? In short, human rights will not happen if illiteracy is prominent. Human rights cannot be effectively promoted if the people do not know how to write and read the word 'human rights.'

In addition, those who do receive an education are also facing many challenges; there is a big problem in the quality of education. For instance, it is stated in the Arab Human Development Report that "[t]hree primary factors are usually cited in accounting for the Arab countries slumping employment trends... and third, the quality and type of education generally provided, which does not stress technical or vocational skills in demand."[965] The report also mentions that "political, economic and social policies must be geared toward mobilizing the potential labour force, a reorientation that is taking place rather slowly. As several studies point out, Arab policies will have to focus on revamping education to close skills

---

963 *Minister of Education and Chairman of the Parliamentary Education Committee at the Egyptian Parliament: planning to reduce the proportion of illiterate 50% in 2015 and more than 90% in 2020*, AHRAM.ORG, http://www.ahram.org.eg/Youth-Education/News/150447.aspx (last visited May 21, 2012).
964 *CBC Channel and ON TV Channel: Masr Tantakheb* (May 6, 2014).
965 ARAB HUMAN DEVELOPMENT REPORT, *supra* note 3, at 111.

gaps, respond to labour market signals and stimulate knowledge-based capabilities matching opportunities in the global, as well as regional economy."[966]

There is a direct link between poverty and education. In other words, as poverty increases, illiteracy also increases. The Arab Human Development report mentioned:

> In particular, human poverty affects children's attendance at elementary school and their levels of continuation at post-elementary stages. In Egypt, the percentage of poor children in elementary school is 7 per cent lower than that for better-off children, 12 per cent lower at intermediate level, and 24 per cent lower at secondary level. In Morocco, around a quarter of children aged ten to fifteen years have not completed elementary school because of poverty. Many poor children are withdrawn from school to work at an early age to help support their families. In all cases, low school completion rates perpetuate the insecurity of the poor.[967]

The right to education is directly connected to all human rights. For example, people who are not educated usually do not know their human rights. Their rights may be violated because they do not know what rights they have and how to claim for their rights. The Egyptian National Council for Human Rights expressed this in its report on Egypt. It states that "the prevailing culture in the society is not cognizant of human rights and freedoms. Promoting a culture of human rights and raising societal awareness of the principle of freedom; such notions are, unfortunately, still unfamiliar in many institutions, particularly in the educational, mass media…"[968]

The Sharia opinion regarding the eradication of illiteracy is stated clearly in that first word of the Quran that was revealed to Prophet Mohammed was *'read'*.[969] The Quran states: "Read! In the Name of your Lord Who has created (all that exists). He has created man from a clot (a piece of thick coagulated blood). Read! And your Lord is the Most Generous. Who has taught (the writing) by the pen. He has taught man that which he knew not."[970] Sharia law is enthusiastic about the

---

966   *Id.* at 111.
967   *Id.* at 116.
968   EGYPTIAN NATIONAL COUNCIL FOR HUMAN RIGHTS, THIRD ANNUAL REPORT, 2006/2007 http://nchr-egypt.org/en/images/files/3rd%20Annual%20Report(1).pdf (last visited Feb. 6, 2013).
969   Knowledge and Action, AHL-ALQURAN.COM, http://www.ahl-alQuran.com/English/show_article.php?main_id=2890 (last visited May 01, 2012).
970   QURAN 96: 1, 2, 3, 4, 5.

eradication of illiteracy; many Quranic verses and hadith call for education and encourage believers who gain knowledge. For example, the Quran proclaims, "Allah will exalt in degree those of you who believe, and those who have been granted knowledge. And Allah is Well-Acquainted with what you do."[971] In addition, the Quran states,

> "Allah bears witness that La ilaha illa Huwa (none has the right to be worshipped but He), and the angels, and those having knowledge (also give this witness); (He always) maintains His creation in Justice. La ilaha illa Huwa (none has the right to be worshipped but He), the All-Mighty, the All-Wise."[972]

Furthermore, the Quran explains, "It is only those who have knowledge among His slaves that fear Allah..."[973]

There is a *hadith* that shows that God gives rewards to the people who teach and advise people. The *hadith* provides that

> "Abu Huraira reported Allah's Messenger (may peace be upon him) as saying: He who called (people) to righteousness, there would be reward (assured) for him like the rewards of those who adhered to it, without their rewards being diminished in any respect. And he who called (people) to error, he shall have to carry (the burden) of its sin, like those who committed it, without their sins being diminished in any respect."[974]

In addition, there is the following *hadith*:

> Narrated Abud Darda': Kathir Ibn Qays said: I was sitting with AbudDarda' in the mosque of Damascus. A man came to him and said: AbudDarda, I have come to you from the town of the Apostle of Allah (peace_be_upon_him) for a tradition that I have heard you relate from the Apostle of Allah (peace_be_upon_him). I have come for no other purpose. He said: I heard the Apostle of Allah (peace_be_upon_him) say: If anyone travels on a road in search of knowledge, Allah will cause him to travel on one of the roads of Paradise. The angels will lower their wings in their great pleasure with one who seeks knowledge, the inhabitants of the heavens and the Earth and the fish in the deep

---

971 *Id.* at 58:11.
972 *Id.* at 3:18.
973 *Id.* at 35:28.
974 *Sahih Muslim, Book 34, Hadith 6470*, SEARCHTRUTH.COM, http://www.searchtruth.com/book_display.php?book=034&translator=2&start=28&number=6469 (last visited Apr. 27, 2012).

waters will ask forgiveness for the learned man. The superiority of the learned man over the devout is like that of the moon, on the night when it is full, over the rest of the stars. The learned are the heirs of the Prophets, and the Prophets leave neither dinar nor dirham, leaving only knowledge, and he who takes it takes an abundant portion.[975]

There is a very important practice that was done by Prophet Mohammed during wars, which clearly shows that Sharia law encourages the eradication of illiteracy. After the war of Badr, Prophet Mohammed released the prisoners of war on one condition: that each prisoner succeeded in assisting ten people to become literate.[976] This example shows clearly that Sharia law advocates the seeking of knowledge.

All of the previous *hadith* and Quranic verses show clearly that Sharia law encourages the seeking of knowledge, education, and the eradication of illiteracy. The Arab Charter is aligned with both Sharia law and international human rights law. However, there are no effective supervisory mechanisms to guarantee the implementation of the rights in the Charter. In other words, the right to education is fully covered by the Arab Charter, but an effective supervisory mechanism should exist to monitor the implementation of this protected right.

---

975 *Sunan Abu-Dawud, Book25, Hadith 3634,* SEARCHTRUTH.COM, http://www.searchtruth.com/book_display.php?book=25&translator=3&start=0&number=0 (last visited Apr. 27, 2012).

976 HELALY, *supra* note 273, at 395.

E. Private and Family Rights[977]

---

[977] Article 17 of the International Covenant on Civil and Political Rights states: "No one shall be subjected to arbitrary or unlawful interference with his privacy, family, home or correspondence, nor to unlawful attacks on his honour and reputation. Everyone has the right to the protection of the law against such interference or attacks." (ICCPR, *supra* note 63, at art 17) Article 8 of the European Convention on Human Rights states: "Everyone has the right to respect for his private and family life, his home and his correspondence. There shall be no interference by a public authority with the exercise of this right except such as is in accordance with the law and is necessary in a democratic society in the interests of national security, public safety or the economic well-being of the country, for the prevention of disorder or crime, for the protection of health or morals, or for the protection of the rights and freedoms of others." (ECHR, *supra* note 497, at art. 8)
Article 12 of the European Convention on Human Rights states: "Men and women of marriageable age have the right to marry and to found a family, according to the national laws governing the exercise of this right." (ECHR, *supra* note 497, at art 12).
Article 5 of Protocol 7 to the European Convention on Human Rights states: "Spouses shall enjoy equality of rights and responsibilities of a private law character between them, and in their relations with their children, as to marriage, during marriage and in the event of its dissolution. This Article shall not prevent States from taking such measures as are necessary in the interests of the children." (ECHR, *supra* note 497, Protocol 7, at art 12).
Article 18 of the African Charter on Human and peoples' Rights states: "1. The family shall be the natural unit and basis of society. It shall be protected by the State which shall take care of its physical health and moral. 2. The State shall have the duty to assist the family which is the custodian of morals and traditional values recognized by the community. 3. The State shall ensure the elimination of every discrimination against women and also ensure the protection of the rights of the woman and the child as stipulated in international declarations and conventions. 4. The aged and the disabled shall also have the right to special measures of protection in keeping with their physical or moral needs." (African Charter, *supra* note 127 at art. 18)
Article 11 of the American Convention on Human Rights states: "1. Everyone has the right to have his honor respected and his dignity recognized. 2. No one may be the object of arbitrary or abusive interference with his private life, his family, his home, or his correspondence, or of unlawful attacks on his honor or reputation. 3. Everyone has the right to the protection of the law against such interference or attacks." (Organization of American States, American Convention on Human Rights, "Pact of San Jose", Costa Rica, art. 11, Nov. 22, 1969, http://www.unhcr.org/refworld/docid/3ae6b36510.html (last visited Feb. 6, 2013).
Article 17 of the American Convention on Human Rights states: "1. The family is the natural and fundamental group unit of society and is entitled to protection by society and the state. 2. The right of men and women of marriageable age to marry and to raise a family shall be recognized, if they meet the conditions required by domestic laws, insofar as such conditions do not affect the principle of nondiscrimination established in this Convention. 3. No marriage shall be entered into without the free and full consent of the intending spouses. 4. The States Parties shall take appropriate steps to ensure the equality of rights and the adequate balancing of responsibilities of the spouses as to marriage, during marriage, and in the event of its dissolution. In case of dissolution, provision shall be made for the necessary protection of any children solely on the basis of their own best interests. 5. The law shall recognize equal rights for children born out of wedlock and those born in wedlock." (Organization of American

1. The Legal Framework

The right to private life has extremely different interpretations from one system to another; even within the same convention and the same court the definition changes from time to time. For instance, the European Court on Human Rights did not provide an exhaustive definition of the right to private life.[978] In the *Pretty Case* it stated, "As the Court had previous occasions to remark, the concept of 'private life' is a broad term not susceptible to exhaustive definition. It covers the physical and psychological integrity of a person."[979] Article 8 of the European Convention on Human Rights requires negative and positive obligations regarding the right to private life. It imposes obligations on countries to stop anyone from interfering with or violating the right to private life. In addition, it requests that countries take the necessary steps and measures to safeguard and protect this right from any violation.[980] In the case of *X and Y vs. Netherlands*,[981] a complaint was made on behalf of a sixteen year old girl who was mentally disabled. She was raped while in a private home for people with special needs. Her family complained that the law of Netherlands violates the right to private life. This law does not accept any complaint unless the victim makes it in person. Therefore, the girl's family could not submit a complaint under the Netherlands law, which they sought to do as the girl lacked capacity to do so herself. The European Court found that this law violated Article 8. The Court added:

> "Although the object of article 8 is essentially that of protecting the individual against arbitrary interference by public authorities, it does not merely compel the State to abstain from such interference: in addition to this primarily negative undertaking, there may be positive obligations inherent in an effective respect for private or family life."[982]

Article 9 of the Arab Charter on Human Rights states:

> No one shall be subjected to medical or scientific experimentation or to the use of his organs without his free consent and full awareness of the consequences and provided that ethical, humanitarian and pro-

---

States, American Convention on Human Rights, "Pact of San Jose", Costa Rica, art. 17, Nov. 22, 1969, http://www.unhcr.org/refworld/docid/3ae6b36510.html (last visited (last visited Feb. 6, 2013).

[978] See, e.g., judgment of 16 December 1992, Niemietz, para. 29; judgment of 28 January 2003, peck, para. 51.

[979] Judgment of 29 April 2002, para. 60.

[980] JACOBS & WHITE, *supra* note 566, at 24.

[981] Judgment of 26 March 1985, Series A, No.91; (1986) 8 EHRR 235.

[982] Para. 23 of the Judgment.

fessional rules are followed and medical procedures are observed to ensure his personal safety pursuant to the relevant domestic laws in force in each State party. Trafficking in human organs is prohibited in all circumstances.[983]

Article 14 (1) of the Arab Charter on Human Rights states:

> 1. Everyone has the right to liberty and security of person. No one shall be subjected to arbitrary arrest, search or detention without a legal warrant.[984]

Article 21 of the Arab Charter on Human Rights states:

> 1. No one shall be subjected to arbitrary or unlawful interference with regard to his privacy, family, home or correspondence, nor to unlawful attacks on his honour or his reputation.
>
> 2. Everyone has the right to the protection of the law against such interference or attacks.[985]

Article 33 of the Arab Charter on Human Rights states:

> 1. The family is the natural and fundamental group unit of society; it is based on marriage between a man and a woman. Men and women of marrying age have the right to marry and to found a family according to the rules and conditions of marriage. No marriage can take place without the full and free consent of both parties. The laws in force regulate the rights and duties of the man and woman as to marriage, during marriage and at its dissolution.
>
> 2. The State and society shall ensure the protection of the family, the strengthening of family ties, the protection of its members and the prohibition of all forms of violence or abuse in the relations among its members, and particularly against women and children. They shall also ensure the necessary protection and care for mothers, children, older persons and persons with special needs and shall provide adolescents and young persons with the best opportunities for physical and mental development.
>
> 3. The States parties shall take all necessary legislative, administrative and judicial measures to guarantee the protection, survival, develop-

---

[983] ACHR, *supra* note 126, at art. 9.
[984] *Id.* at art 14 (1).
[985] *Id.* at art. 21.

ment and well-being of the child in an atmosphere of freedom and dignity and shall ensure, in all cases, that the child's best interests are the basic criterion for all measures taken in his regard, whether the child is at risk of delinquency or is a juvenile offender.

4. The States parties shall take all the necessary measures to guarantee, particularly to young persons, the right to pursue a sporting activity.[986]

The Cairo Declaration on Human Rights in Islam provides:

Everyone shall have the right to privacy in the conduct of his private affairs, in his home, among his family, with regard to his property and his relationships. It is not permitted to spy on him, to place him under surveillance or to besmirch his good name. The State shall protect him from arbitrary interference.

A private residence is inviolable in all cases. It will not be entered without permission from its inhabitants or in any unlawful manner, nor shall it be demolished or confiscated and its dwellers evicted.[987]

Islamic law strikes a balance between, on the one hand, protecting society from crime and, on the other, ensuring an individual's personal security.[988] It restrains those state activities that curtail the right to privacy, such as obtaining entry into a dwelling without the consent of the owner. On the other hand, the inviolability of the dwelling is not absolute; it is subject to certain exceptions necessary to maintain public order and safety. In addition, state officials, through the procedures prescribed by law and after having a warrant, may search an individual if such activity is clearly for the protection of public order.[989]

The right to privacy is a fundamental right in Islam. This right is stated in Sharia law several times. The Quran explains,

"O you who believe! Enter not houses other than your own, until you have asked permission and greeted those in them, that is better for you, in order that you may remember. And if you find no one therein, still, enter not until permission has been given. And if you are asked to go

---

986 *Id.* at art. 33.
987 Cairo Declaration on Human Rights in Islam, *supra* note 423, art. 18 (b) & (c).
988 HUMAN RIGHTS AND DEMOCRACY THE ROLE OF THE SUPREME CONSTITUTIONAL COURT OF EGYPT 211 (Kevin Boyle & Adel Omar Sherif eds., 1996).
989 *Id.*

back, go back, for it is purer for you, and Allah is All-Knower of what you do".[990]

In another verse the Quran states, "Avoid much suspicions, indeed some suspicions are sins. And spy not, neither backbite one another…"[991] Sharia law gives great concern to the right of private life of women. Sharia law threatens husbands who disclose the secrets of their wives. Even after the dissolution of marriage, husbands are forbidden to reveal the private life of their wives. There is a hadith for the Prophet Mohammed in which he said, "The most wicked among the people in the eye of Allah on the Day of Judgment is the man who goes to his wife and she comes to him, and then he divulges her secret."[992] This hadith clearly shows that God threatens the husband that divulges any of his wife's secrets. Also, the hadith shows the justice toward women within Sharia law.

Under Islamic law, only state officials with the necessary jurisdiction can interfere in the private life and they can only do so according to the rule of law.[993] The story of the Caliphate of Omar Ibn El-Khattab[994] clearly ensures that Sharia law guarantees, respects, and protects the right to privacy.[995] The right to privacy is recognized in the constitutions of the countries of the Arab League. For example, the Constitution of the United Arab Emirates mentions the freedom of postal and telegraphic correspondence and other means of communication.[996] The United Arab Emirates Constitution also provides for the sanctity of dwelling and prohibits entry without the consent of the occupants.[997] The Bahrain Constitution explains, "Dwellings are inviolate. They cannot be entered or searched without the permission of their occupants exception in cases of maximum necessity as laid down and in the manner provided by law."[998] This Constitution states, "The freedom of postal, telegraphic, telephonic and electronic communication is safeguarded and its confidentiality is guaranteed. Communications shall not be censored or their confidentiality breached except in exigencies specified by law and in accordance with procedures and under guarantees prescribed by law."[999] The

---

990 QURAN 24:27-28.
991 *Id.* at 49:12.
992 *Sahih Muslim, Book 8, Hadith 3369*, SEARCHTRUTH.COM, http://www.iium.edu.my/deed/hadith/muslim/008_smt.html (last visited Apr. 24, 2012).
993 BADERIN, *supra* note 138, at 116.
994 BADERIN, *supra* note 385, at 117.
995 *Id.*
996 U.A.E. Const., art. 31.
997 *Id.* at art. 36.
998 Bahrain Const., art 25.
999 *Id.* at art. 26.

Algerian Constitution guarantees the secrecy of communication and the home inviolability by stating, "The private life and the honour of the citizen are inviolable and protected by the law. The secrecy of private correspondence and communication, in any form, is guaranteed."[1000] This Constitution continues, "The State guarantees home inviolability. No thorough search can be allowed unless in pursuance of the law and in compliance with the latter. The thorough search can only be in pursuance of a search warrant emanating from the competent judicial authority."[1001]

Similarly, the Egyptian Constitution explicitly states the right to private life. It provides that,

> "The right to privacy may not be violated, shall be protected and may not be infringed upon.
>
> Postal, telegraphic and electronic correspondences, telephone calls, and other means of communication are inviolable, and their confidentiality is guaranteed. They may not be confiscated, revealed or monitored except by virtue of a reasoned judicial order, for a definite period, and only in the cases defined by Law.
>
> The State shall protect citizens' right to use all forms of public means of communications. Interrupting or disconnecting them, or depriving the citizens from using them, arbitrarily, is impermissible. This shall be regulated by Law."[1002]

Concerning dwellings it states,

> "Privacy of homes is inviolable. Except for cases of danger or call for help, homes may not be entered, inspected, monitored or eavesdropped except by a reasoned judicial warrant specifying the place, the time and the purpose thereof. This is to be applied only in the cases and in the manner prescribed by Law. Upon entering or inspection, the residents of houses must be apprised and have access to the warrant issued in this regard."[1003]

1000 Algerian Const. art. 39 para. 1 & 2.
1001 *Id.* at art. 40.
1002 Unofficial translation of the Egyptian Const, art. 57, http://www.sis.gov.eg/Newvr/Dustor-en001.pdf (last visited May 14, 2014).
1003 *Id.* at art. 58.

Article 57 of the Egyptian Constitution goes further by stating that the interference in the private life is considered a crime; it provides,

> "Any violation of personal freedom, or the sanctity of the private life of citizens, or any other public rights and freedoms which are guaranteed by the Constitution and the Law is a crime. The criminal and civil lawsuit arising of such crime shall not abate by prescription. The affected party shall have the right to bring a direct criminal action. The State shall guarantee fair compensation for the victims of such violations. "[1004]

The provisions of the constitutions referred to above, which either explicitly establish the sanctity of private life or implicitly create zones of privacy, demonstrate the importance of constitutional guarantees that embrace all aspects of this right.[1005]

The Egyptian Supreme Constitutional Court has issued many decisions with regard to family and private life. One of the popular cases[1006] is regarding the constitutionally of the law prohibiting members of the State Council[1007] from marrying non-Egyptian Women. Article 73 (6) of the Law No 47 of the 1972 regarding the State Council (Egypt's Administrative Judicial Body) states that a person assigned to be a member of the Council "must not be married to a foreign wife."[1008] The law adds that the previous condition can be waived upon the approval of the President of Egypt only if the non-Egyptian wife is holding the nationality of an Arab country.[1009] The applicant in this case was a former judge at the State Council. He was married to a non-Egyptian woman. In order not to be dismissed from his work in the judicial service, he requested to be transferred to another judicial body that does not prohibit marrying non-Egyptian women. A presidential decree transferred him to the Administrative Prosecution Body. After that, he submitted a case before the High Administrative Court requesting the

---

1004 *Id.* at art. 99.

1005 HUMAN RIGHTS AND DEMOCRACY THE ROLE OF THE SUPREME CONSTITUTIONAL COURT OF EGYPT, *supra* note 988.

1006 Case No 23, Judicial Year 16, Decided on 18th March 1995, [Official Gazette, No 14, 6th April 1995].

1007 The State Council is a judicial body. Article 172 of the Egyptian Constitution of 1971 provides, "The State Council shall be an independent judiciary organization competent to take decisions in administrative disputes and disciplinary cases. The law shall determine its other competences" see http://www.sis.gov.eg/en/LastPage.aspx?Category_ID=208 (last visited Feb. 6, 2013).

1008 Article 73 (6) of the Law No 47 of the 1972 regarding the State Council.

1009 HUMAN RIGHTS AND DEMOCRACY THE ROLE OF THE SUPREME CONSTITUTIONAL COURT OF EGYPT, *supra* note 988, at 235-236.

invalidation of this presidential decree. He added that his request to be transferred was not made by his free will, but made to avoid being dismissed from the judicial service. He added that article 73 (6) is unconstitutional.[1010]

The Supreme Constitutional Court states:

> Personal liberty is fundamental. Many essential rights are derived from it, including the rights to marry and raise a family. Freedom of choice is essential for exercising these rights. Its denial violated both ethical principles that underpin a free society, and the due process of law as guaranteed by constitution. Intrinsic to the right to marry is the right to choose a spouse. This is not only a vital personal right in itself, but is also essential to the formation of the secure family unit which, as Article 9 of the Constitution makes clear, is the foundation of society.'[1011]

The Court also added:

> Islamic Sharia principles recognize the right to privacy and encourage marriage for many social, psychological and religious reasons. Moreover, several international agreements accepted or ratified by Egypt support the right to choose a spouse (Article 16 of the Universal Declaration of Human Rights; Article 5 of the International Convention on Elimination of all Forms of Racial Discrimination; Article 23 (2) of the International Covenant on Civil and Political Rights; Article 16 of the Convention on Elimination of All Forms of Discrimination against Women). It is therefore widely accepted that the right to choose a spouse is a civil right and an essential component of personal privacy. Consequently, the legislature must not use a discretionary power to determine who may be married and to whom. The right to marriage and the right to choose a spouse are further protected by the Egyptian Constitution, which provides that 'The law shall protect the inviolability of the private life of citizen.'[1012] The fact that the rights to marry or choose a spouse are not specifically mentioned in... the Constitution does not mean that they are not constitutionally guaranteed. Rather they are embodied in the spirit of the Constitution, reflecting its true intentions, in a similar manner to the United States Constitution which, although not explicitly mentioning the right to privacy, was interpreted

---

1010 *Id.*
1011 *Id.*
1012 Egyptian Const., art. 45, http://www.sis.gov.eg/Newvr/Dustor-en001.pdf (last visited May 14, 2014).

by the American judiciary to encompass private life. The Egyptian Constitution, by providing for the right to privacy in Article 45, implicitly also guarantees the right to marry and choose a spouse as an essential component of upholding the sanctity of private life. [1013]

The Court also mentioned that the members of the Supreme Constitutional Court are permitted to marry non-Egyptians even though the Supreme Constitutional Court examines more sensitive cases than those being dealt with by the State Council.[1014] The Court stated that Article 73 (6) violated Article 40 of the Constitution,[1015] because it discriminates between State Council members and other judicial bodies. The Court also found a violation of the right to work and to occupy public jobs because those who marry non-Egyptian women will be dismissed from work.[1016]

2. Parental Rights

For some people the word "*Sharia*" means inequality, injustice, and discrimination against Muslim women, be she a daughter, sister, mother, or wife. These rights are placed at the top of the hierarchy of rights that must be respected and protected. In this hierarchy, it is placed directly after believing in God.

The Prophet Mohammed stated a lot of *hadith* in favor of parental rights. For instance, the Prophet said:

> While three persons were walking, rain began to fall and they had to enter a cave in a mountain. A big rock rolled over and blocked the mouth of the cave. They said to each other, 'Invoke Allah with the best deed you have performed (so Allah might remove the rock)'. One of

---

[1013] HUMAN RIGHTS AND DEMOCRACY THE ROLE OF THE SUPREME CONSTITUTIONAL COURT OF EGYPT, *supra* note 988.

[1014] *Id.*

[1015] Article 40 of the Egyptian Constitution of 1971 provides, "All citizens are equal before the law. They have equal public rights and duties without discrimination due to sex, ethnic origin, language, religion or creed." Unofficial translation of Article 53 of the Egyptian Constitution of 2014 provides that "All citizens are equal before the Law. They are equal in rights, freedoms and general duties, without discrimination based on religion, belief, sex, origin, race, color, language, disability, social class, political or geographic affiliation or any other reason. Discrimination and incitement of hatred is a crime punished by Law. The State shall take necessary measures for eliminating all forms of discrimination, and the Law shall regulate creating an independent commission for this purpose." http://www.sis.gov.eg/Newvr/Dustor-en001.pdf (last visited May 14, 2014).

[1016] HUMAN RIGHTS AND DEMOCRACY THE ROLE OF THE SUPREME CONSTITUTIONAL COURT OF EGYPT, *supra* note 988.

them said, 'O Allah! My parents were old and I used to go out for grazing (my animals). On my return I would milk (the animals) and take the milk in a vessel to my parents to drink. After they had drunk from it, I would give it to my children, family and wife. One day I was delayed and on my return I found my parents sleeping, and I disliked to wake them up. The children were crying at my feet (because of hunger). That state of affairs continued till it was dawn. O Allah! If You regard that I did it for Your sake, then please remove this rock so that we may see the sky.' So, the rock was moved a bit...[1017]

In the Quran, Jesus said, "And dutiful to my mother, and made me not arrogant, unblest."[1018] When asked about the great sins, the Prophet Mohammed said, "They are: To join in worshipping others with Allah, To be undutiful to one's parents, To kill a person (which Allah has forbidden to kill) And to give a false witness."[1019] In another *hadith,* Prophet Mohammed said, "Allah postpones the punishment for one's sins till the Day of Judgment if He so desires. But He awards the punishment for disobeying the parents during this life, before his death."[1020] This previous *hadith* means that due to the graveness of the sin of being undutiful to one's parent, a person will be punished two times; first, during the person's lifetime and, second, in the hereafter.[1021] The Quran also speaks to parental rights and in Islam these rights are superior over any other right. Parental rights are extremely important in Islam, they are highly ranked and they are also written in the Quran just after the mandate to believe in God. The parents rights is the highest right according to Sharia Law. It comes just after servitude to God. "The mention of servitude to parents follows immediately after servitude to God. This is repeated throughout the Qur'an."[1022] In the Quran it states:

> And (remember) when Luqman said to his son when he was advising him: "O my son! Join not in worshipping others with Allah. Verily joining others in worship with Allah is a great Zulm (wrong) indeed. And We have enjoined on man (to be dutiful and good) to his parents. His mother bore him in weakness and hardship upon weakness and hard-

---

1017 *Parent's Rights in Islam,* QURANANDSCIENCE.COM http://www.Quranandscience.com/fakes-about-islam/171-parents-rights-in-islam.html (last visited Mar. 9, 2012) (citing (Bukhari-3:418)).

1018 QURAN 32:19.

1019 *Parent's Rights in Islam, supra* note 1017 (citing (Bukhari 3-821)).

1020 *Ideal Muslim Teenager,* THE-IDEAL-TEENAGER.BLOGSPOT.CA, http://the-ideal-teenager.blogspot.com/2010/08/did-you-know-that-disobeying-parents.html (last visited Mar. 28, 2012).

1021 *Id.*

1022 *Islams Women,* ISLAMSWOMEN.COM, http://www.islamswomen.com/articles/mothers_in_islam.php (last visited Jan. 6, 2013).

ship, and his weaning is in two years — give thanks to Me and to your parents. Unto Me is the final destination."[1023]

Also, the Quran states, "And your Lord has decreed that you worship none but Him. And that you be dutiful to your parents. If one of them or both of them attain old age in your life, say not to them a word of disrespect, nor shout at them but address them in terms of honour."[1024]

Muslims must be kind to their parents even if the parents do not believe in God or they want their son or daughter to not believe in God. It is said in Quran: "But if they [both] strive with you to make you join in worship with Me others that of which you have no knowledge, then obey them not; but behave with them in the world kindly, and follow the path of him who turns to Me in repentance and in obedience. Then to Me will be your return, and I shall tell you what you used to do."[1025]

In Islam, mothers are given more care than fathers. Mother bears the baby and suffers during pregnancy and at the time of delivering the baby. A Companion asked the Prophet, "'Who deserves my good treatment most?' 'Your mother,' said the Prophet. 'Who next?' 'Your mother.' 'Who next?' 'Your mother.' 'Who after that?' 'Your father.'"[1026] Therefore, mothers are giving higher degrees of care than fathers. According to Sunnah, mothers have three times the care from their sons and daughters, which is more than the care deserved by the father.[1027] It is also stated in the Quran that, "[a]nd when We made a covenant with the children of Israel: You shall not serve any but Allah and (you shall do) good to (your) parents, and to the near of kin and to the orphans and the needy, and you shall speak to men good words and keep up prayer and pay the poor-rate. Then you turned back except a few of you and (now too) you turn aside."[1028] Furthermore, the Quran outlines, "And lower unto them the wing of submission and humility through mercy," and say: "My Lord! Bestow on them Your Mercy as they did bring me up when I was young."[1029]

There is a hadith for Prophet Mohammed in which he asked his companion to request from a man from Yemen to pray for them whenever they meet him. If this

---

1023 QURAN 31:13-14.
1024 *Id.* at 17:23.
1025 *Id.* at 31:15.
1026 Dr. I. A. Arshed. *Parents Rights Relationship in Islam*. ISLAM101.COM, http://www.islam101.com/sociology/parchild.htm (last visited May 8, 2014).
1027 *Id.*
1028 QURAN 2:82.
1029 *Id.* at 17:24.

man prays to God, God will fulfill his wishes. This is because he is very dutiful to his parents.[1030] Prophet said,

> "There will come to you with reinforcements from Yemen a man called Uways ibn 'Âmir of the clan of Murâd from the tribe of Qaran…He has a mother and he has always treated her with kindness and respect. If he prays to Allah, Allah will fulfill his wish. If you can ask him to pray for forgiveness for you, then do so."[1031]

The previous story shows the importance of being dutiful to one's parents. God fulfills his wishes because he was respectful, kind, and caring towards his mother. Taking care of one's parents is more highly ranked than making *hajj*. The prophet never met this man because the man preferred to stay in Yemen taking care of his mother and not go to Mekka to make *hajj* which is the fifth pillar of Islam. He traveled to make *hajj* after his mother died.[1032]

Parental rights extend not only during their lifetime, but also after their death. There is another hadith for the Prophet that states,

> "While we were with the Apostle of Allah! (peace be upon him) a man of Banu Salmah came to Him and said: Apostle of Allah is there any kindness left that I can do to my parents after their death? He replied: Yes, you can invoke blessings on them, forgiveness for them, carry out their final instructions after their death, join ties of relationship which are dependent on them, and honor their friends."[1033]

The Arab Charter should reflect the cultures and traditions of the Arab region. In addition, it is inspired by Sharia law. The Arab Charter highlights the importance of family rights in general; it is stated in Article 33 (2) that:

> The State and society shall ensure the protection of the family, the strengthening of family ties, the protection of its members and the prohibition of all forms of violence or abuse in the relations among its members, and particularly against women and children. They shall also ensure the necessary protection and care for mothers, children, older persons and persons with special needs and shall provide adolescents

---

1030 *Uways Qarany*, YOUTUBE.COM, http://www.youtube.com/watch?v=7v35nIqZKdM (last visited Jan. 6, 2013).

1031 Islams women, http://www.islamswomen.com/articles/mothers_in_islam.php (last visited Jan. 6, 2013).

1032 *Id.*

1033 *Parent's Rights in Islam, supra* note 1017 (citing (Abu Dawood 2440)).

and young persons with the best opportunities for physical and mental development.[1034]

I do not know why the Arab Charter in Human Rights did not include an article for parental rights.

Sharia law is not limited to the relationship between man and woman or husband and wife. Sharia law goes beyond that to include other values that strengthen the bonds of family through love and care. The Arab Charter should not clone other intentional conventions, but should reflect its region. Saudi Arabia stated in its report submitted to the CEDAW:

> Islam affirms many values which promote the family, which is not limited to husband and wife but extends to include children, siblings, parents and relatives. These values include filial piety, the bond of kinship and the raising of children. Women enjoy a more favourable share of these than men: the Islamic Shariah has more to say about the virtue of caring for daughters than for sons, a mother's right over her children is three times that of a father's and a woman's right to custody of her infant child takes precedence over a man's, in principle.[1035]

People from the Eastern cultures should not impose their beliefs regarding the unique and high respect for their parents on Western society. There should be a constructive dialogue. Vice-versa, people from Western cultures should not impose their beliefs and traditions on Eastern society.

3. Homosexuality

Some scholars support the legality of homosexuality. They think that criminalizing homosexuality in general, and specifically homosexual marriage, will significantly violate the right of homosexuals to fulfill their sexual desires. In addition, they believe that the criminalization of homosexuality will lead to the prosecution of homosexual people. Furthermore, the prohibition of homosexuality will affect the employment of homosexuals because employers will be unwilling to hire them. In short, there will be a discrimination against homosexual people in all fields of life, such as housing, employment, etc.[1036] For example, in case of

---

1034 ACHR, *supra* note 126, at art. 33 (2).

1035 U.N. Committee the Elimination of All Forms of Discrimination against Women, U.N. Committee on the Elimination of Discrimination against Women: Combined Initial and Second Periodic Reports of States Parties, Saudi Arabia, *supra* note 6.

1036 *The Constitutionality of Laws Forbidding Private Homosexual Conduct*, 72 MICH. L. REV. 1613, 1614 (1974), http://www.jstor.org/discover/10.2307/1287691?uid=2129&uid=2&uid=70&uid=4&sid=56228708163 (last visited Jun. 3, 2012).

Schware vs. Board of Bar Examiners, the applicant stated that he was dismissed from joining the bar because he was a homosexual.

Homosexuality was prohibited and not given any justification by law in order to protect health and morals. "General sodomy statutes prohibit 'unnatural' acts between heterosexuals and homosexuals alike in twenty-seven states and the District of Columbia. The statutes impose criminal sanctions..."[1037] "Most of the statutes describe the act as a 'crime against nature.'"[1038] In the United States of America:

> Legal punishments often included heavy fines and/or life prison sentences, with some states (Illinois being the first in 1827) specifically denying other rights, such as suffrage, to anyone convicted of the crime of sodomy. In the late 19th and early 20th centuries, several states imposed various eugenics laws against anyone deemed to be a "sexual pervert." As late as 1970, Connecticut denied a driver's license to a man for being an 'admitted homosexual.'[1039]

In the early 1970's, John Singer and Paul Barwick, two homosexuals, requested a marriage license in Seattle, Washington, but it was rejected. In a similar case (*Singer vs. Hara*), the Court did not accept giving a marriage license not "because of sex discrimination but because of the very definition of marriage as between a man and a woman."[1040] This has begun to change and Western states have started to decriminalize homosexuality because of a change in morals. It was only in late 1973 that the Board of Trustees of the American Psychiatric Association (APA) removed homosexuality from the list of mental diseases.[1041] The Board of the APA stated, "The Board's action was approved by a general vote of the APA membership in April 1974, although only about one half of the membership voted, and of that group two fifths disagreed."[1042] Furthermore:

> In *Lawrence vs. Texas*, the Supreme Court of the United States of America struck down the sodomy law in Texas and, by extension, invalidated sodomy laws in thirteen other states, making same-sex sexual activity legal in every U.S. state and territory. The court overturned its previous

---

1037 *Homosexuality and the Good Morals*, 56 U. Det. J. Urb. L. 129 (1978-1979).
1038 *Id.*
1039 *Lawrence vs. Texas*, Wikipedia.org, http://en.wikipedia.org/wiki/Lawrence_v._Texas (last visited Jun. 7, 2012).
1040 William Stacy Johnson, A Time To Embrace 30 (2006).
1041 *The Constitutionality of Laws Forbidding Private Homosexual Conduct, supra* note 1036.
1042 *Id.* (citing N.Y. Times, April 9, 1974, at 12, col. 4 (late city ed.)).

ruling on the same issue in the 1986 case *Bowers vs. Hardwick*, where it upheld a challenged Georgia statute and did not find a constitutional protection of sexual privacy. *Lawrence* explicitly overruled *Bowers*, holding that it had viewed the liberty interest too narrowly... The Court held that intimate consensual sexual conduct was part of the liberty protected by substantive due process under the Fourteenth Amendment.[1043]

In the United Kingdom, homosexuality was a crime in civil society and the military until 1967, when the Sexual Offence Act was adopted. This act does criminalize homosexual acts in the Air Force and the Army. This act also does not criminalize homosexuality in civil society on the condition that it is committed in private between consenting people, who are twenty one years and older.[1044] In 1994, the Ministry of Defense in the United Kingdom decriminalized homosexuality in the Armed Forces. It made amendments to the Armed Forces Policy and Guidelines regarding Homosexuality. The amendments prohibited the prosecution of homosexuals under military law for the reason of their homosexuality. However, the military still had the right to administratively discharge homosexuals from the military. The guidelines stressed that homosexuality was not aligned with service in the Military "because of the close physical conditions in which personnel often have to live and work, [and] also because homosexual behaviour can cause offence, polarise relationships, induce ill-discipline, and... damage morale and unit effectiveness."[1045]

In *Lustig-Prean & Beckett vs. United Kingdom*,[1046] Mr. Lustig-Prean (who was an officer) was discharged from the Navy in 1995 because he was a homosexual.[1047] The European Court of Human Rights rendered a decision stating that preventing people who are homosexual from joining the armed forces constitutes a violation to Article 8 (Private Life) of the European Convention for the Protection of Human Rights and Fundamental Freedoms. A similar decision was also rendered in *Smith*

1043 *Lawrence vs. Texas*, Wikipedia.org, *Cf.* Lawrence vs. Texas, 539 U.S. 558 (2003). *supra* note 1039.

1044 Sameera Dalvi, *Homosexuality and the European Court of Human Rights: Recent Judgments Against the United Kingdom and Their Impact on Other Signatories to the European Convention on Human Rights*, 15 U. Fla. J.L. & Pub. Pol'y 481 (2004).

1045 *Id.; see also* Richard Kamm, *European Court of Human Rights Overturns British Ban on Gays in the Military*, wcl.american.edu, http://www.wcl.american.edu/hrbrief/v7i3/european.htm (last visited Mar. 11, 2012).

1046 Sameera Dalvi, *supra* note 1044 (citing Lustig-Prean & Beckett vs. United Kingdom, 29 Eur. H.R. Rep. 548 (1999)).

1047 Richard Kamm, *supra* note 1045.

& Grady vs. United Kingdom.[1048] In 2000, the United Kingdom Ministry of Defense made the necessary amendments in the laws. Homosexuals were permitted to serve in the military.[1049] This was the first case of a complaint against the application of the English Sexual Offences Act, which criminalizes homosexual intercourse with male persons under twenty one years old. Both the Commission and the Committee of Ministers found that the criminalization, prosecution, and punishment were justified on the ground of "the protection of rights and freedoms of others."[1050]

In 1981, the case of *Dudgeon vs. the United Kingdom* before the European Court on Human Rights.[1051] The case was submitted against the United Kingdom of Great Britain and Northern Ireland by Mr. Dudgeon, who is a homosexual. He complained against the laws in Northern Ireland that consider a homosexual act between consenting adult males to be a criminal offence. The Court concluded that Mr. Dudgeon was suffering from an unjustified interference with his right to respect for his private life. The Courts held by fifteen votes to four that this constituted a breach of Article 8 of the Convention regarding private life.[1052]

In *Toonen vs. Australia*[1053] the Human Rights Committee of the ICCPR observed:

> In so far as article 17 is concerned, it is undisputed that adult consensual sexual activity in private is covered by the concept of 'privacy.' The court rejected the State Party's argument that the law was justified on the grounds of public morals, which must be left to domestic law of the state. It held that it "cannot accept…for the purpose of article 17 of the covenant [that] moral issues are exclusively a matter of domestic concern, as this would open the door to withdrawing from the Committee's security a potentially large number of statutes interfering with privacy."[1054]

Also, on 5 December 2011, the first ever United Nations report on the human rights of lesbian, gay, bisexual, and transgender (LGBT) people detailed "how

---

1048 Sameera Dalvi, *supra* note 1044, at 469 (citing Smith & Grady vs. United Kingdom, 29 Eur. H.R. Rep. 493 (1999)).

1049 Richard Kamm, *supra* note 1045; *see also* Sameera Dalvi, *supra* note 1044, at 488.

1050 Report of the 12 October 1978, X vs. the United Kingdom, D&R 19 (1980), p.66 (75).

1051 Dudgeon vs. the United Kingdom, no. 7525/6, ECHR 1981 http://hudoc.echr.coe.int/sites/eng/pages/search.aspx?i=001-57473 (last visited Mar. 11, 2012).

1052 Dudgon vs. the United Kingdom, no. 7525/6, *supra* note 1051.

1053 Toonen vs. Australia, Comm. No. 488/1992, Human Rights Committee (04 April 1994), U.N. Doc. CCPR/C/50/D/488/1992.

1054 *Id.* para. 8.6.

around the world people are killed or endure hate-motivated violence, torture, detention, criminalization and discrimination in jobs, health care and education because of their real or perceived sexual orientation or gender identity."[1055]

Having sexual relations with a person of the same sex is still illegal in seventy-six countries and at least five countries apply the death sentence to homosexuals.[1056] Homosexuality is completely forbidden in Islam. According to the Islamic view, homosexuality is not a natural activity.[1057] For instance, it is stated in the Quran: "And (remember) Lout (Lot), when he said to his people: 'Do you commit the worst sin such as none preceding you has committed in the Alameen (mankind and jinns)?' Verily, you practice your lusts on men instead of women. Nay, but you are a people transgressing beyond bounds (by committing great sins)."[1058] Also, it was explained in the Quran that God punished the people who are doing this act

> "And when Our Messengers came to Ibrahim (Abraham) with the glad tidings they said: 'Verily, we are going to destroy the people of this (Louts (Lots)) town (i.e. the town of Sodom in Palestine). Truly, its people have been Zalimoon (wrong-doers, polytheists and disobedient to Allah and have also belied their Messenger Lout (Lot)).'"[1059]

Islam only permits traditional marriage between men and women. The Quran states:

> Made lawful to you this day are AtTayyibat (all kinds of Halal (lawful) foods, which Allah has made lawful (meat of slaughtered eatable animals, etc., milk products, fats, vegetables and fruits, etc.). The food (slaughtered cattle, eatable animals, etc.) of the people of the Scripture (Jews and Christians) is lawful to you and yours is lawful to them. (Lawful to you in marriage) are chaste women from the believers and chaste women from those who were given the Scripture (Jews and Christians) before your time, when you have given their due Mahr (bridal money given by the husband to his wife at the time of marriage), desiring chastity (i.e. taking them in legal wedlock) not committing illegal sexual intercourse, nor taking them as girl-friends. And whosoever disbelieves

---

1055 U.N. News Center, *U.N. Issues First Report on Human Rights of Gay and Lesbian People*, http://www.un.org/apps/news/story.asp?NewsID=40743 (last visited Mar. 11, 2012).

1056 *Id.*

1057 *Sodomy*, WIKIPEDIA.COM, http://en.wikipedia.org/wiki/Sodomy#Islamic_views (last visited May 8, 2014).

1058 QURAN 7:81-82.

1059 *Id.* at 7:31.

in the Oneness of Allah and in all the other Articles of Faith (i.e. His (Allah's), Angels, His Holy Books, His Messengers, the Day of Resurrection and AlQadar (Divine Preordainments)), then fruitless is his work, and in the Hereafter he will be among the losers.[1060]

According to Sharia law, in order to apply *hodood* punishments on homosexuals, the people who commit this crime in private cannot be arrested while they are committing their crime unless the law enforcement officers know for certain that the people are currently involved in the acts. As I explained before, the right to private life is protected, no one can search a home without enough grounds that there is a crime. Furthermore, Sharia law requires that, for prosecution and accusation, four witnesses who must have seen the accused people while they were having sex. According to Sharia law, if they are arrested without four witnesses seeing them having sex, the law enforcement officer who arrested them should be punished. As previously mentioned the Caliphate of Muslims' Omar Ibn El-Khattab asked a question to Aly Ibn Aby Talb, who is considered to be one of the closest relatives and companions of Prophet Mohammed. He asked Aly whether is it legitimate to punish people who commit illegal sexual relations if the sexual intercourse was watched by the Caliph himself. Aly replied by saying to him that you will be punished if you did not get another three witnesses to also see the act.[1061] It should be noted that during the life of the Prophet, no one was punished for having illegal sexual relations, except peoples who admitted to committing the crime and requested that the Prophet punish them.[1062] For instance, a woman came to the Prophet admitting to having committed adultery and requesting from him to be punished by *hodood*. The Prophet did not ask her who her partner was and did not even send someone to follow her to investigate and arrest her partner. Furthermore, the Prophet did not arrest her, he left her until she delivered and breastfed her baby. After this, the woman came to him on her own will, requesting to be punished by *hodood*. This clearly shows that the people who were punished by *hodood* were punished after admitting to having committed their crimes.[1063] It is difficult, if not impossible, to gather the evidence required by Sharia law. The aim of Sharia law is that private life should be respected as long as the sins are being done in private, not in public. Sharia law does not intend to name and shame people.

1060 *Id.* at 5:5.
1061 MANSOUR, *supra* note 755, at 69.
1062 *Id.* at 75.
1063 Telephone interview with Sheikh Khaled Al-Gendy (Aug. 29, 2012).

On the other hand, it is considered a crime if people gather in a specific home or place to commit an act of prostitution or homosexuality because the owner of the house or the place is encouraging people to come and do these acts.[1064] Therefore, it is not considered an issue of private life, but it is considered a business that is selling bodies.

As I mentioned in Chapter 2, the Quran is the primary source of Sharia law. Therefore, the Quran should be respected and protected. In the Quran, Allah said, "Allah does not like that the evil should be uttered in public... "[1065] The goal of Sharia law is not to name and shame. The door of repentance is open to people until the last second of their lives. Sharia law encourages people to ask forgiveness from God.[1066] For instance, Egypt, as an example of a state party to the Arab League that signed the Arab Charter on Human Rights, criminalizes people who habitually and repeatedly commit promiscuity or prostitution with different people indiscriminately. In regards to prostitution, Article 9(c) of the law number 10 of the year 1961 stated that, "who habitually commits promiscuity or prostitution shall be imprisoned not less than three months and not more than three years and fined not less than twenty five pounds and not more than three hundred pounds or one of these two penalties."[1067] Article 1 (a) of the same law stated that, "Each person who incites a male or female to commit prostitution or debauchery or assists … to commit promiscuity or prostitution is punishable by imprisonment for not less than one year and not exceeding three years and a fine not less than a hundred pounds and not exceeding three hundred pounds." As can be seen from both Articles 1 and 9, it is clear that the Egyptian Law does not criminalize homosexuality as a crime in and of itself unless it is done habitually and repeatedly with different people indiscriminately. Therefore, no person, male or female, can be accused of being guilty of something because of his or her sexual interest. The Egyptian law criminalizes people who habitually and repeatedly commit promiscuity or prostitution with different people indiscriminately. The Supreme Egyptian Court commented on Article 9 (c) by saying that, "This provision criminalizes promiscuity whether committed by a female (prostitution) or by a male (promiscuity)."[1068] According to Article 9, private sexual relations are permitted if it is not done indiscriminately but prohibited it if it includes sexual

---

1064 Telephone interview with the academic counselor of the Egyptian Mufti (March 3, 2012).

1065 QURAN 4:148.

1066 *Satr al-muslim* (Lester Muslims), ALUKAH.NET, http://www.alukah.net/Sharia/0/10221/ (last visited Mar. 3, 2012).

1067 Article 9(c) of the law number 10 of the year 1961.

1068 Case number 24450 for the Judicial Year 59, 5/12/1994.

acts that are done in exchange for money. It should be noted that Egypt applies criminal law, not *hodood* punishments, in the cases of such crimes.

In addition, homosexuality in public or in private if it is committed by a group of people (in cases that could be considered selling one's body) should be prohibited because it could be considered to be human trafficking in certain cases. Article 10 of the Arab Charter provides that "All forms of slavery and trafficking in human beings are prohibited and are punishable by law... Trafficking of human beings for the purpose of prostitution or sexual exploitation... are prohibited."[1069] Criminalizing promiscuity and prostitution helps in preventing and combating human trafficking. Due to its geographical location between Asia, Europe, and Africa, Egypt is considered to be a transit country for human and sex trafficking. It has been stated, "Egypt is a transit country for women trafficked from Eastern Europe...for the purpose of sexual exploitation"[1070] and that "Egypt is a source, transit, and destination country for women and children who are subjected to conditions of forced labor and sex trafficking."[1071] Therefore, if Egypt does not have effective laws for combating prostitution and promiscuity, it will be a country of destination for sex trafficking.

In the case of *Norris vs. Ireland*, the European Court on Human Rights "struck down Ireland's sodomy law under Article 8 finding that the vast majority of member states no longer prohibited sodomy – and thus prosecutions for sodomy are not necessary to protect morals in a democratic society."[1072] If this had happened in an Arab country, the decision of the Arab Court would be that homosexuality is prohibited because it is against Sharia law. In addition, the Arab Court would similarly say that all of the member states prohibited sodomy and thus prosecutions for sodomy are significantly necessary to protect morals in a democratic society. The important question that should be raised by the Arab Court is that it should examine whether the convicted persons enjoyed the right to a fair trial and were given their full rights to defend themselves.

Homosexuality is against *fitrah*, which advocates traditional marriage between a man and a woman. It is also against the order of nature. In addition, men and women are encouraged to marry in order for reproduction to continue and for subsequent generations to continue. In the case of *Singer vs. Hara*, the homo-

---

1069 ACHR, *supra* note 126, at art. 10.

1070 U.S. DEPARTMENT OF STATE, TRAFFICKING IN PERSONS REPORT (2006), http://www.state.gov/g/tip/rls/tiprpt/2006/65988.htm (last visited Mar. 3, 2012).

1071 U.S. DEPARTMENT OF STATE, TRAFFICKING IN PERSONS REPORT (2011), http://www.state.gov/documents/organization/164454.pdf (Last visited March 3, 2012).

1072 Brauch, *supra* note 555.

sexual applicants were not given a marriage license, not "because of sex discrimination but because of the very definition of marriage as between a man and a woman."[1073] On the other hand, it should be noted that the United States of America Supreme Court's decision in *United States vs. Windsor* declared the federal Defense of Marriage Act unconstitutional. The Supreme Court held that restricting United States of America federal interpretation of "marriage" and "spouse" to apply only to heterosexual unions, by Section 3 of the Defense of Marriage Act (DOMA), violates the Due Process Clause of the Fifth Amendment.[1074]

God is the only one who created people and who also created *fitrah*. Therefore, the religions cannot be against *fitrah*; they have to comply with *fitrah*. Judge Zekia said in his dissenting to the case of *Dudgeon vs. the United Kingdom*, "Christian and Moslem religions are all united in the condemnation of homosexual relations and of sodomy. Moral conceptions to a great degree are rooted in religious beliefs. All civilised countries until recent years penalised sodomy and buggery and akin unnatural practices."[1075] Judge Zekia also added:

> We must not forget and must bear in mind that respect is also due to the people holding the opposite view, especially in a country populated by a great majority of such people who are completely against unnatural immoral practices. Surely the majority in a democratic society are also entitled under Articles 8, 9 and 10 (art. 8, art. 9, art. 10) of the Convention and Article 2 of Protocol No. 1 (P1-2) to respect for their religious and moral beliefs and entitled to teach and bring up their children consistently with their own religious and philosophical convictions.

A democratic society is governed by the rule of the majority. It seems to me somewhat odd and perplexing, in considering the necessity of respect for one's private life, to underestimate the necessity of keeping a law in force for the protection of morals held in high esteem by the majority of people.

A change of the law so as to legalise homosexual activities in private by adults is very likely to cause many disturbances in the country in question. The respondent Government were justified in finding it necessary to keep the relevant Acts on the

---

1073 WILLIAM STACY JOHNSON, A TIME TO EMBRACE 30 (2006).
1074 United States vs. Windsor http://www.supremecourt.gov/opinions/12pdf/12-307_6j37.pdf (last visited May 8, 2014).
1075 Dudgeon v the United Kingdom, no. 7525/6; *see also* Dudgeon v the United Kingdom, WIKIPEDIA.ORG, *supra* note 1051.

statute book for the protection of morals as well as for the preservation of public peace.[1076]

Because of the fact that homosexuality is against *fitrah* and the nature of God, it is still illegal in seventy-six countries. Even in the countries that consider homosexuality to be legal, there are many people living in these countries who still consider homosexuality to be an unnatural act. Therefore, it is impossible for homosexuality to be a major human rights principle, because there is no international consensus on this issue. Of the seventy-six countries against this issue, twenty-two of them are Arab countries. The Arab countries are not the only countries against this change; there are also many other countries that are opposed. For instance, in May 2012, North Carolina voters "approved a state constitutional amendment that bans same-sex marriage and civil unions… Twenty-eight other states have voter-approved constitutional bans on same-sex marriages, according to the National Conference of State Legislatures."[1077] As I previously mentioned, however, the United States of America Supreme Court's decision in *United States vs. Windsor* declared the federal Defense of Marriage Act unconstitutional. This example clearly shows that there is no international consensus on the approval of same sex marriage. Even in the United States of America, more than 50% of the American states voted for constitutional bans on same-sex marriage. This is because homosexuality is against *fitrah* and the law of nature. The legislators can permit homosexuality, however, when the public votes on the issue, they usually vote against homosexuality, because they are affected by *fitrah*. The Quran explains, "And that He (Allah) creates the pairs, male and female."[1078] In all human beings, animals, and plants there are male and female pairs. The Quran explains, "And of everything We have created pairs, that you may remember (the Grace of Allah)."[1079]

I agree entirely with Judge Zekia, who stated that the opinion of the majority in a certain country should be respected because the democratic society is governed by the rule of the majority. The parliament represents the majority and they adopt legislation that is not contrary to the morals, public order, and fundamental principles of the majority. Any legalization of homosexuality in the Arab countries

---

1076 Dudgeon v the United Kingdom, European Court of Human Rights, http://cmiskp.echr.coe.int/tkp197/view.asp?action=html&documentId=695350&portal=hbkm&source=externalbydocnumber&table=F69A27FD8FB86142BF01C1166DEA398649 (last visited Mar. 11, 2012).

1077 Wade Rawlins, *North Carolina Voters Approve Same-Sex Marriage Ban*, REUTERS.COM, http://www.reuters.com/article/2012/05/09/us-usa-campaign-northcarolina-gays-idUSBRE8470LT20120509 (last visited May 9, 2012).

1078 QURAN 53:45.

1079 *Id.* at 51:49.

is against the will of the majority and will cause disturbance in the public order. Also, due to the fact that homosexuality is against nature it can cause a lot of diseases. In 1994, the United Kingdom Armed Forces Policy and Guidelines stated that "homosexual behaviour can cause offence, polarise relationships, induce ill-discipline, and...damage morale and unit effectiveness."[1080] We can see clearly that prohibiting homosexuality helps the Arab Charter in maintaining public order and protecting human rights for the people within its jurisdiction. The principle of the margin of appreciation should be applied in order to accept the criminalization of homosexuality in Arab countries. In addition, it can be criminalized easily because it is a debatable issue and there is no international consensus on its decriminalization. As a result, each region can do whatever is needed by the public order and by its democratic society. This way, it can be criminalized in some regions and decriminalized in other regions. People living in each region should respect the law.

Sharia law can be used to promote the Arab Charter for better protection of human rights. For instance, the Arab Charter can be used to request that the states parties fulfill the human rights requirements of Sharia law. For example, if a country is applying *hodood* punishments in cases of prostitution, it can be requested that the country not apply *hodood* on those committing prostitution unless he or she is seen by four witnesses while engaging in the sexual act.

1080 Sameera Dalvi, *supra* note 1044, at 481; *see also* Richard Kamm, *supra* note 1045.

F. Torture and Cruel, Inhuman, or Degrading Treatment or Punishment

1. Introduction

In this section, I will explain how the Arab Charter treats torture through a comparative evaluation, whereby I will examine the approach taken to torture by different international and regional conventions in order to demonstrate its similarities with the Arab Charter. Furthermore, I will briefly give examples of international governmental committees, such as the concluding observations of the Human Rights Committee regarding some Arab countries. In addition, I will explain the Sharia law point of view regarding torture to show that it is compatible with international human rights. I will also explain the '*hodood*' punishments (the criminal punishments of Sharia law) to point out that Sharia law does not want to torture people. Also, I will explain different opinions between Islamic jurisprudential schools and scholars regarding the interpretation of the verses of the Quran.

The right to not be subjected to torture inhuman or degrading treatment is a fundamental right that is stated in all international and regional human rights instruments.

Article 1 of the Convention against Torture and other Cruel, Inhuman or Degrading Treatment or Punishment (1984), defined the term 'torture' as follows:

> For the purposes of this Convention, the term "torture" means any act by which severe pain or suffering, whether physical or mental, is intentionally inflicted on a person for such purposes as obtaining from him or a third person information or a confession, punishing him for an act he or a third person has committed or is suspected of having committed, or intimidating or coercing him or a third person, or for any reason based on discrimination of any kind, when such pain or suffering is inflicted by or at the instigation of or with the consent or acquiescence of a public official or other person acting in an official capacity. It does not include pain or suffering arising only from, inherent in or incidental to lawful sanctions.[1081]

There are many international and regional instruments that are concerned with this issue.[1082]

1081 Convention against Torture and Other Cruel, Inhuman or Degrading Treatment or Punishment art. 1, June 12, 2002, U.N. Doc. CAT/C/CR/28/5, http://www.unhchr.ch/tbs/doc.nsf/(Symbol)/CAT.C.CR.28.5.En?Opendocument (last visited Jan. 4, 2010).

1082 International instruments include:
Article 2 of the Convention against Torture and Other Cruel, Inhuman or Degrading Treatment

or Punishment 1984, which states: "1. Each State Party shall take effective legislative, administrative, judicial or other measures to prevent acts of torture in any territory under its jurisdiction. 2. No exceptional circumstances whatsoever, whether a state of war or a threat of war, internal political in stability or any other public emergency, may be invoked as a justification of torture. 3. An order from a superior officer or a public authority may not be invoked as a justification of torture." (Convention against Torture and Other Cruel, Inhuman or Degrading Treatment or Punishment, *supra* note 1081, art. 5).

Article 5 of the Universal Declaration of Human Rights, which states, "No one shall be subjected to torture or to cruel, inhuman or degrading treatment or punishment." (UDHR, *supra* note 106, at art. 5).

Article 7 of the International Covenant on Civil and Political Rights 1966, which states, "No one shall be subjected to torture or to cruel, inhuman or degrading treatment or punishment. In particular, no one shall be subjected without his free consent to medical or scientific experimentation." (ICCPR, *supra* note 63, at art 3).

Article 1 of the Declaration on the Protection of All Persons from Being Subjected to Torture and Other Cruel, Inhuman or Degrading Treatment or Punishment, which states: "1. For the purpose of this Declaration, torture means any act by which severe pain or suffering, whether physical or mental, is intentionally inflicted by or at the instigation of a public official on a person for such purposes as obtaining from him or a third person information or confession, punishing him for an act he has committed or is suspected of having committed, or intimidating him or other persons. It does not include pain or suffering arising only from, inherent in or incidental to, lawful sanctions to the extent consistent with the Standard Minimum Rules for the Treatment of Prisoners. 2. Torture constitutes an aggravated and deliberate form of cruel, inhuman or degrading treatment or punishment." (Article 1 of The UNGA Res. 3452 (XXX) of 9 December 1975, Declaration on the protection of all persons from being subjected to torture and other cruel, inhuman or degrading treatment or punishment.)

Article 7 (Crimes against Humanity) of the Rome Statute of International Criminal Court 1998, which states: "For the purpose of this Statute, "crime against humanity" means any of the following acts when committed as part of a widespread or systematic attack directed against any civilian population, with knowledge of the attack: (…) (f) Torture.

2. For the purpose of paragraph 1: (…) (e) "Torture" means the intentional infliction of severe pain or suffering, whether physical or mental, upon a person in the custody or under the control of the accused; except that torture shall not include pain or suffering arising only from, inherent in or incidental to, lawful sanctions. (U.N. General Assembly, Rome Statute of the International Criminal Court (last amended 2010) art. 7, July 17 1998, ISBN No. 92-9227-227-6, http://www.unhcr.org/refworld/docid/3ae6b3a84.html (last visited Feb. 6, 2013).

Article 7 (1) (f) of the International Criminal Court Element of Crimes 2000, which states: "1. The Perpetrator inflicted severe physical or mental pain or suffering upon one or more persons. 2. Such person or persons were in the custody or under the control of the perpetrator. 3. Such pain or suffering did not arise only from, and was not inherent in or incidental to, lawful sanctions. 4. The conduct was committed as part of a widespread or systematic attack directed against a civilian population. 5. The perpetrator knew that a conduct was part of or intended the conduct to be part of a widespread or systematic attack directed against a civilian population." (International Criminal Court (ICC), Report of the Preparatory Commission for the International Criminal Court. Addendum. Part II, Finalized draft text of the Elements of Crimes art. 7 (1) (f), Nov. 2, 2000, PCNICC/2000 /1/Add.2 http://www.unhcr.org/refworld/docid/46a5fd2e2.html (last visited Feb. 6, 2013).

Article 8 (War crimes) of the Rome Statute of the International Criminal Court 1998, which states: "'War crimes' means: (a) Grave breaches of the Geneva Conventions of 12 August 1949, namely, any of the following acts against persons or property protected under the provisions of the relevant Geneva Convention:(…) (ii) Torture or inhuman treatment, including biological experiments; (…) (b) Other serious violations of the laws and customs applicable in international armed conflict, within the established framework of international law, namely, any of the following acts: (…) (xxi) Committing outrages upon personal dignity, in particular humiliating and degrading treatment; (…) (c)In the case of an armed conflict not of an international character, serious violations of article 3 common to the four Geneva Conventions of 12 August 1949, namely, any of the following acts committed against persons taking no active part in the hostilities, including members of armed forces who have laid down their arms and those placed hors de combat by sickness, wounds, detention or any other cause: (i) Violence to life and person, in particular murder of all kinds, mutilation, cruel treatment and torture; (ii) Committing outrages upon personal dignity, in particular humiliating and degrading treatment; (…) (d) Paragraph 2 (c) applies to armed conflicts not of an international character and thus does not apply to situations of internal disturbances and tensions, such as riots, isolated and sporadic acts of violence or other acts of a similar nature." (U.N. General Assembly, Rome Statute of the International Criminal Court (last amended 2010) art. 8, July 17 1998, ISBN No. 92-9227-227-6, http://untreaty.un.org/cod/icc/statute/english/rome_statute(e).pdf (last visited July 31, 2013).

Regional instruments include:

Article 3 of the European Convention for the Protection of Human Rights and Fundamental Freedoms 1950, which states that, "No one shall be subjected to torture or to inhuman or degrading treatment or punishment." (Council of Europe, European Convention for the Protection of Human Rights and Fundamental Freedoms, as amended by Protocols Nos. 11 and 14, art. 3, Nov. 4, 1950, ETS 5, http://www.unhcr.org/refworld/docid/3ae6b3b04.html (last visited Feb. 6, 2013).

Article 1 of the European Convention for the Prevention of Torture and Inhuman or Degrading Treatment or Punishment 1987, which states, "There shall be established a European Committee for the Prevention of Torture and Inhuman or Degrading Treatment or Punishment (hereinafter referred to as "the Committee"). The Committee shall, by means of visits, examine the treatment of persons deprived of their liberty with a view to strengthening, if necessary, the protection of such persons from torture and from inhuman or degrading treatment or punishment." (Convention against Torture and Other Cruel, Inhuman or Degrading Treatment or Punishment, *supra* note 1081, art. 1).

Article 5 (2) of the American Convention on Human Rights, which states, "No one shall be subjected to torture or to cruel, inhuman, or degrading punishment or treatment. All persons deprived of their liberty shall be treated with respect for the inherent dignity of the human person." (Organization of American States, American Convention on Human Rights, "Pact of San Jose", Costa Rica, art. 5 (2), Nov. 22, 1969, http://www.unhcr.org/refworld/docid/3ae6b36510.html (last visited Feb. 6, 2013).

Article 2 of the Inter-American Convention to Prevent and Punish Torture, which states: "For the purposes of this Convention, torture shall be understood to be any act intentionally performed whereby physical or mental pain or suffering is inflicted on a person for purposes of criminal investigation, as a means of intimidation, as personal punishment, as a preventive measure, as a penalty, or for any other purpose. Torture shall also be understood to be the use of methods upon a person intended to obliterate the personality of the victim or to diminish

For example, the Cairo Declaration on Human Rights in Islam provides,

> "It is not permitted to subject him to physical or psychological torture or to any form of humiliation, cruelty or indignity. Nor is it permitted to subject an individual to medical or scientific experimentation without his consent or at the risk of his health or of his life. Nor is it permitted to promulgate emergency laws that would provide executive authority for such actions."[1083]

Article 8 of the Arab Charter on Human Rights states:

> No one shall be subjected to physical or psychological torture or to cruel, degrading, humiliating or inhuman treatment. Each State party shall protect every individual subject to its jurisdiction from such practices and shall take effective measures to prevent them. The commission of, or participation in, such acts shall be regarded as crimes that are punishable by law and not subject to any statute of limitations. Each

---

his physical or mental capacities, even if they do not cause physical pain or mental anguish. The concept of torture shall not include physical or mental pain or suffering that is inherent in or solely the consequence of lawful measures, provided that they do not include the performance of the acts or use of the methods referred to in this article." (Organization of American States, *Inter-American Convention to Prevent and Punish Torture*, Dec. 9, 1985, OAS Treaty Series, No. 67, art. 2, http://www.unhcr.org/refworld/docid/3ae6b3620.htmt (last visited Feb. 6, 2013).

Article 3 of the same Convention states, "The following shall be held guilty of the crime of torture: (A) A public servant or employee who acting in that capacity orders, instigates or induces the use of torture, or who directly commits it or who, being able to prevent it, fails to do so. (B) A person who at the instigation of a public servant or employee mentioned in subparagraph (a) orders, instigates or induces the use of torture, directly commits it or is an accomplice thereto" (*Id.* at art. 3).

Article 4 of the same Convention states, "The fact of having acted under orders of a superior shall not provide exemption from the corresponding criminal liability" (*Id.* at art. 4).

Article 5 of the same Convention states: "The existence of circumstances such as a state of war, threat of war, state of siege or of emergency, domestic disturbance or strife, suspension of constitutional guarantees, domestic political instability, or other public emergencies or disasters shall not be invoked or admitted as justification for the crime of torture. Neither the dangerous character of the detainee or prisoner, nor the lack of security of the prison establishment or penitentiary shall justify torture." (*Id.* at art. 5).

Article 5 of the African Charter on Human and Peoples' Rights states, "Every individual shall have the right to the respect of the dignity inherent in a human being and to the recognition of his legal status. All forms of exploitation and degradation of man particularly slavery, slave trade, torture, cruel, inhuman or degrading punishment and treatment shall be prohibited. (African Charter, *supra* note 127, at art. 5).

1083 Cairo Declaration on Human Rights in Islam, *supra* note 423, art. 20.

State party shall guarantee in its legal system redress for any victim of torture and the right to rehabilitation and compensation.

Article 9 of this Charter states:

No one shall be subjected to medical or scientific experimentation or to the use of his organs without his free consent and full awareness of the consequences and provided that ethical, humanitarian and professional rules are followed and medical procedures are observed to ensure his personal safety pursuant to the relevant domestic laws in force in each State party. Trafficking in human organs is prohibited in all circumstances.

The previous articles from different conventions outlined in the footnote show that all of the international conventions, including the Arab Charter, are very similar in regards to the prohibition of torture. I will explain the nature of torture from the Sharia law point of view later.

The United Nations General Assembly's definition of torture in its 1975 declaration stated, "Torture constitutes an aggravated and deliberate form of cruel, inhuman and degrading treatment or punishment."[1084] The prohibition of torture is considered to be an essential basic right and no derogation from it is accepted. The prohibition of torture is considered to be a peremptory norm of international law.[1085] The absolute prohibition of torture was clearly stressed in the *Chahal* case,[1086] concerning the intent of the United Kingdom to deport Chahal, a Sikh separatist, to India by arguing that he had been involved in terrorist activities and posed a risk to the national security of the United Kingdom. The European Court of Human Rights emphasized,

"Article 3 enshrines one of the most fundamental values of democratic society. The Court is well aware of the immense difficulties faced by States in modern times in protecting their communities from terrorist violence. However, even in these circumstances, the Convention prohibits in absolute terms torture or inhuman or degrading treatment or punishment, irrespective of the victim's conduct."[1087]

1084 Article 1 of The UNGA Res. 3452 (XXX) of 9 December 1975, Declaration on the protection of all persons from being subjected to torture and other cruel, inhuman or degrading treatment or punishment.

1085 BADERIN, *supra* note 138.

1086 Chahal vs. United Kingdom (App. 22414/93), Judgment of 15 November 1996; (1997) 23 E.H.R.R. 413.

1087 Para. 80 of the judgment.

In the *Greek* case concerning the alleged violation of Article 3 by the Greek Government after the revolution of April 21, 1967,[1088] the Commission explained and analyzed the meaning of Article 3 by saying:

> It is plain that there may be treatment to which all these descriptions apply, for all torture must be inhuman and degrading treatment covers at least such treatment as deliberately causes severe suffering, mental or physical, which, in the particular situation, is unjustifiable. The word 'torture' is often used to describe inhuman treatment, which has a purpose, such as the obtaining of information or confessions, or the infliction of punishment, and it is generally an aggravated form of inhuman treatment. Treatment or punishment of an individual may be said to be degrading if it grossly humiliates him before others or drives him to act against his will or conscience.[1089]

In *Il vs. Bulgaria*,[1090] the Court stated that "the Court considers that the conditions of detention of the applicant amounted to inhuman and degrading treatment contrary to Article 3 of the Convention..."[1091] and that:

> The Court further notes that the sanitary conditions in which the applicant was kept were very unsatisfactory. The cell was dark, poorly ventilated and apparently damp... The Court considers that the fact that the applicant had to spend practically twenty-four hours a day during nearly three months in an overcrowded cell without exposure to natural light and without any possibility for physical and other out-of-cell activities must have caused him intense suffering. The Court is of the view that in the absence of compelling security considerations there was no justification for subjecting the applicant to such limitations.[1092]

It was also stated, "The Court considers that the applicant has undoubtedly suffered non-pecuniary damage as a result of his detention for approximately three months in conditions which were inhuman and degrading ..."[1093] The Court added that this constitutes a violation of Article 5 (paragraph 1, 3, 4).[1094] The Court also mentioned that the act of the detention of an individual for three months in

---

1088 The Greek Case, Report of 5 November 1969, (1969) 12 Yearbook 186-510.
1089 *Id.* at 186.
1090 Il vs. Bulgaria (App. 44082/98), Judgment of 9 June 2005. http://hudoc.echr.coe.int/sites/eng/pages/search.aspx?i=001-69313 (last visited Feb. 6, 2013).
1091 *Id.*
1092 *Id.*
1093 *Id.*
1094 *Id.*

a very small cell, without any natural light or satisfactory ventilation, coupled with poor sanitary facilities and no provision for spending time out of his cell, is considered inhuman and degrading treatment. The Court differentiated between torture and inhuman and degrading treatment. The Court outlined that torture is usually distinguished from 'cruel, inhuman or degrading treatment and punishment' in areas of severity, intent, and the intensity of suffering or pain. In *Ireland vs. UK*, the European Court stated that, "'torture' attaches 'a special stigma to deliberate inhuman treatment causing very serious and cruel suffering.'"[1095]

The circumstances of a case are the main way through which it can be determined whether torture or inhuman or degrading treatment has occurred.[1096] In the case of *Ireland vs. United Kingdom*, the Court mentioned that some factors that can lead to determining the existence of inhuman treatments include: the age, sex, and health of the victim; the duration of the treatment; and its physical or mental effects.[1097] The concluding observations of the Human Rights Committee regarding Kuwait provide:

> The Committee is concerned about alleged practices of torture and inhumane or degrading treatment of prisoners in police custody and in detention centres. (arts. 7, 10). The State party should ensure independent and prompt investigation and prosecution of State officials responsible for alleged acts of torture or inhumane or degrading treatment, and grant compensation to victims of such acts. The State party should also guarantee full respect for the United Nations Standard Minimum Rules for the Treatment of Prisoners.[1098]

The concluding observations of the Human Rights Committee regarding Jordan provide:

> The Committee is concerned at the high number of reported cases of torture and ill-treatment in detention centres, particularly in the General Intelligence Directorate facilities. It also notes with concern the absence of a genuinely independent complaints mechanism to deal with cases of alleged torture or ill-treatment by public officials, as well as the low number of prosecutions of such cases. The Committee is further

---

1095 Tyrer vs. United Kingdom, 25 April 1978, (1979-80) 2 E.H.R.R. at series a, No. 3, para. 167.
1096 JACOBS & WHITE, *supra* note 566, at 77.
1097 Ireland vs. United Kingdom, Judgment of 18 January 1978, series A, No. 25; (1979-80) 2 E.H.R.R. 25, para. 162 of Judgment.
1098 U.N. Human Rights Committee, Concluding Observations, Kuwait, 103rd Session, Oct. 17-Nov. 4 2011, http://www.ohchr.org/EN/countries/MENARegion/Pages/KWIndex.aspx (last visited Mar. 26, 2012).

concerned at information that the right to prompt access to a lawyer and an independent medical examination is not granted to detainees (arts. 7 and 9).[1099]

The concluding observations of the Committee against Torture regarding Syria provide:

> The Committee is deeply concerned at numerous reports of torture, ill treatment, death in custody and incommunicado detention of people belonging to the Kurdish minority, in large part stateless, in particular political activists of Kurdish origins. The Committee is further concerned that convictions to some Kurdish detainees pronounced by military courts have been passed on vague charges of "weakening national sentiment" or "spreading false of exaggerated information." Moreover, the Committee notes with concern reports of growing trend of deaths of Kurdish conscripts who have died whilst carrying out their mandatory military service and whose bodies were returned to the families with evidence of severe injuries (arts. 1, 2, 12 and 16).[1100]

The concluding observations of the Human Rights Committee on Algeria, provide, "the Committee is concerned that confessions obtained under torture are not explicitly prohibited and excluded as evidence under the State party's legislation (Covenant, arts. 7and 14)."[1101]

Many of the laws of the states parties of the Arab League stress the issue of prohibiting torture. For instance, in the United Arab Emirates, the federal law on the organization of penal institutions stated, "It is prohibited any act of cruelty or beatings or torture or other manifestations of physical assault on the prisoner, also prohibits any form of psychological oppression. The discipline penalties assessed in accordance with the provisions of the law and this chapter."[1102]

1099 U.N. Human Rights Committee, Concluding Observations, Jordan, 100th Session, Geneva, Oct. 11-29, 2010, http://daccess-dds-ny.un.org/doc/UNDOC/GEN/G10/467/05/PDF/G1046705.pdf?OpenElement (last visited Feb. 10, 2013).

1100 Committee against Torture, Concluding Observations, Syrian Arab Republic, 44th Sess. April 26-May 14, 2010, http://www2.ohchr.org/english/bodies/cat/docs/CAT.C.SYR.CO.1.pdf (last visited Mar. 26, 2012).

1101 U.N. Human Rights Committee, Concluding Observations, Algeria, 91st Sess.Oct. 15-Nov.2, 2007, http://daccess-dds-ny.un.org/doc/UNDOC/GEN/G07/457/74/PDF/G0745774.pdf?OpenElement (last visited Feb. 10, 2013).

1102 The Ministry of Interior Resolution number 471 for the year 1995, article 86 (1) of the executive regulation of the federal law 43 for the year 1992 on the organization of penal institutions.

The Egyptian Constitution not only prohibits torture but also provides that the crime of torture is not subject to any statute of limitations. The Constitution provides that "Torture in all forms and types is a crime that is not subject to prescription."[1103] Furthermore, the Consitution states,

> Every person who is either arrested, detained, or his freedom is restricted shall be treated in a manner that maintains his dignity. He/she may not be tortured, intimidated, coerced, or physically or morally harmed; and may not be seized or detained except in places designated for that purpose, which shall be adequate on human and health levels. The State shall cater for the needs of people with disability.[1104]

Article 126 of the Egyptian Penal Code penalizes acts of civil servants or public employees who commit torture or order acts of torture for the purpose of obtaining confession. The sentence of doing this crime of torture is imprisonment of not less than three years and not exceeding ten years. If the person who was tortured died, then the punishment will be the same as in cases of murder. The Egyptian Supreme Court has not given a detailed definition of torture and it has not mentioned the exact limit beyond which an act is considered torture. The Supreme Court stated that it is left up to the discretion of the authority of the Court to decide depending on the circumstances of the case.[1105] In one case, the Egyptian Supreme Court stated that if a person was tortured in order to force him to confess to committing a certain crime, the torture would be recognized as a crime even if the tortured person did not confess to anything. The law enforcement officer will be accused of committing torture as long as his or her act of torture was inflicted for the purpose of obtaining a confession.[1106]

Sharia law prohibits any kind of torture or cruel, inhuman, or degrading treatment and prohibits the subjection of a human being to scientific experimentation without his or her consent. It has been reported that Prophet Mohammed said, "God will torture, in the hereafter, those who torture people in life."[1107] Sharia law prohibits torture not only on human beings, but also on animals. Prophet Mohammed said,

---

1103 Egyptian Const. art. 52. http://www.sis.gov.eg/Newvr/Dustor-en001.pdf (last visited May 14, 2014).
1104 Egyptian Const. art. 55. http://www.sis.gov.eg/Newvr/Dustor-en001.pdf (last visited May 14, 2014).
1105 Case No. 1314 for the Judicial year 36 K, Decided in 28/11/1966.
1106 Case No 5732 for the Judicial year 63 K, Decided in 08/03/1995.
1107 BADERIN, *supra* note 138, at 76.

> "A woman was tortured and was put in Hell because of a cat which she had kept locked till it died of hunger. Allah's Apostle further said, (Allah knows better) Allah said (to the woman), You neither fed it nor watered when you locked it up, nor did you set it free to eat the insects of the earth."[1108]

The conclusions and recommendations of the Committee against Torture on Yemen welcomed "The establishment of the Human Rights Ministry in 2003 aimed at promoting and ensuring respect for human rights, including consideration of individual complaints."[1109] The Committee stated that there is "lack of a comprehensive definition of torture in the domestic law."[1110] Furthermore, the Committee added that, "The nature of some criminal sanctions, in particular flogging and amputation of limbs, which may be in breach of the Convention."[1111] The Committee requested that the states parties "Take all appropriate measures to ensure that criminal sanctions are in full conformity with the Convention."[1112] In 2002, the conclusions and recommendations of the Committee against Torture on Egypt welcomed "Decisions taken by the Egyptian courts to refuse any confession made under duress as evidence."[1113] It stated:

> The establishment in 2000 of the Directorate-General for Human Rights Affairs at the Ministry of Justice, whose functions are to assume responsibility for the fulfillment of the legal aspects of international obligations arising from human rights instruments, including the preparation of replies to international bodies, promote greater public awareness and provide training on these matters for members of the judiciary and the Department of Public Prosecutions.[1114]

The Committee was concerned about "The fact that a state of emergency has been in force since 1981, hindering the full consolidation of the rule of law in

---

1108 *Narrated 'Abdullah bin 'Umar, Sahih Muslim, Book 40, Hadith 553*, SEARCHTRUTH.COM, http://www.searchtruth.com/searchHadith.php?keyword=cat&translator=1&search=1&book=&start=0&records_display=10&search_word=exact (date last visited).

1109 Committee against Torture, Conclusions and Recommendations, Yemen, U.N. Doc. CAT/C/CR/31/4 (Feb. 5, 2004) http://www.unhchr.ch/tbs/doc.nsf/(Symbol)/e8ad754e16566e4fc1256e6800349a5c?Opendocument (last visited Mar. 18, 2012).

1110 *Id.*

1111 *Id.*

1112 *Id.*

1113 Committee against Torture, Conclusions and Recommendations, Egypt, U.N. Doc. CAT/C/CR/29/4 (Dec. 23, 2002), http://www.unhchr.ch/tbs/doc.nsf/(Symbol)/4db43a0eb288d650c1256dc60037256c?Opendocument (last visited Mar. 18, 2012).

1114 *Id.*

Egypt, the excessive length of many of the proceedings initiated in cases of torture and ill-treatment, and the fact that many court decisions to release detainees are not enforced in practice."[1115] The Committee recommended that Egypt "Adopt a definition of torture which fully corresponds to the definition in article 1, paragraph 1, of the Convention."[1116] The situation in Egypt changed after the Egyptian revolutions. The state of emergency, which had been active for more than thirty years, was deactivated on June 1, 2012. For the first time the new Egyptian Constitution highlights the human rights treaties, the constitution provides that "The State shall be bound by the international human rights agreements, covenants and conventions ratified by Egypt, and which shall have the force of law after publication in accordance with the prescribed conditions."[1117] With time, the situation in Egypt is improving.

In the conclusions and observations of the Committee against Torture on Qatar, "the Committee notes the creation of the Qatari Institution for the Protection of Women and Children in 2003 as well as the establishment of a set of telephone hotlines to aid persons complaining of abuse."[1118] It added, "The State party should adopt a definition of torture in domestic penal law consistent with article 1 of the Convention, including the differing purposes set forth therein, and should ensure that all acts of torture are offences under criminal law, and that appropriate penalties are established for those responsible for such acts."[1119]

In this context, it is often assumed that Sharia law, in particular its *hodood* punishments, constitutes or promotes torture. It is therefore apposite to address those punishments in greater detail.

2. *Hodood* Islamic Punishments

Before explaining *hodood* according to Sharia law, it is important to examine some of the Western points of views regarding *hodood*. It is important to know whether or not *hodood* is considered a problem with respect to the protection of human rights. For instance, an Amnesty International report released in 2003 stated,

---

1115 *Id.*

1116 *Id.*

1117 Unofficial translation of the Egyptian Const., art. 93, http://www.sis.gov.eg/Newvr/Dustor-en001.pdf (last visited May 14, 2014).

1118 Committee against Torture, Conclusions and Observations, Qatar, U.N. Doc. CAT/C/QAT/CO/1, (July 25, 2006), http://www.unhchr.ch/tbs/doc.nsf/898586b1dc7b4043c1256a450044f331/4b6bc620e633dfd1c12571ee00286e7f/$FILE/G0643239.pdf (last visited Mar. 18, 2012).

1119 *Id.*

> "The Sudanese Penal Code, which is partly based on interpretation of Islamic legal doctrines, allows for penalties including flogging and amputations ... Amnesty International does not take a position on Islamic or any other religious law, but does consider such penalties to be cruel, inhuman and degrading punishments which are inconsistent with Sudan's obligations under international human rights law (Sudan is a state party to the International Covenant on Civil and Political Rights)."[1120]

There are four kinds of principles related to Islamic punishments: *Qisas, Diyyah, hodood,* and *Ta'zir*.[1121] *Qisas* is the famous principle that means the "Law of equality in punishment."[1122] The Quran explains, "And We ordained therein for them: 'Life for life, eye for eye, nose for nose, ear for ear, tooth for tooth, and wounds equal for equal.' But if anyone remits the retaliation by way of charity, it shall be for him an expiation. And whosoever does not judge by that which Allah has revealed, such are the Zalimun (polytheists and wrong-doers – of a lesser degree)."[1123]

Diyyah is the blood money paid to the victim's family.[1124] For instance, the Quran states:

> It is not for a believer to kill a believer except (that it be) by mistake; and whosoever kills a believer by mistake, (it is ordained that) he must set free a believing slave and a compensation (blood-money, i.e. Diya) be given to the deceased's family unless they remit it. If the deceased belonged to a people at war with you and he was a believer, the freeing of a believing slave (is prescribed); and if he belonged to a people with whom you have a treaty of mutual alliance, compensation (blood-money – Diya) must be paid to his family, and a believing slave must be freed. And whoso finds this (the penance of freeing a slave) beyond his means, he must fast for two consecutive months in order to seek repentance from Allah. And Allah is Ever All-Knowing, All-Wise.[1125]

1120 Amnesty Int'l, Sudan: 16-year-old Girl to be Flogged for 'Crime' of Adultery http://www.amnesty.org.uk/news_details.asp?NewsID=15053 (last visited Sep. 5, 2013).
1121 *Hudud*, WIKIPEDIA.ORG, http://en.wikipedia.org/wiki/Hudud (last visited June 9, 2012).
1122 Eye for an eye, http://en.wikipedia.org/wiki/Eye_for_an_eye (last visited May 9, 2014)
1123 QURAN 5:45.
1124 *Id.* at 4:92.
1125 *Id.* at 4:92.

Ta'zir means "punishment, usually corporal, administered at the discretion of the judge."[1126] *Ta'zir* is very broad-ranging authority given to the judge to choose whatever punishment, depending on the gravity of the crime and the circumstances of the case. It can include verbal threatening, imprisonment, expulsion, the death sentence, etc. In addition, crimes that are punished by *Ta'zir* do not have the same evidence requirements as those punished by hodood. For instance, it is not required that there were four witnesses or that there was a confession in order for a criminal to be punished under *Ta'zir*.[1127] In short, *Ta'zir* is like any penal code that includes different categories of punishments.

The fourth category of punishments is hodood. *Hodood* is the plural form, its singular form is 'hadd,' which means limit or the limit beyond which no one should go.[1128] *Hodood* punishments include stoning, hand cutting, and lashing.[1129] *Hodood* punishments are applied to very few crimes, including theft and sexual relations between unmarried couple. For instance the Quran explains, "The fornicatress and the fornicator, flog each of them with a hundred stripes…"[1130] *Hodood* punishments include lashing for cases of adultery; but if the person accused of committing adultery is married and committed adultery with someone else, then the punishment would be stoning. The Quran explains:

> The fornicatress and the fornicator, flog each of them with a hundred stripes. Let not pity withhold you in their case, in a punishment prescribed by Allah, if you believe in Allah and the Last Day. And let a party of the believers witness their punishment. (This punishment is for unmarried persons guilty of the above crime, but if married persons commit it (illegal sex), the punishment is to stone them to death, according to Allah's Law).[1131]

May I clarify at this point that the State of Egypt, in its system of criminal law, does not apply *hodood* punishments. Egypt applies Sharia law mainly in family matters. According to Sharia law, however, *hodood* punishment falls in the category of lawful sanctions. Article 1 of the Declaration on the Protection of All Persons from Being Subjected to Torture and Other Cruel, Inhuman or Degrading Treatment

---

1126 *Hudud, supra* note 1121.
1127 Telephone interview with Prof. Saad al-Din Helaly, Professor of Comparative Islamic Jurisprudence at Al-Azhar University (March 20, 2012).
1128 *Hudud, supra* note 1121.
1129 *Id.*
1130 QURAN 24:2.
1131 *Id.*

or Punishment stated that torture "does not include pain or suffering arising only from, inherent in or incidental to, lawful sanctions ... "[1132]

I will analyze the objectives and purposes of Islam in relation to these crimes. The aim of *hodood* is to prevent crimes from being committed. It is stated, "The main objective of *hudud* is not to punish, but to deter man from committing crime. To achieve this objective, *hudud* is daunting and intimidating, so that man will be frightened of the crime and will stay away from it."[1133] *Hodood* punishment is not applied to certain categories of people, such as those who are mad or insane. There is a *hadith* which states,

> "Once a Muslim man went to see the Rasulullah in a mosque and said: 'O Rasulullah! I have committed adultery.' Rasulullah turned away from the man until the man confessed four times. Then the Prophet called him and asked: 'Are you mad?' The man replied: 'No.' 'Are you married?' The man replied: 'Yes.' The Prophet then said: 'Take him and stone him.'"[1134]

The previous *hadith* shows that *hodood* are usually applied on people that confess to having committed the crime because it is difficult to fulfill the requirement of evidence of *hodood*. Even the Prophet was not willing to apply *hodood* punishment on a person who has admitted committing a crime. The Prophet turned away from the man three times until the man insisted and stated a fourth time that he had committed adultery.

The objectives and purposes of the *hodood* punishment are not to execute the person who committed murder or cut the hand of the thief. The objectives and purposes of *hodood* punishment are to deter the criminal from committing these kinds of crimes.[1135] If the objective was to torture people, Sharia law would not require that at least four witnesses saw the crime in order for criminals to be punished by *hodood*. If the goal was to cut as many hands as possible, Sharia law would state that only one witness was required for *hodood* punishment to be used. Even in cases where all of the evidence is gathered and all the requirements are fulfilled (and four witnesses have been found), Sharia law requests forgiveness

---

1132 Article 1 of The UNGA Res. 3452 (XXX) of 9 December 1975, Declaration on the protection of all persons from being subjected to torture and other cruel, inhuman or degrading treatment or punishment.

1133 Hafiz Firdaus Abdullah, *Characteristics of Hudud, The Islamic Criminal Law*, Muslimvillage.com, http://muslimvillage.com/forums/topic/60736-hudud-offenses-and-punishments/ (last visited Jun. 9, 2012).

1134 *Id.*

1135 Mansour, *supra* note 755, at 84-85.

of the criminal from either the victim or the victim's family. If the objective was to torture people, it would be easy for Sharia law to not encourage forgiveness from the victim or the victim's family. Sharia law always encourages victims and heir(s) to forgive the criminal, and when this occurs, *hodood* punishment should be not used. Even in cases of murder, which is considered one of the gravest crimes on earth, Sharia law encourages forgiveness or paying blood money to the heir. The Quran states:

> O you who believe! Al-Qisas (the Law of Equality in punishment) is prescribed for you in case of murder: the free for the free, the slave for the slave, and the female for the female. But if the killer is forgiven by the brother (or the relatives, etc.) of the killed against blood-money, then adhering to it with fairness and payment of the blood-money to the heir should be made in fairness. This is an alleviation and a mercy from your Lord. So after this whoever transgresses the limits (i.e. kills the killer after taking the blood-money), he shall have a painful torment.[1136]

Crimes cannot be combated by *Hodood* punishments alone. *Ta'zir* punishments must also be used because the objectives and purpose of *hodood* is to deter people. Suppose a case where a person has committed robbery of 5000 pounds and all of the evidence is gathered and the victim refuses to forgive the criminal. Let us assume that the court renders its judgment that the criminal will have his hand cut off. If the victim told the court that he believed that the money he had stolen was owed to him and he stole it from the victim because the victim refused to return it back to him and if this were true, the court should withdraw its punishment. In this case, the court can apply *Ta'zir*, but not *hodood*.[1137]

We should look not only at the graveness of the punishment, but also at the gravity of the crime. Furthermore, *hodood* punishment can only be applied when a significant amount of proof has been shown. It is stated that, "[t]here were very exacting standards of proof that had to be met if hudud punishments were to be implemented."[1138] This significant degree of proof is not used in any other legal system worldwide because if were to be used, it would be very difficult to accuse anyone. For instance, "the stoning is imposed for the married adulterer and his partner only if the crime is proven, either by four male adults eye witnessing the actual sexual intercourse at the same time or by self-confession."[1139] It is very difficult, if not impossible, to have four witnesses in cases of illegal sexual intercourse

---

1136 *Id.* at 2:178.
1137 Helaly, *supra* note 267.
1138 Hudud, *supra* note 1121.
1139 *Id.*

unless this sexual act is committed on the street or in a public place. The objective of *hodood* punishment is not to punish, but to deter.

Sharia law places several restrictions that limit the application of *hodood* punishments. It should be noted that *hodood* punishments cannot be applied on petty crimes. For instance, robbery cannot be punished by *hodood* if only a little amount of money was stolen, even if all the evidence is gathered and even if the criminal confesses to having committing the crime. The Islamic schools of jurisprudence have different opinions regarding the amount of money that is sufficient for the application of *hodood* punishment.[1140] In addition, some schools of Islamic jurisprudence state that the punishment of *hodood* cannot be applied if the crime of robbery is committed on something that is not protected in a storage place (for example, in the case of someone stealing gold or silver that was not in a safety box, but rather was left in an open public place).[1141] Furthermore, *hodood* punishment was not applicable during famines. Omar Ibn El-Khattab, who was one of the companions of Prophet Mohammed and one of the famous caliphs of Muslims, "did not allow the punishment of cutting a thief's hand valid during famines."[1142] Professor Mabrook Ateya, who is a professor of Sharia at Al-Azhar University and one of the popular Islamic scholars in Egypt, noted that Omar Ibn El-Khattab did not suspend the implementation of *hodood* during famines. He added that *hodood* is not applicable during famines. He added that *hodood* is not to be applied to a sick person until they have recovered.[1143] The example of not implementing *hodood* during famines clearly shows that *hodood* cannot be applied on unemployed person who has no fixed salary and does not have money to buy food. In addition, some Islamic scholars say that *hodood* punishments should not be implemented on a person who steals unless he/she committed this crime more than one time, in other words, the crime became a habit.[1144] All of these examples are clear evidence that Sharia law does not seek to torture people or apply *hodood* punishments rampantly. The objective of *hodood* is deterrence, not punishment.

Hodood is also not applied if the killer is the father or the grandfather of the murdered person.[1145] If there is no evidence that proves the guilt of the accused

---

1140 Mansour, *supra* note 755, at 329.

1141 *Id.* at 328-329.

1142 *Balance and Justice on Earth*, Esscr.org, http://www.esscr.org/g205_4.htm (last visited June 9, 2012); *see also* Mansour, *supra* note 755, at 326.

1143 *Dream One Channel: Al-Maw'aza Al-Hassana* (November 3, 2012).

1144 Interview with the Prof. Magdy Ashore, the academic advisor of the Egyptian Mufti (Sep. 23, 2012).

1145 *Al mawso'aa Al-shamlah* (comprehensive encyclopedia), Islamport.com, http://islam-

with certainty, he would not be punished by *hodood*, but would only receive punishment by *Ta'zir*. Sharia law does not list all the kinds of *Ta'zir* punishments, which could include verbal threatening, imprisonment, expulsion, etc. Sharia law leaves this to the legislators and judges to decide. For example, if a person stole money, after the court rendered its decision of the cutting off of his hand, the criminal could say that some of the money that he stole was his own. He could attempt to convince the court that he decided to steal the money because the victim refused to pay him back. In this case, he cannot be punished by *hodood*[1146] and the court would have to withdraw its previous decision of the cutting of his hand. Instead, the court's decision could be his imprisonment (*Ta'zir*). As another example, if a man was arrested while he was having sexual intercourse with a woman, the court might render a decision of lashing him. He could state that he thought that he was going to marry her. In this case, the court would have to withdraw its decision and could render a decision of imprisonment (*Ta'zir*).[1147]

Ta'zir punishments can play a very important role, as, with respect to them, the legislator and the judge have the right to choose the kind of punishments that will be implemented case by case. *Ta'zir* is vital and important as it shows that there are different kinds of punishments; this gives more flexibility to combat crimes. *Ta'zir* punishments show clearly that Sharia law does not seek to torture people. However, if there is any uncertainty about a case, the application of *hodood* would be stopped automatically and the judge would be given the flexibility to apply any other sanction that he or she determines. Dr. Saad Al-Din Helaly, who is a famous professor of Islamic comparative jurisprudence at Al-Azhar University, said that *Ta'zir* punishment cannot be replaced by *hodood*. He said that *Ta'zir* is important to combat crimes in the society. He added that the requirement for evidence is greater in cases punished by *hodood* than in crimes punished by *Ta'zir*. Dr. Saad also outlined the following example in relation to *hodood* crimes: if a person is killed and the family of the victim forgives the criminal, the accused will not be punished by the death sentence. Therefore, *hodood* will not be applied. However, the accused can be imprisoned by *Ta'zir* or the death penalty can even be applied in some cases even if the family of the victim forgives the accused.[1148]

---

port.com/w/fqh/Web/2793/1939.htm?zoom_highlight=%C7%E1%DA%DD%E6 (last visited Aug. 14, 2013).

1146 MANSOUR, *supra* note 755, at 328.
1147 Helaly, *supra* note 267.
1148 *Id.*

Many people and even scholars mistakenly think that Sharia law is seeking torture. However, this is totally wrong. Caliph Omar Ibn El-Khattab said that it is better for *hodood* not to be applied when a case is based only on suspicion or circumstantial evidence.[1149]

According to Sharia law, judges are required to attempt to find any evidence that could prove innocence. For instance, I asked a highly ranked judicial officer from Saudi Arabia to give brief examples on the implementation of Islamic punishments in Saudi Arabia. I asked him about the crime of adultery, in the case of a confession made by the accused woman and there being no other evidence except her confession. He answered that according to Sharia law judges and prosecutors are requested to attempt to locate any suspicion of innocence. *Hodood* punishment will not be implemented in Saudi Arabia on the accused women who admitted committing adultery unless she admitted four repetitive times that she committed adultery. He gave me another example by saying that if a women was found pregnant although she is divorced or her husband was absent from home for a long time (e.g traveling abroad), *Hodood* punishment will not be implemented in Saudi Arabia on the accused women if she said that she was raped and forced to have sex. He added that *hodood* will not be implemented on the accused woman even if she did not say that she was raped except after she was found pregnant. I asked him whether *hodood* punishment can be suspended in murder crimes. He said that the heirs will be asked whether they want retribution or want to pardon the criminal. He added that they may request being paid blood money or pardon without being paid blood money. The heirs can request to stop the implementation of the death sentence at any time even after the court renders its final decision of death sentence. Finally he commented by saying that mercy is integral to Islamic punishment. For instance, imprisonment has side effects on the family of the imprisoned person and on the society. On the other hand, lashing can be painful but has no side effects on society and the family of the accused.

Sheikh Khaled Al-Gendy, who is a famous Islamic scholar in Egypt and the Arab world, said that judges are requested to attempt to locate any suspicion of innocence such that the application of hodood can be suspended. If there is a suspicion, it should not be applied as was articulated by Prophet Mohammed. Sheikh Khaled added that *hodood* punishment is applied only if the criminal admits to having committed the crime. He mentioned an example that happened during the life of Prophet Mohammed, whereby a woman came to the Prophet admitting to having committing adultery. The Prophet did not ask her with whom

---

1149 *Al mawso'aa Al-shamlah, supra* note 1145.

she had committed this crime; the Prophet did not ask about the name of the criminal or where he lived. The Prophet told her to come again to him after she had delivered her baby. He did not imprison her until after she had delivered her baby. She came after the delivery of her baby, and the Prophet requested that she return after she had completed breastfeeding her baby, which can take around two years. The Prophet did not imprison her until after she had finished breastfeeding her baby. After she breastfed her child, he applied *hodood* on her and she was stoned. The previous example shows that Sharia law applies *hodood* punishment only on people that admit to having committing the crime. The woman could have escaped and not returned to the Prophet. The Prophet did not take any measures to prevent the woman from escaping away from the city. In short, *hodood* punishment is not enacted out of a desire to torture people, rather it is a kind of deterrent.[1150]

Regarding the gravity of the *hodood* punishments, Sheikh Khaled commented that any punishment in the world that does not include a kind of moral and/or material torture is not a punishment. Imprisonment is a kind of torture. The *hodood* crimes are only applied to serious crimes.[1151]

As previously mentioned, the Arabic translation of *hodood* is limited. In other words, there is a limit beyond which no one should go. For instance, imagine a criminal that insists on entering a military base that has signs indicating not to trespass. If the criminal were killed or injured by an electric fence surrounding the military area, would we claim that this was torture and insist that the military should remove the electric fence? Why do we not feel sympathy toward the criminal and accuse the military base of torturing the victim? The answer is that the military base put a limit beyond which no one should enter and this was indicated at the entrance to the military base. In this way, *hodood* punishment threatens and deters those who commit these kinds of crimes in that they know that they will be punished if four witnesses see them while they are committing such a crime. A very weak point of the international human rights system is that the drafters of these treaties focus more on rights and not on duties. In addition, the drafters focus on the criminals and not on the victims or the society. However, Sharia law recognizes both the rights of the victim and the right of the suspect to a fair trial.

In light of my proposed theory, which is based on Sharia law and gradualism, *hodood* punishment should not be abolished absolutely even if some Western

---

1150 Telephone interview with Sheikh Khaled Al-Gendy (Aug. 29, 2012).
1151 *Id.*

scholars think that it violates *jus cogens* rights. In fact, *hodood* punishment is not a violation of *jus cogens* rights. *Jus cogens* prohibits torture, and torture does not include "pain or suffering arising only from, inherent in or incidental to, lawful sanctions."[1152] *Hodood* punishment addresses only the crimes considered most serious by Islamic society, and it is applied only under extremely strict evidentiary requirements. Furthermore, Islamic countries are gradually abandoning the actual application of *hodood* punishment. This process of abandonment should be allowed to proceed to its conclusion without the disrupting attempt to abolish *hodood* punishment by an abrupt mandate. The absolute abolition of the death penalty in the European Convention of Human Rights was not applied immediately after the entry into force of the European Convention rather it was applied gradually. It took more than fifty years for this idea to become legally binding. Even *hodood* punishments were not implemented immediately. The verses of the Quran with respect to *hodood* punishments were revealed to Prophet Mohamed after more than seventeen years since the start of the Islamic religion.[1153] It is preferable to encourage all of the state parties to ratify the Arab Charter without any reservation rather than to have many countries place reservations on it. In the light of my proposed theory, the death penalty should be applied even if it faces some criticism. However, it should be left for the Arab Court to decide when *hodood* punishments should be applied. The Arab Court can play an important role to monitor its implementation and decide whether it is compatible with Sharia law or not. In addition, the Court can examine whether it is implemented for the most serious crimes and after fair trial in the light of Sharia law. For instance, the Arab Court should be examining whether the accused person, by a free will, confesses and admits to having committed the crime. In modern times, it is tough to get a confession out of a suspect. Another example, the Arab Court should examine, in crimes of theft, if the criminal has no job or a fixed salary enough to cover the living expenses. In addition, the Arab Court can use Sharia law to reduce its implementation by encouraging pardoning and forgiveness from the victim's family. Furthermore, the giving of blood money can also be encouraged in order to reduce the implementation of some of the *hodood* punishment. Therefore, my proposed theory, gradualism can play a key role as I explained.

Sheikh Shahat Al-Azazy said that the priority should be given to the interest of the society and the victim more than the interest of the criminal. He added that

---

1152 CAT, *supra* note 1081.
1153 Telephone interview with Shekh/ Fekry Hassan Ismail, the former under Minster of Awqaf in the Ministry of endowments, which is in charge of religious endowments (Sep. 8, 2013).

hodood punishments during the life of Prophet Mohammed over a period of twenty three years was not applied except two times in crimes of adultery and one time in crime of robbery although Muslims population at these era were around one hundred and twenty thousand. He added that the misinterpretation of the versus of Quran and the abuse of powers from those who are authorized to implement Islamic laws result in the corrupted picture that we see erupting in part of the Islamic world. For instance, a corrupted judge does not mean that the judiciary is corrupted. The abuse of power of a law enforcement official does not mean that the agency that he/she belongs to is corrupted."[1154]

Sheikh Khaled Al-Gendy explained his point of view regarding *hodood* punishments by giving an example of robbery crime. He said that we should look whether the following requirements are established: First, a significant amount of proof has been shown in the light of Sharia law that request from judges to attempt to locate any suspicion of innocence. Second, the criminal records show that the accused person committed theft more than one time. Third, the investigation and prosecution obtained proof that the accused is not poor and has enough money to satisfy his needs. Fourth, the crime is not committed during a famine. Fifth, the crime is not a petty crime. Sixth, the robbery concerned something that was protected in a storage place, not in an open public place. He added that if all the previous requirements are fulfilled and there is no doubt, the *hodood* punishment should be applied on the criminal in order to protect the public order. He added that according to the jurisprudence of the conflict of interests, if there is a conflict of interests between the society and the individual, the priority should be given to the society. In other words, if there is a conflict of interests between applying *hodood* punishment on a criminal and the interest of the society, the priority should be given to the interest of the society and public order as long as the right to fair trial is implemented. He said that public order differs from one society to another. For instance, bribery is punished by death sentence in China although it is punished by imprisonment in the Arab World. He pointed out that we should not turn blind eyes to the human rights of the victim. He explained that Sharia law balances between the rights of the society, the criminal and the victim. The victim has the full human rights to live peacefully. He ended by saying that if all the previous requirements are fulfilled but *hodood* punishment is still not applied, corruption will break out and spread dramatically in the society. He said the non-implementation of *hodood* punishments in several Arab Countries does not mean that these countries deny its existence.[1155]

1154 Telephone interview with Sheikh/ Shahat Al-Azazy (Sep. 8, 2013).
1155 *Id.*

There should be a constructive dialogue between the East and the West, For instance, the Eastern people cannot force the Western people to prohibit prostitution and homosexuality. On the other hand, the Western people cannot force the Eastern people to prohibit *hodood*. It should be noted, also, that *hodood* punishment is applied very rarely due to the very strict requirements of evidence. *Hodood* strikes a balance between the criminal, the victim, and society. We should look not only at the gravity of the punishment, but also at the gravity of the crime. In addition, *hodood* punishment is a deterrent in order to protect the society and even to protect the criminal and the victim. In other words, the criminal will think many times before committing *hodood* crimes because the criminal knows the punishments that may be imposed on him/her if the crime is committed. Therefore, the life of the victim and the criminal is protected because the criminal is deterred and the crime is not committed. In addition, society is protected because the punishment is a deterrent. The Quran explains this idea by stating, "And there is (a saving of) life for you in Al-Qisas (the Law of Equality in punishment)."[1156] Furthermore, if the criminal committed *hodood* crimes, he/she will not be punished unless the judge is entirely certain that the criminal committed the crime. The judge can be entirely certain only if the accused person confesses and admits to having committed the crime. According to Sharia law, confession must be by a free will. A confession is null and void if it is brought about by torture. In other words, *hodood* punishments are not applied except if the criminal confesses to having committing the crime. During the life of the Prophet Mohammed, *hodood* punishment was not applied except after the confession of the criminal.[1157] Even if the criminal admitted to having committed the crime, *hodood* punishment can be waived, such as in crimes of theft if the criminal has no job or a fixed salary to buy items of basic need such as the food, medicine, etc.

Professor Abdel Aziz Mohamed Sarhan,[1158] who was a professor of international law, published a book in 1987 stating that some people criticize the application of some Islamic punishments such as the death penalty and the cutting off of hands.[1159] The criticizers claim that these kinds of punishments can only be

---

1156 QURAN 2:179.
1157 Telephone Interview with the Islamic scholar Khaled Al-gendy (Aug. 29, 2012).
1158 Prof. Abdel Aziz Mohamed Sarhan was professor of international law at the head of the International Law department at Ain Shams University, Cairo Egypt. In addition, he was also the head of the International Law department at the School of Law and Sahria at the University of Kuwait.
1159 PROF. ABDEL AZIZ MOHAMED SARHAN, THE LEGAL FRAMEWORK OF HUMAN RIGHTS IN INTERNATIONAL LAW IN COMPARISON WITH ISLAMIC SHARIA, ARAB CONSTITUTIONS, INTERNATIONAL TREATIES, RESOLUTIONS OF INTERNATIONAL ORGANIZATIONS, THE REVIEW MECHANISMS OF HUMAN RIGHTS AND THE NATIONAL COURTS, 238 (1st ed. 1987).

applied in a barbaric society. He commented on this saying that the success of any punishment depends on its effect on the crime and the criminals. If the statistics show that the rate of crime and the number of criminals is decreasing, it is considered an effective punishment. However, if the number of crimes and criminals is increasing, it is not considered an effective punishment and the legislators should reconsider the kinds of punishments to find an effective one. He gave the example of the rate of crimes in the United States of America by saying that stealing and murder are increasing in the United States of America. On the other hand, he said that the statistics of 1975 have shown that in the last twenty-four years there were only sixteen cases of the cutting off of hands in Saudi Arabia.[1160]

Professor Abdel Aziz said that the commonality between Sharia law and man-made laws is that they both seek to protect the interests of the community. On the one hand, Sharia law has two additional goals. First, Sharia law believes that norms and morals are the first pillars that build the community. Therefore, Sharia law always aims to protect and safeguard the morals of society. On the other hand, man-made laws completely ignore moral issues unless some material harm directly affects the security of the country, the people, or the public order. He gave an example of man-made laws by saying that illegal sexual relations are not prohibited unless someone involved is forced to have sex or it was without his/her consent. Another example of man-made laws is that homosexuality is permitted unless one of them is forced to have sex or it was without his/her consent. By contrast, Sharia law prohibits homosexuality and illegal sexual relations because Sharia law aims to protect morals and norms.[1161]

Hodood punishments have a very strict requirement for the presence of evidence; in fact, this requirement is stricter than in any other legal system. We should not make a hasty decision about the legitimacy of *hodood*; instead, we should reflect deeply about it. One of the main reasons for *hodood* punishments is to threaten people who commit such crimes. The evidence required for the enactment of *hodood* punishment is very hard to establish. For instance, it is very difficult, if not impossible, to have four people witness a couple committing adultery, unless it is being committed in a public place. *Hodood* will not absolutely prevent people from committing crimes, but it will help limit it as much as possible. The severity of *Hodood* punishment helps prevent a person from even thinking of committing a crime. The Quran states, "And indeed We have created man, and We know what his ownself whispers to him..."[1162]

1160 *Id.* at 238-239.
1161 *Id.*
1162 QURAN 50:16.

I will give an example of a *hodood* punishment and explain some of the opinions of Islamic jurists to show that there are strict conditions on applying *hodood*. The Quran explains, "The only reward of those who make war upon Allah and His messenger and strive after corruption in the land will be that they will be killed or crucified, or have their hands and feet on alternate sides cut off, or will be expelled out of the land. Such will be their degradation in the world, and in the Hereafter theirs will be an awful doom."[1163] This Quranic verse is referring to gangsters who bully and terrorize people through the use of violence. The Islamic scholars focused on the meaning of gangsters in order to determine to whom *hodood* could be applied. For instance, the Hanafi and Hanbali Schools said that this verse will be applied only to people who commit their crimes while in possession of a weapon. In addition, they added that the crime must be committed in the desert or in a place where very few people are located. In another words, it must be committed in an uncontrolled place where there is no police. The punishment of *hodood* will not be applied if the crime is committed in a city. The Hanafi School said that the punishment of *hodood* will not be applied on a woman because the Prophets told Muslims to not kill non Muslims women in times of war. Therefore, women who are nationals will not be killed even if they are criminals.

The Islamic scholars tried to interpret the word 'or' which is stated several times in the previous verse "will be killed *or* crucified, *or* have their hands and feet on alternate sides cut off, *or* will be expelled out of the land" in the following way:[1164] The Malik School said that the word 'or' means to choose between any of these punishments, in other words, to be killed through crucifixion, to have alternate hands and feet cut off, or will be expelled from the land. He added that this can be chosen freely, regardless of the crime committed. Malik said that even if the criminal committed murder, robbery, and rape, the judge has discretionary authority to choose between any of the punishments. The only condition is that the judge's choice of punishment should be based on wisdom and legitimate policy. For instance, a war between the two countries could be sparked if an accused from another country was killed. The Hanafi, Shafi, and Hanbali Schools said the word 'or' means diversification. In other words, the judge can choose between these punishments depending on the crime committed. For example, if the crime was murder then the accused should be killed. In this way, if the crime was serious then the punishment should be serious.[1165]

1163 *Id.* at 5:33.
1164 Helaly, *supra* note 267.
1165 *Id.*

Furthermore, Islamic jurists have different interpretations of the meaning of the word 'expelled' in the previous verse from the Quran. Does it mean being expelled to another country or to another city in the same country? Can expelling mean imprisonment? Islamic scholars have different opinions on this matter. For instance, the Hanbali School said that a woman cannot be expelled and if she is expelled, her husband, brother, father, mother's brother, or father's brother should go with her. The opinion of the Malik School was that, instead of sending someone with the woman, the expulsion should be cancelled.[1166] The previous examples clearly show that there is diversity in Sharia law and that this diversity gives legislators the flexibility to choose different options. Within this diversity, there is a framework for justice.

The Quran requests believers not to follow lusts. The Quran states, "O you who believe! Stand out firmly for justice, as witnesses to Allah, even though it be against yourselves, or your parents, or your kin, be he rich or poor, Allah is a Better Protector to both (than you). So follow not the lusts (of your hearts)..."[1167] According to the Sharia, on the Day of Judgment everyone will stand alone in front of God to be questioned in regards to all what he or she did and will be requested to justify their actions. The Quran describes what people will do on Day of Judgment by stating, "That Day shall a man flee from his brother, And from his mother and his father, And from his wife and his children. Everyman that Day will have enough to make him careless of others."[1168] The Quran also states, "And We have made every man's actions to cling to his neck, and We will bring forth to him on the resurrection day a book which he will find wide open: Read your book; your own self is sufficient as a reckoner against you this day."[1169]

1166 *Id.*
1167 Quran 4:135.
1168 *Id.* at 80:34, 35, 36, 37
1169 *Id.* at 17:13, 14.

G. The Right to Freedom of Thought, Conscience and Religion

1. Introduction

The right to freedom of thought, conscience, and religion is a basic fundamental right and principle that must be protected and guaranteed. This right is stated in all the international and regional conventions of human rights of people.[1170] With respect to the restrictions placed on a religion, the General Comment on Article 18 of the ICCPR provides:

> Article 18.3 permits restrictions on the freedom to manifest religion or belief only if limitations are prescribed by law and are necessary to protect public safety, order, health or morals, or the fundamental rights and freedoms of others. The freedom from coercion to have or to adopt a religion or belief and the liberty of parents and guardians to ensure religious and moral education cannot be restricted. In interpreting the scope of permissible limitation clauses, States parties should proceed from the need to protect the rights guaranteed under the Covenant, including the right to equality and non-discrimination on all grounds specified in articles 2, 3 and 26. Limitations imposed must be established by law and must not be applied in a manner that would vitiate the rights guaranteed in article 18. The Committee observes that paragraph 3 of article 18 is to be strictly interpreted: restrictions are not allowed on grounds not specified there, even if they would be allowed as restrictions to other rights protected in the Covenant, such as national security. Limitations may be applied only for those purposes for which they were prescribed and must be directly related and proportionate to the specific need on which they are predicated. Restrictions may not be imposed for discriminatory purposes or applied in a discriminatory manner…[1171]

1170 For instance, Article 18 of the International Covenant on Civil and Political Rights provides: "1. Everyone shall have the right to freedom of thought, conscience and religion. This right shall include freedom to have or to adopt a religion or belief of his choice, and freedom, either individually or in community with others and in public or private, to manifest his religion or belief in worship, observance, practice and teaching. 2. No one shall be subject to coercion which would impair his freedom to have or to adopt a religion or belief of his choice. 3. Freedom to manifest one's religion or beliefs may be subject only to such limitations as are prescribed by law and are necessary to protect public safety, order, health, or morals or the fundamental rights and freedoms of others. 4. The States Parties to the present Covenant undertake to have respect for the liberty of parents and, when applicable, legal guardians to ensure the religious and moral education of their children in conformity with their own convictions." (ICCPR, *supra* note 63, at art 18).

1171 High Commissioner for Human Rights, General Comment No. 22: The right to freedom of

The Arab Charter on Human Rights ensures the right of every person to freely choose his or her own religion by his or her own will. Article 30 of the Charter provides:

> Everyone has the right to freedom of thought, conscience and religion and no restrictions may be imposed on the exercise of such freedoms except as provided for by law. The freedom to manifest one's religion or beliefs or to perform religious observances, either alone or in community with others, shall be subject only to such limitations as are prescribed by law and are necessary in a tolerant society that respects human rights and freedoms for the protection of public safety, public order, public health or morals or the fundamental rights and freedoms of others.[1172]

The Arab Charter on Human Rights and the International Covenant on Civil and Political Rights are very similar with respect to the right to religion. They guarantee the right to freedom of religion and place limitations on the violation of these rights, such as through the protection of public order. However, the Arab Charter needs to have General Comments like the ICCPR in order to create a frame for these limitations.

The Egyptian Constitution respect the freedom of religion, article 3 states, "The canon principles of Egyptian Christians and Jews are the main source of legislation for their personal status laws, religious affairs and the selection of their spiritual leaders."[1173] In addition the constitution totally respects the freedom of religion and thought, the Constitution provides, "Freedom of belief is absolute. The freedom of practicing religious rituals and establishing worship places for the followers of Abrahamic religions is a right regulated by Law."[1174]

The Egyptian Constitution goes further, the preamble of the Constitution provides great respect to all divine religions, the Constitution provides,

> Egypt is the cradle of belief and the banner of glory of the revealed religions.

---

thought, conscience and religion, Doc. CCPR/C/21/Rev.1/Add.4, (July 30, 1993) http://www.unhchr.ch/tbs/doc.nsf/(Symbol)/9a30112c27d1167cc12563ed004d8f15?Opendocument (last visited Mar. 24, 2012).

1172 ACHR, *supra* note 126, at art. 30.
1173 Unofficial translation of the Egyptian Const., art. 3, http://english.ahram.org.eg/NewsContent/1/0/88644/Egypt/0/Egypts-constitution--vs--A-comparison.aspx (last visited May 14, 2014).
1174 Unofficial translation of the Egyptian Const., art. 64, http://www.sis.gov.eg/Newvr/Dustor-en001.pdf (last visited May 14, 2014).

> On its land, Prophet Moses – to whom Allah spoke – grew up and on Mount Sinai, the Revelation of Allah shone on his heart and Divine message descended.
>
> On its land, Egyptians harbored in their bosoms Virgin Mary and her baby and offered thousands of martyrs in defense of the Church of Jesus, Peace Be Upon Him.
>
> When the Seal of the Messengers Mohammad (Peace and Blessings Be Upon Him) was sent to all mankind to perfect the sublime morals, our hearts and minds were opened to the light of Islam, and we, labeled the best soldiers on Earth fighting for the cause of Allah, disseminated the message of truth and sciences of religion across the world.[1175]

Sharia law is the foundation of the Arab Charter. In addition, Sharia law is the standard used to evaluate the rights mentioned in the Arab Charter. Therefore, it is important to explain the Sharia point of view regarding the right to religion. Sharia law encourages the freedom to choose religion and states that anyone can choose his or her religion by his or her own will. There is a clear-cut verse in Quran that says, "There is no compulsion in religion."[1176] This verse indicates and assures that religion is not compulsory. The reason for the previous verse was that a Muslim came to the Prophet complaining that his two sons were Christians. He told the Prophet that he wanted to force them to convert to Islam. As a result, God put this verse in the Quran to ensure that no one can be forced to convert to another religion.[1177] If God wanted all of the people on earth to believe in one religion, He could do that. However, God created human beings with minds to think and choose the right religion for them. The Quran explains, "And had your Lord willed, those on earth would have believed, all of them together. So, will you (O Muhammad) then compel mankind, until they become believers."[1178] The Quran also states that "[i]f Allah had willed, He would have made you one nation, but that (He) may test you in what He has given you; so compete in good deeds.

1175 Unofficial translation of the Egyptian Const., preamble, http://www.sis.gov.eg/Newvr/Dustor-en001.pdf (last visited May 14, 2014).

1176 QURAN 2:256.

1177 Mohamed Al-Ameen Alshankeety, *Daf'a Ihaam Al'id'drabaat an Ayaat Al-ketaab* [Push the turmoil from the verses of the book], ISLAMPORT.COM http://islamport.com/d/1/qur/1/72/493.html?zoom_highlightsub=%22%E1%C7+%C5%DF%D1%C7%E5+%DD%ED+%C7%E1%CF%ED%E4+%22 (last visited Mar. 21, 2012); *see also* Abo-Alfedaa Islamil Abn-Omar Alkorashy, *Tafseer Alkoran Al-Azeem*, [The Interpretation of Great Quran] (2nd ed. 1999), ISLAMPORT.COMhttp://islamport.com/d/1/tfs/1/27/1161.html?zoom_highlightsub=%22%E1%C7+%C5%DF%D1%C7%E5+%DD%ED+%C7%E1%CF%ED%E4+%22 (last visited Mar. 21, 2012).

1178 QURAN 10:99.

The return of you (all) is to Allah; then He will inform you about that in which you used to differ."[1179] The previous verses of the Quran are very important because they are the roots of the freedom of religion. These verses ensure the respect for the dignity of human beings. It guarantees that the freedom of religion is a peremptory norm that must be respected. The Quran explains, "And indeed We have honoured the Children of Adam…"[1180] As Sharia law is the foundation of the Arab Charter, it can be an important instrument for the interpretation of the Charter. The Arab Charter, and its general comments, conclusions and court decisions that will be developed in the future should use this verse as the key for the freedom of religion. The Arab Charter is compatible with the verses of the Quran regarding the freedom of religion; Article 30 of the Charter states:

> 1. Everyone has the right to freedom of thought, conscience and religion and no restrictions may be imposed on the exercise of such freedoms except as provided for by law.
>
> 2. The freedom to manifest one's religion or beliefs or to perform religious observances, either alone or in community with others, shall be subject only to such limitations as are prescribed by law and are necessary in a tolerant society that respects human rights and freedoms for the protection of public safety, public order, public health or morals or the fundamental rights and freedoms of others.
>
> 3. Parents or guardians have the freedom to provide for the religious and moral education of their children.[1181]

This Article is entirely compatible with the verses of the Quran with respect to the freedom of religion.

Sharia law does not seek to force people to convert to Islam. The Sharia law looks for true believers who fully believe in Allah. The objectives of Sharia law with respect to the freedom of religion are clear. God does not look to what is written in the official governmental documents regarding the religion of people. God judges people by looking to their hearts; the Quran explains, "And whoever does righteous good deeds, male or female, and is a (true) believer [in the Oneness of Allah (Muslim)], such will enter Paradise and not the least injustice, even to the size of a speck on the back of a date-stone, will be done to them."[1182] Also, the Quran states, "O mankind! We have created you from a male and a female, and

---

1179 *Id.* at 5:48.
1180 *Id.* at 17:70.
1181 ACHR, *supra* note 126, at art. 30.
1182 QURAN 4:124.

made you into nations and tribes, that you may know one another. Verily, the most honourable of you with Allah is that (believer) who has At-Taqwa [i.e. he is one of the Muttaqun (the pious. See V.2:2)]. Verily, Allah is All-Knowing, All-Aware."[1183]

Allah requests that people not just be Muslims, but also do and believe in certain things. The Quran interpreted the word 'Muttaqun' mentioned in the previous verse, by stating:

> This is the Book (the Qur'an), whereof there is no doubt, a guidance to those who are Al-Muttaqun [the pious believers of Islamic Monotheism who fear Allah much (abstain from all kinds of sins and evil deeds which He has forbidden) and love Allah much (perform all kinds of good deeds which He has ordained)]. Who believe in the Ghaib and perform As-Salat (Iqamat-as-Salat), and spend out of what We have provided for them [i.e. give Zakat, spend on themselves, their parents, their children, their wives, etc., and also give charity to the poor and also in Allah's Cause — Jihad]. And who believe in (the Qur'an and the Sunnah) which has been sent down (revealed) to you (O Muhammad) and in that which was sent down before you [the Taurat (Torah) and the Injeel (Gospel), etc.] and they believe with certainty in the Hereafter. (Resurrection, recompense of their good and bad deeds, Paradise and Hell). They are on (true) guidance from their Lord, and they are the successful.[1184]

If a person is not a true believer, he or she cannot do or believe in the requirements that are mentioned in the previous verse. Therefore, Sharia law prohibits forcing or threatening people to convert to Islam.

Sharia law considers the freedom of religion as a main principle to be respected. The Quran is the main source of Sharia law and the Quran and the Sunnah of Prophet Mohammed are considered to be the constitution of Islam. The story in the Quran of an Egyptian king called Pharaoh who claimed to be God and massacred many Jewish people is a clear demonstration that Sharia law is very clear with respect to the respect of the religions of others. This story took place during the life of Prophet Moses. The Quran states that Pharaoh claimed that he is God, "Fir'aun (Pharaoh) said: 'O chiefs! I know not that you have an ilah (a god) other than me.'"[1185] Also, Quran states "Then he gathered (his people) and cried

---

1183 *Id*.at 49:13.
1184 *Id*. at 2:2, 3, 4, 5.
1185 *Id*. at 28:38.

aloud, Saying: 'I am your lord, most high.'"[1186] Also, with respect to Pharaoh, the Quran states:

> Verily, Fir'aun (Pharaoh) exalted himself in the land and made its people sects, weakening (oppressing) a group (i.e. Children of Israel) among them: killing their sons, and letting their females live. Verily, he was of the Mufsidun (i.e. those who commit great sins and crimes, oppressors, tyrants). And We wished to do a favour to those who were weak (and oppressed) in the land, and to make them rulers and to make them the inheritors.[1187]

The Quran also states, "And (remember) when We delivered you from Fir'aun's (Pharaoh) people, who were afflicting you with a horrible torment, killing your sons and sparing your women, and therein was a mighty trial from your Lord."[1188] God did not tell Prophet Moses to go and kill Pharaoh. God did not tell Moses to not speak with this person because he is a criminal. In the Quran, God said to Moses, "Go, both of you, to Fir'aun (Pharaoh), verily, he has transgressed (all bounds in disbelief and disobedience and behaved as an arrogant and as a tyrant). And speak to him mildly, perhaps he may accept admonition or fear (Allah)."[1189] As another example, as I explained before, Muslims must be kind to their parents, even if their parents do not believe in Islam. A clear example is the story of Prophet Ibrahim and his father, who believed in idols. It is said in Quran,

> And mention in the Book (the Qur'an) Ibrahim (Abraham). Verily he was a man of truth, a Prophet. When he said to his father: O my father! Why do you worship that which hears not, sees not and cannot avail you in anything? O my father! Verily there has come to me of the knowledge that which came not unto you. So follow me, I will guide you to the Straight Path. O my father! Worship not Shaitan (Satan). Verily Shaitan (Satan) has been a rebel against the Most Gracious (Allah). O my father! Verily I fear lest a torment from the Most Gracious (Allah) should overtake you, so that you become a companion of Shaitan (Satan) (in the Hell-fire). He (the father) said: Do you reject my gods, O Ibrahim (Abraham)? If you stop not (this), I will indeed stone you. So get away from me safely (before I punish you). Ibrahim (Abraham) said: Peace be on

---

1186 *Id.* at 79:23,24.
1187 *Id.* at 28:4,5.
1188 *Id.* at 2:49.
1189 *Id.* at 20:43,44.

you! I will ask Forgiveness of my Lord for you. Verily He is unto me Ever Most Gracious."[1190]

All of the previous examples from the Quran clearly show that Sharia law requests that believers speak mildly and wisely to others. Sharia law encourages this form of speaking even with a person who is claiming to be God.

Sharia law respects the freedom of religion of people during their life and even after their death because it considers that everyone is a human being regardless of their religion. Sharia law does not discriminate between people on the basis of religion. There is a *hadith* from Prophet Mohammed that proves clearly that Sharia law respects the freedom of religion even after a person dies. The *hadith* states,

> "Sahl bin Hunaif and Qais bin Sad were sitting in the city of Al-Qadisiya. A funeral procession passed in front of them and they stood up. They were told that funeral procession was of one of the inhabitants of the land i.e. of a non-believer, under the protection of Muslims. They said, 'A funeral procession passed in front of the Prophet and he stood up. When he was told that it was the coffin of a Jew, he said, 'Is it not a living being (soul)?'"[1191]

Another *hadith* states, "A funeral procession passed in front of us and the Prophet stood up and we too stood up. We said, 'O Allah's Apostle! This is the funeral procession of a Jew.' He said, 'Whenever you see a funeral procession, you should stand up.'"[1192] The two previous *hadith* show that the Sharia is not discriminatory. Prophet Mohammed did not say, I will stand up only for the funeral procession of a Muslim.

There is another example, which also happened during the life of the Prophet, which is the Hodybaya treaty,[1193] a treaty between Prophet Mohammed and Quraysh (non Muslims believers in Makkah). Prophet Mohammed requested that one of the Muslims write at the beginning of the treaty 'In the Name of Allah, the Most Gracious, the Most Merciful.' Quraysh refused and requested to amend this sentence. The Prophet Mohammed's companions felt oppressed and objected

---

1190 *Id.* at 19: 41-47.

1191 *Sahih Bukaria, volume 2, book 23, number 399*, HADITSBUKHARIONLINE.BLOGSPOT.CA, http://hadits-bukharionline.blogspot.com/2010/10/funerals-al-janaaiz.html (last visited June 13, 2012).

1192 *Sahih Bukari, volume 2, book 23, number 398*, HADITSBUKHARIONLINE.BLOGSPOT.CA, http://hadits-bukharionline.blogspot.com/2010/10/funerals-al-janaaiz.html (last visited June 13, 2012).

1193 *Solh Hodybaya* (Hodybaya Reconciliation), WIKIPEDIA.ORG, http://ar.wikipedia.org/wiki/%D8%B5%D9%84%D8%AD_%D8%A7%D9%84%D8%AD%D8%AF%D9%8A%D8%A8%D9%8A%D8%A9 (last visited June 14, 2012).

but the Prophet accepted. In addition, the title of Mohammed was written in the treaty as 'Mohammed the God's messenger.'[1194] Quraysh refused and requested that he should write his name without title, claiming that they do not know that he is a prophet. Mohammed accepted all their requests and the treaty was written as they wanted. He did not force them that it must be written in the treaty that he is the prophet of God. He was very peaceful. He respected their thoughts and beliefs.

2. Apostasy

The Islamic punishment for apostasy in case where a person converts from Islam to another religion is a very controversial issue. On the other hand, Sharia law requests that Muslims treat non-Muslims who do not believe in Islam kindly, with equality and justice, as long as they are peaceful. The Quran explains, "Allah does not forbid you to deal justly and kindly with those who fought not against you on account of religion nor drove you out of your homes. Verily, Allah loves those who deal with equity."[1195] The previous verse clearly shows that Islam does not advocate fighting other religions. Islam advocates treating everyone with peace and justice. Furthermore, the believers of Islam should treat people nicely even if they themselves are treated badly. The Quran states, "The good deed and the evil deed cannot be equal. Repel (the evil) with one which is better (i.e. Allah orders the faithful believers to be patient at the time of anger, and to excuse those who treat them badly) then verily he, between whom and you there was enmity, (will become) as though he was a close friend."[1196] All of the Quranic verses that I have quoted throughout this book show that the objectives and purposes of the Quran are not to call for revenge or commit terrorist attacks. Sharia law calls for peace and justice.

There is an important point called 'red'dah,' which means apostasy including conversion from Islam to any other different religion.[1197] It has been stated that, "Islamic scholarship differs on its punishment, ranging from execution – based on an interpretation of certain hadiths – to no punishment at all as long as they 'do not work against the Muslim society or nation.'"[1198] Islamic scholars hold different

---

1194 *Id.*
1195 QURAN 60:8.
1196 *Id.* at 41:34.
1197 *Al mawso'aa Al-shamlah* (comprehensive encyclopedia), ISLAMPORT.COM, http://islamport.com/w/fqh/Web/2793/2007.htm?zoom_highlight=%C7%E1%D1%CF%C9 (last visited May 9, 2014).
1198 *Apostasy in Islam*, WIKIPEDIA.ORG http://en.wikipedia.org/wiki/Apostasy_in_Islam (last visited Jun. 10, 2012).

opinions in this issue. Professor Saad Al-Din Helaly said that there are four Islamic jurisprudential opinions regarding the Islamic punishment for apostasy.[1199] The first opinion states that the person who converted from Islam to another religion should be killed. The second opinion is that the person who converted from Islam to another religion should not be killed. The third opinion is that the person who converted from Islam to another religion should not be killed unless he joined the army of an enemy country and started to fight his country. The fourth opinion is that the person who converted from Islam to another religion should not be killed, unless it is in the case of the simultaneous conversion from Islam to another religion being made by large group of people (such as an entire city).[1200]

Sheikh Mohammed Metwally Shaarawy, who is one of the most popular Egyptian and Arab Islamic religious Imams, said that Islamic punishment for apostasy clearly shows that Islam does not seek to proselytize people to convert to Islam. However, apostasy is a kind of alienation that prevents people from converting to Islam unless they are very true believers in Islam. He added that the Islamic punishment of apostasy is not against personal liberty; rather Islam requests that people only convert to Islam after profound reflection. [1201]

The opinion that the person who converts from Islam to another religion should not be killed is based on many verses from the Quran and *hadith* of the Prophet.[1202] For instance, the Quran states, "Verily, those who believe, then disbelieve, then believe (again), and (again) disbelieve, and go on increasing in disbelief; Allah will not forgive them, nor guide them on the (Right) Way."[1203] The previous verse did not say that they should be killed. In another verse, the Quran explains, "So remind them (O Muhammad) – you are only one who reminds. You are not a dictator over them."[1204] Another verse in the Quran says, "And say: 'The truth is from your Lord.' Then whosoever wills, let him believe; and whosoever wills, let him disbelieve."[1205] The previous verse is a very clear indication that Muslims cannot force anyone to believe in Islam. In addition, the previous verses are from the Quran, which is the first main source in Sharia law. As such, freedom of religion is a main principle in Islam.

1199 Telephone interview with Prof. Saad Al-Din Helaly, professor of Comparative Islamic Jurisprudence at Al-Azhar University (June 10, 2012).

1200 *Id.*

1201 *Abdalla Mohamen*, YOUTUBE.COM, http://www.youtube.com/watch?v=IF473164Z R0&feature=related (last visited Jun. 14, 2012).

1202 Makased Al-Sharia Al-Islameyah wa Kadayaa Al-Asr, *supra* note 784, at 498-499.

1203 QURAN 4:137.

1204 *Id.* at 88:21-22.

1205 *Id.* at 18:29.

The Arab Charter on Human Rights: A Voice for Sharia in the Modern World

Dr. Abdel Mejeed Abel Bary, the Minister of Islamic Affairs in the Republic of Maldives, mentioned that, according to Islam, God did not request that his prophets and messengers force people to believe. God requested that his prophets invite people to Islam with wisdom and fair preaching.[1206] The Quran explains, "Invite (mankind, O Muhammad) to the Way of your Lord (i.e. Islam) with wisdom (i.e. with the Divine Revelation and the Qur'an) and fair preaching, and argue with them in a way that is better. Truly, your Lord knows best who has gone astray from His Path, and He is the Best Aware of those who are guided."[1207] If God wanted people to follow one religion, He could do so immediately.[1208] The Quran states, "And had your Lord willed, those on earth would have believed, all of them together. So, will you (O Muhammad) then compel mankind, until they become believers."[1209] Also the Quran states "To each among you, We have prescribed a law and a clear way. If Allah had willed, He would have made you one nation, but that (He) may test you in what He has given you; so compete in good deeds. The return of you (all) is to Allah; then He will inform you about that in which you used to differ."[1210] Dr. Abdel Mejeed added that, although there is freedom of religion and belief, Sharia law creates regulations in order to protect the public order, public morals, and security of the society.[1211]

The Egyptian former *Mufti* Sheikh Aly Gomma stated that apostasy is a very controversial issue in Western perception, as it is perceived that believers are forced to follow Islam. This approach does not recognize the impact of the constitution of Muslims with respect to the freedom of belief and freedom of thought, which is stated in the verse of Quran that says, "There is no compulsion in religion. Verily, the Right Path has become distinct from the wrong path... "[1212] The *Mufti* mentions several names of Muslims who disbelieved after accepting Islam whom the Prophet did not kill.[1213] Furthermore, both the *Mufti* and Dr. Tarek Al-Swidan, a famous Islamic scholar in Kuwait and the Arab world, state that killing the person who convert from Islam to another religion is not done because of the conversion to another religion. It was because of the acts done by some groups

---

1206 Makased Al-Sharia Al-Islameyah wa Kadayaa Al-Asr, *supra* note 784, at 535.
1207 QURAN 16:125.
1208 Makased Al-Sharia Al-Islameyah wa Kadayaa Al-Asr, *supra* note 784, at 535..
1209 QURAN 10:99.
1210 *Id.* at 5:48.
1211 Makased Al-Sharia Al-Islameyah wa Kadayaa Al-Asr, *supra* note 784, 531.
1212 QURAN 2:256.
1213 ALY GOMMA, AL-BAYAN LMAA YASH'GAL AL-AZ'HAAN [Addressing Issues that Cccupy the Mind] 81-82 (11th ed. 2009); *see also* DAR-ALIFTA.ORG, http://www.dar-alifta.org/ViewBayan.aspx?LangID=1&ID=257 (last visited June 11, 2012).

of people do after claiming that they have converted to Islam in order to lead other Muslims to disbelieving in Islam.[1214] He mentioned the following verse of the Quran that supports this idea; "And a party of the people of the Scripture say; 'Believe in the morning in that which is revealed to the believers (Muslims), and reject it at the end of the day, so that they may turn back.'"[1215]

The *Mufti* mentioned an opinion of a former Sheikh Azhar, Sheikh Shaltoot,[1216] who said that non-believing is not a reason for killing unless the person who converted from Islam to another religion started to use aggression against and fight Muslims.[1217] Professor Kamal Abo Al-Magd, who is member of the Islamic Research Academy, said that former Sheikh Azhar, Sheikh Shaltoot said that apostasy is not punishable by death sentence. Sheikh Shaltoot mentioned the verse of the Quran that states, "There is no compulsion in religion..."[1218] Professor Kamal Abo Al-Magd said that he also holds this opinion.[1219]

The Academic Advisor of the Egyptian *Mufti* stated that one of the important examples that clearly shows that Prophet Mohammed did not apply the death penalty to apostasy is the Hodybaya treaty,[1220] which was a treaty between Prophet Mohammed and *Quraysh* (non-Muslim believers in Makkah). Quraysh wrote an article of the treaty that Muslims should return to Quraysh any Quraysh citizen who converted to Islam. On the other hand, Quraysh will not return any Muslim who converted from Islam to Quraysh. Although many Muslims opposed this treaty and requested that the Prophet Mohammed not sign it, the Prophet insisted on signing the treaty.[1221] The previous example shows how peaceful the Prophet was. He could easily have refused signing the treaty and claimed that any person who converted from Islam to another religion should be killed.

Both Sheikh Yousef Alkaradawy, and Sheikh Magdy Ashore the Academic Advisor of the Egyptian *Mufti* stated that, according to Sharia law, the person who converts from Islam to another religion should not be killed. However, killing this

---

1214 GOMMA, *supra* note 1213; *see also* Dr. Tarek Al-Swidan, YOUTUBE.COM, http://www.youtube.com/watch?v=VKXIJxs5XLY&feature=related (last visited Jun. 14, 2012).

1215 QURAN 3:72.

1216 Mahmoud Shaltoot, WIKIPEDIA.ORG, http://ar.wikipedia.org/wiki/%D9%85%D8%AD%D9%85 %D9%88%D8%AF_%D8%B4%D9%84%D8%AA%D9%88%D8%AA (last visited June 20, 2012).

1217 GOMMA, *supra* note 1213.

1218 QURAN 2:256.

1219 Interview with Prof. Kamal Abo Al-Magd (June 20, 2012).

1220 Telephone interview with the Academic Advisor of the Egyptian *Mufti* (Jun. 11, 2012).

1221 *Solh Hodybaya* [Hodybaya treaty], WIKIPEDIA.ORG, http://ar.wikipedia.org/wiki/%D8% B5% D9%84%D8%AD_%D8%A7%D9%84%D8%AD%D8%AF%D9%8A%D8%A8%D9%8A %D8%A9 (last visited Jun. 11, 2012).

person can only happen if the person loudly criticizes Islam and seeks to disturb the public order of the country by being aggressive against Muslims.[1222] In addition, there is an Islamic jurisprudential opinion that states that if the person who converted from Islam to another religion should not be killed if she is a female. The Islamic school of jurisprudence that supports this opinion used the principle of *Qiyas*,[1223] which is based on a hadith for Prophet Mohammed in which he prohibited killing non-Muslim women in times of war.[1224] Professor Yousef Alkaradawy stated that Omar Ibn El-Khattab, the Caliph of Muslims, did not think that a person who converted from Islam should always be killed. He mentioned a case in which Omar criticized the killing of a person who converted from Islam to another religion.[1225]

Professor Saad Al-Din Helaly said that all of these opinions are correct and any one of them can be applied. He added that all of the opinions of Islamic scholars are based on legal reasoning. Therefore, it is not required that all Muslims be forced to believe in a single opinion and disregard the rest. In other words, it should be left for each nation to choose between opinions according to the public interest of each country.[1226] He stated that Islamic scholars should rethink their jurisprudence regarding apostasy without being affected by any jurisprudence that was implemented in any previous period.[1227]

It should be noted, as I said before, that Sharia law is aligned with *fitrah* and the natural law theory. For instance, the understanding that no one should be forced to believe in a certain religion comes from *fitrah* because if we look at the world we can easily see that there is no dominant religion. There are many religions and even there are also those who do not believe in any religion. Therefore, it is *fitrah* not to force a person to believe in another religion; this is the freedom of religion. In addition to all the verses that I have mentioned, there are many different verses that state that many people are non-believers. For example, the Quran states, "And most of them believe not in Allah except that they attribute partners unto

---

1222 Telephone interview with the Academic Advisor of the Egyptian *Mufti* (June 11, 2012); *see also* Makased Al-Sharia Al-Islameyah wa Kadayaa Al-Asr, *supra note* 784, at 506. (citing Prof. Yousef Alkaradawy).
1223 See pages 182 and 183, notes 784 and 785.
1224 Makased Al-Sharia Al-Islameyah wa Kadayaa Al-Asr, *supra note* 784, at 507; *see also* HELALY, *supra* note 273, at 225.
1225 HELALY, *supra* note 273, at 409 (citing Prof. Yousef Alkaradawy); *see also* GOMMA, *supra* note 1213, at 83.
1226 Telephone interview with Prof. Saad Al-Din Helaly (June 10, 2012).
1227 Makased Al-Sharia Al-Islameyah wa Kadayaa Al-Asr, *supra* note 784.

Him [i.e. they are Mushrikun i.e. polytheists...]"[1228] In another verse the Quran states, "No doubt, surely, all that is in the heavens and the earth belongs to Allah. No doubt, surely, Allah's Promise is true. But most of them know not."[1229] The Quran does not request that his Prophet or his believers force others to believe in it. The Quran explains, "And had your Lord willed, those on earth would have believed, all of them together. So, will you (O Muhammad) then compel mankind, until they become believers."[1230]

3. The Headscarf

There are several cases regarding different issues related to the wearing of the headscarf, for instance, the cases of *Dogru vs. France*[1231] and *Kervanci vs. France*.[1232] These cases were examined before the European Court and other regional and international courts. The applicants are Muslim French nationals who were born 1987 and 1986 in France. The two cases were regarding the applicants' exclusion from school because they refused to remove their headscarves in physical education and sports classes. Article 9 of the European Convention on Human Rights states:

> Everyone has the right to freedom of thought, conscience and religion; this right includes freedom to change his religion or belief, and freedom, either alone or in community with others and in public or private, to manifest his religion or belief, in worship, teaching, practice and observance.
>
> Freedom to manifest one's religion or beliefs shall be subject only to such limitations as are prescribed by law and are necessary in a democratic society in the interests of public safety, for the protection of public order, health or morals, or the protection of the rights and freedoms of others.[1233]

The European Court "observed that the purpose of the restriction on the applicants' right to manifest their religious convictions was to adhere to the require-

---

1228 QURAN 12:106.
1229 *Id.* at 10:55.
1230 *Id.* at 10:99.
1231 Dogru vs. France, App. no. 27058/05, Eur. Ct H. R. (2009), http://cmiskp.echr.coe.int/tkp197/view.asp?item=30&portal=hbkm&action=html&highlight=Islam&sessionid=89457595&skin=hudoc-en (last visited Mar. 24, 2012).
1232 Kervanci vs. France, App. no. 31645/04, Eur. Ct H. R. http://hudoc.echr.coe.int/sites/eng/pages/search.aspx?i=001-90047 (last visited Feb. 10, 2013).
1233 ECHR, *supra* note 497, at art. 9.

ments of secularism in state schools."[1234] The court rendered a decision that there is not a violation of Article 9 of the European Convention on Human Rights.[1235]

Another example regarding the wearing of the Islamic headscarf by Muslim women is the case of *Leyla Sahin vs. Turkey*,[1236] which was a case against the Republic of Turkey. The applicant was Leyla Sahin who complained that banning wearing Islamic headscarf in higher-education institutions constituted a violation of her rights and freedoms as per the European Convention of Human Rights. She was born in 1973 and lived in Vienna. In 1997 she was in her fifth year at the faculty of medicine at Istanbul University and was prohibited from wearing a headscarf at the university. The applicant alleged that the prohibition of wearing headscarves obliged students to choose between education and religion. She added that the prohibition discriminated between believers and non-believers. She explained that Muslim women are required to cover their heads and necks. The government replied by saying:

> The applicant's argument that the Koran imposed a duty to wear the Islamic headscarf…As to the headscarf, the form it took for Muslim women varied according to the country and regime. The bandanna, which left the hair partly visible…The burka (full veil covering the entire body and face)…The chador or abaya (a black veil which covered the entire body from head to ankles)…It was difficult to reconcile all those different forms of dress derived from the same religious rule with the principle of neutrality in State education.[1237]

The government also mentioned that banning the headscarf in educational institutions is compatible with the principle of secularism. The restriction was foreseeable to those concerned and pursued the legitimate aims of protecting the rights and freedoms of others and maintaining public order. The obvious purpose of the restriction was to preserve the secular character of educational institutions.[1238] The court added that, "[a]lthough a margin of appreciation is thereby left to the national authorities, their decision remains subject to review

---

1234 Dogru v. France and Kervanci v. France http://hudoc.echr.coe.int/sites/eng-press/pages/search.aspx?i=003-2569490-2781270 (last visited May 9, 2014).

1235 *Id.*

1236 Leyla Sahin vs. Turkey, App. no. 44774/98, Eur. Ct H. R. (2005), http://cmiskp.echr.coe.int/tkp197/view.asp?item=2&portal=hbkm&action=html&highlight=Islam&sessionid=89457595&skin=hudoc-en (last visited Mar. 24, 2012).

1237 *Id.*

1238 *Id.*

by the court for conformity with the requirements of the Convention."[1239] The judgment of the Chamber was that there was not a violation of Article 9 of the Convention (freedom of thought, conscience, and religion) and not a violation of Articles 8, 10, or 14, and no violation to Article 2 of Protocol No.1. The case was referred to the Grand Chamber, which rendered its decisions by confirming that there is not a violation to Articles 8, 9, 19, or 12 or Article 2 of Protocol number 1.

Another example, also from the European Court of Human Rights, is the case of *Dahlab vs. Switzerland*,[1240] which is the case of a Swiss woman who used to work as a primary school teacher. After she converted to Islam, the school prevented her from teaching because she wore a headscarf, although there were never any complaints from the students' parents.[1241] The applicant complained to the court, saying that she had worn the headscarf for four years and there had been no problems within the school. The government and the Court were concerned with the impact of the headscarf as a "powerful religious symbol" on very young students.[1242] The applicant mentioned that none of the parents of the students complained:

> The secular nature of State schools meant that teaching should be independent of all religious faiths, but did not prevent teachers from holding beliefs or from wearing any religious symbols whatever. She argued that the measure prohibiting her from wearing a headscarf amounted to manifest interference with her right to freedom of conscience and religion... [H]er teaching, which was secular in nature, had never given rise to the slightest problem or to any complaints from pupils or their parents.[1243]

The court declared the case inadmissible.[1244]

I will mention the opinion of the Quran and the interpretations of some scholars of the Islamic jurisprudence regarding the headscarf. The difference between the *niqab* and *hijab* should be noted. The *niqab* is a covering for the face, regardless

---

1239 *Id.*
1240 Dahlab vs. Switzerland, App. no. 42393/98, Eur. Ct H. R. (2001), http://baer.rewi.hu-berlin.de/w/files/l_adr/dahlab_echr_2001_4239398.pdf (last visited Mar. 24, 2012).
1241 *Id.*
1242 *Id.; see also Dahlab vs. Switzerland*, MINORITYRIGHTS.ORG, http://www.minorityrights.org/1275/minority-rights-jurisprudence/dahlab-v-switzerland.html (last visited Mar. 24, 2012).
1243 Dahlab vs. Switzerland, *supra* note 1240.
1244 *Id.*

of whether or not the eyes are covered. The *hijab*, or the headscarf, is a covering for the hair. The Quran states:

> And say to the believing women that they cast down their looks and guard their private parts and do not display their ornaments except what appears thereof, and let them wear their head-coverings over their bosoms, and not display their ornaments except to their husbands or their fathers, or the fathers of their husbands, or their sons, or the sons of their husbands, or their brothers, or their brothers' sons, or their sisters' sons, or their women, or those whom their right hands possess, or the male servants not having need (of women), or the children who have not attained knowledge of what is hidden of women; and let them not strike their feet so that what they hide of their ornaments may be known; and turn to Allah all of you, O believers! so that you may be successful.[1245]

In the previous verse, the Quran did not specify what could be made apparent. It is left for interpretation. The Quran requires that people think and use their minds.

From my research, based on many of the opinions of Islamic scholars regarding *niqab*, we can come to the conclusion that there is not a unanimous opinion regarding the *niqab*. However, there is a unanimous opinion regarding the headscarf.[1246] The interpretations of Islamic schools aim to leave the door open for

---

1245 QURAN 24:31.

1246 The former Egyptian Mufti said that the Shafi and Hanafi requested women to wear *niqab* as a habit not as a form of worship. The Hanafi, Shafi, and Hanbali scholars said that wearing the *niqab* is a habit. A thorough analysis of the books of the previous three authors leads to the conclusion that wearing the *niqab* is a habit. The former Egyptian Mufti added that Imam Malik mentioned that *niqab* is a disliked practice unless used in one of two situations. First, it is not hated if it is a habit in a certain country. For instance, in some Gulf countries women wear *niqab*, in which case it is not a hated habit. Second, it is not hated if it is worn to prevent temptation by a beautiful and attractive woman. The former Mufti said that the Prophet requested women to not cover their face in Hajj. The former Mufti added that the Islamic Research Academy at Al-Azhar analyzed this issue and declared that it is a habit, not a form of worship. The former Mufti mentioned a Prophet *hadith* saying that a woman can show only her face and hands once she becomes mature. He also mentioned a *hadith* for the Prophet saying that in Hajj women must not cover their face. The former Mufti said as there are different opinions from scholars and Islamic schools of jurisprudence, we should not dismiss any of the opinions. For instance, we should not say one opinion is correct and all the other opinions are wrong. (*The Egyptian Mufti*, YOUTUBE.COM, http://www.youtube.com/watch?v=OjcCXAQ1jQA&feature=related (last visited March 22, 2012); *see also Is the niqab Habit or Worship?*, YOUTUBE.COM, http://www.youtube.com/watch?v=6brANqi0cRo&feature=related (last visited Mar. 23, 2012); *see also Niqab*, YOUTUBE.COM, http://www.youtube.com/watch?

different cultures and traditions. For instance, in Egypt the majority of women wear a headscarf only. In Saudi Arabia, the majority of women wear the *niqab*. One is not better than the other; both approaches are outlined within the opinions of Islamic scholars. For instance, the jurisprudence of a scholar would certainly be affected by being born and growing up in a city where the majority of women wear a *niqab*. However, this does not mean that there is confusion in the interpretations, because all of the scholars have unanimously said that the hair must be covered. Muslim women have the right to choose between these opinions. Mr. Nisar Mohammed bin Ahmad has stated:

> Nevertheless, it is fundamental to remember that, to a Muslim woman, the wearing of the headscarf is not merely a personal display of faith — it is an obligation imposed by her religion. Proponents of the ban claim that the headscarf cannot be tolerated in a secular state educational system because the mere fact of wearing it amounts to proselytism. Yet for those who wear it, it is simply a matter of personal obedience to God. It is also imperative to remember that even if evidence is adduced to show that the headscarf amounts to proselytism — this is not a legitimate reason under international human rights law to ban it from being worn. In fact, such a manifestation of one's religion would be protected under ECHR provisions relating to freedom of expression.

---

v=3XNe21mQxTc&feature=related (last visited Mar. 23, 2012).

Professor Saad, who is a famous Professor of Islamic jurisprudence at Al-Azhar University, said that there are different opinions regarding what can be seen of women. With respect to what can be seen of a woman in front of a stranger man, he answered: "The first, all the woman is roughness and must not be seen at all. Hanbali and some opinions of the Shafi School and some opinions of Maliki School. There are exceptions, like her eyes she cannot cover. The second opinion is the hand and faces are the only things that can be seen of her body. This opinion is supported by the majority of scholars Shafi, Hanafi and Maliki. In addition, the Hanafi added that the feet of the woman can be seen. Abo Yousef added that the arms can also be seen.. The third opinion is that covering the face is hated. This is the opinion of some of Maliki. (*Prof. Saad el din Helaly*, YOUTUBE.COM, http://www.youtube.com/watch?v=PAKHVqyVkUE&feature=related (last visited Mar. 22, 2012)).

Furthermore, Professor Saad said that these are different opinions of scholars and we cannot say there is a one that is the best or that another one is wrong. In all of his speeches, he always mentions that people should think wisely and choose what they think is better. He mentioned the verse of Quran which says "And We have also sent down unto you (O Muhammad) the Dhikr [reminder and the advice (i.e. the Qur'an)], that you may explain clearly to men what is sent down to them, and that they may give thought." (QURAN 16:44). Professor Saad added that if covering faces is mandatory, then why have we witnessed a woman removing the headscarf in front of the judge. All of the scholars, except some of the hanafi, said that a woman must uncover her face in front of the judge in order for the judges and the parties of the case to be able to see her. (Prof. Sald el din Helal, YOUTUBE.COM, http://www.youtube.com/watch?v=PAKHVqyVkUE&feature=related (last visited Mar. 22, 2012))

Article 10 of the ECHR provides that this right includes, freedom to hold opinions and to receive and impart information and ideas without interference.[1247]

From the above analysis, we can come to the conclusion that the headscarf is not optional; rather it is an obligation for Muslim women. However, a woman could not be forced to wear the headscarf. It is a relationship between a person and God. It is the responsibility of the woman herself, if she does not want to wear the headscarf that is her decision. On the other hand, if a woman chooses to wear a headscarf, she cannot be forced to remove the headscarf. It is important to say that the court decisions and laws of countries should be respected and implemented. It is important to note that it is unrealistic to force women in universities to remove their headscarf because they belong to the religion of the greater majority of the population in Turkey. In addition, the principle of secularism should safeguard the freedom of religion and conscience. It should be noted,

> "There are significant problems with the principle of secularism as a ground for restriction of religious liberty, and with the Council of Europe's enforcement of the principle. The first, and most obvious, is that neither the ICCPR nor the ECHR list defending secularism in principle as a ground upon which the manifestation of religious belief may be restricted."[1248]

It should also be noted that the General Comment of the Office of the High Commission for Human Rights explains:

> The fact that a religion is recognized as a state religion or that it is established as official or traditional or that its followers comprise the majority of the population, shall not result in any impairment of the enjoyment of any of the rights under the Covenant, including articles 18 and 27, nor in any discrimination against adherents to other religions or non-believers. In particular, certain measures discriminating against the latter, such as measures restricting eligibility for government service to members of the predominant religion or giving economic privileges to them or imposing special restrictions on the practice of other faiths, are not in accordance with the prohibition of discrimination based on

---

1247 Mr. Nisar Mohammed bin Ahmad, *The Islamic and International Human Rights Law Perspectives of Headscarf: the Case of Europe* 2 INTERNATIONAL JOURNAL OF BUSINESS AND SOCIAL SCIENCE, 161, 169 (2011), http://www.ijbssnet.com/journals/Vol_2_No_16_September_2011/18.pdf (last visited Mar. 24, 2012).

1248 M. Todd Parker, *The Freedom to Manifest Religious Belief: An Analysis of the Necessity Clauses of the ICCPR and the ECHR*, 17 DUKE J. COMP. & INT'L L. 121 (2006).

religion or belief and the guarantee of equal protection under article 26.[1249]

In 2004, a French law entered into force regarding secularism. This law stated, "In public [primary and secondary schools], the wearing of symbols or clothing through which the pupils ostensibly manifest a religious appearance is prohibited."[1250] All Muslim girls who refused to remove their headscarves were expelled from school.[1251] It was stated, "The French Education Minister's claim that the law calls for 'mutual respect' assumes that France can show that religious symbols worn by public school students in France cause others to feel disrespected"[1252] and that:

> Even if France could show that wearing such symbols caused others to feel disrespected, to justify the blanket ban France must then show that: (1) causing another to feel disrespected by wearing a religious symbol is a violation of a fundamental right to not feel disrespected (a difficult showing); (2) the alleged disrespect caused by the religious symbols was stirring up the school so as to create a threat to public order; or (3) wearing religious symbols violated some well-ensconced moral order in France. Obviously, such a showing would be nearly impossible. The EC's acceptance of the principle of secularism as a justification for restricting religious liberty is not a faithful reading of the ICCPR and the ECHR, and improperly makes room for illegitimate justifications for those restrictions.[1253]

Both Article 18 of the International Covenant on Civil and Political Rights and Article 9 of the European of Human Rights do not prohibit the existence of a country or state religion as long as that religion does not by any means discriminate or put limitation on religious freedoms.

The democratic countries that always call for the equality for women and non-discrimination should do more with respect to respecting the rights of women that live in their countries. Furthermore, banning Muslim girls who wear a headscarf from school will increase rates of women's illiteracy. Women that wear headscarves did not do anything wrong, rather they are fulfilling their religious obligations. There should be no kind of discrimination against women due to

---

1249 High Commissioner for Human Rights, General Comment No. 22, *supra* note 1171, at art. 18.
1250 Parker, *supra* note 1248, at 115.
1251 *Id.*
1252 *Id.* at 124-125.
1253 *Id.* at 125.

their religion. The Convention on the Elimination of All Forms of Discrimination against Women determined that

> "the term 'discrimination against women' shall mean any distinction, exclusion or restriction made on the basis of sex which has the effect or purpose of impairing or nullifying the recognition, enjoyment or exercise by women, irrespective of their marital status, on a basis of equality of men and women, of human rights and fundamental freedoms in the political, economic, social, cultural, civil or any other field."[1254]

After analyzing the cases related to the wearing of the headscarf, I have come to the conclusion that the headscarf was banned in France and the case of *Dahlab vs. Switzerland* because Muslims are a minority in Switzerland and in order to protect the secular state in France. On the other hand, the headscarf was banned in the case of *Leyla Sahin vs. Turkey* because the religious freedoms of the minority and non-practicing Muslim women were being protected. It should be noted that, in a country like Egypt women have the choice of whether or not to wear the headscarf. There are millions of Egyptian Muslim women who do not wear the headscarf and there are millions of Egyptian Muslim women who do wear the headscarf. On the other hand, there are millions of Egyptian women who believe in Christianity, a large number of whom wear religious symbols. All Egyptian people, regardless of their religion, sex, color, race, etc., live together peacefully and happily. No one can force them to wear or not to wear a religious symbol. It is a relationship between a person and God in which no one can interfere. This is the correct definition of a secular state. The religious rights are protected of everyone, even people who will be executed by death sentence. According to the Egyptian law, no one can be executed during the official holidays or the holidays of his or her religion.[1255]

We can come to conclusion that there are different interpretations of this issue within the 'secular states.' The first interpretation is the one followed by the European Court of Human Rights. The second approach, which is followed in Egypt and other countries, was explained by the applicant of the case of *Dahlab vs. Switzerland*, who stated understanding of a secular state by saying that "the secular nature of State schools meant that teaching should be independent of all religious faiths, but did not prevent teachers from holding beliefs or from wearing any religious symbols whatever…"[1256] The courts and governments that think that the first approach is correct cannot force other countries and courts to use

---

1254 United Nations Division for the Advancement of Women, *supra* note 134, art. 1.
1255 Egyptian Criminal Procedural Law, art 475.
1256 Dahlab vs. Switzerland, *supra* note 1240.

this approach. On the other hand, the courts and countries that apply the second approach cannot force other countries and courts to use this second approach. Each approach must be respected.

One of the main reasons for banning the wearing of the headscarf in Europe is because the majority of European governments and people do not know that wearing the headscarf is a religious obligation.[1257] The Arab Charter on Human Rights, which is inspired by Sharia law, can play an important role in improving women rights not only within its region, but also beyond its regional boundaries. The potential future General Comments of the Arab Charter and the potential decisions of a future Arab Court on Human Rights will certainly improve the understanding of Sharia law by regional courts. The Arab Charter always provided, "The States parties to the present Charter shall take the requisite measures to guarantee effective equality in the enjoyment of all the rights and freedoms… [and] Men and women are equal in respect of human dignity, rights and obligations within the framework of the positive discrimination established in favour of women by the Islamic Shariah…"[1258]

H. The Right to a Fair Trial and the Rule of Law

The right to a fair trial is one of the core fundamental supreme rights in any international, regional, or domestic human rights treaty or law. The right to a fair trial and the rule of law are at the heart of human rights. Human rights cannot be established without fair trial and the rule of law. All human rights would vanish if the right to a fair trial and the rule of law did not exist. For instance, we cannot stop incidents of torture without a fair trial for the criminal committing torture. We cannot guarantee women's rights without fair trial. The right to life would be more likely to be violated without a fair trial to punish the criminal and deter others from committing crime. In short, the right to a fair trial is an important right that protects the international human right system. The right to a fair trial is considered the gauge for the presence of justice in any country and region. All of the international and regional treaties include the right to a fair trial and the rule of law.[1259]

1257 bin Ahmad, *supra* note 1247.

1258 ACHR, *supra* note 126, at art. 3(2) & (3).

1259 For instance, Article 14 of the ICCPR states: "1. All persons shall be equal before the courts and tribunals. In the determination of any criminal charge against him, or of his rights and obligations in a suit at law, everyone shall be entitled to a fair and public hearing by a competent, independent and impartial tribunal established by law. The press and the public may be excluded from all or part of a trial for reasons of morals, public order (ordre public) or national security in a democratic society, or when the interest of the private lives of the parties so

More than ten of the fifty-three articles of the Arab Charter are dealing with the right to fair trial and the rule of law. For example, Article 11 states, "All persons are equal before the law and have the right to enjoy its protection without discrimination."[1260] Article 12 of the Charter states, "All persons are equal before the courts and tribunals. The States parties shall guarantee the independence of the judiciary and protect magistrates against any interference, pressure or threats. They shall also guarantee every person subject to their jurisdiction the right to seek a legal remedy before courts of all levels."[1261] The previous two articles guarantee that all people are equal before the law and also are equal before courts. The examples that I stated clearly show that the Arab Charter is similar to other conventions with respect to the right to a fair trial. Furthermore, the General Comment number 13 regarding Article 14 of the ICCPR provides:

> requires, or to the extent strictly necessary in the opinion of the court in special circumstances where publicity would prejudice the interests of justice; but any judgement rendered in a criminal case or in a suit at law shall be made public except where the interest of juvenile persons otherwise requires or the proceedings concern matrimonial disputes or the guardianship of children. 2. Everyone charged with a criminal offence shall have the right to be presumed innocent until proved guilty according to law. 3. In the determination of any criminal charge against him, everyone shall be entitled to the following minimum guarantees, in full equality: a. To be informed promptly and in detail in a language which he understands of the nature and cause of the charge against him; b. To have adequate time and facilities for the preparation of his defence and to communicate with counsel of his own choosing; c. To be tried without undue delay; d. To be tried in his presence, and to defend himself in person or through legal assistance of his own choosing; to be informed, if he does not have legal assistance, of this right; and to have legal assistance assigned to him, in any case where the interests of justice so require, and without payment by him in any such case if he does not have sufficient means to pay for it; e. To examine, or have examined, the witnesses against him and to obtain the attendance and examination of witnesses on his behalf under the same conditions as witnesses against him; f. To have the free assistance of an interpreter if he cannot understand or speak the language used in court; g. Not to be compelled to testify against himself or to confess guilt. 4. In the case of juvenile persons, the procedure shall be such as will take account of their age and the desirability of promoting their rehabilitation. 5. Everyone convicted of a crime shall have the right to his conviction and sentence being reviewed by a higher tribunal according to law. 6. When a person has by a final decision been convicted of a criminal offence and when subsequently his conviction has been reversed or he has been pardoned on the ground that a new or newly discovered fact shows conclusively that there has been a miscarriage of justice, the person who has suffered punishment as a result of such conviction shall be compensated according to law, unless it is proved that the non-disclosure of the unknown fact in time is wholly or partly attributable to him. 7. No one shall be liable to be tried or punished again for an offence for which he has already been finally convicted or acquitted in accordance with the law and penal procedure of each country. (ICCPR, *supra* note 63, at art 14).

1260 ACHR, *supra* note 126, at art. 11.
1261 *Id.* at art. 12.

> The Committee would find it useful if, in their future reports, States parties could provide more detailed information on the steps taken to ensure that equality before the courts, including equal access to courts, fair and public hearings and competence, impartiality and independence of the judiciary are established by law and guaranteed in practice. In particular, States parties should specify the relevant constitutional and legislative texts which provide for the establishment of the courts and ensure that they are independent, impartial and competent, in particular with regard to the manner in which judges are appointed, the qualifications for appointment...[1262]

Many member states of the Arab League have articles in their constitution that guarantee the rule of law, fair trial, and the separation of power. This has an important significance for this book because it is evidence to show that the Arab countries, like many other countries around the world, apply the right to a fair trial. For instance, the Egyptian Constitution, which was adopted in January 2014, states,

> All citizens are equal before the Law. They are equal in rights, freedoms and general duties, without discrimination based on religion, belief, sex, origin, race, color, language, disability, social class, political or geographic affiliation or any other reason.
>
> Discrimination and incitement of hatred is a crime punished by Law.
>
> The State shall take necessary measures for eliminating all forms of discrimination, and the Law shall regulate creating an independent commission for this purpose.."[1263]

Also, this Constitution guarantees the independence of the judicial authority and judges, stating, "The Judiciary is an autonomous authority that carries out its tasks through courts of all types and degrees. Courts shall issue their rulings in accordance with the law..."[1264] and "Judges are independent and immune to

---

[1262] High Commissioner for Human Rights, General Comment No. 13, Equality before the courts and the right to a fair and public hearing by an independent court established by law (art. 14), 21st Sess. (Apr, 13, 1984), http://www.unhchr.ch/tbs/doc.nsf/(Symbol)/9a30112c27d1167cc12563ed004d8f15?Opendocument (last visited Mar. 24, 2012), http://www.unhchr.ch/tbs/doc.nsf/(Symbol)/bb722416a295f264c12563ed0049dfbd?Opendocument (last visited Mar. 26, 2012).

[1263] Egyptian Const., art. 53, http://www.sis.gov.eg/Newvr/Dustor-en001.pdf (last visited May 14, 2014).

[1264] Egyptian Const., art. 184, http://www.sis.gov.eg/Newvr/Dustor-en001.pdf (last visited May 14, 2014).

dismissal, are subject to no other authority but the law, and are equal in rights and duties."[1265]

In some member states of the Arab League, the laws permit the trial of civilians by military courts. For instance, before the Egyptian revolutions, civilians could be tried by military courts. However, since the revolutions the situation started to change and legislators are currently working on amending the laws in order to prevent referral of civilians to the military courts. The new Egyptian Constitution of 2014 provides,

> The Military Court is an independent judicial body exclusively competent to adjudicate on all crimes pertaining to the Armed Forces, the officers and personnel thereof, and their equivalents, and on the crimes committed by the personnel of the General Intelligence while and by reason of performing their duties.

> No civilian shall face trial before the Military Court, except for crimes that constitute a direct assault against military facilities or camps of the Armed Forces, or their equivalents, against military zones or border zones determined as military zones, against the Armed Forces' equipment, vehicles, weapons, ammunition, documents, military secrets, or its public funds, or against military factories; crimes pertaining to military service; or crimes that constitute a direct assault against the officers or personnel of the Armed Forces by reason of performing their duties.

> The law shall define such crimes, and specify the other competences of the Military Court.

> Members of the Military Court shall be independent and shall be immune to dismissal. They shall have all the guarantees, rights and duties stipulated for the members of other judicial bodies.[1266]

The United Nations General Comment number 13 regarding Article 14 of the ICCPR speaks to the military courts, stating:

> The provisions of article 14 apply to all courts and tribunals within the scope of that article whether ordinary or specialized. The Committee notes the existence, in many countries, of military or special courts which try civilians. This could present serious problems as far as the

---

1265 Egyptian Const., art. 186, http://www.sis.gov.eg/Newvr/Dustor-en001.pdf (last visited May 14, 2014).

1266 Egyptian Const., art. 204. http://www.sis.gov.eg/Newvr/Dustor-en001.pdf (last visited May 14, 2014).

equitable, impartial and independent administration of justice is concerned. Quite often the reason for the establishment of such courts is to enable exceptional procedures to be applied which do not comply with normal standards of justice. While the Covenant does not prohibit such categories of courts, nevertheless the conditions which it lays down clearly indicate that the trying of civilians by such courts should be very exceptional and take place under conditions which genuinely afford the full guarantees stipulated in article 14. The Committee has noted a serious lack of information in this regard in the reports of some States parties whose judicial institutions include such courts for the trying of civilians. In some countries such military and special courts do not afford the strict guarantees of the proper administration of justice in accordance with the requirements of article 14 which are essential for the effective protection of human rights. If States parties decide in circumstances of a public emergency as contemplated by article 4 to derogate from normal procedures required under article 14, they should ensure that such derogations do not exceed those strictly required by the exigencies of the actual situation, and respect the other conditions in paragraph 1 of article 14.[1267]

The countries that did not previously have an independent judiciary have started to work toward developing such a judiciary. For instance, the Public Prosecution was not independent in Oman until the adoption of a new law in 2011, which gave full independence to the Public Prosecution in Oman. The countries whose constitution includes articles stating that judges and prosecutors are independent have the challenge of ensuring the implementation of these articles. The Arab Charter can play an important role in developing the independence of the judiciary in its states parties. Even the countries that have an independent judiciary still need the support of the Arab Charter to guarantee its independence.

The human rights of criminals must be respected. For instance, the concluding observations of the Human Rights Committee regarding Kuwait stated,

> "The State party should adopt legislation to ensure that anyone arrested or detained on a criminal charge is brought before a judge within 48 hours. The State party should also guarantee that all other aspects of its law and practice on pre-trial detention are harmonized with the requirements of article 9 of the Covenant, including by providing

---

1267 High Commissioner for Human Rights, General Comment No. 13, *supra* note 1262.

detained persons with immediate access to counsel and contact with their families."[1268]

Also, the concluding observations of the Human Rights Committee regarding Jordan provide:

> The State party should establish an effective and independent mechanism to deal with allegations of torture. It should also ensure that all cases of torture and ill-treatment are properly investigated and prosecuted, that the perpetrators are sentenced by ordinary civilian courts and that victims of torture and ill-treatment receive adequate reparation and compensation. The State party should further ensure that all detainees can have immediate access to a lawyer of their choice and an independent medical examination.[1269]

The concluding observations of the Committee against Torture states in its report on Jordan:

> The State party should strengthen its measures to ensure prompt, thorough, impartial and effective investigations into all allegations of torture and ill-treatment of convicted prisoners and detainees and to bring to justice law enforcement, security, intelligence, and prison officials who carried out, ordered or acquiesced in such practices. In particular, such investigations should be undertaken by an independent body. In connection with prima facie cases of torture and ill-treatment, the alleged suspect should as a rule be subject to suspension or reassignment during the process of investigation, to avoid any risk that he or she might impede the investigation, or continue any reported impermissible actions in breach of the Convention.[1270]

Similarly, the concluding observations of the Committee against Torture states in its report on Yemen that: "The State party should ensure that all allegations of torture and ill-treatment are investigated promptly, effectively and impartially, and that the perpetrators are prosecuted and convicted in accordance with the gravity of the acts, as required by article 4 of the Convention."[1271] The concluding

---

1268 U.N. Human Rights Committee, Concluding Observations, Kuwait, *supra* note 1098.

1269 U.N. Human Rights Committee, Concluding Observations, Jordan, *supra* note 1099.

1270 Committee against Torture, Concluding Observations, Jordan, 44th Session, (April 26-May 14, 2010), http://www2.ohchr.org/english/bodies/cat/docs/CAT.C.JOR.CO.2.pdf (last visited Mar. 26, 2012).

1271 Committee against Torture, Concluding Observations, Yemen, 44th Session, (April 26-May 14, 2010), http://www2.ohchr.org/english/bodies/cat/docs/CAT.C.YEM.CO.2.pdf (last visited

observations of the Committee against torture states in its report on Syria that: "The State party should take urgent measures to ensure prompt, thorough, impartial and effective investigation into all allegations of torture, ill-treatment, death in custody, death during military service and incommunicado detention..."[1272] Lastly, the concluding observation of the Human Rights Committee on Algeria listed as important the "[g]uarantee that all allegations of torture and cruel, inhuman or degrading treatment are investigated by an independent authority and that the perpetrators of such acts are duly prosecuted and punished."[1273]

The European Convention on Human Rights protects the right of fair trial. It states:

> In the determination of his civil rights and obligations or of any criminal charge against him, everyone is entitled to a fair and public hearing within a reasonable time by an independent and impartial tribunal established by law. Judgement shall be pronounced publicly by the press and public may be excluded from all or part of the trial in the interest of morals, public order or national security in a democratic society, where the interests of juveniles or the protection of the private life of the parties so require, or the extent strictly necessary in the opinion of the court in special circumstances where publicity would prejudice the interests of justice. Everyone charged with a criminal offence shall be presumed innocent until proved guilty according to law. Everyone charged with a criminal offence has the following minimum rights:
>
> a. to be informed promptly, in a language which he understands and in detail, of the nature and cause of the accusation against him;
>
> b. to have adequate time and the facilities for the preparation of his defence;
>
> c. to defend himself in person or through legal assistance of his own choosing or, if he has not sufficient means to pay for legal assistance, to be given it free when the interests of justice so require;

March 26, 2012).

1272 Committee against Torture, Concluding Observations, Syrian Arab Republic, 44th Session, (April 26-May 14, 2010), http://www2.ohchr.org/english/bodies/cat/docs/CAT.C.SYR.CO.1.pdf (last visited March 26, 2012).

1273 Human Rights Committee, Concluding Observation, Algeria, 91st Sess, Oct.15-Nov. 2, 2007), http://daccess-dds-ny.un.org/doc/UNDOC/GEN/G07/457/74/PDF/G0745774.pdf?OpenElement (last visited Mar. 26, 2012).

d. to examine or have examined witnesses against him and to obtain the attendance and examination of witnesses on his behalf under the same conditions as witnesses against him;

e. to have the free assistance of an interpreter if he cannot understand or speak the language used in court.[1274]

This previous article outlines many different rights. The first right listed in the article is that of the right to access to court. The European Court defined this right in the following way:

The Court first recognized this right in Golder v United Kingdom (1975), where it held that the detailed fair trial guarantees under Article 6 would be useless if it were impossible to commence court proceedings in the first place. The applicant was detained in an English prison where serious disturbances broke out. He was accused of assault by a prison officer and wished to bring proceedings for defamation in order to have his record cleared, but this was precluded by the Prison Rules. Though not without limitation, the Court concluded that Article 6(1) contained an inherent right of access to a court, alongside the principle of international law which forbids the denial of justice.[1275]

Sharia law is both the standard upon which the Arab Charter is based and also is the mechanism used to evaluate the rights within the Arab Charter. Sharia law considers that justice is more than just a right. *Fitrah* and natural law theory advocate for fair trial and justice; it is recognized that even young children can feel jealous if their parents have a discriminatory approach toward any of them. Justice is not merely mentioned, but is also particularly emphasized, in many Quranic verses and many *hadith*. It is explicitly clear within the Quran and *hadith* that God loves people who apply justice and gives them great rewards. The Quran states, "And if you judge, judge with justice between them. Verily, Allah loves those who act justly."[1276] For instance, there is a *hadith* from the Prophet stating, "There are seven categories of people whom God will shelter under His shade on the Day when there will be no shade except His. [One is] the just

---

1274 ECHR, *supra* note 497, at art. 6.

1275 InterRights, *Right to a Fair Trial Under the European Convention on Human Rights (Article 6)*. http://www.google.com.eg/url?sa=t&rct=j&q=fair+trial+EUROPEAN+COURT&source=web&cd=3&ved=0CD4QFjAC&url=http%3A%2F%2Fwww.interights.org%2Ffiles%2F107%2FFINTERIGHTS%2520Article%25206%2520Manual.pdf&ei=YaBwT8z4HaX44QTEw7W_Ag&usg=AFQjCNFV8q4Erl7DWPXX13znvH3bYaNhIQ (last visited Mar. 26, 2012).

1276 Quran 5:42.

leader."[1277] Also, there is a *hadith* wherein God states, "O My slaves, I have forbidden injustice for Myself and forbade it also for you. So avoid being unjust to one another."[1278] On the other hand, the Quran proclaims, "O you who believe! Stand out firmly for Allah as just witnesses; and let not the enmity and hatred of others make you avoid justice. Be just: that is nearer to piety; and fear Allah. Verily, Allah is Well-Acquainted with what you do."[1279] Also, the Quran states:

> Verily, Allah enjoins Al-'Adl (i.e. justice and worshipping none but Allah Alone – Islamic Monotheism) and Al-Ihsan [i.e. to be patient in performing your duties to Allah, totally for Allah's sake and in accordance with the Sunnah (legal ways) of the Prophet in a perfect manner], and giving (help) to kith and kin (i.e. all that Allah has ordered you to give them e.g., wealth, visiting, looking after them, or any other kind of help), and forbids Al-Fahsha' (i.e all evil deeds, e.g. illegal sexual acts, disobedience of parents, polytheism, to tell lies, to give false witness, to kill a life without right), and Al-Munkar (i.e all that is prohibited by Islamic law: polytheism of every kind, disbelief and every kind of evil deeds), and Al-Baghy (i.e. all kinds of oppression). He admonishes you, that you may take heed.[1280]

The Quran also mentions that one of the reasons for sending messengers is to ensure the application of justice. The Quran states, "Indeed We have sent Our Messengers with clear proofs, and revealed with them the Scripture and the Balance (justice) that mankind may keep up justice."[1281] There is another *hadith* of Prophet Mohammed in which he says, "What destroyed the nations preceding you, was that if a noble amongst them stole, they would forgive him, and if a poor person amongst them stole, they would inflict Allah's Legal punishment on him. By Allah, if Fatima, the daughter of Muhammad stole, I would cut off her hand."[1282]

There is also an important *hadith* regarding the right to fair trial. Prophet Mohammed advised a judge not to come to a quick decision until he had listened to the all the parties of a case. According to this *hadith*:

1277 *Justice in Islam*, ISLAMRELIGION.COM, http://www.islamreligion.com/articles/376/ (last visited Mar. 25, 2012).
1278 *Id.*
1279 QURAN 5:8.
1280 *Id.* at 16:90.
1281 *Id.* at 57:25.
1282 Raghed El-Sergany, *supra* note 251 (citing Al Bukhari: Kitab Al Anbiyaa (Book of the Prophets)).

Narrated Ali ibn AbuTalib: The Apostle of Allah (peace_be_upon_him) sent me to the Yemen as judge, and I asked: Apostle of Allah, are you sending me when I am young and have no knowledge of the duties of a judge? He replied: Allah will guide your heart and keep your tongue true. When two litigants sit in front of you, do not decide till you hear what the other has to say as you heard what the first had to say; for it is best that you should have a clear idea of the best decision. He said: I had been a judge (for long); or he said (the narrator is doubtful): I have no doubts about a decision afterwards.[1283]

A case happened during the life of Prophet Mohammed that is the story of a stolen shield.[1284] A Muslim man named Rafa'ah owned the shield that was stolen. Rafa'ah's nephew, Qatadah, went to the Prophet and told him that another Muslim man named Bashir from the Al-Khazraj tribe had stolen the shield. Yet, three Muslim men came to the Prophet and told him that Bashir had not stolen the shield, that, instead, a Jewish man named Zayed had stolen the shield. The Prophet sent a group of people to search Zayed's house and found the shield planted in the garden surrounding the house. Prophet Mohammed declared that the Muslim was innocent and the Jew was guilty. Yet, that same day, Gabriel, the messenger of God, came to the Prophet and told him that the Jew was innocent and that the Muslim man, Bashir, was the one who had stolen the shield. The truth was that Bashir had decided to play a trick after he found out that Qatadah had informed the Prophet that he had stolen the shield. Bashir and Zayed were neighbors and Bashir jumped over the wall and planted the shield in Zayed's garden. After that, Bashir told the three men to inform the Prophet that Zayed was the one who had stolen the shield.[1285]

This story was mentioned in the Quran although the person who had done the crime was a Muslim and all the witnesses were Muslims. This story was not mentioned in a *hadith*, but in the Quran, which demonstrates the importance of justice outlined in this story. Chapter Four of the Quran, which is entitled 'The Women,' states, "Surely, We have sent down to you (O Muhammad) the Book (this Qur'an) in truth that you might judge between men by that which Allah has shown you (i.e. has taught you through Divine Revelation), so be not a pleader for

---

1283 *Sunan Abu-Dawud, book number 24, hadith number 3575*, SEARCHTRUTH.COM, http://www.searchtruth.com/book_display.php?book=24&translator=3&start=0&number=3575#3575 (last visited Apr. 27, 2012).

1284 *The story of stolen shield*, YOUTUBE.COM, http://www.youtube.com/watch?v=Gnr9znaOgO8&feature=relmfu (last visited Mar. 26, 2012).

1285 *Id.*

the treacherous."[1286] The Quran uses the word 'treacherous' to refer to Bashir and the three witnesses and, also in relation to this story, states:

> And seek the Forgiveness of Allah, certainly, Allah is Ever Oft-Forgiving, Most Merciful. And argue not on behalf of those who deceive themselves. Verily, Allah does not like anyone who is a betrayer, sinner. They may hide (their crimes) from men, but they cannot hide (them) from Allah; for He is with them (by His Knowledge), when they plot by night in words that He does not approve. And Allah ever encompasses what they do. Lo! You are those who have argued for them in the life of this world, but who will argue for them on the Day of Resurrection against Allah, or who will then be their defender? And whoever does evil or wrongs himself but afterwards seeks Allah's Forgiveness, he will find Allah Oft-Forgiving, Most Merciful. And whoever earns sin, he earns it only against himself. And Allah is Ever All-Knowing, All-Wise. And whoever earns a fault or a sin and then throws it on to someone innocent, he has indeed burdened himself with falsehood and a manifest sin.[1287]

In the same chapter and with respect to the story of the stolen shield, the Quran also contains a wonderful short condensed verse that covers all of the things that may lead people to be unjust. It states, "O you who believe! Stand out firmly for justice, as witnesses to Allah, even though it be against yourselves, or your parents, or your kin, be he rich or poor, Allah is a Better Protector to both (than you). So follow not the lusts (of your hearts), lest you avoid justice; and if you distort your witness or refuse to give it, verily, Allah is Ever Well-Acquainted with what you do."[1288] This verse not only orders believers to apply justice in general, but also emphasizes some issues that may lead to injustice. It orders believers to apply equality and justice for any person regardless of their religion, sex, race, friends, enemies, etc. In addition, it goes beyond this and orders believers to apply justice to themselves. Although parents are given a unique status, Sharia law requests that justice should even be applied against ones parents or close relatives and friends.[1289] The verse uses the term 'witnesses to Allah,' which means to not witness falsely, by favoritism, or take something in return for what say you have seen. The Quran wants people to witness in favor of God (Iwa'gh Allah), not

---

1286 QURAN 4:105.
1287 *Id.* at 4:105-112.
1288 *Id.* at 4:135.
1289 Dr. Zaglol Al-Nagar, *Interpretation of QURAN 4:135*, DIGITAL.AHRAM.ORG. http://digital.ahram.org.eg/Religion.aspx?Serial=800453 (last visited Mar. 25, 2012).

in favor of anyone else. In another words, because God loves justice, the witness will tell the truth voluntarily, by his or her own will. Similarly, he or she will not lie either because they hate or love the other person. Instead, they will tell the truth regardless of the color, sex, religion, and nationality of the parties involved. Rather, they will tell the truth without waiting for a reward or something in return from anyone. Instead, people are taught to want only the reward of God. All of this is included in the meaning of 'witnesses to Allah.'

The verse also stated "be he rich or poor, Allah is a Better Protector to both (than you)"[1290], which means to apply justice regardless of whether the parties are rich or poor. It also means to not feel either compassion or arrogance towards the poor or feel either courtesy or hatred towards the rich. The Quran requests that people apply justice and not be lead by their emotions. The last part of the verse is a threat from God, reminding those who mislead justice that He knows and sees everything.[1291] In another verse God states "Allah wishes to accept your repentance, but those who follow their lusts, wish that you (believers) should deviate tremendously away (from the Right Path)."[1292] Furthermore, God criticizes people that follow their own desires in another verse wherein he states, "Have you (O Muhammad) seen him who has taken as his ilah (God) his own vain desire? Would you then be a Wakil (a disposer of his affairs or a watcher) over him?"[1293]

At the very beginning of Islam, new Muslims were distressed and feared torture. The Prophet suggested that some of his companions travel to Ethiopia, as there was a just king there who would reliably apply justice. This king, who was Christian, created the first asylums in Islam.[1294] The Muslims were very safe; while even non-believers of Islam requested their deportation, the King of Ethiopia refused and protected them. After Prophet Mohammed gave them permission to return back home, some of them even choose to stay in Ethiopia. From the previously mentioned Quranic verses and *hadith*, we can see that the Arab Charter can use the soft power[1295] of Sharia law to influence states parties of the Arab League. The soft power is effective because the majority of the people of these countries believe in, and love, Sharia law. Therefore, through using the influence of Sharia

---

1290 QURAN 4:135.

1291 Dr. Zaglol Al-Nagar, *supra* note 1289.

1292 QURAN 4:27.

1293 *Id.* at 25:43.

1294 *The King of Ethiopia*, YOUTUBE.COM, http://www.youtube.com/watch?v=4hYcGUEXlfU (last visited Mar. 25, 2012).

1295 Joseph Nye defined soft power as "It is the ability to get what you want through attraction rather than coercion or payments." (JOSEPH NYE, SOFT POWER THE MEANS TO SUCCESS IN WORLD POLITICS x (2004)).

law, governments can be pushed towards the implementing and guaranteeing the right of fair trial, the independence of judges, and the rule of law. The right to fair trial and rule of law cannot be accomplished without the presence of independent judges and prosecutors. The Arab Charter can play an important role in improving and implementing the separation of powers by ensuring the independence of the judiciary (both the judges and prosecutors). The Arab Charter can limit or prevent the referral of civilians to the military courts and ensure the right to fair trial and rule of law without the need for a national revolution The Arab Charter can play a more effective role in this regard than other international human rights treaties as most of the Arab countries made reservations on international human rights treaty because of Sharia law. On the other hand, the Arab Charter can effectively use Sharia law to improve the human rights situations in the states parties to the Arab Charter.

In the previous paragraph, I emphasized that the Arab Charter 'can' do this effectively. I did not say the Arab Charter 'does' this currently. The reason for this is because the Arab Charter cannot do anything without effective mechanisms for, and instruments of, supervision. For example, there is a need for an effective committee to supervise and examine the state reports, mechanisms that permit individuals to express complaints against countries in the case of the violation of any right, and an effective court. In short, there is a need for effective supervisory mechanisms. I will further explain all of this in greater detail in the next chapter and will also offer recommendations for how to move ahead on these issues.

I. The Right to Freedom of Movement and the Right to Seek Asylum

The right to freedom of movement and the right to seek asylum are directly connected to human dignity. Freedom of movement has several affiliated rights, including the right not to be arbitrary expelled from, or prevented from entering, a country; the right to choose to live in any city; and the right to seek asylum if one fears persecution. The right to freedom of movement is mentioned in all human rights treaties because it is a basic fundamental right.[1296] The ICCPR Gene-

---

1296 Article 13 of the Universal Declaration on Human Rights states, "(1) Everyone has the right to freedom of movement and residence within the borders of each state. (2) Everyone has the right to leave any country, including his own, and to return to his country." Article 14 states, "(1) Everyone has the right to seek and to enjoy in other countries asylum from persecution. (2) This right may not be invoked in the case of prosecutions genuinely arising from non-political crimes or from acts contrary to the purposes and principles of the United Nations." (UDHR, *supra* note 106, at art. 13).
Article 12 of the International Covenant on Civil and Political Rights states: "1. Everyone lawfully within the territory of a State shall, within that territory, have the right to liberty of movement and freedom to choose his residence. 2. Everyone shall be free to leave any country,

ral Comment No. 27 regarding the freedom of movement explains that, "[l]iberty of movement is an indispensable condition for the free development of a person. It interacts with several other rights enshrined in the Covenant, as is often shown in the Committee's practice in considering reports from States parties and communications from individuals."[1297]

There was a case before the European Court of Human Rights entitled *Baumann vs. France*,[1298] which is a case regarding a seizure for considerable amount of time of a German passport by the French authorities. Subsequent to the passport seizure, the holder of the German passport was arrested in Germany and sentenced to imprisonment. The French authorities claimed that there are no restric-

---

including his own. 3. The above-mentioned rights shall not be subject to any restrictions except those which are provided by law, are necessary to protect national security, public order (ordre public), public health or morals or the rights and freedoms of others, and are consistent with the other rights recognized in the present Covenant. 4. No one shall be arbitrarily deprived of the right to enter his own country." (ICCPR, *supra* note 63, at art 12).

Article 13 of the International Covenant on Civil and Political Rights states: "An alien lawfully in the territory of a State Party to the present Covenant may be expelled therefrom only in pursuance of a decision reached in accordance with law and shall, except where compelling reasons of national security otherwise require, be allowed to submit the reasons against his expulsion and to have his case reviewed by, and be represented for the purpose before, the competent authority or a person or persons especially designated by the competent authority." (ICCPR, *supra* note 63, at art 13).

Article 2 of Protocol No. 4 of the European Convention on Human Rights states: "1. Everyone lawfully within the territory of a State shall, within that territory, have the right to liberty of movement and freedom to choose his residence. 2. Everyone shall be free to leave any country, including his own. 3. No restrictions shall be placed on the exercise of these rights other than such as are in accordance with law and are necessary in a democratic society in the interests of national security or public safety, for the maintenance of *ordre public*, for the prevention of crime, for the protection of health or morals, or for the protection of the rights and freedoms of others. 4. The rights set forth in paragraph 1 may also be subject, in particular areas, to restrictions imposed in accordance with law and justified by the public interest in a democratic society. (ECHR, *supra* note 497, Protocol 4, at art 2).

Article 3 of Protocol No. 4 of the European Convention on Human Rights states: "1. No one shall be expelled, by means either of an individual or of a collective measure, from the territory of the State of which he is a national. 2. No one shall be deprived of the right to enter the territory of the state of which he is a national." (ECHR, *supra* note 497, Protocol 4, at art 3). Article 4 of Protocol No. 4 of the European Convention on Human Rights states, "Collective expulsion of aliens is prohibited." (ECHR, *supra* note 497, Protocol 4, at art 4).

1297 U.N. Human Rights Committee, General Comment No. 27: Freedom of movement (art. 12) (Nov. 2, 1999), http://www.unhchr.ch/tbs/doc.nsf/(Symbol)/6c76e1b8ee1710e380256824005a10a9?Opendocument (last visited Jun. 12, 2012).

1298 Baumann vs. France, App. no. 33592/96, (May 22, 2001), http://hudoc.echr.coe.int/sites/eng/pages/search.aspx?i=001-59470 (last visited Feb. 10, 2013).

tions on the freedom of movement placed by the French authorities because he was arrested and imprisoned in Germany. The Court stated:

> The Government cannot rely on circumstances posterior and external to the decision taken *ab initio* by the authorities, which gave rise to the impugned measure, to justify its consequences with regard to the complaint lodged by the applicant under Article 2 of Protocol No. 4 to the Convention. Furthermore, having regard to the fact that there was no judicial co-operation with the German authorities in the instant case, the Court cannot take into consideration the applicant's arrest by those authorities in assessing the legitimacy of the impugned restriction on the applicant's freedom of movement... Accordingly, the Court considers that a measure by means of which an individual is dispossessed of an identity document such as, for example, a passport, undoubtedly amounts to an interference with the exercise of liberty of movement.[1299]

Freedom of movement is not an absolute right without restrictions and limitations. In *Ciancimino vs. Italy*,[1300] the applicant complained that Italy violated his right to freedom of movement because Italian police restricted his freedom of movement while he was under police supervision. The European Commission stated that, although this constitutes an interference with freedom of movement, these measures are necessary in a democratic society and prescribed by law in order to combat and prevent crimes.[1301]

The Arab Charter on Human Rights protected the right to freedom of movement in details. Article 26, 27, and 28 discuss this issue, as follows:

> Article 26
>
> 1. Everyone lawfully within the territory of a State party shall, within that territory, have the right to freedom of movement and to freely choose his residence in any part of that territory in conformity with the laws in force.
>
> 2. No State party may expel a person who does not hold its nationality but is lawfully in its territory, other than in pursuance of a decision reached in accordance with law and after that person has been allowed to submit a petition to the competent authority, unless compelling

---

1299 *Id.*
1300 Ciancimino vs. Italy, App. No. 12541/86 (May 27, 1991).
1301 JACOBS & WHITE, *supra* note 566, at 403.

reasons of national security preclude it. Collective expulsion is prohibited under all circumstances.

Article 27

1. No one may be arbitrarily or unlawfully prevented from leaving any country, including his own, nor prohibited from residing, or compelled to reside, in any part of that country.

2. No one may be exiled from his country or prohibited from returning thereto.

Article 28

Everyone has the right to seek political asylum in another country in order to escape persecution. This right may not be invoked by persons facing prosecution for an offence under ordinary law. Political refugees may not be extradited.

The Cairo Declaration on Human Rights in Islam states,

> "Every man shall have the right, within the framework of Shari'a, to free movement and to select his place of residence whether inside or outside his country and if persecuted, is entitled to seek asylum in another country. The country of refuge shall ensure his protection until he reaches safety, unless asylum is motivated by an act which Shari'a regards as a crime."[1302]

The Egyptian Supreme Constitutional Court has also rendered many decisions confirming the freedom of movement. For instance, this Court rendered several judgments stating that the resolution of the Minister of Interior regarding banning some people from traveling is considered a violation to the freedom of movement. Thus, limiting or banning the freedom of movement cannot be done by an administrative decision. The Court added that every person is entitled to the freedom of movement. Derogation from this right can be done only in limited cases by a competent judicial authority (a judge or a public prosecutor) for a legitimate goal in order to protect the state security. The Court stated that freedom of movement is protected and safeguarded by articles 41, 50, 51, and 52 of the Egyptian Constitution.[1303] The Egyptian Supreme Constitutional Court rendered another decision stating that the rights of a person holding a passport

---

1302 Cairo Declaration on Human Rights in Islam, *supra* note 423, art. 12.
1303 Case No. 44, Judicial Year 44, appeal no. 2297, 17th Mar. 2001; *see also* appeal no. 243, Judicial Year 21, 4th Nov. 2000.

include not only those connected with being Egyptian but those connected with his personal freedom. The Court added that the right to personal freedom is protected by Article 41 of the Egyptian Constitution of 1971, which provides:

> Individual liberty is a natural right and shall not be touched. Except in cases of in flagrante delicto no person may be arrested, inspected, detained or his freedom restricted or freedom of movement curtailed except by judicial warrant required for the purpose of an investigation or the preservation of the security of the society. This warrant shall be issued by the competent judge or the Public Prosecutor in accordance with the provisions of the law. The law shall determine the period of custody.[1304]

The 2014 Egyptian Constitution protects the right to freedom of movement from any violation, the Constitution provides,

> Freedom of movement, residence and emigration shall be guaranteed. No citizen may be expelled from the State territory or prevented from returning thereto. No citizen may be prevented from leaving the State territory, placed under house arrest or prevented from residing in a

---

[1304] Egyptian Const. art. 41. After amending the Egyptian Constitution in 2014, article 41 become article 54. Article 54 read as follow "Personal freedom is a natural right, shall be protected and may not be infringed upon. Except for the case of being caught in flagrante delicto, it is not permissible to arrest, search, detain, or restrict the freedom of anyone in any way except by virtue of a reasoned judicial order that was required in the context of an investigation.
Every person whose freedom is restricted shall be immediately notified of the reasons therefore; shall be informed of his/her rights in writing; shall be immediately enabled to contact his/her relatives and lawyer; and shall be brought before the investigation authority within twenty four (24) hours as of the time of restricting his/her freedom.
Investigation may not start with the person unless his/her lawyer is present. A lawyer shall be seconded for persons who do not have one. Necessary assistance shall be rendered to people with disability according to procedures prescribed by Law.
Every person whose freedom is restricted, as well as others, shall have the right to file grievance before the court against this action. A decision shall be made on such grievance within one (1) week as of the date of action; otherwise, the person must be immediately released. The Law shall regulate the provisions, duration, and causes of temporary detention, as well as the cases in which damages are due on the state to compensate a person for such temporary detention or for serving punishment thereafter cancelled pursuant to a final judgment reversing the judgment by virtue of which such punishment was imposed.
In all events, it is not permissible to present an accused for trial in crimes that may be punishable by imprisonment unless a lawyer is present by virtue of a power of attorney from the accused or by secondment by the court." http://www.sis.gov.eg/Newvr/Dustor-en001.pdf (last visited May 14, 2014).

certain place except by a reasoned judicial order for a specified period of time and in the cases as defined by the Law."[1305]

Sharia law respects and protects the right to freedom of movement. The Quran states, "O mankind! We have created you from a male and a female, and made you into nations and tribes, that you may know one another. Verily, the most honourable of you with Allah is that (believer) who has At-Taqwa [i.e. he is one of the Muttaqun (the pious. See V.2:2)]. Verily, Allah is All-Knowing, All-Aware."[1306] There are several verses that request that people move freely, including the following, "Say (O Muhammad): 'Travel in the land...'"[1307] and "... so travel through the earth..."[1308] and "Say: 'Travel in the land and see how (Allah) originated the creation, and then Allah will bring forth the creation of the Hereafter (i.e. resurrection after death). Verily, Allah is Able to do all things,'"[1309] as well as "And verily, We have sent among every Ummah (community, nation) a Messenger (proclaiming): 'Worship Allah (Alone), and avoid (or keep away from) Taghut (all false deities i.e. do not worship Taghut besides Allah).' Then of them were some whom Allah guided and of them were some upon whom the straying was justified. So travel through the land and see what was the end of those who denied (the truth)."[1310]

Sharia law gives the right to believers to move from the place they are living or even leave the country of residence in cases of persecution or ill-treatment. The Quran states,

"When angels take the souls of those who die in sin against their souls,

they say: 'In what (plight) Were ye?' They reply: 'Weak and oppressed Were we in the earth.' They say: 'Was not the earth of Allah spacious enough for you to move yourselves away (From evil)?' Such men will find their abode in Hell, What an evil refuge! "[1311]

However, the right to freedom of movement is not an absolute right without any limitations. Sharia law requests that believers not move to any place without requesting the permission of the hosting person and hosting country. This

---

1305 Egyptian Const. art. 62. http://www.sis.gov.eg/Newvr/Dustor-en001.pdf (last visited May 14, 2014).
1306 QURAN 49:13.
1307 *Id.* at 6:11.
1308 *Id.* at 3:137.
1309 *Id.* at 29:20.
1310 *Id.* at 16:36.
1311 *Id.* at 4:97.

permission can be sought, for example, through an asylum request or through a visa application. The Quran states, "O you who believe! Enter not houses other than your own, until you have asked permission and greeted those in them; that is better for you, in order that you may remember. And if you find no one therein, still, enter not until permission has been given. And if you are asked to go back, go back, for it is purer for you. And Allah is All-Knower of what you do."[1312] When he decided to emigrate from Makka to Madina, Prophet Mohammed only travelled when the people of Madina accepted to host him. Before traveling to Madina, he requested to travel to *Ta'ef*, but the people of *Ta'ef* did not grant him permission to do so.[1313] This demonstrates that Sharia law requests that believers seek the permission from the hosting person before traveling to their location. As demonstrated in an example that was previously mentioned, during the very beginning of Islam, when new Muslims faced oppression, persecution, and torture, Prophet Mohammed suggested that some of his companions travel to Ethiopia. The Prophet told them there was a king in Ethiopia who was never unjust. This king was Christian, yet he created the first asylums in Islam.[1314] The Muslims did not travel until they received the permission of the King of Ethiopia.[1315] In short, Sharia law accepts, and even encourages, people to seek freedom of movement, the right to seek asylum, and the right to travel when they fear human rights violations. However, in such situations, the laws and regulations of the hosting countries must be respected and fulfilled.

The right to not be expelled from a country is extended to a child born out of wedlock. For example, according to Sharia law, an infant found on the street whose family is not known, he or she should not be expelled from the country. There are several Quranic verses and *hadith* the encourage believers to be helpful and generous. For instance, Quran states, "Help ye one another in righteousness and piety…"[1316] Also, the Quran explains "and if any one saved a life, it would be as if he saved the life of the whole people."[1317]

From these Quranic verses, we can come to conclusion that the Quran seeks to respect and protect the life of all people. Thus, Sharia law is against the extradi-

---

1312 *Id.* at 24:27-28.
1313 HELALY, *supra* note 273, at 194.
1314 *Id.* at 195; *see also The King of Ethiopia*, YOUTUBE.COM, http://www.youtube.com/watch?v=4hYcGUEXIfU (last visited Mar. 25, 2012).
1315 HELALY, *supra* note 273, at195.
1316 QURAN 5:2.
1317 *Id.* at 5:32.

tion or expulsion of anyone to a country where he or she may fear persecution or oppression.

Sharia law encourages freedom of movement not only to escape persecution, but also for touristic reasons. God requested that people travel and see other places and while doing so think about how God created the Earth. The Quran states,

> "See they not how Allah originates the creation, then repeats it. Verily, that is easy for Allah. Say: 'Travel in the land and see how (Allah) originated the creation, and then Allah will bring forth the creation of the Hereafter (i.e. resurrection after death). Verily, Allah is able to do all things.'"[1318]

Sharia law establishes the connection between travel and a belief in God. In other words, when people travel and see different places, they are supposed to think about how there must be a creator for the earth and the universe. This will make believers that much more certain that God is the creator for the universe. The Quran states, "Thus did we show Ibrahim (Abraham) the kingdom of the heavens and the earth that he be one of those who have Faith with certainty."[1319] Furthermore, the Quran poses the question, "Have they not travelled through the land, and have they hearts wherewith to understand and ears wherewith to hear? Verily, it is not the eyes that grow blind, but it is the hearts which are in the breasts that grow blind."[1320] In this way, Sharia law protects and respects freedom of movement and the capacity to travel from a place to another. The Quran states,

> "See you not that Allah sends down water (rain) from the sky, and We produce therewith fruits of various colours, and among the mountains are streaks white and red, of varying colours and (others) very black. And likewise of men and Ad-Dawabb [moving (living) creatures, beasts], and cattle, are of various colours. It is only those who have knowledge among His slaves that fear Allah. Verily, Allah is All-Mighty, Oft-Forgiving."[1321]

In addition, Sharia law encourages travel for other purposes, such as gaining money. For instance, a person can travel to another city or country seeking a better position, better salary, or for the purposes of being within nature. The Quran states, "He it is Who has made the earth subservient to you (i.e. easy for

---

1318 *Id.* at 29:19-20.
1319 *Id.* at 6:75.
1320 *Id.* at 22:46.
1321 *Id.* at 35:27-28.

you to walk, to live and to do agriculture on it); so walk in the path thereof and eat of His provision. And to Him will be the Resurrection."[1322] The Arab Charter is aligned with both Sharia law and international human rights standards. Like international human rights law, the Arab Charter also protects the right to the freedom of movement. However, in order to increase the effectiveness of the Charter in the protection of human rights, effective supervisory mechanisms must be created to monitor the implementation of the rights, such as that of the freedom of movement, mentioned in the Charter.

J. Prohibition of Slavery

The right to not be subject to slavery is a fundamental right that must be respected. There is an international consensus of all international human rights treaties on the prohibition of slavery.[1323] The Arab Charter on Human Rights states,

> "All forms of slavery and trafficking in human beings are prohibited and are punishable by law. No one shall be held in slavery and servitude under any circumstances [and] Forced labor, trafficking in human beings for the purposes of prostitution or sexual exploitation, the ex-

---

1322 *Id.* at 67:15.

1323 The ICCPR states: "1. No one shall be held in slavery; slavery and the slave-trade in all their forms shall be prohibited. 2. No one shall be held in servitude. 3. (a) No one shall be required to perform forced or compulsory labour; (b) Paragraph 3 (a) shall not be held to preclude, in countries where imprisonment with hard labour may be imposed as a punishment for a crime, the performance of hard labour in pursuance of a sentence to such punishment by a competent court; (c) For the purpose of this paragraph the term "forced or compulsory labour" shall not include: (i) Any work or service, not referred to in subparagraph (b), normally required of a person who is under detention in consequence of a lawful order of a court, or of a person during conditional release from such detention; (ii) Any service of a military character and, in countries where conscientious objection is recognized, any national service required by law of conscientious objectors; (iii) Any service exacted in cases of emergency or calamity threatening the life or well-being of the community; (iv) Any work or service which forms part of normal civil obligations." (ICCPR, *supra* note 63, at art. 8).

The European Convention on Human Rights prohibits slavery. It states: "1. No one shall be held in slavery or servitude. 2. No one shall be required to perform forced or compulsory labour. For the purpose of this article the term "forced or compulsory labour" shall not include: a) any work required to be done in the ordinary course of detention imposed according to the provisions of Article 5 of this Convention or during conditional release from such detention; b) any service of a military character or, in case of conscientious objectors in countries where they are recognised, service exacted instead of compulsory military service; c) any service exacted in case of an emergency or calamity threatening the life or well-being of the community; d) any work or service which forms part of normal civic obligations. (ECHR, *supra* note 497, at art 4).

ploitation of the prostitution of others or any other form of exploitation or the exploitation of children in armed conflict are prohibited."[1324]

The Cairo Declaration on Human Rights in Islam explains:

> a) Human beings are born free, and no one has the right to enslave, humiliate, oppress or exploit them, and there can be no subjugation but to God the Most-High.
>
> b) Colonialism of all types being one of the most evil forms of enslavement is totally prohibited. Peoples suffering from colonialism have the full right to freedom and self-determination. It is the duty of all States and peoples to support the struggle of colonized peoples for the liquidation of all forms of colonialism and occupation, and all States and peoples have the right to preserve their independent identity and exercise control over their wealth and natural resources.[1325]

Sharia law applied a strategy of gradualism in relation to the issue slavery. Sharia law did not prohibit slavery explicitly; however, it encouraged setting slaves free. In other words, Sharia law closed the doors of slavery gradually. According to Sharia law, to set a slave free was considered to be a good deed. In addition, if a person did certain mistakes, he or she could free a slave as one of the ways of seeking God's forgiveness.[1326] For example, as cited above, the Quran states:

> It is not for a believer to kill a believer except (that it be) by mistake; and whosoever kills a believer by mistake, (it is ordained that) he must set free a believing slave and a compensation (blood-money, i.e. Diya) be given to the deceased's family unless they remit it. If the deceased belonged to a people at war with you and he was a believer, the freeing of a believing slave (is prescribed); and if he belonged to a people with whom you have a treaty of mutual alliance, compensation (blood-money – Diya) must be paid to his family, and a believing slave must be freed. And whoso finds this (the penance of freeing a slave) beyond his means, he must fast for two consecutive months in order to seek repentance from Allah. And Allah is Ever All-Knowing, All-Wise. [emphasis added][1327]

1324 ACHR, *supra* note 126, at art. 10.
1325 Cairo Declaration on Human Rights in Islam, *supra* note 423, art. 11.
1326 An interview with Prof. Magdi Ashore, the Academic Consultant of the Egyptian Mufti (February 15, 2012); *see also Gradualism in Applying Shari'ah*, ISLAMAWARENESS.NET, http://www.islamawareness.net/Shariah/sh_fatwa010.html (last visited Apr. 20, 2012).
1327 QURAN 4:92.

In another example, the Quran explains:

> Allah will not call you to account for what is futile in your oaths, but He will call you to account for your deliberate oaths: for expiation, feed ten indigent persons, on a scale of the average for the food of your families; or clothe them; or give a slave his freedom. If that is beyond your means, fast for three days. That is the expiation for the oaths ye have sworn. But keep to your oaths. Thus doth Allah make clear to you His signs, that ye may be grateful.[1328]

Furthermore, the Quran emphasizes, "And those who make unlawful to them their wives by Zihar and wish to free themselves from what they uttered, (the penalty) in that case is the freeing of a slave before they touch each other. That is an admonition to you (so that you may not repeat such an ill thing). And Allah is All-Aware of what you do."[1329]

Sharia law encourages treating slaves well with respect to human rights and dignity. For example, there is a *hadith* in which "The Prophet said, 'He who has a slave-girl and teaches her good manners and improves her education and then manumits and marries her, will get a double reward; and any slave who observes Allah's right and his master's right will get a double reward.'"[1330] The previous *hadith* not only shows respect to slaves and to their dignity, but it also shows that Sharia law advocates equality between people. In other words, the previous *hadith* did not prohibit the slaves could marry if they are of different races. This indicates that all, according to Sharia law, people are all equal before the law.

The principle of gradualism was used to abolish slavery in United States of America. This strategy, used by the world's first antislavery organization, the Pennsylvania Abolition Society:

> Emphasized that government and its representative legal and political institutions should gradually attack the institution of slavery. By pressuring state and federal officials to craft abolitionist statutes, and by challenging courts to hand down pro-abolitionist decisions... The PAS viewed litigation against masters as another important way to strike at bondage gradually. By representing kidnapped free blacks in court, by bargaining with slaveholders for a fugitive slave's freedom, and by requiring northern courts to protect the constitutional rights of blacks,

---

[1328] *Id.* at 5:89.
[1329] *Id.* at 58:3.
[1330] Sahih Bukharia, Book 46, Hadith 723, Searchtruth.com, http://www.searchtruth.com/book_display.php?book=46&translator=1&start=28&number=720 (last visited (May 5, 2012).

the PAS hampered slavery's legal protections nationally – turning bondage into a distinctly sectional institution with different legal sanctions in northern and southern courts. Pennsylvania abolitionists spent most of their time and money planning legal tactics and achieved a national reputation as blacks' legal representatives.[1331]

The previous example shows that gradualism was used not only in Sharia law but also in the United States of America as a way of abolishing slavery. Gradualism is a very effective and successful way in abolishing slavery.

Gradualism is not only successful with respect to combating slavery but also is considered the main key to the success of any human rights system. In the next chapters, gradualism will play an important role in improving the effectiveness of the supervisory role of the Arab human rights system.

[1331] RICHARD S. NEWMAN, THE TRANSFORMATION OF AMERICAN ABOLITIONISM: FIGHTING SLAVERY IN THE EARLY REPUBLIC (2002), http://www.ibiblio.org/uncpress/chapters/newman_transformation.html (last visited Apr. 21, 2012).

Chapter 6: An Evaluation of the Procedural Human Rights Protections Through the Existing Arab Committee

A. Introduction

In 1968, the Arab League established the Permanent Arab Committee for Human Rights.[1332] This Permanent Committee was established before the adoption of the Arab Charter. The Permanent Arab Committee for Human Rights is a permanent Committee not related to the Arab Committee on Human Rights which is established under the Arab Charter.

The Permanent Arab Committee for Human Rights is one of the permanent technical committees that were established in compliance with Article 4 of the Pact of the Arab League. The duty of the Permanent Committee is broad, covering all human rights issues in the Arab League. In addition, it adopts principles of human rights in the Arab League. Furthermore, the Permanent Committee is also concerned with the implementation of the treaties and resolutions that are concerned with human rights in the Arab League. All the states parties to the Arab League are members of the Permanent Arab Committee for Human Rights.[1333]

In contrast, the Arab Committee on Human Rights is the committee established by the Arab Charter on Human Rights in compliance with Article 45 of the Arab

---

1332 Permanent Arab Committee for Human Rights, http://www.lasportal.org/wps/portal/las_ar/inner/!ut/p/c5/vZLLjoJAFES_hS-4twVBlxhAu7F77Iev3hhMDAEfGDWO8vVCMsms1I3x1rJS99SiwEKjQ3Yt8uxSVIdsBwuw_irqSzXzlItofnyknVGkBBFub-A3_vK5z8ib9BwW6K10eT_Selur MICcl2yijfzl44SLMr7zKElFjLWZVjdhaH0OFOUmScm5T2aJjMOUcUFzB3R2av7ZV8S2T-vjkwsRlmCD__xQph5SqbuC6QkJhwjmg41fszpfZLIfZJGPshjYfFet26UOQIyq_QaO--m1UD3yJzcPHecBqiPYzw!!/dl3/d3/L2dBISEvZ0FBIS9nQSEh/?pcid=9b27da0049c42042a5f5bd526698d42c (last visited Aug. 16, 2013).

1333 The Permanent Arab Committee for Human Rights has several duties stated in its rules of procedures. For instance: i) Establish rules of cooperation between the Arab countries in the field of human rights. ii) Write draft charters and treaties related to the protection of human rights. iii) Evaluate Arab conventions that are related to human rights for the purpose of measuring whether they apply the minimum standards and principles of human rights. iv) Cooperate with other international and regional organizations related to human rights. v) Encourage work on the development and promotion of and respect for and protection of human rights in the Arab world. http://www.lasportal.org/wps/wcm/connect/3153d4004a7c51248bf79f526698d42c/%D8%A7%D9%84%D9%84%D8%A7%D8%A6%D8%AD%D8%A9+%D8%A7%D9%84%D8%AF%D8%A7%D8%AE%D9%84%D9%8A%D8%A9+%D9%84%D9%84%D8%AC%D9%86%D8%A9+%D8%A7%D9%84%D8%B9%D8%B1%D8%A8%D9%8A%D8%A9+%D8%A7%D9%84%D8%AF%D8%A7%D8%A6%D9%85%D8%A9+%D9%84%D8%AD%D9%82%D9%88%D9%82+%D8%A7%D9%84%D8%A5%D9%86%D8%B3%D8%A7%D9%862%5B1%5D.pdf?MOD=AJPERES (last visited Aug. 16, 2013).

Charter. It consists of seven members.[1334] These members should be elected for a four-year term.[1335] They can be re-elected for one time only in order to give due regard for the principle of rotation.[1336] It is very wise that the Arab Charter states that no State party can have more than one member in the Committee.[1337] It also states that the members of the Committee consist of nationals of the states parties to the Charter.[1338] It is very important that the members should be nationals of the states parties in order to give their nationals experience and to have a generation that is capable of dealing with human rights cases. The Arab Charter is also effective in its limitation of re-election to one time only. This will help ensure that the Charter is a living instrument to promote human rights. Changing the members of the Committee will also help ensure that the Charter is a living instrument, because every new member will come with new ideas and high levels of motivation to promote and protect human rights. In addition, the former members will be able to write books or articles or give lectures on their experiences. Therefore, the use of rotation also results in increasing the knowledge and awareness of Arab nations. The Arab Committee can promote the rights within the Arab Charter because of the factors outlined above.

The Arab Charter is also well designed in that it outlines that members of the Committee shall be elected for a four-year term, as opposed to the six-year term stated in the African Charter. This will definitely help expose large numbers of people to work within the Committee. Furthermore, it will guarantee the independence of the Committee because they know they are there for limited time and that other members will be appointed. Therefore, the Arab Charter will be more efficient.

The State reporting mechanism in the Arab Charter is the only monitoring supervisory system within the Charter. Unlike the African Charter, the Arab Charter was clear and precise in stating that the Arab Committee is the only body that is responsible to examine the reports and write the observations and recommendations. Article 48 of the Arab Charter provides, "The States parties undertake to submit reports to the Secretary-General of the League of Arab States on the measures they have taken to give effect to the rights and freedoms recognized in this Charter and on the progress made towards the enjoyment thereof. The Secretary-General shall transmit these reports to the Committee for its considera-

---

1334 ACHR, *supra* note 126, at art. 45 (1).
1335 *Id.* at art. 45 (4).
1336 *Id.* at art. 45 (3).
1337 *Id.*
1338 *Id.* at art. 45 (2).

tion."[1339] In addition to the initial report and the periodical report once every two years, the Committee has the right to request that the states parties submit additional information related to the implementation of the Charter. The Charter provides, "Each State party shall submit an initial report to the Committee within one year from the date on which the Charter enters into force and a periodic report every three years thereafter. The Committee may request the States parties to supply it with additional information relating to the implementation of the Charter."[1340] The Arab Committee is responsible for writing observations and recommendations on the reports. The Charter provides, "The Committee shall submit an annual report containing its comments and recommendations to the Council of the League, through the intermediary of the Secretary-General."[1341] The Charter did not state that the reports are submitted directly from the states to the Committee. However, it should be submitted to the Committee through the Secretary General. The reason behind this is maybe because of the power of the Secretary General and the corresponding influence to put pressure on states to submit their reports on time. In addition, the reason for submitting the recommendation and observations to the Secretary General and not directly to the states is to put pressure on states by informing the Secretary General of the conclusions of the Committee. On the other hand, the disadvantage of submitting the reports through the Secretary General is that it may be politically motivated. In other words, the semi-judicial structure of the Committee may collapse. The Committee must be separated and isolated from the Secretary General of the Arab League in order to avoid any intentional or non-intentional delay in submitting the reports to the Committee. The best way is to submit the report first to the Committee and then send a copy to the Secretary General.

In Chapters 6, 7, 8 and 9, I will seek to show how the Arab Charter can promote human rights, primarily through an evaluative process. I will also use a comparative approach insofar as it helps strengthen the understanding of this evaluation. In addition, I will suggest what can be done to promote human rights through the Arab Charter.

In Chapters 6, 7, 8 and 9, I will focus on this procedural aspect of the Charter because rights are useless if there are no effective supervisory mechanisms. The success being achieved by the European Convention is primary due to its effective supervisory mechanisms. The European system has an effective Court. The Inter-American system of human rights protection, which I will not discuss

---

1339 *Id.* at art. 48(1).
1340 *Id.* at art. 48(2).
1341 *Id.* at art. 48(5).

in detail due to reasons of space and relative remoteness of connection to the Arab system, consists of a Commission and a Court. The African system has both a Court and a Commission. On the other hand, the Arab system only has a Committee. The role of the existing Arab Committee is to receive periodic annual reports from states parties and subsequently to write recommendations to concerned states. The Arab Committee is not permitted to receive complaints from individuals or states, nor is the Arab Committee independent, as some of its members are diplomats and hold governmental positions. Also, there is no Arab Court. I will suggest how to amend the structure of the Arab Committee to make it more effective and efficient. In addition, I will suggest two optional protocols; the first of which is to increase the effectiveness of the Arab Committee through the amendment of its structure and function, such as the creation of a mechanism through which the Committee can receive both individual and state complaints. The second protocol would ultimately establish an effective Arab Court.

Best practices of other regional courts should be examined in order to promote the effectiveness and efficiency of the decisions made by the Arab Court. It should be noted that even if there are several Arab countries that have efficient judicial systems, the Arab Court should be structured as the guaranteed protector of the judicial systems. In other words, if there is any misuse of justice, the Arab Court should be the last shield of protection.

Chapters 6, 7, 8 and 9 are directed towards people working on establishing the Arab Human Rights system and people living in Arab countries, such that they can expand their knowledge regarding regional human rights systems. One of the main aims of the Arab Charter is to develop and promote the culture of human rights protection in the Arab countries that have ratified the Charter.

B. The Composition and Structure of the Existing Arab Human Rights Committee

The Arab Charter established an Arab Committee on Human Rights. The Committee is composed of seven members who are elected by secret ballot by the states parties to the Charter. Article 45 (1) of the Arab Charter on Human Rights provides, "Pursuant to this Charter, an 'Arab Human Rights Committee,' hereinafter referred to as 'the Committee' shall be established. This Committee shall consist of seven members who shall be elected by secret ballot by the states parties to this Charter."[1342] The Arab Charter states that the members of the Com-

---

1342 *Id.* at art. 45 (1).

mittee are nationals of the States parties to the Charter.[1343] Furthermore, the members of the Committee are elected for four years and can be re-elected only once.[1344] The Arab Charter provides, "The Committee shall include among its members not more than one national of a State party; such member may be re-elected only once. Due regard shall be given to the rotation principle."[1345] The Arab Charter stated that the members of the Committee must be highly experienced, independent, and impartial. In addition, they shall serve only in their personal capacity.[1346] Furthermore, states parties shall ensure that immunities are given to the members of the Arab Committee. The Arab Charter provides, "The States parties undertake to ensure that members of the Committee shall enjoy the immunities necessary for their protection against any form of harassment or moral or material pressure or prosecution on account of the positions they take or statements they make while carrying out their functions as members of the Committee."[1347] A seat is declared vacant in case of death or resignation or if, in the unanimous opinion of the other members, a member of the Committee has ceased to perform his functions without offering an acceptable justification or for any reason other than a temporary absence. The Arab Charter provides that:

> The Secretary-General shall declare a seat vacant after being notified by the Chairman of a member's:
> (a) Death;
> (b) Resignation; or
> (c) If, in the unanimous, opinion of the other members, a member of the Committee has ceased to perform his functions without offering an acceptable justification or for any reason other than a temporary absence.[1348]

The seat of the Committee is at the headquarters of the Arab League in Cairo, Egypt. The Arab Charter provides, "The Committee shall hold its meetings at the headquarters of the League of Arab States. It may also meet in any other State party to the present Charter at that party's invitation."[1349]

1343 *Id.* at art. 45 (2).
1344 *Id.* at art. 45 (3) & (4).
1345 *Id.* at art. 45 (3).
1346 *Id.* at art. 45 (2).
1347 *Id.* at art. 47.
1348 *Id.* at art. 46 (1).
1349 *Id.* at art. 45 (7).

1. The Members of the Arab Committee on Human Rights

It should be noted that Article 45 (5) of the Arab Charter provides, "Six months prior to the date of the election, the Secretary-General of the League of Arab States shall invite the States parties to submit their nominations within the following three months." The Arab Charter entered into force in March 2008, and the members of the Arab Committee were elected on March 5, 2009. The Arab Charter provides, "Each State party shall submit an initial report to the Committee within one year from the date on which the Charter enters into force and a periodic report every three years thereafter."[1350] Article 45 (4) of the Arab Charter provides, "The members of the Committee shall be elected for a four-year term, although the mandate of three of the members elected during the first election shall be for two years and shall be renewed by lot."[1351] It should be noted that there is a mistake in Article 45 (4). The word "renewed" should be deleted. The real meaning of this article is that three of the members of the Committee should be chosen by lot in order to be replaced by another new three members. Therefore, the word *"renewed"* should be replaced with the word *"chosen."* The article should be written as follow "The members of the Committee shall be elected for a four-year term, although the mandate of three of the members elected during the first election shall be for two years and shall be *chosen* by lot." The Arab League stated clearly that this is a mistake, recommending that the Arab Committee on Human Rights should correct the word "renewed."[1352] On March 5, 2009, the seven members of the Committee were elected. In 2011, three new members were elected, replacing the other three members in compliance with Article 45 (4). The members of the Arab Committee should be highly experienced and serve in their personal capacity. Article 45 (2) of the Arab Charter provides, "The Committee shall consist of nationals of the states parties to the present Charter, who must be highly experienced and competent in the Committee's field of work. The members of the Committee shall serve in their personal capacity and shall be fully independent and impartial."[1353] The official website of the league of Arab States published the curriculum vitae of the members of the Arab Committee on Human Rights.[1354] Some of the members of the Arab Committee are highly

---

1350 *Id.* at art. 48 (2).

1351 *Id.* at art. 45 (4).

1352 The title of the book is "The Mechanisms for Reviewing the Arab Charters and Treaties That Are Related to Human Rights, The Secretariat of the Arab League", Department of Social Affairs, Office of Human Rights, The Technical Secretariat of the Permanent Arab Committee on Human Rights page 63. (2006).

1353 ACHR, *supra* note 126, at art. 45 (2).

1354 *The official website of the League of Arab States*, http://www.lasportal.org/ (last visited October

experienced professionally and academically. For instance, the former Chairman of the Committee, Dr. Abdel Reheem Al-Awady, graduated from the Faculty of Law, Cairo University. He also completed his Master's degree in Law from the University of Georgia in the United States of America. In addition, he earned his Ph.D. in International Law from the University of Exeter in the United Kingdom. Professionally, he was a prosecutor at the Ministry of Justice in the United Arab Emirates, currently working at its office of legal and media affairs, studies and research. He represented the United Arab Emirates at several international and regional conferences. He is a member of a number of international committees.

It should be noted that most of the members of the Arab Committee hold governmental positions. Several members are diplomats. For instance, the representatives of Syria and Bahrain are diplomats from the Ministries of Foreign Affairs in Syria. The representative of Libya is a diplomat from the Ministry of Foreign Affairs in Libya.

2. The Secretariat of the Arab Committee on Human Rights

In 2010, the Arab Committee put out a newspaper advertisement requesting human rights experts to apply for positions at the Secretariat of the Arab Committee. The newspaper advertisement stated that the Arab Human Rights Committee requests experts in the field of human rights. The Committee mentioned the required qualifications of the applicants as the following:

- The applicant should have undertaken post graduate studies in international law, especially in the field of human rights.
- At least 10 years professional background in the field of analyzing and examining human rights reports in international or regional organizations either governmental or nongovernmental.
- The applicant should have very good knowledge of a foreign language.[1355]

C. The State Reporting Mechanism

The state reporting mechanism in the Arab Charter is the only monitoring/supervisory system within the Charter. The Arab Charter provides, "The States parties undertake to submit reports to the Secretary-General of the League of Arab States on the measures they have taken to give effect to the rights and freedoms reco-

---

5, 2012).

1355 The Office of Human Rights at the League of Arab States provided me with a copy of the newspaper advertisement.

gnized in this Charter and on the progress made towards the enjoyment thereof. The Secretary-General shall transmit these reports to the Committee for its consideration."[1356] Each state party is requested to submit an initial report within one year from the date on which the Charter enters into force. After that, each state party should submit an annual report every three years. Once the Committee receives the state's report, the members of the Committee start examining the report and then draft the challenges, conclusions, and recommendations. The Arab Committee should submit an annual report to the Council of the League. This report should includes comments and recommendations. This report should be a public document. The Arab Charter provides:

> 1. The States parties undertake to submit reports to the Secretary-General of the League of Arab States on the measures they have taken to give effect to the rights and freedoms recognized in this Charter and on the progress made towards the enjoyment thereof. The Secretary-General shall transmit these reports to the Committee for its consideration.
>
> 2. Each State party shall submit an initial report to the Committee within one year from the date on which the Charter enters into force and a periodic report every three years thereafter. The Committee may request the States parties to supply it with additional information relating to the implementation of the Charter.
>
> 3. The Committee shall consider the reports submitted by the States parties under paragraph 2 of this article in the presence of the representative of the State party whose report is being considered.
>
> 4. The Committee shall discuss the report, comment thereon and make the necessary recommendations in accordance with the aims of the Charter.
>
> 5. The Committee shall submit an annual report containing its comments and recommendations to the Council of the League, through the intermediary of the Secretary-General.
>
> 6. The Committee's reports, concluding observations and recommendations shall be public documents which the Committee shall disseminate widely.[1357]

1356 ACHR, *supra* note 126, at art. 48 (1).
1357 *Id.* at art. 48.

The official website of the League of Arab States briefly explains the mechanism of the work of the Arab Committee. It details the steps that should be followed from the moments of writing the report until its publication as follows:

> – The Arab Committee gives states parties guidelines to guide them in writing the states reports. These guiding principles help to establish a unified shape of the report. In addition, the guidelines help to ensure a full picture explaining the human rights situation in the country in order to evaluate its compatibility with the provisions of the Charter.[1358]
>
> – After the Secretary General receives the report from the State party he forwards it to the Arab Committee for examination. The Committee starts writing its notes on the report in order to prepare for its final examination.[1359]
>
> – The Arab Committee discusses the report with the State Party concerned. After that, the Committee writes its conclusions and observations.[1360]
>
> – On a yearly basis, the Committee sends a report to the Council of the Arab League through the Secretary General of the Arab League. This report includes its recommendations and conclusions to the Arab Committee.[1361]
>
> – The Committee reports, including the conclusions and recommendations, should be published widely.[1362]

In 2012, the Arab Committee examined the first country report submitted by Jordan. The Committee is currently working on examining the rest of the reports of the State Parties. Jordan's report was the first report to be examined by the Arab Committee. Algeria was the second country to submit its report to the Arab Committee on April 28, 2011. Bahrain was the third country to submit its report on August 25, 2012. The Chairman of the Arab Committee declared that the report by Algeria would be the second report to be examined by the Arab Committee.[1363] The reports submitted by states parties and the final recommen-

---

1358 The official website of the League of Arab States, http://www.lasportal.org (last visited October 6, 2012).
1359 *Id.*
1360 *Id.*
1361 *Id.*
1362 *Id.*
1363 *The Arab Committee on Human Rights*, ALITTIHAD.AE http://www.alittihad.ae/details.php?id=33085&y=2012 (last visited Apr. 23, 2012).

dations and conclusions of the Arab Committee on the reports are published on the website of the Arab League.[1364]

D. Documents Published by the Arab Committee on Human Rights to Guide the Committee and the Reviewed States

The Arab Committee on Human Rights published documents that can help guide the Arab Committee when reviewing states reports. In addition, these documents also guide the reviewed states when writing its reports and discussing it with the Committee. In addition, the Committee published the Temporary Rules of Procedure of the Arab Committee.

1. Temporary Rules of Procedure of the Arab Committee on Human Rights

The Arab Charter provides that the Arab Committee on Human Rights should establish its own rules of procedure. Article 45 (7) of the Arab Committee states,

> "The Committee's first meeting shall be convened by the Secretary General. During this meeting, the Committee shall elect its chairman from its members, for a two-year term renewable for one further term of two years. The Committee shall establish its own statute and rules of procedure and shall determine how often it shall meet. The Committee shall hold its meetings at the headquarters of the League of Arab States. It may also meet in any other State party to the present Charter at that party's invitation."[1365]

In light of the previous article, the Arab Committee established its own rules of procedure.[1366] However, it is written on the official website of the League of Arab States that these rules are temporary. It seems that the Committee is seeking to amend these rules in the future.[1367] The Temporary Rules of Procedure are com-

---

1364 *The Arab Human Rights Committee, Countries reports, supra* note 958.
1365 ACHR, *supra* note 126, at art. 45 (7).
1366 Temporary Rules of Procedure of the Arab Committee on Human Rights, http://www.lasportal.org/wps/wcm/connect/a0d151004a6cd7e39dfe9d526698d42c/%D8%A7%D9%84%D9%86%D8%B8%D8%A7%D9%85+%D8%A7%D9%84%D8%AF%D8%A7%D8%AE%D9%84%D9%8A+%D8%A7%D9%84%D9%85%D8%A4%D9%82%D8%AA+%D9%84%D9%84%D8%AC%D9%86%D8%A9+%D8%AD%D9%82%D9%88%D9%82+%D8%A7%D9%84%D8%A5%D9%86%D8%B3%D8%A7%D9%86+%D8%A7%D9%84%D8%B9%D8%B1%D8%A8%D9%8A%D8%A9.pdf?MOD=AJPERES (last visited Feb. 10, 2013).
1367 *Id.*

posed of twenty articles.[1368] There is no English version of these rules. I will provide rough translations of the main content of the articles as follows:

1. The first article defines the terms used:[1369]
   - "Committee:" The Arab Committee on Human Rights.
   - "President:" The President of the Arab Committee.
   - "Vice-President:" The Vice-President of the Arab Committee.
   - "Rapporteur:" The Rapporteur of the Arab Committee.
   - "Technical Secretariat:" The Technical Secretariat of the Arab Committee.
   - "Rules:" The Rules of Procedure of the Arab Committee.
   - "League:" The League of Arab States.
   - "Council:" The Council of the Arab League.
   - "Secretary General:" The Secretary General of the Arab League.
   - "General Secretariat:" The General Secretariat of the Arab League.
   - "Charter:" The Arab Charter on Human Rights.
   - "States Parties:" The States Parties of the Arab Charter on Human Rights.

2. The second article of the Rules of Procedure states that the Committee has its own Chairman, Vice-Chairman, and Rapporteur.[1370]

3. Article 3 of the Rules of Procedure states that the Chairman is the one that invites the members of the Committee to its meetings. At least two weeks before the meeting, the Technical Secretariat should inform the members of the Committee of the invitation of the Chairman. The agenda of the meeting should be attached to the invitation.

4. The Committee holds four regular meetings a year and can hold extraordinary meetings if the need arises at the invitation of the chairman, after consultation with members.

5. The quorum of the Committee is filled if there are at least five members of the Committee, including the Chairman or the Vice-Chairman.

6. The Committee meetings are held at the headquarters of the General Secretariat of the League of Arab States. The Committee may hold meetings in any State Party to the Charter at the invitation of this State Party.

1368 *Id.*
1369 *Id.*
1370 *Id.*

7. The Committee recognizes the agenda at the beginning of each meeting and prepares a report on its work and its decisions.

8. Decisions of the Committee are made by consensus and if this is not possible, decisions are made by a majority vote of those present. The President casts the decisive vote in the case of a tie.

9. The Chairman of the Committee chairs the meetings. In his absence, the meeting is chaired by the Vice-Chairman.

10. The Committee exercises its functions in conformity with the Charter and in accordance with the criteria laid down in this particular provision.

11. The Chairman of the Committee and the members of the Committee enjoy the immunities provided for in Article 47 of the Arab Charter on Human Rights and Article 25 of the Convention on the Privileges and Immunities of the Arab League.

12. The Chairman and members of the Committee take their bonuses and compensation for expenses in accordance with the Charter.

13. The Chairman is the spokesman of the Committee. The Chairman represents the Committee at the General Secretariat and at other agencies.

14. The Committee members have the right to express their opinions in the framework of their duties as members of Committee.

15. For the Committee to carry out its functions it may request any information from the League of Arab States and other various Arab joint institutions.

16. The Committee opens a special bank account, funded from the following financial resources on the condition that it is not inconsistent with the objectives and purposes of the Pact of the League of Arab States and the Arab Charter on Human Rights:
 - The financial resources that are provided by the Secretary General to the Committee.
 - The voluntary contributions from states parties to support the Committee's activities.
 - Allocations from international donor agencies to support or implement programs or projects or joint activities related to the competence of the Committee or to promote the capabilities of the Committee.

– Donations from natural persons and juridical persons.

17. For the Committee to perform its functions it can hold private meetings, seminars, and conferences on issues related to human rights, so as to serve the goals and purposes of the Arab Charter.

18. The Committee should have a Technical Secretariat under the supervision of the Committee's Rapporteur.

19. The tasks and duties of the Technical Secretariat are to:
- Prepare for committee meetings, prepare minutes, and provide the necessary requirements for the meetings.
- Prepare studies relating to the functions of the Committee.
- Build an integrated database of human rights in Arab countries to assist the Commission in the performance of its mission.
- Collect states parties' reports and regional and international conventions and UN interpretations of the concepts and charters of human rights.

20. The provisions of the Charter shall prevail regarding the issues that are not covered by the Rules of Procedure.[1371]

2. The Mechanism to Examine the States Parties' Reports in the Arab Charter on Human Rights

The Office of Human Rights at the Arab League provided me with a copy of the document entitled "mechanism of examining the states parties reports in the Arab Charter on Human Rights." It is written in Arabic. This mechanism provides guidelines to the members of the Arab Committee as they examine the states reports. I will briefly highlight the main points that are mentioned in this mechanism:

The goal of examining the states reports is to:
- Recognize the human rights violations of all of the states parties.
- Improve the situation of human rights by encouraging states parties to fulfill their obligations and commitments with respect to human rights contained in the Charter.
- Assess the positive developments and challenges faced by states.
- Provide technical assistance to states parties with respect to the application of the terms of the Charter.

1371 *Id.*

- Share best practices among states parties to implement the Arab Charter on Human Rights.

The mechanism for reviewing and examining the states parties reports should be guided by:

- The Arab Charter on Human Rights.
- The Mechanism of examining the states parties reports in the Arab Charter on Human Rights.
- The guidelines.
- The notes of Arab Committee on Human Rights.

While examining the states reports, the Arab Committee should make sure that the state party report cover all of the rights mentioned in the Arab Charter.

While examining the states parties reports the Committee should:

- Make sure there are no deficiencies in the national constitution and legislation regarding the protection of the rights contained Charter.
- Examine human rights situations through monitoring practices for violations of the rights contained in the Charter.
- Examine the measure being taken by the states parties to achieve best practices and how to overcome challenges and obstacles.

The Arab Committee should choose a rapporteur from among its members to examine the state report. The rapporteur must not hold the nationality of the state party concerned.

The state party concerned should sent its report to the Arab Committee through the Secretary General of the League of the Arab States.

The Arab Committee receives reports from nongovernmental organizations (NGOs).

The Secretariat of the Arab Committee should prepare a report regarding the observations of the NGOs.

During the examination of the state report, the Committee has the right to raise any question and discuss with the state concerned any issue mentioned in the NGOs reports.

The Arab Committee should inform the state concerned when it will discuss its report.

The Committee has the right to request additional information from the state party concerned .

The examination process of each state party report should be as follows:
- The discussion of the states report should be in open session. Nongovernmental organizations have the right to be observers during the discussion of the report.
- The examination of each state party report should be through an interactive dialogue for two days between the state party and the Arab Committee on Human Rights.
- The head of the delegation of the State party that is being reviewed should provide an opening statement presenting the report.
- The Rapporteur of the Arab Committee should make general observations regarding the report of the state party concerned.
- The members of the Arab Committee on Human Rights should present their observations and questions.
- The state party concerned should reply to the questions of the members of the Committee. The state party concerned has the right to answer some of the questions the subsequent day.
- The meetings should continue the following day. The state party has the right to present a final statement.
- The Arab Committee deliberates in closed sessions to draft the concluding observations and recommendations.
- The conclusions, observations, and recommendations of the Arab Committee are sent to the State party concerned, through the Secretary General within two weeks of the end of examination of the report. The state concerned should send its feedback and observations within one month from the date of dispatch to the Secretary General of the League of Arab States.
- The Committee should send a copy of the report and the concluding observations and recommendations to the Secretary General and should publish the report widely. In addition, the Committee should publish the final conclusions and observations on the official website of the Arab Committee.[1372]

1372 Temporary Rules of Procedure of the Arab Committee on Human Rights, http://www.lasportal.org/wps/wcm/connect/a0d151004a6cd7e39dfe9d526698d42c/%D8%A7%D9%84%D9%86%D8%B8%D8%A7%D9%85+%D8%A7%D9%84%D8%AF%D8%A7%D8%AE%D9%84%D9%8A+%D8%A7%D9%84%D9%85%D8%A4%D9%82%D8%AA+%D9%84%D9%84%D8%AC%D9%86%D8%A9+%D8%AD%D9%82%D9%88%D9%82+%D8%A7%D9%84%D8%A5%D9%86%D8%B3%D8%A7%D9%86+%D8%A7%D9%84%D8%B9%D8%B1%D8%A8%D9%8A%D8%A9.pdf?MOD=AJPERES (last visited Feb. 10, 2013).

3. The Guidelines Regarding the Form and Content of Reports to Be Submitted by States Parties to the Arab Charter on Human Rights

The Arab Committee issued guidelines to the state parties. These principles can guide states in writing their reports in compliance with the requirements requested by the Arab Committee. The guidelines focus on the shape and content of the state's report. The introduction of the guidelines refers to Article 48 (1) of the Arab Charter, which states, "The States parties undertake to submit reports to the Secretary-General of the League of Arab States on the measures they have taken to give effect to the rights and freedoms recognized in this Charter and on the progress made towards the enjoyment thereof. The Secretary-General shall transmit these reports to the Committee for its consideration."[1373] I will highlight the main points to be made and the guidelines that states should follow when writing their reports:

- Each State party shall submit an initial report to the Committee within one year from the date on which the Charter enters into force.
- Each State party shall submit a periodic report every three years. In addition, the Arab Committee may request the states parties to supply it with additional information relating to the implementation of the Charter.
- The report should show the extent of the practical implementation of the rights in the country concerned and should also show the progress achieved.
- The guidelines is divided into two parts. The first is the format of the report. The second is the content of the report as follows:
  First, the format of the report should include:
  - The name of the institutions that wrote the report.
  - Whether the report includes information from nongovernmental sources.
  - Whether or not the state report is published. The guidelines state also that the Arab Committee will publish its conclusions and recommendations in conformity with Article 48 (6) of the Charter.
  - The guidelines mention the Arabic font style and size and add that the report should not exceed 100 pages.
  - The state's report should be sent to the Secretary General of the Arab League. The Secretary General should forward the

---

1373 ACHR, *supra* note 126, at art. 48(1).

report to the Arab Committee within three months from the date of receiving the report.
- The Committee will inform the concerned state of the date of examining and discussing the report.

Second, with respect to the content of the report
- The first part of the content should include:
  - General information about the country and the population.
  - The political structure of the country.
  - The legal framework of human rights protection.
- The second part of the content should state, regarding each right of the Charter:
  - Legislative and administrative measures.
  - The derogating measures imposed on the rights.
  - Any obstacles that can affect the enjoyment of the rights.
  - The progress achieved in the enjoyment of each right.

The state concerned should attach the necessary documents that support and ensure the accuracy of the information given in the report. The state concerned should mention how each right is protected and guaranteed from violation. Also, the state concerned should explain the efforts being undertaken to safeguard each right.

E. The States Reports Submitted to and Examined by the Arab Committee on Human Rights

1. Jordan

a. The Report

Jordan was the first State party to submit its report to the Arab Committee. The report was submitted to the Arab Committee on Human Rights on October 28, 2010.[1374] The members of the Arab Committee examined Jordan's report in April 1 and 2, 2012, and their concluding observations and recommendations were sent to Jordan.[1375] The examination of the Jordanian report started with an opening speech by the Chairman of the Arab Committee. I will highlight the main issues he covered as follows: [1376]

1374 *The Arab Human Rights Committee, Countries reports, supra* note 958.
1375 *Id.; see also Arab committee to discuss Jordan's report on human rights,,* EL-BALAD.COM, http://www.el-balad.com/125069/lgnh-arbyh-tnaksh-tkryr.aspx (last visited Apr. 23, 2012).
1376 The Office of Human Rights at the Arab League provided me with a copy of the speech of the Chairman of the Arab Committee.

We stated that the committee applies the principle of transparency.

The Committee has its own website on the Internet through which it publishes all of the state reports it receives.

The aim of the publication of these reports is to give NGOs the opportunity to evaluate and examine the reports and then send their comments and shadow reports to the Committee regarding the concerned State Party. The comments and shadow reports will be used by the Committee when discussing the State report with the delegation of the State concerned.

This mechanism is only the first step in a long journey that requires us to show a clear view of the facts and excel in patience and objectivity in our evaluation and analysis of events.

While we are opening the first day of our meeting, the Arab world is witnessing significant changes. We hope that one of the fruits of this change is the full respect for human rights. The full respect should not only cover those rights that are called basic rights such as the right to life and the freedom of speech but also other rights such as the right to development.

The work of the Arab Committee should not be isolated from other regional and international mechanisms especially the mechanisms that are established by the United Nations. The Arab Committee complements other mechanisms. In other words, Arab countries are still obliged to submit their periodic reports to the these mechanisms according to the treaties that each country ratified.

The added value by the Arab Charter that distinguishes it from other regional and international mechanisms stems from the fact that the mandate of the Arab Charter is not limited to the protection of certain rights, such as the treaties that focus on specific issues.

The Charter also differs in its philosophy from some international mechanisms that apply the universal periodic review to the human rights situation.

The review mechanism of the Arab Charter is made by experts that are characterized by objectivity and neutrality, impartiality and expertise. The review is not made by politicization and courtesy like some peer review mechanisms through which states parties review each other.

An Arab mechanism of human rights is not contrary to the universality of human rights. The Arab countries are part of the universality of human rights. The principle of universality of human rights is mentioned in the constitutions of the Arab countries. The Vienna Declaration of 1993 stated that the principle of universality does not prevent any group from adopting regional treaties that reflect the special nature of that group.

Finally, the Chairman of the Arab Committee invited the Arab countries that did not ratify the Arab Charter to ratify it. He hoped that the Committee's work will be extended to include all Arab countries and their populations, which exceeds 300 million people.[1377]

In a press release, the Committee stated that it discussed the report with the delegation of Jordan. The Committee added that the members of the Jordanian delegation replied to all of the questions that were raised by the Committee. The Committee added that it met with the Jordanian nongovernmental organizations regarding their shadow reports that were submitted to the Committee.[1378] In addition, it was written on the Arab League website that the Arab Committee received shadow reports on Jordan.[1379] The Head of the Arab Committee declared that the Arab Committee on Human Rights examined shadow reports submitted by NGOs as the Committee met with Jordanian non-governmental organizations.[1380]

I will highlight some of the main issues addressed in the introduction of the report that was submitted by Jordan:

- Jordan is submitting its reports in compliance with Article 48 (1) of the Arab Charter.
- Jordan was the first country to ratify the Arab Charter in 2004.
- Jordan did not have any reservations on any article of the Arab Charter.

1377 *Id.*
1378 *The Activities of the Arab Committee on Human Rights, press release*, http://www.lasportal.org/wps/portal/las_ar/inner/!ut/p/c5/vZJPj4IwEMU_C59gphZRjzWglt1W2-IfejEYNwREIazRXT69kJh4cr1snHeZ5M2b3-WBhVan5JKIyTkrT0kBG7De1h8pvXI1RYzm HvLezNeSSDoce60fP_dD8iK9hjgAk9TtYv867R51Pj4ZhhCDHTzyU_XhIlemL0OzIGyKEMEG3a3JfyveHBqdDxTKQyFFza4iKOYytwuRGyI-GUZ-_PPtj4WpOYpmSYkYkdVEBYxX7I5w5wWr90YWfSOL_CsrBJsW5a6r2ATkrDx-QXVcXjI9JHfRIDnODSVVDIA!/dl3/d3/L2dBISEvZ0FBIS9nQSEh/?pcid=934eb0804cc37b158091c4081bb96571 (last visited Feb. 10, 2013).
1379 *The Arab Human Rights Committee, Countries reports, supra* note 958.
1380 *The Arab Committee on Human Rights,* ALITTIHAD.AE, http://www.alittihad.ae/details.php?id=33085&y=2012 (last visited Apr. 23, 2012).

- Human Rights are universal, inherent, and indivisible.
- Jordan took significant strides in order to promote the concepts of human rights in Jordanian society.
- Jordan ratified the main international human rights treaties. For instance, Jordan ratified the ICCPR, ICESCR, CEDAW, etc. On the regional level, Jordan ratified the Arab Charter on Human Rights and accepted the Cairo Declaration on Human Rights in Islam.
- The treaties that are ratified by Jordan are parts of Jordanian legislation but on a higher level than national law.

Jordan's report explained, article by article, the steps taken by Jordan to implement the articles of the Charter. I will highlight from the report some of the efforts being done by Jordan to implement these rights:

Article 3 of the Arab Charter (Right to Equality): the right to equality is stated in the Jordanian constitution explicitly. Article 6 of the Jordanian Constitution provides, "(i) Jordanians shall be equal before the law. There shall be no discrimination between them as regards to their rights and duties on grounds of race, language or religion. (ii) The Government shall ensure work and education within the limits of its possibilities, and it shall ensure a state of tranquillity and equal opportunities to all Jordanians."[1381]

Article 6 of the Arab Charter (Right to Life): The death sentence is applied only on the most serious crimes such as murder, raping juveniles, and terrorist activities. In addition, the death penalty has been applied in only a few cases, as several amendments were made to Jordanian laws in order to replace the death penalty punishment with life imprisonment. Furthermore, it is not applied except after a series of other measures. In addition, the Jordanian penal law requests the judge to appoint a lawyer for the convicted person if the convicted person has no lawyer. In addition, if the Court rendered its judgment of a death sentence, the case is automatically appealed to the Supreme Court even if the accused person did not appeal. Furthermore, the King of Jordan has the legal authority to give a pardon and to reduce the punishment. The death sentence has not been implemented in Jordan since 2006.

The death sentence is not applied to juveniles. The death sentence is replaced by life imprisonment if the accused person is pregnant.

1381 Jordanian Constitution art. 6.

Article 12 of the Arab Charter (the Independence of the Judiciary): The Jordanian constitution protects the independence of the judiciary. The Constitution provides, "Judges are independent, and in the exercise of their judicial functions they are subject to no authority other than that of the law."[1382]

Article 13 of the Arab Charter (Right to Fair Trail): The Jordanian law requests the judge to appoint lawyers for accused persons who cannot afford to pay lawyers. The Jordanian Constitution guarantees the right to fair trail to every person. Article 101 of the Constitution provides, "The courts shall be open to all and shall be free from any interference in their affairs. The sittings of the courts shall be public unless the court considers that it should sit in camera in the interest of public order or morals."[1383]

Article 14 of the Arab Charter (Right to Liberty and Security of Person): The Jordanian Constitution safeguard the right to liberty and security of person. The Constitution provides, "Personal freedom shall be guaranteed. No person may be detained or imprisoned except in accordance with the provisions of the law."[1384]

Article 15 of the Arab Charter (No Crime or Penalty without Prior Provision of Law): Article 3 of the Jordanian penal law provides that no crime and no penalty can be established without a prior provision of the law.

Article 19 of the Arab Charter (No One May Be Tried Twice for the Same Offence): Article 58 (1) of the Jordanian penal law provides that the accused will be tried only once for the same offence.

Article 21 of the Arab Charter (Right to Privacy): The Jordanian Constitution protects the right to privacy. The constitution provides, "No property of any person may be expropriated except for purposes of public utility and in consideration of a just compensation, as may be prescribed by law."[1385] Also, the Constitution states, "All postal, telegraphic and telephonic communications shall be treated as secret and as such shall

---

1382 *Id.* at art 97.
1383 *Id.* at art. 101.
1384 *Id.* at art. 7, 8.
1385 *Id.* at art. 10.

not be subject to censorship or suspension except in circumstances prescribed by law."[1386]

Article 25 (Right of Minorities) and Article 30 of the Arab Charter (Right to Freedom of Thought, Conscience, Religion): The Jordanian Constitution safeguards the freedom of religion and the right to belief. In addition, the constitution protects the rights of congregations to establish and maintain their own schools. Article 14 of the Constitution provides, "The State shall safeguard the free exercise of all forms of worship and religious rites in accordance with the customs observed in the Kingdom, unless such is inconsistent with public order or morality."[1387] Also, the Constitution provides, "Congregations shall have the right to establish and maintain their own schools for the education of their own members provided that they comply with the general provisions of the law and be subject to the control of Government in matters relating to their curricula and orientation."[1388] Furthermore, the different religious groups have the right to be governed by their religion regarding family affairs. The law gives the right to each religious group to establish family courts regarding their family matters such as marriage, divorce, and inheritance. For instance, Christians have their own law on family matters. On the other hand, the Jordanian report referred to two Quranic verses that clearly show that Islam advocates the freedom of religion. The Quran states, "There is no compulsion in religion."[1389] In addition, the Quran provides, "So, will you (O Muhammad) then compel mankind, until they become believers."[1390]

Article 27 of the Arab Charter (Right to Freedom of Movement): Every Jordanian person has the right to freedom of movement; he cannot be deported arbitrary. Article 9 of the Jordanian constitution provides, "No Jordanian may be deported from the territory of the Kingdom. No Jordanian may be prevented from residing at any place, or be compelled to reside in any specified place, except in the circumstances prescribed by law."[1391]

1386 *Id.* at art. 18.
1387 *Id.* at art. 14.
1388 *Id.* at art. 19.
1389 QURAN 2:256.
1390 *Id.* at 10:99.
1391 Jordanian Const. *supra* note 1381, at art. 9.

Article 28 of the Arab Charter (Right to Seek Political Asylum): The Jordanian constitution protects the right to seek political asylum. In addition, all of the bilateral and multilateral judicial cooperation treaties that are ratified by Jordan include an explicit provision prohibiting extradition of criminals if they are accused of political offences. The Jordanian Constitution provides, "Political refugees shall not be extradited on account of their political beliefs or for their defence of liberty. Extradition of ordinary criminals shall be regulated by international agreements and laws."[1392]

Article 33 of the Arab Charter (Family Rights): The Jordanian law of personal affairs explicitly states that a contract of marriage is between a man and woman in order to establish a family and have offspring. Therefore, both the man and the woman are parties to the contract. In other words, the consent of the woman and the man is a precondition for the validity of the contract. Each woman has the full right to freely choose her husband.

Article 41 (Right to Education): Jordan is achieving good progress in the eradication of illiteracy. The percentage of illiteracy in Jordan is 7.3 %. The report added that this percentage is very low compared to the percentage of illiteracy in the Arab world, which is 25%. The Ministry of Education is promoting the concepts of human rights in school curricula and textbooks.

Finally, in the conclusion of the report it is written that Jordan does not claim that it has reached the stage of perfection and ideal performance. Jordan emphasizes that there it harbors a a sincere desire to reach the desired change. Jordan believes in the importance of human rights and the role of human rights in maintaining the dignity of the individual and the community.

b. Conclusions and Observations of the Arab Human Rights Committee

After Jordan submitted its report, the Arab Human Rights Committee examined the report and wrote a report that includes final observations and recommendations to Jordan. I will highlight the conclusions, recommendations, and observations of the Committee on Jordan's report:[1393]

1392 *Id.* at art. 21.
1393 *The Arab Human Rights Committee, Countries reports, supra* note 958.

The Committee is thankful to Jordan because it is the first country to ratify the Arab Charter and the first country to submit a state report.

The Committee mentioned the good progress done by Jordan in the field of human rights, especially with respect to the eradication of illiteracy and combating domestic violence.

The Committee notes that the report does not show that non-governmental organizations participated in enriching its content.

The Committee notes that in some rights the Jordanian report did not comply with the guidelines stated by the Arab Committee. For instance, it did not state the obstacles that face the implementation of rights.

The Committee notes that Article 6 of the Jordanian Constitution did not state explicitly "the right to equality between men and women." Therefore, Article 6 of the Constitution is not in compliance with the Arab Charter and many international human rights treaties.

Regarding the prohibition of torture, the Committee notes that the Jordanian report did not explain the extent of the implementation of this right in reality. In addition, there is no explicit provision in the Jordanian law concerning the compensation and damages given to the victims who suffered from torture. There is a general article in the civil law for the compensation, but are no special articles for the victims of torture.

The Committee notes that the Jordanian report did not explain the problems arising from not granting equal rights to women and men with respect to the nationality of their children. Children of Jordanian women that are not married to Jordanian men are not granted the Jordanian nationality. This raises the issue of discrimination between men and women.

The Committee notes that the report did not examine in depth the issue of sexual harassment at work.

The Committee notes that the Jordanian report did not refer to the polices of tackling the issue of overcrowding in public schools. In addition, the Committee notes that non-Jordanians have a low degree of opportunity to join public schools.

Finally, the Arab Committee provides recommendations to the Jordanian authorities. I will highlight some of the important comments:

> The Arab Committee recommends amending Article 6 of the Jordanian constitution in order to state explicitly the right to equality between men and women.
>
> The Committee recommends amending the Jordanian law of nationality in order to grant Jordanian nationality to the children of Jordanian women that are not married to Jordanian men.
>
> The Committee recommends issuing special legislation concerning the compensation of the victims of torture, arbitrary detention, and cruel treatment.
>
> The Committee recommends that Jordan must take more effective steps to entrench a culture of human rights. The inclusion of the concepts of human rights system should be included in the curriculum of schools and universities in order to promote the culture of human rights.

After the Arab Committee discussed the Jordanian report with the Jordanian delegation, the Chairman of the Arab Committee said made the following main points:[1394]

> Discussing States reports is not a goal in itself for the Arab Committee. The real work starts after discussing the report. In other words, it is important to see how the states parties will deal with the conclusions and observations of the Committee.
>
> He added that he hoped that the Committee will not be disappointed. He hoped that all states parties give the attention needed to carry out their obligations to pursue and accomplish the agreed upon goals.
>
> He also hoped that all the states parties widely publish the recommendations and conclusions of the Arab Committee using audiovisual, traditional, and modern ways. The publication will make the conclusions easily accessible by both governmental and nongovernmental organizations.
>
> He urged all of the agencies, each according to its specialty, to participate in implementing the recommendations and conclusions of the Committee. All of these efforts will lead to promoting the culture of human rights in the Arab world. In addition, it will raise awareness among Arab citizens.

1394 The Office of Human Rights at the Arab League provided me with a copy of the speech of the Chairman of the Arab Committee.

2. Algeria

Algeria was the second country to submit its report to the Arab Committee. The report was submitted to the Arab Committee on Human Rights on April 28, 2011.[1395] The members of the Arab Committee examined the Algerian report on October 15 and 16, 2012.[1396] In addition, the Arab Committee received shadow reports during the period of March 15 until April 15 2012.[1397]

I will highlight some of the main issues addressed in the introduction of the report submitted by Algeria:

> Algeria is submitting its reports in compliance with Article 48 of the Arab League.
>
> Algeria ratified the Arab Charter in 2006.
>
> This report shows a sincere picture of the achievements and challenges.
>
> Algeria ratified many international human rights treaties. For instance, Algeria ratified the ICCPR; the first protocol to the ICCPR; the ICESCR; CEDAW; the United Nations Convention on the Rights of the Child; the United Nations Convention against Torture and Other Cruel, Inhuman, or Degrading Treatment or Punishment; etc. On the regional level, Algeria ratified the Arab Charter on Human Rights, the African Charter on Human and Peoples' Rights, the African Charter on the Rights and Welfare of the Child, and the Protocol to the African Charter on Human And Peoples' Rights on the Establishment of an African Court on Human and Peoples' Rights.
>
> The treaties that are ratified by Algeria are parts of Algerian legislations but on a higher level than national law.

The Algerian report explained, article by article, the steps taken by Algeria to implement the articles of the Charter. I will highlight from the report some of the efforts being undertaken by Algeria to implement these rights:

> Article 3 of the Arab Charter (Right to Equality without Discrimination): The Algerian report stated that discrimination between nationals and foreigners is prohibited by the Algerian Constitution. Article 29 of the Constitution states, "All citizens are equal before the law. No discrimination shall prevail because of birth, race, sex, opinion or any other per-

---

1395 *The Arab Human Rights Committee, Countries' Reports, supra* note 958.
1396 *Id.*
1397 *Id.*

sonal or social condition or circumstance."[1398] In addition, the constitution also states, "Algeria associates itself with all the peoples fighting for their political and economic liberation, for the right of self-determination and against any racial discrimination."[1399] Furthermore, Algerian legislations focuses on the principle of non-discrimination between people.

Algeria aims to ensure the principle of equality between men and women in their rights and duties. Article 31 of the Algerian Constitution states, "The aim of the institutions is to ensure equality of rights and duties of all citizens, men and women, by removing the obstacles which hinder the progress of human beings and impede the effective participation of all in the political, economic, social and cultural life."[1400] In 2008, a new constitutional amendment added Article 31 bis in order to give women more political rights. The article provides, "The State works for the promotion of the political rights of women by increasing their chances of access to representation in elected assemblies..."[1401] Furthermore, the Algerian nationality law gives Algerian women that are married to non-Algerian nationals the right to grant their children Algerian nationality. In addition, non-Algerian women are granted Algerian nationality if they are married to Algerian men. In short, the Algerian laws give people the right to submit complaints if they are discriminated against.

Article 4 of the Arab Charter (the Situation of Emergency): The status of emergency ceased in Algeria in February 2011.

Article 5 of the Arab Charter (Right to Life): The right to life is one of the main principles of the Algerian Constitution. Article 32 of the Algerian Constitution states, "The fundamental human and citizen's rights and liberties are guaranteed. They are a common heritage of all Algerians, men and women, whose duty is to transmit it from generation to another in order to preserve it and keep it inviolable."[1402] In addition, the Algerian constitution provides, "The State guarantees the inviol-

---

1398 Algerian Const. *supra* note 1000, art. 29,
1399 *Id.* at art. 27.
1400 *Id.* at art. 31.
1401 *Id.* at art. 31.
1402 *Id.* at art. 32.

ability of the human entity. Any form of physical or moral violence or breach of dignity is forbidden."[1403]

Regarding the death sentence, the penal law was amended in order to reduce the number of crimes that are punishable by death sentence. The death penalty is not applied except to the most serious crimes (blood crimes). The criminal who is punished by the death sentence has the right to request a pardon or reduction of punishment. In addition, the death penalty has not been applied since 1993. Furthermore, all of the legislations adopted after 1993 did not include capital punishment.

Regarding pregnant women, the death sentence is not applied to nursing women until the baby is two years old. The death sentence is not applied to persons who are eightteen years old and younger.

Article 8 (Right to Prohibition of Torture): Algeria ratified the United Nations Convention against Torture. In addition, Algeria accepted the jurisdiction of the United Nations Committee against Torture. Therefore, people in Algeria can submit complaints to the Committee against Torture if they are subjected to any kind of torture or cruel or inhuman treatment. Furthermore, the Algerian Constitution prohibits any kind of violation of the human rights of persons. The Constitution states, "The State guarantees the inviolability of the human entity. Any form of physical or moral violence or breach of dignity is forbidden."[1404]

Article 11 (Right to Equality Before Law): The right to equality before law is one of the fundamental principles that are protected by the Algerian Constitution. Article 29 of the Constitution provides, "All citizens are equal before the law. No discrimination shall prevail because of birth, race, sex, opinion or any other personal or social condition or circumstance."[1405]

Article 12 (Independence of the Judiciary and Equality before the Law): The Algerian Constitution protects the independence of the judiciary. The constitution provides, "The judicial power is independent. It is exercised within the framework of the law."[1406] In addition, the Constitution safeguards the principle of equality before law. The Constitution provides, "Justice is founded on the principles of lawfulness and equality.

1403 *Id.* at art. 34.
1404 *Id.*
1405 *Id.* at art. 29.
1406 *Id.* at art. 138.

It is the same for all, accessible for all and is expressed by the respect for the law."[1407] Furthermore, Articles 147 and 148 of the Constitution provide, "The judge obeys the law exclusively. The judge is protected against any form of pressure, interventions or maneuvers that prejudice his mission or the respect of his free will."[1408]

Article 13 of the Arab Charter (Right to Fair Trial): The Algerian Constitution ensures the principle of equality. Article 47 of the Constitution provides, "No one can be pursued, arrested or detained unless within the cases defined by the law and in accordance with the forms prescribed."[1409] Also the Constitution provides, "The right to a defense is recognized. In penal matters, it is guaranteed."[1410] In addition, the Constitution provides, "Justice decisions are justified and pronounced in public hearing."[1411] Furthermore, the judiciary protects the rights of the society and of individuals. The Constitution states, "The judicial power protects the society and the liberties. It guarantees, to all and to everyone, the safeguarding of their fundamental rights."[1412] It is important to note that the law protects the public from any abuse by judges. The Constitution provides, "The law shall protect the parties to the judicial proceedings against any abuse or misconduct by the judge."[1413]

Article 15 of the Arab Charter (No Crime or Penalty without Prior Provision of Law): The Algerian Constitution explicitly protects this right. The Constitution provides, "No one is guilty unless it is in accordance with a law promulgated law prior to the incriminated action."[1414]

Article 16 of the Arab Charter (Everyone Charged with a Criminal Offence Shall be Presumed Innocent until Proved Guilty): The Algerian Constitution protects this right. Article 45 of the Algerian Constitution provides, "Any person is presumed not guilty until his culpability is

---

1407 *Id.* at art. 140.
1408 *Id.* at art. 147, 148.
1409 *Id.* at art. 47.
1410 *Id.* at art. 151, 148.
1411 *Id.* at art. 144.
1412 *Id.* at art. 139.
1413 *Id.* at art. 150.
1414 *Id.* at art. 46.

established by a regular court of jurisdiction in conformity with all the guarantees required by the law."[1415]

Article 21 of the Arab Charter (Right to Privacy): The Algerian Constitution respects the private life of individuals. Article 39 of the Constitution provides, "The private life and the honour of the citizen are inviolable and protected by the law. The secrecy of private correspondence and communication, in any form, is guaranteed."[1416] In addition, the Constitution provides, "The State guarantees the inviolability of the home. No thorough search can be allowed unless in pursuance of the law and in compliance with the latter. Thorough searches can only be conducted pursuant to a search warrant emanating from the competent judicial authority."[1417] Furthermore the Constitution provides, "All the individual liberties are carried out within the respect of the rights of others recognized by the Constitution, in particular, the respect of the right for honour, intimacy and the protection of the family, the youth and children."[1418]

Article 25 of the Algerian Constitution (Rights of Minorities): The report states that the Algerian people are united, there is no minority or majority. However, the Algerian Constitution assures the principle of equality and non-discrimination. For instance, the constitution provides, "All citizens are equal before the law. No discrimination shall prevail because of birth, race, sex, opinion or any other personal or social condition or circumstance."[1419]

Article 28 of the Arab Charter (Right to Seek Political Asylum): The Algerian Constitution protects the right to seek political asylum. The Constitution provides, "In no case, a political refugee having legally the right of asylum can be delivered or extradited."[1420] In addition, Algeria ratified the United Nations Refugee Convention and its additional protocol.

Article 29 (Right to Nationality): Algerian women have the same rights as men with respect to granting Algerian nationality to their children.

1415 *Id.* at art. 45.
1416 *Id.* at art. 39.
1417 *Id.* at art. 40.
1418 *Id.* at art. 63.
1419 *Id.* at art. 29.
1420 *Id.* at art. 69.

Article 6 of the Algerian nationality law states that Algerian nationality is granted to any child if his father or his mother have Algerian nationality.

Article 30 (Freedom of Thought, Conscience, and Religion): The Algerian Constitution protects the freedom of religion and conscience. The Constitution provides, "Freedom of creed and opinion is inviolable."[1421] Furthermore, there are national laws that protect and safeguard the freedom of religion and conscience.

Article 41 of the Arab Charter (Eradication of Illiteracy): Despite the efforts being done in combating illiteracy, this issue still presents a challenge. Algeria took a significant steps forward in the eradication of illiteracy and improving the quality of education. When Algeria gained its independence, illiteracy was 85%. In 2002, illiteracy was 25%. In 2005, there were more than 6 million illiterate people. It is important to note that the Algerian population is more than 34 million.

F. Implementation Review Mechanisms in the Arab League

The Council of the Arab League established a Committee of legal experts and experts from the Secretariat to gather all of the Arab treaties and charters that are related to human rights, such as the Arab Charter on Child Rights. The Arab League published a book on the mechanisms of reviewing the Arab charters and treaties that are related to human rights.[1422] This book is an important document that sheds light on the significant importance of the supervisory/monitoring review mechanisms. I will highlight some of the important points that are mentioned in this book:

> The main responsibility of respecting human rights is on each country. Each country should formally adopt human rights guarantees. Then, each country should establish supervisory mechanisms in order to guarantee the implementation of these rights. In addition, each country should develop a culture of human rights.
>
> Despite the fact that there are human rights provisions in the national laws and supervisory mechanisms to guarantee their implementation,

---

1421 *Id.* at art. 36.
1422 The title of the book is "The Mechanisms to Review the Arab Charters and Treaties That Are Related to Human Rights," The Secretariat of the Arab League, Department of Social Affairs, Office of Human Rights, The Technical Secretariat of the Permanent Arab Committee on Human Rights (2006).

this is not enough to stop human rights violations. The national supervisory mechanisms may not be efficient.

International efforts cannot replace national efforts, but they are an important supplement to guaranteeing the protection of human rights.

International treaties are no more than "ink on paper"[1423] if there is no suitable means to supervise their implementation. Each state party to a treaty has the main responsibility to protect and implement the rights stated in the treaty. In addition, each state party should make the rights included in the treaty accessible to people living in the territory of that state party. People should be able to claim these rights before the national courts.

There is a big problem regarding the implementation of the rights protected in the Arab League. This problem is widespread with respect to most of the resolutions, treaties, and charters of the Arab League. There is a big gap between the decisions taken by the Arab League and what is implemented in reality. Regarding the review mechanism, it is almost exclusively undertaken by the Council of the Arab League and the Secretary General. The Council is a political body that did not take any practical measures to find effective solutions to this problem. The Council only urges States parties to implement and fulfill their duties. It is surprising and interesting to know that the problem of implementation exists despite the fact that most of the resolutions and treaties were enacted through a majority vote. In other words, although there are no objections with respect to the resolutions and treaties, they are not implemented.

The power or the weakness of any organization depends on whether the States Parties are willing to implement and respect the decisions of the organization.

Since the beginning of this century there has been a strong collective will in the Arab world to push forward in the field of human rights.

The Arab League focused extensively on human rights norms and principles but the same focus was not directed to the mechanisms of their implementation.

1423 "Ink on paper" is an expression that means it is useless and not effective.

G. Activities of the Arab Committee on Human Rights

1. Algeria

Despite the fact that the Arab Charter did not mention any duties for the Arab Committee except examining state reports, the Arab Committee took significant steps forward in developing the culture of human rights in the Arab world. Article 17 of the Rules of Procedure of the Arab Committee gives the committee the right to organize seminars, conferences, etc. The Committee started its introductory visits to states parties to introduce the Arab Charter to both governmental and nongovernmental bodies. This is a very effective gradual step forward in the protection of human rights because the Committee is trying to find new ways and ideas to promote human rights in the Arab world. For instance, the Arab Committee organized a two-day workshop in Algeria in 2012. In the first day, the Arab Committee met with the Algerian governmental institutions that wrote the report that was submitted by Algeria to the Arab Committee on Human Rights. Also in the first day, the Committee met many Algerian diplomats. The second day was an introductory workshop. The Committee met nongovernmental organizations and the media. The workshop included an introductory presentation on the Arab Charter as the first Arab regional treaty on Human Rights. The workshop also included an explanation of the implementation review mechanism and the guidelines. In addition, the workshop explained the important role of the shadow reports that are submitted by nongovernmental organizations in parallel to the official report that is submitted by the government.[1424]

It is unclear whether the Committee will visit each State Party before the Committee examines the report of the State Party concerned or whether this visit to Algeria that happened before examining the Algerian report is a coincidence. It seems that the Committee is trying to establish a custom of visiting each State Party before examining its report. The Committee mentioned that it decided to organize an introductory workshop in the states parties regarding the Arab Charter on Human Rights. This would be a significant step forward.

2. Libya

On September 3, 2011, the Arab Committee issued a press release regarding the severe human rights violations in Libya. The Committee stated that Libya had already ratified the Arab Charter on Human Rights. Therefore, the Committee requested that the Libyan authorities stop using weapons against innocent

---

1424 *Activities of the Arab Committee on Human Rights: The visit of the Arab Committee to Algeria,* http://www.lasportal.org/ (last visited September 30, 2012).

civilians. The Committee added that the human rights infringements are considered a very extreme violation of international law, international humanitarian law, and the Arab Charter on Human Rights. The Committee welcomed the Security Council resolution of the referral of the case of Libya to the International Criminal Court.[1425] The Committee requested that the Arab countries implement the Security Council resolution number 1970 concerning Libya by freezing the assets of the former regime of Libya.

The Committee requested that international and humanitarian organizations provide humanitarian assistance to the Libyan people. In addition, the Committee requested that the United Nations take the necessary measures in order to make sure that humanitarian assistance is transferred safely to Libya.[1426] The Arab Committee welcomed the decision of the League of Arab States of suspending the participation of the Libyan delegations in the meetings of the Arab League. The Committee requested that the League of Arab States consider freezing the membership of Libya in the Arab League if the Libyan authorities did not stop the extreme human rights violations.[1427]

3. Syria

In the light of the protocol signed between the Arab League and Syria, the Arab League sent a delegation to Syria to monitor the human rights situation in Syria. One of the duties of the delegation is to ensure the release of innocent civilian detainees. Two of the members of the delegations are members of the Arab Committee on Human Rights. The Arab Human Rights Committee mentioned that Syria ratified the Arab Charter on Human Rights. Therefore, the Arab Human Rights Committee is monitoring any violation to the rights under the Arab Charter. In addition, the Arab Human Rights Committee urged Syria to implement the Arab Charter on Human Rights.[1428]

4. United Nations Human Rights Council

On 2012, the Chairman of the Arab Human Rights Committee, Mr. Abdel Reheem Al-Awady, and the Vice-Chairman of the Committee, Mr. Hady Al-Yamy, met with the President of the United Nations Human Rights Council in Geneva. Mr. Al-Awady explained the duties and importance of the Arab Committee. He explained that it is considered the first Arab Committee to review the implementation

---

1425 *Activities of the Arab Committee on Human Rights, press release, supra* note 1378.
1426 *Id.*
1427 *Id.*
1428 *Id.*

by the states parties of the Arab Charter. Ambassador Lora, the President of the Human Rights Council, stated that the Council is keen to cooperate with all regional human rights bodies. She added that she can offer technical assistance and an exchange of experience in order to enrich human rights protection.[1429]

5. Introductory Visits

The Arab Human Rights Committee stated that it is going to arrange country visits to the states parties to present the duties of the Arab Committee of Human Rights and its role.[1430] In light of the brief highlighting of the activities of the Arab Committee on Human Rights, we can see clearly that the role being played by the Arab Committee is developing. For instance, the Committee made a visit to Algeria as it met with governmental and nongovernmental bodies. This visit was made before the examination of the Committee of the Algerian report that was submitted to the Committee. The Committee is demonstrating a solid effort to explain the role that can be played by the Charter and its monitoring body in improving the human rights situation in Algeria to the Algerian people. The Rules of Procedure of the Committee increased its role in the field of human rights. For instance, Article 17 of the Rules of Procedure provides that the Committee can hold private meetings, seminars and conferences on issues related to human rights, so as to serve the goals and purposes of the Arab Charter. Therefore, the Rules of Procedure extended the role of the Committee from just receiving and examining states' reports to promoting human rights. The Committee has the right to attend and/or organize seminars, private meetings, and conferences on issues related to human rights. This new role of the Committee is a good start on the way of promoting human rights in the Arab world.

The role of the Technical Secretariat of the Arab Committee is very important. For instance, some of the functions of the Technical Secretariat stated in Article 19 of the Rules of Procedure include that the Technical Secretariat may build an integrated database of human rights in Arab countries to assist the Committee in the performance of its mission. In addition, it collects the states parties' reports and regional and international conventions and United Nations interpretations of the concepts and charters of human rights. This role means that the Arab Committee wants to expand its knowledge in the field of human rights.

1429 *Id.*
1430 *Id.*

H. Evaluation

One of the major limitations of the Arab Charter is the absence of effective mechanisms to supervise the implementation of the rights in the Arab Charter. It is not sufficient to have a regional group of countries that are parties to a human rights treaty. There must be an effective supervisory body to monitor the implementation of the treaty.

The Arab Charter cannot achieve such success without having an efficient and effective supervisory mechanism. The key criterion for success of the Arab Charter is its implementation, which will ensure that the Charter protects, respects, and fulfills human rights. My goal is to outline the best practices to make the Arab Court more efficient. This will include the development of mechanisms through which the Arab Court and the Arab Committee can receive complaints from individuals and states parties that have ratified the protocols establishing the Court and the Committee, respectively.

The human rights articles in the Arab Charter are very good, but rights are useless if there are no means for implementation. Professor Abdallah Al-Nagar, a member of the Islamic Research Academy[1431] commented that the former Egyptian Constitution of 1971 was suspended in 2011.[1432] He said that the former constitution had nice-looking articles for the protection of human rights. However, it was useless as it was not implemented. He added that there must be mechanisms in the new constitution in order to implement and guarantee its human rights articles. The new Egyptian Constitution of 2014 is very good compared to the Consition of 1971. For the first time, the Egyptian Consitution give very good concern to international human rights treaties, the Constitution states "The State shall be bound by the international human rights agreements, covenants and conventions ratified by Egypt, and which shall have the force of law after publication in accordance with the prescribed conditions."[1433] However, this is not enough, a supervisory mechanisms of implementation and follow up is very important to be adopted.

Currently, there are no effective supervisory mechanisms or follow-up mechanisms within the Arab Charter. The Arab Charter permits neither individuals nor

---

1431 *Dream 2 Channel: Al'Ashira Masa'an* (April 3, 2012).
1432 The Egyptian Constitution of 1971 was enforced from 1971 until its suspension after the Egyptian revolution in 2011. After that, a new constitution was adopted in 2012 then suspended in 2013 until the adoption of the amended constitution of 2014.
1433 Unofficial translation of the Egyptian Const, art. 93. http://www.sis.gov.eg/Newvr/Dustor-en001.pdf (last visited May 14, 2014).

states to submit complaints to the Arab Committee against any human rights violations. Similarly, there is no real independence for the members of the Arab Committee and no effective enforcement mechanism. Most of the members of the Committee are either diplomats or hold government positions. The Arab Charter did not mention any promotional role for the Committee. In Chapter 7, I will examine how the Arab Committee can be modified in order to have an effective and efficient Arab Committee. Chapter 8 deals with the ultimate goal of establishing an Arab Court on Human Rights.

Although I suggested that the Arab Court should receive individual complaints, it is also important that the Arab Committee receive complaints until the Court replaces it. With respect to a ratifying state, the second protocol should replace the first protocol regarding the individual and state complaints. I propose that the Court's decisions be binding. On the other hand, the decisions of the Committee would only be recommendatory. My key proposal is to now amend the jurisdiction, structure, and functions of the present Arab Committee; then, after a period of time of adjustment to human rights supervision, the Committee should stop working and be replaced by a Court. The Arab Court would replace the Arab Committee for the countries that ratified the second protocol establishing the Arab Court. The second protocol will be applicable for those member states that ratify it. On the other hand, the Arab Committee should continue its work in receving individual and state complaints for the countries that ratified only the first protocol. It is strongly expected that not all of the Arab countries will smoothly and quickly accept to ratify the second protocol establishing the Arab Court. The European Court of Human Rights faced similar challenges. For instance, Protocol 14, which amended the structure of the European Court, did not enter into force for several years. This delay in the entry into force is due to article 19, which states that the protocol will not enter into force unless all the states Parties to the Convention have expressed their consent to be bound by the Protocol.[1434] Therefore, in order to overcome this challenge another Protocol was in order to get around the problem. Protocol 14 bis states, "This Protocol shall enter into force on the first day of the month following the expiration of a period of three months after the date on which three High Contracting Parties to the Convention have expressed their consent to be bound by the Protocol ...."[1435]

1434 Article 19 of Protocol 14 to the Convention for the Protection of Human Rights and Fundamental Freedoms, http://conventions.coe.int/Treaty/EN/Treaties/Html/194.htm (last visited Jan. 6, 2013).

1435 Article 6 of Protocol 14 bis to the Convention for the Protection of Human Rights and Fundamental Freedoms, http://conventions.coe.int/Treaty/EN/Treaties/Html/204.htm (last visited Jan. 6, 2013).

The new structure of the European Court introduced by Protocol 14 bis is applied only regarding the states that ratified exclusively the protocol. Protocol 14 bis provides, "This Protocol shall not apply in respect of any individual application brought against two or more High Contracting Parties unless, in respect of all of them, either the Protocol is in force or applied on a provisional basis, or the relevant corresponding provisions of Protocol No. 14 are applied on a provisional basis."[1436]

It is important to understand the circumstances and situations of each region. In other words, that which fits a certain region may not necessary fit other regions. For instance, in the European system, people can submit cases directly to the Court. In the African system, there is both a Court and a Commission. The Inter-American human rights system does not permit individuals to submit complaints directly to the Court. In the American system, people have no direct access to the Court. The Court can only be accessed by the Commission if the violating state did not comply with the recommendatory opinion of the Commission. The American Convention on Human Rights states, "Only the States Parties and the Commission shall have the right to submit a case to the Court."[1437]

The Arab Committee should be able to receive individual and state complaints because some countries may refrain from ratifying the protocol establishing the Arab Court. As long as the suggested second protocol is not in force for them, they should still be subject to the jurisdiction of the Committee as enhanced by the suggested first protocol. Currently several Arab Countries are still in transitional periods. In fact, still several member states of the Arab League are not even members of the Arab Charter. Egypt, Somalia, and Sudan are subject to the African Charter on Human and Peoples' Rights, which receives complaints from individuals through the African Commission.[1438] On the other hand, they did not ratify the protocol establishing the African Court on Human and Peoples' Rights, which entered into force in 2004.[1439] If they were not member states of the African

---

1436 Article 8 (2) of Protocol 14 bis to the Convention for the Protection of Human Rights and Fundamental Freedoms, http://conventions.coe.int/Treaty/EN/Treaties/Html/204.htm (last visited Jan. 6, 2013).

1437 (Organization of American States, American Convention on Human Rights, "Pact of San Jose", Costa Rica, art. 61 (1), Nov. 22, 1969, http://www.unhcr.org/refworld/docid/3ae6b36510.html (last visited Feb. 10, 2013).

1438 List of the States parties to the African Charter on Human and Peoples' Rights can be found here: http://www.au.int/en/sites/default/files/African%20Charter%20on%20Human%20and%20Peoples'%20Rights.pdf (last visited June 20, 2012).

1439 Protocol to the African Charter on Human And Peoples' Rights on the Establishment of an African Court on Human and Peoples' Rights, http://www.au.int/en/sites/default/files

Charter and its Commission, it would not be possible to receive complaints because they did not ratify the protocol establishing the African Court on Human and Peoples' Rights.

In light of the previous example, if the African Commission did not permit individuals to submit complaints to it, people in Egypt, Somalia, and Sudan would not be able to submit complaints anywhere as they are not subject to the jurisdiction of the African Court. If the Arab Committee focuses only on state reports, it may take a very long time for the Arab countries to ratify the optional protocol establishing the Arab Court. Therefore, the right to submit individual complaints to the Committee and after that to the Court is essential in order to make the states parties familiar with, and respect, the regional human rights culture. In this way, gradualism is important in order to improve the culture of human rights.

It is necessary to apply the principle of gradualism. In other words, the first protocol to the Arab Charter should be the protocol amending the Arab Committee. After a period of time, the Arab countries will get familiar with the procedure of individual complaints to the Arab Committee. In addition, after the culture of regional human rights and compliance with human rights grow in states members of the Arab Charter, the members of states parties to the Arab Charter and its first optional protocol amending the Arab Committee will increase slowly and smoothly. After reaching a critical mass of seven states adopting the first protocol, the second optional protocol establishing an Arab Court on Human Rights should be opened for signature. The second protocol should enter into force after being ratified by only five countries (approximately a quarter of all Arab Countries). Once it entered into force, the second optional protocol should replace the first optional protocol. In other words, the Court, which issues binding decisions, replaces the Committee, which only gives recommendations for those countries that have adopted the second protocol; the others who did not adopt the second protocol still retain their subjection to the Committee, which retains its functions as to them. Therefore, a new era of human rights protection in the Arab world should start and human rights protection would be promoted through the principle of gradualism. After the Arab Court starts working, the Arab Committee should stop examining state and individual complaints as to the countries which adopted the second protocol. As to them, it should focus on other things, such as examining state reports and what is referred to it by the Court. For instance, if the Arab Court declared that a case is inadmissible because

---

/achpr.pdf (last visited Feb. 10, 2013). The list of countries that ratified the protocol on the statute of the African Court of Justice and Human Rights can be found here: http://www.au.int/en/sites/default/files/Protocol%20on%20Statute%20of%20the%20African%20Court%20of%20Justice%20and%20HR_1.pdf (last visited June 20, 2012).

the person who submitted the complaint is not a victim, but it considers the law or state practice involved as violating Arab human rights, the Court has the right to refer that case to the Arab Committee. The Arab Committee can examine this law while examining the state report of the State concerned and issue pertinent recommendations, including the indication of preventive measures.

Chapter 7: Recommendations for a Reformed Arab Committee on Human Rights Based on a Comparison with the African Commission on Human and Peoples' Rights

A. Creation and Composition

The African Charter provides, "An African Commission on Human and Peoples' Rights, hereinafter called 'the Commission', shall be established within the Organization of African Unity to promote human and peoples' rights and ensure their protection in Africa."[1440] Furthermore the Charter provides, "1- The Commission shall consist of eleven members chosen from amongst African personalities of the highest reputation, known for their high morality, integrity, impartiality and competence in matters of human and peoples' rights; particular consideration being given to persons having legal experience. 2- The members of the Commission shall serve in their personal capacity."[1441] No country can have more than one national member on the Commission.[1442]

Concerning the Arab Charter and my proposed articles regarding the Arab Court and the Arab Committee, both the Court and the Committee can receive communications from states parties and individuals. However, the Arab Committee with enhanced powers should be established first (Protocol one) and, then a few years later, a Court should replace the Committee with respect to those countries that recognize its jurisdiction (Protocol two). The major difference between Court and the Committee is that the Court's judgments are entirely binding for the concerned states. The Court's judgment can include compensation that should be paid by the state concerned to the victim. In addition, the Court's judgment also can include an order to the state concerned to amend the laws that constitute violations to human rights protected by the Charter. It should be noted that states are obliged to implement the Court's decision. On the other hand, the Committee cannot render a decision of compensation to the victim to be paid by the state concerned. It issues recommendations, it does not render judgments. In addition, the Committee has the right to follow up on the implementation of its recommendations. For instance, the Committee can submit a report to the summit of the Arab League informing states parties of the failing states that are unwilling to implement the Committee's decisions.

Applying the principle of gradualism is very important. Some Arab countries will refrain, for a long time, from ratifying both the first and the second optional

---

1440 African Charter, *supra* note 127, at art. 30.
1441 *Id.* at art. 31.
1442 *Id.* at art. 32.

protocol. In addition, some Arab countries will take a long time to ratify Protocol 1 until they become familiar with the new structure and duties of the Arab Committee. Furthermore, some Arab countries will not accept the idea of establishing an Arab Court. They will claim that they already have domestic courts that work efficiently, so there is no need for a regional court. In addition, they will claim, before and after the entry into force of protocol 1, that the Committee is working efficiently, so there is no need for an Arab Court. For these countries, the first protocol is suitable for them until the achievements of the three following goals. First, the culture of human rights develops further in these countries. Second, the governmental officials of these countries who make decisions on human rights issues are able to demonstrate an academic and professional background in this field. Third, they begin having the good will and the motivation to accept the idea of adopting a second protocol establishing an Arab Court and comply with the articles of the Arab Charter and its protocol. After achievement of the three goals and also after these countries start complying with the first optional protocol, it is hoped and expected that the culture of human rights will further develop and, after several years, they will ratify the second optional protocol. Therefore, it is important to have the Committee, which, after a period of time, will be replaced by a Court in order for the principle of gradualism to be applied smoothly. After the Arab Court starts working, the Committee should stop receiving communications from states parties and individuals with respect to those countries that have ratified the second protocol establishing the Arab Court. The Committee should focus on the states parties annual reports and on the prevention measures. The prevention measures require that the Arab Committee work on avoiding human rights violations from happening the first place. To that end, for instance, the Committee evaluates the national laws and constitutions in order to examine whether or not they are safeguarding and protecting human rights.

I suggest that the number of the members of the Arab Committee be increased in order to face the large number of human rights issues that are facing the states parties. The Committee should be given the right to increase the number of judges at any time during the year to be able accommodate the expected increase in the number of cases. All of these suggestions and recommendations will help in promoting the Arab Charter and its Committee.

The African Commission faced criticism because some of members of the Commission were holding other positions at the national level that are incompatible with their work at the African Commission. For example, some of the members of the Commission are simultaneously acting as ministers and ambassadors of their country of origin. The former Chairperson of the Commission of the African Union, Professor Alpha Omar Konara, mentioned explicitly the need to put an end to this problem.[1443] The Arab Charter gave immunity to the members of the Committee in order to work more independently. The Arab Charter provides, "The Committee shall consist of nationals of the states parties to the present Charter, who must be highly experienced and competent in the Committee's field of work. The members of the Committee shall serve in their personal capacity and shall be fully independent and impartial."[1444] Also, the Charter provides, "The States parties undertake to ensure that members of the Committee shall enjoy the immunities necessary for their protection against any form of harassment or moral or material pressure or prosecution on account of the positions they take or statements they make while carrying out their functions as members of the Committee."[1445] Some of the members of the Arab Human Rights Committee hold other governmental positions. We cannot expect great steps forward in the success of the Arab Committee if the members of the Committee are not independent. This is one of the main challanges facing the Arab Charter.

The existing articles of the Arab Charter should be applied strictly in order not to run into the same problem that is happening with the members of the African Commission. In order to have an effective Arab Charter the members of the Committee should be very independent and at the same time very specialized. For instance, some of the members of the Committee should be judges, as judges are supposed to have a high degree of experience in the field of human rights. In addition, judges are used to working in an independent environment and are used to having immunity (i.e. they cannot be fired from their positions as judges). In addition to judges, other members of the committee can be independent persons who are very qualified and have outstanding experience in the field of human rights and regional human rights systems. It is impossible to promote human rights of the countries that are member of the Arab Charter without having independent committee members.

In order to promote the Arab Charter, the members of the Committee should be judges because they are independent and also, judges are not allowed to work in another job that is incompatible with their positions. The Arab Committee cannot immediately change and dismiss the members of the Arab Committee who are assistant ministers and are holding governmental positions. In addition, the culture of human rights is not fully mature in the Middle East, and governments are conservative regarding regional human rights systems. Therefore, half

---

1443 Germain Baricako, *The African Charter and African Commission on Human and Peoples' Rights, The System in Practice, in* THE AFRICAN CHARTER ON HUMAN AND PEOPLES' RIGHTS: THE SYSTEM IN PRACTICE 1986- 2006, 1, 9-10 (Malcolm Evans & Rachel Murray eds., 2nd ed. 2008).

1444 ACHR, *supra* note 126, at 45 (2).

1445 *Id.* at art. 47.

the members of the Arab Committee should be judges. After several years and after the culture of human rights further develops in the Arab world, all the members of the Arab Committee should be judges. In addition, in order to guarantee the independence of the judges, they should be elected by the presidents of the Supreme Judicial Council or the equivalent body of each state party. This will definitely ensure their independence because all of the members of this Council are highly ranked judges who are presumed to be entirely independent. Furthermore, in order to ensure justice, it is prohibited for any member of the Committee to examine any case to which his state is party. In short, if there are no guarantees for the independence and high-ranking experience of the members of the Committee, it is impossible to expect that the Arab Charter can promote human rights effectively.

Proposed articles regarding the Arab Committee of the Arab Charter on Human Rights:

> The Committee shall consist of a number of members equal to that of the High Contracting Parties. The members of the Committee can be increased by simple majority of votes of the members of the Arab Committee.
>
> Half the members of the Committee must be judges.
>
> The members of the Committee must be nationals of the countries members of the League of Arab States, persons of high moral character, and they must possess the qualifications required in their respective countries for appointment to the highest judicial offices.
>
> The members of the Committee shall be elected for a period of four years and may not be re-elected; provided, however, that of the members elected at the first election, the terms of half number of the members shall expire at the end of their second year and the terms of the rest of them shall expire at the end of their fourth year.
>
> The judges are elected by the Supreme Judicial Council of each State party.
>
> The presidents of the Supreme Judicial Councils sit together to interview all of the judges and exclude the judges that are not suitable for that position.
>
> It is prohibited for any member of the Committee to sit on any case that his state is party to.

The members of the Committee shall serve in their personal capacity and shall be fully independent and impartial.

The states parties undertake to ensure that members of the Committee shall enjoy the immunities necessary for their protection against any form of harassment or moral or material pressure or prosecution on account of the positions they take or statements they make while carrying out their functions as members of the Committee.

B. Mandate and Organization

The African Charter states that the Commission shall elect its Chairman and Vice-Chairman for a two-year period. in those positions, they can be re-elected.[1446] In the case of equal votes for two candidates, the Chairman breaks the tie.[1447] The Arab Charter effectively promotes the work of the Commission through limiting the re-election of the Chairman to only one time.[1448] However, it is always better if they are being elected for one period without the possibility of re-election. This will help to increase the rotation of the position of the Chairman. This may help in promoting and protecting human rights.

The Arab Charter gives the right to the Committee to establish its own rules of procedure and methods of work.[1449] The Rules of Procedure are important as they further detail the procedures, such as the ones on voting and electing the Chairman. Unlike the African Charter, the Arab Charter did not mention that there will be a Vice-Chairman. This will create a problem if the Chairman is absent. The temporary Rules of Procedure of the Arab Committee on Human Rights state in Article 2 that the Committee has a Chairman, aVice-Chairman, and a Rapporteur. It will be very important that the permanent Rules of Procedure deal with this issue. This is a big challenge that will face the Arab Committee; it must work independently in order to guarantee effective protection of the rights.

Proposed articles regarding the mandate and organization of the Arab Committee of the Arab Charter on Human Rights:

> The Committee shall elect its Chairman and Vice Chairman for a two-year period. They cannot be re-elected.

1446 African Charter, *supra* note 127, at art. 42 (1).
1447 Id. at art. 42 (4).
1448 Id. at art. 45 (7).
1449 ACHR, *supra* note 126, at art. 45 (7).

C. Seat

Both the African Charter and the Rules of Procedure did not mention the seat of the Commission. The African Commission decided that it is important to have its seat outside of the country hosting the African Union. This will keep the Commission away from any influence or pressure.[1450] In the 14th session of the African Union Assembly of Heads of the State and Government held in Addis Ababa, Ethiopia, it was decided that the seat of the African Commission should be in Banjul, The Gambia.[1451]

Unlike the African Charter, the Arab Charter was not silent regarding the seat. The Arab Charter provides, "The Committee shall hold its meetings at the headquarters of the League of Arab States. It may also meet in any other State party to the present Charter at that party's invitation."[1452] In addition, Article 6 of the temporary Rules of Procedure of the Arab Committee states that the Committee shall hold its meetings at the headquarters of the League of Arab States. It may also meet in any other State party to the present Charter at that party's invitation.

It would be better if the seat of the Committee was in another country, another city, or even in a separate building other than the headquarter building that hosts the administrative and political organs of the League of Arab States. This will help the Committee be a fully independent body, shielded from any pressure or influence. The Committee may also face financial difficulties, such as was experienced by the African Commission. Therefore, the Committee and the Court should be assigned a specific percentage of the budget of the Arab League.

The Arab League should choose a country or a city that provides great facilities, privileges, and immunity from any interference for the Committee and the Court. The city that hosts the Court and Commission will definitely affect the success of the Charter. For instance, a nice beautiful city on the sea or the ocean would provide a good environment for the members of the Court and Commission. At the same time, the city should have libraries and facilities that can help the judges. For instance, Alexandria, which is about 200 kilometer from Cairo, would be an ideal city for the Court. It is a beautiful city on the Mediterranean Sea. It has the biggest library in Egypt and one of the biggest libraries in the Middle East, called the Alexandria Library. This environment can definitely help in promoting the work of both the Committee and the Court. Furthermore, it is very inexpensive city relative to cities in Gulf countries and other Arab countries. In

---

1450 Baricako, *supra* note 1443, at 11.
1451 *Id.* at 11-12.
1452 ACHR, *supra* note 126, at art. 45 (7).

other words, it will not be expensive for the parties of a case if they wish to come to the Court or if the Court requested to hear them or hear other witnesses. This way, the Arab Charter could properly protect human rights for the people within its jurisdiction. On September, 2013 the League accepted the request of Bahrain to host the Arab Court on Human Rights in Manama.[1453] Bahrain is a very beautiful Gulf country.

Proposed articles regarding the seat of the Arab Committee and the Arab Court of the Arab Charter on Human Rights:

The Committee shall have its seat in Alexandria, Egypt.

The seat may be changed after consultation with the Committee and states parties.

The Court shall have its seat in Alexandria, Egypt.

The seat of the Court may be changed after consultation with the Court and states parties.

D. Functions

1. The Promotional Task[1454]

The Commissioners of the African Commission have a duty to promote the Charter. They visit African states and must write a report on their activities at each session.[1455] The Rules of Procedure of the African Commission provide, "Each member of the Commission shall file a written report on his/her activities at each session including countries visited and organisations contacted."[1456] The Commissioners have the right to also visit African states that did not ratify the Charter.[1457] The Commission organized several seminars in cooperation with different institutions, such as the United Nations and NGOs.[1458]

The Arab Charter should give the members of the Arab Committee the same authority that is given to the members of the African Commission. It is very wise

---

1453 The Kingdom of Bahrain hosts the Arab Court on Human Rights, http://62.3.35.36/Human-RightsOffice/index.php?action=News&Sub=ShowOne&ID=8 (last visisted May 19, 2014).
1454 Baricako, *supra* note 1443, at 14, 15, 16.
1455 *Id.* at 14-15.
1456 Rule 87 (3) of the Rules of Procedure of the African Commission on Human and Peoples' Rights.
1457 Baricako, *supra* note 1443, at 14-15.
1458 *Id.* at 15.

that the members of the African Commission have the authority to also visit countries that did not yet ratify the Charter. Although nearly all of the African countries have now ratified the Charter, it was vital at the beginning to encourage states that had not yet ratified the Charter to do so or at least abide by its principles and norms.

The members of the Arab Committee have an important role to play with respect to promotion, especially because many countries have not yet ratified the Arab Charter on Human Rights. Therefore, it will be very important for the members of the Committee to arrange visits and conferences in coordination with governmental and nongovernmental organizations and in collaboration with the hosting government. This will certainly increase awareness of human rights, if not encourage the hosting state to ratify the Charter. Also the seminars, conferences, and even the regular meetings of the Committee (when they are organized in more than one country) will render the work of the Committee both more effective and more attractive. For example, if the Committee were examining the report of Country 'A,' then it would be better to organize meetings within this country. In addition, it is important to organize conferences in this country that focus on finding solutions to the deficiencies found in its report. This will lead to focusing closely on the problem and hearing different opinion from people, NGOs, and governmental personnel of Country 'A,' and will definitely help in improving human rights protection. Article 17 of the temporary Rules of procedure of the Arab Committee states that the Committee can hold special sessions, seminars, and conferences regarding human rights in order to serve the goals and purposes of the Charter. The Arab Committee is already doing a great job. For instance, it visited Algeria before examining its first report. During this visit, the Committee explained the importance of the Charter to the government and civil society. The Committee made several other visits. For instance, some of its members visited Syria to monitor human rights violations. The Committee also requested that Libya stop human rights violations. In short, the visits and the activities of the Committee can be considered a good start.

Proposed articles regarding the promotional task of the Arab Committee of the Arab Charter on Human Rights:

The promotional task of the Committee shall be:

1) To promote human and rights and in particular:
(a) To collect documents, undertake studies and research on Arab problems in the field of human rights; organize seminars, symposia and conferences; disseminate information; encourage national and local institutions concerned with human rights; and, should the

case arise, give its views or make recommendations to States and the Arab League.

(b) To formulate and present principles and rules aimed at solving legal problems relating to human rights and fundamental freedoms upon which Arab governments may base their legislations.

(c) To cooperate with other Arab and international institutions concerned with the promotion and protection of human and peoples' rights.

(d) To organize, seminars, workshops, and conferences regarding human rights in order to serve the goals and purposes of the Charter.

2) Ensure the protection of human rights under conditions laid down by the present Charter.

3) Perform any other tasks that may be entrusted to it by the Assembly of Heads of State and Government.

2. The State Reporting System

The African Charter provides, "Each state party shall undertake to submit every two years, from the date the present Charter comes into force, a report on the legislative or other measures taken with a view to giving effect to the rights and freedoms recognized and guaranteed by the present Charter."[1459] Article 62 neither clarified to whom the states parties will submit the report, nor stated who is responsible for examining these reports.[1460] However, in 1988, at the third Ordinary Session, the Commission took the view that "the African Commission is the only appropriate organ of the African Union capable not only of studying the said periodic reports but also of making pertinent observations to States Parties" and recommended that the OAU provide it with the power to examine them.[1461] Not only did the Assembly of Heads of State and Government of the African Union do so, but it also entrusted the Commission with the responsibility for preparing guidelines with respect to the form and content of the periodic reports.[1462] The Commission's Reporting Guidelines states the goal of the

---

1459 African Charter, *supra* note 127, at art. 62.

1460 Baricako, *supra* note 1443, at 52.

1461 *Id.* at 52 (citing the Recommendation on Periodic Reports, First Annual Activity Report of the African Commission on Human and Peoples' Rights 1987-1988, ACHPR/RTP/1st, Annex IX, *in* DOCUMENTS OF THE AFRICAN COMMISSION 168 (Murray and Evans eds., 2001)).

1462 *Id.* at 52 (citing 24th Ordinary Session. See Second Annual Activity Report of the African

reporting procedure as to "create a channel for constructive dialogue between the States and [the Commission] on Human and Peoples' rights."[1463]

According to Article 62 of the African Charter, State parties will submit an initial report to be followed every two years by periodic reports that provide updates on the progress and on obstacles encountered. The reporting guidelines state:

> In the following periodic reports the governments would indicate the measures taken, the progress made in achieving the observance of the rights and duties in the Charter, and spell out the difficulties limiting success which they encountered in their efforts. A report on the new measures such as new legislations, new administrative decisions or judicial judgments passed to uphold these rights since the submission of the initial report would also be added. This means that the subsequent reports will follow the topics as discussed in the initial reports.[1464]

After submitting the report, states will be invited to send representatives to the next session of the Commission, where the report will be examined in public.[1465] The Commission mandated itself to examine the reports and send questions to the State party concerned. The representative will then present the report to the Commission at its next session.[1466] The reason behind this is to create a 'constructive dialogue' between the Commission and the state.[1467] However, in practice, the question may not be sent in time and representatives may not appear, thus postponing examination for up to several years. As a result, at the twenty-third session the Commission decided that those reports of states that failed to send representatives would be examined in absentia.[1468]

It is important that, to ensure the effectiveness of the Arab Charter, each state send a periodic report every two years, not every three years. Article 48 of the

---

Commission on Human and Peoples Rights, para. 31 (Murray and Evans (eds.), *Documents of the African Commission*, p. 176)).

1463 *Id.* at 56 (citing Guidelines for National Periodic Reports, Second Annual Activity Report of the African Commission on Human and Peoples' Rights 1988-1989, ACHPR/RPT/2ND, Annex XII in DOCUMENTS OF THE AFRICAN COMMISSION 168 (Murray and Evans eds., 2001)).

1464 *Id.* at 58 (citing Guidelines for National Periodic Reports, Second Annual Activity Report of the African Commission on Human and Peoples' Rights 1988-1989, ACHPR/RPT/2ND, Annex XII in DOCUMENTS OF THE AFRICAN COMMISSION 168 (Murray and Evans eds., 2001)).

1465 *Id.* at 54.

1466 MURRAY, *supra* note 715, at 17.

1467 *Id.* (citing Guidelines for National Periodic Reports, Second Annual Activity Report of the African Commission on Human and Peoples' Rights (1988-9)).

1468 MURRAY, *supra* note 715, at 17.

Arab Charter should be amended in order to require the submission of the periodic report every two years. This will definitely help the Committee in its preventive role. In addition, for the Arab Charter to be more effective, each country should send a representative while the Committee is examining the report. The representative is supposed to help the Committee by giving clarification and explanations. In addition, the attendance of a representative gives more importance to the report. The important aim behind the reports is not only to collect data, but also to improve and protect human rights. In addition, the goal is to find solutions for the human rights challenges that are facing countries. Sometimes it is better to hear, rather than read, about the problem. However, in order to be a constructive representation and examination of the report, the Committee should read the report and then send questions to the country. After that, there should be a joint meeting with the representatives. This will definitely help to ensure a constructive dialogue between the Committee and each State party. In addition, like in the African system, if the representative did not come, the Committee should examine the report in absentia.

States do not always comply with the time limit with respect to submitting their reports to the Commission. For example, at the 40th Ordinary Session in November 2006, fifteen states had not submitted any reports at all. Only eleven states had submitted and presented all of their reports.[1469] In order to face the backlog of the overdue reports it was decided by the Commission in 1995, that several reports could be combined into one.[1470] Some of the Arab countries that are parties to the African Charter on Human and Peoples' Rights submitted combined reports, for example, Algeria, Egypt, Libya, Sudan, and Mauritania.[1471] The experience of some Arab countries in the African Commission will help these Arab countries in complying with the procedural requirement of the Arab Committee. Algeria submitted its third report in 2006 (combining the 2003-2005 overdue reports). Egypt submitted its second report in 2000 (combining its overdue reports since 1994). Libya submitted its second report in 2000 (combining 1993, 1995, 1997, and 1999 overdue reports).[1472] The African Commission's response to

---

1469 MURRAY, *supra* note 715, at 54 (citing the Twenty-First Activity Report of the African Commission on Human and Peoples' Rights 2006, para. 63).

1470 MURRAY, *supra* note 715, at 54-55.

1471 *Id.* at 54 (citing the *Status on Submission of State Periodic Reports to the African Commission*, ACHPR.ORG, http://old.achpr.org/english/_info/status_submission_en.html (last visited May 9, 2014).

1472 *Status on Submission of State Initial/Periodic reports to the African Commission*, ACHPR.ORG, http://old.achpr.org/english/_info/status_submission_en.html (last visited April 5, 2012).

this situation is to adopt resolutions calling on states to submit their reports and to write letters to countries who have failed to do so.[1473]

The Arab Charter entered into force in 2008. The Arab Committee started the process of examining the states reports in 2012. Therefore, with time the work of the Committee will be more harmonized and more efficient. From my professional experience as an expert nominated by the Egyptian Public Prosecution to participate in the implementation review mechanism of the United Nations Convention Against Corruption, some states' reports took more than two years to evaluate.[1474] Furthermore, from the experience of some Arab countries in the African Commission, we can easily recognize that state reports are not an effective mechanism. State reports are not submitted on time. There must be an opportunity for both individual and state complaints. In addition, there must be an effective Court.

In light of Article 45 (1) (a) of the African Charter,[1475] the Commission encouraged working relationship with either African or international NGOs. More than three hundred NGOs have been granted observer status, which has the effect of creating a formal relationship between the NGOs and the Commission. The

---

1473 MURRAY, *supra* note 715, at 54.

1474 I served as an expert nominated by the Government of Egypt to participate in the Implementation Review Mechanism of the United Nations Convention against Corruption ("the UNCAC"). I was one of the Egyptian experts that reviewed the reports submitted by three states parties to the UNCAC. As one of the experts in the review process, I was responsible for helping to complete the Self-Assessment Checklist during which the State party under review reports on its compliance with the articles of the Convention.
The Review Mechanism was adopted by the Conference of the States Parties to the UNCAC in Doha, Qatar in 2009. With over 160 State parties to the Convention, the Convention against Corruption is rapidly nearing universal ratification. In 2009, the Conference decided that more efforts were needed to ensure that the Convention was being implemented by ratifying States, and so adopted the Review Mechanism to ensure a level of accountability to States that have ratified the Convention. The Review Mechanism is conducted on a peer-review basis, meaning that States under review are reviewed by two other States parties to the Convention – one State from the same region, and one State from anywhere in the world. The completion of the Self-Assessment Checklist will be followed by an analysis by the experts from the reviewing States parties and then further discussed among all of the experts assigned to the review, concluding in a comprehensive report and Executive Summary containing observations, conclusions, and recommendations.

1475 Article 45 (1) (a) of the African Charter on Human and Peoples' Rights provides that the Commission is "To collect documents, undertake studies and researches on African problems in the field of human and peoples' rights, organize seminars, symposia and conferences, disseminate information, encourage national and local institutions concerned with human and peoples' rights, and should the case arise, give its views or make recommendations to Governments." (African Charter, *supra* note 127, at art. 45 (1) (a)).

Commission encourages national NGOs to prepare alternate or shadow reports or commentaries to their country reports, and to make these available to the Commission.[1476]

The state reporting mechanism is used in all of the principal United Nations human rights treaties. It is considered the only compulsory mechanism in all instruments. The reporting system has been regarded as the lowest minimum standard for supervising the human rights treaties. It has been derided for being inadequate in forcing states to comply with their treaty obligations. Such criticisms miss the point. The reporting system is intended to monitor compliance, not intended to be an enforcement mechanism. The essence of this process lies in the state presenting its records in compliance with the monitoring body and receiving the benefit of external scrutiny.[1477] The in-depth examinations of the United Nations reporting systems have shown the corrosive effects of the backlog of reports that are still awaiting submission to the supervisory bodies and the time it takes these bodies to consider reports.[1478]

Even though there are many disadvantages in the reporting system, there are still aspects of this system that are helpful. The reporting system has acquired strength that can help in bringing out compliance with human rights standards and treaty obligations. In addition, some international experts believe that the process of the reporting system, although it contains bureaucratic baggage, should be treated as an opportunity rather than a chore or formality. In this way, it is an opportunity to reaffirm a government's commitment to respecting the human rights of its own citizens and to reassert that commitment in the domestic political forum.[1479]

While acknowledging that the reporting system can be time-consuming and expensive, an effective reporting system that enables periodic evaluation and examination of the human rights situation within a country against the backdrop of specific set of legally framed obligations can hardly fail to enhance the degree of protection accorded to those within the scope of the African Charter.[1480] The Arab Committee can use the same ideas used in the African System, such as the combined reporting system, in order to encourage countries to submit their

---

1476 MURRAY, *supra* note 715, at 71.
1477 *Id.* at 50-51.
1478 *Id.* at 51.
1479 *Id.* (citing P. Alston, 'Purposes of Reporting' in United Nations Manual on Human Rights Reporting Under Six Major International Human Rights Instruments, U.N. DOC. HR/PUB/91/1 (1991), 19-24, p. 13).
1480 MURRAY, *supra* note 715, at 51.

reports. The Arab Committee should also think of new ideas to force the countries that did not submit reports to submit them on time. For example, they can organize international conferences inviting all the international media, NGOs, etc. These conferences can be arranged not only on a regular basis, but also whenever it is necessary. At this conference, they can publish the work of the Committee and its recommendations and observations on the annual reports of the states. The Committee should divide the conference into four parts: First, the positive side, which includes the achievement of the Committee and the states with respect to the protection and promotion of human rights. Second, the challenges facing the countries that did not fulfill some of their obligations in protecting and promoting human rights. Third, it should name the countries that did not submit their reports or that did not fulfill the recommendations of the Committee. Fourth, the Committee should outline its short, medium, and long-term plans for the future. This kind of international conference may help to force the countries that are members of the Arab Charter to comply with the obligations under the Charter. In addition, countries may be forced by these kinds of conferences to submit their reports on time. The African Charter gave the African Commission the authority to do many things to improve and protect human rights in Africa. For example, "To collect documents, undertake studies and researches on African problems in the field of human and peoples' rights, organize seminars, symposia and conferences, disseminate information, encourage national and local institutions concerned with human and peoples' rights, and should the case arise, give its views or make recommendations to Governments."[1481] The Arab Committee should have similarly wide authority, which, if used in a good way, can be a key for the success of the Committee.

Another way of achieving success for the Charter and its Committee is that the subject of human rights should be fixed in the agenda of the annual Arab League Summit.[1482] On yearly basis, presidents, kings, and ministers should discuss the success and challenges of the human rights issue of the states parties to the Arab Charter. For example, in these summits the Arab Committee can mention the countries that did not submit its reports or submitted a minimal and insufficient report. Therefore, this summit can be a golden opportunity for the Committee to achieve its goals.

1481 African Charter, *supra* note 127, at art. 45(1)(a).
1482 The Arab League summit is an important summit that occurs yearly in one of the Arab States. This summit gains its importance from the highly ranked Arab States delegation who attend this summit. They are usually presidents, kings, and ministers.

Despite the fact that the Arab Charter does not state that the Arab Committee must receive shadow reports, the Committee already received reports from NGOs. The Arab Committee is doing a good job in finding ways to improve the effectiveness of the Arab Charter. The amended Arab Charter and/or the Rules of Procedure should give the right to the Committee to receive shadow reports. It is very important for the effectiveness of the Arab Committee to receive shadow reports from NGOs and potential victims. This will be very helpful, especially because there are only seven members of the Committee, each of whom have a lot of work to do. The shadow reports will help the Committee understand different opinions regarding the human rights situation. Therefore, the committee can request more clarifications and explanations from the state. In addition, these shadow reports will make the recommendations and observations of the Committee more constructive.

If the Committee did not publish its conclusions and observations widely, it will be difficult to achieve the expected success from the Charter. One of the very positive things in the Arab Charter is that it emphasized the publication of the reports. The Charter provides, "The Committee's reports, concluding observations and recommendations shall be public documents which the Committee shall disseminate widely."[1483] The Committee is already publishing on the website of the Arab League both the state reports and the conclusions and observations of the Committee. This step will significantly improve the efficiency of the promoting and protecting the rights in the Charter.

As previously mentioned, the amended Arab Committee will start its work once the first optional protocol enters into force. After the Arab Committee is successful and the culture of human rights starts to develop and flourish, the Arab Court should be adopted by Protocol 2. The Arab Court should then replace the Arab Committee. After the entry into force and operation of the Arab Court, the Arab Committee will refrain from receiving complaints from individuals and states. In other words, the Court will render its judgments on complaints submitted to the Court. On the other hand, the Committee will work as a preventive mechanism. It will examine the domestic law and write recommendations. Then, the Committee will follow up on the measures taken by the state parties regarding the Committee's recommendations. At the same time, the Committee will receive shadow reports from international and regional organizations including NGOs. Furthermore, it will receive shadow reports from individuals and even potential victims. In addition, the Committee can examine any report published regarding human rights in Arab countries. Furthermore, the Committee should analyze the

---

1483 ACHR, *supra* note 126, at art. 48(6).

judgments of the Arab Court and the reports of United Nations Committees regarding any human rights violations in the laws of Arab countries. It can point out the domestic laws and regulations that violate the human rights. The Arab Committee can also request further information from the country concerned and submit recommendations to that country regarding amending these laws and measures. These recommendations will make the work of the Committee more effective and efficient.

The Committee should not wait for the three-year periodic report. Rather, it should be given the right to request additional information anytime. For instance, if the Committee found that a certain country adopted a law that is violating human rights, it should be able to immediately request further information from the country concerned and give recommendations. In addition, the Arab Committee should submit a yearly report on the work that it did during the year. This report should include an analysis of the judgments of the Arab Courts. In another words, if the Court found that a certain law violated human rights, the Committee should include this finding in the report. This report should be published and also submitted to the Summit of the Arab League. This summit is organized on a yearly basis and is attended by high-ranking officials, such as presidents, kings, and prime ministers. Therefore, the Committee can play a vital role in prevention, without waiting for further violations of human rights to occur. In short, the Arab Charter can be a great step forward in the protection of human rights.

Proposed articles regarding the Arab Committee of the Arab Charter on Human Rights:

> In its annual report, the Committee shall include a summary of its activities under the present Protocol. The Committee may take this report to the Council of the Arab League and the state concerned with respect to particular recommendations, as it deems useful. In addition, the Committee should present its annual report to the Council of Arab League and the Summit of Ministers.
>
> The High Contracting Parties undertake to abide by the recommendations of the Committee in any case to which they are parties.
>
> The Committee must follow up on the implementation of its recommendations.
>
> The recommendations of the Committee shall be transmitted to both the Summit of Ministers of Justice, which shall supervise its execution and the Supreme Judicial Councils of states parties.

If the Summit of Ministers and Supreme Judicial Councils fail to execute the recommendations of the Committee, the case shall be transmitted to the Council of the Arab League to take all the necessary adequate measures.

The Court has the discretionary authority, after deciding a case inadmissible, to transfer it to the Committee to consider the case as a shadow report.

Proposed articles regarding article 48 of the Arab Charter on Human Rights:

The existing article 48 provides:

1. The States parties undertake to submit reports to the Secretary-General of the League of Arab States on the measures they have taken to give effect to the rights and freedoms recognized in this Charter and on the progress made towards the enjoyment thereof. The Secretary-General shall transmit these reports to the Committee for its consideration.

2. Each State party shall submit an initial report to the Committee within one year from the date on which the Charter enters into force and a periodic report every two years thereafter. The Committee may request the States parties to supply it with additional information relating to the implementation of the Charter.

3. The Committee shall consider the reports submitted by the States parties under paragraph 2 of this article in the presence of the representative of the State party whose report is being considered.

4. The Committee shall discuss the report, comment thereon and make the necessary recommendations in accordance with the aims of the Charter.

5. The Committee shall submit an annual report containing its comments and recommendations to the Council of the League, through the intermediary of the Secretary-General.

6. The Committee's reports, concluding observations and recommendations shall be public documents which the Committee shall disseminate widely.[1484]

Article 48 (2) of the Arab Charter should be amended to read as follows:

1484 *Id.* at art. 48.

"Each State party shall submit an initial report to the Committee within one year from the date on which the Charter enters into force and a periodic report every *two years* thereafter. The Committee may request the States parties to supply it with additional information relating to the implementation of the Charter."

A new paragraph 4 shall be inserted which shall read as follows:

"4. The Committee Shall receive shadow reports from the Arab Court, and also from governmental or nongovernmental organizations, potential victims, group individuals and any individual."

Paragraphs 4, 5, and 6 shall become paragraphs 5, 6, and 7, respectively.

E. Jurisdiction of the Arab Committee

The state reporting system is the main function of the Committee. In order to protect and promote human rights, the duties of the Arab Committee should be amended. The Arab Committee, as it is currently, does not receive any communications from individuals. Therefore, it is not expected to achieve success in promoting human rights in the Middle East. We should have an effective state reporting system. The Arab Committee must be given more flexibility in its work. In other words, it should be allowed to make country visits, examine witnesses, and receive complaints. Similar to the African Commission, it should be given the right to conduct investigations. It should also be given the right to receive communications, not only from individuals but also from states, against other states that violated the provisions of the Charter. Furthermore, in the situation where the Arab Court considers a case inadmissible because, for example, there is no victim or the application is against a law that may violate human rights, the Arab Court can forward the case to the Arab Committee as a shadow report to be examined while it examines other state reports. In addition, while examining the state reports, the Arab Committee can make use of shadow reports submitted by states, governmental, and nongovernmental organizations, as well as complaints submitted by individuals. This will definitely help in preventing violations from happening. In this way, the Arab Charter can be more effective. In the example that I mentioned regarding the Austrian who submitted a complaint against the abortion law in Austria, instead of declaring this case inadmissible, such as did the European Court, the Arab Court has the right to forward the case to the Arab Committee. The Arab Committee can consider this a shadow report when examining the annual report of the state concerned. The Committee will efficiently play its preventive role. Therefore, the Committee should exist even while the Arab

Court is working efficiently. The Arab Committee will help to reduce the number of cases before the Arab Court because it plays this preventive role.

We should neither undermine the reporting system nor have a negative view about it. Although the reporting system is not the best supervisory system, it can still help in promoting and protecting human rights in the Middle East and North Africa. The reporting system will be one of the important things that will help in having an overall picture of the human rights background, challenges, and prospects in the Middle East and North Africa. The most important thing that will affect the efficiency of the reporting system is the will and motivation of the states parties to the Charter. These countries should have a strong will and motivation to cooperate with the Arab Committee and submit fully detailed reports to them. The countries should submit the reports on time without delays in order to help the Committee achieve its work efficiently. It will then be the turn of the Arab Committee to immediately examine the reports. The reporting system of the Arab Committee is currently very weak. After the Committee submits its recommendations on the state reports, it should at least have the right to follow up. Article 48 (3) of the Charter provides, "The Committee shall consider the reports submitted by the States parties under paragraph 2 of this article in the presence of the representative of the State party whose report is being considered."[1485] Article 48 (4) provides, "The Committee shall discuss the report, comment thereon and make the necessary recommendations in accordance with the aims of the Charter."[1486] From the previous article, we can see that there are no follow up mechanisms in the Arab Charter. In order for the Committee to protect the human rights in the Charter, it must have a follow up mechanism. Through such a mechanism, it can examine the measures being taken by the concerned country in response to the recommendation of the Committee.

Proposed articles regarding the Arab Committee of the Arab Charter on Human Rights:

> A state party to the Charter that becomes a party to the present Protocol recognizes the competence of the Committee to receive and consider communications from states and from individuals subject to its jurisdiction who claim to be victims of a violation by that state party of any of the rights set forth in the Charter. The Committee shall receive no communication if it concerns a State party to the Charter that is not a Party to the present Protocol.

1485 *Id.* at art. 48(3).
1486 *Id.* at art. 48(4).

Subject to the provisions of Article 1, individuals who claim that any of their rights enumerated in the Charter have been violated and who have exhausted all available domestic remedies may submit a written communication to the Committee for consideration.

If a State party to the present Charter has good reasons to believe that another State party to this Charter has violated the provisions of the Charter, it may submit a written communication to the Committee for consideration.

The Committee shall consist of a number of members equal to that of the High Contracting Parties. The members of the Committee can be increased by majority of votes of the members of the Arab Committee.

If the communication that is considered inadmissible refers to a law that is considered violating human rights, the Committee shall convert this inadmissible communication to a shadow report during its examination to the annual periodic report of the state concerned.

The Court has the discretionary authority after deciding a case inadmissible to transfer it to the Committee to consider the case as a shadow report.

The Committee must follow up on the implementation of its recommendations.

It shall, with a view to ascertaining the facts, undertake together with the representatives of the parties an examination of the petition and, if need be, an investigation, for the effective conduct of which the states concerned shall furnish all necessary facilities, after an exchange of views with the Committee.

The Committee may resort to any appropriate method of investigation; it may hear any person capable of enlightening it.

Proposed amendment to article 48(1) of the Arab Charter on Human Rights:

The existing article provides, "1. The states parties undertake to submit reports to the Secretary-General of the League of Arab States on the measures they have taken to give effect to the rights and freedoms recognized in this Charter and on the progress made towards the enjoyment thereof. The Secretary-General shall transmit these reports to the Committee for its consideration."[1487]

1487 *Id.* at art. 48(1).

Article 48 (1) of the Arab Charter shall be amended to read as follows: "1. The states parties undertake to submit reports to the *Committee on Human Rights* on the measures they have taken to give effect to the rights and freedoms recognized in this Charter and on the progress made towards the enjoyment thereof. The State concerned shall *submit a copy of this report to the Secretary-General of the League of Arab States.*"

F. Further Recommendations for the Arab Committee on Human Rights

As I stated before, Dr. Nabil Al-Araby informed me that the State of Bahrain submitted a proposal on establishing an Arab Court of Human Rights. The Arab League established a committee of experts that is examining this proposal. A draft statute was written and and the Arab League is organizing several meetings with a view toward drafting further amendments. The Arab League is keen is establish this Court. The idea of establishing an Arab Court is a significant step forward with respect to promoting and protecting human rights in the Middle East. However, this Court is expected to face many challenges and obstacles that will prevent its establishment or prevent it from becoming an effective Court. The Court will be either ineffective, or if it is effective, the protocol establishing the Court will not be ratified by many of the countries of the region. In order to establish an Arab Court, there must be a collective will of the states parties to establish an effective Arab Court. The principle of gradualism should be applied smoothly. In other words, the Arab Committee should be able to receive state and individual reports. After that, the Court can be established after the governments gain confidence in the regional human rights protection and the collective will increases.

In order for the Arab Charter to achieve success in protecting and promoting human rights, it must accept individual and state complaints. This cannot be done immediately, but, rather, must be done gradually and smoothly. The individual complaints were not compulsory on the states parties to the European Convention. However, over time this situation changed. The European states did not accept individual petitions immediately. However, this procedure was gradually applied; it took approximately fifty years until it achieved success. It takes a long time for the states to gain confidence in the work of the Commission and until the culture of human rights protection in their countries has developed and matured. It has been recognized that "[t]he Commission became legally competent to receive individual petitions pursuant to Article 25 in 1955. It takes around 40 years for all the States parties to the Convention to recognize the admissibility of private complains. All the twenty-two countries by 1 January, 1990 had agreed to recognize the admissibility of private complaints."[1488]

The states parties to the Arab Charter should take steps gradually. However, the environment is suitable for the Arab Charter to achieve success. There are many reasons for that, for example, many of the Arab countries signed and ratified international and regional human rights treaties. In addition, many of them are already members of regional or international commissions. For example, Egypt is member of the African Charter on Human and Peoples' Rights. In addition, Egypt is member of the African Commission on Human Rights. Therefore, many of the countries of the Arab League are familiar and experienced with international and regional human rights protection systems.

The role of the Committee of Ministers that was applied prior to the entry into force of Protocol 11 to the European Convention on Human Rights should not be applied at all within the Arab human rights system. This is because of the political role of the Committee. The former Secretary of the Committee criticized the role of the Committee. He said, "the members of the Committee whom are Permanent Representative of Member States at the Council of Europe are generally career diplomats. They act on human rights cases on instruction of their capitals. They have no experience or training to deal with human rights issues."[1489] He also added that "they are trained to defend State interests or what their central authority regards as interests of their State."[1490] He further stated that "when their own State is 'in the dock' they will have a natural inclination to defend it. When other States are concerned they may find it inappropriate to judge their human rights performance, unless it is considered as being in the interest of their own State to do so."[1491]

I agree entirely with the opinion of the former Secretary of the Committee, not only because the Deputy Ministers are lacking experience and do not have background knowledge of human rights, but also, as he mentioned, because they defend the interest of their states. Therefore, the rights provided in the Convention will be only theoretically and not practically protected and safeguarded. The Summit of Ministers of Justice of the States members of the Arab League and the

---

1488 JANIS & KAY, *supra* note 45, at 42.
1489 ALASTAIR MOWBRAY, CASES AND MATERIALS ON THE EUROPEAN CONVENTION ON HUMAN RIGHTS 13-14 (2007); *see also* Peter Leuprecht, The Protection of Human Rights by Political Bodies: The Example of the Committee of Ministers of the Council of Europe, 98 & 106-107, *in* PROGRESS IN SPIRIT OF HUMAN RIGHTS (M. Nowak & D. Steurer eds.1998).
1490 *Id.*
1491 *Id.*

Supreme Judicial Councils of states parties to the Arab League should supervise the implementation of the recommendations of the Arab Committee. As previously mentioned, the members of the Arab Committee must be independent in order to protect the human rights that are stated in the Charter.

Proposed articles regarding the Arab Committee of the Arab Charter on Human Rights:

> Individuals who claim that any of their rights enumerated in the Charter have been violated and who have exhausted all available domestic remedies may submit a written communication to the Committee for consideration.
>
> The members of the Committee must be nationals of the countries members of the League of Arab States, persons of high moral character, and they must possess the qualifications required in their respective countries for appointment to the highest judicial offices.
>
> The members of the Committee shall be elected for a period of four years and may not be re-elected; provided, however, that of the members elected at the first election, the terms of half number of the members shall expire at the end of their second year and the terms of the rest of them shall expire at the end of their fourth year.
>
> The members of the Committee shall serve in their personal capacity and shall be fully independent and impartial.
>
> The states parties undertake to ensure that members of the Committee shall enjoy the immunities necessary for their protection against any form of harassment or moral or material pressure or prosecution on account of the positions they take or statements they make while carrying out their functions as members of the Committee.
>
> The High Contracting Parties undertake to abide by the recommendations of the Committee in any case to which they are parties.
>
> The recommendations of the Committee shall be transmitted to both the Summit of Ministers of Justice, which shall supervise its execution and the Supreme Judicial Councils of states parties.
>
> If the Summit of Ministers and Supreme Judicial Councils fail to execute the recommendations of the Committee, the case shall be transmitted to the Council of the Arab League to take all the necessary adequate measures.

Chapter 8: An Arab Court of Human Rights Based on a Comparison with the European Court of Human Rights

A. Institutional Structure and Composition

1. Gradualism Within the European and Arab Courts of Human Rights

A regional court of human rights should be able to receive complaints from both individuals and states. However, it is important to know that if we want to establish an effective court for the states parties to the Arab Charter on Human Rights, the establishment of such mechanisms should be done gradually. The development of the Arab Court of Human Rights could be stated in an additional optional protocol, which states would be encouraged to ratify smoothly. However, if the court was mentioned in the Charter itself, many countries would refrain from ratifying the Charter or make reservations to the article pertaining to the creation of the Court. It should be noted that it will take time for the popularity of the Arab Court of Human Rights to increase from the perspective of Arab governments. We must be patient with respect to the development of the Arab Court, because as it currently stands the Arab Charter is useless without the inclusion of an effective mechanism such as the Court. We should apply the principle of gradualism that I mentioned both in the chapter focused on Sharia law and the chapter outlining my proposed theory.

It should be noted that the shift from complaints being an optional to a compulsory process took many years within the European system.

Judgments from the Court were optional for Contracting States until 1998, when the ECHR's jurisdiction became compulsory and binding for all Member States of the Council of Europe. Finally, prior to 1994, applicants could not submit their claims directly to the Court. Instead, complaints were lodged with the Commission, who then attempted to broker a friendly settlement between the parties concerned. If this proved impossible, the Commission would draw up a report stating its opinion of the case. The opinion would then be given to the Committee of Ministers to decide whether or not a violation of the Convention had occurred. If so, the Committee of Ministers was responsible for ensuring "just satisfaction" to the victim. The Commission and Contracting States had a three-month period after the transmission of the report to the Committee of Ministers in which to bring the case before the ECHR instead, in order to obtain a binding judgment. If a judgment was given, the Committee of Ministers was responsible for ensuring its execution. This system was reformed in 1994, when the Court allowed cases to be brought directly to it for screening (rather than to the Commission), and further reformed in 1998 when the ECHR became a permanent court, the Commission was dismantled, and the Committee of Ministers' adjudicative function was eliminated.[1492]

In this way, it has taken the European Court of Human Rights a long time to achieve its current incarnation. The European Convention on Human Rights was not immediately effective and efficient upon its adoption. Rather, it took a long time for the Convention to develop into its present harmonious and efficient structure. The principle of gradualism was patiently applied throughout the development of the European Court of Human Rights. I will highlight the importance of this principle of gradualism in relation to the promotion and development of the Arab Charter.

The Council of Europe drafted the European Convention in 1949 and 1950. It was signed on November 4, 1950 and entered into force on September 3, 1950, after the ratification by eight countries.[1493] As of January 1, 1990, twenty-two countries had become parties to the Convention.[1494] As of April 1, 2012, forty-seven countries have become parties to the Convention.[1495] The European Convention on Human Rights is not only one of the most successful human rights systems in the world, but is also one of the most advanced and efficient forms of international legal process.[1496] In short, "the Court monitors respect for the human rights of 800 million Europeans in the 47 Council of Europe member States that have ratified the Convention."[1497] The number of cases before the European Courts on Human Rights increased rapidly in the 1980s. In 1990, sixty-one referrals were made to the European Court, which is almost equal to the number of cases that the European Court dealt with in the first twenty-four years of its existence.[1498] In 1999, the Court delivered 177 judgments. In 2011, the Court delivered 1,157 judgments.[1499]

1492 *The European Court of Human Rights*, GLOBALGOVERNANCEWATCH.ORG, http://www.globalgovernancewatch.org/security/the-european-court-of-human-rights (last visited Jan. 4, 2013).

1493 These eight countries were Denmark, the Federal Republic of Germany, Iceland, Ireland, Luxembourg, Norway, Sweden, and the United Kingdom.

1494 JANIS & KAY, *supra* note 45.

1495 *Convention for the Protection of Human Rights and Fundamental Freedoms,* Council of Europe, http://conventions.coe.int/Treaty/Commun/ChercheSig.asp?NT=005&CM=8&DF=&CL=ENG (last visited Apr. 1, 2012).

1496 JANIS & KAY, *supra* note 45.

1497 The European Court of Human Rights, *The Court in Brief,* http://www.echr.coe.int/NR/rdonlyres/DF074FE4-96C2-4384-BFF6-404AAF5BC585/0/Brochure_en_bref_EN.pdf (last visited Apr. 2, 2012).

1498 HARRIS, O'BOYLE, & WARBRICK, *supra* note 712, at 648.

1499 The ECHR in Facts & Figures 2011, http://www.echr.coe.int/NR/rdonlyres/4ACC88A2-0336-415D-A904-061BE63EDE8D/0/FAITS_CHIFFRES_EN_JAN2012_VERSION_WEB.pdf (last visited Feb. 10, 2013).

On September 18, 2008, the Court delivered its 10,000th judgment.[1500] Since the establishment of the Court in 1959, the Court has rendered more than 15,000 judgments[1501] and "approximately 151,600 applications were pending before a judicial formation on 1 January 2012."[1502]

I am looking forward to a drastic increase in the efficiency of the Arab Charter within the next few years. The steps towards improving the Arab Charter should be taken gradually, such as was the case with the European Court. Many Arab countries ratified both international and regional instruments for human rights. In addition, some of the Arab states that are members of the Arab Charter are already members of the African human rights system. Furthermore, the media and both governmental and nongovernmental organizations can play an important role in increasing public awareness of issues of human rights and the corresponding systems. The popularity of the Arab human rights system will depend largely on its efficiency, effectiveness, and its compulsory jurisdiction. In short, if we want to have an effective Arab Court it must be introduced gradually.

2. Judges

It is not sufficient to simply install an Arab Court. The judges within the Court must also, by necessity, be independent and impartial. I will evaluate the independence of judges in the European Court and then suggest how to ensure the effectiveness of the Arab Charter in this regard.

The number of judges of the European Court is equal to the number of states parties. The European Convention provides, "The Court shall consist of a number of judges equal to that of the High Contracting Parties."[1503] Currently, they are forty-seven judges on the European Court.[1504] Each State party submits a list of three candidates. While it is not necessary that these candidates hold the nationality of the state electing them, this is normally the case.[1505] The Parliamentary

---

1500 *The Court in Brief, supra* note 1497.
1501 The European Court of Human Rights, *Overview 1959-2011*, http://www.echr.coe.int/NR/rdonlyres/8031883C-6F90-4A5E-A979-2EC5273B38AC/0/APERCU_19592011_EN.pdf (last visited May 15, 2012).
1502 The European Court of Human Rights, *The ECHR in Facts and Figures 2011*, http://www.echr.coe.int/NR/rdonlyres/4ACC88A2-0336-415D-A904-061BE63EDE8D/0/FAITS_CHIFFRES_EN_JAN2012_VERSION_WEB.pdf (last visited May 15, 2012).
1503 ECHR, *supra* note 497, at art. 20.
1504 The European Court of Human Rights, *Organization of the Court*, http://www.echr.coe./ECHR/EN/Header/The+Court/The+Court/Organisation+of+the+Court/ (last visited May 9, 2014).
1505 JACOBS & WHITE, *supra* note 566, at 473.

Assembly, the body responsible for electing judges, appoints experts to interview all of the candidates. After the candidates are interviewed, the experts write a report and submit it to the Parliamentary Assembly,[1506] which then elects one of the three candidates. The election of judges is done by a majority of votes. The European Convention states, "The judges shall be elected by the Parliamentary Assembly with respect to each High Contracting Party by a majority of votes cast from a list of three candidates nominated by the High Contracting Party."[1507]

The European Convention provides the following criteria for judges:

– The judges shall be of high moral character and must either possess the qualifications required for appointment to high judicial office or be jurisconsults of recognised competence.

– The judges shall sit on the Court in their individual capacity.

– During their term of office the judges shall not engage in any activity that is incompatible with their independence, impartiality or with the demands of a full-time office; all questions arising from the application of this paragraph shall be decided by the Court.[1508]

To ensure its effectiveness, the Arab Charter must have independent judges within the Arab Court. These judges must be highly qualified and their decisions must be impartial. Judges at the European Court are elected for nine years. The European Convention states, "The judges shall be elected for a period of nine years. They may not be re-elected."[1509] It is important that judges not be re-elected as this may affect their decisions and equality. Each state nominates three candidates for their national seat. Therefore, the judges may try to influence the countries to re-nominate them again. Therefore, it is better not to re-elect judges in order to avoid anything that may lead to the lack of fairness of the judges or the appearance thereof. Similarly, to ensure the independence of the judges within the Arab Court, they should not be re-elected.

The European Convention states, "The terms of office of judges shall expire when they reach the age of seventy."[1510] The age of retirement of the Egyptian judicial system in domestic courts is seventy years; as is the case within the European system and the Egyptian system, the Arab Court should require that the age limit

---

1506 *Id.*
1507 ECHR, *supra* note 497, at art. 22 (1).
1508 *Id.* at art. 21.
1509 *Id.* at art. 23(1).
1510 *Id.* at art. 23(2).

for terms of office for judges be seventy years. According to the former law of the Egyptian judicial system, the retirement age was sixty years, but, due to the large increase in the number of cases, the law was amended to set the retirement age at seventy years. However, it should be noted that there will be a limited number of judges within the Arab Court, unlike within the Egyptian judicial system which consists of more than ten thousand judges. Therefore, it is important that the few judges within the Arab Court are very qualified, efficient and in good health, especially because of the large number of cases that are expected to be brought to the Court. It is important to ensure that the judges have enough experience and, at the same time, are in good health, such that they can complete their work efficiently.

Just as the judges must be very qualified, the lawyers should also be very qualified. It should be noted that in Egypt, there is no bar exam for a law graduate to be a lawyer. Every graduate can easily apply for the membership of the bar and become a lawyer in a few weeks. Therefore, in order for the Court to be effective and efficient and for the victims to achieve success in their cases, the lawyers must be qualified. This can be done by several ways. For instance, the Court can have a list of approved lawyers. This list should be based on a written and even an oral exam for the lawyers. The lawyers that pass the exam can then defend victims before the Arab Court. In other words, the victims must choose a lawyer from the list of the registered lawyers in the Court.

Another important point that was considered a big challenge with respect to the independence of the judges was mentioned in Article 26 (4) of the ECHR, which states, "There shall sit as an ex-officio member of the Chamber and the Grand Chamber the judge elected in respect of the State Party concerned or, if there is none or if he is unable to sit, a person of its choice who shall sit in the capacity of judge."[1511] According to this Article, a judge will automatically sit as a member of the Chamber or the Grand Chamber if he holds the nationality of a state that is party to a case. Clare Ovey and Robin White have outlined that "it is arguable that greater independence would be achieved by excluding the national judge, but inclusion of the judge of the respondent State has the advantage of ensuring acquaintance with the legal system and the background to the case."[1512] No one can deny that a judge of the same nationality as the State party would best know the national laws, legal system, and the background of the case. However, we should not forget that the judge who holds the nationality of the state party was nominated by his country. His country is the one who submitted his name.

1511 ECHR, *supra* note 497, at art. 26(4).
1512 JACOBS & WHITE, *supra* note 566, at 474.

Therefore, in order to protect and strengthen the independence of the Court a compromise solution is preferable. The judge can automatically be a member of the Chamber or the Grand Chamber, but he should have no right to vote in such a case and is not permitted to deliver a separate or dissenting opinion. In other words, the judge will guide and help the other judges become more well-informed about the background of the case and the legal system of the country that elected him, but it would be better for a judge, and for the reputation of the Court, that the judge in question be excluded from rendering decisions in cases where his country is party to the case. The Arab Court should not invite the judge who represents a state party in the case or is a national of that country. This is currently the case in Egypt, where judges and public prosecutors are not allowed to work in any governorate that he is originally from. For example, if a judge is originally from Luxor or Hurgada, he or she cannot work in this governorate. This is to ensure independence and impartiality. This should also be applied by the Arab Court in order to make it more effective and ensure that it properly protects the human rights of the people within its jurisdiction.

It is very important that the judges not be engaged in any activity incompatible with their independence, impartiality, or the demands of a full time office. Judges at the European Court are prohibited from taking on any activity that is incompatible with the full time responsibilities of their office.[1513] Nearly all of the member countries of the Arab League impose the same obligations on the judges working at the national court.

One of the main criteria that should exist for judges of the Arab Court is a proficient understanding of English or French. This will ensure that they are able to read more cases from other international and regional courts. Also, it will ensure that they are able to read international law journals, books, and reports in foreign languages in order to stay up to date.

In order to ensure the effective and efficient rendering of decisions, there should be no maximum number of judges in the Arab Court. There must be flexibility for the Court to appoint as many judges as needed, depending on the number of cases under review. For instance, the number of cases in the first year of the Court may be low compared to the following years. This is certainly true from my experience as a Chief prosecutor in the Egyptian judicial system. An increasingly large number of cases must be anticipated and in order to ensure that cases are not delayed, a correspondingly large number of judges must be available. There should even be flexibility to allow the Court to appoint more judges at any point throughout the year. At the beginning of this century, due to the huge number

---

1513 MOWBRAY, *supra* note 1489, at 7.

of cases, the Egyptian Supreme Court of Cassation failed to render decisions in hundreds of thousands of cases before the court. Cases were delayed for many years. This situation remained until the law was changed. The temporary new law allows for the appointment of judges from the Appeals Court to work as if they were judges of the Supreme Court and to render decisions in a large number of these cases.

The Arab Court of Human Rights should take the equality of states between countries in the appointment of judges into consideration. For instance, each country member of the Arab League should be able to appoint one judge regardless of whether the judges hold the nationality of the country that appointed them or the nationality of a country member to the Arab League.

We may compare this issue with the situation in the European Court of Human Rights based on Protocol 11.[1514] The idea of a full-time European court began to develop in the 1980s. It was necessary to replace the previous court system with a full time court due to the large number of cases and the delay in rendering decisions.[1515] In fact, "the number of applications increased from 5,279 in 1990 to 10,335 in 1994 (+96%), 18,164 in 1998 (+76%) and 34,546 in 2002 (+90%)."[1516] Although there was great need for Protocol 11 within the European human rights system, this Protocol did not enter into force immediately. Instead, it took four years for it to enter into force. Protocol 11 "was opened for signature on 11 May 1994 and came into force on 1 November 1998."[1517] The old Courts ceased to exist at the end of October 1998. The former admissibility criteria were retained in the new full time Court.[1518] Also, the Committee of Ministers retains responsibility for supervising the execution of the new court's judgment.[1519]

Gradualism is necessary in the process of improving the effectiveness of the Arab Court. The Arab Court will not be made efficient overnight. It has been recognized:

> The European Court at its beginning was very slow. In the first seventeen years of its existence [1959 to 1975], it had had an average of only one case a year. Like the International Court of Justice, it had a

---

1514 MOWBRAY, *supra* note 1489, at 14-15.
1515 *Id.*
1516 Explanatory Report of Protocol 14 to the European Court of Human Rights, at http://conventions.coe.int/Treaty/EN/Reports/Html/194.htm (last visited May 15, 2012).
1517 *Id.*
1518 MOWBRAY, *supra* note 1489, at 14-15; See also ECHR, *supra* note 497, at art. 35.
1519 *Id.*; See also ECHR, *supra* note 497, at art. 46.

period of three bleak years (March 1962-June 1965) with a total absence of cases. In the 17 years from 1959 to 1975, only 20 judgments were delivered. Yet, by 1988, the annual number of cases referred to it had risen to about 20 and, in 1991, was just under one hundred.[1520]

In fact, due to the very slow rate of its beginning, one of the leading judges of the Court published an article in which he asked, "Has the European Court of Human Rights a Future?"[1521] This shows clearly that steps to develop a Court of Human Rights should be taken gradually.

I am certain that the Arab Court of Human Rights will face the same problem of an increase in the number of cases and applications. However, there are many solutions to tackle this problem before it occurs. One of the key answers is that the number of judges should be equal to the number of states parties to the Arab League. For instance, if the Arab Court entered into force after the fifth ratification of the Protocol establishing the Court, the number of judges should not be five but should be twenty two which is equal to the number of the state parties to the Arab League. In other words, the judges' members to the Arab Court should represent all the Arab countries member to the Arab League. This idea was followed by the European Court of Human Rights. The European Convention on Human Rights which entered into force in 1953 stated in article 38 that "The European Court of Human Rights shall consist of a number of judges equal to that of the Members of the Council of Europe. No two judges may be nationals of the State." This idea will increase the number of judges and at the same time will encourage the non-ratifying states to join the Arab Court. Professor Dr. Herbert Petzold, who is a Professor of Law and the former long-time Registrar of the European Court of Human Rights, informed me that the first French judge René Samuel Cassin to the European Court of Human Rights was a judge and even the Vice President (1959-1965) and President of the European Court (1965–1968), although France was not a member of the Court as it ratified the Convention only in 1974.[1522] He added that Judge Cassin did a great effort to push France to ratify

---

1520 NADASIRI JASENTULIYANA, PERSPECTIVES ON INTERNATIONAL LAW 314 (1995).

1521 Henri Rolin, *Has the European Court of Human Rights a Future?*, HOW. L.J. 442 (1965); *see also* HARRIS ET AL, *supra* note 712, at 624.

1522 Chart of signatures and ratifications of the European Convention for the Protection of Human Rights and Fundamental Freedoms, http://conventions.coe.int/Treaty/Commun/ChercheSig.asp?NT=005&CM=7&DF=03/09/2013&CL=ENG (last visited Sep. 3, 2013).

the Convention.[1523] Therefore, this idea will help in encouraging non-ratifying Arab states to join the Arab Charter and the Arab Court.

Furthermore, one of the key answers to tackle the increase in the number of cases and applications is to increase the number of judges. In Article 20, the European Convention stated that the number of judges should be equal to the number of state parties to the Convention. The Arab Charter should not follow the same approach. The Supreme Judicial Councils should be given the right to increase the number of judges upon the request of the majority of the presidents of the Supreme Judicial Councils. In addition, the plenary of the Arab Court should be given the right to increase the number of judges of the Court upon the request of the majority of judges of the Court. For instance, instead of appointing one judge, each state party of the Arab Charter should appoint five judges. This will definitely help in having enough judges on the Court. Therefore, they will be able to face the large number of anticipated cases. It is not practical at this point to indicate a finite number of judges on the Court. This will ensure that the Arab Court will be able to promote human rights effectively. The Arab Committee can take the same approach.

Proposed articles regarding the number of Judges of the Arab Court:

> Each state party of the Arab League should appoint one judge that hold the nationality of the country that appointed them or the nationality of a country member to the Arab League.

> The Supreme Judicial Councils can increase the number of judges upon the request of the majority of the presidents of the Supreme Judicial Councils. The plenary of the Arab Court can increase the number of judges upon the request of the majority of judges of the Court.

> Each country should have an equal number of judges under conditions to be set out in the Rules of Procedure.

a. *Structure of the Arab Court*

We may compare the structure of the potential Arab Court with the situation in the European Court of Human Rights based on Protocol 14 and 14 bis amended the structure of the European Court. The current structure of the Court is single-

---

[1523] Telephone interview with Professor Dr. Herbert Petzold, Professor of Public International Law, Saarbrücken University; Former Registrar, European Court of Human Rights (Sep. 3, 2013).

judge formation, committees, Chambers, and Grand Chamber.[1524] Protocol 14 explains a committee of three judges may, by unanimous vote:

> (a) declare it inadmissible or strike it out of its list of cases, where such decision can be taken without further examination; or
>
> (b) declare it admissible and render at the same time a judgment on the merits, if the underlying question in the case, concerning the interpretation or the application of the Convention or the Protocols thereto, is already the subject of well-established case-law of the Court.[1525]

Also, it is outlined, "'Well established case-law' means case law that has been consistently applied by a Chamber. However, in some exceptional cases, a single judgment can be a 'well established case law', particularly if it was rendered by the Grand Chamber. This new competence will apply, specially, to repetitive cases."[1526] According to Protocol 14, the case should be referred to the Chamber if the Committee does not reach a unanimous decision.[1527]

If no decision is taken by the single judge or the Committee of the European Court "a Chamber shall decide on the admissibility and merits of individual applications submitted under Article 34. The decision on admissibility may be taken separately."[1528] On the other hand, the interstate applications go directly to the Chamber.[1529]

The Chamber relinquishes a case to the Grand Chamber of the European Court if it "raises a serious question affecting the interpretation of the Convention or the Protocols thereto, or where the resolution of a question before the Chamber might have a result inconsistent with a judgment previously delivered by the Court, the Chamber may, at any time before it has rendered its judgment, relinquish jurisdiction in favour of the Grand Chamber, unless one of the parties to the case objects."[1530]

The power of the Grand Chamber is explained in the explanatory report of the European Convention on Human Rights which states that it is "to have competence both with regard to inter-State applications referred to it under Article

---

1524 ECHR, *supra* note 497, at art. 26.
1525 New article 28 (4) (a) (b) of Protocol 14 bis to the European Convention on Human Rights.
1526 THEORY AND PRACTICE OF THE EUROPEAN CONVENTION ON HUMAN RIGHTS 107 (Pieter Van Dijk et. al. eds., 4th ed., 2006).
1527 Article 9 of Protocol 14 amends article 29 (1) of the European Convention on Human Rights.
1528 ECHR, *supra* note 497, at art. 29 (1).
1529 *Id.* at art. 29 (2).
1530 *Id.* at art. 30.

30 or 43 as well as individual applications when they are referred to it under Article 30 or 43. The Grand Chamber is also to consider requests for advisory opinions, a function which the plenary Court carried out under the former system."[1531]

The structure of the Arab Court should include Chamber, Grand Chamber, and Plenary. The Arab Court should be set up such that it is effective from its inception. In other words, the right of submitting a case to the court should be given to states parties and to individuals. This will definitely improve the efficiency of the Court and promote human rights protection in the Arab world. Similarly, the Arab Charter should establish an effective Court that, from its beginning, can bear the increase in the number of cases. The increase of the number of cases in the European Court was caused by three reasons, in addition to the increase in the population of the European countries. First, an increased culture of knowing human rights resulted in an increase in people claiming their rights. Second, people began to trust the effectiveness and the credibility of the European Court and that they could use the Court as a last resort to safeguard their rights. Third, an increased willingness on the part of the states parties to respect the decisions of the Court and implement them definitely resulted in an increase of power and effectiveness of the Court.

The majority of people in the Arab world have started to know and claim their rights. The major important thing is their 'collective will' and their motivation. The Arab Court cannot be effective and credible unless the states parties of the Arab League have the good will, motivation, and intention to respect and implement the decisions of the Court. The collective will of the Arab countries increased with respect to achieving human rights and justice. The secret of the success of the European Court is the collective will and motivation of the High Contracting Parties to abide by the final judgment of the Court in any case to which they are parties. This will is not only reflected in the European Convention,[1532] but also in their intention to respect and implement the decisions of the Court. The states parties of the European Convention on Human Rights are keen to keep up the work of the Court and its effectiveness. They are always adopting new protocols and thinking of new ways to improve the effectiveness of the Convention.

1531 Explanatory Report of Protocol 11 to the European Convention on Human Rights is available at http://conventions.coe.int/Treaty/EN/Reports/Html/155.htm (last visited May 9, 2014).

1532 Article 16 of Protocol 14 amending Article 46 of the European Convention. New Article 46 (1) provides, "The High Contracting Parties undertake to abide by the final judgment of the Court in any case to which they are parties."

To improve its effectiveness, the Arab Charter should not copy entirely the number of judges used in the European Convention. Article 20 of the European Convention states , "The Court shall consist of a number of judges *equal* to that of the High Contracting Parties. [emphasis added]"[1533] Each state party of the Arab League should initially appoint one judge. In addition, the Supreme Judicial Councils can increase the number of judges upon the request of the majority of the presidents of the Supreme Judicial Councils. Also, the plenary of the Arab Court should be able to increase the number of judges upon the request of the majority of judges of the Court. The number of judges should be compatible to the number of cases before it. For example, the explanatory report of the European Convention on Human Rights states that "the number of applications increased from 5,279 in 1990 to 10,335 in 1994 (+96%), 18,164 in 1998 (+76%) and 34,546 in 2002 (+90%)."[1534] This surge had to be accommodated.

Although Protocol 14 was a major step forward, it is only a partial remedy. With Protocol 14, the Court still cannot deal with the large number of applications that increases daily in the Strasbourg Court. In his speech at the Third Summit of the Council of Europe held in Warsaw in May 2005, the President of the European Court said:

> We therefore need to look beyond Protocol No. 14 and address the issue of the long-term future of the system, and we should start doing so now. What kind of international protection mechanism do we need in the Europe of the twenty-first century? Are the present procedures still adjusted to the pan-European character which the system has acquired? What will be the impact of the projected accession of the European Union to the Convention? These are some of the crucial questions which we urgently need to start addressing, if we want to have a chance to enable the system to face up in time to the new challenges awaiting it. Now is not the time for a quick fix, but for vision. A vision on how to ensure that the European Court of Human Rights remains what it has been since its creation, for the benefit of nearly two generations of citizens: the tangible symbol of the effective pre-eminence on our continent of human rights and the rule of law.[1535]

1533 ECHR, *supra* not 497, at art. 20.
1534 Explanatory Report of Protocol 14 to the European Court of Human Rights, *supra* note 1516.
1535 Prof. Dr. Luzius Wildhaber, President of the European Court, at the Third Summit of the Council of Europe held in Warsaw (May 2005), https://wcd.coe.int/ViewDoc.jsp?id=930555&Site=COE&BackColorInternet=DBDCF2&BackColorIntranet=FDC864&BackColorLogged=FDC864 (last visited May 9, 2014); *see also* JACOBS & WHITE, *supra* note 566, at 524.

In order to ensure the effectiveness of the Arab Court, a maximum number of judges should not be set at the beginning. The Court could also have a provision that permits increasing the number of judges in the future. As the main language of the twenty-two member states of the Arab League is Arabic, they will not face the problem experienced in the European countries with respect to translation of the documents and the simultaneous translation of the oral speeches of the parties of the case. As I mentioned previously, the drafters of the potential Arab Human Rights Court should study the European system in order not to repeat the same mistakes, as it would be better to establish an effective Arab system from the beginning.

Proposed articles regarding the Arab Court:

> To consider cases brought before it, the Court shall sit in Chambers of five judges, in a Grand Chamber of thirteen judges and a plenary of all the judges of the Court.
>
> The following are entitled to submit cases to the Court:
>
> - Any High Contracting Party may refer to the Court any alleged breach of the provisions of the Charter and the protocols thereto by another High Contracting Party.
>
> - The Court may receive applications from any person or group of individuals claiming to be the victim of a violation by one of the High Contracting Parties of the rights set forth in the Convention or the protocols thereto provided that they have exhausted all available domestic remedies. The High Contracting Parties undertake not to hinder in any way the effective exercise of this right.
>
> When a State Party has an interest in a case, it may submit a request to the Court to be permitted to join. The Court has full discretionary authority to accept or reject the request.
>
> The Chamber, by a majority of votes, may:
>
> - Declare a case inadmissible or strike it out of its list of cases, where such decision can be taken without further examination; or
>
> - Declare it admissible and render, at the same time, a judgment on the merits, if the underlying question in the case, concerning the interpretation or the application of the Charter or the Protocols thereto, is already the subject of well-established case-law of the Court.

If a solution is not reached, the Chamber shall draw up a Report on the facts and state its opinion as to whether the facts found disclose a breach by the State concerned of its obligations under the Charter. The Report shall be transmitted to the Grand Chamber.

If the appeal is accepted by the panel of five judges or if no decision is taken by the Chamber, the Grand Chamber shall decide on the admissibility and merits of individual applications.

The Grand Chamber shall decide on the admissibility and merits of inter-State applications. The decision on admissibility shall be taken by majority of votes. If the appeal is accepted by the panel of five judges or if no decision is taken by the Grand Chamber, the plenary of the Court shall decide on the admissibility and merits of inter-state applications.

If a judge is a national of any state that is a party to a case submitted to the Court, that judge shall not hear the case. In addition, a judge shall not examine any application against a state party to a case in respect of which that judge has been elected. The Court can invite the concerned judge to give an advisory or explanatory opinion. However, his or her voice should not be counted and he or she should have no right to vote in such a case.

b. *Immunity*

It is important that there be no external influences affecting the judge's decisions. The United Nations Commentary on the Bangalore Principles of Judicial Conduct states:

> It is essential to judicial independence and to maintaining the public's confidence in the justice system that the executive, the legislature and the judge do not create a perception that the judge's decisions could be coloured by such influences. The variety of influences to which a judge may be subjected are infinite. The judge's duty is to apply the law as he or she understands it, on the basis of his or her assessment of the facts, without fear or favour and without regard to whether the final decision is likely to be popular or not.[1536]

1536 U.N. Office on Drugs and Crime, Commentary on the Bangalore Principles of Judicial Conduct, September 2007, at 42 http://www.unodc.org/documents/corruption/publications_unodc_commentary-e.pdf (last visited May 9, 2014)..

The Universal Declaration on the Independence of Justice (Montreal Declaration) provides, "Judges individually shall be free, and it shall be their duty, to decide matters before them impartially, in accordance with their assessment of the facts and their understanding of the law without any restrictions, influences, inducements, pressures, threats or interferences, direct or indirect, from any quarter or for any reason."[1537]

The Fourth Protocol to the General Agreement on Privileges and Immunities of the Council of Europe states the immunities and privileges of judges as follows:

> Immunity from personal arrest or detention and from seizure of their personal baggage, and, in respect of words spoken or written and all acts done by them in their official capacity, immunity from legal process of every kind;

> Exemption in respect of themselves and their spouses as regards any restrictions on their freedom of movement on exit from and return to their country of residence, and entry into and exit from the country in which they exercise their functions; and from aliens' registration in the country which they are visiting or through which they are passing in the exercise of their functions.[1538]

Furthermore, judges are given "by their own government the same facilities as those accorded to senior government officials travelling abroad on temporary official duty."[1539] In addition, other governments of States parties give them "the same facilities as those accorded to heads of diplomatic missions."[1540] Also, judges are given "complete freedom of speech and complete independence in the discharge of their duties, the immunity from legal process in respect of words spoken or written and all acts done by them in discharging their duties shall continue to be accorded, notwithstanding that the persons concerned are no longer engaged in the discharge of such duties."[1541] In order to be effective, the judges of the Arab Court must have immunities and privileges that are no less than the immunities mentioned above. In addition, their salaries should be in the highest category of the salaries of government officials. During their stay in the country

---

1537 Article 2: 02 of the Universal Declaration on the Independence of Justice (Montreal Declaration); see also ABIMBOLA A. OLOWOFOYEKU, SUING JUDGES: A STUDY OF JUDICIAL IMMUNITY, 1 (1993).
1538 European Court of Human Rights, Fourth Protocol to the General Agreement on Privileges and Immunities of the Council of Europe, art. 2 (Dec. 16, 1961).
1539 *Id.* at art. 3(a).
1540 *Id.* at art. 3(b).
1541 *Id.* at art. 5.

that hosts the Court, judges of the Arab Court should be exempt from paying taxes.

Judges of the European Court on Human Rights cannot be dismissed unless it is decided by a two-thirds majority of the other judges that a particular judge has ceased to fulfill the required conditions of the office. The European Convention provides, "No judge may be dismissed from his office unless the other judges decide by a majority of two-thirds that he has ceased to fulfil the required conditions."[1542] I agree entirely with providing immunity and privileges to the judges, in order for them to engage in their work freely and independently. However, this right should be limited to that which is related to exercising their work effectively, efficiently and independently. The Fourth Protocol to the European Convention on Human Rights insists on this, stating:

> Privileges and immunities are accorded to judges not for the personal benefit of the individuals themselves but in order to safeguard the independent exercise of their functions. The Court alone, sitting in plenary session, shall be competent to waive the immunity of judges; it has not only the right, but is under a duty, to waive the immunity of a judge in any case where, in its opinion, the immunity would impede the course of justice, and where it can be waived without prejudice to the purpose for which the immunity is accorded.[1543]

For this reason, the only entity that can waive the immunity of the judges should be the judges of the Court themselves in order to prevent the intervention of a third party in their work. In order to ensure that they are able to work more independently, many of the states parties to the Arab League, including Egypt, not only give immunity to the judges working in their national courts, but also to their prosecutors. This is in compliance with the United Nations Convention against Corruption, as it states,

> "Bearing in mind the independence of the judiciary and its crucial role in combating corruption, each State Party shall, in accordance with the fundamental principles of its legal system and without prejudice to judicial independence, take measures to strengthen integrity and to prevent opportunities for corruption among members of the judiciary…"[1544]

1542 ECHR, *supra* note 497, at art. 24.
1543 ECHR, *supra* note 497, Protocol 4, at art 6.
1544 U.N. Office on Drugs and Crime, United Nations Convention against Corruption, art. 11 (1) (2004).

A protocol establishing an Arab Court of Human Rights should state the same privileges and immunities as outlined in the Fourth Protocol to the General Agreement on Privileges and Immunities of the Council of Europe. Also, it should state the duties of the judges working in the court. This will increase the efficiency and effectiveness of the Court considerably. With the independence and immunities of the judges comes a large degree of responsibility; this responsibility relates to making decisions without hesitation or fear and demonstrating both wisdom and discretion in their statements. The Protocol can include an article similar to Article 21 of the European Court on Human Rights,[1545] which is focused on not discussing the work of the Court with the media.

The protocol adopting the Arab Court should state the major rights that are mentioned by the United Nations, for example, in the Basic Principles on the Independence of the Judiciary that was adopted by the Seventh United Nations Congress on the Prevention of Crime and the Treatment of Offenders, which stated, "The judiciary shall decide matters before them impartially, on the basis of facts and in accordance with the law, without any restrictions, improper influences, inducements, pressures, threats or interferences, direct or indirect, from any quarter or for any reason"[1546] and that "[t]he judiciary shall have jurisdiction over all issues of a judicial nature and shall have exclusive authority to decide whether an issue submitted for its decision is within its competence as defined by law."[1547] Furthermore, the Basic Principles on the Independence of the Judiciary outlined, "There shall not be any inappropriate or unwarranted interference with the judicial process, nor shall judicial decisions by the courts be subject to revision. This principle is without prejudice to judicial review or to mitigation or commutation by competent authorities of sentences imposed by the judiciary, in accordance with the law."[1548]

1545 Article 21 of the European Court of Human Rights states, "1-The judges shall be of high moral character and must either possess the qualifications required for appointment to high judicial office or be jurisconsults of recognised competence. 2- The judges shall sit on the Court in their individual capacity. 3- During their term of office the judges shall not engage in any activity which is incompatible with their independence, impartiality or with the demands of a full-time office; all questions arising from the application of this paragraph shall be decided by the Court."

1546 Article 2 of the Basic Principles on the Independence of the Judiciary, which was adopted by the Seventh United Nations Congress on the Prevention of Crime and the Treatment of Offenders; see http://www2.ohchr.org/english/law/indjudiciary.htm (last visited Feb. 14, 2013).

1547 *Id.* at art. 3.

1548 *Id.* at art. 4.

Proposed articles regarding the judges of the Arab Court:

The judges are elected by the Supreme Judicial Council of each State Party concerned.

The presidents of each Supreme Judicial Council shall sit together to interview all of the judges and exclude the judges that are not suitable for that position.

The judges of the Court shall be elected for a period of five years and may not be re-elected provided, however, that, of the judges elected at the first election, the terms of half of the judges shall expire at the end of three years and the terms of the remaining half shall expire at the end of five years.

The Supreme Judicial Councils can increase the number of judges upon the request of the majority of the presidents of the Supreme Judicial Councils. The plenary of the Arab Court can increase the number of judges upon the request of the majority of judges of the Court.

A judge shall not be suspended or removed from office unless, by the decision of a two-thirds majority of the votes of the other judges of the Court, the concerned judge has been found to be no longer fulfilling the required conditions of the Court.

The Court shall be composed of a body of independent judges who are nationals of the countries members of the League of Arab States, from among persons of high moral character who possess the qualifications required in their respective countries for appointment to the highest judicial offices.

The judges shall sit on the Court in an individual capacity.

The Court shall act impartially, fairly, and justly.

In performance of the judicial functions and duties, the Court and its judges shall not be subject to the direction or control of any person or body.

The judiciary shall decide on matters before them impartially, on the basis of facts and in accordance with the law, without any restrictions, improper influences, inducements, pressures, threats or interferences, direct or indirect, from any quarter or for any reason.

No member of the Court may exercise any political or administrative function or engage in any other occupation of a professional nature.

During their term of office the judges shall not engage in any activity that is incompatible with their independence, impartiality, or the demands of a full-time office; the Court shall decide all questions arising from the application of this article.

The judges of the Court shall enjoy the immunities extended to diplomatic agents in accordance with international law from the moment of their election and throughout their term of office.

At no time shall the judges of the Court be held liable for any decision or opinion issued in the exercise of their functions.

Judges shall be granted immunity from personal arrest or detention and from seizure of their personal baggage and immunity from legal process of every kind in respect to words spoken or written and all acts done by them in their official capacity.

Judges shall have complete freedom of speech and complete independence in the discharge of their duties, immunity from legal process in respect of words spoken or written, and all acts done by them in discharging their duties shall continue to be accorded, notwithstanding that the persons concerned are no longer engaged in the discharge of such duties.

Judges and their spouses shall receive exemption with respect to any restrictions on their freedom of movement in exiting from and returning to their country of residence and entering into and exiting from the country in which they exercise their functions, as well as exemption from aliens' registration in the country they are visiting or through which they are passing in the exercise of their functions.

Judges are given by their own government the same facilities as those accorded to senior government officials travelling abroad on temporary official duty. Privileges and immunities are accorded to judges not for the personal benefit of the individuals themselves, but in order to safeguard the independent exercise of their functions. The Court alone, sitting in plenary session, shall be competent to waive the immunity of judges; it has not only the right, but is under a duty to waive the immunity of a judge in any case where, in its opinion, the immunity would impede the course of justice and where it can be waived without prejudice to the purpose for which the immunity is accorded.

The independence of the judges shall be fully ensured in accordance with international law.

c. President and Vice-President of the Court

The Arab Charter must have an effective judicial Court in order to truly protect the human rights of people in the Arab world. In the case of the European Court, "The plenary Court shall elect its President, two Vice-Presidents ... The elections referred to in this Rule shall be by secret ballot."[1549] The winning judge is the one who achieves an absolute majority of votes.[1550] In order to promote the effectiveness of the Arab Court, the President should refrain from being involved in any case related to the country of his of her nationality or that of the country that elected him or her to the Court.

Proposed articles regarding the President of the Court and the two Vice-Presidents of the Arab Court:

> The Court shall elect its President and two Vice-Presidents for a period of three years. They cannot be re-elected.

> The President of the Court and the two Vice-Presidents of the Court shall be elected by the plenary of the Court. The election is conducted by secret ballot. The winning seat is given to the judge by who received the absolute majority of votes.

> The functions of the President and the Vice-Presidents shall be set out in the Rules of Procedure of the Court.

> If the President of the Court or the two Vice-Presidents of the Court are a national of any state that is a party to a case submitted to the Court, that judge shall not hear that particular case.

3. The Registry

The European Court has a registry,[1551] which includes approximately 540 clerical employees from the member states including administrators, translators and lawyers.[1552] The Secretary General of the Council of Europe appoints the members of the registry.[1553]

1549 European Court of Human Rights, Rules of the Court at Rule 8, http://www.echr.coe.int/NR/rdonlyres/D1EB31A8-4194-436E-987E-65AC8864BE4F/0/RulesOfCourt.pdf (last visited May 15, 2012).
1550 *Id.*
1551 E.C. at art. 25.
1552 JACOBS & WHITE, *supra* note 566, at 475.
1553 Rule 18(3) of the Rules of procedure. http://www.echr.coe.int/NR/rdonlyres/6AC1A02E-9A3C-4E06-94EF-E0BD377731DA/0/REGLEMENT_EN_2012.pdf (last visited Feb. 14, 2013).

According to the Rules of Procedure, "The Registry shall consist of Section Registries equal to the number of Sections set up by the Court and of the departments necessary to provide the legal and administrative services required by the Court."[1554] The duties of the registry are very important. The Rules of Procedure of the Court state:

> The Registrar shall assist the Court in the performance of its functions and shall be responsible for the organisation and activities of the Registry under the authority of the President of the Court ... have the custody of the archives of the Court and shall be the channel for all communications and notifications made by, or addressed to, the Court in connection with the cases brought or to be brought before it ... reply to requests for information concerning the work of the Court, in particular to enquiries from the press...[1555]

In addition, the registry plays a vital role as it provides the Court with answers regarding any questions of national law. Furthermore, the registry assists in drafting judgments and decisions. In short, the registry helps in improving the effectiveness of the Court.[1556]

The existing Arab Committee appointed experts in the field of human rights to help the members of the Committee analyze and examine the states parties' reports. The Committee made a newspaper advertisement requesting human rights experts to apply for positions of Technical Secretariat at the Arab Committee. The Committee requested experts in the field of human rights who had no less than ten years experience. This is a good step forward. The potential Arab Court must become effective not only by having independent judges, but also by having an outstanding staff of registry.

The Arab Court of Human Rights should take great care when choosing the registry. The registry in the Arab Court should have an even greater role than the registry of the European Court. In addition to the duties mentioned above from Article 286 of the Rules of Procedure, there should be more duties for the registry in the Arab Court. The members of the registry should be geographically distributed, taking into account the number of cases of each country and its population. Furthermore, the members should have great deal of experience with regard to national laws and national courts procedures and a high level of knowledge of international human rights laws, especially the work of other regional courts.

1554 *Id.* at Rule 18 (1).
1555 *Id.* at Rule 17.
1556 JACOBS & WHITE, *supra* note 566, at 475.

The international and regional human rights bodies, including courts, are dealing with very similar rights that are mentioned in the Arab Charter of Human Rights. Therefore, speaking and reading English or French fluently would be an important asset for at least some of the members of the registry. It is important that the registry provide assistance to the judges by giving advice regarding the latest decisions taken by international and other regional courts. This will help ensure that the judges will be up to date with respect to decisions taken by all the courts, including European Court. This up-to-date knowledge will help ensure that the court is a living instrument and will also help ensure that the judges to know how other regional courts are dealing with cases. Furthermore, some of the registry must have graduated from Al-Azhar Law School, which will be necessary in order to ensure the presence of some professional lawyers who can use Sharia law as a standard for interpretation of human rights. Furthermore, these lawyers will be able to evaluate the articles of the Arab Charter from the point of view of Sharia law. In addition, they can help judges by expanding the interpretation of the human rights articles through the inclusion of the perspective of Sharia law.

Some of the members of the registry and the deputy registry should be judges or prosecutors. However, they should be highly qualified not only with respect to professional experience, but also regarding their knowledge of other international and regional courts. It would be best if these members have both academic and professional experience at one of the regional or international courts. In addition, they should be able to speak, write, and read English and/or French fluently.

The translation department is one of the most important departments within the Arab Court of Human Rights. This department is necessary as it will be the vital link between the Arab Court and other international and regional courts. One of the main duties of this department will be assisting in translating and summarizing cases and court decisions from other regional courts and international courts. For instance, when dealing with a case concerning the violation of certain rights, the Arab Court can request the help of the translation department in locating a case from a different court concerning the same right. This will help the judges be informed about how other courts are examining the violation of this right. Therefore, this may lead to an increased development of the skills and experience of the judges. All these advantages will definitely facilitate the work of the Arab Court.

Proposed articles regarding the Registry of the Arab Court:

> The Court shall appoint its own Registrar and the other members of staff of the registry from among nationals of member Arab states according to the Rules of Procedure.
>
> The office and residence of the Registrar shall be situated at the location where the Court has its seat.
>
> The Registrar shall assist the Court in the performance of its functions and shall be responsible for the following:
> - The organization and activities of the Registry under the authority of the President of the Court.
> - The custody of the archives of the Court and for acting as the channel for all communications and notifications made by, or addressed to, the Court in connection with the cases brought, or to be brought, before it.
> - Providing the Court with answers regarding any questions of national law.
> - Assisting the judges by providing advice regarding the latest decisions taken by international and other regional courts.
>
> The members of the Registry should be geographically distributed taking into account the number of cases of each country and its population.
>
> The members of the Registry should have a high degree of experience with regard to national laws and national courts procedures as well as knowledge of international human rights laws.
>
> The members of the Registry should be able to speak, write, and read fluently in English and/or French.
>
> Some of the members of the registry and the deputy registry should be judges and/or prosecutors.
>
> The functions and organization of the registry shall be laid down in the rules of the Court.

4. Public Nature of the Proceedings

The proceedings of the European Court are public. However, the Rules of Procedure of the Court state, "The press and the public may be excluded from all or part of a hearing in the interests of morals, public order or national security in a democratic society, where the interests of juveniles or the protection of the private life of the parties so require, or to the extent strictly necessary in the opinion of the Chamber in special circumstances where publicity would prejudice the interests of justice."[1557] European Court documents are generally accessible, but access may be restricted in exceptional cases. The Rules of Procedure state:

> All documents deposited with the Registry by the parties or by any third party in connection with an application, except those deposited within the framework of friendly settlement negotiations as provided for in Rule 62, shall be accessible to the public in accordance with arrangements determined by the Registrar, unless the President of the Chamber, for the reasons set out in paragraph 2 of this Rule, decides otherwise, either of his or her own motion or at the request of a party or any other person concerned. Public access to a document or to any part of it may be restricted in the interests of morals, public order or national security in a democratic society, where the interests of juveniles or the protection of the private life of the parties or of any person concerned so require, or to the extent strictly necessary in the opinion of the President of the Chamber in special circumstances where publicity would prejudice the interests of justice.[1558]

In order to promote the Arab Court, the nature of the proceeding (hearing and documents) in the Arab Court and Commission should be also of public nature. Only in very exceptional cases should public access be restricted. However, the reasons for such restriction should be stated in law, exactly as is done in the European system.

Proposed articles regarding the public nature of proceedings before the Arab Court:

> The Court shall conduct its proceedings in public. The press and the public may be excluded from all or part of a hearing in the interests of morals, public order, or national security in a democratic society, where the interests of juveniles or the protection of the private life of the parties so require, or to the extent strictly necessary in the opinion of the judges in special circumstances where publicity would prejudice the interests of justice.

1557 Rule 63 (2) of the Rules of the Court.
1558 Rule 33 (1) and (2) of the Rules of Procedure.

Public access to a document or to any part of it may be restricted in the interests of morals, public order, or national security in a democratic society, where the interests of juveniles or the protection of the private life of the parties or of any person concerned so require, or to the extent strictly necessary in the opinion of the judges in special circumstances where publicity would prejudice the interests of justice.

5. Admissibility

a. Who Can be Considered a Victim?

It is important to differentiate between inter-state applications and individual. In the individual applications, the person submitting the complaint must be victim of a specified violation. The European Convention explains, "The Court may receive applications from any person, non-governmental organisation or group of individuals claiming to be the victim of a violation by one of the High Contracting Parties of the rights set forth in the Convention or the protocols thereto."[1559] On the other hand, in the inter-state application, any state can submit a complaint, even if the state is not a victim. The European Convention provides, "Any High Contracting Party may refer to the Court any alleged breach of the provisions of the Convention and the protocols thereto by another High Contracting Party."[1560] For instance, an individual from Austria submitted a complaint against the abortion legislation of Austria, stating that it violates Articles 2 and 8 of the Convention. His application was not accepted. The Commission stated that it "was not competent to examine in *abstracto* its [the disputed legislation's] compatibility with the Convention."[1561]

Many steps must be taken to ensure the development of supervisory mechanisms for the Arab Charter. For example, the Arab Court should give the right to any State party to lodge an application against another State party with regard to any violation of any of the articles of the Convention. The purpose of the Arab Charter is not only to criminalize, but also to prevent violations. Therefore, it is important to accept cases from states against other states. The Arab Committee, which is stated in the Arab Charter and in my proposed protocol one, should be given the right to accept complaints against a another member state's law that on its face violates human rights, not only against a state's individual act that concretely violated the rights of a person. On the other hand, the Arab Court should give

---

1559 ECHR, *supra* note 497, at art. 34.
1560 *Id.* at art. 33.
1561 X vs. Austria, Appl. 7045/75, D & R 7 (1977), P. 87 (88); *see also* THEORY AND PRACTICE OF THE EUROPEAN CONVENTION ON HUMAN RIGHTS, *supra* note 1526, at 59.

individuals the right to submit an application before the Court only if they claim to be victims of a concrete state action, since submission by individuals of applications that are of abstract character will increase the workload of the Court intolerably.

Proposed articles regarding the Arab Court:

> Any High Contracting Party may refer to the Court any alleged breach of the provisions of the Charter and the protocols thereto by another High Contracting Party.

> The Court may receive applications from any person or group of individuals claiming to be the victim of a violation by one of the High Contracting Parties of the rights set forth in the Convention or the protocols thereto provided that they have exhausted all available domestic remedies. The High Contracting Parties undertake not to hinder in any way the effective exercise of this right.

> The Court has the discretionary authority after holding a case to be inadmissible to transfer it to the Committee to consider the case as a shadow report.

b. Exhaustion of Domestic Remedies

The European Court on Human Rights is a last resort for the protection of human rights. In this way, the first and the main judicial bodies implementing and enforcing human rights are the national domestic courts.[1562] One of the main reasons behind the need to ensure that all domestic remedies are exhausted before moving to the European Court is to safeguard the domestic legal order of each State party.[1563] Article 35 (1) of the European Convention states, "The Court may only deal with the matter after all domestic remedies have been exhausted, according to the generally recognised rules of international law, and within a period of six months from the date on which the final decision was taken."[1564] In *Akdivar and others vs. Turkey* the court explained the rule of exhaustion of domestic remedies by stating:

> The rule of exhaustion of domestic remedies referred to in Article 26 obliges those seeking to bring their case against the State before an international judicial or arbitral organ to use first the remedies provided

---

1562 REID, *supra* note 817, at 29.
1563 LOUIS B. SOHN AND THOMAS BUERGENTHAL, INTERNATIONAL PROTECTION OF HUMAN RIGHTS 1109 (1973).
1564 ECHR, *supra* note 497, at art. 35 (1).

by the national legal system. Consequently, States are dispensed from answering for their acts before an international body before they have had an opportunity to put matters right through their own legal system. The rule is based on the assumption, reflected in Article 13 of the Convention – with which it has close affinity – that there is an effective remedy available in respect of the alleged breach in the domestic system whether or not the provisions of the Convention are incorporated in national law. In this way, it is an important aspect of the principle that the machinery of protection established by the Convention is subsidiary to the national systems safeguarding human rights.[1565]

The Court also stressed that the domestic remedy should be available in practice, not only in theory.

As such, the State party concerned should prove the existence of domestic remedies in theory and in practice; thereafter, the burden of proof shifts to the applicant. The applicant must either prove the exhaustion of all domestic remedies or that domestic remedies are not effective and do not exist in theory and in practice.[1566] In *Akdivar and others vs. Turkey*, the Court stated:

> The existence of the remedies in question must be sufficiently certain not only in theory but in practice, failing which they will lack the requisite accessibility and effectiveness. Article 26 also requires that the complaints intended to be made subsequently at Strasbourg should have been made to the appropriate domestic body, at least in substance and in compliance with the formal requirements and time-limits laid down in domestic law and, further, that any procedural means that might prevent a breach of the Convention should have been used.[1567]

The Court added:

> There is a distribution of the burden of proof. It is incumbent on the Government claiming non-exhaustion to satisfy the Court that the remedy was an effective one available in theory and in practice at the relevant time, that is to say, that it was accessible, was one which was capable of providing redress in respect of the applicant's complaints and offered reasonable prospects of success. However, once this burden has been satisfied it falls to the applicant to establish that the remedy advanced

---

1565 Akdivar vs. Turkey, App. No. 21893/93, Judgment of 16 September 1996, (1997) 23 E.H.R.R. 143.
1566 REID, *supra* note 817, at 29.
1567 Akdivar vs. Turkey, *supra* note 1565.

by the Government was in fact exhausted or was for some reason inadequate and ineffective in the particular circumstances of the case, or that there existed special circumstances absolving him or her from the requirement.[1568]

Furthermore, the Court stated, "The domestic remedies will be considered unexhausted if the applicant failed to comply with the domestic formal regulations, requirements, and time limits. The applicant must raise before the domestic courts the complaints that he wants to raise before the European Court."[1569] The European Court will consider the complaints inadmissible if identical complaints were already raised before the domestic courts. However, if the complaints are inadequate or ineffective, the applicant has the right not to exhaust domestic remedies and directly raise the complaints before the European Court.[1570] In other words, if the State party concerned is not willing or unable to protect the applicant rights, therefore, the applicant can go directly to the European Court. The domestic remedies required to be exhausted must be stated in the law. If the remedies are exceptional or discretionary, the applicant has the right to go directly to the European Court without a need to go first to the domestic courts.[1571] Jacobs and White explain:

> The domestic remedies rule applies also to inter-state applications which are confined with to particular individual. In this case, all the domestic remedies have to be exhausted. On the other hand, the rule of domestic remedies is not applicable if the application is to determine the compatibility with the convention of legislative measures and administrative practice in general. However, it is not sufficient to claim the existence of such legislative or administrative measures; their existence must be shown by substantial evidence.[1572]

For instance, in *Ireland vs. United Kingdom*,[1573] "the Irish Government complained concerning the treatment of persons in custody in North Ireland. The Court rejected the complaint because there was no sufficient evidence of this practice."[1574]

1568 *Id.*
1569 JACOBS & WHITE, *supra* note 566, at 486.
1570 *Id.* at 486.
1571 *Id.*
1572 *Id.*
1573 Ireland vs. United Kingdom, (App. 5310/71) Judgment October 1, 1972.
1574 JACOBS & WHITE, *supra* note 566, at 486.

The Additional Protocol that will establish the Arab Court on Human Rights should apply the same rule that is applied by the European Court of Human Rights regarding the exhaustion of domestic remedies. The Arab Court on Human Rights should be subsidiary. People should go to the Arab Court only after exhausting all of the remedies at the national level. At the national level individuals should comply with the regulations and time limitations used at the domestic level. If they fail to comply with the domestic regulations then the case should be considered inadmissible before the Arab Court. The burden of proof of the existence of effective remedies, in theory and practice, is on the government. After this has been established, the burden to proof should shift to the applicant, who must demonstrate that domestic remedies were exhausted. However, there is no need to exhaust the domestic remedies if they are not accessible, effective, or adequate.

Proposed articles regarding the Arab Court:

> The Court may receive applications from any person or group of individuals claiming to be the victim of a violation by one of the High Contracting Parties of the rights set forth in the Convention or the protocols thereto provided that they have exhausted all available domestic remedies within a period of four months from the date on which the final decision was taken. The High Contracting Parties undertake not to hinder in any way the effective exercise of this right.

c. *Sixth Month Limitation*

The European Convention imposed a specified limitation as to the point in time by which cases must be submitted. Article 35 (1) states, "The Court may only deal with the matter .... within a period of six months from the date on which the final decision was taken."[1575] In light of this rule, the Court will declare all cases inadmissible unless they are submitted to the Court within a period of six months from the date on which the final decision was taken. In other words, cases must be submitted before the completion of six months.

On the other hand, if there is no domestic remedy, the sixth months start from the date on which the act of human rights violation occurred.

> The sixth months start running from the day after the applicant became aware of the act or decision of which he/she complains. If there is no domestic remedy available, the sixth month start running from the date

---

1575 ECHR, *supra* note 470, at art. 35 (1).

of the act alleged to constitute the violation of the convention. The applicant cannot reopen the period by, for example, applying for a retrial. However, the time is running as long as the complain concern a continuing situation. The sixth months start running only after the end situation concerned.[1576]

Furthermore, "The rule of sixth month cannot be waived by the Court or by the respondent government. It is strictly applied by the Court. Even if the respondent government does not raise it, the Court has to apply it by its own motion."[1577]

When adopting a protocol on the Arab Court of Human Rights, the time limit procedure of the European Court should be followed. Such a time limit must be in place in order to promote human rights through the Arab Charter, as this will help ensure that the judges reach the right decisions easily before the evidence diminishes. However, the time limit should be shorter than sixth months. Four months or an even shorter period of time may be sufficient because, as I mentioned before, this court is subsidiary to the national court. Therefore, in order to assure the certainty and finality of the national courts, it is better to have a shorter time limit.

Proposed articles regarding the Arab Court:

> The Court may receive applications from any person or group of individuals claiming to be the victim of a violation by one of the High Contracting Parties of the rights set forth in the Convention or the protocols thereto provided that they have exhausted all available domestic remedies within a period of four months from the date on which the final decision was taken. The High Contracting Parties undertake not to hinder in any way the effective exercise of this right.

6. Handling of the Case After Registering the Application

According to the rules of procedure of the European Court on Human Rights:

> If the judge elected in respect of the Contracting Party concerned is not a member of the Committee, the Committee may at any stage of the proceedings before it, by a unanimous vote, invite that judge to take the place of one of its members, having regard to all relevant factors,

---

1576 REID, *supra* note 817, at 25.
1577 REID, *supra* note 817, at 25 (citing *Walker vs. United Kingdom* (App. 34979/97), Judgment of January 25, 2000, in which the Court dismissed the complaint even though the country did not make any objection regarding the six months limit).

including whether that Party has contested the application of the procedure under Article 28 § 1 (b) of the Convention.[1578]

In order to ensure its effectiveness, the Arab Court should not invite the judge who represents a state party in the case or is a national of that country. If the judge is invited his or her voice should not be counted. In addition, if the judge is already in the Chamber that examines the case, he or she should be replaced by another judge. In other words, the opinion of the judge should be no more than an advisory or explanatory opinion by giving explanation or presentation about the legal system of his country and an overview of his opinion orally under conditions to be set out in the Rules of Procedure. In addition, the judge should not be permitted to deliver a separate or dissenting opinion.

If the European Committee did not make a decision in a case, the case is to be forwarded to the Chamber.[1579] The Chamber can "declare the application inadmissible or strike it out of the Court's list of cases."[1580] On the other hand, the Chamber can request from the parties of the case to submit further information or documents, etc.[1581] In addition, if the case is admissible and no friendly settlement is reached, the Chamber has the right to adopt a judgment in the case.[1582] In this way, "The decision of the Chamber shall state whether it was taken unanimously or by a majority and shall be accompanied or followed by reasons."[1583] On the other hand, in Inter-State applications, the case goes directly to the Chamber, not the Committee. The judge rapporteur shall prepare and submit a report on the admissibility. According to the Rules of Procedure, "… the Chamber constituted to consider the case shall designate one or more of its judges as Judge Rapporteur(s), who shall submit a report on admissibility when the written observations of the Contracting Parties concerned have been received."[1584]

In the case of both the inter-state and individual complaints, the Chamber has the right to request any further documents, information, or other material from state concerned or the applicant.[1585] The Chamber may also "give notice of the application to the respondent Contracting Party and invite that Party to submit written observations on the application and, upon receipt thereof, invite the applicant

---

1578 Rule 53 (3) of the Rules of procedure of the Court.
1579 *Id.* at rule 53(6).
1580 *Id.* at rule 54(1).
1581 *Id.* at rule 54(2).
1582 *Id.* at rule 54A(2).
1583 *Id.* at rule 56(1).
1584 *Id.* at rule 48(1).
1585 *Id.* at rule 54(2)(a).

to submit observations in reply."[1586] Furthermore, the Chamber may "invite the parties to submit further observations in writing."[1587] This invitation happens after the judge rapporteur finishes examining the case and submits the report on its admissibility. The Chamber can decide to hold a hearing, as the Rules of Procedure of the Court provides that "the Chamber may decide, either at the request of a party or of its own motion, to hold a hearing if it considers that the discharge of its functions under the Convention so requires. In that event, unless the Chamber shall exceptionally decide otherwise, the parties shall also be invited to address the issues arising in relation to the merits of the application."[1588]

Cases can be relinquished to the Grand Chamber. The European Convention provides:

> Where a case pending before a Chamber raises a serious question affecting the interpretation of the Convention or the protocols thereto, or where the resolution of a question before the Chamber might have a result inconsistent with a judgment previously delivered by the Court, the Chamber may, at any time before it has rendered its judgment, relinquish jurisdiction in favour of the Grand Chamber, unless one of the parties to the case objects.[1589]

The right to relinquish a case is not absolute; rather, it depends on the discretionary authority of the Court. The right to relinquish a case is on condition that none of the parties to the case submit reasoned objections. The European Convention on Human Rights states, "The Registrar shall notify the parties of the Chamber's intention to relinquish jurisdiction. The parties shall have one month from the date of that notification within which to file at the Registry a duly reasoned objection. An objection which does not fulfil these conditions shall be considered invalid by the Chamber."[1590] In exceptional cases, any party to the case can request the referral of a case to the Grand Chamber within a period of three month from the date of rendering the decision of the Court if the case raises either a serious question affecting the interpretation or application of the Convention or the protocols thereto or a serious issue of general importance. A panel

---

1586 *Id.* at rule 54(2)(b).
1587 *Id.* at rule 54(2)(c).
1588 *Id.* at rules 54(3) and 54(A).
1589 ECHR, *supra* note 497, at art. 30.
1590 Rule 72 (2) of the Rules of procedure of the Court.

of five judges will examine the request and if the conditions are fulfilled, the Grand Chamber will examine the case by means of a judgment.[1591]

The Arab Court can choose between any of the best practices outlined above with respect to ways to improve the Court under conditions to be set out in the Rules of Procedure. For instance, the structure of the Arab Court should include Chamber, Grand Chamber and Plenary. The Arab Court shall sit in five Chambers. Each Chamber should be composed of five judges and two substitute judges. There should be an equal distribution of judges, i.e. each Chamber should include a judge from North Africa, Gulf countries, etc. In addition, different legal systems should be represented in each Chamber. The Grand Chamber should be composed of thirteen judges and one substitute judge.

As I explained before, a judge shall not examine any application against a state party to a case in respect of which that judge has been elected or is a national of that country. However, the Court can invite the concerned judge to give advisory or explanatory opinion. However, his or her voice should not be counted and should have no right to vote in such a case and is not permitted to deliver a separate or dissenting opinion.

The Grand Chamber shall include the President and the Vice-Presidents of the Court and the Presidents of the Sections. Any Vice-President of the Court or President of a Section who is unable to sit as a member of the Grand Chamber shall be replaced by the Vice-President of the relevant Section. The judges and substitute judges who are to complete the Grand Chamber in each case referred to it shall be designated from among the remaining judges by a drawing of lots. The modalities for the drawing of lots shall be laid down by the Plenary Court, having due regard to the need for a geographically balanced composition reflecting the different legal systems among the Contracting Parties. In case of appeal, the Grand Chamber shall not include any judge who sat in the Chamber which rendered the judgment in the case so referred.

Chamber of the Arab Court can render a decision in individual cases by majority of votes, if the underlying question in the case, concerning the interpretation or the application of the Charter or the Protocols thereto, is already the subject of well-established case-law of the Court. However, it always has the right to refer the case to the Grand Chamber. On the other hand, inter-state applications go directly to the Grand Chamber. There should be no process of appeal in the Arab Court. The decision of the Arab Court should be final. However, the right of appeal or withdrawal of the Court's decision can be done in very rare cases during

---

1591 ECHR, *supra* note 497, at art. 43.

which the Grand Chamber of the Court may review the Court's decision in light of new evidence under conditions to be set out in the Rules of Procedure and/or if the decision of the Court was violating the human rights principles protected by the Arab Charter and its protocols. In addition, the judgment of the Chamber of the Arab Court shall be final. However, in very rare cases it can be subject to appeal if the Chamber rendered a judgment on the merits, but the underlying question in the case, concerning the interpretation or the application of the Charter or the Protocols thereto, is not already the subject of well-established case-law of the Court. A panel of five judges of the Grand Chamber shall decide if the case raises a serious question affecting the interpretation or application of the Convention or the Protocols thereto, or a serious issue of general importance. If the appeal is accepted by the panel of five judges or if no decision is taken by the Chamber, the Grand Chamber shall decide on the admissibility and merits of individual applications. In addition, the Grand Chamber shall decide on the admissibility and merits of individual applications if the underlying question in the case, concerning the interpretation or the application of the Charter or the Protocols thereto, is not the subject of well-established case-law of the Court. Furthermore, the Grand Chamber shall decide on the admissibility and merits of inter-state applications. The decision on admissibility shall be taken by majority of votes.

The Chamber and the Grand Chamber should apply the friendly settlement on the basis of respect for human rights. If a friendly settlement is effected, the Court shall strike the case out of its list by means of a decision which shall be confined to a brief statement of the facts and of the solution reached.

The Arab Court may at any stage of the proceedings decide to strike an application out of its list of cases under conditions to be set out in the Rules of Procedure. For instance, where the circumstances of the case lead to the conclusion that the applicant does not intend to pursue his application; or the matter has been resolved; or for any other reason established by the Court, it is no longer justified to continue the examination of the application.

Finally, the plenary of the all the judges of the Court should be given the right to elect the President and one or two Vice-Presidents of the Court. In addition, it shall set up Chambers, and Grand Chamber of the Court. Also, the plenary adopts the Rules of the Court. The plenary may, at the request of the Arab League or any country member to the Arab League, give advisory opinions on legal questions concerning the interpretation of the Convention and the Protocols thereto. In addition, the plenary of the Court shall decide on the admissibility and merits of inter-state applications. As I mentioned before, the judgment of the Grand Chamber is final. However, if the appeal is accepted by the panel of five judges or if no decision is taken by the Grand Chamber, the plenary of the Court shall decide on the admissibility and merits. Finally, the plenary of the Arab Court can increase the number of judges upon the request of the majority of judges of the Court.

Proposed articles regarding the Arab Court:

A Chamber, by a majority of votes, may:

- Declare a case inadmissible or strike it out of its list of cases, where such decision can be taken without further examination; or
- Declare it admissible and render, at the same time, a judgment on the merits, if the underlying question in the case, concerning the interpretation or the application of the Charter or the Protocols thereto, is already the subject of well-established case-law of the Court.

The judgment of the Court decided by majority shall be final and not subject to appeal.

Without prejudice to the previous point, in very rare cases, the judgment of the Chamber can be subject to appeal by the Grand Chamber. In addition, the judgment of the Grand Chamber can be subject to appeal by the plenary. A panel of five judges of the Grand Chamber of the Court may review the Chamber's and the Grand Chamber's decisions, upon the request of the parties or by unilateral decision of the Court, in the light of new evidence under conditions to be set out in the Rules of Procedure and/or if the decision of the Court was violating the human rights principles protected by the Arab Charter and its protocols and/or if the case raises a serious question affecting the interpretation or application of the Convention or the Protocols thereto, or a serious issue of general importance.

If a solution is not reached, the Chamber shall draw up a report on the facts and state its opinion as to whether the facts found disclose a breach by the state concerned of its obligations under the Charter. The Report shall be transmitted to the Grand Chamber.

If the appeal is accepted by the panel of five judges or if no decision is taken by the Chamber, the Grand Chamber shall decide on the admissibility and merits of individual applications. If the appeal is accepted by the panel of five judges or if no decision is taken by the Grand Chamber, the plenary of the Court shall decide on the admissibility and merits.

The Grand Chamber shall decide on the admissibility and merits of inter-state applications. The decision on admissibility shall be taken by majority of votes. If the appeal is accepted by the panel of five judges or if no decision is taken by the Grand Chamber, the plenary of the Court shall decide on the admissibility and merits of inter-state applications.

If a judge is a national of any state that is a party to a case submitted to the Court, that judge shall not hear the case. In addition, a judge shall not examine any application against a state party to a case in respect of which that judge has been elected. The Court can invite the concerned judge to give advisory or explanatory opinion. However, his or her voice should not be counted and should have no right to vote in such a case.

The Court may interpret its own decision unilaterally or upon the request of the State party concerned or the request of the Arab Committee. For instance, the state party concerned can request further clarification from the court on how to implement the court's decisions.

The plenary of all the judges of the Court should be given the right to elect the President and one or two Vice-Presidents of the Court. In addition, it shall set up Chambers, and the Grand Chamber of the Court. Furthermore, the plenary shall adopt the Rules of the Court. The plenary may, at the request of the Arab League or any country member to the Arab League, give advisory opinions on legal questions concerning the interpretation of the Charter and the Protocols thereto. The plenary of the Arab Court can increase the number of judges upon the request of the majority of judges of the Court. In addition, the plenary of the Court shall decide on the admissibility and merits of inter-state applications. The judgment of the Grand Chamber is final. However, if the appeal is accepted by the panel of five judges or if no decision is taken by the Grand Chamber, the plenary of the Court shall decide on the admissibility and merits. Finally, the plenary of the Arab Court can increase the number of judges upon the request of the majority of judges of the Court.

The Arab Court may at any stage of the proceedings decide to strike an application out of its list of cases under conditions to be set out in the Rules of Procedure.

The Chamber and the Grand Chamber should apply the procedure of friendly settlement on the basis of respect for human rights.

7. Judgment

Regarding the judgment, the European Convention provides:

    1. The judgment of the Grand Chamber shall be final.

    2.. The judgment of a Chamber shall become final

    (a) when the parties declare that they will not request that the case be referred to the Grand Chamber; or

    (b) three months after the date of the judgment, if reference of the case to the Grand Chamber has not been requested; or

    (c) when the panel of the Grand Chamber rejects the request to refer under Article 43.

    3. The final judgment shall be published.[1592]

There is an important point mentioned by the European Convention, which is that "[i]f a judgment does not represent, in whole or in part, the unanimous opinion of the judges, any judge shall be entitled to deliver a separate opinion."[1593] To ensure the effectiveness of the Arab Court, the Court and the judges must not let the judges deliver separate opinions if the judgment did not reach a unanimous decision. As previously mentioned, each judge in the Court was chosen from a list of three candidates nominated by the High Contracting Party. Therefore, any Contracting Party may use its soft power on the judge that was elected by the country. In other words, a judge may render a decision that is welcomed by his own government in order to encourage the government to re-elect him. Even if the country that elected the judge is not a party to the case, this country may still have an interest in that case. In short, judges will not be working freely in an independent environment.

In order for the Arab Court to be more independent, it should not follow the approach taken by the European Court. Judges of the Arab Court should deliver a judgment by the majority of votes. The judge who does not agree on the judgment should not write any separate opinion. Even the judgment of the Court should not mention that there is one or more judges who disagree with the majority of votes. According to my knowledge, states parties to the Arab League do not currently allow separate opinions in their domestic courts. Therefore, they are not even familiar with this procedure.

1592 *Id.* at art. 44.
1593 *Id.* at art. 45(2).

Proposed articles regarding the Arab Court:

If the judgment of the Court does not represent, in whole or in part, the unanimous decision of the judges, no judge is permitted to deliver a separate or dissenting opinion.

8. Enforceability – Comparison with the European Court of Human Rights

a. *Remedies Under Article 41*

Jacobs and White have stated, "In general, the contracting States have discretionary authority to choose the means by which they can comply with a judgment in which a court has found a breach."[1594] Also, Article 1 of the European Convention provides, "The high Contracting Parties shall secure to everyone within their jurisdiction the rights and freedoms defined in Section I of this Convention."[1595] On the other hand, if the domestic national law either does not allow any remedies or allows for only partial reparation of the damages, the European Court on Human Rights is given the right to afford the victim just satisfaction. Article 41 of the European Convention provides, "If the Court finds that there has been a violation of the Convention or the protocols thereto, and if the internal law of the High Contracting Party concerned allows only partial reparation to be made, the Court shall, if necessary, afford just satisfaction to the injured party."[1596] Article 41 is criticized because it does not specifically explain the damages that should be awarded in more detail, nor does it explain when and how these damages should be measured.[1597] Jacobs and White further stated, "Awards of financial satisfaction can be made under three heads: pecuniary loss, non pecuniary loss, and costs and expenses. The most frequent award of just satisfaction beyond the declaration of violation is the award of costs and expenses incurred in the case, either in the domestic proceedings or in Strasbourg."[1598]

In order to promote the human rights in the Arab Charter, the Arab Court affords each country the right to find the best means of complying with judgment of the Court. The Arab Charter provides, "Each State party to the present Charter undertakes to ensure to all individuals subject to its jurisdiction the right to enjoy the rights and freedoms set forth herein, without distinction on grounds of race, colour, sex, language, religious belief, opinion, thought, national or social origin,

---

1594 JACOBS & WHITE, *supra* note 566, at 491.
1595 ECHR, *supra* note 497, at art.1.
1596 *Id.* at art. 41.
1597 JACOBS & WHITE, *supra* note 566, at 491.
1598 *Id.* at 492.

wealth, birth or physical or mental disability."[1599] The potential Arab Court should have the right to give reparation as stated in Article 41 of the European Court. Then, after the Arab Charter gains more popularity and both Arab governments and Arab nation gain confidence in the Charter, the protocol can be amended to state the damages to be awarded in more detail, as well as the timing and their valuation.

Proposed articles regarding the Arab Court:

> If the Court finds that there has been a violation of the Charter or the protocols thereto, and if the internal law of the High Contracting Party concerned allows only partial reparation to be made, the Court shall, if necessary, afford just satisfaction to the injured party.

> The court's judgment varies from paying damages to the victim to amending domestic law that constitutes a violation to the human rights protected by the Charter.

> In cases of extreme gravity and urgency, and when necessary to avoid irreparable harm to persons, the Court shall adopt such provisional measures as it deems necessary.

b.   Committee of Ministers

The decisions of the European Court on Human Rights are final.[1600] The Committee of Ministers guarantees the implementation of the decisions of the Court. The success of the European Court is based the implementation of the Court's decisions. The European Convention provides:

> The High Contracting Parties undertake to abide by the final judgment of the Court in any case to which they are parties. The final judgment of the Court shall be transmitted to the Committee of Ministers, which shall supervise its execution. If the Committee of Ministers considers that the supervision of the execution of a final judgment is hindered by a problem of interpretation of the judgment, it may refer the matter to the Court for a ruling on the question of interpretation. A referral decision shall require a majority vote of two thirds of the representatives entitled to sit on the Committee. If the Committee of Ministers considers that a High Contracting Party refuses to abide by a final judgment in a case to which it is a party, it may, after serving formal notice on that

---

1599 ACHR, *supra* note 126, at art. 3 (1).
1600 ECHR, *supra* note 497, at art. 44.

Party and by decision adopted by a majority vote of two thirds of the representatives entitled to sit on the Committee, refer to the Court the question whether that Party has failed to fulfil its obligation under paragraph 1. If the Court finds a violation of paragraph 1, it shall refer the case to the Committee of Ministers for consideration of the measures to be taken. If the Court finds no violation of paragraph 1, it shall refer the case to the Committee of Ministers, which shall close its examination of the case.[1601]

The Committee of Ministers is not set up by the European Convention. The Council of Europe is the body that established the Committee of Ministers. The Statute of the Council of Europe provides:

Each member shall be entitled to one representative on the Committee of Ministers, and each representative shall be entitled to one vote. Representatives on the Committee shall be the Ministers for Foreign Affairs. When a Minister for Foreign Affairs is unable to be present or in other circumstances where it may be desirable, an alternate may be nominated to act for him, who shall, whenever possible, be a member of his government.[1602]

Furthermore, it has been noted:

In accordance with Article 46 of the Convention as amended by Protocol No. 11, the Committee of Ministers supervises the execution of judgments of the European Court of Human Rights. This work is carried out mainly at four regular meetings (DH meetings) every year. Documentation for these meetings takes the form of the Annotated Order of Business. The content of this document is made public, as are, in general, the decisions taken in each case. The Committee of Ministers' essential function is to ensure that member states comply with the judgments and certain decisions of the European Court of Human Rights. The Committee completes each case by adopting a final resolution. In some cases, interim resolutions may prove appropriate. Both kinds of Resolutions are public.[1603]

[1601] *Id.* at art. 46.

[1602] Article 14 of the Statute of the Council of Europe http://conventions.coe.int/Treaty/en/Treaties/html/001.htm (last visited May 14, 2012).

[1603] Supervision and execution of judgments of the European Court of Human Rights, http://www.coe.int/t/cm/humanRights_en.asp (last visited August 1, 2013).

The effectiveness of the Arab Charter requires effective supervisory mechanisms. The mechanisms currently used by the European system are effective, because of their efficiency. The Arab Charter should follow that same rule. However, Dr. Nabil Al-Araby, the Secretary General of the Arab League, said in the interview that I conducted with him that there is a weakness in the international judicial system. He mentioned that there is no effective judicial way to force a country to implement an international or regional court decision. The Arab system should apply a new creative judicial mechanism in order to enforce the decisions of the Arab Court. For instance, in the Arab League there is a regular meeting for the Ministers of Justices of the Arab League. In addition, in March 2012, as a member of the Egyptian delegation, I attended the Summit of the Arab Public Prosecutors and Attorney Generals, which was organized for the first time by the Arab League. For instance, if a Court decision is not implemented, the summit of both Ministers of Justice and Prosecutors General, in addition to the Supreme Judicial Council of States parties, should all meet to find ways to execute the judgments. Combined, these summits would have the power to force the implementation of a Court decision by a country that refrained from doing so. In addition, if the country insisted on not implementing the Court decision, the situation could be forwarded to the Summit of Presidents, Kings, and Prime Ministers in order to suspend the membership of the concerned country in the Arab League or to take other measures. This may help in ensuring the effectiveness of the Arab Charter. There should be creativity and flexibility given to the Arab League and the Arab Charter in cases where a state does not implement a Court decision and/or Committee recommendation. For instance, steps that could be taken include the following:

1. Serving formal notice to the concerned party.

2. Referring to the Court a question as to whether the state concerned has failed to fulfill its obligation.

3. After Steps 1 and 2, the Summit of the Ministers of Justice and Ministers of foreign Affairs and/or the Summit of Prosecutors General could be permitted to suspend the rights of representation in any meetings organized by the Arab League from the concerned state and withhold the right to vote in any meeting organized by the Arab League from the concerned state.

4. In addition to the previous measures the Arab League should be given the right to take any further decision or action.

If the judgments of the Arab Court are not binding, its decisions will be useless. As a result, the Court itself will be useless. If the states parties of the Arab Charter want to have effective Arab Court, the Court must have the power to issue binding decisions. It is important that the potential Arab Court follow the strategy taken by the African Court with respect to the use of sanctions in cases where countries fail to execute a Court decisions. It would be wise to include an implementation office in the Arab human rights system responsible for monitoring and supervising the execution of the judgments of the Court. If this Committee finds that any state did not execute a Court decision, it should refer the case to the Council of the League of the Arab States. Each State party would be represented in this Council and each state has one vote. The legislators of the Arab Court should think of further more effective ways in order to ensure the implementation of the judgments.

Proposed articles regarding the Arab Court:

> If the Court finds that there has been a violation of the Charter or the protocols thereto, and if the internal law of the High Contracting Party concerned allows only partial reparation to be made, the Court shall, if necessary, afford just satisfaction to the injured party.

> The parties to the case shall be notified of the judgment of the Court and it shall be transmitted to the states parties and the Committee.

> The Summit of both Ministers of Justice and Prosecutors Generals in addition to the Supreme Judicial Council of states parties shall be notified of the judgment and shall monitor its execution.

> If the Summit of Ministers of Justice, the Supreme Judicial Council of states parties, and the Committee fail to execute the judgment, the Council of League of Arab States should be notified to take necessary measures.

> The states parties to the present Protocol undertake to comply with the judgment in any case to which they are parties within the time stipulated by the Court and to guarantee its execution.

> The Court shall submit a report on its work during the previous year to each regular session of the Council of League of Arab States. The report shall specify, in particular, the cases in which a state has not complied with the Court's judgment. In addition, the report should mention best practices, challenges that faced the Court, and the recommendations of the Court in order to promote human rights in the Arab world.

c. General Measures

The Arab Charter should not only deliver decisions in regards to paying damages to victims, but it should also push states parties to make necessary changes by amending laws and regulation. In this way, the main purpose of the Arab Charter is to prevent damages from happening. This approach will definitely help with respect to the promotion of the Arab Charter. According to Protocol 14, the European Committee can request the Court to interpret any of its judgments.[1604] The Explanatory Report to Protocol 14 provides:

> The aim of the new paragraph 3 is to enable the Court to give an interpretation of a judgment, not to pronounce on the measures taken by a High Contracting Party to comply with that judgment. No time-limit has been set for making requests for interpretation, since a question of interpretation may arise at any time during the Committee of Ministers' examination of the execution of a judgment. The Court is free to decide on the manner and form in which it wishes to reply to the request. Normally, it would be for the formation of the Court which delivered the original judgment to rule on the question of interpretation. More detailed rules governing this new procedure may be included in the Rules of Court.[1605]

The Arab Charter should follow the European system in this regard. It should give the Committee the right to request an interpretation of the decision. This will definitely help in improving the human rights system. In this way, the League of Arab States should give the Arab Court and Committee more rights and privileges in order to do its job efficiently. In other words, the respect that will be given to the Committee and Court decisions is the key parameter for success of the Arab System. The success will increase as long as the respect for the system increases. The Arab League should put a lot of measures into action to ensure that member countries that have signed onto the Arab Charter respect and implement its decisions.

There should be a separate office in the Arab Charter whose only duty is to analyze the Court decisions and Committee reports, the name of which could be the 'implementation office.' This office should be responsible to follow up on the implementation of the Court judgments and Committee recommendations. The

---

1604 New article 46 (3) http://conventions.coe.int/Treaty/Commun/QueVoulezVous.asp?NT=194& CL=ENG (last visited Feb. 14, 2013).

1605 Explanatory Report of Protocol 14 to the European Convention on Human Rights, *supra* note 1516.

office would not only follow up on the implementation of remedies of the victims, but also focus on preventative measures. It would analyze the Court decision in order to find the reasons behind the violations and how to prevent future violations. In addition, there should be a brief recommendations section in every Court judgment. This section should recommend what could be done in the future in order to prevent similar violations from happening again in the future. The implementation office should analyze the recommendations of the section and follow up with the state concerned to determine what can be done in order to prevent future violations. If this advice is followed, the Arab Charter will be very efficient.

Proposed articles regarding the Arab Court and the new role of the Arab Committee:

> An 'implementation office' is an office at the Arab Court that is responsible to follow up on the implementation of the Court judgments.

> The office should analyze the Court's decision in order to find the reasons generating the violations and how to prevent them.

B. The Jurisprudence of the European Court on Human Rights, the African Court and Commission on Human and Peoples' Rights as a Possible Guiding Light to the Functioning of the Arab Committee and Court

1. The Principles Applied in the European Court on Human Rights

Karen Reid has outlined, "The Court, when deciding a case, should take into account relevant rules of international law that are applicable to the case. Also the Court should interpret the Convention as far as possible in harmony with other rules of international law."[1606] The Arab Court should certainly receive complaints from individuals and states parties to the protocol establishing the Arab Court. The Arab Charter should be interpreted, as much as possible, in harmony with other international and regional charters and conventions. For instance, it should be interpreted in light of the Vienna Convention on the Law of Treaties. I will mention some of important principles applied in the European Court, which can be applied in the Arab system in order to make it more effective.

1606 REID, *supra* note 817, at 44.

2. Subsidiarity

The European Court is subsidiary to domestic judicial systems. The European Court exists to guarantee the protection of human rights in states parties. On the other hand its decisions prevail over domestic court decisions. The Explanatory Report of Protocol no 14 to the European Convention of Human Rights explains:

> The principle of subsidiarity underlies all the measures taken to increase the effectiveness of the Convention's control system. Under Article 1 of the Convention, it is with the High Contracting Parties that the obligation lies 'to secure to everyone within their jurisdiction the rights and freedoms' guaranteed by the Convention, whereas the role of the Court, under Article 19, is 'to ensure the observance of the engagements undertaken by the High Contracting Parties in the Convention'. In other words, securing rights and freedoms is primarily the responsibility of the Parties; the Court's role is subsidiary.[1607]

The Arab Charter is also subsidiary in this sense. The amended Arab Committee will be subsidiary. Furthermore, the Arab Court that will replace the Arab Committee will also be subsidiary. The Charter provides:

> 1. Each State party to the present Charter undertakes to ensure to all individuals subject to its jurisdiction the right to enjoy the rights and freedoms set forth herein, without distinction on grounds of race, colour, sex, language, religious belief, opinion, thought, national or social origin, wealth, birth or physical or mental disability.
>
> 2. The States parties to the present Charter shall take the requisite measures to guarantee effective equality in the enjoyment of all the rights and freedoms enshrined in the present Charter in order to ensure protection against all forms of discrimination based on any of the grounds mentioned in the preceding paragraph.[1608]

The Arab Charter also provides, "The states parties undertake to adopt, in conformity with their constitutional procedures and with the provisions of the present Charter, whatever legislative or non-legislative measures that may be necessary to give effect to the rights set forth herein."[1609] Therefore, like the European Convention, the Arab Charter is both subsidiary and supervisory. Article 35 of the

---

1607 Explanatory Report of Protocol 14 to the European Convention on Human Rights, *supra* note 1516.
1608 ACHR, *supra* note 126, at art. 3(1 & 2).
1609 *Id.* at art. 44.

European Convention states, "The Court may only deal with the matter after all domestic remedies have been exhausted, according to the generally recognised rules of international law…"[1610] This clearly ensures that the European system is both subsidiary and supervisory.

In order to be an effective Charter, the Arab Court should only examine cases after the exhaustion of all domestic remedies.

Proposed articles regarding the Arab Court and the Arab Committee on Human Rights:

> Individuals who claim that any of their rights enumerated in the Charter have been violated and who have exhausted all available domestic remedies may submit a written communication to the Committee for consideration.
>
> The Court shall consider cases received from individuals inadmissible if:
>
> - It is anonymous, or which it considers to be an abuse of the right of submission of such cases or to be incompatible with the provisions of the Charter.
> - The individual has not exhausted all available domestic remedies, according to the generally recognized rules of international law, unless it is obvious to the Court that the procedure of achieving these remedies would be unduly prolonged.
> - The case is submitted to the Court after the completion of four months from the date of the exhaustion of all domestic remedies.
>
> The Committee shall consider communications received from individuals inadmissible if the individual has not exhausted all available domestic remedies unless it is obvious to the Committee that the procedure of achieving these remedies would be unduly prolonged.

3. Living Instrument

The term 'living instrument,' which was defined in the *Tyrer vs. United* case, means the interpretation of the European Convention according to present-day conditions.[1611] In *Ocalan vs. Turkey*, the Court provided that "the Convention is a living instrument and must be interpreted in the light of present day conditions. This

---

1610 *Id.* at art. 35.
1611 Tyrer vs. United Kingdom, *supra* note 1095.

may result (and, in fact, has on numerous occasions resulted) in judicial modifications of the original meaning of the Convention... the Court may so proceed when its interpretation remains in harmony with the values and standards that have been endorsed by the Member States."[1612] It should be noted that living instrument does not mean expanding the interpretation of a decision rendered. In *Johnston vs. Ireland*, it was explained, "It is true that the Convention and its Protocols must be interpreted in the light of present-day conditions. However, the Court cannot, by means of an evolutive interpretation, derive from these instruments a right that was not included therein at the outset."[1613]

In order to improve, the Arab Court and the Arab Committee should follow the principles stated above. The concept of a living instrument should be followed and applied in order to be in harmony with other international and regional bodies and treaties. The living instrument does not mean that the interpretation can be extended to create rights not intended to be included in the Arab Charter. For instance, the concept of a living instrument does not mean that the interpretation of the right to private life should be extended to include homosexuality. The living instrument idea does mean increasing the flexibility of the protection of the rights of individuals within the framework of the objectives and purposes of the Arab Charter. One of the examples of the flexibility of the Arab Court would be to increase the number of judges at any time during the year, depending on the number of cases.

The African Charter on Human and Peoples' Rights gives the African Commission the right to draw inspiration from other human rights instruments other than the African Charter in order to be a living instrument in harmony with other human rights bodies. The African Charter states:

> The Commission shall draw inspiration from international law on human and peoples' rights, particularly from the provisions of various African instruments on human and peoples' rights, the Charter of the United Nations, the Charter of the Organization of African Unity, the Universal Declaration of Human Rights, other instruments adopted by the United Nations and by African countries in the field of human and peoples' rights as well as from the provisions of various instruments

---

1612 Ocalan vs. Turkey, 46221/99, 12 May 2005, (2005) 41 E.H.R.R. 45.
1613 Johnston vs. Ireland, 9697/82, 18 December 1986, (1987) 9 E.H.R.R. 203. The Court thus concludes that the applicants cannot derive a right to divorce from Article 12 as it is not intended by the drafters.

adopted within the Specialized Agencies of the United Nations of which the parties to the present Charter are members.[1614]

In order to be promoted, the amended Arab Committee and the Arab Court that will replace the Committee should draw inspiration from other human rights instruments. However, this inspiration should not contradict the objectives and purposes of the Arab Charter.

Proposed articles regarding the Arab Court and the Arab Committee on Human Rights:

> The Supreme Judicial Councils can increase the number of judges upon the request of the majority of the presidents of the Supreme Judicial Councils. The plenary of the Arab Court can increase the number of judges upon the request of the majority of judges of the Court.
>
> The Arab Court shall draw inspiration from international human rights law, particularly from the provisions of various Arab instruments on human rights, the Charter of the United Nations, the Universal Declaration of Human Rights, and other instruments adopted by the United Nations in the field of human rights, as well as from the provisions of various instruments adopted within the Specialized Agencies of the United Nations of which the parties to the present Charter are members.
>
> The Committee shall draw inspiration from international human rights law, particularly from the provisions of various Arab instruments on human rights, the Charter of the United Nations, the Universal Declaration of Human Rights, and other instruments adopted by the United Nations in the field of human rights, as well as from the provisions of various instruments adopted within the Specialized Agencies of the United Nations of which the parties to the present Charter are members.
>
> Inspiration must not contradict the objectives and purposes of the Arab Charter.

1614 African Charter, *supra* note 127, at art. 60.

C. Relationship with Other Human Rights Systems

An important question may arise with respect to the body to which complaints should be addressed. For instance, if an individual living in Europe found that his protected rights are being protected by both the European Convention and the ICCPR, is he or she allowed to choose freely the body to which he or she will submit the complain? Can the same complaint be lodged subsequently or be placed the same time before both of them? Any victim is completely free to choose to lodge a complaint either before the European Convention or the ICCPR as long as both bodies protect the violated rights. However, in inter-state applications, states do not have a right to choose. Article 55 of the European Convention provides,

> "The High Contracting Parties agree that, except by special agreement, they will not avail themselves of treaties, conventions or declarations in force between them for the purpose of submitting, by way of petition, a dispute arising out of the interpretation or application of this Convention to a means of settlement other than those provided for in this Convention."[1615]

Also, Article 35 (2) (b) of the European Convention provides, "[The] Court shall not deal with any application submitted under Article 34 that is substantially the same as a matter that has already been examined by the Court or has already been submitted to another procedure of international investigation or settlement and contains no relevant new information."[1616] Furthermore, Article 5 (2) (a) of the Optional Protocol to the International Covenant on Civil and Political Rights provides, "The Committee shall not consider any communication from an individual unless it has ascertained that: The same matter is not being examined under another procedure of international investigation or settlement."[1617]

If we suppose that a victim lodged two identical complaints at the same time before the European Convention and the ICCPR, these complaints may be postponed to enable the applicant to withdraw one of the applications or the two applications may be declared inadmissible and rejected by both of them.[1618] The reason behind this is that the European Court will not examine applications that *have already been submitted* to another procedure of international inves-

---

1615 ECHR, *supra* note 497, at art. 55.
1616 *Id.* at art. 35(2)(b).
1617 Article 5(2)(a) of the Optional Protocol to the International Covenant on Civil and Political Rights, at http://www2.ohchr.org/english/law/ccpr-one.htm (last visited Feb. 14, 2013).
1618 THEORY AND PRACTICE OF THE EUROPEAN CONVENTION ON HUMAN RIGHTS, *supra* note 1526, at 89-90.

tigation or settlement, as long as this application has no relevant new information.[1619] Also, the ICCPR will declare the application inadmissible because it *is being examined* under another procedure of international investigation or settlement.[1620]

If the application is first lodged to the ICCPR, after which point the applicant decided to lodge application before the European Court because he or she was not satisfied by the outcome, the European Court will declare the application inadmissible. This is because the Court will implement article 35 (2) (b) of the European Convention. In other words, the Court will not deal with any application that *has been already submitted* to another procedure of international investigation or settlement.

On the other hand, if the application is lodged first to the European Court, but the applicant was not satisfied by the outcome and decided to lodge an application before the ICCPR, the ICCPR will not declare that the case is inadmissible merely on the account that the fact of this case has already been examined in another procedure. The reason behind this is that the ICCPR will declare applications inadmissible only if they are 'being examined' by another body. In this way, the ICCPR can examine any case after that case being examined by another body.

In order to overcome the issue that many cases may be examined by the ICCPR after examination by the European Court, in 1970 the Committee of Ministers urged states parties ratifying the Optional Protocol to the United Nations Covenant on Civil and Political Rights to make a declaration denying the competence of the Human Rights Committee to receive any communications from any individuals concerning matters that have been already examined or are being examined by the European Convention, unless rights and/or freedoms not set forth in the Convention are invoked or being invoked in such communications.[1621] Several states parties made this declaration or a reservation.[1622]

Another problem will arise in the Arab Charter, which will not only be the issue of the Arab Court decision and the ICCPR, but also the African Commission on Human Rights will be the third party. Some countries that are member to the Arab League are located in Africa, such as in Egypt, Tunisia, and Libya. Therefore, there is a possibility that a country can be party to three human rights charters,

---

1619 ECHR, *supra* not 497, at art. 35 (2) (b).
1620 Article 5 (2) (a) of the Optional Protocol to the International Covenant on Civil and Political Rights.
1621 THEORY AND PRACTICE OF THE EUROPEAN CONVENTION ON HUMAN RIGHTS, *supra* note 1526, at 90; *see also* Yearbook XIII (1970), 74-76.
1622 THEORY AND PRACTICE OF THE EUROPEAN CONVENTION ON HUMAN RIGHTS, *supra* note 1526, at 90-91.

i.e. the African Charter on Human and Peoples' Rights and the Arab Charter on Human Rights, in addition to the ICCPR. The Protocol of the Arab Charter is not yet adopted, so we cannot expect what the Charter is going to say with regard to the possibility of submitting applications to the Arab Charter before or after submitting the same application to the ICCPR or the African Charter. The African Charter stated that communications will be considered if they "[d]o not deal with cases which *have been settled* by these States involved in accordance with the principles of the Charter of the United Nations, or the Charter of the Organization of African Unity or the provisions of the present Charter. [emphasis added]"[1623] This means that it will not deal with any applications that have been examined by the ICCPR.

The question arises if an applicant submitted an application before the ICCPR first and later decided to submit another application before the African Commission. In this case, the African Court will not consider the application because the case is already examined in accordance with the principles of the Charter of the United Nations. On the other hand, if the applicant lodged an application before the African Commission and subsequently, because the applicant is not satisfied with the outcome, decides to lodge an application before the ICCPR, the application will not be rejected just because the African Commission examined it.

Proposed articles regarding the Arab Committee and the Arab Court on Human Rights:

> The Committee shall consider communications received from individuals inadmissible if the same matter has be examined before by the Arab Human Rights Committee or is *being examined* under another procedure of international investigation or settlement under another procedure of international or regional investigation or settlement and if it contains no relevant new information.

> The same matter has been examined before by the Arab Court on Human Rights or is *being examined* under another procedure of international or regional investigation or settlement and if it contains no relevant new information.

1623 African Charter, *supra* note 127, at art. 56 (7).

Chapter 9 : Conclusion

A. The Arab Charter

Human rights situations in the Arab World face many challenges in most of the states parties of the Arab League. There is a need to have a minimum floor of human rights below which no country should go. There were several efforts to adopt an Arab Charter on Human Rights for the twenty-two countries that are members of the Arab League. The idea of having an Arab Charter sparked in 1969, then, after several meeting the old Arab Charter on Human Rights, was adopted in 1994. However, no country ratified this Charter. Iraq was the only country that signed the Charter. The old Charter was replaced by a new Charter, which was adopted in 2004 and entered into force in 2008. As of August 2014, fourteen countries have ratified this Charter.

It is not unfortunate that the first Arab Charter (1994) was not ratified; rather, the Arab countries insisted on a new Arab Charter so another Charter was adopted. The most important thing is the collective will and the motivation to have a regional Charter for the Arab countries. The European human rights system also faced a lot of obstacles. Although the European Convention is currently the best regional Charter, it is still facing some challenges. For instance, Protocol 14 of the European Convention did not enter into force for several years, so another Protocol was needed to get around the problem. Protocol 14 was first issued in 2004 and in May 2009 Protocol 14 bis was opened for signature. In October 2009, it entered into force.[1624] After that in June 2010, protocol 14 entered into force.[1625] This example clearly shows that the presence of motivation and will can result in success.

In this book I showed that nearly all of the Arab countries have articles in their constitution declaring that Sharia law is the main source of legislation. Therefore, in order to understand the use of the Sharia as a legal system, it was necessary to have a full chapter dedicated to explaining Sharia law and its origins, objectives, and purposes. My aim was to make it easy for scholars and even lay-people to be able to easily understand the Sharia legal framework, such that they could evaluate the Arab Charter from the Sharia law point of view and comprehend why its articles were written as they were. I examined different human rights theories after which I developed and explained my proposed theory. I stated that it is not practical to have a nice theory that remains on a shelf but, rather, that it

---

1624 Protocol 14 bis signatures and ratifications, http://conventions.coe.int/Treaty/Commun/ChercheSig.asp?NT=204&CM=7&DF=&CL=ENG (last visited Jan. 6, 2013).

1625 *Protocol 14 signatures and ratifications,* http://conventions.coe.int/Treaty/Commun/ChercheSig.asp?NT=194&CM=7&DF=&CL=ENG *(last visited Jan. 6, 2013).*

is wise to have a moderate theory that can be applied and welcomed by Arab countries. It is important to keep that in mind as a possibility in the future. Therefore, it is wise to encourage and respect my proposed theory as long as it strikes a balance between cultures, traditions, and religious beliefs of the region while complying with the main principles of international human rights law. My theory is grounded in a belief that there is the presence of universal human rights that need to be protected everywhere. On the other hand, this theory is based on a perspective that we should leave a lot of room for the culture and traditions of each region to determine the details.

I also mentioned the history of the Arab Charter and the Arab League. I explained the many steps taken for the Charter to get to where it is currently. Then I explained the supervisory mechanisms of the Arab Charter. I also mentioned the efforts being taken to establish an Arab Court of Human Rights. I mentioned Bahrain's proposal regarding the establishment of an Arab Court. This proposal was submitted to the Arab League in 2011. I conducted an interview with the Secretary General of the Arab League who stated his frank opinion regarding the lack of effectiveness of the international judicial system.[1626] I stated that both the Secretary General of the Arab League and the Bahrain's proposal mentioned that the Arab Court will not be established overnight rather it will take time.[1627] I referred to the principle of gradualism and mentioned that even the European human rights system, which is the most effective regional system, took time to develop. I explained the substantive rights protected by the Charter from the perspective of Sharia law in order to show why the articles were written as they were and also to evaluate the rights from the Sharia perspective. I concluded that the Sharia legal system is in compliance with the international human rights system.

We should not criticize the Charter all of the time, nor should we say that it is the best human rights instrument in the world. The Charter does not have efficient supervisory mechanisms and some of the rights in the Charter could be more effective. On the other hand, no one can deny that the Charter is an important step toward the protection of human rights in the Arab world. The Arab Charter on Human Rights is a good evolutionary start in the Arab region. For the first time ever in the Middle East and North Africa, an Arab Charter on Human Rights has entered into force. This Charter is compatible with international human rights treaties and at the same time it respects Sharia law and the cultures of the Arab countries. The Charter is inspired by Sharia law. Sharia law is not just mentioned in the Charter as a legal system to be applied; instead Sharia law is used as a

---

1626 *See* chapter 4.
1627 *See* chapter 4.

standard to evaluate the Arab Charter and as a reason to explain why the Arab Charter was written as it was.

In this book I hope I succeeded in establishing a common ground between the Arab Charter and international human rights principles. I explained the objectives and purposes of Sharia law in order to show how it is aligned with international law.[1628] In addition, I examined different theories of human rights and then suggested a new proposed theory.[1629] I stated that many of the theories that were written by different scholars either focusing on the Western concept of human rights as the base which the Islamic concept should follow or focusing on the Islamic concept of human rights and ignoring the Western approach. My proposed theory establishes a common ground for shared principles. In my theory, Sharia law is implemented and the international human rights principles are respected. The theory understands the objectives and purposes of Sharia law and then examines the articles of the domestic laws to see whether they are in alignment with, or contrary to, Sharia law. Furthermore, the theory examines Islamic jurisprudence to determine whether there is any Islamic interpretation that is compatible with the international human rights standards. These previous studies help to establish a common ground for shared values and principles that should not be derogated.

My theory is based on several principles. I mentioned the possibilities of reconciliation between Sharia law and international law. For instance, I explained Islam's *Zakat* and the International Right to Social Security. I showed that *Zakat*, which is part of the four pillars of Islam, matches succinctly with social security.[1630] I also mentioned the existence of duties and rights in Islam.[1631] I explained how Sharia law strikes a balance between duties and rights. I showed that we could not have rights if there are no duties. The primary international human rights treaties do not balance duties and rights. Instead, they focus mainly on rights. The Arab Charter followed the international human rights treaties in this way, yet, as it is inspired by Sharia law, the Arab Charter should also balance duties and rights. In the future, the Charter could be amended or additional protocols could be adopted in order to reflect and emphasize duties in the Charter. The Charter is inspired more by the international human rights treaties as there is no balance between rights and duties. As I explained in detail before, Sharia law strikes a balance between duties and rights. Without duties, rights will not be fulfilled. In

---

1628 *See* pages 52-61.
1629 *See* Chapter 3.
1630 *See* pages 89-95.
1631 *See* pages 95-99.

addition, for Muslims, the Quran is the Word of God, therefore Muslims are supposed to happily implement and fulfill the obligations stated in the Quran. I also mentioned the principle of gradualism in Sharia law and international human rights law.[1632] I showed that the Arab Charter can be promoted through applying the principle of gradualism. I gave different examples regarding the principle of gradualism. I stated that the European Convention on Human Rights, which is currently the most effective regional human rights instrument, applied the principle of gradualism. I mentioned that it took many years until the European Convention made the jurisdiction of the European Court compulsory on all states parties to the Convention. I concluded that the Arab Charter cannot achieve full success immediately. Rather, it will take time until the Arab Charter is promoted smoothly. I referred to my interview with Dr. Nabil Al-Araby, the Secretary General of the Arab League, who said that it will take time until the Arab League can succeed in establishing an Arab Court.

In addition, I mentioned the relationship between individual and 'umma (nation) in Sharia law.[1633] I explained that Sharia law balances between 'umma and the individual. I stated that, recently, international human rights become more similar to Sharia law in recognizing group rights or 'umma rights. I also explained the relationship between *fitrah* and natural law.[1634] I explained that Sharia law as a legal system is based on *fitrah* or natural law. I tried to clearly show that the roots of Sharia law come from *fitrah*. In other words, Sharia law is aligned with natural law. I showed that Sharia law is in compliance with the order of nature. I gave examples of Western law articles that criminalized some acts because they are against the "order of nature."

In addition, I explained the principle of equality to show the Sharia law point of view on this issue.[1635] I mentioned that Sharia law is compatible with international law. However, I added that, according to Sharia law, in the relationship between a husband and wife, the husband has lot of responsibilities towards his wife. The husband is financially responsible for his wife even if she is working. I concluded that Sharia law approaches the relationship between a man and woman differently than is done from by the Western perspective. I conducted a comparison between the human dignity as perceived in Islam and in international law.[1636] I stated that Sharia law respects the dignity of the human being very much. I men-

---

1632 *See* pages 99-105.
1633 *See* pages 105-111.
1634 *See* pages 111-113.
1635 *See* pages 113-120.
1636 *See* pages 121-126.

tioned that human rights of people exist because of the human dignity. I provided several Quranic verses and *hadith* that show the respect of Sharia law for human dignity. I briefly mentioned the successful efforts of the Arab states in establishing an Arab League and then an Arab Charter of Human Rights. I also explained the ongoing efforts to establish an Arab Court.[1637]

I stated the rights that are mentioned in the Charter and showed that the rights in the Arab Charter are aligned, and consistent, with Sharia law. I gave examples of rights protected by the Charter, such as the right to life, right to private life, prohibition of torture, right to education, and freedom of movement. I evaluated the Charter from the Sharia law point of view. I showed the Sharia law opinion with respect to each of the rights that I explained. I stated the different opinions of Islamic scholars. I concluded that the Charter is compatible with both Sharia law and international law.[1638]

I evaluated the supervisory mechanism of the Arab Charter through comparing it with the African and European Charters. I explained and suggested what can be done to improve the work of the Committee to make it more effective and efficient. I evaluated the procedural human rights protections in the Arab Charter through an Arab Court on Human Rights.[1639] The main reason for this comparison was not to determine which regional system is the best. I concluded that the Arab Charter does not yet efficiently promote human rights and I provided details to suggest how it can promote human rights. I noted that the majority of the Arab countries, if not all of them, have very nice sounding articles in their domestic laws related to human rights. I also said that the majority of the Arab countries ratified the main international human rights treaties. In my opinion, the major deficiency and weakness of the Charter is not in the rights themselves, but in the implementation of the rights. There should be effective and efficient supervisory mechanisms for the Arab Human Rights Charter.

I proposed two optional protocols to the Arab Charter on Human Rights. The first protocol suggests establishing an effective Arab Committee and the second protocol proposes establishing an effective Arab Court. I agree entirely with the opinion of Professor Mohammed Mattar, the Executive Director of the Protection Project at Johns Hopkins University, who said that the Arab Charter imposes obligations on Arab countries regarding human rights.[1640] In addition, the Charter is aligned, and consistent, with Sharia law. He said that the most important thing

---

1637 *See* chapter 4.
1638 *See* chapter 5.
1639 *See* chapters 6, 7, and 8.
1640 *See* chapter 4.

is the implementation and application of the articles of the Charter and added that this implementation and application is more important than the wording of the phrases of the articles of the Charter.[1641] Instead of focusing on mere criticism of the Arab Charter, we should emphasize constructive criticism. In other words, it is better not to focus on whether the rights should be criticized or welcomed. Instead, we should focus on the implementation of the rights.

Regional human rights systems are probably more effective with respect to regional human rights, as countries in the same region share the same cultures and traditions and are fewer in number than the countries in universal systems. This illustrates some of the advantages that enable regional systems to have a greater capacity to apply pressure and ensure the protection of human rights more successfully than the international legal systems. The Arab Charter is well suited to the Arab region. If it is promoted by an effective supervisory mechanism, it can play an important role in improving human rights in the Middle East. The Arab Charter reflects the religion, culture, and traditions of the Arab countries because it is issued, adopted, and implemented by the region. No one from the Arab region will fear it because it has been issued by them. In addition, the members of the supervisory mechanism (the Committee and the Court) are nationals of Arab countries nominated by Arab states parties to the Convention.

B. Redefining Human Rights in the Arab Charter

The human rights principles stated in the Arab Charter should balance rights and duties. This can be redefined to reflect Islamic principles. Individual's and state duties should be added to the Arab Charter on Human Rights. This can happen either by amending the existing Charter or adopting additional protocols to the Arab Charter on Human Rights in order to strike a balance between duties and rights.

We should not only look to points of divergence, but we should also focus on points of convergence. There is a common ground of shared values and principles between international human rights and Sharia law. Even the Quran explains that the reason why people are from different cultures and countries is in order to know each other. The Quran states, "O mankind! We have created you from a male and a female, and made you into nations and tribes, that you may know one another..."[1642] Prophet Mohammed called for peace and signed international treaties with others. It has been noted, "The beginning of the first Islamic state

---

1641 *See* chapter 4.
1642 QURAN 49:13.

resulted from the Medina Constitution, in which Mohammed entered into agreements with other tribes in order to provide for collective security and form a united front against invaders from Mecca."[1643]

C. The Door of *Ijtihad* is Open[1644]

The door of *ijtihad* is still open and was never closed. The real question is not whether the door of *ijtihad* is still open or closed; the question that needs to be answered is who can make this *ijtihad*. When we read the jurisprudence of the four Islamic schools and the reasons for each opinion, we will find that they offer very profound reflection. They analyzed every issue very deeply. These days, it is not easy to find a scholar who possesses this great knowledge and very deep analysis. However, during the current century we have more privileges than were experienced in previous centuries. We have technology with which we can access data in a single click. For instance, we can get access to books and libraries, including the Islamic jurisprudence of the four popular Islamic schools, very easily.

As I mentioned, we need a qualified trusted academic institution that can apply *ijtihad*. I suggested Al-Azhar, which is one of the moderate institutions, which does not support any particular Islamic school and teaches all of the different schools from a position of neutrality.

D. The Arab Committee

Concerning the Arab Committee, the state reporting mechanism in the Arab Charter is the only monitoring supervisory system in the Arab Charter. It should be noted that the reporting system of the Arab Committee, which is even weaker than the African Commission, cannot effectively promote Arab human rights. From the experience of some Arab countries in the African Commission, we can easily recognize that state reports are not an effective mechanism and are not submitted on time. In my book, I suggested a first Optional Protocol to the Arab Charter on Human Rights to amend the structure and function of the present Arab Committee on Human Rights. There should be opportunities for individual and state complaints. The Arab Committee, as it is, does not receive any communications from individuals. The efficiency of the reporting system will be affected by the *will* and *motivation* of the states parties to the Charter. These countries should have a strong will and motivation to cooperate with the Arab Committee

---

1643 Jordan, *supra* note 141, at 70 (citing Jorgen S. Nielsen, *Contemporary Discussions on Religious Minorities in Islam*, 2002 BYU L. Rev. 353, 362 (2002) (discussing the origins of the first Islamic state and the Medina Constitution)).

1644 *See* pages 62-73.

by submitting fully detailed reports to them. The countries should submit the reports on time without delays in order to help the Committee achieve its work efficiently. It will then be the turn of the Arab Committee to examine the reports without delay. The reporting system of the Arab Committee is currently very weak. The important aim behind the reports is not only to collect data but also to improve and protect human rights. In the future, the Charter should be amended or additional protocols should be added in order to promote the work of the Committee. After the Committee submits its recommendations on the state report, the Committee should at least have the right to follow up on the implementation of its recommendations. Regarding the state reporting system, each State party should summit the annual report every two years, instead of every three years. This will definitely help the Committee in its preventive role.

In addition, the members of the Committee should be independent. It cannot be expected to have an independent and efficient Arab Committee if its members are holding positions that are incompatible with the function of the Committee. At least half of the members of the Committee should be judges. The former Secretary of the European Committee criticized the role of the Committee. He said,

> "[The] Ministers' Deputies [who are members of the Committee] are generally career diplomats. They act, in human rights cases as in other matters, on instructions from their capitals. They usually have no special training or competence to deal with human rights issues. They are trained to defend State interests or what their central authority regards as the interests of their state."[1645]

I agree entirely with the opinion of the former Secretary of the Committee, not only because the Deputy Ministers are lacking experience and do not have background knowledge of human rights issues, but also, as he explained, because they defend the interests of their states.

On the other hand, the members of the Committee should be given flexibility to travel and visit Arab countries either that have or have not yet ratified the Arab Charter. Currently, the members of the Arab Committee are doing a good promotion of the Charter. They travel to different countries in the Arab world to introduce the Charter to the people and the governments. However, their travels should not only focus on the ratifying countries to the Charter but also on the

---

1645 MOWBRAY, *supra* note 1489, at 13-14; *see also* Peter Leuprecht, *The Protection of Human Rights by Political Bodies-The Example of the Committee of Ministers of the Council of Europe*, 98, 106-107 *in* PROGRESS IN SPIRIT OF HUMAN RIGHTS (M Nowak & D Steurer eds., 1998).

non-ratifying countries in order to increase public awareness and encourage non-ratifying states to ratify the Charter. For instance, the Arab Charter does not give them the right to travel and organize promotional visits to ratifying or non-ratifying countries. The promotional role of the Committee is very important to improving the efficiency of the Charter. It will definitely increase human rights awareness, if not encourage the hosting state to ratify the Charter. In addition, if there are no guarantees for the independence and experience of the members of the Committee, it is impossible to expect that the Arab Charter can promote human rights. The Arab Committee should give the state parties to the Arab Charter the right to complain about the conduct of any other state Party, regardless of the nationality of the victims of the violation. In addition, it is very important for the Arab Committee to receive shadow reports from NGOs and potential victims. Currently, the Committee is cooperating with different NGOs. Before examining each state report, the Committee gives a long period of time for the NGOs to submit their shadow reports. All of the previous recommendation should promote the work of the Arab Committee.

The Arab Committee should be creative and effective. The Committee should not wait for the three years periodic report. Instead, it should be given the right to request additional information anytime. For instance, if the Committee found that a certain country adopted a law that is in violation of human rights, it should immediately request further information from the country concerned and give recommendations. The Committee should then follow up on the measures taken by the state party concerned regarding the Committee's recommendations. The Arab Committee should welcome receiving shadow reports from international and regional organizations, whether governmental or nongovernmental bodies. In addition, it should also welcome receiving shadow reports from individuals and even potential victims. In addition, the Committee should analyze the judgments of the Arab Court regarding any human rights violations in the laws of Arab countries. It can determine the domestic laws and regulations that violate the human rights. The Arab Committee can then request further information from the country concerned and submit recommendations to that country regarding amending these laws and measures. In addition, similar to the African Charter, the Arab Committee should draw inspiration from other human rights instruments in order to be promoted. However, this inspiration should not contradict the objectives and purposes of the Arab Charter.

All of the previous ideas will make the work of the Committee more effective and efficient. This will improve the preventive role of the Arab Committee in improving human rights protection in the Arab Charter. In addition, the Arab Committee should submit a yearly report on the work that it accomplished during the year. This report should include an analysis of the judgments of the Arab Court.

In another words, if the Court found that a certain law violates human rights, the Committee should include this note in the report. Furthermore, the Committee should be given the right to request an interpretation of the of the Court's decisions in order to facilitate to the Committee to follow up the implementation of the Court's decisions.

One of the very positive things in the Arab Charter is that it emphasizes the publication of the reports. The Charter provides, "The Committee's reports, concluding observations and recommendations shall be public documents which the Committee shall disseminate widely."[1646] Publishing the reports will definitely improve the protection of human rights in the Arab region. Currently, both the states reports and the conclusions and observations of the Committee are published on the website of the Arab League.

At the end of the book I attached an optional additional protocol to the Arab Charter on Human Rights (first Optional Protocol). This protocol suggests how to make the Arab Committee more effective and efficient.

E. An Arab Court

The Arab Charter on Human Rights did not mention the possibility of establishing an Arab Court on Human Rights. I propose a second Optional Protocol to the Arab Charter establishing an Arab Court on Human Rights. Regarding the potential Arab Court on Human Rights, the jurisdiction of the Court should be limited to all Arab human rights treaties that are issued by the League of Arab States. The mechanism of the Court must be completely independent. Even the way of choosing judges should be independent. There should be strict competitive regulations for choosing judges. They should have high degree of experience in judging cases related to human rights violations. In addition, priority should be given to judges who have completed graduate studies on different regional human rights systems or have previous experience in this field. Furthermore, at least a few members of the judges of the Court should have a competent knowledge of English and/or French in order to be able to expand his or her knowledge by reading the decisions of other regional and international courts. If these criteria for choosing highly qualified judges are followed we can have judges who are academically and practically efficient. Furthermore, to guarantee independence, the vote of the judge who holds the nationality of a state party to a case should not be counted when rendering a decision in that case. The lawyers that

---

1646 ACHR, *supra* note 126, at art. 48 (6).

represent victims before the Court should be very qualified. There should be special exams for them or special qualifications for choosing the lawyers.

The structure of the Arab Court should be left to the drafters of the additional protocol of the Court. However, there should be flexibility in amending the structure to be prepared for the large number of anticipated cases submitted to the Court. In addition, there should be a flexibility to be able to increase the number of judges depending on the number of cases. The potential Arab Court must be effective, not only by having independent judges but also by having an outstanding staff in its registry. The role of the registry is very important in improving the quality of the Court decision.

The most important thing is that the jurisdiction of the Court should exist only after the exhaustion of all domestic remedies. In other words, the Arab Court must be subsidiary, just as is the case for other regional courts. Furthermore, the right to submit a case before the Arab Court after the exhaustion of domestic remedies should not be open forever. Rather, it should be possible only for a period of four months from the date of the exhaustion of domestic remedies. The burden of proof of the existence of effective remedies, in theory and practice, is on the government. Once the government has demonstrated the burden of proof, the applicant must prove that all other remedies have been exhausted. On the other hand, there is no need to exhaust the domestic remedies if they are not accessible, or effective or adequate.

The right to appeal the decision of the Arab Court should be limited; it should not be given automatically to the parties of the cases. The judgment of the Chamber can be subject to appeal to the Grand Chamber. In addition, the judgment of the Grand Chamber can be subject to appeal to the plenary. A panel of five judges of the Grand Chamber of the Court may review the Chmaber's and the Grand Chamber's decisions, upon the request of the parties or by unilateral decision of the Court, in the light of new evidence under conditions to be set out in the Rules of Procedure and/or if the decision of the Court was violating the human rights principles protected by the Arab Charter and its protocols and/or if the case raises a serious question affecting the interpretation or application of the Convention or the Protocols thereto, or a serious issue of general importance.

There should be no separate judgment than that of the Arab Court in cases where the judges did not reach a unanimous decision. This will be better for the independence of the Arab Court. The decision should be by the majority of votes without any dissenting opinion. Also, regarding the Court's judgment, it should be noted that the purpose of establishing the Arab Court is not for the purposes of a criminal investigation; it is established to ensure that the minimum human rights standards established are respected and protected. The Arab Court should examine whether or not the domestic court or other governmental bodies protected and respected the rights stated in the Charter.

The proceedings before the Court should generally be public in character. This will give more confidence in the Court. In addition, this will increase the popularity of the Court. In exceptional cases, the public nature of the proceeding may be restricted. States should have the right to lodge applications against each other, regardless of the nationality of the victim or the relationship between the alleged violation and the applicant country. The Arab Court should apply the friendly settlement on the basis of respect for human rights. The aim of the Court is not to name and shame, but to promote human rights. Therefore, if a friendly settlement is reached with respect to human rights, the file of the case should be closed. In order to hasten the speed of cases, the Court should be given the right to make the decision on the merits and admissibility jointly. This will certainly help reduce the number of pending cases in the Court. Therefore, it will promote the efficiency of the Arab Charter.

The Arab Court should put conditions in order to prevent people from playing with the regional courts and international courts. For instance, some Arab countries are member to the ICCPR and its protocols and also are members to both the Arab and the African Charter. People can use different regional and international human rights instrument to submit the same case. The Arab Charter should regulate this issue.

In order to promote the Arab system of the protection of human rights the Arab Court should be given the right to receive requests for advisory opinions. In other words, the League of Arab States, in addition to the Arab states should be able to request an advisory opinion from the Court. It is important to encourage countries to get in contact with the Court by giving these countries the right to request advisory opinions from the Court. The goal of the Arab system is to spread, promote, and protect human rights in the region.

At the end of this book, I attach a second additional optional protocol to the Arab Charter on Human Rights. This protocol will suggest the structure, functions, and duties of the Arab Court on Human Rights.

F. Summary

The supervisory mechanism of the Arab Charter should be effective and creative; it can be constituted by both a Court and a Committee. However, complaints should be submitted to the Committee, first. After a period of time, the Court should replace the Committee, with respect to the countries that join the second protocol establishing the Court. In addition, another supervisory mechanism can be Special Rapporteurs. Rapporteurs can be appointed for specific duties or for specific countries. The Arab Committee cannot do the job of the rapporteur at the same level of efficiency. The rapporteur should be an expert in his or her field.

The Court and the Committee should work together. Both of them should receive individual and state complaints. As I explained, many Arab countries will be unwilling to ratify the protocol establishing the Arab Court. Therefore, the Arab Committee should first receive individual and state complaints, in accordance with the first additional protocol. After that, with time, Arab countries will gain confidence in the Court and they will begin to ratify its second protocol. After the Court enters into force, the Committee should stop receiving state and individual complaints as to the countries that ratify the second protocol. I gave the example of Egypt, which is party to the African Commission on Human and Peoples' Rights. The African Commission accepts individual complaints. Although Egypt is member to the African Commission, it is not a member to the African Court on Human and Peoples' Rights. In short, we should accept having an Arab Court and Committee at the same time. States should be given the right to ratify the protocol establishing the reformed Committee and the protocol establishing the Court. With time, the states that did not ratify the protocol establishing the Court initially will ratify this protocol in the future.

The supervisory mechanism (whether committee, court, or rapporteurs) should be established gradually. For instance, the Arab Court can be established by an additional protocol. The states parties that wish to be members of the Court can ratify the additional protocol. It took the European Convention around forty years to make the optional jurisdiction of the European Court compulsory. In addition, the European Court did not start as a full time court. Rather, it started as a part time body that held sessions each month. Furthermore, it took approximately thirty years until countries were prohibited to join the Council of Europe unless they agreed to ratify the Convention. In short, states parties to the Charter cannot be forced to comply with a specific supervisory mechanism. However, after the Arab Charter and the Arab Court gain in popularity and after the Arab countries gain more confidence in the Court's decisions, the number of ratifying countries to the court jurisdiction will increase gradually. It took many years until we saw a significant increase in the member states of the European Convention. As of January 1, 1990, twenty-two countries were parties to the Convention. As of April 1, 2012, forty-seven countries were parties to the Convention. This is evidence that gradualism is important to achieving success.

It will take a few years for the Arab Court to gain popularity and a good reputation, as is currently experienced by the European Court. At its beginning, the European Court was very slow and did not receive a large number of cases. In the first seventeen years of its existence (1959 to 1975), on average one case per year was brought before the Court. Between March 1962 and June 1965, there were no pending cases. However, with time, the number of cases gradually began to increase. Nowadays, the large number of cases is a threat to the efficiency of the Court. Therefore, in order to promote the efficiency of the Arab Court we need to be patient and, with time, the Court will achieve success.

The success of both the Court and the Committee will depend on the will and motivation of the states parties to the Charter. The member states should not wait for a problem to happen and then find the solution. Instead, they should learn from the experience of others, expect problems and find solutions before they happen. In addition, the people who work in the Court and the Committee must be highly qualified. We cannot expect success from people who are not qualified for their positions. In addition, we cannot expect success in the Court and the Committee if their members are not fully independent.

Many steps can be taken to promote the Arab Court and the Arab Committee. For example, the Arab Committee and the Arab Court should give the right to any State party to lodge an application against another State party with regard to any violation of any of the articles of the Convention. The purpose of the Arab Charter is not only to criminalize, but also to prevent bad conduct. Therefore, it is important to accept cases from states against other states. The Arab Committee should be given the right to accept complaints that are against a law, not only concrete cases involving a person. On the other hand, the Arab Court should give individuals the right to submit an application before the Court only if they are victims of an alleged violation.

One of the important challenges of the Arab human rights system is the implementation of the decisions of the Arab Court and the implementation of the Arab Committee's recommendations. As Dr. Nabil Al-Araby, the Secretary General of the Arab League, said in the interview that I conducted with him, there is a weakness and deficiency in the international judicial system. He mentioned that there is no effective judicial way to force a country to implement international or regional court decisions.[1647] The Arab system should apply a new creative judicial mechanism in order to enforce the decisions of the Arab Court. For instance, the subject of human rights should be fixed in the agenda of the yearly Arab League Summit, which is the primary yearly summit of the Arab League. On a yearly basis, presidents, kings, and ministers should discuss the success and challenges of the human rights issue in the countries members of the Arab Charter. For example,

---

1647 *See* chapter 4.

in these summits the Arab Committee should be able to mention the countries that did not submit its reports or submitted a minimal insufficient report. Therefore, this summit can be a golden opportunity for the Committee to achieve its goals.

One of the best practices for achieving success is planting the culture of human rights in the states parties to the Arab Charter. In other words, after the Arab Court and the Committee achieve great success and the majority of the member states to the Arab League gain confidence in it, the situation should change. No Arab countries should be allowed to join the Arab League unless they agree to ratify the Charter. Then, after a while, the situation should change again. In other words, no Arab countries should be allowed to join the Arab League unless they agree to ratify the Arab Charter and all its protocols. This is the principle of gradualism that I mentioned in my theory. With time, everything can change smoothly. For instance, the European Convention applied the principle of gradualism. Not all rights, including the right to property, were initially mentioned in the main convention. However, many of the rights were subsequently added via additional protocols. Furthermore, it took approximately thirty years until countries were prohibited to join the Council of Europe unless they agreed to ratify the Convention. Before 1980, it was optional for the European Countries to ratify the European Convention. Therefore, by applying the principle of gradualism the Arab Charter will be better in protecting the human rights in the Arab countries.

The culture of human rights cannot be improved in one day. Building the culture of respect for human rights can be achieved gradually through different means. For instance, increasing the awareness of people regarding their rights can be done in different ways. For example, there is a direct link between education and human rights. Eradication of illiteracy is important in the improvement of human rights; illiteracy should be reduced in the Arab countries. We cannot expect a revolutionary improvement in human rights if there are millions of people in each Arab country who still cannot read or write. In addition, improvement of human rights should be a basic subject for students in schools and universities. Passing human rights courses should be a precondition for the promotion of people working in law enforcement. In addition, after human rights begin to develop in the community, passing human rights exams should be a precondition for people working in both the private and public sector. Furthermore, one of the major ways to achieve respect of human rights is the role being played by the media. The media has to improve public awareness of human rights issues and remedies. All of these suggestions will definitely improve and promote the awareness and culture of human rights, and will do gradually.

It is impossible to list all the creative ways of achieving success in the Arab Court. By practice, after the Court starts working, we will get to know how we can make it better. The members of the Committee and the Court, in addition to the League of Arab States will face challenges and will try to find solutions for them. They are the best people to devise solutions because they will be working in the field. If they proposed a solution and it is not successful, they should try another approach and not expect to succeed always and immediately. Professor Dr. Herbert Petzold who is a Professor of Law and the former long-time Registrar of the European Court of Human Rights, informed me that the European Convention on Human Rights, after it entered into force, stated that the Court sit in Chamber only. Article 43 of the European Court states, "For the consideration of each case brought before it the Court shall consist of a Chamber composed of seven judges ..."[1648] He added that the judges of the European Court found it difficult to decide as seven judges, so the Court drafted its own rules of procedure which were technically violating Article 43 of the European Convention in that they added that the European Court sit as Grand Chamber as well, which was a healthy development.[1649]

The most important thing is not to start off by saying that the Arab Charter does promote human rights effectively from the first day. In fact, the important thing is not the immediate achievement of success, but its long-term acceptance and enforcement. Furthermore, it is not important to push all the twenty-two members states to the Arab League to ratify the potential Protocol that will establish the Arab Court. The most important thing is that the States parties to the Protocol should be willing to respect and implement the decisions of the Court. If the judgments of the Arab Court are not binding, the decisions will be useless and the court itself will be useless. I did not suggest an outstanding and efficient Court from the beginning because states may refrain from ratifying the protocol establishing the Court. I am applying the principle of gradualism. The goal is to encourage countries to ratify smoothly and fully respect and safeguard human rights. With time, the culture of human rights will be promoted. In addition, governments will gain confidence in regional human rights protection. Until we have collective will and the motivation to achieve human rights protection, gradualism should be applied very smoothly. The most important major thing is to say that states parties to the Charter should be highly motivated to achieve success in human rights. In addition, it is very vital that the State parties should appoint highly qualified members to the Court and the Committee. I suggested

---

1648 ECHR, *supra* note 497, at art. 43.

1649 Telephone Interview with Professor Dr. Herbert Petzold, Professor of Public International Law, Saarbrücken University; former Registrar, European Court of Human Rights (Sep. 3, 2013).

two optional protocols to the Arab Charter on Human Rights in order to promote and protect human rights of the Arab Charter.

In this book, I succeeded in explaining the concepts of Western society and Western views on human rights in a way that would be understood by Arab countries. In addition, I highlighted the Arab view of human rights and explained the cultures, traditions, and religious beliefs that are related to human rights such that this could be understood by Western countries. I briefly mentioned the human rights violations in Arab states in order to clarify the importance of the Arab Charter on Human Rights in promoting the human rights situation. However, the Arab Charter as it is cannot promote or protect human rights; it needs to be amended to be more effective.

The book is intended to help states parties of the Arab Charter understand the rights protected by the Arab Charter in order to apply them on the national level as long as they are in alignment with Sharia law. In addition, I explained the different substantive matters and mechanisms that supervise the protection of human rights in detail in order to help legislators of the issue additional optional protocols for the improvement of the Arab Charter.

I hope I achieved one of my main goals, i.e. highlighting the main challenges that threaten the protection of human rights in the Arab world, such as illiteracy. I also gave a condensed explanation of human rights in order to help people in the Middle East expand their knowledge of human rights and understand their rights and duties. In addition, I succeeded in explaining the Arab Charter and its objectives and purposes to Western people. Finally, I am looking forward to this book being a positive contribution to both the literature on human rights and a guiding light for professionals seeking the improvement of the Arab Charter on Human Rights. I quote three verses from the Quran: "And mankind have not been given of knowledge except a little."[1650] "My Lord! Increase me in knowledge."[1651] "And We have enjoined on man to be dutiful and kind to his parents. His mother bears him with hardship. And she brings him forth with hardship, and the bearing of him, and the weaning of him is thirty months, till when he attains full strength and reaches forty years, he says: "My Lord! Grant me the power and ability that I may be grateful for Your Favour which You have bestowed upon me and upon my parents, and that I may do righteous good deeds, such as please You, and make my offspring good. Truly, I have turned to You in repentance, and truly, I am one of the Muslims (submitting to Your Will).""[1652]

1650 QURAN 17:85.
1651 *Id.* at 20:114.
1652 *Id.* at 46:15.

Annex

1. Arab Charter on Human Rights

League of Arab States
adopted 22 May 2004
entered into force 15 March 2008

Based on the faith of the Arab nation in the dignity of the human person whom God has exalted ever since the beginning of creation and in the fact that the Arab homeland is the cradle of religions and civilizations whose lofty human values affirm the human right to a decent life based on freedom, justice and equality,

In furtherance of the eternal principles of fraternity, equality and tolerance among human beings consecrated by the noble Islamic religion and the other divinely-revealed religions,

Being proud of the humanitarian values and principles that the Arab nation has established throughout its long history, which have played a major role in spreading knowledge between East and West, so making the region a point of reference for the whole world and a destination for seekers of knowledge and wisdom,

Believing in the unity of the Arab nation, which struggles for its freedom and defends the right of nations to self-determination, to the preservation of their wealth and to development; believing in the sovereignty of the law and its contribution to the protection of universal and interrelated human rights and convinced that the human person's enjoyment of freedom, justice and equality of opportunity is a fundamental measure of the value of any society,

Rejecting all forms of racism and Zionism, which constitute a violation of human rights and a threat to international peace and security, recognizing the close link that exists between human rights and international peace and security, reaffirming the principles of the Charter of the United Nations, the Universal Declaration of Human Rights and the provisions of the International Covenant on Civil and Political Rights and the International Covenant on Economic, Social and Cultural Rights, and having regard to the Cairo Declaration on Human Rights in Islam,

The States parties to the Charter have agreed as follows:

Article 1

The present Charter seeks, within the context of the national identity of the Arab States and their sense of belonging to a common civilization, to achieve the following aims:

1. To place human rights at the centre of the key national concerns of Arab States, making them lofty and fundamental ideals that shape the will of the individual in Arab States and enable him to improve his life in accordance with noble human values.

2. To teach the human person in the Arab States pride in his identity, loyalty to his country, attachment to his land, history and common interests and to instill in him a culture of human brotherhood, tolerance and openness towards others, in accordance with universal principles and values and with those proclaimed in international human rights instruments.

3. To prepare the new generations in Arab States for a free and responsible life in a civil society that is characterized by solidarity, founded on a balance between awareness of rights and respect for obligations, and governed by the values of equality, tolerance and moderation.

4. To entrench the principle that all human rights are universal, indivisible, interdependent and interrelated.

Article 2

1. All peoples have the right of self-determination and to control over their natural wealth and resources, and the right to freely choose their political system and to freely pursue their economic, social and cultural development.

2. All peoples have the right to national sovereignty and territorial integrity.

3. All forms of racism, Zionism and foreign occupation and domination constitute an impediment to human dignity and a major barrier to the exercise of the fundamental rights of peoples; all such practices must be condemned and efforts must be deployed for their elimination.

4. All peoples have the right to resist foreign occupation.

Article 3

1. Each State party to the present Charter undertakes to ensure to all individuals subject to its jurisdiction the right to enjoy the rights and freedoms set forth herein, without distinction on grounds of race, colour, sex, language, religious belief, opinion, thought, national or social origin, wealth, birth or physical or mental disability.

2. The States parties to the present Charter shall take the requisite measures to guarantee effective equality in the enjoyment of all the rights and freedoms enshrined in the present Charter in order to ensure protection against all forms of discrimination based on any of the grounds mentioned in the preceding paragraph.

3. Men and women are equal in respect of human dignity, rights and obligations within the framework of the positive discrimination established in favour of women by the Islamic Shariah, other divine laws and by applicable laws and legal instruments. Accordingly, each State party pledges to take all the requisite measures to guarantee equal opportunities and effective equality between men and women in the enjoyment of all the rights set out in this Charter.

Article 4

1. In exceptional situations of emergency which threaten the life of the nation and the existence of which is officially proclaimed, the States parties to the present Charter may take measures derogating from their obligations under the present Charter, to the extent strictly required by the exigencies of the situation, provided that such measures are not inconsistent with their other obligations under international law and do not involve discrimination solely on the grounds of race, colour, sex, language, religion or social origin.

2. In exceptional situations of emergency, no derogation shall be made from the following articles: article 5, article 8, article 9, article 10, article 13, article 14, paragraph 6, article 15, article 18, article 19, article 20, article 22, article 27, article 28, article 29 and article 30. In addition, the judicial guarantees required for the protection of the aforementioned rights may not be suspended.

3. Any State party to the present Charter availing itself of the right of derogation shall immediately inform the other States parties, through the intermediary of the Secretary-General of the League of Arab States, of the provisions from which it has derogated and of the reasons by which it was actuated. A further communication shall be made, through the same intermediary, on the date on which it terminates such derogation.

Article 5

1. Every human being has the inherent right to life.

2. This right shall be protected by law. No one shall be arbitrarily deprived of his life.

Article 6

Sentence of death may be imposed only for the most serious crimes in accordance with the laws in force at the time of commission of the crime and pursuant to a final judgment rendered by a competent court. Anyone sentenced to death shall have the right to seek pardon or commutation of the sentence.

Article 7

1. Sentence of death shall not be imposed on persons under 18 years of age, unless otherwise stipulated in the laws in force at the time of the commission of the crime.

2. The death penalty shall not be inflicted on a pregnant woman prior to her delivery or on a nursing mother within two years from the date of her delivery; in all cases, the best interests of the infant shall be the primary consideration.

Article 8

1. No one shall be subjected to physical or psychological torture or to cruel, degrading, humiliating or inhuman treatment.

2. Each State party shall protect every individual subject to its jurisdiction from such practices and shall take effective measures to prevent them. The commission of, or participation in, such acts shall be regarded as crimes that are punishable by law and not subject to any statute of limitations. Each State party shall guarantee in its legal system redress for any victim of torture and the right to rehabilitation and compensation.

Article 9

No one shall be subjected to medical or scientific experimentation or to the use of his organs without his free consent and full awareness of the consequences and provided that ethical, humanitarian and professional rules are followed and medical procedures are observed to ensure his personal safety pursuant to the relevant domestic laws in force in each State party. Trafficking in human organs is prohibited in all circumstances.

Article 10

1. All forms of slavery and trafficking in human beings are prohibited and are punishable by law. No one shall be held in slavery and servitude under any circumstances.

2. Forced labor, trafficking in human beings for the purposes of prostitution or sexual exploitation, the exploitation of the prostitution of others or any other form of exploitation or the exploitation of children in armed conflict are prohibited.

Article 11

All persons are equal before the law and have the right to enjoy its protection without discrimination.

Article 12

All persons are equal before the courts and tribunals. The States parties shall guarantee the independence of the judiciary and protect magistrates against any interference, pressure or threats. They shall also guarantee every person subject to their jurisdiction the right to seek a legal remedy before courts of all levels.

Article 13

1. Everyone has the right to a fair trial that affords adequate guarantees before a competent, independent and impartial court that has been constituted by law to hear any criminal charge against him or to decide on his rights or his obligations. Each State party shall guarantee to those without the requisite financial resources legal aid to enable them to defend their rights.

2. Trials shall be public, except in exceptional cases that may be warranted by the interests of justice in a society that respects human freedoms and rights.

Article 14

1. Everyone has the right to liberty and security of person. No one shall be subjected to arbitrary arrest, search or detention without a legal warrant.

2. No one shall be deprived of his liberty except on such grounds and in such circumstances as are determined by law and in accordance with such procedure as is established thereby.

3. Anyone who is arrested shall be informed, at the time of arrest, in a language that he understands, of the reasons for his arrest and shall be promptly informed of any charges against him. He shall be entitled to contact his family members.

4. Anyone who is deprived of his liberty by arrest or detention shall have the right to request a medical examination and must be informed of that right.

5. Anyone arrested or detained on a criminal charge shall be brought promptly before a judge or other officer authorized by law to exercise judicial power and shall be entitled to trial within a reasonable time or to release. His release may be subject to guarantees to appear for trial. Pre-trial detention shall in no case be the general rule.

6. Anyone who is deprived of his liberty by arrest or detention shall be entitled to petition a competent court in order that it may decide without delay on the lawfulness of his arrest or detention and order his release if the arrest or detention is unlawful.

7. Anyone who has been the victim of arbitrary or unlawful arrest or detention shall be entitled to compensation.

Article 15

No crime and no penalty can be established without a prior provision of the law. In all circumstances, the law most favorable to the defendant shall be applied.

Article 16

Everyone charged with a criminal offence shall be presumed innocent until proved guilty by a final judgment rendered according to law and, in the course of the investigation and trial, he shall enjoy the following minimum guarantees:

1. The right to be informed promptly, in detail and in a language which he understands, of the charges against him.

2. The right to have adequate time and facilities for the preparation of his defense and to be allowed to communicate with his family.

3. The right to be tried in his presence before an ordinary court and to defend himself in person or through a lawyer of his own choosing with whom he can communicate freely and confidentially.

4. The right to the free assistance of a lawyer who will defend him if he cannot defend himself or if the interests of justice so require, and the right to the free assistance of an interpreter if he cannot understand or does not speak the language used in court.

5. The right to examine or have his lawyer examine the prosecution witnesses and to on defense according to the conditions applied to the prosecution witnesses.

6. The right not to be compelled to testify against himself or to confess guilt.

7. The right, if convicted of the crime, to file an appeal in accordance with the law before a higher tribunal.

8. The right to respect for his security of person and his privacy in all circumstances.

Article 17

Each State party shall ensure in particular to any child at risk or any delinquent charged with an offence the right to a special legal system for minors in all stages of investigation, trial and enforcement of sentence, as well as to special treatment that takes account of his age, protects his dignity, facilitates his rehabilitation and reintegration and enables him to play a constructive role in society.

Article 18

No one who is shown by a court to be unable to pay a debt arising from a contractual obligation shall be imprisoned.

Article 19

1. No one may be tried twice for the same offence. Anyone against whom such proceedings are brought shall have the right to challenge their legality and to demand his release.

2. Anyone whose innocence is established by a final judgment shall be entitled to compensation for the damage suffered.

Article 20

1. All persons deprived of their liberty shall be treated with humanity and with respect for the inherent dignity of the human person.

2. Persons in pre-trial detention shall be separated from convicted persons and shall be treated in a manner consistent with their status as unconvicted persons.

3. The aim of the penitentiary system shall be to reform prisoners and effect their social rehabilitation.

Article 21

l. No one shall be subjected to arbitrary or unlawful interference with regard to his privacy, family, home or correspondence, nor to unlawful attacks on his honour or his reputation.

2. Everyone has the right to the protection of the law against such interference or attacks.

Article 22

Everyone shall have the right to recognition as a person before the law.

Article 23

Each State party to the present Charter undertakes to ensure that any person whose rights or freedoms as herein recognized are violated shall have an effective remedy, notwithstanding that the violation has been committed by persons acting in an official capacity.

Article 24

Every citizen has the right:

1. To freely pursue a political activity.

2. To take part in the conduct of public affairs, directly or through freely chosen representatives.

3. To stand for election or choose his representatives in free and impartial elections, in conditions of equality among all citizens that guarantee the free expression of his will.

4. To the opportunity to gain access, on an equal footing with others, to public office in his country in accordance with the principle of equality of opportunity.

5. To freely form and join associations with others.

6. To freedom of association and peaceful assembly.

7. No restrictions may be placed on the exercise of these rights other than those which are prescribed by law and which are necessary in a democratic society in the interests of national security or public safety, public health or morals or the protection of the rights and freedoms of others.

Article 25

Persons belonging to minorities shall not be denied the right to enjoy their own culture, to use their own language and to practice their own religion. The exercise of these rights shall be governed by law.

Article 26

1. Everyone lawfully within the territory of a State party shall, within that territory, have the right to freedom of movement and to freely choose his residence in any part of that territory in conformity with the laws in force.

2. No State party may expel a person who does not hold its nationality but is lawfully in its territory, other than in pursuance of a decision reached in accordance with law and after that person has been allowed to submit a petition to the competent authority, unless compelling reasons of national security preclude it. Collective expulsion is prohibited under all circumstances.

Article 27

1. No one may be arbitrarily or unlawfully prevented from leaving any country, including his own, nor prohibited from residing, or compelled to reside, in any part of that country.

2. No one may be exiled from his country or prohibited from returning thereto.

Article 28

Everyone has the right to seek political asylum in another country in order to escape persecution. This right may not be invoked by persons facing prosecution for an offence under ordinary law. Political refugees may not be extradited.

Article 29

1. Everyone has the right to nationality. No one shall be arbitrarily or unlawfully deprived of his nationality.

2. States parties shall take such measures as they deem appropriate, in accordance with their domestic laws on nationality, to allow a child to acquire the

mother's nationality, having due regard, in all cases, to the best interests of the child.

3. Non one shall be denied the right to acquire another nationality, having due regard for the domestic legal procedures in his country.

Article 30

1. Everyone has the right to freedom of thought, conscience and religion and no restrictions may be imposed on the exercise of such freedoms except as provided for by law.

2. The freedom to manifest one's religion or beliefs or to perform religious observances, either alone or in community with others, shall be subject only to such limitations as are prescribed by law and are necessary in a tolerant society that respects human rights and freedoms for the protection of public safety, public order, public health or morals or the fundamental rights and freedoms of others.

3. Parents or guardians have the freedom to provide for the religious and moral education of their children.

Article 31

Everyone has a guaranteed right to own private property, and shall not under any circumstances be arbitrarily or unlawfully divested of all or any part of his property.

Article 32

1. The present Charter guarantees the right to information and to freedom of opinion and expression, as well as the right to seek, receive and impart information and ideas through any medium, regardless of geographical boundaries.

2. Such rights and freedoms shall be exercised in conformity with the fundamental values of society and shall be subject only to such limitations as are required to ensure respect for the rights or reputation of others or the protection of national security, public order and public health or morals.

Article 33

1. The family is the natural and fundamental group unit of society; it is based on marriage between a man and a woman. Men and women of marrying age have the right to marry and to found a family according to the rules and conditions of marriage. No marriage can take place without the full and free consent of both parties. The laws in force regulate the rights and duties of the man and woman as to marriage, during marriage and at its dissolution.

2. The State and society shall ensure the protection of the family, the strengthening of family ties, the protection of its members and the prohibition of all

forms of violence or abuse in the relations among its members, and particularly against women and children. They shall also ensure the necessary protection and care for mothers, children, older persons and persons with special needs and shall provide adolescents and young persons with the best opportunities for physical and mental development.

3. The States parties shall take all necessary legislative, administrative and judicial measures to guarantee the protection, survival, development and well-being of the child in an atmosphere of freedom and dignity and shall ensure, in all cases, that the child's best interests are the basic criterion for all measures taken in his regard, whether the child is at risk of delinquency or is a juvenile offender.

4. The States parties shall take all the necessary measures to guarantee, particularly to young persons, the right to pursue a sporting activity.

Article 34

1. The right to work is a natural right of every citizen. The State shall endeavor to provide, to the extent possible, a job for the largest number of those willing to work, while ensuring production, the freedom to choose one's work and equality of opportunity without discrimination of any kind on grounds of race, colour, sex, religion, language, political opinion, membership in a union, national origin, social origin, disability or any other situation.

2. Every worker has the right to the enjoyment of just and favourable conditions of work which ensure appropriate remuneration to meet his essential needs and those of his family and regulate working hours, rest and holidays with pay, as well as the rules for the preservation of occupational health and safety and the protection of women, children and disabled persons in the place of work.

3. The States parties recognize the right of the child to be protected from economic exploitation and from being forced to perform any work that is likely to be hazardous or to interfere with the child's education or to be harmful to the child's health or physical, mental, spiritual, moral or social development. To this end, and having regard to the relevant provisions of other international instruments, States parties shall in particular:

(a) Define a minimum age for admission to employment;

(b) Establish appropriate regulation of working hours and conditions;

(c) Establish appropriate penalties or other sanctions to ensure the effective endorsement of these provisions.

4. There shall be no discrimination between men and women in their enjoyment of the right to effectively benefit from training, employment and job protection and the right to receive equal remuneration for equal work.

5. Each State party shall ensure to workers who migrate to its territory the requisite protection in accordance with the laws in force.

Article 35

1. Every individual has the right to freely form trade unions or to join trade unions and to freely pursue trade union activity for the protection of his interests.

2. No restrictions shall be placed on the exercise of these rights and freedoms except such as are prescribed by the laws in force and that are necessary for the maintenance of national security, public safety or order or for the protection of public health or morals or the rights and freedoms of others.

3. Every State party to the present Charter guarantees the right to strike within the limits laid down by the laws in force.

Article 36

The States parties shall ensure the right of every citizen to social security, including social insurance.

Article 37

The right to development is a fundamental human right and all States are required to establish the development policies and to take the measures needed to guarantee this right. They have a duty to give effect to the values of solidarity and cooperation among them and at the international level with a view to eradicating poverty and achieving economic, social, cultural and political development. By virtue of this right, every citizen has the right to participate in the realization of development and to enjoy the benefits and fruits thereof.

Article 38

Every person has the right to an adequate standard of living for himself and his family, which ensures their well-being and a decent life, including food, clothing, housing, services and the right to a healthy environment. The States parties shall take the necessary measures commensurate with their resources to guarantee these rights.

Article 39

1. The States parties recognize the right of every member of society to the enjoyment of the highest attainable standard of physical and mental health and the right of the citizen to free basic health-care services and to have access to medical facilities without discrimination of any kind.

2. The measures taken by States parties shall include the following:

(a) Development of basic health-care services and the guaranteeing of free and easy access to the centres that provide these services, regardless of geographical location or economic status;

(b) Efforts to control disease by means of prevention and cure in order to reduce the morality rate;

(c) Promotion of health awareness and health education;

(d) Suppression of traditional practices which are harmful to the health of the individual;

(e) Provision of the basic nutrition and safe drinking water for all;

(f) Combating environmental pollution and providing proper sanitation systems;

(g) Combating drugs, psychotropic substances, smoking and substances that are damaging to health.

Article 40

1. The States parties undertake to ensure to persons with mental or physical disabilities a decent life that guarantees their dignity, and to enhance their self-reliance and facilitate their active participation in society.

2. The States parties shall provide social services free of charge for all persons with disabilities, shall provide the material support needed by those persons, their families or the families caring for them, and shall also do whatever is needed to avoid placing those persons in institutions. They shall in all cases take account of the best interests of the disabled person.

3. The States parties shall take all necessary measures to curtail the incidence of disabilities by all possible means, including preventive health programmes, awareness raising and education.

4. The States parties shall provide full educational services suited to persons with disabilities, taking into account the importance of integrating these persons in the educational system and the importance of vocational training and apprenticeship and the creation of suitable job opportunities in the public or private sectors.

5. The States parties shall provide all health services appropriate for persons with disabilities, including the rehabilitation of these persons with a view to integrating them into society.

6. The States parties shall enable persons with disabilities to make use of all public and private services.

Article 41

1. The eradication of illiteracy is a binding obligation upon the State and everyone has the right to education.

2. The States parties shall guarantee their citizens free education at least throughout the primary and basic levels. All forms and levels of primary education shall be compulsory and accessible to all without discrimination of any kind.

3. The States parties shall take appropriate measures in all domains to ensure partnership between men and women with a view to achieving national development goals.

4. The States parties shall guarantee to provide education directed to the full development of the human person and to strengthening respect for human rights and fundamental freedoms.

5. The States parties shall endeavour to incorporate the principles of human rights and fundamental freedoms into formal and informal education curricula and educational and training programmes.

6. The States parties shall guarantee the establishment of the mechanisms necessary to provide ongoing education for every citizen and shall develop national plans for adult education.

Article 42

1. Every person has the right to take part in cultural life and to enjoy the benefits of scientific progress and its application.

2. The States parties undertake to respect the freedom of scientific research and creative activity and to ensure the protection of moral and material interests resulting form scientific, literary and artistic production.

3. The state parties shall work together and enhance cooperation among them at all levels, with the full participation of intellectuals and inventors and their organizations, in order to develop and implement recreational, cultural, artistic and scientific programmes.

Article 43

Nothing in this Charter may be construed or interpreted as impairing the rights and freedoms protected by the domestic laws of the States parties or those set force in the international and regional human rights instruments which the states parties have adopted or ratified, including the rights of women, the rights of the child and the rights of persons belonging to minorities.

Article 44

The states parties undertake to adopt, in conformity with their constitutional procedures and with the provisions of the present Charter, whatever legislative or non-legislative measures that may be necessary to give effect to the rihts set forth herein.

Article 45

1. Pursuant to this Charter, an "Arab Human Rights Committee", hereinafter referred to as "the Committee" shall be established. This Committee shall consist of seven members who shall be elected by secret ballot by the states parties to this Charter.

2. The Committee shall consist of nationals of the states parties to the present Charter, who must be highly experienced and competent in the Committee's field of work. The members of the Committee shall serve in their personal capacity and shall be fully independent and impartial.

3. The Committee shall include among its members not more than one national of a State party; such member may be re-elected only once. Due regard shall be given to the rotation principle.

4. The members of the Committee shall be elected for a four-year term, although the mandate of three of the members elected during the first election shall be for two years and shall be renewed by lot.

5. Six months prior to the date of the election, the Secretary-General of the League of Arab States shall invite the States parties to submit their nominations within the following three months. He shall transmit the list of candidates to the States parties two months prior to the date the election. The candidates who obtain the largest number of votes cast shall be elected to membership of the Committee. If, because two or more candidates have an equal number of votes, the number of candidates with the largest number of votes exceeds the number required, a second ballot will be held between the persons with equal numbers of votes. If the votes are again equal, the member or members shall be selected by lottery. The first election for membership of the Committee shall be held at least six months after the Charter enters into force.

6. The Secretary-General shall invite the States parties to a meeting at the headquarters the League of Arab States in order to elect the member of the Committee. The presence of the majority of the States parties shall constitute a quorum. If there is no quorum, the secretary-General shall call another meeting at which at least two thirds of the States parties must be present. If there is still no quorum, the Secretary-General shall call a third meeting, which will be held regardless of the number of States parties present.

7. The Secretary-General shall convene the first meeting of the Committee, during the course of which the Committee shall elect its Chairman from among its members, for a two-year term which may be renewed only once and for an identical period. The Committee shall establish its own rules of procedure and methods of work and shall determine how often it shall meet. The Committee shall hold its meetings at the headquarters of the League of Arab States. It may also meet in any other State party to the present Charter at that party's invitation.

Article 46

1. The Secretary-General shall declare a seat vacant after being notified by the Chairman of a member's:

(a) Death;

(b) Resignation; or

(c) If, in the unanimous, opinion of the other members, a member of the Committee has ceased to perform his functions without offering an acceptable justification or for any reason other than a temporary absence.

2. If a member's seat is declared vacant pursuant to the provisions of paragraph 1 and the term of office of the member to be replaced does not expire within six months from the date on which the vacancy was declared, the Secretary-General of the League of Arab States shall refer the matter to the States parties to the present Charter, which may, within two months, submit nominations, pursuant to article 45, in order to fill the vacant seat.

3. The Secretary-General of the League of Arab States shall draw up an alphabetical list of all the duly nominated candidates, which he shall transmit to the States parties to the present Charter. The elections to fill the vacant seat shall be held in accordance with the relevant provisions.

4. Any member of the Committee elected to fill a seat declared vacant in accordance with the provisions of paragraph 1 shall remain a member of the Committee until the expiry of the remainder of the term of the member whose seat was declared vacant pursuant to the provisions of that paragraph.

5. The Secretary-General of the League of Arab States shall make provision within the budget of the League of Arab States for all the necessary financial and human resources and facilities that the Committee needs to discharge its functions effectively. The Committee's experts shall be afforded the same treatment with respect to remuneration and reimbursement of expenses as experts of the secretariat of the League of Arab States.

Article 47

The States parties undertake to ensure that members of the Committee shall enjoy the immunities necessary for their protection against any form of harassment or moral or material pressure or prosecution on account of the positions they take or statements they make while carrying out their functions as members of the Committee.

Article 48

1. The States parties undertake to submit reports to the Secretary-General of the League of Arab States on the measures they have taken to give effect to the rights and freedoms recognized in this Charter and on the progress made towards the enjoyment thereof. The Secretary-General shall transmit these reports to the Committee for its consideration.

2. Each State party shall submit an initial report to the Committee within one year from the date on which the Charter enters into force and a periodic report every three years thereafter. The Committee may request the States parties to supply it with additional information relating to the implementation of the Charter.

3. The Committee shall consider the reports submitted by the States parties under paragraph 2 of this article in the presence of the representative of the State party whose report is being considered.

4. The Committee shall discuss the report, comment thereon and make the necessary recommendations in accordance with the aims of the Charter.

5. The Committee shall submit an annual report containing its comments and recommendations to the Council of the League, through the intermediary of the Secretary-General.

6. The Committee's reports, concluding observations and recommendations shall be public documents which the Committee shall disseminate widely.

Article 49

1. The Secretary-General of the League of Arab States shall submit the present Charter, once it has been approved by the Council of the League, to the States members for signature, ratification or accession.

2. The present Charter shall enter into effect two months from the date on which the seventh instrument of ratification is deposited with the secretariat of the League of Arab States.

3. After its entry into force, the present Charter shall become effective for each State two months after the State in question has deposited its instrument of ratification or accession with the secretariat.

4. The Secretary-General shall notify the States members of the deposit of each instrument of ratification or accession.

Article 50

Any State party may submit written proposals, though the Secretary-General, for the amendment of the present Charter. After these amendments have been circulated among the States members, the Secretary-General shall invite the States parties to consider the proposed amendments before submitting them to the Council of the League for adoption.

Article 51

The amendments shall take effect, with regard to the States parties that have approved them, once they have been approved by two thirds of the States parties.

Article 52

Any State party may propose additional optional protocols to the present Charter and they shall be adopted in accordance with the procedures used for the adoption of amendments to the Charter.

Article 53

1. Any State party, when signing this Charter, depositing the instruments of ratification or acceding hereto, may make a reservation to any article of the Charter, provided that such reservation does not conflict with the aims and fundamental purposes of the Charter.

2. Any State party that has made a reservation pursuant to paragraph 1 of this article may withdraw it at any time by addressing a notification to the Secretary-General of the League of Arab States.

2. Proposed First Optional Protocol to the Arab Charter on Human Rights

The States Parties to the present Protocol,

Considering that in order further to achieve the purposes of the Arab Charter on Human Rights (hereinafter referred to as the Charter) and the implementation of its provisions it would be appropriate to enable the "Arab Human Rights Committee", hereinafter referred to as "the Committee", **to receive and consider**, as provided in the present Protocol, **communications from States and from individuals that claim to be victims of violations of any of the rights set forth in the Charter.**

Have agreed as follows:

Article 1

A State Party to the Charter that becomes a Party to the present Protocol recognizes the competence of the Committee to receive and consider communications from States and from individuals subject to its jurisdiction who claim to be victims of a violation by that State Party of any of the rights set forth in the Charter. The Committee shall receive no communication if it concerns a State Party to the Charter that is not a Party to the present Protocol.

Article 2

1. Subject to the provisions of Article 1, individuals who claim that any of their rights enumerated in the Charter have been violated and who have exhausted all available domestic remedies may submit a written communication to the Committee for consideration.

2. If a State party to the present Charter has good reasons to believe that another State party to this Charter has violated the provisions of the Charter, it may submit a written communication to the Committee for consideration.

Article 3

1. The Committee shall consist of a number of members equal to that of the High Contracting Parties. The members of the Committee can be increased by majority of votes of the members of the Arab Committee.

2. Half of the members of the Committee must be judges.

3. The members of the Committee must be nationals of the Countries member to the League of Arab States, persons of high moral character, and possess the qualifications required in their respective countries for appointment to the highest judicial offices.

4. The members of the Committee shall be elected for a period of four years and may not be re-elected; provided, however, that of the members elected at the first election, the terms of half of the members shall expire at the end of their second year and the terms of the rest of them shall expire at the end of their fourth year.

5. The judges are elected by the Supreme Judicial Council of each State Party.

6. The presidents of the Supreme Judicial Councils sit together to interview all of the judges and exclude the judges that are not suitable for that position.

Article 4

1. The members of the Committee shall serve in their personal capacity and shall be fully independent and impartial.

2. The States parties undertake to ensure that members of the Committee shall enjoy the immunities necessary for their protection against any form of harassment or moral or material pressure or prosecution on account of the positions they take or statements they make while carrying out their functions as members of the Committee.

Article 5

The Committee shall elect its Chairman and Vice Chairman for a two-year period. They cannot be re-elected.

Article 6

It is prohibited for any member of the Committee to sit on any case that his state is party to.

Article 7

The Committee shall consider inadmissible any communication under the present Protocol which is anonymous, or which it considers to be an abuse of the right of submission of such communications or to be incompatible with the provisions of the Charter.

Article 8

1. The Committee shall bring any communications submitted to it under the present Protocol to the attention of the State Party to the present Protocol alleged to be violating any provision of the Charter.

2. The Committee may ask the States concerned to provide it with all relevant information.

3. When the Committee is considering the matter, States concerned may be represented before it and submit written or oral representation.

Article 9

1. The Committee shall consider communications received under the present Protocol in the light of all written information made available to it by the individual and by the State Party concerned.

2. The Committee shall consider communications received from individuals inadmissible if:

(a) It is anonymous, or which it considers to be an abuse of the right of submission of such communications or to be incompatible with the provisions of the Charter.

(b) The same matter has been examined before by the Arab Human Rights Committee or being examined under another procedure of international investigation or settlement under another procedure of international or regional investigation or settlement and if it contains no relevant new information.

(c) The individual has not exhausted all available domestic remedies unless it is obvious to the Committee that the procedure of achieving these remedies would be unduly prolonged.

(d) The communication is submitted to the Committee after the completion of four months from the date of the exhaustion of all domestic remedies.

(e) The communication is written in disparaging or insulting language directed against the State concerned and its institutions or to the Arab League.

(f) Are based exclusively on news disseminated through the mass media.

3. The Committee shall hold closed meetings when examining communications under the present Protocol.

4. The Committee shall forward its views to the State Party concerned and to the individual.

Article 10

If the communication that is considered inadmissible refers to a law that is considered violating human rights, the Committee shall convert this inadmissible communication to a shadow report during its examination to the annual periodic report of the State concerned.

Article 11

If the communications apparently relate to special cases which reveal the existence of a series of serious or massive violations of human rights, the Committee shall draw the attention of the Council of Arab League and the Secretary General.

Article 12

In the event of the Committee accepting a communication referred to it:

1. It shall, with a view to ascertaining the facts, undertake together with the representatives of the parties an examination of the petition and, if need be, an investigation, for the effective conduct of which the states concerned shall furnish all necessary facilities, after an exchange of views with the Committee;

2. The Committee may resort to any appropriate method of investigation; it may hear any person capable of enlightening it;

3. It shall place itself at the disposal of the parties concerned with a view to securing a friendly settlement of the matter on the basis of respect for Human Rights as defined in this Charter.

Article 13

If the Committee succeeds in effecting a friendly settlement in accordance with Article 8, it shall draw up a Report which shall be sent to the States concerned, and to the Secretary-General of the League of Arab States for publication. This Report shall be confined to a brief statement of the facts and of the solution reached.

Article 14

The Commission must continue its examination of the case based on the documents available if within three months from the date on which the original communication is received by the State to which it is addressed:

(a) The issue is not settled by friendly settlement based on respect for Human Rights;

(b) The State concerned did not submit to the Committee the required documents without acceptable reason;

(c) If the Committee found that the individual who submitted the communication is trying to delay the work of the Committee without acceptable reasons.

Article 15

After having obtained from the States concerned and from other sources all the information it deems necessary and after having tried all appropriate means to reach an amicable solution based on the respect of human rights, the Committee shall prepare, within three months after the end of the four months in article 9, a report stating the facts and its findings. This report shall be sent to the States concerned and communicated to the Council of Arab League.

Article 16

1. The Committee shall take its decisions by a majority of its members.

2. If the opinion of the majority of judges of the Committee does not represent, in whole or in part, the unanimous decision of the judges, no judge is permitted to deliver a separate or dissenting opinion.

Article 17

The Committee should do a promotional task in order to promote and protect human rights.

The Promotional task of the Committee shall be:

1. To promote human and rights and in particular:

(a) To collect documents, undertake studies and research on Arab problems in the field of human rights; organize seminars; symposia and conferences; disseminate information; encourage national and local institutions concerned with human and rights; and, should the case arise, give its views or make recommendations to States and the Arab League;

(b) To formulate and present, principles and rules aimed at solving legal problems relating to human rights and fundamental freedoms upon which Arab Governments may base their legislation;

(c) To cooperate with other Arab and international institutions concerned with the promotion and protection of human and peoples' rights;

(d) To organize, seminars, workshops and conferences regarding human rights in order to serve the goals and purposes of the Charter.

2. Ensure the protection of human rights under conditions laid down by the present Charter.

3. Perform any other tasks that may be entrusted to it by the Assembly of Heads of State and Government.

Article 18

In its annual report, the Committee shall include a summary of its activities under the present Protocol. The Committee may take this report to the Council of the Arab League and the State concerned with respect to particular recommendations, as it deems useful. In addition, the Committee should present its annual report to the Council of Arab League and the Summit of Ministers.

Article 19

1. The High Contracting Parties undertake to abide by the recommendations of the Committee in any case to which they are parties.

2. The Committee must follow up on the implementation of its recommendations.

Article 20

1. The recommendations of the Committee shall be transmitted to both the Summit of Ministers of Justice, which shall supervise its execution and the Supreme Judicial Councils of States parties.

2. If the Summit of Ministers and Supreme Judicial Councils fail to execute the recommendations of the Committee, the case shall be transmitted to the Council of the Arab League to take all the necessary adequate measures.

Article 21

An 'implementation office' is an office at the Arab Committee that is responsible to follow up the implementation of the Committee's recommendations.

Article 22

1. The Committee shall draw inspiration from international human rights law, particularly from the provisions of various Arab instruments on human rights, the Charter of the United Nations, the Universal Declaration of Human Rights, and other instruments adopted by the United Nations in the field of human rights, as well as from the provisions of various instruments adopted within the Specialized Agencies of the United Nations of which the parties to the present Charter are members.

2. Inspiration must not contradict the objectives and purposes of the Arab Charter.

Article 23

1. The Committee shall have its seat in Alexandria, Egypt.

2. The seat may be changed after consultation with the Committee and States Parties.

Article 24

Article 48 of the Arab Charter shall be amended as follows:

Article 48 (1) of the Arab Charter shall be amended to read as follows:

"1. The States parties undertake to submit reports to the Committee on Human Rights on the measures they have taken to give effect to the rights and freedoms recognized in this Charter and on the progress made towards the enjoyment thereof. The State concerned shall submit a copy of this report to the Secretary-General of the League of Arab States."

Article 48 (2) shall be amended to read as follows:

"2. Each State party shall submit an initial report to the Committee within one year from the date on which the Charter enters into force and a periodic report every *two years* thereafter. The Committee may request the States parties to supply it with additional information relating to the implementation of the Charter."

A new paragraph 4 shall be inserted which shall read as follows:

"4. The Committee shall receive shadow reports from the Arab Court, and also from governmental or nongovernmental organizations, potential victims, group individuals and any individual."

Paragraphs 4, 5 and 6 shall become paragraphs 5, 6 and 7 respectively.

Article 25

The provisions of the present Protocol shall extend to all parts of States territories without any limitations or exceptions.

Article 26

1. The present Protocol is open for signature by any State which has signed the Charter.

2. The present Protocol is subject to ratification by any State which has ratified or acceded to the Charter. Instruments of ratification shall be deposited with the secretariat of the League of Arab States.

3. The present Protocol shall be open to accession by any State which has ratified or acceded to the Charter.

4. Accession shall be effected by the deposit of an instrument of accession with the secretariat of the League of Arab States.

5. The Secretary-General shall inform all States which have signed the present Protocol or acceded to it of the deposit of each instrument of ratification or accession.

Article 27

1. Subject to the entry into force of the Charter, the present Protocol shall enter into force three months after the date of the deposit with the Secretary-General of the third instrument of ratification or instrument of accession.

2. For each State ratifying the present Protocol or acceding to it after the deposit of the third instrument of ratification or instrument of accession, the present Protocol shall enter into force two months after the date of the deposit of its own instrument of ratification or instrument of accession.

Article 28

1. Any State Party to the present Protocol in addition to the Arab Human Rights Committee may submit written proposals. After these amendments have been circulated among the States members, the Secretary-General shall invite the States parties to consider the proposed amendments before submitting them to the Council of the League for adoption.

2. The amendments shall take effect, with regard to the States parties that have approved them, once they have been approved by majority of votes of the States Parties to the Protocol.

3. When amendments come into force, they shall be binding on those States Parties which have accepted them, other States Parties still being bound by the provisions of the present Protocol and any earlier amendment which they have accepted.

Article 29

1. Any State Party may denounce the present Protocol at any time by written notification addressed to the Secretary-General. Denunciation shall take effect three months after the date of receipt of the notification by the Secretary-General.

2. Denunciation shall be without prejudice to the continued application of the provisions of the present Protocol to any communication submitted under article 2 before the effective date of denunciation.

3. Proposed Second Optional Protocol to the Arab Charter on Human Rights

The States Parties to the present Protocol,

BASED on the faith of the Arab nation that justice must be guaranteed;

RECALLING the objectives and principles enunciated in Arab Charter on Human Rights and the Pact of the League of Arab States in particular Article 19 (the idea of strengthening the ties between Arab States by creating an Arab Court);

BEARING IN MIND their commitment to promote peace, Justice, and security and to protect human rights in accordance with the Arab Charter on Human Rights and other relevant instruments relating to human rights;

FIRMLY CONVINCED that the **establishment of an Arab Court of Justice and Human Rights** shall assist in the achievement of the goals and purposes of the Arab League and the Arab Charter on Human Rights.

Article 1

To ensure the protection of human rights by the High Contracting Parties in the Arab Charter and the Protocols thereto, there shall be set up an Arab Court on of Justice and Human Rights, hereinafter referred to as "the Court". It shall function on a permanent basis.

Article 2

1. Each state party of the Arab League should appoint one judge that hold the nationality of the country that appointed them or the nationality of a country member to the Arab League.

2. The Court shall consist of a number of judges at least equal to that of the States Parties to the Arab League. Each country should have the same equal number of judges under conditions to be set out in the Rules of Procedure.

3. The judges of the Court shall be elected for a period of five years and may not be re-elected provided, however, that, of the judges elected at the first election, the terms of half of the judges shall expire at the end of three years and the terms of the remaining half shall expire at the end of five years.

4. The judges are elected by the Supreme Judicial Council of each State Party concerned.

5. The presidents of each Supreme Judicial Council shall sit together to interview all of the judges and exclude the judges that are not suitable for that position.

6. The Supreme Judicial Councils can increase the number of judges upon the request of the majority of the presidents of the Supreme Judicial Councils. The

plenary of the Arab Court can increase the number of judges upon the request of the majority of judges of the Court.

7. The terms of office of judges shall expire when they reach the age of 70.

8. The judges shall hold office until replaced. They shall, however, continue to deal with such cases as they already have under consideration.

9. In the case of the resignation of a member of the Court, the resignation shall be addressed to the President of the Court. This last notification makes the place vacant.

10. A judge shall not be suspended or removed from office unless, by the decision of a two-thirds majority of the votes of the other judges of the Court, the concerned judge has been found to be no longer fulfilling the required conditions of the Court.

Article 3

1. The Court shall be composed of a body of independent judges, who are nationals of the Countries member to the League of Arab States, from among persons of high moral character, who possess the qualifications required in their respective countries for appointment to the highest judicial offices.

2. The judges shall sit on the Court in their individual capacity.

3. The Court shall act impartially, fairly and justly.

4. In performance of the judicial functions and duties, the Court and its Judges shall not be subject to the direction or control of any person or body.

5. The judiciary shall decide on matters before them impartially, on the basis of facts and in accordance with the law, without any restrictions, improper influences, inducements, pressures, threats or interferences, direct or indirect, from any quarter or for any reason.

6. No member of the Court may exercise any political or administrative function, or engage in any other occupation of a professional nature.

7. During their term of office the judges shall not engage in any activity that is incompatible with their independence, impartiality, or the demands of a full-time office; the Court shall decide all questions arising from the application of this article.

Article 4

After their election, the judges of the Court shall make a solemn declaration to discharge their duties impartially and faithfully.

Article 5

1. The independence of the judges shall be fully ensured in accordance with international law.

2. No judge may hear any case in which the same judge has previously taken part as agent, counsel or advocate for one of the parties or as a member of a national or international court or a commission of enquiry or in any other capacity. Any doubt on this point shall be settled by decision of the Court.

3. The judges of the Court shall enjoy the immunities extended to diplomatic agents in accordance with international law from the moment of their election and throughout their term of office.

4. At no time shall the judges of the Court be held liable for any decision or opinion issued in the exercise of their functions.

5. Judges shall be granted immunity from personal arrest or detention and from seizure of their personal baggage and immunity from legal process of every kind in respect to words spoken or written and all acts done by them in their official capacity.

6. Judges shall have complete freedom of speech and complete independence in the discharge of their duties, immunity from legal process in respect of words spoken or written, and all acts done by them in discharging their duties shall continue to be accorded, notwithstanding that the persons concerned are no longer engaged in the discharge of such duties.

7. Judges and their spouses shall receive exemption with respect to any restrictions on their freedom of movement in exiting from and returning to their country of residence and entering into and exiting from the country in which they exercise their functions, as well as exemption from aliens' registration in the country they are visiting or through which they are passing in the exercise of their functions.

8. Judges are given by their own government the same facilities as those accorded to senior government officials travelling abroad on temporary official duty. Privileges and immunities are accorded to judges not for the personal benefit of the individuals themselves, but in order to safeguard the independent exercise of their functions. The Court alone, sitting in plenary session, shall be competent to waive the immunity of judges; it has not only the right, but is under a duty to waive the immunity of a judge in any case where, in its opinion, the immunity would impede the course of justice and where it can be waived without prejudice to the purpose for which the immunity is accorded.

Article 6

To consider cases brought before it, the Court shall sit in Chambers of five judges, in a Grand Chamber of thirteen judges and a plenary of all the judges of the Court.

Article 7

If a judge is a national of any State that is a party to a case submitted to the Court, that judge shall not hear the case. In addition, a judge shall not examine any application against a state party to a case in respect of which that judge has been elected. The Court can invite the concerned judge to give advisory or explanatory opinion. However, his or her voice should not be counted and he or she should have no right to vote in such a case.

Article 8

1. The following are entitled to submit cases to the Court:

(a) Any High Contracting Party may refer to the Court any alleged breach of the provisions of the Charter and the protocols thereto by another High Contracting Party.

(b) The Court may receive applications from any person or group of individuals claiming to be the victim of a violation by one of the High Contracting Parties of the rights set forth in the Convention or the protocols thereto provided that they have exhausted all available domestic remedies. The High Contracting Parties undertake not to hinder in any way the effective exercise of this right.

(c) The State Party whose citizen is a victim of human rights violation.

2. When a State Party has an interest in a case, it may submit a request to the Court to be permitted to join. The Court has full discretionary authority to accept or reject the request.

Article 9

1. The Court shall appoint its own Registrar and the other members of staff of the registry from among nationals of member Arab states according to the Rules of Procedure.

2. The office and residence of the Registrar shall be situated at the location where the Court has its seat.

3. The Registrar shall assist the Court in the performance of its functions and shall be responsible for the following:

(a) The organization and activities of the Registry under the authority of the President of the Court;

(b) The custody of the archives of the Court and for acting as the channel for all communications and notifications made by, or addressed to, the Court in connection with the cases brought, or to be brought, before it;

(c) Providing the Court with answers regarding any questions of national law;

(d) Assisting the judges by providing advice regarding the latest decisions taken by international and other regional courts.

4. The members of the Registry should be geographically distributed taking into account the number of cases of each country and its population.

5. The members of the Registry should have a high degree of experience with regard to national laws and national courts procedures as well as knowledge of international human rights laws.

6. The members of the Registry should be able to speak, write, and read fluently in English and/or French.

7. Some of the members of the registry and the deputy registry should be judges and/or prosecutors.

8. The functions and organization of the registry shall be laid down in the rules of the Court.

Article 10

1. The Court shall elect its President and two Vice-Presidents for a period of three years. They cannot be re-elected.

2. The President and the two Vice-Presidents of the Court shall be elected by the plenary of the Court. The election is conducted by secret ballot. The winning seat is given to the judge by who received the absolute majority of votes.

3. The functions of the President and the two Vice-Presidents shall be set out in the Rules of Procedure of the Court.

4. If the President or one of the two Vice-Presidents of the Court is a national of any state that is a party to a case submitted to the Court, that judge shall not hear that particular case. In addition, a judge shall not examine any application against a state party to a case in respect of which that judge has been elected. The Court can invite the concerned judge to give advisory or explanatory opinion. However, his or her voice should not be counted and should have no right to vote in such a case and is not permitted to deliver a separate or dissenting opinion.

Article 11

1. The jurisdiction of the Court shall extend to all cases and disputes submitted to it concerning the interpretation and application of the Charter, this Protocol and any other relevant Human Rights instrument ratified by the States concerned.

2. In the event of a dispute as to whether the Court has jurisdiction, the Court shall decide.

Article 12

1. At the request of a Member State of the Arab Charter or the Arab League, the Court may provide an opinion on any legal matter relating to the Charter or any other relevant human rights instruments, provided that the subject matter of the opinion is not related to a matter being examined by the Commission.

2. The Court shall give reasons for its advisory opinions.

Article 13

1. The Court, when deciding on the admissibility of a case instituted may request the opinion of the Committee which shall give it as soon as possible.

2. The Court may consider cases or transfer them to the Committee.

3. The Court shall rule on the admissibility of cases.

Article 14

1. The Chamber, by a majority of votes, may:

(a) Declare a case inadmissible or strike it out of its list of cases, where such decision can be taken without further examination; or

(b) Declare it admissible and render, at the same time, a judgment on the merits, if the underlying question in the case, concerning the interpretation or the application of the Charter or the Protocols thereto, is already the subject of well-established case-law of the Court.

2. If a solution is not reached, the Chamber shall draw up a report on the facts and state its opinion as to whether the facts found disclose a breach by the state concerned of its obligations under the Charter. The Report shall be transmitted to the Grand Chamber.

Article 15

1. If the appeal is accepted by the panel of five judges or if no decision is taken by the Chamber, the Grand Chamber shall decide on the admissibility and merits of individual applications. If the appeal is accepted by the panel of five judges or if

no decision is taken by the Grand Chamber, the plenary of the Court shall decide on the admissibility and merits.

2. The Grand Chamber shall decide on the admissibility and merits of inter-state applications. The decision on admissibility shall be taken by majority of votes. If the appeal is accepted by the panel of five judges or if no decision is taken by the Grand Chamber, the plenary of the Court shall decide on the admissibility and merits of inter-state applications.

3. The Court has the discretionary authority after holding a case to be inadmissible to transfer it to the Committee to consider the case as a shadow report.

Article 16

The Court shall consider a case received from one or more individuals inadmissible if:

(a) It is anonymous, or which it considers to be an abuse of the right of submission of such cases or to be incompatible with the provisions of the Charter.

(b) The same matter has been examined before by the Arab Court on Human Rights or is being examined under another procedure of international or regional investigation or settlement and if it contains no relevant new information.

(c) The individual has not exhausted all available domestic remedies, according to the generally recognized rules of international law, unless it is obvious to the Court that the procedure of achieving these remedies would be unduly prolonged.

(d) The case is submitted to the Court after the completion of four months from the date of the exhaustion of all domestic remedies from the date on which the final decision was taken.

e) The complaint is written in disparaging or insulting language directed against the State concerned and its institutions or to the Arab League.

(f) It is based exclusively on news disseminated through the mass media.

Article 17

1. The plenary of all the judges of the Court should be given the right to:

(a) Elect the President and one or two Vice-Presidents of the Court. In addition, it shall set up Chambers, and the Grand Chamber of the Court.

(b) Adopt the Rules of the Court. The plenary may, at the request of the Arab League or any country member to the Arab League, give advisory opinions on legal questions concerning the interpretation of the Charter and the Protocols thereto.

(c) Increase the number of judges upon the request of the majority of judges of the Court.

(d) Decide on the admissibility and merits of inter-state applications.

Article 18

1. The Court shall apply the provisions of the Arab Charter on Human Rights and any other relevant human rights instruments ratified by the States concerned.

2. The Arab Court shall draw inspiration from international human rights law, particularly from the provisions of various Arab instruments on human rights, the Charter of the United Nations, the Universal Declaration of Human Rights, and other instruments adopted by the United Nations in the field of human rights, as well as from the provisions of various instruments adopted within the Specialized Agencies of the United Nations of which the parties to the present Charter are members.

3. Inspiration must not contradict the objectives and purposes of the Arab Charter.

Article 19

The Rules of Procedure of the Court shall lay down the detailed conditions under which the Court shall consider cases brought before it, bearing in mind the complementarity between the Committee and the Court.

Article 20

The Arab Court may at any stage of the proceedings decide to strike an application out of its list of cases under conditions to be set out in the Rules of Procedure.

The Chamber and the Grand Chamber should apply the procedure of friendly settlement on the basis of respect for human rights.

Article 21

1. The Court shall conduct its proceedings in public. The press and the public may be excluded from all or part of a hearing in the interests of morals, public order or national security in a democratic society, where the interests of juveniles or the protection of the private life of the parties so require, or to the extent strictly necessary in the opinion of the judges in special circumstances where publicity would prejudice the interests of justice.

2. Public access to a document or to any part of it may be restricted in the interests of morals, public order, or national security in a democratic society, where the interests of juveniles or the protection of the private life of the parties or of any person concerned so require, or to the extent strictly necessary in the opinion of the judges in special circumstances where publicity would prejudice the interests of justice.

3. Any party to a case shall be entitled to be represented by a legal representative of the party's choice. Free legal representation may be provided where the interests of justice so require.

4. Any person, witness or representative of the parties, who appears before the Court, shall enjoy protection and all facilities, in accordance with international law, necessary for the discharging of their functions, tasks and duties in relation to the Court.

Article 22

1. The Court shall hear submissions by all parties and if deemed necessary, hold an enquiry. The States concerned shall assist by providing relevant facilities for the efficient handling of the case.

2. The Court may receive written and oral evidence including expert testimony and shall make its decision on the basis of such evidence.

Article 23

The Court must continue its examination of the case based on the document available if within six months from the date on which the original communication is received by the State to which it is addressed:

(a) The issue is not settled by friendly settlement based on respect for Human Rights.

(b) The State party did not submit to the Court the required documents without acceptable reason.

(c) If the Court found that the individual who submitted the complain is trying to delay the judgment without acceptable reasons.

Article 24

1. If the Court finds that there has been a violation of the Charter or the protocols thereto, and if the internal law of the High Contracting Party concerned allows only partial reparation to be made, the Court shall, if necessary, afford just satisfaction to the injured party.

2. The court's judgment varies from paying damages to the victim to amending domestic law that constitutes a violation of the human rights protected by the Charter.

3. In cases of extreme gravity and urgency, and when necessary to avoid irreparable harm to persons, the Court shall adopt such provisional measures as it deems necessary.

Article 25

1. The Court shall render its judgment within four month of having completed its deliberations.

2. The Court may interpret its own decision unilaterally or upon the request of the State party concerned or the request of the Arab Committee.

3. The judgment of the Court shall be read in open court, due notice having been given to the parties.

4. Reasons shall be given for the judgment of the Court.

5. If the judgment of the Court does not represent, in whole or in part, the unanimous decision of the judges, no judge is permitted to deliver a separate or dissenting opinion.

6. If the Court found that its decision will be in contradiction with previous similar cases by the Court, it has the right to request all the judges of the Arab Court to sit together and render a judgment in the case.

Article 26

1. The judgment of the Court decided by majority shall be final and not subject to appeal.

2. Without prejudice to sub-article 1 above, in very rare cases, the judgment of the Chamber can be subject to appeal by the Grand Chamber. In addition, the judgment of the Grand Chamber can be subject to appeal by the plenary. A panel of five judges of the Grand Chamber of the Court may review the Chamber's and the Grand Chamber's decisions, upon the request of the parties or by unilateral decision of the Court, in the light of new evidence under conditions to be set out in the Rules of Procedure and/or if the decision of the Court was violating the human rights principles protected by the Arab Charter and its protocols and/or if the case raises a serious question affecting the interpretation or application of the Convention or the Protocols thereto, or a serious issue of general importance.

Article 27

1. The parties to the case shall be notified of the judgment of the Court and it shall be transmitted to the States parties and the Committee.

2. The Summit of both Ministers of Justice and Prosecutors Generals in addition to the Supreme Judicial Council of States parties shall be notified of the judgment and shall monitor its execution.

3. If the Summit of Ministers of Justice, the Supreme Judicial Council of states parties, and the Committee fail to execute the judgment, the Council of League of Arab States should be notified to take necessary measures.

Article 28

The States parties to the present Protocol undertake to comply with the judgment in any case to which they are parties within the time stipulated by the Court and to guarantee its execution.

Article 29

An "implementation office" is an office at the Arab Court that is responsible to follow up the implementation of the Court judgments.

The office should analyze the Court's decision in order to find the reasons generating the violations and how to prevent them.

Article 30

The Court shall submit a report on its work during the previous year to each regular session of the Council of League of Arab States. The report shall specify, in particular, the cases in which a state has not complied with the Court's judgment. In addition, the report should mention best practices, challenges that faced the Court, and the recommendations of the Court in order to promote human rights in the Arab world.

Article 31

The Court shall draw up its Rules and determine its own procedures. The Court shall consult the Commission as appropriate.

Article 32

1. The Court shall have its seat in Alexandria, Egypt.

2. The seat of the Court may be changed after consultation with the Court and States Parties.

Article 33

1. The present Protocol is open for signature by any State which has signed the Charter.

2. The present Protocol is subject to ratification by any State which has ratified or acceded to the Charter. Instruments of ratification shall be deposited with the secretariat of the League of Arab States.

3. The present Protocol shall be open to accession by any State which has ratified or acceded to the Charter.

4. Accession shall be effected by the deposit of an instrument of accession with the secretariat of the League of Arab States.

5. The Secretary-General shall inform all States which have signed the present Protocol or acceded to it of the deposit of each instrument of ratification or accession.

Article 34

1. Subject to the entry into force of the Charter, the present Protocol shall enter into force six months after the date of the deposit with the Secretary-General of the fifth instrument of ratification or instrument of accession.

2. For each State ratifying the present Protocol or acceding to it after the deposit of the fifth instrument of ratification or instrument of accession, the present Protocol shall enter into force six months after the date of the deposit of its own instrument of ratification or instrument of accession.

Article 35

The provisions of the present Protocol shall extend to all parts of States territories without any limitations or exceptions.

Article 36

1. Any State Party to the present Protocol in addition to the Arab Human Rights Committee may propose may submit written proposals. After these amendments have been circulated among the States members, the Secretary-General shall invite the States parties to consider the proposed amendments before submitting them to the Council of the League for adoption.

2. The amendments shall take effect, with regard to the States parties that have approved them, once they have been approved by majority of votes of the States Parties to the Protocol.

3. When amendments come into force, they shall be binding on those States Parties which have accepted them, other States Parties still being bound by the provisions of the present Protocol and any earlier amendment which they have accepted.

Article 37

1. Any State Party may denounce the present Protocol at any time by written notification addressed to the Secretary-General. Denunciation shall take effect three months after the date of receipt of the notification by the Secretary-General.

2. Denunciation shall be without prejudice to the continued application of the provisions of the present Protocol to any communication submitted under article 2 before the effective date of denunciation.

Bibliography

A. Books and Independent Publications

Al-Faruqi, Lois Lamya & Ismail Raji' Al-Faruqi: The Cultural Atlas of Islam (1986)

Abdal-Haqq, Irshad: Islamic Law: An Overview of its Origin and Elements (2002)

Alkaradawy, Yousf: Derasah Fi Fkh Makasd Alsharia [Study in the Jurisprudence of the Purposes of Sharia] (3rd ed. 2008)

Alkorashy, Abo-Alfedaa Islamil Abn-Omar: Tafseer Alkoran Al-Azeem [The Interpretation of Great Quran] (2nd ed. 1999)

Al-Magd, Kamal Abo: Hewar la Mowagaha [Dialogue, Not Confrontation] (3rd ed. 2006)

Allam, Wael: Al Mesaq Al Aaby Lehokook Al En'saan Derasaah Hwl Dor El Mesaq Fi Tazez Hkook Al En'saan Fi Gamet Al Dewal Al Arabeyah [The Arab Charter on Human Rights, Study on its Role in Strengthening Human Rights in the Arab League] (2005)

Alshankeety, Mohamed Al-Ameen: Daf'a Ihaam Al'id'drabaat an Ayaat Al-ketaab [Push the Turmoil from the Verses of the Book] (1996)

Amara, Mohamed: Shobohat Wa Igabat Hawl Makant Al-mar'aa Fi Al-islam [Suspicions and Answers About the Status of Women in Islam] (2001)

Baderin, Mashood A.: International Human Rights and Islamic Law (2005)

Bassiouni, M. Cherif: The Protection of Human Rights in the Administration of Criminal Justice: a Compendium of United Nations Norms and Standards (1994)

Bassiouni, M. Cherif: A Compilation of Arab Constitutions, a Comparative Study of International Human Rights Standards (2005)

Bassiouni, M. Cherif: Introduction To International Criminal Law (2nd ed. 2012)

Bassiouni, M. Cherif & Khaled M. Ahmed: International and Regional Instruments on Criminal Justice, Part II, International Crimes and Cooperation in Criminal Matters (2007)

Brownile, Ian: Principles of Public International Law (6th ed. 2003)

Buergenthal, Thomas & Janusz Symonides: Human Rights Concept and Standards (2000)

Christou, Theodora & Keir Starmer: Human Rights Manual and Sourcebook for Africa (2005)

Cryer, Robert: An Introduction to International Criminal Law and Procedure (2nd ed. 2010)

Dalacoura, Katerina: Islam, Liberalism and Human Rights (3rd ed. 2007)

Decasa, George C.: Svd, the Quranic Concept of Umma and its Function in Philippine Muslim Society (1999)

Dembour, Marie-Benedicte: Who Believes in Human Rights, Reflection on the European Convention (2006)

Doi, Abdur Rahman I.: Shariah: the Islamic Law (1984)

Donnelly, Jack: International Human Rights (1998)

Eaton, Charles Le Gai: The Concept of Justice in Islam (2010)

El-Sergany, Raghed: Justice in Islam – Its Importance and Reality (2010)

English, Kathryn & Adam Stapleton: The Human Rights Handbook: a Practical Guide to Monitoring Human Rights (1995)

Gomma, Aly: Al-Bayan Lmaa Yash'gal Al-Az'haan [Addressing Issues that Occupy the Mind] (11th ed. 2009)

Harris, David, Michael O'Boyle, Colin Warbrick, & Ed Bates, Law of the European Convention on Human Rights (1995)

Helaly, Saad Al-Din: Hokook Alinsan Fi Alislam [Human Rights in Islam] (2010)

Jacobs, Francis G. & Robin C. A. White: The European Convention on Human Rights (4th ed. 2006)

Janis, Mark W. & Richard S. Kay, European Human Rights Law (1990)

Jayawickrama, Nihal: The Judicial Application of Human Rights Law: National, Regional and International Jurisprudence (2002)

Kamali, Mohammad Hashim: Principles of Islamic Jurisprudence (2005)

Khaled, Amr: Akhlaak Almo'men [Ethics of Believers] (5th ed. 2005)

Khaleel, Rashad Hassan: Nazareyt Al-Mosawah Fi Al-Sharia Al-Islameyah [Theory of Equality in Islamic Sharia, part two] (2007)

Korff, Douwe: The Right to Life: a Guide to the Implementation of Article 2 of the European Convention on Human Rights (2006)

Mansour, Aly Aly: Nezam Al-Tagreem Wa Al-Akaab Fi Al-Islam Mokaranan Bel Kawaneen Al- Wad'iyaa [The System of Criminsalization and Punishment in Islam Comparing to Manmade Law] (1976)

Mowbray, Alastair: Cases and Materials on the European Convention on Human Rights (2007)

Moxley, B.: Capital Punishment: Right or Wrong? (1995)

Murray, Rachel: The African Commission on Human and Peoples' Rights and International Law (2000)

Newman, Richard S.: The Transformation of American Abolitionism: Fighting Slavery in the Early Republic (2002)

Nowak, Manfred: Introduction to the International Human Rights Regime (2003)

Orakhelashvili, Alexander: Peremptory Norms in International Law (2006)

Price, Daniel E.: Islamic Political Culture, Democracy, and Human Rights: a Comparative Study (1999)

Ramadan, Hisham M., Irshad Abdal-Haqq, Hisham M. Ramadan, Ahmed Zaki Yamanai, Noor Mohammed, Mahmoud Hoballah, Hafiz Nazeem Goolam & Ali Khan: Understanding Islamic Law: from Classical to Contemporary (2006)

Reid, Karen: A Practitioner's Guide to the European Convention on Human Rights (3rd ed. 2008)

Rembe, N.S.: The System of Protection of Human Rights Under the African Charter on Human and Peoples' Rights: Problems and Prospects (1991)

Robertson, A. H.: Human Rights in National and International Law (1968)

Sarhan, Abdel Aziz Mohamed: The Legal Framework of Human Rights in International Law in Comparison with Islamic Sharia, Arab Constitutions, International Treaties, Resolutions of International Organizations, the Review Mechanisms of Human Rights and the National Courts (1987)

Schabas, William A.: The Death Penalty as Cruel Treatment and Torture (1996)

Schabas, William A.: An Introduction to the International Criminal Court (4th ed. 2011)

Shwkey, Ahmed et al.: La Hemayah L'ahad Door Gamet Al Dewal Al Arabeyah Fi Hemayat Hkook Al En'saan [No Protection for Any One, Role of the Arab League in Protecting Human Rights] (2006)

Sohn, Louis B. & Thomas Buergenthal, International Protection of Human Rights (1973)

Steiner, Henry J., Philip Alston & Ryan Goodman, International Human Rights in Context – Law, Politics, Morals (3rd ed. 2007)

Van Dijk, Pieter et. Al.: Theory and Practice of the European Convention on Human Rights (4th ed. 2006)

Viljoen, Frans: International Human Rights Law in Africa (2007)

Villiger, Mark: Customary International Law and Treaties, a Manual on the Theory and Practice of Interrelation of Sources (2nd ed. 1997)

Vitzthum, Wolfgang Graf: Begriff, Geschichte und Quellen des Völkerrechts, in Wolfgang Graf Vitzthum ed., Völkerrecht (3rd ed. 2004)

Articles and Contributions to Edited Works

Abdal-Haqq, Irshad: Islamic Law: An Overview of its Origin and Elements, 1 J. ISLAMIC L. 7 (1996)

Alford, Roger P.: In Search of a Theory for Constitutional Comparativism, 52 UCLA L. REV. 639 (2005)

Al-Hibri, Azizah: Islam, Law and Custom: Redefining Muslim Women's Rights, 12 AM. U. J. INT'L L.& POL'Y 4 (1997)

An-Naim, Abdullahi Ahmed: Human Rights in Muslim World: Socio-Political Conditions and Scriptural Imperatives, A Preliminary Inquiry, 3 HARV. HUM. RTS. J. 13 (1990)

Baderin, Mashood A.: Human Rights and Islamic Law: The Myth of Discord, 10 EUR. HUM. RTS. L. REV. 168 (2005)

Baricako, Germain: The African Charter and African Commission on Human and Peoples' Rights, The System in Practice, in Malcolm Evans & Rachel Murray eds., The African Charter on Human and Peoples' Rights: the System in Practice 1986-2006, 1 (2nd ed. 2008)

Bassiouni, M. Cherif: The Proscribing Function of International Criminal Law in the Processes of International Protection of Human Rights, 9 YALE J. WORLD PUB. ORD. 195 (1982)

Bin Ahmad, Nisar Mohammed: The Islamic and International Human Rights Law Perspectives of Headscarf: the Case of Europe 2 INTERNATIONAL JOURNAL OF BUSINESS AND SOCIAL SCIENCE 161 (2011)

Brauch, Jeffrey A.: The Margin of Appreciation and the Jurisprudence of the European Court of Human Rights: Threat to the Rule of Law, 11 COLUM. J. EUR. L. 113 (2004)

Buergenthal, Thomas: The Evolving International Human Rights System, 100 AJIL 783 (2006)

Corwin, Edwin S.: The Higher Law Background of American Constitutional Law, 42 HARVARD LAW REV. 149 (1928)

Dalvi, Sameera: Homosexuality and the European Court of Human Rights: Recent Judgments Against the United Kingdom and Their Impact on Other Signatories to the European Convention on Human Rights, 15 U. FLA. J.L. & PUB. POL'Y 481 (2004)

Dammann, Jens C.: The Role of Comparative Law in Statutory and Constitutional Interpretation, 14 ST. THOMAS L. REV. 513 (2002)

Donnelly, Jack: Human Rights and Human Dignity: An Analytical Critique of Non-Western Conceptions of Human Rights, 76 AM. POL. SCI. REV. 303 (1982)

El-Awa, Muhammed Selim: Approaches to Shari'a: A Response to N. J. Coulson's 'A History of Islamic Law', 2 J. ISLAMIC STUDIES 143 (1991)

Entelis, Joëlle: International Human Rights: Islam's Friend Or Foe? 20 FDMILJ 1267 (1997)

George, Robert P.: Natural Law, The Constitution, and the Theory and Practice of Judicial Review, 69 FORDHAM L. REV. 2269 (2001)

Grant, Evadne: Dignity and Equality, H.R.L REV. 304 (2007)

Greenberg, David F. & Valerie West, Siting the Death Penalty Internationally, 33 LAW & SOC. INQUIRY 295 (2008)

Harris, Seth R.: Asian Human Rights: Forming a Regional Covenant, 1 ASIA-PACIFIC L. & POL'Y J. 17, 2 (2000)

Jordan, David A.: The Dark Ages of Islam: Ijtihad, Apostasy, and Human Rights in Contempo- rary Islamic Jurisprudence, 9 WASH. & LEE RACE & ETHNIC ANC. L.J. 68 (2003)

Joseph, Sarah: Human Rights Committee: Recent Cases, 5 HUMAN RIGHTS LAW REVIEW 105 (2005)

Khadduri, Majid: Towards an Arab Union: The League of Arab States, 40 AM. POL. SCI. REV. 90 (1946)

Khan, Hamid M.: Nothing Is Written: Fundamentalism, Revivalism, Reformism and the Fate of Islamic Law, 24 MICH. J. INT'L L. 276 (2002)

Leuprecht, Peter: The Protection of Human Rights by Political Bodies: The Example of the Committee of Ministers of the Council of Europe, 98 , in M. Nowak & D. Steurer eds., Progress in Spirit of Human Rights (1998)

Mohammed, Yasien: Fitrah and its Bearing on the Principles of Psychology, 12 THE AM. J. OF ISLAMIC SOC. SCI. 1 (1995)

Morgan, Wayne: Sexuality and Human Rights: The First Communication by an Australian to the Human Rights Committee under the Optional Protocol to the International Covenant on Civil and Political Rights, 14 AUSTRALIAN Y.B. INT'L L. 277 (1992)

Morgan-Foster, Jason: A New Perspective on the Universality Debate: Reverse Moderate Relativism in the Islamic Context, 10 ILSA J. INT'L & COMP. L. 35 (2003)

Morgan-Foster, Jason: Reverse Moderate Relativism Applied: Third Generation International Human Rights from an Islamic Perspective, BEPRESS LEGAL SERIES 5 (2004)

Morgan-Foster, Jason: Third Generation Rights: What Islamic Law Can Teach the International Human Rights Movement, 8 YALE HUM. RTS. & DEV. L.J. 103 (2005)

Mugwanya, George William: Realizing Universal Human Rights Norms Through Regional Human Rights Mechanisms: Reinvigorating the African System, 10 IND. J. GLOBAL LEGAL STUD. 35 (1999)

Parker, M. Todd: The Freedom to Manifest Religious Belief: An Analysis of the Necessity Clauses of the ICCPR and the ECHR, 17 DUKE J. COMP. & INT'L L. 121 (2006)

Pogany, I.: The League of Arab States: An Overview, 21 BRACTON L. J. 43 (1989)

Radacic, Ivana: Gender Equality Jurisprudence of the European Court of Human Rights, 19 EUR. J. INT'L L. 841 (2008)

Reichert, Elisabeth: Human Rights: An Examination of Universalism and Cultural Relativism, J. COMP. SOC. WELFARE 22 (2006)

Rishmawi, Mervat: The Revised Arab Charter on Human Rights: A Step Forward? 5 HUM. RTS. L. REV 361-376 (2005)

Robbins, Melissa: Powerful States, Customary Law and the Erosion of Human Rights Through Regional Enforcement, 35 CAL. W. INT'L L.J. 275 (2005)

Rolin, Henri: Has the European Court of Human Rights a Future?, HOW. L.J. 442 (1965)

Sayeht, Leila P. & Adriaen M. Morse, Jr: Islam and the Treatment of Women: An Incomplete Understanding of Gradualism, 30 TEX. INT'L L. J. 311 (1995)

Schumm, Walter R. & Alison L. Kohler: Muslims Social Cohesion and the Five Pillars of Islam: A Comparative Perspective, 23 AMERICAN JOURNAL OF ISLAMIC SOCIAL SCIENCES (2006)

Sinnott, Robert E.: Universalism and Cultural Relativism in Roper vs. Simmons, 14 WILLAMETTE J. INT'L L. & DISPUTE RES. 136 (2006)

Tibi, Bassam: International Law and Islamic Law, Islamic Law/Shari'a, Human Rights, Universal Morality and International Relations, 16 HUM. RTS. Q. 278 (1994)

Wilner, Gabriel M.: Status and Future of the Customary International Human Rights Law: Reflections on Regional Human Rights Law, 25 GA. J. INT'L & COMP. L. 407 (1996)

Younce Schooley, Kimberly: Cultural Sovereignty, Islam, and Human Rights – Toward a Communitarian Revision, 25 CUMB. L. REV. 661 (1994-1995)

Documents

American Law Institute, Third Restatement of the Foreign Relations Law of the United States, § 103 Reporters' Notes No. 1 (1987)

Amnesty Int'l, Middle East and North Africa, Human Rights Report (2008)

Cairo Declaration on Human Rights in Islam, Aug. 5, 1990, U.N. GAOR, World Conf. on Hum. Rts., 4th Sess., Agenda Item 5, U.N. Doc. A/CONF.157/PC/62/Add.18 (1993)

The Casablanca Declaration of the Arab Human Rights Movement, 17(3) N.Q.H.R. 363-369, (1999)

Committee against Torture, Conclusions and Recommendations, Egypt, U.N. Doc. CAT/C/CR/29/4 (Dec. 23, 2002)

Committee against Torture, Conclusions and Observations, Qatar, U.N. Doc. CAT/C/QAT/CO/1 (July 25, 2006)

Committee against Torture, Concluding Observations, Jordan, 44th Session, (April 26-May 14, 2010)

Committee against Torture, Concluding Observations, Yemen, 44th Session, (April 26-May 14, 2010)

Committee against Torture, Concluding Observations, Syrian Arab Republic, 44th Sess. April 26 - May 14, 2010, http://www2.ohchr.org/english/bodies/cat/docs/CAT.C.SYR.CO.1.pdf

Conclusions by the General Rapporteur, Mary Robinson, President of Ireland, Human Rights at the Dawn of the 21st Century, Council of Europe Doc. CE/CMDH (93), (citing World Conference on Human Rights, Status of Preparation of Publications, Studies and Documents for the World Conference, U.N. Doc. A/CONF.157/PC/62/Add.11/Rev.1 (Apr. 22, 1993)

Council of Europe, European Convention for the Protection of Human Rights and Fundamental Freedoms, as amended by Protocols Nos. 11 and 14, 4 November 1950, ETS 5

Council of the League of Arab States, Arab Charter on Human Rights, 15 September 1994, reprinted in 18 HUM. RTS. L.J., 151 (1997)

Human Rights Watch, World Report, Tunisia (2008)

International Committee of the Red Cross, Agreement for the Prosecution and Punishment of the Major War Criminals of the European Axis, and Charter of the International Military Tribunal. London, (8 Aug. 1945)

United Nations, Charter of the United Nations, 1 UNTS XVI, 24 October 1945

United Nations, International Covenant on Economic, Social and Cultural Rights, G.A. Res. 2200A (XXI), entered into force 3 Jan. 1976

United Nations, Statute of the International Court of Justice, 18 April 1946

U.N. Committee on the Elimination of All Forms of Discrimination Against Women (CEDAW), Concluding Observations, Egypt, CEDAW A/39/45 (1984), 34th and 39th mtgs (Mar. 30 & Apr. 3, 1984)

U.N. Committee on the Elimination of All Forms of Discrimination Against Women (CEDAW), Responses to the List of Issues and Questions with Regard to the Consideration of the Combined 6th and 7th Periodic Reports: Egypt, 23 Nov. 2009, CEDAW/C/EGY/Q/7/Add.1

U.N. Committee on the Elimination of All Forms of Discrimination Against Women (CEDAW), Concluding Comments of the Committee on the Elimination of Discrimination against Women: Morocco, U.N. Doc. CEDAW/C/SMOR/CO/4

U.N. Committee on the Elimination of All Forms of Discrimination Against Women (CEDAW), Combined Initial and Second Periodic Reports of States Parties, Saudi Arabia,,U.N. Doc. CEDAW/C/SAU/2

U.N. Committee the Elimination of All Forms of Discrimination Against Women (CEDAW), Concluding Comments of the Committee on the Elimination of Discrimination against Women: Saudi Arabia, U.N. Doc. CEDAW/C/SAU/CO/2 (Apr. 8, 2008), http://www2.ohchr.org/english/bodies/cedaw/docs/ CEDAW.C.SAU.CO.2_en.pdf

U.N. Committee on the Elimination of Racial Discrimination (CERD), U.N. Committee on the Elimination of Racial Discrimination: Concluding Observations, Oman, U.N. Doc. CERD/C/OMN/CO/1 (Oct. 19, 2006)

U.N. Convention against Torture and Other Cruel, Inhuman or Degrading Treatment or Punishment, Conclusions and recommendations of the Committee against Torture: Qatar, U.N. Doc. CAT/C/QAT/CO/1 (July 25, 2006)

U.N. Convention against Torture and Other Cruel, Inhuman or Degrading Treatment or Punishment, Conclusions and Recommendations of the Committee against Torture: Saudi Arabia, U.N. Doc. CAT/C/CR/28/5 (June 12, 2002)

U.N. General Assembly, Declaration on the Right and Responsibility of Individuals, Groups and Organs of Society to Promote and Protect Universally Recognized Human Rights and Fundamental Freedoms G.A. Res. 53/144 U.N. Doc. A/RES/53/144 (Mar. 8, 1998)

U.N. Human Rights Committee, General Comment No. 13, Equality Before the Courts and the Right to a Fair and Public Hearing by an Independent Court Established by Law (art. 14), 21st Sess. (1984)

U.N. Human Rights Committee, General Comment No. 22: The Right to Freedom of Thought, Conscience and Religion, Doc. CCPR/C/21/Rev.1/Add.4 (30 July 1993)

U.N. Human Rights Committee, General Comment No. 24: Issues Relating to Reservations Made upon Ratification or Accession to the Covenant or the Optional Protocols Thereto, or in Relation to Declarations Under Article 41 of the Covenant, U.N. Doc. CCPR/C/21/Rev.1/Add.6 (1994)

U.N. Human Rights Committee, General Comment No. 28: Equality of Rights Between Men and Women (art. 3), para. 5, U.N. Doc. CCPR/C/21/Rev.1/Add.10 (2000)

U.N. Human Rights Committee, Concluding Observations, Algeria, 91st Sess.Oct. 15-Nov.2, (2007)

U.N. Human Rights Committee, Concluding Observations, Jordan, 100th Session, Geneva, Oct. 11-29, 2010, http://daccess-dds-ny.un.org/doc/UNDOC/GEN/G10/467/05/ PDF/G1046 705.pdf?OpenElement

U.N. Human Rights Committee, Concluding Observations, Kuwait, 103rd Session, Oct. 17-Nov. 4 2011, http://www.ohchr.org/EN/countries/MENARegion/Pages/KWIndex.aspx

U.N. International Covenant on Civil and Political Rights, Concluding Observations of the Human Rights Committee on Egypt, U.N. Doc. CCPR/CO/76/EGY (28 Nov. 2002)

U.N. International Covenant on Civil and Political Rights, 82th Sess. Concluding Observations of the Human Rights Committee on Morocco, U.N. Doc. CCPR/CO/82/MAR (1 Dec. 2004)

U.N. International Covenant on Civil and Political Rights, Concluding Observations of the Human Rights Committee on Libya, U.N. Doc. CCPR/C/DZA/CO/3 (15 Nov. 2007)

U.N. International Covenant on Civil and Political Rights, Concluding Observations of the Human Rights Committee on Algeria, U.N. Doc. CCPR/C/DZA/CO/3 (12 Dec. 2007)

U.N. Office of the High Commissioner for Human Rights, The Report of the Special Rapporteur on the Human Rights Aspects of the Victims of Trafficking in Persons, Especially Women and Children (2005)

U.N. Office on Drugs and Crime, Commentary on the Bangalore Principles of Judicial Conduct, September 2007, http://www.unodc.org/documents/corruption/publications_unodc_commentary-e.pdf

United Nations Special Rapporteur on the Study Requested by the Commission in its Resolution 2000/63 and Submitted Pursuant to Economic and Social Council Decision 2002/277, Promotion and Protection of Human Rights. U.N. Doc. E/CN.4/2003/105 (17 Mar. 2003) (by Miguel Alfonso Martínez)

U.N. Human Rights Council, Report of the Special Rapporteur on Torture and Other Cruel, Inhuman or Degrading Treatment or Punishment, U.N. Doc. A/HRC/10/44/Add.2 (18 February 2009)

U.S. Department of State, Country Report on Human Rights Practices Djibouti (2007)

U.S. Department of State, Country Report on Human Rights Practices Morocco (2007)

U.S. Department of State, Trafficking in Persons Report 2006 http://www.state.gov/g/tip/rls/tiprpt/2006/65988.htm

U.S. Department of State, Trafficking in Persons Report 2011 http://www.state.gov/documents/organization/164454.pdf

Websites

Abdullah, Hafiz Firdaus: Characteristics of Hudud, The Islamic Criminal Law, Muslimvillage.com, http://www.ahlalhdeeth.com/vb/showthread.php?t=103280

Ahas, Hlayhel: Did Egypt Customs Lead to a New Shafi'i School?, muslimmatters.org, http://muslimmatters.org/2010/04/19/did-egyptian-customs-lead-to-a-new-shafii-school/

AL-ISLAM.ORG, http://www.al-islam.org/al-tawhid/ijtihad/2.htm

al-Kawthari, Shaykh Muhammad ibn Adam: Purpose and Benefit of Zakat, QIBLA.COM, http://islamqa.org/hanafi/qibla-hanafi/43514

Al-Nagar, Zaglol: Interpretation of QURAN 4:135, DIGITAL.AHRAM.ORG. http://digital.ahram.org.eg/Religion.aspx?Serial=800453

Amnesty International, Death Sentences and Executions in 2007, http://www.amnesty.org/en/death-penalty/death-sentences-and-executions-in-2007

Arshed, I.A.: Parents Rights Relationship in Islam. ISLAM101.COM

Council of Europe, Manual on Human Rights Education with Young People, The Evolution of Human Rights, http://eycb.coe.int/compass/en/chapter_4/4_2.html

Egyptian National Council for Human Rights, Third Annual Report, 2006/2007 http://www.nchregypt.org/media/ftp/report3.pdf

Egyptian Society for Spiritual and Cultural Research, Balance and Justice on Earth, ESSCR.ORG, http://www.esscr.org/g205_4.htm

European Parliament Directorate-General for External Policies, Policy Department: The Role of Regional Human Rights Mechanisms (Nov. 2010) http://www.europarl.europa.eu/RegData/etudes/etudes/join/2010/410206/EXPO-DROI_ET(2010)410206_EN.pdf

HIDAYA.ORG, http://www.hidaya.org/publications/zakat-information/how-should-i-calculate-zakathttp://www.hidaya.org/publications/zakat-information/how-should-i-calculate-zakat

Human Rights in the Middle East and North Africa, http://www.derechos.org/human- rights/mena/

Human Rights Education: Lessons from History, http://www.euroclio.eu/down-load/bulletin/Bulletin_25_Human_Rights_Lessons_from_History.pdf

ISLAMAWARENESS.NET, http://www.islamawareness.net/Shariah/sh_fatwa010.html

Islams Women, ISLAMSWOMEN.COM, http://www.islamswomen.com/articles/mothers_in_islam.php

ISLAMWEB.NET, http://www.islamweb.net/fatwa/printfatwa.php?Id=125360&lang=A Kamm, Richard: European Court of Human Rights Overturns British Ban on Gays in the Military, WCL.AMERICAN.EDU, http://www.wcl.american.edu/hrbrief/v7i3/european.htm

Kuwaiti Jurisprudence Encyclopedia (comprehensive encyclopedia), ISLAMPORT.COM Quran: An electronic version of the Quran and its English translation is available at http://www.searchtruth.com

QURANANDSCIENCE.COM http://www.Quranandscience.com/fakes-about-islam/171- parents-rights-in-islam.html

Tharoor, Shashi: Are Human Rights Universal?, NEW INTERNATIONALIST MAGAZINE, Mar. 2001, http://www.thirdworld- traveler.com/Human_Rights/Are_HR_Universal%3F.html

U.N. Development Programme, Regional Bureau for Arab States (RBAS), Challenges to Human Security in the Arab Countries, Arab Human Development Report (2009), http://www.arab-hdr.org/contents/index.aspx?rid=5

U.N. Office on Drugs and Crime, Sixth Session of the Conference of the Parties to the United Nations Convention Against Transnational Organized Crime, Vienna, 15-19 October 2012, http://www.unodc.org/unodc/en/treaties/CTOC/CTOC-COP-session6.html

WIKIPEDIA.COM, http://en.wikipedia.org/

WISEGEEK.COM, http://www.wisegeek.com/what-is-natural-law-theory.htm

Yasien, Mohamed: The Definition of Fitrah, ANGELFIRE.COM, http://www.angelfire.com/al/islamicpsychology/fitrah/fitrah.html

Yousif, Abdelwahid Abdalla: Adult Literacy and Adult Education in the Arab States: Bahrain, Egypt, Oman, Saudi Arabia, Sudan, Syria and Yemen 2 (2007). Research paper prepared for the UNESCO Regional Conferences in Support of Global Literacy (Doha, 12 – 14 March 2007), http://unesdoc.unesco.org/images/0016/001611/161145e.pdf

Zakat and Social Justice, ZAKAT.ORG, http://www.zakat.org/zakat-and-beyond/zakat-social-justice/

Index

abortion 75, 88, 191-195
adult education 230-231, 233
adultery, see -> Hodood punishments
affirmative action in favor of women, see -> positive discrimination
African Charter on Human and People's Rights. 9, 32, 35
- African Commission on Human and People's Rights 370
- living instrument. 438-440
- privacy and family life 238
- right to life 170
- system of protection 164-167
- torture 263
Aisha 119
alcohol, see -> prohibition of alcohol
Alexandria Protocol 131
Allah
- revelation of the Quran. .... 41 et seq.
Algeria
- allegations of torture 268
- Constitutional protection of privacy and family rights 243
- death penalty no longer applied. 179
- initial report to the Arab Committee on Human Rights (2011) 355-360
- violation of human rights. 3
- visit by the Arab Committee on Human Rights (2012). 362, 364
alimony, see -> child support
Al Muttaqun, see -> Muttaqun
American Convention on Human Rights, see -> Inter-American Convention
American Law Institute
- Third Restatement of Foreign Relations Law. 27
Amnesty International
- Middle East and North Africa Human Rights Report 2008.. .... 3, 7, 10
analogical reasoning, see -> Qiyas
apostasy 293-298
Arab Charter of People's and Human Rights
- abortion 191-195
- additional protocol pursuant to Art. 52 155
- adequate standard of living 95, 144
- amendment 155
- and Sharia. 37-38
- annual reporting system 148-150
- asylum 143, 321
- binding nature 141
- Committee on Human Rights. 30, 139, 148, 156, 330-369

Arab Charter of People's and Human Rights (cont'd)
- comparison with African Charter and European Convention 163-167
- consistency with Sharia 160
- criticism 160
- death penalty 174
- dignity 123, 143, 147
- disabled persons 142, 144
- duties of men and women 164-165
- duties to balance rights in a future redefinition of the Charter . . . . 448 et seq.
- education 144
- enforcement 158, 161
- equality in general 114, 141, 145-146, 307
- equality of men and women 114-115, 140-141, 146
- eradication of poverty 95
- exceptions 142-143
- fair trial . . . . 143, 307 et seq.
- family rights . . . . 146-147, 239 et seq., 249
- first generation rights 141
- freedom of movement and residence 320
- freedom of religion 287, 289
- freedom of thought 141, 143, 287
- gradualism in implementation 103, 145, 370
- history . . . . xiii, xiv, 7-9, 130-139
- human trafficking 142
- illiteracy 35-36
- independence of the judiciary 146
- inhuman treatment 264
- liberty 141
- living instrument 438-440
- medical experiments 239-240, 265
- nationality of children 198
- ne bis in idem 143
- organ trafficking 240
- positive discrimination in favor of women 35, 38, 199
- preamble 166
- privacy and family life . . . . 239 et seq.
- prohibition of prostitution and sexual exploitation 148
- prohibition of forced labor 148
- prohibition of slavery 143, 326-329
- prohibition of torture and cruel or inhuman treatment 142, 264
- proposal for individual complaint procedure 366
- protection of children 148, 240-241
- ratifications 138
- relationship with other human rights systems 442-443
- reporting system 148-150, 157

- right to an adequate standard of living 95, 144
- right to basic nutrition 103
- right to clean water 103
- right to development 95, 142, 145
- right to education. 36, 144, 212, 231
- right to fair trial . . . . 143, 307 et seq.
- right to food 144
- right to health care 103, 144
- right to healthy environment 95, 104, 144
- right to housing 95
- right to liberty and security of person 240
- right to life 141, 169-195
- right to social security 95, 142
- right to work 142, 147
- rule of law . . . . 307 et seq.
- second generation rights 141
- shortcomings of supervisory system 365-369
- supervisory mechanism . . . . 148-150, 331 et seq.
- third generation rights 142
- torture prohibition 264
- Umma 108
- universal human rights 139

Arab Committee on Human Rights. 30, 139, 148, 156, 330-369, 450-453
- guidelines for state reports 345-346
- history . . . . 330 et seq.
- jurisdiction 387-390
- lack of independence 333, 366, 371-372
- mechanisms to examine state reports 342-344
- membership . . . . 331, 333-336, 372 et seq.
- press release about severe human rights violations in Libya (2011) 362-363
- proposal for individual complaint procedure 366
- reform proposals for the Arab Committee 370-392
- report by Algeria (2011) 355-360
- report by Jordan (2010) 149, 346-354
- rules of procedure 339-342
- secretariat 336
- seat 334, 375
- shortcomings of supervisory system 365-369
- state reporting system 332-333, 336-339, 378-387
- tasks 331-333, 376-387
- tools for promotion of human rights in the region 364, 376-378
- visit to Algeria (2012) 362, 364
- visit to Syria 363
- visit to UN Human Rights Council (2012) 363-364

Arab Court of Human Rights 154-160, 393-443, 453-455
- admissibility of complaints 417-422
- Bahrein's Proposal 156, 390
- Committee of Ministers 431-434
- damage awards 435
- enforcement of decisions 430-436
- exhaustion of domestic remedies 418-421, 438
- gradual implementation 390, 393
- history 154-160
- immunity of judges 406-412
- individual complaints 158, 366, 417
- institutional structure and composition .... 393 et seq.
- judges .... 395 et seq.
- judgments 429-430
- legislative changes in response to decisions 435
- prevention of future human rights violations 435
- proposal by this author 366
- procedure 422-428
- public proceedings 415-417
- registry 412-415
- Sharia law 158
- standing before the Court 417
- structure 401-406
- subsidiarity 437-438
- time limits 421-422
Arab Human Development Report 2009... 1, 5
Arab League, see -> League of Arab States
Arab Spring 162
asylum, see -> right to asylum

Bahrain
- Constitutional protection of privacy and family rights 242
- proposal for the establishment of an Arab Court of Human Rights 156-159
- reservation to Article 2 of CEDAW 197
- Sharia as basis of legislation 179
Bahrain Independent Committee of Inquiry. xiv
Banjul Charter, see -> African Charter on Human and People's Rights
Bassiouni, Cherif.. xiii-xvii, 14, 87, 134
blood money, see -> Diyah

Cairo Declaration on Human Rights in Islam. .... xiii, 96, 134, 140
- dignity 124
- equality of men and women 200
- freedom of movement and residence 321
- right to life 176

- right to privacy and family life 241
- right to self-determination 327
- slavery prohibition 327
- torture prohibition 264

Casablanca Declaration of the Arab Human Rights Movement.. 6
CAT, see -> United Nations Convention Against Torture and Other Cruel,
    Inhuman or Degrading Treatment or Punishment
CEDAW, see -> United Nations Committee on the Elimination of All Forms of
    Discrimination Against Women
CERD, see -> United Nations Committee on the Elimination of Racial
    Discrimination
charity in Islam, see also -> Zakat, and see -> Sadaqah
- generosity towards neighbors, the poor .... 60-61, 89 et seq.

Charter of the United Nations see -> United Nations Charter
child support 208-209
collective rights, see -> human rights, and see -> Umma
Committee on Human Rights under the ACHR, see -> Arab Committee
    on Human Rights
Committee on the Elimination of Discrimination Against Women
    see -> United Nations Convention on the Elimination of All Forms
    of Discrimination Against Women (CEDAW)
community, see -> Umma
Comoros, see -> Union of the Comoros
Convention Against Torture and Other Cruel, Inhuman or Degrading
    Treatment or Punishment (CAT) see -> United Nations Convention
    Against Torture and Other Cruel, Inhuman or Degrading Treatment
    or Punishment
Convention on Rights of the Child, see -> United Nations Convention
    on Rights of the Child
corporal punishment, see -> Hodood punishments
Council of Europe
- Report on Human Rights at the Dawn of the 21st Century 1993.................. 10

crimes of passion 224-225
cruel and unusual punishment 261-285
cultural relativism
- in the protection of human rights................................ 8, 20, 74 et seq.
- moderate cultural relativism 76, 79-80
- reverse moderate relativism 80
- strict cultural relativism 76, 78

customary international law. 20, 24-26
cutting of the hand, see -> Hodood punishments

death penalty 76, 88, 170–190
- blood money 181, 183-184

death penalty (cont'd)
- for renouncing Islam, see -> apostasy
- gradualism in abolition 171
- minors 174-175, 178
- nursing mothers 175-176
- pregnant women 174
- reporting requirements 189
- women in general 182

digital illiteracy, see also -> right to eduction 233
dignity, see -> human rights
Discrimination, see also -> women; see also -> equality; and
  see -> United Nations Convention on the Elimination of
  All Forms of Discrimination Against Women (CEDAW)
- divorce 226-229
- equality as a principle in Sharia and international law .... 113 et seq.
- homosexuals .... 250 et seq.
- inheritance 52-53, 204-205
- justice vs discrimination 57
- on grounds of religion 303-304
- polygamy 215-224
- positive discrimination in favor of women 35, 38, 53, 199
- punishment for adultery 5, 85, 225

divine revelation, see -> Quran
divorce .... 209 et seq., 226-229
Diyah 108, 181, 183-184, 272
dowry 116-119
Dudgeon v. United Kingdom 253, 258
duties
- as a corollary of rights 96
- duties and rights of men and women 117-119
- Universal Declaration of Human Responsibilities 98

education, see also -> right to education
- importance of education for girls .... 211 et seq., 230
- specifically encouraged in Islam 120, 235-237
- technical and vocational training 234

Egypt
- abortion as crime 192
- Constitution 125
- Constitutional protection of privacy and family rights .... 243 et seq.
- Constitutional right to equality 308
- Constitutional right to freedom of movement 321-323
- crimes of passion 224
- custody of children 202-203
- death penalty 173, 179, 186

- divorce initiated by the wife ... 202
- freedom of religion ... 287, 305
- independence of the judiciary ... 308
- military courts ... 309
- National Council for Human Rights ... 7
- nationality of children ... 214
- prohibition of torture ... 269
- reservations to Articles 2 and 16 of CEDAW ... 213
- right to education ... 233
- right to fair trial ... 308
- Sharia as basis of legislation ... 179
- state of emergency ... 270-271
- violation of human rights ... 3

El Araby, Nabil ... 150-154, 156
embryo, see -> unborn child
equality, see also -> discrimination
- between men and women ... 113 et seq., 195-229
- in Islamic law ... 96, 113-115
- polygamy ... 215-224
- positive discrimination in favor of women ... 35, 38, 53, 199

ethics in Islam ... 54
European Convention for the Prevention of Torture and Inhuman
   or Degrading Treatment or Punishment ... 263
European Convention on Human Rights ... 20, 163-164
- access to court ... 313
- death penalty ... 170
- enforcement ... 164
- equality of men and women ... 114, 196
- fair trial ... 312
- freedom of movement and residence ... 318
- freedom of thought, conscience and religion ... 298
- individual complaints to the European Court of Human Rights ... 32
- living instrument ... 438-440
- privacy and family life ... 238-239
- prohibition of slavery and forced labor ... 326
- right to life ... 169
- torture ... 263

European Court of Human Rights
- jurisprudence ... 436-440
- relationship with other human rights systems ... 441-443
- slow start ... 399 et seq.
- subsidiarity ... 437-438

fair trial, right to 76, 306-318
family
- blood money in compensation for the killing of a relative 187-190
- importance for society as a whole 200-201, 220
- roles of men and women 200, 219
- special protection by the Arab Charter .... 146-147, 239 et seq.
- status in Sharia 38
- vendettas 184
Fasting, see -> Ramadan
Fatwa, see also -> Ijtihad
- definition 73
- not legally binding 73
Fiqh, see also -> Islamic law
- definition. 39, 47-49
- diversity 61, 72-73
Fitrah 69, 99, 104, 111-113, 126, 146, 201, 257, 297, 313
Five Pillars of Islam. 53-56
food, see -> human rights
forced labor. 148, 257, 326
freedom of movement, see -> human rights
freedom of speech, see -> human rights
freedom of religion, see also -> human rights
- apostasy 293-298
- freedom of thought, conscience and religion 286-306
- religious dress, incl. headscarf 298-306

general principles of law.. 27
gender equality, see -> equality between men and women
Genocide Convention, see -> United Nations Convention on the
       Prevention and Punishment of the Crime of Genocide
good morals, see also -> ordre public
- ethical foundations of Islam.. 54
Golder v United Kingdom (access to court) 313
Gospel. 41-42
gradualism. 99-105
- in abolition of the death penalty 171
- in implementation of the Arab Charter on Human Rights 103, 145, 370
- with regard to the rights of women 119-120
greed, consequences of 91-93
group rights, see -> human rights, and see -> Umma
guests, treatment of 60

Hadd punishment, see -> Hodood punishments
Hadith, see also -> Sunnah; and see -> Prophet Mohammed (PBUH)
- chain of transmission (isnad)... 46
- five hundred ahkam 65
- Six Books... 47
Hajj.. 46, 56
Hanafi School of Islamic jurisprudence.. 49
Hanbali School of Islamic jurisprudence... 49
Handyside v. United Kingdom 127
headscarf
- freedom of thought, conscience and religion 298-306
- prohibition in Turkey 196, 299
Henkin, Louis 74
Hijab, see -> headscarf
Hodood punishments 271-285
- Amnesty International assessment of hodood punishments 271-272
- blood money instead of punishment 271, 275
- deterrent 281-284
- evidence requirements 274, 278
- for adultery 255
- for homosexual acts 255
- for prostitution 260
- limitations 276
- objective 276
- types of Hodood punishments 273
- violation of International ius cogens? 280
homosexuality 75, 88, 113, 250-260
- *Dudgeon v. United Kingdom* 253, 258
- *Lawrence v. Texas* 251
- marriage rights .... 251 et seq.
- *United States v. Windsor* 258
human rights
- apostasy 293-298
- asylum 318-326
- choice of spouse 245
- collective rights of the -> Umma .... 105 et seq.
- cruel and unusual punishment 261-285
- definition... 19 et seq
- degrading treatment .... 261 et seq.
- dignity... 22, 121-126, 140
- disabled persons 142
- enforcement... 33, 148-154
- equality of men and women .... 113 et seq., 195-229
- evolution 87

human rights (cont'd)
- fair trial 306-318
- family rights 238-260
- first generation rights 109
- freedom of speech 122
- freedom of movement 318-326
- freedom of thought, conscience and religion 286-306
- gradualism in implementation 99-105
- importance of regional protection .... 1, 7, 31 et seq.
- individual complaints to international bodies..................... 31-32
- individual rights 109
- inviolability of the home 122, 182, 241, 324
- limitations 95, 142-143
- minimum standards 19
- parental rights 58-59, 70, 246-250
- privacy 122, 238-260
- prohibition of slavery 143, 326-329
- regional protection systems .... 74 et seq., 85 et seq.
- right to education 36, 144, 212, 229-237
- right to food 125
- right to life 169-195
- second generation rights 109
- sources .... 19 et seq
- stages of evolution 87
- torture 261-285
- treaties... 20
- universal vs culturally determined 74, 111, 139
- Western concepts 20, 85-86, 121

Human Rights Committee, see -> International Covenant on Civil
   and Political Rights
Human Rights Watch
- World Report Tunisia 2008.. 6
human trafficking 142, 240, 257

ICC, see -> International Criminal Court
ICCPR, see -> International Covenant on Civil and Political Rights
ICESCR, see -> International Covenant on Economic, Social and Cultural Rights
ICJ, see -> International Court of Justice
Iddah 226
Ijma, see also -> Islamic law
- definition 49
Ijtihad, see also -> Islamic law
- at Al-Azhar 72
- closing the door to Ijtihad 61-62
- definition 41, 47-50, 69

- during the lifetime of the Prophet? 67
- individual vs collective Ijtihad 71-72
- the door is still open? 61-73

illiteracy, see also -> right to education
- consequences 234
- link to poverty 235
- rewards for those who fight illiteracy 237

individual reasoning, see -> Ijtihad

inheritance rights of sons and daughters .... 204 et seq.

inhuman or degrading treatment, see -> torture

Injeel, see -> Gospel

Inter-American Convention on Human Rights. 32
- death penalty 173
- privacy and family life 238
- right to life 169
- torture 263

Inter-American Convention to Prevent and Punish Torture 263

Inter-American Court of Human Rights
- Advisory Opinion on the Rights of Undocumented Migrants 2003............... 25

International Court of Justice (ICJ).. 22

International Covenant on Civil and Political Rights (ICCPR). 21, 28
- Concluding Observations of the Human Rights Committee Algeria 2007. 5
- Concluding Observations of the Human Rights Committee Egypt 2002... 4, 5, 225
- Concluding Observations of the Human Rights Committee Libya 2007. 6
- death penalty 170-173
- dignity 124
- equality of men and women 113, 195
- fair trial 306-308
- First Optional Protocol... 30, 31
- freedom of movement and residence 318
- freedom of thought, conscience and religion 286
- gradualism in implementation 102
- Human Rights Committee. 30
- individual complaints... 30, 31
- individual rights 109
- military courts 309
- polygamy. 216
- privacy and family life 238
- prohibition of slavery and forced labor. 326
- ratifications by Arab countries 161
- right to life 171
- second optional protocol on death penalty 170
- torture 262

International Covenant on Economic, Social and Cultural Rights (ICESCR)............ 28
- dignity... 124-125
- Economic and Social Council... 30
- equality of men and women.. 114
- freedom from hunger... 94
- gradualism in implementation.. 102
- ratifications by Arab countries.. 161
- right to education... 229
- right to social security... 94
International Criminal Court (ICC)... 14, 262-263
International Criminal Tribunal for the Former Yugoslavia......................... 25
International Institute of Higher Studies in Criminal Science (ISICS)................. xiii
international law
- customary international law... 20, 24
- general principles of law... 27
- ius cogens... 24
- sources.. 22-27
- treaty law... 23
- Vienna Convention on the Law of Treaties................................... 23
International League for Human Rights.. 20
inviolability of the home... 241 et seq.
in vitro fertilization... 128
Iraq
- reservation to Article 2 of CEDAW... 199
Iraq conflict... xvi, 3
ISICS... xiii
ISIL, see -> ISIS
ISIS... xvi
Islam
- and human dignity... 121-126
- definition.. 39
- Five Pillars.. 53-56
- religion of Fitrah... 111-113
Islamic law, see also -> Sharia
- as a living instrument... 62-73
- gradualism in implementation....................................... 99-105
- interpretation... 64-73
- punishment for crimes... 271-285
- sources... 40 et seq.
- step-by-step implementation.. 99
Islamic schools of jurisprudence.. 48-49
Islamic State of Iraq and Syria (ISIS)... xvi
Isnad, see -> Hadith
Istihsan... 50-51
Istishab... 50-51

ius cogens.. 24, 34, 83
- prohibition of torture 265

Jihad... 47
Jordan
- allegations of torture in detention centers of the General
  Intelligence Directorate 267, 311
- conclusions and recommendations by the Arab Committee
  on Human Rights 352-354
- initial report to the Arab Committee on Human Rights 149, 346-354
- UN Human Rights Committee Observations 2010 267-268
judgment day.. 43, 93, 106-107, 285
justice
- justice of judges and leaders .... 313 et seq.
- peace and justice in Islam... 56-58

Khul 228
Kurdish people
- treatment in Syria 268
Kuwait
- abortion as crime 192
- crimes of passion 224
- fair trial 310-311
- reservation to Article 16 of CEDAW 199
- Sharia as basis of legislation 179

lashing as a punishment, see -> Hodood punishments
Lawrence v. Texas 251
League of Arab States... 11, 37, 130-133
- Alexandria Protocol 131
- Permanent Arab Committee for Human Rights........................... 330
- human rights treaty implementation review 360-361
- member states 133
- Pact of Arab States 133, 154
Lebanon
- Constitution 125
- independence 132
LGBT rights 253-254
Libya
- case against Libya in the International Criminal Court 363
- polygamy... 216
- press release by the Arab Committee on Human Rights about severe human
  rights violations (2011) 362-363
- reservation to Article 16 of CEDAW 199

Mahr 69, 203
Maliki School of Islamic jurisprudence... 49
margin of appreciation 85, 126-129, 191, 224, 229
marriage rights, see -> private and family rights, see also -> homosexuality
Mary, mother of Jesus 116
Mattar, Mohamed 160
Mavrommatis Palestine Concession Case... 12
McCann and Others v. United Kingdom 170
medical or scientific experiments on human subjects 239-240, 265
messengers of God, see -> prophets
military courts 309-310
moderate cultural relativism, see -> cultural relativism
monotheism. 45
morals -> see ordre public
Morgan-Foster, Jason 76, 80, 89, 94, 98
Morocco
- abortion as crime 192
- death penalty no longer applied 179
- education of girls and women 230
- report by the CEDAW Committee 211
- women's rights in family affairs 204
Mot'aa 226
motherhood
- rights of mothers... 58
Muhkam (entirely clear verses in the Quran) 63-66
Muslim
- definition. 39
Mutashabih (verses in the Quran requiring interpretation) 63-66
Muttaqun 55, 290

nationality of children 197, 214
natural law 111-113, 126, 146
natural rights... 22
neighbors, treatment of 60
Niqab, see also -> headscarf 300-301
Nisab, see also -> Zakat 90
Norris v. Ireland 257
Nuremberg Tribunal.. 12-13

ordre public.. 26, 128
Oman
- independence of the judiciary and public prosecution 310
organ trafficking 240
orphans, treatment of 60, 97

pacta sunt servanda 122
Palestine
- history 132
parental rights.. 58-59, 70, 246-250
peace, see also -> Salaam
- peace and justice in Islam... 56-58
peremptory norm -> see ius cogens
Permanent Arab Committee for Human Rights 330
Permanent Court of International Justice
- Mavrommatis Palestine Concession Case....................................... 12
pilgrimage, see -> Hajj
Plyler v. Doe 231
privacy, see -> human rights, and see -> private and family rights
polygamy 215-224
positive discrimination in favor of women 35, 38, 53, 199
poverty
- cause for low school attendance 235
- link to illiteracy 235
private and family rights 238-260
- freedom to chose a spouse 245
- homosexuality .... 252 et seq.
- inviolability of the home 241-242
- protection of postal- and tele-communication 242
prohibitions
- alcohol 100
- gambling 100
- homosexual acts 254
- prostitution 148, 219-222, 256
promiscuity 256-257
promises, keeping of 122
Prophet Mohammed (PBUH).. 41
- exemplary life... 44
- Hadith. .... 44 et seq.
- Sunnah. 44-47
prophets before Mohammed. 43
prostitution 148, 219-222, 256
public order, see -> ordre public
punishment for crimes specified in Islamic law 271-285

Qisas (equality in punishment). 177
Qiyas, see also -> Islamic law
- definition. 49-50

Quran
- actual word of God.. 41 et seq.
- as primary source of Islamic law................................ 40 et seq., 256
- citation format. xi

Ramadan.. 46, 54-56
regional systems for the protection of human rights, see -> human rights
religious freedom, see -> human rights; and see -> freedom of religion
renouncing Islam, see -> apostasy
responsibilities, see -> duties
Restatement of Foreign Relations Law... 27
Resurrection Day 107
revelation of the Quran, see -> Quran
reverse moderate relativism, see -> cultural relativism
Riba 100
right to asylum 318-326
right to education. 36, 144, 212, 229-237
right to family life 238-260
right to food, see -> human rights
Rome Statute of the International Criminal Court. 14-15
- prohibition of torture 262
rule of law in Islamic law 306-318

Sadaqah, see also -> Zakat 91, 100
Sahin v. Turkey (headscarf) 196, 299
Salaam.. 56
same sex marriage, see also -> homosexuality .... 147, 250 et seq.
Sanad, see -> Hadith
sanctity of the home, see -> inviolability of the home, and
    see -> private and family rights
Saudi Arabia
- CEDAW Report.. 2, 38, 81, 197, 205, 250
- Constitution 125
- equality of men and women 200-201, 205
- nationality of children follows the father 197
- reservations to Articles of CEDAW 38, 199
scientific or medical experiments on human subjects 239-240
search of private dwellings and homes, see -> inviolability of the home
secrecy of private communications, see -> private and family rights
self-determination, right to 103
separation of powers 318
sex discrimination, see also -> discrimination; and
    see -> equality between men and women 196
sexual exploitation, see -> human trafficking
Shafii School of Islamic jurisprudence. 49, 73

Sharia
- abortion 191
- and Fitrah 111-113, 313
- as a living instrument 62-73
- as the foundation of the Arab Charter of Human Rights 168
- as part of constitutional law 37
- before an Arab Court of Human Rights 158
- compatible with international human rights law 84, 88
- custom as a source of Sharia 89
- definition 39
- discrimination of women? .... 197 et seq.
- divorce .... 209 et seq.
- encourages thinking and reasoning 68
- equality before the law .... 313 et seq.
- freedom of movement 323
- freedom of religion 288-292
- headscarf 298-306
- inheritance rights of sons and daughters .... 204 et seq.
- inviolability of the home 122, 182, 241, 324
- justice and equality before the law 313-314
- objectives 52
- parental rights 58-59, 70, 246-250
- polygamy .... 216 et seq.
- privacy as a fundamental right in Islam .... 241 et seq.
- prohibition of homosexual acts 254
- prohibition of slavery 327-329
- prohibition of torture 269
- protection of animal rights 270
- protection of the family .... 38, 239 et seq.
- right to education 120, 235-237
- right to life 176
- sources .... 40 et seq., 256
- transliteration 8
- veil for women 298-306
Shestack, Jerome 20
Siracusa Draft 135
Siracusa International Institute of Higher Studies in Criminal Science (ISICS) ..... xiii, 134
slavery 143, 326-329
sodomy statutes, see -> homosexuality
State Department, see -> US Department of State
Stoic philosophy 126
stoning to death, see -> Hodood punishments
strict cultural relativism, see -> cultural relativism

Sudan
- death penalty 181
Sunnah, see also -> Sharia; and see -> Islamic law
- definition. .... 40 et seq.
- words and practices of Prophet Mohammed (PBUH). 44
Sunni Schools of Islamic jurisprudence. 49
Syria
- Committee Against Torture (CAT) Report 2010 312
- treatment of Kurdish minority 268
- visit by the Arab Committee on Human Rights 363
Syria conflict. .... xv, 152

Takaful 96
Taurat, see -> Torah
Ta'zir punishment 273, 277
Torah. 41
trafficking in human beings, see -> human trafficking
trafficking in human organs 142, 240
transliteration of Arabic words. 8
treaty law -> see international law
torture
- definition 261, 265-267
- prohibition 76, 261-285
Tunisia
- death penalty no longer applied 179

Uganda
- polygamy. 220
Umma 105-108, 144, 187
unborn child
- inheritance 194
- right to life 194
UNHCR, see -> United Nations High Commissioner for Human Rights
Union of the Comoros
- Sharia as basis of legislation 179
United Arab Emirates (UAE)
- Constitutional protection of postal- and tele-communication 242
- privacy rights 242
- prohibition of torture 268
- Sharia as basis of legislation 178
United Nations Charter. 13, 29
- dignity 124
United Nations Committee on the Elimination of Racial Discrimination (CERD)
- Concluding Observations Oman 2006. 5

United Nations Convention Against Torture and Other Cruel, Inhuman
   or Degrading Treatment or Punishment (CAT) 261
- Concluding Observations Algeria 2007 312
- Concluding Observations Jordan 2010 311
- Concluding Observations Syria 2010 312
- Concluding Observations Yemen 2010 311
- Conclusions and Recommendations Egypt 2002 270
- Conclusions and Recommendations Qatar 2006 . . . . 6, 271
- Conclusions and Recommendations Saudi Arabia 2002 6
- Conclusions and Recommendations Yemen 2004 270
United Nations Convention Against Transnational Organized Crime 154
United Nations Convention on Rights of the Child
- right to life 170
United Nations Convention on the Elimination of All Forms of
   Discrimination Against Women (CEDAW)
- adultery 225
- Committee on the Elimination of Discrimination Against Women. 30
- crimes of passion 224-225
- education of girls and women . . . . 230 et seq., 305
- Morocco Report 2008 . . . . 204, 211, 230
- polygamy 215-224
- reservations by certain Arab states 37, 196-197
- Saudi Arabia Report 2007 . . . . 2, 16
United Nations Convention on the Prevention and Punishment
   of the Crime of Genocide 172
United Nations Declaration on the Right and Responsibility of Indivi-
   duals, Groups and Organs of Society to Promote and Protect
   Universally Recognized Human Rights and Fundamental Freedoms 98
United Nations First Report on Human Rights of Gay and Lesbian People 254
United Nations General Assembly Declaration on the Protection of
   All People from Being Subjected to Torture and Other Cruel,
   Inhuman or Degrading Treatment or Punishment 262
United Nations High Commissioner for Human Rights
- Agreement with the League of Arab States 149
- Report of the Special Rapporteur on Trafficking of Women and Children. 4
United Nations Human Rights Committee
- Concluding Observations Algeria 2007 268
- Concluding Observations Jordan 2010 268
- Concluding Observations Syria 2010 268
United Nations Human Rights Council
- Report of the Special Rapporteur on Torture and Cruel, Inhuman
   or Degrading Treatment. 5
United Nations Resolution on Human Rights and Human Responsibilities 98
Universal Declaration of Human Responsibilities 98

Universal Declaration of Human Rights (UDHR). 7, 15, 20, 28-30, 78
- dignity 124
- freedom of movement and residence 318
- gradualism in implementation 102
- right to asylum 318
- right to life 171
- torture 262
universalism
- based on natural law 111-113
- in the Arab Charter on Human Rights 139
- in the protection of human rights. . . . . 8, 74 et seq., 77
- universal vs regional protection of human rights. . . . . 32 et seq., 74 et seq.
- vs sovereignty 75
US Department of State
- Country Report on Human Rights Practices Djibouti 2007. 4
- Country Report on Human Rights Practices Morocco 2007. 4

veil, see -> headscarf; and see -> freedom of religion
Vienna Convention on the Law of Treaties. 23, 83

Western tradition of human rights protection 85-86
Women
- adultery 225
- crimes of passion 224-225
- discrimination. 2, 3, 5, 30, 52-53, 115-117
- divorce 226-229
- education . . . . 120, 230 et seq.
- equality . . . . 113 et seq., 195-229
- headscarf 298-306
- in Arab countries before Islam 115-117
- in Saudi Arabia 81
- polygamy 215-224
- positive discrimination in favor of women. 35, 38, 53, 199
- privacy 123, 242
- roles in the family 200, 219
- special role of mothers 38, 58, 116, 190, 203, 227, 248
- veil 298-306

Yemen
- Concluding Observations by Committee Against Torture 270, 311

Zakat.. 46, 53-55
- building a model and ideal society... 93
- eight forms of zakat 89-90
- percentage 90
- social security 89

Also published by the Council on International Law and Politics:

Corporate Social Responsibility in Comparative Perspective

edited by
Prof. Dr. Frank Emmert, LL.M.

Corporate Social Responsibility in Comparative Perspective brings together academics and practitioners from around the world in an analysis of CSR as currently understood in different legal systems and legal cultures. The authors also explore how CSR – as a global phenomenon – should be applied and advanced in future for the greatest common good.

Frank Emmert introduces the subject with a historic review and offers a critical outlook in *Corporate Social Responsibility - Quo Vadis?*

Dr. Yilmaz Argüden, the Founder and Chairman of ARGE Consulting in Turkey, explores *Civil Society for Good Governance*.

Peter Gjørtler presents *European Union and Danish Perspectives on CSR*.

Angélique Devaux demonstrates the leading role of France in the EU in her contribution on *Corporate Social Responsibility in France*.

Ying Chen analyses *Corporate Social Responsibility from the Chinese Perspective*.

Salma Taman explores *The Concept of Corporate Social Responsibility in Islamic Law*.

Elie Abouaoun discusses specifically *Arab Perspectives on Corporate Social Responsibility and Human Rights*.

Jeffrey Avina, the Citizenship and Community Affairs Director for Microsoft Middle East and Africa, explains *The Evolution of Corporate Social Responsibility During the Arab Spring and Beyond*.

Finally, Mohamed 'Arafa elaborates on *Corporate Social Responsibility and the Fight Against Corruption*, with specific references to the 2011 Revolution in Egypt.

The contributions were originally presented for discussion at conferences organized by the Robert H. McKinney School of Law and its Indiana International & Comparative Law Review and by the Protection Project of the School of Advanced International Studies of Johns Hopkins University. They have been expanded and updated for this publication.

www.ingramcontent.com/pod-product-compliance
Lightning Source LLC
Chambersburg PA
CBHW080529300426
44111CB00017B/2661